VISUAL AND W
       ANCI

Visual and written culture in ancient Egypt

JOHN BAINES

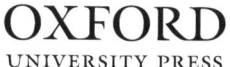
UNIVERSITY PRESS

OXFORD
UNIVERSITY PRESS

Great Clarendon Street, Oxford OX2 6DP

Oxford University Press is a department of the University of Oxford.
It furthers the University's objective of excellence in research, scholarship,
and education by publishing worldwide in

Oxford New York

Auckland Cape Town Dar es Salaam Hong Kong Karachi
Kuala Lumpur Madrid Melbourne Mexico City Nairobi
New Delhi Shanghai Taipei Toronto

With offices in

Argentina Austria Brazil Chile Czech Republic France Greece
Guatemala Hungary Italy Japan Poland Portugal Singapore
South Korea Switzerland Thailand Turkey Ukraine Vietnam

Oxford is a registered trade mark of Oxford University Press
in the UK and in certain other countries

Published in the United States
by Oxford University Press Inc., New York

© John Baines 2007

The moral rights of the author have been asserted
Database right Oxford University Press (maker)

First published 2007
First published in paperback 2009

All rights reserved. No part of this publication may be reproduced,
stored in a retrieval system, or transmitted, in any form or by any means,
without the prior permission in writing of Oxford University Press,
or as expressly permitted by law, or under terms agreed with the appropriate
reprographics rights organization. Enquiries concerning reproduction
outside the scope of the above should be sent to the Rights Department,
Oxford University Press, at the address above

You must not circulate this book in any other binding or cover
and you must impose the same condition on any acquirer

British Library Cataloguing in Publication Data

Data available

Library of Congress Cataloging-in-Publication Data

Data available

Typeset by SPI Publisher Services, Pondicherry, India
Digitally printed and bound in Great Britain by
CPI Antony Rowe, Chippenham and Eastbourne

ISBN 978–0–19–815250–7 (Hbk.)
978–0–19–957799–6 (Pbk.)

1 3 5 7 9 10 8 6 4 2

Preface

This volume collects related studies that I have published over many years, together with three hitherto unpublished or partly published pieces. The newly composed introductory essay is intended to supply an overall theoretical and comparative context, draw together threads, and point toward future questions.

Although I am an Egyptologist, only two of the essays included here first appeared in publications addressed to Egyptologists. As a whole they were written for interested readers and colleagues in various related subject areas, including Egyptology, which in this perspective has the character of a representative of area studies rather than of an autonomous discipline. The essays were thus composed in order to address at least two types of non-specialist: non-Egyptologists who have a cross-cultural interest in one or other of the issues and phenomena that I study; and Egyptologists who wish to explore broader theoretical and interpretive frameworks in relation to their interests within Egyptology.

I have assembled these studies for two main reasons. First, colleagues within and outside Egyptology have remarked that it is difficult to find such widely scattered but related publications and have encouraged me to bring my work together. Second, I have increasingly perceived connections among topics on which I have published and have concluded that an intellectual gain should result from gathering them in a single publication. I shall not have the opportunity to rework this material into a full synthesis. Such an exercise would in any case be rather artificial, because I addressed the subjects singly, not as part of an overall design even when they were quite closely related. It is therefore appropriate to present the articles more or less as they were first published and to allow readers to make any connections they wish among them, with the introductory essay (Prologue, Ch. 1) and the introductory note to the third part (Ch. 8) serving as linking elements. I also give quite numerous cross-references between chapters. I have not removed duplications between the chapters, because to do so would have compromised their integrity as arguments.

Most of the republished articles are presented with only minor changes. Details of the original publication are given in a note at the start of each. The existing titles are retained for consistency, even though the words 'ancient Egypt' are dispensable here. By keeping close to the previous versions, I hope to remove the need to search them out. The order of Chapters 2–7 and 8–14, which mostly follows dates of first publication, may also give some sense of how my work, as well as that of others on whom I draw and with whom I am in dialogue, has developed. Clear errors have been corrected and some references to recent publications inserted; the way this is done varies and is indicated in the initial note to each chapter. All references that were present in the original versions are retained. For the oldest study of literacy that I include (Ch. 2, first published in 1983), both the theoretical framework and the documentary basis have moved forward to some extent. I do not, however, believe that those developments invalidate the approach offered there. Rather, that article provided an initial survey of relevant materials and presented a discussion of some core questions, while later work addresses other issues. For that chapter, I offer additional material both in the chapters which follow and in the Appendix to the most recent, hitherto unpublished essay (Ch. 6).

'Four notes on literacy' (Ch. 3) was written with Christopher Eyre, who has graciously agreed to its republication here and has checked the slightly revised version for me. Because this was the most specialized article and was published in a condensed formulation in an Egyptological journal whose audience would be familiar with much of the material cited, I have expanded it slightly, inserting a short prefatory discussion and adding some factual information about the topics covered. I have not changed the content and argument, but I have added a few observations in footnotes.

The references for the whole book are consolidated into a single list. I hope that this will be a useful resource in itself, but it cannot be used as a bibliography of research on the topics covered (except in part in the appendices to Chs. 6 and 11), because the updatings of individual chapters are not comprehensive.

In preparing these studies, in presenting many of them in various forums, and in revising them subsequently for publication and republication, I have incurred more debts of gratitude than I can enumerate or indeed recall. Below I bring together names from the separate publications, as well as acknowledging further debts. I should like to add that my research is done in the belief that intellectual disciplines cannot prosper in isolation. However imperfect work that reaches across different fields may be, it constitutes the best way forward, not only for the comprehension of individual societies, their institutions, and their material products, but also more broadly for research on general social phenomena to which data from single societies contribute essential evidence. It has been my good fortune to work with colleagues, in many disciplines and institutions, who have shared such a vision with me.

I am grateful to many friends and colleagues—these are not mutually exclusive categories—as well as to various institutions for help received while writing these studies. Those who have read drafts have been particularly kind, since they have tolerated partly considered and obscurely expressed materials and helped them toward a more passable state. Here I list, in alphabetical order, those to whom I owe thanks most directly, noting with melancholy the significant number who are now deceased: James P. Allen, Jon W. Anderson, Jan Assmann, Robert Bagley, J. C. A. and J. E. Baines, Klaus Baer (†), Jonathan Benthall, Carole Biggam, Jeremy Black (†), John Boardman, John A. Brinkman, Edward Brovarski, John Callender (†), Christopher Chippindale, Jerrold Cooper, Marion Cox, Graham Cunningham, Véronique Dasen, Vivian Davies, Thierry De Putter, Rosemarie Drenkhahn, Marianne Eaton-Krauss, Sylwia Ejmont, Roland Enmarch, Christopher Eyre, Gerhard Fecht, Erika Feucht, Marjorie Fisher, Rita Freed, Norman Freeman, Elizabeth Frood, David Gimbel, Jack Goody, Erhart Graefe, Waltraud Guglielmi, Heike Guksch, Dieter Hagedorn, Michael Harbsmeier, Yvonne Harpur, Stephen Harvey, Daniel Herwitz, Stephen Houston, Barbara Hufft, Friedrich Junge, Friederike Kampp-Seyfried, Christina Karlshausen, Barry Kemp, Rolf Krauss, Mogens Trolle Larsen, Robert Layton, Anthony Leahy, Sandra Lippert, Lisa Montagno-Leahy, Antonio Loprieno, Judith Lustig, Peter Machinist, Jaromir Malek, Peter der Manuelian, Joyce Marcus, Donald Matthews, Gerlinde Mauer, Peter McLeod, Liam McNamara, Piotr Michalowski, Alan Millard, David O'Connor, Hans-Ulrich Onasch, Richard Parkinson, Alex Potts, Pat Rabbitt, Janet Richards, Michèle Germon Riley, Michael Roaf, Kim Ryholt, Wolfgang Schenkel, Stephan Seidlmayer, Andrew Sherratt (†), JJ Shirley, Peter Shore (†), Charles Shute (†), Kay Simpson, Robert Simpson, Bert Smith, Mark Smith, Patricia Spencer, Martin Stadler, William Stini, Timothy Taylor, Raymond Thompson, Francesco Tiradritti, Thomas Trautmann, Lana Troy, S. P. Tulante, M. C. Tulante, Peter Ucko, Cherie Wendelken, David Wengrow, Helen Whitehouse, Terry Wilfong, Carl Widstrand, Irene Winter, Zeno Wionzek, Norman Yoffee, Christiane Zivie-Coche. I am especially grateful to Gay Robins for reading the entire text and pointing out inconsistencies, as well as suggesting many further directions in which the work could be taken.

My institutional home for most of my career has been the Faculty of Oriental Studies in the University of Oxford. Many people there have helped me in the most various ways. I have also received financial support for my research from several bodies in the University. A number of the studies gathered here were begun or completed while I was on sabbatical leave, and I owe an enormous amount to Oxford for granting periods of leave and to the institutions at which I have been a visitor while working on these topics. Again in alphabetical order, these are the Alexander von Humboldt-Stiftung (Bonn: periods at the universities of Heidelberg and Münster), the Ecole Pratique des Hautes Etudes in Paris (5ème section), Harvard University, the

University of Arizona, the University of Basel, and the University of Michigan. I have presented versions of these studies in numerous additional places. While I cannot list these here, I am no less grateful to them for the interest they have shown in my work and the stimuli I have received from discussions.

Finally, I owe much to Hilary O'Shea of Oxford University Press for encouraging me to publish this book and for being far more patient than she should have been over the delivery of its text.

J.B.

Oxford, January 2006

Contents

List of figures	x
Conventions	xv
Chronological table	xvi
Map	xvii

PROLOGUE

1 Visual, written, decorum	3

WRITTEN CULTURE

2 Literacy and ancient Egyptian society	33
3 Four notes on literacy	63
4 Literacy, social organization, and the archaeological record: the case of early Egypt	95
5 Writing and society in early Egypt	117
6 Orality and literacy	146
Appendix: Updates to Chapters 2–5; comparative studies	170
7 Ancient Egyptian concepts and uses of the past: third to second millennium evidence	179

VISUAL CULTURE

8 Introductory note	205
9 Theories and universals of representation: Heinrich Schäfer and Egyptian art	207
10 Schäfer's mottoes and the understanding of representation	236
11 Colour terminology and colour classification: ancient Egyptian colour terminology and polychromy	240
12 Stone and other materials: usages and values	263
13 Communication and display: the integration of early Egyptian art and writing	281
14 On the status and purposes of ancient Egyptian art	298
References	338
Index	407

List of figures

The number inbrackets [ ] at the end of each entry is the number of the page on which the figure is sited.

Map of Egypt and adjacent regions, with names of places cited in the text, by JJ Shirley. [xvii]

1. Stela with hymn to the deified king Amenhotep II. Above the figure of the king in his baldachin is a half winged disk, and above the lost figure of the owner is a *wedjat* eye. Name of owner erased. 18th dynasty. Limestone. Height 52 cm, width 84 cm. From Abydos. Cairo, Egyptian Museum, CG 34170. After Lacau (1909: pl. lxii). [22]

2(a) Tomb of Amenemhab at Thebes (TT 85), lintel of entrance from transverse hall into long hall. 18th dynasty, reign of Amenhotep II. Metropolitan Museum of Art, Egyptian Expedition, negative T2576. Courtesy Metropolitan Museum of Art. [27]

(b) Same, interior lintel of doorway. Metropolitan Museum of Art, Egyptian Expedition, negative T2599. Courtesy Metropolitan Museum of Art. [27]

3. Attestation of major scripts and languages in ancient Egypt. Only Egyptian and Greek are discussed in the text; the others are tabulated for completeness. [34]

4. Spoken and written Egyptian compared; adapted from Stricker (1944: 47 fig. 3). [47]

5. Selection of bone tags from tomb U-j at Abydos. Naqada IIIa period. Average height *c*.1.5 cm. Courtesy Deutsches Archäologisches Institut. [119]

6. Two wavy-handled pots with ink inscriptions from tomb U-j at Abydos. The sign on the left pot (height of vessel 25.7 cm) represents a scorpion and that on the right pot (height of vessel 33.5 cm) a bucranium on a pole with a palm frond or similar ornament. Naqada IIIa period. Vessel nos. 5/8 (left), 2/1 (right). Courtesy Deutsches Archäologisches Institut. [120]

7. Narmer Macehead, from the Hierakonpolis Main Deposit, drawing of decoration. Limestone, raised relief. Height 19.8 cm. Dynasty 0, *c*.3000 BCE. Oxford, Ashmolean Museum E.3631. Drawing by Pat Jacobs; courtesy Ashmolean Museum. [123]

8. Cylinder of Narmer with scene of the king as the catfish of his name smiting Libyan enemies, from the Hierakonpolis Main Deposit. Dynasty 0, *c*.3000 BCE. Ivory, raised relief. Height *c*.5.7 cm. Dynasty 0, *c*.3000 BCE. Oxford, Ashmolean Museum E.3915. Drawing courtesy Ashmolean Museum. [123]

9. Tag with the name of Aha from his tomb complex in Cemetery B at Abydos, bearing three registers of pictorial materials and one of information about products. Wood. 1st dynasty. After Petrie (1901: pl. iiia no. 5; dimensions not given). [124]

List of figures xi

10 Old Kingdom annal stone (the Palermo Stone), front, with line of 'predynastic' names of kings (line 1) followed by year boxes for dynasties 1–3 (lines 2–5) and much larger entries for three years of the reign of Snofru (4th dynasty, line 6). Probably inscribed in the 5th dynasty. Museo Archeologico Regionale di Palermo. After Schäfer (1902: pl. 1). [126]

11 Seals with names of kings from Narmer to Den and Narmer to Qaʿa. Patterns reconstructed from mud impressions. The upper sequence reads left to right and the lower one right to left. From Abydos, necropolis of 1st dynasty kings at Umm el-Qaʿab. After Dreyer (1987: 36 fig. 3: 12a); Dreyer et al. (1996: 72 fig. 26: 12b). Courtesy Deutsches Archäologisches Institut. [127]

12 Stela of the priest Imti with offering list, from excavations of Walter B. Emery at North Saqqara. 2nd or 3rd dynasty. Limestone, painted. Dimensions not known. Location of original and source of photograph unknown. After Smith (1958: pl. 13). [129]

13 Mud sealing of Peribsen, probably from the closure of a jar; from Abydos, royal cemetery of Umm el-Qaʿab. 2nd dynasty. After Petrie (1901: pl. viiia no. 7). [130]

14(a) Fragment of a bowl with inscription of King Anedjib, 'Uniter of the Two Lands', with an image of a royal statue to the left. 1st dynasty. From Abydos, Umm el-Qaʿab. Siltstone. Width 11.8 cm. Drawing: Baines (1985c: 69 fig. 42). Oxford, Ashmolean Museum E.137. Courtesy Ashmolean Museum. [132]

 (b) Fragment of bowl with partly erased inscription including the name of King Reneb, reinscribed for his successor Ninetjer. 2nd dynasty. From Abydos, Umm el-Qaʿab, tomb of Peribsen (perhaps secondary location). Siltstone. Height 5 cm, width 9.5 cm. London, British Museum EA 35556. Courtesy British Museum. [132]

15 Vessel for liquid in the form of the hieroglyphs $k\!\!\!3$ enveloping ʿnḥ. 1st dynasty, perhaps reign of Den. Provenance unknown, perhaps Saqqara. Siltstone. Height 17.5 cm, width 14.5 cm. New York, Metropolitan Museum of Art, Rogers Fund, 1919 (19.2.16). Courtesy Metropolitan Museum of Art. [133]

16 Grave stela of a man named Nefer, seemingly a dwarf. 1st dynasty. From Abydos, Umm el-Qaʿab, around the tomb of Semerkhet. About half the height was probably a plinth sunk in the ground. Limestone. Height 45 cm, width 24 cm. British Museum EA 35018. After Spencer (1980: no. 12, pl. 6); see also Dasen (1993: 252 no. 8). Courtesy British Museum. [134]

17 Stela of King Wadj from his tomb at Abydos, Umm el-Qaʿab. 1st dynasty. Limestone. Height 250 cm (150 cm shown; about 100 cm more sunk as plinth into the ground), width 65 cm. Paris, Musée du Louvre E11007. Photo John Baines. [134]

18 Stela of Merika from Tomb 3505 at North Saqqara. 1st dynasty. Limestone. Height 173 cm, width 54 cm. In storage in Egypt. After Emery (1949–58: iii, pl. 39). Courtesy Egypt Exploration Society. [136]

19 Early Dynastic royal relief from Gebelein. Limestone. Raised relief. Turin, Museo Egizio S. 12341. Height c.85 cm, width c.45 cm. After Scamuzzi (n.d.: pl. viii). Copyright Fondazione Museo delle Antichità Egizie di Torino. [136]

List of figures

20 Seal of Peribsen with text that forms a continuous sentence, pattern reconstructed from several mud impressions excavated at Abydos, Umm el-Qaʿab. 2nd dynasty. Petrie (1901: pl. xxii no. 190); Kaplony (1963: III, pl. 95 fig. 368; II, 1143). Redrawn by Liam McNamara from Petrie. [138]

21 Final form of the Horus-and-Seth name of Khasekhemwy, on a sealing from his tomb at Abydos. 2nd dynasty. Pattern reconstructed from several mud impressions. Petrie (1901: pl. xxiii no. 197). Redrawn by Liam McNamara from Petrie. [138]

22 Relief fragments from shrine of Djoser from Heliopolis. Limestone, raised relief. 3rd dynasty. Reconstructed width c.40 cm. Donadoni Roveri (1998: 55 fig. 2, with nos. 239–41; Morenz 2002). Turin, Museo Egizio. Copyright Fondazione Museo delle Antichità Egizie di Torino. [139]

23 Second hour and opening four columns of the third hour of the Amduat as painted on the wall of the burial chamber in the tomb of Amenhotep II in the Valley of the Kings at Thebes. The headline running along the top reads continuously in retrograde writing from left to right. Mid-18th dynasty. Perspective montage by Liam McNamara after Bucher (1932: pls. xxvii–xxviii). [164]

24 Transfer document of Neskhons in favour of her son, in which she willed her property to him in return for his care of her until she died. Four witness copies are written below and to the left of the main text, which is the upper block on the right (sixteen witness signatures are on the back). Papyrus, length of preserved part 191.5 cm, height 39.5 cm; about 100 cm estimated missing from a total length of c.3 metres (Andrews 1990: 16). From Thebes, 265 BCE. British Museum EA 10026. Photograph courtesy British Museum. [165]

25 Colour encoding sequence (after Turton 1980: 313 fig. 2); schematic version of data in, for example, Kay (1975: 260–1); Kay and McDaniel (1978: 639 fig. 13). [241]

26 False door in the tomb of Mehu at Saqqara, painted with a speckled pattern in imitation of granite. 6th dynasty. After Altenmüller (1998: pl. 96). Courtesy Deutsches Archäologisches Institut. [267]

27 Monolithic granitoid naos in the sanctuary of the temple of Edfu. Reign of Nectanebo I (380–362 BCE). Photograph from the 1890s, showing the naos in its original location in the north-west corner. Griffith Institute archive nos. 759/6276. Reproduced with permission of the Griffith Institute, Oxford. [268]

28 Barque shrine of Hatshepsut at Karnak: granodiorite base course, with yellow paint on the sunk relief figures to signify gilding. 18th dynasty, 15th century BCE. Karnak, Open-air Museum. Photograph John Baines. [274]

29 Relief of Ramesses III in the temple of Medinet Habu on the West Bank at Thebes, showing the king's kilt depicted in inlay. Sandstone with fragments of blue glass paste. 20th dynasty. Courtesy Thierry De Putter and Christina Karlshausen. [278]

30 Narmer Palette, from the Hierakonpolis Main Deposit. Dynasty 0, c.3000 BCE. (*left*) Side with smiting scene; (*right*) side with grinding depression. Height 64 cm. Cairo Museum CG 14716. Courtesy Hirmer Fotoarchiv München. [284]

List of figures xiii

31 Emblematic figures on palettes of dynasty 0, *c*.3100–3000 BCE. All siltstone, unknown provenance. After Baines (1985c: 43, fig. 12; drawings by Marion Cox). [286]

   (a) Cities Palette. Height *c*.19 cm. Cairo Museum, CG 14238.

   (b) Battlefield Palette (detail). Detail *c*.12 cm high. Oxford, Ashmolean Museum, 1892.1171.

   (c) Bull Palette (detail). Detail *c*.15 cm high. Paris, Louvre E 11255.

32 The Scorpion Macehead from the Hierakonpolis Main Deposit. Limestone. Dynasty 0. Reconstructed height *c*.32.5 cm. Oxford, Ashmolean Museum E.3632. Courtesy Ashmolean Museum. [287]

33 Selected early examples of the *serekh*, from vase inscriptions of the Naqada III period. (a–b) earliest types; (c) Ro/Irihor; (d) Ka; (e) Narmer; (f) reign of Aha (1st dynasty). After Kaiser and Dreyer (1982: 263 fig. 14), redrawn by Marion Cox. [292]

34 Scenes of sculptors, painters, and carpenters making a bed and smoothing wood, in the tomb of Pepyankh Heny the Black at Meir, room A, north wall, west. 6th dynasty. After Blackman (1914–53: v, pl. 18). [307]

35 Colossal statue of the god Min from Koptos. Limestone. Late fourth millennium, perhaps Naqada IIIa. Height of fragment 1.77 m. Oxford, Ashmolean Museum 1894.105e. Courtesy Ashmolean Museum. [312]

36 Base from statue of Djoser, from the entrance colonnade of the Step Pyramid complex at Saqqara; the inscription on the left names the 'master of sculptors Imhotep'. 3rd dynasty. Painted limestone. Height 14.2 cm, width 48.7 cm, depth 66.3 cm. Cairo Museum JdE 49889. After Firth, Quibell, and Lauer (1935: pl. 58). [314]

37 Reserve head from Giza. Limestone. 4th dynasty. Height 30 cm. Museum of Fine Arts, Boston 14.718 (MFA negative C4362). Courtesy Museum of Fine Arts. [316]

38 The Two Dog Palette from the Hierakonpolis Main Deposit. Naqada III period. (*left*) Side with grinding depression ('recto'); (*right*) side with animal composition and flute player. Siltstone. Height 42.5 cm, width 22 cm. Oxford, Ashmolean Museum E.3924. Courtesy Ashmolean Museum. [317]

39 Three stone vases, provenance unknown. Siltstone. 1st dynasty. Berlin, Ägyptisches Museum 13213, 12778, 12779. Courtesy Ägyptisches Museum Berlin. [319]

40 Ivory statuette of a female dwarf from the Hierakonpolis Main Deposit. 1st dynasty (?). Height 13.3 cm. Oxford, Ashmolean Museum E.298. See Dasen (1993: 274 no. 106). Courtesy Ashmolean Museum. [320]

41 Limestone statue of Khasekhem from the Hierakonpolis Main Deposit. 2nd dynasty. Height 63 cm, width of plinth 17 cm, depth 33 cm. Oxford, Ashmolean Museum E.517. Courtesy Ashmolean Museum. [321]

42 Over-lifesize head of Senwosret III, provenance unknown. Pink granite. 12th dynasty. Height 32.3 cm. Cambridge, Fitzwilliam Museum E.37.1930. Courtesy Fitzwilliam Museum. [322]

xiv *List of figures*

43 Under-lifesize head of Amenemhat III, perhaps from the Aswan area. Dark shelly limestone. 12th dynasty. Height 11.6 cm. Cambridge, Fitzwilliam Museum E.2.1946. Courtesy Fitzwilliam Museum. [322]

44 Head from colossal statue of Amenhotep III, from his mortuary temple on the West Bank at Thebes. 18th dynasty. Quartzite. Height 1.31 m, width 1.02 m across top of crown. British Museum EA7. Courtesy British Museum. [325]

45 Colossal statue of the goddess Sakhmet from the Mut temple complex at Karnak, probably first set up in the mortuary temple of Amenhotep III on the West Bank at Thebes. Granodiorite. 18th dynasty, reign of Amenhotep III. Preserved height 1.98 m, width 48.7 cm. British Museum EA45. Courtesy British Museum. [326]

46 Seated statue of Amenhotep Son of Hapu, pose and iconography inspired by Middle Kingdom models (nose area recarved in antiquity), from Karnak. Granodiorite. 18th dynasty, reign of Amenhotep III. Height 1.42 m. Cairo Museum CG 42127. After Legrain (1906: pl. 76). [327]

47 Stela of the sculptor Bak and his wife Tahere, provenance unknown. Quartzite. 18th dynasty, reign of Akhenaten (Amarna period). Height 67 cm. Berlin, Ägyptisches Museum 1/63. Courtesy Ägyptisches Museum Berlin. [328]

48 Plaster head, possibly of the later King Aya, from the house compound of the sculptor Thutmose at el-Amarna. 18th dynasty, reign of Akhenaten (Amarna period). Berlin, Ägyptisches Museum 21350. Height 27 cm. Courtesy Ägyptisches Museum Berlin. [329]

49 Relief of Sety I offering to Ptah-Sokar, north wall of the Hall of Sokar and Nefertem in his temple at Abydos. 19th dynasty. Photograph by Amice M. Calverley. Courtesy Egypt Exploration Society. [331]

50 Group of offering bearers on the lintel relief of Tjanefer from Heliopolis. Limestone, raised relief. 30th dynasty. Height 30.5 cm, total width 1.14 m. Cairo Museum JdE 29211. After Maspero (1907: pl. 34); see also L. M. Leahy (1988: no. 77). [333]

51 View of the temple complex of Hathor and Isis at Dendara, from west. 1st century BCE – 2nd century CE. After Chassinat (1934: pl. xxv). [334]

TABLE 1 Forms of the script and types of material for which they were used. [46]

TABLE 2 Distribution of Egyptian scripts and text genres in the late New Kingdom (*c.*1200 BCE) and the Graeco-Roman period. [49]

Conventions

Ancient Egyptian texts are generally cited in translation. Unless otherwise stated, translations are mine (as also with modern European languages). Within translated passages, standard conventions for indicating damage and other features are used, as follows:

( )   added to clarify translation or transliteration, not present in original
[ ]   damaged or lost in original, with suggested restorations inside the brackets
⟨ ⟩   erroneously omitted in original, added in translation/transliteration
{ }   superfluous in original

Citations from modern writings use normal present-day conventions, so that [ ] indicates additions to or expansions of what is cited, and ... indicates omissions.

Ancient Egyptian words are cited in consonantal transcription/transliteration. Modern users generally insert *e* between consonants to render words pronounceable. The following rough equivalences apply:

- ꜣ   glottal stop, perhaps originally *l*
- ꜥ   like Arabic/Hebrew ꜥayin, perhaps originally a dental sound
- j   as English *y* or glottal stop, perhaps originally a liquid; often transcribed *i*
- ḏ   *dj*, perhaps originally a palatal sound
- ḥ   emphatic *h*, as in Arabic
- ḫ   *kh*, as in German ach
- ẖ   *kh*, as in German ich
- q   emphatic guttural *k*, as in many Semitic languages
- ṯ   *tj*, perhaps originally a palatal or guttural sound

When Egyptian words are pronounced, ꜥ and ꜣ are often vocalized arbitrarily as *a*, with *w* rendered *u* and *j* as *i*. The reconstruction of Egyptian consonants, and still more of vocalization, is uncertain and disputed. For a summary, see Loprieno (1995b: 15, 28–39).

O in the citation of an ancient manuscript means 'ostracon' and P 'papyrus'.

Ancient Egyptian personal names are generally given in a conventional vocalized form. These forms make no pretense to be close to ancient pronunciation, which in any case varied regionally and changed radically over the millennia. I give preference to conventionalized ancient Egyptian forms over hellenized forms known from classical writers.

Cross-references within the book are to chapters and to sections within them, not to pages. Chapters are cited by number (1, 2, etc.), while sections within them follow the style of the particular chapter. Numbered subsections are preceded by §, so that 'Ch. 2 §2.2' means 'section 2.2 of Chapter 2'.

Chronological table

Predynastic	c.5000–3000
Naqada I (c.4000–3500)	
Naqada II (c.3500–3250)	
Naqada III (late predynastic and dynasty 0; c.3250–3000)	
Early Dynastic	
1st–3rd dynasties	c.2950–2575
Old Kingdom	
4th–8th dynasties	c.2575–2150
First Intermediate period	
9th–11th dynasties	c.2150–1980
Middle Kingdom	
11th–13th dynasties	c.1980–1630
Second Intermediate period	
14th–17th dynasties	c.1630–1520
New Kingdom	
18th–20th dynasties	c.1540–1070
Third Intermediate period	
21st–25th dynasties	c.1070–715
Late period	
25th–30th dynasties, Second Persian period (31st dynasty)	c.715–332
Macedonian period	332–305
Ptolemaic period	305–30
Roman period	30–395 CE
Byzantine period	395–640 CE
Muslim conquest	640 CE

Dates are BCE unless otherwise noted. For earlier periods they are rounded. Overlapping dates are deliberate. For the second millennium I follow the scheme of Rolf Krauss (1985). There is no consensus on Egyptian chronology. Margins of error are around 25 years for the period 2000–715, rising to a century or so at 3000. The time from 332 BCE to 395 CE is very commonly referred to by the broader term 'Graeco-Roman period'.

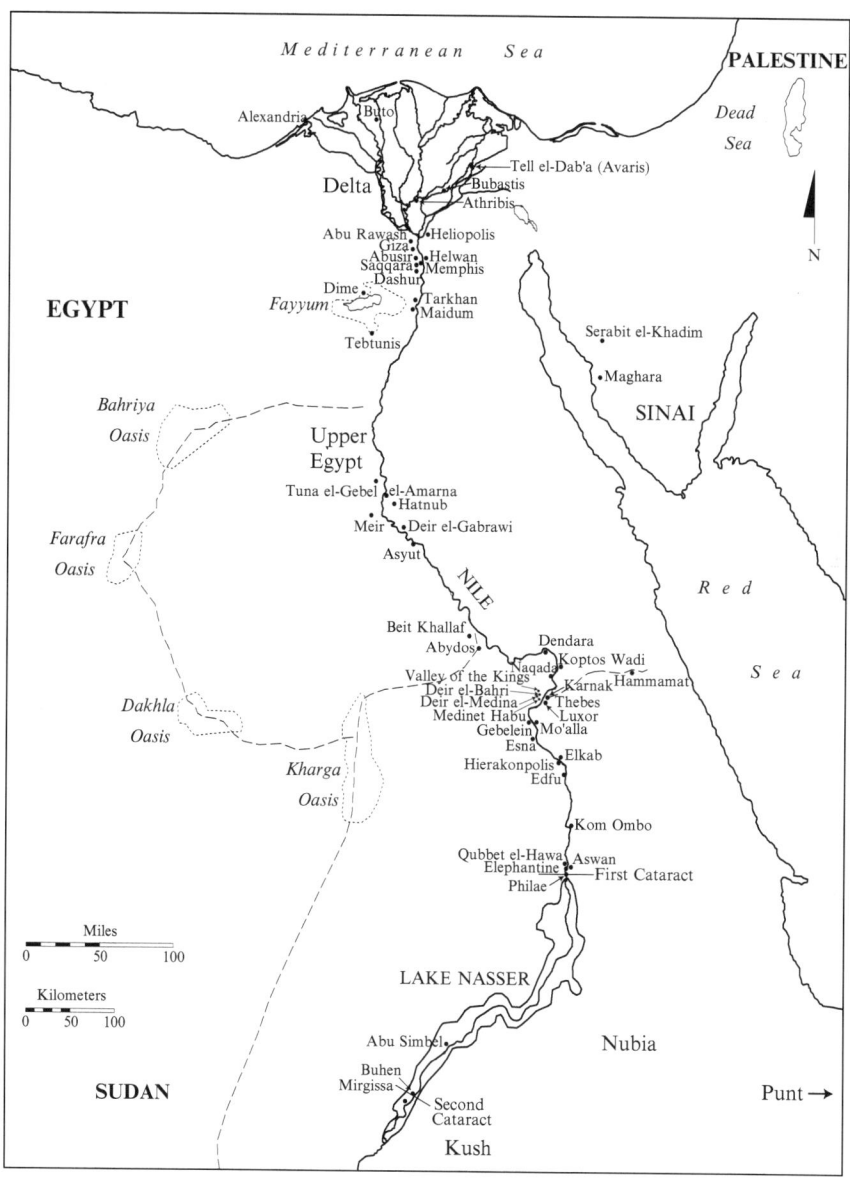

Map of Egypt and adjacent regions, with names of places cited in the text, by JJ Shirley.

Prologue

1

Visual, written, decorum

INTRODUCTION

In this volume I collect studies that focus around two overlapping major institutions of ancient Egyptian civilization. The present, introductory essay begins by setting a theoretical context and goes on to exemplify key questions through a review of the overarching symbolic institution of decorum together with selected domains of the ancient record in which it is manifest. The second part ('Written culture') explores the character and development of writing, its position and functions in society, and some related questions. In the third part ('Visual culture'), I start by focusing on social and cognitive aspects of representational art and connected phenomena, subsequently siting them selectively in relation to institutional context, tradition, architecture, and verbal communication.

In ancient Egypt, artistic production and writing, which cannot be separated from each other, were crucial to the high-cultural core of the civilization (see further Baines and Yoffee 1998). Although evidence from the formative period of the later fourth millennium BCE is limited, it is sufficient for some analysis of the institutions' emergence, so that the phenomena can be viewed from the perspective of their initial scarcity. These modes of representation and recording retained their importance throughout the Egyptian dynastic and Graeco-Roman periods, down to the extinction of the civilization in the early centuries CE (for dates, see table, p. xvi). In several periods, notably that of the great pyramids in the mid-third millennium, much of the civilization's focus was on creating and maintaining its principal forms, which at that time centred around monumental mortuary architecture.

Writing was also of great importance for administration and hence both for organizing state activities and for high-cultural interests. Most writing was no doubt done for administrative purposes, but that does not render its non-administrative uses any less crucial. There has been continuing debate on whether writing was invented for administration or for high-cultural use.

I believe that both were intended from the first and that such an opposition is unnecessary (see Ch. 5). My purpose in this chapter is to supply a conceptual background for studying uses of the two representational modes of pictorial depiction (together with its aesthetic context) and writing in relation to Egyptian society and to its methods of delimiting, sustaining, and transmitting meaning.

MATERIALITY: VISUAL AND WRITTEN

First, I review briefly the modes of the visual and the written together with connections between them. I start by focusing on the visual as a more embracing domain of communication. This initial section is presented in relatively abstract terms; in order to concentrate on broad and basic issues, I give few examples or references. The discussion is intended to introduce a treatment of the ancient Egyptian evidence, which follows in the last part of the chapter as well as the rest of the book. Because the issues reviewed are not specific to Egypt, they are formulated in broader, cross-cultural terms.

It is desirable to address the general category of material culture at the outset. Accompanying the emergence of sedentism from around 15,000 years ago onward, and much later the emergence of civilizations, modes of representation and self-presentation that focused on social institutions which leave no lasting physical trace—notably spoken language—came to be supplemented by increasing numbers of features and domains of material culture. By civilizations, I mean complex societies with overarching ideologies that possess a high-cultural core (compare Yoffee et al. 2005: 253; for the distinctive case of Egypt, see Baines 2003a).

Probably hominids have conveyed social meaning through material culture, both as seen and as experienced dynamically, for hundreds of thousands or millions of years, that is, for as long as their mental processes have been in any way comparable with those of the present human species. The use of physical settings for such purposes could be still older than that of material culture. A fundamental development of sedentization, of the Neolithic, and of the much later emergence of civilizations has been the proliferation of many domains of material culture, leading gradually to the forming of all-encompassing manipulated environments that became a principal focus of structures of meaning for their societies. (The emerging discussion of materiality in archaeology provides a valuable parallel to this argument: DeMarrais, Gosden, and Renfrew 2004.)

Material culture is not a neutral domain; it is subject to aesthetic ordering and it engages the emotions. While it is not possible to specify narrowly what counts as being aesthetic, it is clear that no human group organizes its material culture in exclusively pragmatic or utilitarian ways. Order, as well as criteria such as visual balance, affects choices almost everywhere, as is often remarked for Palaeolithic hand-axes, used for hundreds of thousands of years, whose elegance and symmetry of form cannot well be accounted for exclusively in terms of functional utility (see e.g. Mithen 2005: 188–91; Kohn and Mithen 1999; the aesthetic point remains whether or not their particular interpretation is adopted). A significant visual correlate is the plausible identification of colour manipulation in the form of pigment use in the African Middle Stone Age about 250,000 years ago (Barham 1998). Aesthetic aspects, while fundamental to material culture, are also characteristic of the world of sound, including the realization of language. Language seems to be used universally for more than narrowly functional communication. Moreover, language can hardly operate without metaphor and other complex modes of signification, one of whose characteristics is that they have aesthetic as well as practical and semantic aspects. Sound is the principal medium of music, another universal human institution and channel of transmission which communicates through the corporeal aesthetic exploitation of that medium and of the temporal dimension (see e.g. Nettl 1983; Blacking 1995; Mithen 2005), and is embedded in material culture as well as in socially and visually significant modes of performance that absorb vast resources and are themselves objects of display in many cultures (e.g. ancient China: So 2000; Bagley 2005).

While aesthetic motivations may not be absent from the non-human world (compare Davidson and McGrew 2005 on how far non-human groups may have 'culture'), for human society their importance and distinctive character are too often neglected in the quest to explain how societies 'function'; yet a vital aspect of their functioning is through aesthetically tempered or driven institutions (for aspects of this point as they relate to 'art', compare Morphy and Perkins 2006). Although aesthetics may have some narrowly adaptive advantage in terms of implicit criteria such as balance, their role in human society altogether transcends considerations of that sort (for an action-focused argument along these lines, see Hardin 1993).

Traditional humanistic scholarship tended to focus on text and language. The approach to civilizations through material culture has not advanced as far as have textual and linguistic approaches (for prehistory it is the only possibility), although that difference has become much less marked in recent decades, while the logocentrism typical of some academic disciplines is also less marked than it was. Little would be gained by discussing priority among different modes of transmission of meaning, but it may be useful to consider the following strands among these modes: what might be termed social (and corporeal) representation; language; more narrowly visual forms; and writing.

Social representation includes the social forms through which people interact, encompassing spatial relations among people and attendant visual cues. The human body is a major focus of social representation, and is particularly prominent in societies whose material culture is not strongly elaborated in other domains. While the body is significant for any human group, in sedentary societies and civilizations it is complemented by a vast range of other elements of material culture. The two essential strands of signification that are common to all societies are thus social and strongly visual representation, including meanings conveyed by the body, and sonic communication focused around language; and these are not separate, because the production of spoken language is generally accompanied by visual and other cues. For sedentary societies, and especially civilizations, with complex material cultures and numerous subsystems, these two strands can be related additionally to specialized modes of visual communication, notably through architecture and pictorial representation—the former supplying a context for the latter in addition to enacting its own communication—and in many cases to writing.

Visual and sonic communication are essential to vast numbers of species. Whereas language is necessary to human society and is the feature that sets it off most distinctively from other animal societies, writing, which constitutes a material counterpart of language as a system of communication, came late in social evolution and is in no way necessary to society as such. (All these points relate to human beings in general; where people have such disabilities as blindness or deafness, they do not differ significantly from others in these respects, exemplifying that the characteristics discussed are innate.) The relationship between writing and language is not straightforward and is the subject of much discussion. Furthermore, writing is a system of visual communication as well as a linguistic one. It was invented as the former and became the latter.

These interlocking points give primacy in human symbolization to visual communication, pervasively operating through material culture, and to language, which is what is lost in the historical, and especially the archaeological, record. Visual communication presumably has priority over language, because the latter is a relative latecomer in human evolution, however long it may have existed and been preceded by other forms of auditory communication. Visual communication also necessarily has primacy over writing, not least because writing is present in only a small proportion of societies (even if these encompass the majority of the people now living in the world). Once writing appears, it creates a new channel of transmission and becomes an institution of its own, greatly aided by its status as a domain of material culture and by the heavy societal investment needed to sustain it. Writing constitutes only a tiny proportion of the linguistic communication that takes place, which is no doubt one reason why traditional structural linguistics focused on spoken language. The execution of writing, however, is enveloped by language that is not identical with the words that are written but comments on the creation of written objects and their exploitation, through general setting, reading aloud, explication, and so forth. As spoken and written language develop, they follow parallel, or more commonly diverging, paths, while the significance of writing is in no way exhausted by the fact that it is generally in some sense a representation of language. Language and writing are not a single institution but two connected ones.

Although a language may appear to be a fixed institution if one sets out to learn it as a foreigner, in reality it is unstable and evanescent (the study of child language acquisition is a specialist field that I do not address here). In societies without writing, and thus also in prehistory, it is necessary for significant knowledge that is linguistically formulated and passed down the generations to be intensively tended in memorization and transmission, to be related to cues in the world, or both. 'The world' for these purposes includes the natural landscape, the built environment, or the cultural world of social forms, animate beings, and artefacts. A selected aspect of the world is normally the main vehicle for a specific domain of knowledge, so that different domains can be kept separate and modelled in distinctive ways. Language-based knowledge is often embedded in non-linguistic domains, the classic explicit example familiar from Mediterranean antiquity being the 'art of memory' organized around spatial locations typically in buildings (Yates 1966). Language itself is so all-pervasive that it may not be perceived as being distinct from other aspects of social life. Nonetheless, metalinguistic discourse of one sort or another, and hence reflection on language, may be a universal human trait: from quite early childhood onward, every normal person can formulate the notion that one word 'means' another word or is characterized in terms of a phrase, or more broadly that a word and its referent or referents may be distinct.

Visual representation constitutes a mode of signification that offers analogies with language but differs from it in important ways. The visual dimension of normal social interaction supplies the basis for representation by offering countless models and meanings that it can develop. Here I focus on what is representational in a rather narrower sense. I use 'representation' to mean any use of pigment, line, area, or texture to create pattern, pictorial rendering, or both, as well as three-dimensional modelling of materials to achieve analogous but often markedly different effects. Visual representation can be applied to a vast range of media, among which the human body has a central position, the more so in societies with limited material culture.

Like writing but far more pervasively, visual representation is a second-order activity in which the surface that is used is made to be or to signify something more, or other, than itself (visual mimicry in the animal world shows that such phenomena are still more universal, but generally without inherent intentionality). Like language, visual representation is also readily rendered self-referential and exploited on metalevels. The transformative character of visual representation gives it enormous potential, which is surrounded by restrictions, taboos, and 'magic'. Such attitudes can be seen both in entire cultures, of which well-known examples are the traditional interdiction of representation of the human figure in much of the Islamic world and during one phase in the Byzantine empire, as well as in specific contexts within cultures.

The most important way in which visual representation differs from language is that, although much in it is extremely variable, so that visual forms can differ radically in different cultures and can verge on incomprehensibility between one culture and another, neither representational nor non-representational visual forms are completely arbitrary. Pictorial forms relate ultimately to visual perception and to the phenomenal world, to which cognition and representation respond interpretively and toward which they point. Visual forms that are not pictorial make use of distinctions of line, surface, and so forth, the potential range of which is not infinite and is at least partly anchored in constants of human cognition. This anchoring of visual representation in the world and in cognition may reinforce its symbolic significance.

Language and visual representation should not be separated, not least because language envelops so much of what human beings do. While language is ultimately arbitrary in its relation to the world, this fact is often ignored. Reification of the relation between words and what they denote, or belief that language can influence the world directly, can be compared with the more or less direct relations that exist (or are believed to exist) between visual representations and their referents and/or the surfaces that bear them. As with beliefs relating to language, the interconnections between these domains are powerful motors of symbolic behaviour, of which manifestations that are salient because they have no superficially rational justification are broadly 'magical' in character.

Visual representation and behaviour surrounding it is not just symbolic but also aesthetic. Its aesthetic aspects are closely bound up with values and prestige. The fact that visual representation is generally seen as an embellishment to an underlying reality is very relevant to its social function. Whereas language is so indispensable that there are limits to how far it can be restricted—silent religious orders are extreme cases but they too make use of language if not in acoustic form—visual representation is a little more easily controlled. As material culture becomes more elaborate and society becomes more unequal, in processes that are interrelated in many societies, such control becomes a means of enacting and displaying significant messages, including those of inequality. Visual representation is not merely integrated into social forms but is engaged actively to constitute them.

Perhaps the single most useful point of departure for understanding the use of visual representation in early historic societies and in most premodern ones is to try to envisage a context where decoration, especially pictorial representation, is a scarce resource; this is a difficult task in the modern world where representation is all-pervasive. The myth of Narcissus drowning himself through fixation on his own image in a pool of water reminds us that access to one's own appearance was difficult before mirrors became effective and widely available in relatively modern times. In comprehending visual matters, people were traditionally more dependent on one another than they are now, so that representation was more strongly social. They lived in a world where mechanical reproduction of images was hardly possible, and each visual form was unique even if it represented a familiar type.

Within this context of scarcity and social interdependence for visual resources, complex societies and nascent states of the fourth and early third millennia in Egypt and the Near East further reduced the availability of images, as well as non-pictorial decoration, to all but elites. Since some pigments, as well as suitable surfaces such as textiles, skins, plaster, and ceramic, were fairly widely available, this constituted a significant appropriation of communicative potential. While it cannot be proved that representation was restricted in contexts of which nothing survives, notably the lived and built environment, it is likely that lost domains fitted the patterns of what is attested and so were also subject to restriction. This appropriation was a powerful symbolic element in the creation of structural inequalities in society. As knowledge and wealth became more highly differentiated, so did aesthetic and visual communication.

The emergence of writing provides an obvious parallel for this process of restriction in many, but not all, early civilizations. With exceptions such as Rongorongo on Easter Island, writing is a product only of civilizations or of smaller-scale societies existing on their peripheries. In the ancient Near East and Egypt, it was an instrument of elites who had more interest in appropriating privileged matters than in disseminating them. The purposes to which writing could be put varied widely and cannot always be closely compared from one civilization to another. Writing was probably an effective instrument in administration, but it could equally be integrated deliberately with the domain of pictorial representation and serve intra-elite purposes more than it instituted any wider communication. Here, Mesopotamia and Egypt exemplify two possibilities. The former provides copious evidence for the use of writing in administering large quantities of goods and numbers of people. How 'necessary' writing was for administration is impossible to assess, because such activities can become self-sustaining and self-justifying, but it was compatible with growing social complexity and, for example, with vastly increased settlement size, and it may have contributed significantly to such developments. From Egypt, hieroglyphic writing is inherently pictorial but hardly speaks to wider groups, while the cursive administrative writing that is preserved from early periods relates only to core elite activities and comes from the prestige contexts of royal burials and arrangements surrounding them. How far its use spread into wider spheres is unknown.

Early writing is too often taken as a means of recording language, which it is to only a very limited extent. Rather than being a linguistic system, it is a means of signification that uses language as aid, model, and medium, increasingly so as it develops in range of use (Houston 2004b). This slow development of writing toward operating through language has often been obscured in studies that too readily use a later perspective, as well as having an implicit agenda of promoting the social desirability of writing and literacy for today. The modern perspective also tends to favour the written over the oral (except in linguistics) and to assume that the two are in opposition, perhaps in part because the polarity between the two became a widespread subject of discussion in the 1960s–1970s heyday of structuralism, with its fondness for binary oppositions. In the limited context of early writing, the oral domain will have remained completely dominant, whatever the prestige of the new communicative medium; indeed, because much writing represented its messages in very limited ways, it was not comprehensible without an oral and institutional context.

Despite these strictures, the vast majority of Egyptian writing represents language, if not simply spoken language, but it is important to keep its less linguistic point of departure in mind. More broadly, it is desirable to approach the pictorial representation and writing of early civilizations as two aspects of communicative systems that were rooted in the aesthetically formed oral and ceremonial institutions of small elites.

EXPLOITATION OF THE SYSTEMS

Institutions of visual art and writing need to be investigated in relation to at least three, partly overlapping, themes. I present these briefly here, offer a framework for such investigations, and discuss some implications. The essays

Visual, written, decorum

in the next two parts of this book are organized to focus on the phenomena they address rather than the categories I review here. This difference in orientation exemplifies how phenomena which are taken as objects of study generally intersect with one another and cannot be defined neatly. The framework I propose here addresses in particular the social context of pictorial representation and writing. In several chapters I consider historical aspects of the introduction of visual and representational systems. Although the status of images and writing in later periods was not determined in any straightforward way by their patterns of origin, the perspective of a time when both systems were scarce helps to dispel preconceptions about how they would 'naturally' be used.

The three themes alluded to above are:

1 The structure of the systems; sketched very briefly below.
2 Exploitation as meaningful entities. Relevant topics centre around cross-culturally paralleled ways in which pictorial representation and writing are presented, as well as how they either communicate their content or profess to do so while subverting such communication.
3 Social significance. Under this heading belong such issues as the systems' contribution to the formation and maintenance of the country's administration and of the position of the ruling group.

This book primarily addresses themes 2 and 3. In relation to theme 1, I study pictorial representation from a theoretical perspective in Chapter 9 and its connections with writing in early periods in Chapter 13 (see also Ch. 5). The structure of systems both of pictorial representation and of writing is part of the background to the studies that follow. The basic forms of pictorial representation were analysed in great detail by Heinrich Schäfer, whose fundamental work is discussed in Chapter 9. While significant connections exist between language and script structure, these do not necessarily affect the interplay of script and other modes of representation and so do not need to be considered here. I do not address in detail the make-up of the writing system itself, for which ample literature is available, nor the linguistic character and affinities of the Egyptian language (both of these are excellently treated in Loprieno 1995b).

The Egyptian writing system is complex and incorporates several categories of signs that combine to notate words and grammatical elements such as plural markers and suffixes. The most important distinction is between phonograms, which convey phonemic information of various types, and semograms, which convey meaning. Most words, except for particles and some prepositions, are notated with combinations of these two categories. Three script forms were in use in almost all periods. The hieroglyphic script, the form with the greatest prestige, increased in complexity during the dynastic period, reaching its culmination in Graeco-Roman times, when more signs were used, in more elaborate developments than earlier, while addressing reducing numbers of people as literacy in the Egyptian language became more restricted in the face of the increasingly prevalent Greek.

This complexity has posed problems for sociological interpretation. Champions of the alphabet tend to say that its relative simplicity enables it to be spread widely in society, so that the benefits of a literacy that is ideally universal can be within reach of almost everyone. Scripts such as the Egyptian are seen as deficient because of their greater complexity, rather than, for example, valuing them as elaborate high-cultural creations. As it happens, critics often underestimate its complexity because they do not appreciate that while the Egyptian script had a monumental, 'hieroglyphic' form that is relatively easy to recognize and possessed sign forms that were readily distinguishable from one another, variant sign forms in the altogether more widespread cursive, 'hieratic' script are less memorable and distinct, and some common groups in it are run together into ligatures; such scripts require frequent use to be effective.

In several ways, arguments like these are misdirected. They are also self-evidently Eurocentric and make no attempt to view the matter from the perspective of the actors. Examples like Japanese and Chinese show that the complexity of a script is no barrier to widespread or universal dissemination of writing and literacy. Furthermore, the alphabet's simplicity as a code brings with it a greater abstraction and arbitrariness and a lesser capacity to incorporate cultural meanings (although these remain important, see e.g. Morison 1972; Petrucci 1993). Moreover, alphabets used to write languages, such as French, that have undergone radical phonetic change since their basic orthography was established, or English, for which no unitary phonetic system exists, have to be read logographically, because the shape of written words relates to their history as much as to their pronunciation. What is more relevant here is that the Egyptian script, like many others, was fully functional for the purposes for which it was developed and that, in contrast with alphabets, it could easily be extended when desired. From its earliest forms to its use for an expanded range of purposes including notation of continuous syntax, up to five hundred years later ($c.$3200–2700 BCE), it seems to have developed through several reforms rather than progressively; more reforms followed in the second millennium.

Pictorial representation integrated well with writing principally because the pictorial character of the hieroglyphic script was retained in all periods. I argue that this integration was intended from the beginning (Ch. 5; see also Baines 2004a). One could equally assume that the pictorial, hieroglyphic form was a secondary development from the cursive or less formal as, more conventionally, that the evolution was the other way around. It seems best to posit that the two forms were designed together from the first.

Major difficulties in comprehending the domains of written and artistic culture in ancient civilizations have arisen because it has often been assumed too readily both that sweeping consequences flow more or less automatically from the introduction of writing and that writing and pictorial representation penetrated everywhere in society. Evidence points to the institutions' being confined to relatively small elites, not just in Egypt but in many civilizations. Even though writing could affect nearly everyone through state administration, which aspired to be all-embracing—perhaps to different degrees in different periods (compare O'Connor 1995: 319–21)—it does not follow that most people came near in person to where writing was practised. Rather, many of writing's effects were indirect, with central institutions being pervaded by it while individuals outside provincial centres, especially the majority of the agrarian and pastoral population on the land, may seldom have seen it.

Moreover, writing and artistic culture were instruments of the state and of its principal representative, the king. The extent to which they were used among the wider elite, or more broadly in society as a whole, varied. The overall pattern of development was from a period, lasting perhaps five hundred years, when pictorial representation was confined to more limited domains than it had been before the civilization emerged, to the slow, irregular dissemination of an increasingly large, complex, and multi-layered high-cultural domain. Even so, high culture never pervaded the lives of those far outside elites. Such a pattern cannot be reduced to a single form or focus; nor were trends always in the same direction. The increase in the amount that was written in later periods is clear, although volume need not equate to an increase in the range of uses to which writing was put (on possible change of such a type in a single community, see Haring 2003). Another variable is scale: in later periods, larger compositions were created, up to sizes attested in the Roman period that are perhaps similar to short novels of today (Ryholt 2005). Comparable trends can be sketched for changes in pictorial representation. While there was no overall tendency to increase the amount of images in any one composition—Old Kingdom tombs of the later third millennium have as many as any later ones—pictorial usages did spread to more domains. Such changes need to be examined in detail, while bearing in mind the basic point that the introduction of pictorial representation to a new domain or the application of writing to a new genre were innovations and were not automatic.

Throughout, the pace of change was such that most people, perhaps particularly outside the elite, would not have observed any significant innovation during their lifetimes. The pattern was 'punctuated', with phases of major transformation, during which changes would have been evident, being succeeded by much longer ones when developments were subtle or even indiscernible without close analysis—while still probably very important to the actors.

Elite uses of pictorial representation, and restrictions on its availability to others, relate more widely to the employment of material culture as a whole to incorporate and express social difference. I have emphasized the value of this broader category and the strong association of material culture with aesthetic considerations and distinctions. The acquisition of items of material culture has been argued to be a driving force in radical change, for example in the European Renaissance (e.g. Jardine 1997), but such an approach can be reductive and tends not to use an actors' perspective (I attempt to take such a perspective in Ch. 14). It is probably better to see material culture as something that is exploited in the interests of elites as part of wider motivations, rather along the lines that Pierre Bourdieu (1984) adopted in his analysis of social classes in contemporary France in terms of 'distinction'. Most people naturally respond to the configuration of material culture far more than they personally shape it.

Restrictions like those just mentioned relate to the question of how far the high-cultural complex which provides the core materials for this book was intended to communicate beyond elites, or whether its communicative idiom was rather one of exclusion. Norman Yoffee and I have explored implications of this problem in more detail, primarily on a theoretical level (Baines and Yoffee 1998). Our analysis of high culture pursued one principal aspect of the issue, partly in order to argue against a too-rosy view of the cohesiveness of ancient civilizations (see also Yoffee 2005). The balancing question of how elites communicated with others in Egypt and through what media—whether material culture, social interaction, projects for which the labour and willing or unwilling motivation of non-elites was mobilized, or yet other domains—has hardly been addressed, or has been assumed not to be a problem. It will be difficult to approach this issue, but some model of communication between social groups is necessary to an overall understanding of the society. In the next section of this chapter I argue that a characteristic symbolic feature of Egyptian culture was crucial to distinguishing various domains, including social and hierarchical ones, and so supplies one part of such a model.

DECORUM

The concept

Another approach to studying the structuring of meaningful domains of Egyptian culture is to explore the concept of decorum, which is relevant to questions addressed throughout this book. I argue that the domain of ancient action that I address with this term corresponds with an actors' category, and so opens the way to a relatively close engagement with the material. As a concept, decorum may not correspond with any single word in the Egyptian language. Rather, it is a principle that can be observed in the material, both governing relations between domains and circumscribing modes of action within them. The domains in question are social and pragmatic as well as symbolic and representational. The principle of decorum is expressed in action and representation, and quite probably was so deeply ingrained as not to require explicit formulation. The absence of an ancient term for it is not surprising, because Egyptian generally does not have words for mid-level abstractions.

Decorum has long been a term used widely in art history and related disciplines (e.g. Gombrich 1972b: 7–11), and has been made the subject of conferences and books (e.g. Ames-Lewis and Bednarek 1992). Jørgen Podemann Sørensen (1989) and I seem to have been the first to use it in Egyptology. My application of the term and understanding of the phenomenon have expanded considerably since I first employed them in print in a discussion of temple symbolism thirty years ago (Baines 1976: 14). I begin my review of the topic along the lines on which my approach has developed, with the aim of clarifying the thinking behind several later chapters.

First, I repeat a descriptive definition that I gave in a later article, 'Restricted knowledge, hierarchy, and decorum: modern perceptions and ancient institutions'. Except for the Excursus, 'Decorum and emblematic representation', in *Fecundity figures* (1985c: 277–305) this is my only publication that focuses on decorum, as against using it in analysis:

The decorum found on the monuments, which can be traced from late predynastic times, is a set of rules and practices defining what may be represented pictorially with captions, displayed, and possibly written down, in which context and in what form. It can be related to other constraints on action and reports on action, as when a king says that he killed his opponents while his follower says that he kept them alive [Baines 1986], and was probably based ultimately on rules or practices of conduct and etiquette, of spatial separation and religious avoidance.   (Baines 1990b: 20)

In linking decorum with knowledge and hierarchy, that article addressed its legitimizing function as an institution or network of constraints. But the core of decorum is not about social separation, and Egyptian hierarchies and divisions appear to have been relatively fluid, at least in the third and second millennia BCE; Egypt was not like the hierarchical caste society of India analysed in Louis Dumont's classic work (1970). Parallels between features of decorum and restricted knowledge are important not only in terms of power relations but also because of the sacral character of a great deal of the knowledge in question. Decorum has much to do with enacting and representing the proper order of the world.

I first characterized decorum in terms of distinctions in iconography (1985c: 277–8; developed from Baines 1975). My focus was on interpreting iconographic patterns and finding reasons why some figures—personifications in the original case—are depicted only in specific areas, such as the base registers of walls, as well as why some indirect and metaphorical iconographies, especially of the king, are found mainly in subordinate or outer areas of decorated complexes. I identified comparable treatments of motifs both in the lowest-ranking areas of decoration and in others that are at least two levels above them in a hierarchy of meaning. In other cases, different motifs could occur within the same hierarchical level of decoration, but were incompatible with one another and so could not be placed together. There is thus a complex distribution of material within levels, between one level and another, and between non-contiguous levels. A related iconographic phenomenon, treated in the same study, is the emblematic mode of representation (cognate with emblematic personification: Baines 1985c: 41–63), in which a deity or a king is represented indirectly by an inanimate symbol with limbs attached, or a concept is 'personified' by adding limbs to the hieroglyph or emblem that signifies it. Emblematic figures are diagnostic for distinctions of decorum because, in addition to other functions, they make it possible for entities to be depicted in otherwise inappropriate contexts or for otherwise incompatible iconographic forms to be placed together.

These patterns, as well as others, suggested that the distinctions in question were not just observers' categories and that the actors saw the hierarchy of decoration as a system with a partly positional organization. These last findings, which have not been specifically discussed by later scholars, fit an interpretation of the hierarchies along quasi-linguistic or semiotic lines, so that relations among categories and levels can be seen as ordered 'syntactically'.

While I have not encountered any reason for abandoning those conclusions, the hierarchies of decoration, with their patterns of alternation, are prima facie unlikely to be closely analogous with some of the types of social distinction to which I later applied the term decorum (e.g. Baines 1999c). This difference in character may suggest that my original material, which belonged to a complex, tightly structured symbolic system—stricter in demarcations within unitary compositions than anything familiar from western art—could have been an unsuitable point of departure for approaching broader social issues. Yet this is not necessarily so. While my original context of pictorial representation and writing in 'monumental' contexts is a product of elites, and was focused around a core of deities and the king, it was formulated in the late Predynastic and Early Dynastic periods, during which those elites themselves commissioned and elaborated the social and artistic forms characteristic of Egyptian civilization. The primary social forms to which this secondary one related were in flux at the same time. Neither social nor pictorial and written forms were immutable, but after initial developments the latter two changed slowly, in phases of significant reformulation rather than progressively—which is not to gainsay the central significance of change and motivations toward it (Baines 1997: esp. 215–16; Schneider 2003a). Writing and pictorial representation were probably modelled on analogies with the now inaccessible social forms, integrally including deities in society, which they present at least in part, and the leading members of the society were the prime movers and innovators. Such forms were crucial to elite lives; their monumental analogies were no doubt comparably significant.

Symbolic contexts and their interpretation

Decorum is one means by which people negotiate relations among themselves, between themselves and the royal, and also between themselves and the divine—a connection that is largely presented as passing through the royal. Because so much that related to kings and deities was expressed through representational art, the study of decorum is in part a study of iconography and iconology.

The social forms which were constrained by decorum cannot be reconstructed in any detail, but they seem likely to have been strongly demarcated. The basic formulation of Egyptian iconography, in which only the king could be depicted in direct interaction with deities, separated the human radically from the divine, in a presentation that had meaning in terms of pictorial conventions but did not correspond to the reality of the cult, which was performed by non-royal priestly executants on cult images of different appearance from depictions of deities in temples. The separation of these sacralized images, not just from the world outside but also from most human sight and contact, rendered the depicted role of the king highly salient. From the beginning, this aspect of his position was reinforced through the visual assertion that the gods gave life only to him (e.g. Fig. 8), so that humanity was dependent on him for its dissemination.

Decorum integrates the architectural and pictorial presentation of the world into the context in which it is shown. As has been recognized since the 19th century and is stated explicitly in texts first memorably exploited by Maxence de Rochemonteix (1894 [1885]), architectural forms were cosmological, creating a perfect world for the deity to inhabit. Similar meanings attached to the form of cities and palaces (e.g. O'Connor 1989a; 1993; in preparation), royal and non-royal tombs (e.g. Kamrin 1999), as well as probably with the structure of houses—the last of these being a domain that bears such meanings in many societies (e.g. Tambiah 1970: 19–23; Bourdieu 1979: 133–53 [much reprinted]), and in Egypt most clearly does so in the reflexively designed Middle Kingdom house models of Meketre (Winlock 1955: pls. 9–12; see most recently Dorothea Arnold 2005). Differences between the various domains, all of which can convey similar meanings, exemplify principles of decorum: the identity of a structure's principal inhabitant or the category to which that human or divine person belonged, as well as the regulation of access to the structure, had as much influence on its decoration as did the cosmological notions which were centrally expressed in temples. Temples had ideological primacy because the gods were the ultimate focus of the system and of associated values.

It follows that the decorative system's coverage of royal contexts, such as palaces (of which examples are hardly known from before the New Kingdom), and beyond to non-royal monuments, operated in great measure through exclusion. In locations that were accessible to a wider range of people than were temples, the decoration could not include sacred matter. This principle had significant implications, for example in the exclusion of the king's original and most widespread official title of early times, the Horus name, from the decoration of non-royal tombs of the third millennium (Helck 1974a: 15–16; it occurred rather more widely in purely written contexts). That name was later largely superseded by the less symbolically loaded cartouche names, probably in part for reasons of decorum. Cartouches occur in a very wide range of contexts and on vast numbers of objects, whereas decorative usage of the Horus name were more limited. Since the form of the cartouche encloses the king's name in a protective, 'endless' knotted cord, part of its symbolic intent was probably to protect the name and demarcate it from any environment in which it was sited (compare Barta 1970b). In the period when cartouches were first used for the king's name, they were also depicted as protective amulets worn by people of the highest status, a practice that soon disappeared, probably in part in order to separate the royal symbol from others (Baines 2006b: 7–10). This is a historically traceable example of the kind of symbolic appropriation to the centre and to royalty that must have been widespread in the formative late predynastic period.

Sacred and profane

It is difficult to establish how decorum related to categories such as sacred and profane. The examples evoked above focus around deities and royalty, in an area where the sacred might be a dominant principle. In periods from which evidence is sufficient, rules of purity circumscribed religious action. Side entrances of temples were inscribed with a standard injunction to those who passed through to 'purify four times'. Addresses to the living entering the accessible parts of non-royal tombs—in order to make an offering and perhaps for such purposes as communicating with the deceased—similarly required them to be pure and subjected them to curses and retribution if they were not (Blumenthal 1991; Silverman 2000). These distinctions had moral dimensions. Rules of purity had a negative counterpart in the concept *bwt*, often rendered 'abomination', which was the opposite of order and purity (see studies by Paul John Frandsen, e.g. 1998; 2000: 12 n. 10; 2001). Those who stated their adherence to proper order declared that everything immoral, impure, or forbidden was *bwt* to them (compare Kadish 1978–9). *bwt* is attested principally in funerary literature, but relates to this-worldly as well as next-worldly concerns.

The terms just mentioned had a wider relation with maat (*m₃ꜥt*), the most distinctive Egyptian ideological concept, which encompassed sacred and secular, formal and moral, and is the topic of discourse in literary texts as well as the ultimate, summarizing ritual offering that was depicted as being presented to gods in temples (Teeter 1997; example linking several ethical domains: Fairman 1958). Jan Assmann, who has published the most extensive study of maat (1989; 1990), focuses on its positive and ethical aspects and on the social connectivity, as well as the mutual dependence of living and dead, which the concept fostered. While these aspects are vital, royal inscriptions often have less benign implications. Similarly, the Middle Kingdom Tale of the Eloquent Peasant, the literary text that focuses most strongly on maat, affirms its centrality, but the full force of its implications is voiced by the protagonist after he has been tortured by officials precisely in order to extract all his eloquence from him (Parkinson 2002: 169–74). Such (fictional) measures are justified because so much is at stake in the maintenance of right and order; the issues are more than just this-worldly or straightforwardly moral.

One reason for the importance of maat is the threatened state of order, which requires commitment to it from the king and from human society. When the king comes to the throne, as well as perpetually thereafter, he 'realizes order (maat, *m₃ꜥt*) and destroys disorder (*jzft*)' (Assmann 1970; 1995 [1983]: 20), reaffirming the proper state and wholeness of the cosmos. In some periods a real-world correlate for this ideological statement was that the king should mount a military campaign abroad at the beginning of his reign. Another possibility was that the same affirmation be accomplished through peremptory ritual action. A text that describes the accession of Amenhotep II (*c*.1427–1401) states that he 'bound together the heads' of foreign rulers, an action that preceded their ritual slaughter and is commonly represented on the outer walls of temples (Sethe 1907: 896, 11–14; translation in Burkhardt et al. 1984: 313 incorrect). The point here is not whether Amenhotep II ceremonially executed a group of foreigners to mark his accession and reaffirmation of order—which is possible but could be an ideological fiction—but that such reaffirmation was seen as including acts of violence against potential threats from without or within (compare e.g. Lafages 1992: 34–40 on the medieval and Renaissance French king). The commitment to order was not just focused on solidarity but also adversarial, while the social harmony and generational continuity emphasized by Assmann cannot be generalized beyond the elite, if only because evidence from the wider society is very sparse. As known to us, maat is an elite concept, just as decorum is an elite set of practices; maat may have been exploited as much to delimit and exclude as ethically to include the disadvantaged.

The strong demarcations reinforced by constraints of purity, as well as the emphasis on a hard-won order and harmony, fit well with the system of decorum. While these domains may not have been perceived as unitary (compare Frandsen 2000: 9–13), it is likely that they were mutually reinforcing.

Change

Decorum has a history. In the dynastic period, it changed markedly during some crucial phases of transition, but its conventions continued to operate until the end of Egyptian civilization. The example of the absence of the king's Horus name from Old Kingdom non-royal tombs, cited above, exemplifies how patterns developed. It would be wrong to explain those changes in terms of a single determining factor. Motivations for development may come from various directions, coinciding with considerations of decorum and operating through its framework, rather than being dominated by it. Thus, the exclusion of the Horus name parallels the scarcity of religious material of any type in Old Kingdom tombs. As Jochem Kahl notes (2003b), this practice of exclusion may not have been normal from the beginning because some 3rd dynasty material seems not to fit with it, but it became standard in the 4th dynasty. There is a gap in many types of iconographic evidence between dynasties 0 and 1 (see Ch. 13) and the 4th dynasty. During that period of about three centuries, principles of decorum may have been refined and rendered more stable.

While much of this little-known development can be analysed in terms of decorum—that is, in the establishment of domains and representation of meaning within and across them—other factors must have played a part. In a period culminating in the great 4th dynasty pyramids of Dahshur and Giza, when kings appropriated an unsurpassed proportion of symbolic and material resources to their own monuments, power relations surely contributed to the exclusion of almost everyone, briefly including the highest elite, from the use of more than minimal decoration in their tombs. Since tombs were one of the principal domains of display—the overwhelmingly dominant one in the accessible record until the later second millennium—such a restriction must have made an extremely strong statement, but perhaps not only one of exclusion. Peter der Manuelian (1998: 132–4) has valuably suggested that an aesthetic preference for plainness could have contributed to the direction of change in this period. The short-lived development of an almost completely abstract architectural style during the same two or three generations fits with his interpretation (see Ch. 14).

The reformulation of decorative rules and conventions, together with the elaboration of new architectural forms, from the end of the 4th dynasty to the early 5th may have favoured an understanding of distinctions between contexts and among iconographies as being explicitly rule-bound; decorum would then have been a major factor in the formulation and application of rules.

In the long term, conventions of decorum tended to weaken. But they were so much part of the civilization's forms that their disappearance would be an indicator of its demise. Changes in the rules during the New Kingdom, cited above, exemplify how decorum can usefully be drawn into the interpretation of material that has generally been seen in other terms. I cite only samples; relevant changes are fairly well known, but they have not been studied in detail.

In the early New Kingdom, deities began to be represented on non-royal stelae far more frequently than they had been before (earlier examples, many in special contexts or in the emblematic mode: Malaise 1981; 1984). Some non-royal tombs had images both of the living king (Radwan 1969), also hitherto shown as a name or emblematically, and of deities. Details demonstrate that the new practices pressed at the boundaries of compatibility. Thus, on 18th dynasty round-topped stelae deities are commonly depicted beneath the divine and royal marker of the winged disk, while non-royal individuals, who sometimes stand and offer before the deities, are beneath the more universally applicable *wedjat* eye, the protective whole eye of Horus (Fig. 1; see further e.g. Lacau 1909: nos. 34040, 34058–63, –65, –77, –89, –90, 34140, –70 [king]). The resultant compositions, which show a disk with a single wing, appear rather unbalanced, evidently in order to avoid placing a human figure under the disk. In a sense, these are pairs of half compositions rather than integrated single ones. An alternative treatment was to have a small winged disk with the human figures set outside the area covered by it (e.g. Lacau

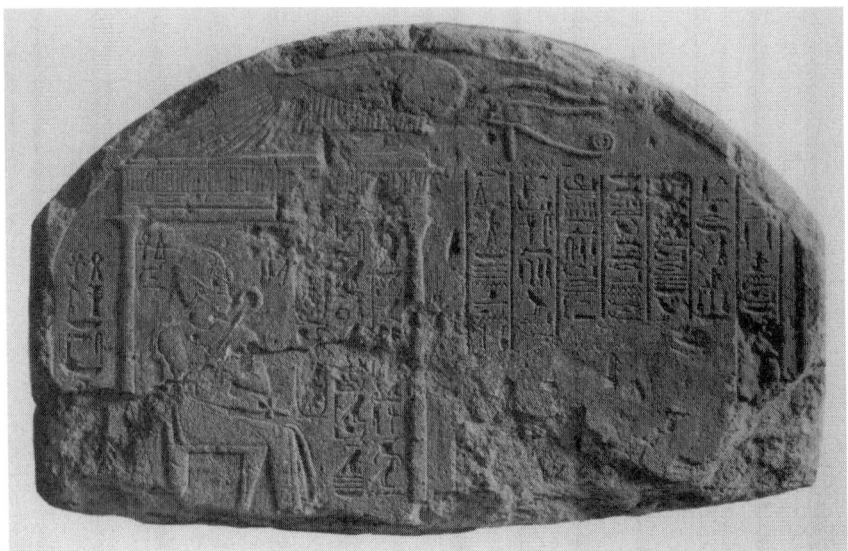

Fig. 1. Stela with hymn to the deified king Amenhotep II. Above the figure of the king in his baldachin is a half winged disk, and above the lost figure of the owner is a *wedjat* eye. Name of owner erased. 18th dynasty. Limestone. Height 52 cm, width 84 cm. From Abydos. Cairo, Egyptian Museum, CG 34170. After Lacau (1909: pl. lxii).

no. 34051). Near the end of the 18th dynasty, the disk with two wings began to be shown above figures of both gods and human beings (e.g. Lacau no. 34185).

In Theban non-royal tombs of the 18th dynasty, figures of deities occur in only a few contexts, notably in depictions of stelae that are generally sited at the ends of the transverse hall (Hermann 1940) and, for example, on lintels. Examples elsewhere in the tombs, or ones where the deity is represented directly rather than in a depiction of a depiction (such as a statue), are often mediated, so that the protagonist does not face the deity directly or, for example, the deity is inside a shrine and thus is clearly demarcated from the surroundings; this latter treatment is common also on stelae.

It might seem possible to interpret these conventions as showing relations between human beings and deities as they actually were, that is, to assume that until a relatively late date people could not approach the gods 'directly', and that when that became possible, they commissioned depictions of themselves performing cult actions. Most people, however, were in any case barred from approaching the physical vehicles of divine manifestation, because cult images were accessible only to those who were initiated as priests and were observing rules of purity (see Robins 2005). Moreover, the iconography of the deities does not depict cult images. So one must ask what status and what reality images like these addressed.

Here, I return to temple iconography. In temple relief and related contexts, the actions of humanity are hardly ever shown, while depictions of cult images of deities are also uncommon. Instead, reliefs in temple interiors show the king before figures of deities that are iconographic abstractions, in the sense that they correspond to no known conception of a deity's appearance, except that of statuary that was intended to be set up in spaces similar to the temple reliefs themselves, that is, in the courts and rooms of temples. Pictures of pictures of deities are relatively common in contexts such as the lunettes of Middle Kingdom non-royal stelae, where they function as enlarged hieroglyphs, interacting in emblematic groupings with royal names, another decorum-influenced mode of presentation (numerous examples in Simpson 1974; see also Morenz 1996: 82). These figures of deities often have an undifferentiated bodily form, which again depicts no particular cult image but is a generalized, archaizing convention common to a number of deities. So deities are visually distinguished from kings by conventionalized iconographies, while they are more absolutely separated from human beings. Yet texts show that people did not only perform the cult themselves but also vaunted their performance as a sign of social and religious privilege (e.g. Roccati 1982: 235).

The dominance of figures of the king in temple relief is as conventionalized and abstract as is the iconography of the gods. It is not a question, as is often asserted, of the king's delegating the practical performance of the cult to priests because he could not be everywhere at once. Rather, rules of decorum govern temple reliefs that depict human interaction with deities. These scenes present an abstract, idealized, cosmological space where the king is the sole hierarchically valid human protagonist because he is a being of a comparable order to the gods. While reliefs mention specific cult actions, these are often tokens of the generality of cult. The selection of actions for depiction in scenes and their ordering into sequences of actions could relate to the space where they were shown and could display relevant rituals, but such instances constitute a minority (see e.g. Arnold 1962, which has been perhaps unduly influential; compare Winter 1968: 13–17). Cases where more extensive information was added to the standard forms are rare before the later New Kingdom. The oldest surviving major example is the representation of episodes of the daily temple ritual in the chapels of the temple of Sety I at Abydos, chiefly through much longer text captions than are normal in temple relief (e.g. Barta 1973).

Thus, consideration of the domain of religious iconography, within which the 18th dynasty forms that show human owners of monuments offering before deities were introduced, does not support reading them as directly representing specific contexts or actions. Rather, changes in access to the display of symbols enabled non-royal owners to depict the king and deities in monumental contexts from which such material had been excluded and gradually to present themselves as protagonists in roles that had been represented exclusively through images of the king. Such changes are changes in decorum. Whether they were also changes in lived practice may never be known. While alterations in decorum were probably so significant as to count as major developments in themselves, they may well also have corresponded to developments in practice.

The pictorial forms and conventions of the revolutionary period of Akhenaten (the Amarna period, c.1350–1335 BCE) in the late 18th dynasty in one sense resacralized the divine by reducing images of the deity to the sun-disk with rays, worshipped only by the king, the queen, and their daughters (see e.g. Davies 1903–8; Freed, D'Auria, and Markowitz 1999). As in other periods, the focus on the deity and the king, as well as Akhenaten's claim in his hymn to the Aten to have exclusive knowledge of his deity, do not indicate whether the non-royal had access to sacred space and religious benefits. As Susanne Bickel has shown (2003), any royal exclusivity was at least in principle circumvented, so that people could address the Aten directly with their personal religious concerns. In the detail of Amarna iconography there are many reversals of existing conventions, in which the vertical ordering of decorative motifs is inverted. These appear to mark a deliberate change in decorum, because the subject matter of the conventions, such as the hieroglyphic group ꜥnḫ ḏdt wꜣs 'life, duration, and power', was ideologically crucial and related to central beliefs both before and during the Amarna period (Baines 1985c: 280 with addendum p. vii).

Because Amarna developments lasted only about fifteen years, no system of conventions crystallized, so that one can hardly study the artistic decorum of the period. Radical changes of subsequent decades, however, may have been triggered by the reversals of Amarna. The most striking development in the extant record is the near-complete sacralization of the decoration of non-royal tombs over about a century, during a time when display of religious matters increased in other domains, extending to texts recounting subjective religious experience on small monuments and in a few tombs that are generally characterized as exhibiting 'personal piety' (e.g. Assmann 1999 [1975]: 369–449). With exceptions such as the tomb of Ipy at Deir el-Medina (Davies 1927), the pictorial decoration of late New Kingdom tombs is if anything less 'personal' than that of earlier ones. The content focuses around relations of the protagonists with the deities who are depicted, as well as on their progress into the next world. The presentation of hitherto restricted religious content culminates in the 20th dynasty inscription, in tombs of leading priests, of texts belonging to the central cult of the sungod (e.g. Seele 1959) that otherwise hardly survive in monumental contexts.

This religious display has generally been read as documenting an increase in 'piety' in the later New Kingdom. While such a development is possible, access to deities and concern with them had been a benefit that was celebrated in biographical texts at least since the later Old Kingdom. More generally, religion is seen as a positive value in the majority of societies; the more religion the better. It is therefore problematic to see the increase in religious display in the late New Kingdom as documenting only a change in values, however much such a development may have contributed to the new patterns. I suggest that it is more plausible to interpret the new forms as at least in part exhibiting a change in decorum and rules of display.

The living context

I proposed above that the ultimate locus of meaning of decorum resided in hypothetical, now largely inaccessible features of lived practice. In studies of non-royal self-presentation and of kingship I have explored aspects of related phenomena that can be inferred from Early Dynastic and Old Kingdom texts and images (Baines 1999a). An example is the elaborate interplay between the king and his doctor Niankhsakhmet over the latter's request for a false door for his tomb (Baines 1999c: 21–5). Materials such as these show a high degree of convention and formality in modes of presentation, in the patterns of action to which they allude, and in the significance attributed to them (compare Baud and Farout 2001), supporting the hypothesis that distinctions of purity and access relating to temples and tombs may have been integrated into patterns of social life.

Such parallels do not help us to understand how far what is shown on the monuments resembles what happened in life. The iconography of clothing and of the human body is relevant here. The generally sparse clothing depicted is unlikely to relate to lived practice in any straightforward way, while discrepancies between what is depicted and rare finds of garments support the assumption that the matter is more complex. This domain seems to be a web of convention, in which garments are organized hierarchically, at least in part according to non-pictorial criteria (Baines in preparation-a). Much in the differentiation of clothing is hierarchical, while important aspects focus around the depiction of an idealized bodily form. Among Old Kingdom monuments, one feature that may be in part decorum-related is the scarcity of bodily ornament and the near-absence of amulets on all but a minority of tomb-owners (Baines 2006b). This case also exemplifies how multiple factors affected changes, because the choices involved were clearly also aesthetic, as well as having correlates in the wider material record.

A significant development in the iconography of clothing exemplifies problems of assessing how pictorial conventions are formulated and what meanings they convey. In the mid-18th dynasty, roughly from the reign of Amenhotep II onward (late 14th century BCE), fuller clothing began to be depicted more widely. Changes over a millennium led to the style of the 4th century BCE and later, when the most characteristic presentation of elite men was in heavy three-layer garment sets (Baines 2004b: 50–2, with refs.). These features have mostly been interpreted in terms of changing fashion, either in clothes worn or in those depicted. But since the relevant Late period monuments—tomb reliefs, and stelae or statuary to be placed in temples—were located in crucial contexts that were in principle the same as earlier, they too may obey conventions that would limit their 'realism'.

The initial stages of the developments just mentioned are broadly parallel in date to the religious changes sketched in the previous section. I suggest that this parallel is not coincidental. I posited that the appearance of non-royal religious activity in a wider range of contexts constitutes a change in rules of decorum. The same reasoning does not apply in a simple way to the iconography of dress: shifts in rules could have led to depictions that were closer to realities of clothing, or new depicted sets of clothing could have been analogous to changes in practice without corresponding closely to them, or both possibilities could be valid.

A clear example of how convention dominates the meaning of dress in a transitional period is in the Theban tomb (no. 85) of the military man Amenemhab and his wife Baki, again from the reign of Amenhotep II (Porter and Moss 1960: 170–5, to be published in full by Heike Guksch; cited from photographs kindly provided by the Metropolitan Museum of Art). The outer face of the doorway into the inner part of the tomb shows the owner and his wife Baki in multilayer garments, being offered to by their son, who is less heavily clad, perhaps marking both his subordinate status and his cult role (Fig. 2a; Porter and Moss no. 19). The lintel on the other side of the doorway bears a double scene of the couple offering to Osiris and the personified West (Fig. 2b). Here their clothing is far scantier, especially for Baki, who wears a dress with thin straps gathered below the breasts; the scene may be envisaged here as being set in the next world, but as often, it is impossible to be sure, and the idea of a specific setting may be inappropriate. The subordinate role of the son on the outside of the lintel also parallels that of Amenemhat on the inside, son to father and father to god (pointed out to me by Gay Robins).

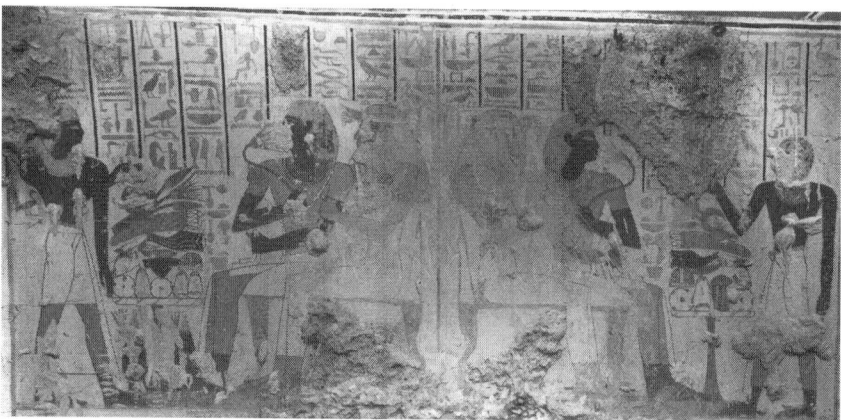

Fig. 2(a) Tomb of Amenemhab at Thebes (TT 85), lintel of entrance from transverse hall into long hall. 18th dynasty, reign of Amenhotep II. Metropolitan Museum of Art, Egyptian Expedition, negative T2576. Courtesy Metropolitan Museum of Art.

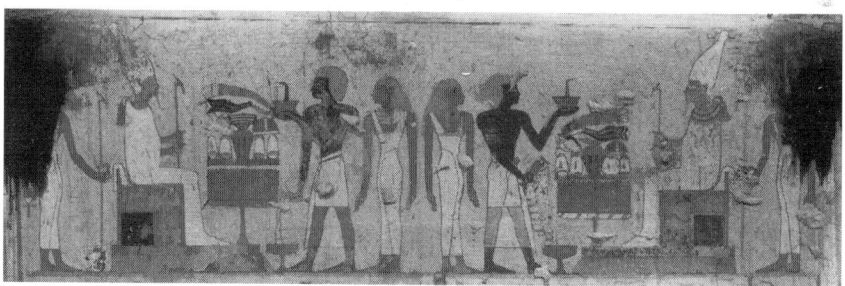

Fig. 2(b) Same, interior lintel of doorway. Metropolitan Museum of Art, Egyptian Expedition, negative T2599. Courtesy Metropolitan Museum of Art.

These aspects may be complementary, and I suggest that the outer scene is more 'secular' and public and the inner one more 'sacred'. The way sparser garments signify greater austerity and sacrality, which applies equally, for example, to Titian's *Sacred and profane love* (e.g. Burke 2001: 38–9), here contrasts with slightly later banquet scenes in Theban tombs, in which high-status women wear more clothing while servants and musical performers are largely nude, with various pointers demonstrating that the nudity has erotic meaning (the exact significance of which is uncertain). The banquets probably have a religious meaning, but in comparison with scenes of people before deities they are relatively 'secular'.

I do not claim that these changes in the treatment of dress relate only to decorum. Rather, their meaning resides within an iconographic tradition that was moulded in part by considerations of decorum. Whereas the formal exchanges presented in the texts of Niankhsakhmet may document real institutions, a more prudent understanding of the iconography of dress is in terms of changing pictorial conventions. Although the later forms appear to be closer to what may have been worn, they could run parallel to actual developments, rather than recording them.

More generally, these strands of change in New Kingdom and later conventions of decorum belong within a stepwise loosening of the system and broader dissemination of sacred content. I have cited counter-examples to such a pattern for the Old Kingdom and characterized them as appropriation to the centre. More generally, those who are subject to a system of which a significant purpose is restriction can be expected to chafe at its limitations, especially since much of the import of rules of decorum is the separation of matters that could be contiguous. Where no alternative existed, it should not be expected that people would wish to break the system down entirely. Decorum was so deeply embedded in the civilization that such an attempt would probably have been unthinkable except from the vantage point of another value system, such as Christianity in the early centuries CE. Moreover, Egyptian decorum, while perhaps unusually all-encompassing, is an instance of a phenomenon that can be paralleled in some form in many or most societies.

The power of rules of decorum consists to a large extent in their integration with high-cultural, aesthetic, and cosmological concerns, through which they resonate with elite commitment to a fragile order. Such connections are part of the legitimation of social inequality and seem intrinsic to civilizations in general. They simplify issues of allegiance in ways that rulers find valuable, while the intricacies of decorum complicate matters in a strongly aesthetic fashion. Egyptian elites may have had a stronger commitment to central values than some others and may have formulated and sacralized their centripetal focus more strongly. They also clothed their commitment in an aura of often bland celebration (Baines 1997), restricting the representation of the untoward to exteriors where it could be dominated and to special zones such as the representation of the underworld (e.g. Hornung 1990). Written literature too incorporated ambivalent themes (Parkinson 2002), probably building upon and extending specialized institutions that existed in oral form (Baines 1999c). The monumental record naturally exhibits a bias toward the positive, because of the large investment in its creation, the intended permanence of the results, and the function of many monuments to commemorate individuals, whether elites or rulers (in addition to deities). It is more clearly appropriate to confront imperfection and disturbances to order in ephemeral performances that are set off from everyday life, and by extension in written works that are in part lasting analogies for such institutions, than to perpetuate such issues in monuments.

CONCLUSION AND INTROIT

The two groups of chapters that follow this essay address Egyptian institutions, categories, and aspects of cognition that can be paralleled cross-culturally and are best studied within comparative frameworks of interpretation. The single most distinctive feature of the Egyptian material is that it derives from a civilization that was centralized in major periods and possessed elites who invested vast central resources in these phenomena; but such investment is by no means unique to Egypt.

The topics focused around literacy that are tackled under the heading 'Written culture' relate to civilizations, which constitute the societal form in which writing is mostly found. The problems of pictorial representation, colour terminology and classification, and stone as a significant material, which are addressed under the heading 'Visual culture', are common to a wider range of societies. They have a distinctive character in civilizations, both because of the same factor of major investment and because in Egypt long, explicit traditions developed particularly complex and reflexive cultural institutions (addressed in part in Ch. 7), while those same traditions make it possible to analyse patterns of change in more ways than can be done for most premodern societies. Another focus of the studies collected under 'Visual culture' is to discuss potential universals that have been widely debated for many different contexts and societies, notably in perceptual psychology (pictorial representation), anthropology, and linguistics (colour).

By contrast, the discussion of what 'art' is and how it relates to its social and intellectual setting has tended to be viewed in the West according to an overevolutionary, Eurocentric perspective, in which relevant institutions are said to have been transformed by aesthetic ideas developed especially since the 18th century and to be characteristic of modern and postmodern societies. Such a view is exemplified by the subtitle of Hans Belting's *Likeness and presence: a history of the image before the era of art* (1994), which alludes to the European later Middle Ages as a period. In part, the last chapter of this book (14) was begun as a response to such ideas, pursuing—as I do in several other chapters—a phenomenon for which explicit verbal evidence hardly survives but for which material evidence both exists in plenty and points toward a greater cultural salience and complexity than is often accepted for premodern times. I also exemplify that human classifications are not bounded by language, so that the absence of terminology in a society is only a very partial guide to that society's institutions, and thus also argue against unduly logocentric approaches (here I owe a debt to the as yet unpublished work of David Gimbel, 2002, on early Mesopotamia). Since 'art', in the broad sense of aesthetic motivations, activities, and products, is a human universal as much as or more than others considered as 'Visual culture', it too offers enormous potential to comparative research.

I suggest that decorum, which underlies a number of the themes I address, also has universal aspects, although its Egyptian forms are compellingly specific. In its lived context, decorum is an example of the social representation with which I began this discussion; evidence for it, however, derives from visual and verbal productions, the large majority of accessible examples of which are works of art. It is thus a 'total social fact' in the sense of Marcel Mauss (1954 [1950]). In presenting the above discussion of decorum as well as in engaging with the other themes of this book, I hope that analysis of the Egyptian instances of the phenomena may contribute to debates within and beyond the study of ancient Egypt. All these topics focus around institutions that both actors and observers see as vital for many human societies and crucial for civilizations.

Written culture

2

Literacy and ancient Egyptian society

1 INTRODUCTION

Literacy is an important, if often tacit, criterion according to which fields of study are categorized, and this corresponds to an evident reality. Societies completely pervaded by writing, such as our own, are very different from non-literate societies. In between these extremes comes a range of possibilities, some of which were placed by Talcott Parsons (1964: 347; 1966: 26–7), to whose ideas later work has referred, in an evolutionary sequence with literacy as a significant element in classification. Against this background, a study of literacy should seek to cross boundaries between disciplines. General works in the field have not been based on detailed studies within the areas they compare, because such studies are mostly lacking. A number of essays on 'traditional' literacy—mostly in a contemporary context, not in dead societies—were gathered by Jack Goody (1968), who has returned to the subject in *The domestication of the savage mind* (1977; compare review by Keith B. Basso, 1980). Here he has useful things to say about modes of analysis, which we take for granted, that are closely related to literacy.

Available discussions are mostly concerned with societies not closely comparable with ancient Egypt, while Egypt is in some ways comparable with non-literate societies. Yet it is necessary here to concentrate on the literacy of my title, for only vague and generalizing statements can be made about ancient Egyptian society as such. In comparison with what has been established for various ancient and oriental societies, and still more for early modern England (Schofield 1968; Cressy 1980), no precise results are available from Egypt; both my survey of the facts about literacy and my

Man NS 18 (1983) 572–99. Most references bearing dates after 1983 are additions of bibliography that do not affect the argument. See Chs. 5 and 6 for later revisions to the factual basis and interpretive consensus on some points covered in this chapter. Updatings here are sparing.
  References to Egyptian texts cite published translations where these are available; the editions of the originals can be found from there.

interpretations are tentative and impressionistic. Basically, I return to questions of stability and change and of the position of writing in society that Kathleen Gough studied in her articles on China and Kerala (1968a; 1968b) and Oswyn Murray considered in *Early Greece* (1980: 91–9). The topic is large and diffuse. In Egypt the largest dimension is temporal, from the latest predynastic period around 3000 BCE to the late Roman period, around 300 CE (Fig. 3).[1] It is necessary to refer to evidence from this entire range, but it is also vital to guard against an Olympian view.

This temporal span presents a fundamental problem. If, as is generally assumed, writing is in itself a stimulus to change, how is it institutionalized in a way that is nonetheless conducive to stability? Or is this the wrong question, because it takes too long a view of the subject and does not see it in terms of the actors? Only a few times in Egyptian history will the system have changed markedly in an average lifetime; in between, the uses of writing and its degree of penetration in society remained similar for very long periods.

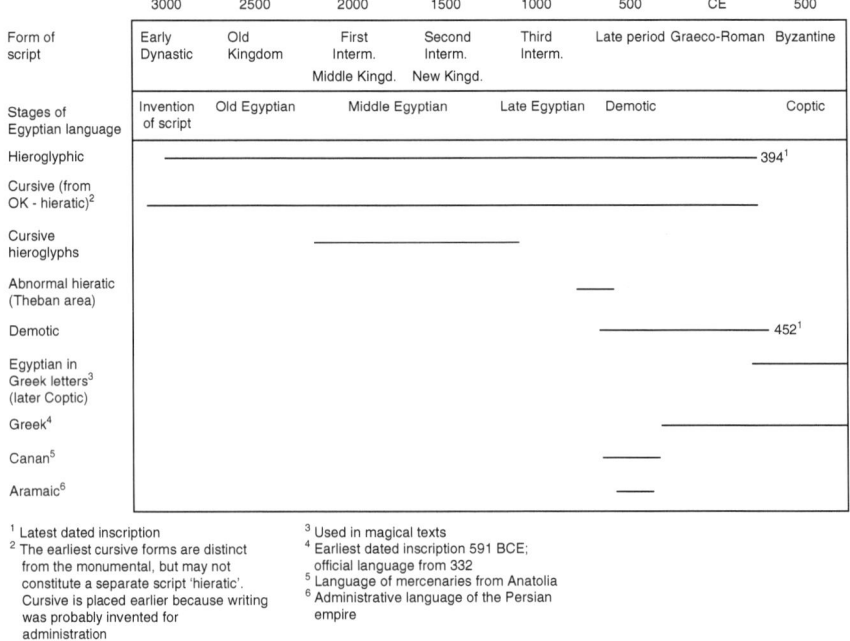

Fig. 3. Attestation of major scripts and languages in ancient Egypt. Only Egyptian and Greek are discussed in the text; the others are tabulated for completeness.

[1] I mostly omit material of the Graeco-Roman period, especially sources in Greek, which are the province of others. Nor do I discuss the principles of the script, which are basically the same in all its forms (Schenkel 1976). That question is tangential to my topic.

To state the matter thus is still to take a broader view than that of the actual users of writing, for whom the addition of a new genre of text to a restricted repertory could be very significant. Because the social background of any such development is very little known, one can often work only from observation of the uses of writing to hypotheses about the range of written genres, and then to the social context to which they belonged. Writing provides direct evidence from a very small proportion of the population, to whom discussion must be largely confined; but this does not necessarily prevent us from achieving some understanding of general developments related to writing, which in all periods except the earliest originated among the literate or among those close to them. Those chiefly responsible were probably the core elite, rather than the 'sub-elite' of scribes (see further Ch. 3 §1).

All these points imply that for most of the time both the literate and the non-literate scarcely perceived writing as a separate element in the social system. Despite its being a latecomer in social evolution, people did not look to a time when it was absent, except perhaps in myth. In almost all periods, the literate used writing for traditional purposes, which may be specifically literate, but are mostly better characterized under general headings such as administration or prestige, and those were activities common to literate and non-literate elites. The circumscription of writing is part of a society's definition of itself, which its members inherit, so that changes in writing often imply or reflect changes in society. Initially, this definition including writing related to the state which formed before writing appeared (see now Chs. 5 and 6). Writing may then change society, but it need not do so in a programme of expansion. More probably, it was devised in response to gaps perceived in the non-literate system.

In order to give a context for these observations, I describe the origins of writing in Egypt and the Near East, its institutional position, and its range of application. I then return to broader issues.

2 DESCRIPTION

2.1 Origins and development

The three transformations associated with the rise of civilization are the development of settled, agricultural communities—the 'Neolithic revolution'; the rise of urban society; and the appearance of complex, centralized states. According to the hypothesis of Denise Schmandt-Besserat (e.g. 1977; 1992), the Neolithic revolution also produced durable accounting systems which were the precursors of writing. These are attested in the Near East from around the eighth millennium BCE, being documented in a series of stages by clay counters of different shapes, figurines, and open (later sealed) containers, sometimes impressed with signs corresponding with their contents. 'Impressed tablets' of clay, the signs on which are the same as the counters used in the previous stage, come shortly before the invention of writing, also on clay tablets, in Mesopotamia—or conceivably Elam—in the late fourth millennium (Schmandt-Besserat 1981). No such tidy development can be demonstrated for Egypt, but some objects of the same general type have been found there and in Sudan (Schmandt-Besserat 1978; omitted from her subsequent presentations). This system of accounting, whose duration was at least as long as that of the writing systems that replaced it, suggests that administration had primacy in the origin of writing, a primacy that most must have acknowledged, but which may not fit the introduction of writing everywhere.[2] Just as writing and developments of it may not be necessary features of the types of society in which they occur, so accounting of this sort is not necessary to Neolithic society: most Neolithic societies appear to have lacked it.

Egyptian writing is first attested in the latest predynastic period, and in the 1st dynasty became a fairly stable system, difficult now to interpret and different from later forms. Most probably, the idea of writing was introduced indirectly by 'stimulus diffusion' from Mesopotamia (but see Ch. 5).[3] The system is fully Egyptian and no more than analogous with the Mesopotamian one, but it is significant that it evolved relatively rapidly. In Mesopotamia, the development of complex society and of the state went hand-in-hand with that of writing and lasted many centuries. In Egypt, complex society and the state formed much faster, before the introduction of writing (Schenkel 1983).

A script can be adequate for some accounting without writing continuous sentences. Because of such a discrepancy, the early administrative writing of Mesopotamia (Green 1981), Elam, and to a lesser extent Egypt, can be partially understood but cannot now be 'read' linguistically, although those who used the accounts will have read them in a language (Hawkins 1979; Nissen, Damerow, and Englund 1993). The influence of accounting on written language is so great that it ostensibly penetrates even the spoken form, producing

---

[2] Wolfgang Schenkel (1983) has an excellent discussion of theories of script origins. Other theories emphasize 'historical consciousness' and cult. On chronological grounds alone the former should be excluded. These issues are discussed at various points in Chs. 5 and 6, where more diverse approaches are introduced.

[3] This is a widespread guess. The discovery of late fourth millennium sites in Syria (Tells Habuba Kabira, Qannas, and Qraya) renders the idea more plausible, but no Egyptian objects have been found there (Kay Simpson, personal communication; Schmandt-Besserat 1981: 323–4).

constructions that depend on tables rather than conventional grammar. In the Egyptian Tale of the Two Brothers (c.1200 BCE), a handsome cowherd, asked how much he is carrying by the evil woman who wishes to seduce him, replies, 'Emmer: 3 sacks; Barley: 2 sacks; Total: 5' (Lichtheim 1976: 204). People may not really come to talk like this, but the influence of tabular presentation on written material involving numbers is profound (Edel 1955–64: §§385–409; Helck 1974a: 87–91). Here the original restriction of writing to tables, marks of ownership, and captions exerted a continuing influence.

Although there may have been cases, such as Aegean Linear B, where writing stayed at the stage of accounting, Egypt was not one of them. Almost from the beginning it served the two purposes of administration and monumental display, but for nearly half a millennium there is no evidence that continuous texts were written. Its non-textual use could not, however, fail to change the existing patterns of activity for which it was devised. In the case of accounting, the result was probably a vast proliferation in the amount done, allowing improved central control of economic activity, as well as a more precisely monitored distribution of royal largesse. Symptomatic of the frequency of writing is the invention within a century or so of the artificial medium of papyrus.[4] Papyrus, which was henceforth the principal writing material, as well as hypotheses about writings on papyrus and their implications, are my chief subject here. It must be borne in mind that only an infinitesimal proportion of what there was has survived: normal writing from administrative buildings or settlements is preserved only in rare cases where these were in the desert.

In the case of monumental display, the new medium of communication was an integral part of an ideologically important system I term decorum, which defines and ranks the fitness of pictorial and written material on monuments, their content, and their captions (see Prologue here). The system is visible on the earliest royal monuments and seems to be inseparable from the first development of writing. On the monuments, writing and pictorial representation are not separate; instead, there is a complex of representational conventions including that of writing (cf. Fischer 1977b: 3–4). Together, these conventions define the Egyptian presentation of the world and have widespread ramifications for the use of writing. Rigid though they are, they were not fixed for all time. Partly because of this flexibility, the system

---

[4] Papyrus from a very high official's tomb of the mid-1st dynasty: Emery (1938: 41 no. 432); later said to be two rolls: Emery (1961: 233–5)—the earlier statement is probably correct. The papyrus, which was in a fine inlaid box, was blank. It is more likely to have been meant for the tomb owner than for a scribal employee of his.

remained in operation as long as monuments continued to be created. The link between iconography and text is visible elsewhere in the later production of 'illustrated books';[5] these are perhaps the most characteristically Egyptian texts.

Later Egyptians, and Egyptologists, define the dynastic period, which began a generation or two after the invention of the system of decorum and perhaps a century after the first writing, as the beginning of history (for which there is no Egyptian word). Written records of the names of regnal years were introduced then. These 'annals' name the years by events that show a conception of the king's historical role comparable to that of later periods, but are expressed in caption-like phrases, not in consecutive texts.[6] Enumerative, chronological lists of them developed together with writing itself and came to have their own ideological purpose, but in origin they were probably administrative aids (see further Ch. 5). 'History' is thus set off from 'prehistory' by an ordering process analogous to the elaboration of decorum and related to accounting conventions, rather than by a specific event. 'History' does not imply a discursive, still less an analytical interest in the past, of which these brief year formulas are all that is accurately retained. Since decorum and writing define 'history', reflect state formation, and constitute the Egyptian presentation of the ordered world, writing acquired great prestige in relation to the country and its boundaries. No explicit comment on such matters is preserved, yet it is clear that Egypt, the largest centralized state of its time, was set off from its neighbours by its writing. The less powerful, closer neighbours were not literate, and powerful but distant states used a different script. The extent to which the script is identified with Egypt is illustrated by the fact that it was never adapted to writing other languages until a few forms were adopted in Sudan for the Meroitic alphabet in the 3rd century BCE (Shinnie 1967: 132–40); in principle it could write other languages.[7]

---

[5] Perhaps significantly, most of these refer to the next life, the depiction of which is not part of the original system of decorum. In chronological order, important compositions include: the Book of Two Ways (c.2000; Faulkner 1978: 127–89); New Kingdom underworld books (Piankoff 1954; Hornung 1984 [1972]); the Book of the Dead (Hornung 1979; Faulkner 1985); mythological papyri (Third Intermediate period; Piankoff 1957); 'Fayyum papyri' (Graeco-Roman: Tait 1977: no. 35; 2003b; Beinlich 1991).

[6] I intend to treat these issues in a future publication; initial discussion: Baines (2003b).

[7] There are insignificant exceptions from the New Kingdom, as well as an Aramaic text in demotic script that dates to the later first millennium BCE (Vleeming and Wesselius 1982; 1985; Nims and Steiner 1983; Steiner and Nims 1984; 1985). In various periods there were different, cumbrous ways of writing foreign words, termed either 'group writing' or 'syllabic orthography'. This situation is quite different from that of the multilingual cuneiform script. (Our alphabet may be derived ultimately from Egyptian writing, but the route of transmission is quite uncertain; see e.g. Zauzich 1980. The origin of the alphabet is not the same as the adoption of a complex script.)

In display, the system of decorum continued to betray its early origin through the lack of extensive texts. It reinforced the prestige of the sparse written word on the monuments. In later periods spaces for captions were often marked out in religious scenes but the captions themselves were not inscribed. In such cases, especially when iconography was enough to convey the meaning, writing could be dispensed with but was too important to be seen to be omitted (the craftsman might also be illiterate).

The early use of writing and the system of decorum exemplify a principle of scarcity. Writing was a centrally controlled facility in a state that was focused on its chief representative, the king, and became ever more highly centralized in its first few centuries. There might have been a strong stimulus to diffuse writing widely had it been necessary for technological purposes, but the most sophisticated crafts, as well as complex techniques such as surveying, will themselves have been organized by the state. For 'pure' administration, the number of literate people needed would be very small. The administrative significance of this scarcity is paralleled in the use of writing in display, which is the more potent for being restricted. The extreme sparsity of writing and decoration in non-royal tombs of the 4th dynasty, the most centralized period of all, is symptomatic of this manipulation of scarcity: one suspects that an attempt was made to stem the proliferation of a much improved system, because the plainest tombs are later than the first longer inscriptions.

The Graeco-Egyptian historian Manetho recorded that under Djoser (3rd dynasty) the culture hero Imhotep 'devoted attention to writing', which corresponds well with advances visible on the monuments of Djoser's time.[8] If these resulted from a definite reform—probably in monumental and administrative writing—this was a significant precursor of later reforms of writing and language; major changes were seldom gradual.

From the 3rd or 4th dynasty continuous texts were written,[9] and the script could in theory have been be used for almost any purpose for which we use writing, yet it was not so used. By the end of the Old Kingdom (c.2150 BCE), attested categories of text include copies of legal decrees and proceedings and important private contracts, which could be displayed in order to make their terms public and operative in perpetuity (Goedicke 1967; 1970); letters

---

[8] Translation of W. G. Waddell (1940: fragment 11, 12a–b). The name Imhotep is a modern emendation in the text, adopted by Waddell.

[9] Possible in principle from the beginning, because many Early Dynastic personal names form sentences (Kaplony 1963: I, 377–672); nonetheless, no text more than a sentence long is preserved. In Mesopotamia, the advent of continuous texts was marked by a decline in tabular presentation, the one compensating for the other (Green 1981; Nissen et al. 1993). In Egypt the monuments always remained 'tabular', as for a long period were public documents (Helck 1974a). This slower victory of language over layout probably related to the prominence of monuments and to decorum. See also Ch. 5.

(Posener-Kriéger 1973; Wente 1990: nos. 62–7, with royal letters inscribed in tombs at nos. 2–5); long religious and magical texts (chiefly the Pyramid Texts: e.g. Faulkner 1969); and 'biographical' inscriptions (compare Spiegel n.d. [1935]; examples: Lichtheim 1973: 15–27; 1988; Roccati 1982). The existence of technical writings can probably be inferred from other evidence, but it is unlikely that any purely literary texts were written down;[10] their oral prototypes are reflected in biographical inscriptions (Baines 1999c). No royal narrative inscription is known, even though the king's 'historical' role was fully defined. For him, the traditional mixture of relief and caption continued to be the norm, while the 'annals' referred to above became more detailed and in some captions recorded matters in sentence form; their function of dating had been lost because years were now identified numerically.

In the expansion of texts, biographical inscriptions are revealing, as well as perhaps reflecting a changing concept of the person. The general context is the search for permanence beyond the initial threshold of death—as Jan Assmann remarks (1983b), the most characteristically Egyptian concern of all. The earliest continuous text on the monuments (early 4th dynasty) appears to be largely legal in import (Helck 1972; see also Baines 1999a), while contemporaneous display materials were restricted to title strings and captions. Only gradually did ethical precepts (also related to the avoidance of litigation), general assertions of conformity to social norms, marks of royal favour, and the actions leading to royal favour come to be recorded, a progressive development that took over two hundred years.[11] The writing of continuous texts was probably a response to requirements of administration, law, and perhaps religion in contexts now lost, but the new possibilities came slowly to be exploited for different purposes. So long as the centralized Old Kingdom state survived, the development of genres seems to have been limited. The succeeding First Intermediate period shows a great broadening in the content of biographical texts, largely independent of royal sanction. Stone stelae, whose only known use in the Old Kingdom was for royal legal decrees, acquired a variety of functions for other people; they could contain biographical texts, suitably captioned commemorative pictures of families, or religious texts.

In the next major period of history, the Middle Kingdom, these changes were consolidated. Two developments are particularly significant. First, kings produced the equivalent of non-royal biographical texts in royal inscriptions

---

[10] Helck (1972), Lichtheim (1973: 5–8), and Assmann (1983b) argue for a later dating of texts ascribed to Old Kingdom authors.

[11] See Schott (1977). Recent studies show that this period was not quite so long; see Baud and Farout (2001).

recording outstanding events according to set schemata. Second, narrowly literary texts appear,[12] and include 'wisdom' texts (instructions on how to get on in society or to live a virtuous life); narrative tales, often with mythological overtones; hymns; and various texts less easily categorized. Medical, magical, mathematical, astronomical, and calendrical texts survive and are also 'literary' material,[13] which therefore constitutes the transmitted body of written high culture as a whole. What is very rare is the systematic treatment of topics; exceptions are a surgical treatise (Westendorf 1966; Bardinet 1995: 493–522; Allen 2005: 70–115) and onomastica—lists of categories which loosely order words as compendia of knowledge.[14] There is nothing popular about the literature.

Monuments of kings and non-royal individuals slowly came to bear more and more writing, often in places to which few had access; changes in decorum also slowly extended the pictorial repertory. Monumental inscriptions show a strong kinship with literary texts, indicating a common milieu and period of origin. Although the two groups are mostly separate, some texts appear both on the monuments and on papyrus or ostraca (potsherds and limestone flakes).

The range of literary texts expanded only slightly after the Middle Kingdom, which later had the status of a classical period. The chief development of the New Kingdom was the addition of superficially popular literary types—various genres of story told in simpler style than in Middle Kingdom texts and using folklore-type motifs, and love poems, which depart from the objectivizing tendencies of other genres. It is, however, uncertain whether such texts were more widely disseminated than their predecessors. This slow expansion, which is our best example of the force of writing as a self-sustaining stimulus to development, has two main features. First, the Old Kingdom use of writing, with its scarce currency of continuous texts, mostly in practical contexts, was superseded only after an extension of the circles of people who set up inscriptions and an increased use of texts for prestige and display. This need not correlate with an increased *rate* of literacy, but it does imply that those who created literature looked to a greater familiarity with texts among the literate. Second, the change followed transitional rather than stable

---

[12] Some texts are ascribed to the First Intermediate period (e.g. Lichtheim 1973: 97–109, 169–84), but, like those ascribed to the Old Kingdom, they could have been composed later.

[13] Shown chiefly by the grouping of texts in finds from the Middle Kingdom to the Roman period (e.g. Gardiner 1935; Smith and Tait 1984). Insofar as finds may attest to 'libraries', they are studied in detail by Burkard (1980).

[14] Gardiner (1947; cf. Goody 1977: 99–103); comparable text of the Graeco-Roman period: Osing (1998). From the latest periods there are some grammatical texts (Kaplony-Heckel 1974), mnemonic texts that appear to help the memorizing of an 'alphabetical' order of consonantal phonemes (Smith and Tait 1984: no. 27), and a herbal (Tait 1977: no. 20; 1991).

periods. Because writing and its uses were part of the system of decorum or extensions of it, the system as a whole had to change if elements within it were to change (for changes in pictorial decorum, see Baines 1985c: Excursus 2–3; Ch. 1 here). A possible corollary of this process is that in literary texts the Old Kingdom has some of the status of a golden age; tales are set in it and famous people of the time have instruction texts ascribed to them.

A notable feature of Egyptian texts is that the majority of those that use continuous syntax are written in a kind of metre.[15] This formalizes the stress patterns of the language into units of two or three stresses, and is in theory easy to learn and apply. Its principles could go back beyond written texts into oral culture, but the system we have is probably a product of dynastic times. The obsession with order it exemplifies is typically dynastic, and its maintenance to the end of Egyptian civilization is paralleled, for example, in the system of decorum; both are normative for the culture. Metrical forms can be extremely complex and ill-suited to long compositions.[16] This, too, suggests that written form is primary, because oral works tend to use simpler, open-ended patterns. The system of metre must nonetheless have antecedents in spoken form.

One familiar concept that developed still more slowly than continuous writing is that of a text itself. In non-literate cultures, traditional formulations will generally be unstable, but there can be an idea of canonical 'texts'. Both in Egypt and in Mesopotamia the recording of traditional continuous texts in set forms came late. In Mesopotamia 'lexical' lists occur in the second preserved period of writing (Uruk III, c.3000), before continuous texts were written (cf. Green 1981: 359–60); literary texts are not known until about 2500. In Egypt the earliest texts in this sense are the Pyramid Texts (from c.2350; Faulkner 1969). These were hidden in the royal burial apartments, and one cannot know how widely such semi-canonical material circulated or when it was fixed. What it does show is that important ritual texts, mainly intended for performance, were among the earliest to be written down, another instance of the principle of scarcity according to which only the most important matters were recorded at first. Religious matter of this sort was almost certainly written as soon as the writing system was sufficiently developed (see further Baines 2004c).

So far, the discussion has mostly related to a small minority of texts. Nothing precise can be said about the frequency of genres, and in any case

---

[15] Numerous publications by Gerhard Fecht (e.g. 1982, citing criticisms), whose views have been disputed (also by Burkard 1983) but I believe to be established beyond serious doubt in their essentials. See also Ch. 6.

[16] e.g. Fecht (1965: no. 9). Compare also the Tale of the Two Brothers, with its 'cantos' and 'cantiche' (Assmann 1977a: 3–5). For arguments for a greater significance for orality, see Ch. 6.

our sample is fatally biased toward the monumental and, among non-monumental sources, toward the literary. Administrative writing, which comprised the vast bulk, is very largely lost. Where it does survive, as at the elite workmen's village of Deir el-Medina (c.1300–1100), it dominates the record;[17] the same is true of demotic and of Greek papyri from Egypt.

Thus, the spread of uses of writing in Egypt—not its frequency of use or its diffusion through society—came very slowly to be comparable with that of the modern world. A possible important exception may be personal diary material. The spread is not a significant indicator of distinctions between literate societies. Despite the unity of Egyptian culture over its huge duration, it is necessary to break development into shorter periods, and to look to other factors at least as much as to writing itself, when analysing developments in its use.

2.2 Status and dissemination; forms of the script

As an administrative device and an element in monumental art, writing could be practised by technicians in these crafts, while the elite who benefited from them might not be literate. This was often true in the Middle Ages, but was probably never the case in Egypt. A 1st dynasty stone vase (Fig. 15) in the form of two hieroglyphs may write the name of its owner and/or allude to the life-giving properties of a libation poured from it, but in either case the user needed to know at least the meaning of these signs (Fischer 1972: 5–15). The titles 'scribe' and 'administrator of scribes' are found in this period and are applied to people of highest status.[18] In the 3rd dynasty the official Hezyre was depicted as a scribe in his wonderful mortuary reliefs (Wood 1978: pls. 1–2); elite status was completely identified with literacy (Janssen 1978: 224). According to later evidence, kings were literate.[19] Writing was presented as the goal of

---

[17] See Ch. 3 §4; Eyre (1980); McDowell (1999). On writing practice in the community, see Donker van Heel and Haring (2003). For ratios in the village, see Ch. 6, Appendix.

[18] Kaplony (1963: II, 1215, with refs.). Matters are complicated by such instances as a granite statue of a shipwright, also a member of the elite, holding his tools (Spencer 1980: no. 1), which implies that any high craftsmanship was worthy of display. Such iconography is absent from later periods. Early Dynastic inscriptions, including that with the name of the famous Imhotep, point in the same direction (cf. Kaplony 1963: I, 364–76). The prestige of crafts and of personal servants of the king seems to have yielded to that of bureaucrats as the latter proliferated, but proximity to the king continued to rank high. (See further Ch. 6, Appendix.)

[19] See Ch. 3 §2. Gods were preliterate; Thoth, the 'lord of divine words (hieroglyphs)' and Seshat are almost the only specifically literate deities. In the Tale of Horus and Seth, Thoth has a joke at the expense of his illiterate master, the sun god Re, by writing in a letter that Re is 'beloved of Thoth' (Lichtheim 1976: 215); only inferiors could be 'beloved' of superiors (see e.g. Simpson 1977).

fine speech. In two tales in which fine words are pronounced, the sayings are written down, in one on the king's instructions, in the other by the king himself.[20] There are similar implications in the framing stories of several other didactic texts and, more broadly, in the respect owed to famous writers of the past.[21] All this contrasts with Plato's views of the dangers of writing 1500 years later,[22] but in a sense reflects the scarcity of writing in Egypt. Plato was emphasizing the hazards of something relatively common.

From very early on, therefore, the social system centred on literate officials under the king, himself referred to as an 'office-holder' in later texts and probably so conceptualized much earlier. This bureaucratic idiom continued in less centralized periods. Like other features already discussed, it is part of the self-definition of Egypt. By the Middle Kingdom, this definition had expanded from being literate to being also literary.

Despite all this, the work of writing may be a chore. The highest officials had statues as scribes, but in reliefs they were not shown writing except in the symbolic scene of depicting the seasons (Sakkarah Expedition 1938: I, pls. 6–7; James and Apted 1953: 20, pl. 10); almost their only activity, as against 'observing' scenes and receiving reports and goods, is the prestigious symbolic pursuit of fishing and fowling. The work of writing is done by other, subordinate scribes (Piacentini 2002). Literacy is thus necessary for high status, but those who achieve that status delegate writing; a polite way of saying 'you' in a letter is 'your scribe', who, this implies, wrote or read out the message (Smither 1942: 16; Wente 1990: no. 67—both render 'you' in their translations; see also Ch. 6). The retention of scribe statues may reflect the conservatism of statuary, but they show status and perhaps learning and do not depict a specific scene (corpus: Scott 1989). These were not the only statues showing their owners, who displayed a variety of attributes, only one of which was literacy.

Evidence for teaching is at first sparse. By the late First Intermediate period there were schools, at which basic literacy was acquired, but their existence is uncertain for the Old Kingdom.[23] The more important part of a scribe's training seems to have been vocational, under a superior in an office.

---

[20] Lichtheim (1973: 172–3, 140). Literary texts cited from Lichtheim (1973) can be found, in much improved renderings, in Parkinson (1998).

[21] Lichtheim (1976: 175–8). For a cryptic allusion to the superiority of written over oral form, see Korostovtsev (1947: 161 line 7).

[22] Phaedrus (274c–275b). Note that this is projected onto Egypt. Theuth (the god of writing, Thoth) wishes to spread writing, but Thamous, the king or perhaps king of the gods, thinks it wise to restrict it.

[23] Brunner (1957: 10–13) stated that there were no Old Kingdom schools, but cited good evidence for the First Intermediate period; the institution could very well go back to the Old Kingdom.

Such early specialization would tend to diminish the common culture even of the literate,[24] except for the core elite; the same basic point is made in the modern world. In such a situation the identity of one's superior is important. The ideal of father and son in Old Kingdom tombs is of a father in the mature prime of life with a young son who is sometimes given a scribal title or scribal gear, and has thus started in a career, probably under his father as his amanuensis.[25] In keeping with this, a scribe's pupil is often called his 'child' (Brunner 1957: 10–11; for a later community, see Ch. 3 §4).

From the Old Kingdom on, selected children of various backgrounds were brought up with the royal sons (Feucht 1995: 266–304). Here, political factors are far more important than literacy, with education involving other activities as well as the imparting of values. Such education may sometimes have generated an inner group around a future king; the king also chose prominent officials, in the New Kingdom especially military ones, from among his close companions. Some people who were educated at court, however, had humbler offices in later life. Sons of foreign vassals were often included, subsequently becoming rulers back at home. In later periods reading and writing were learned by copying, and probably reciting,[26] classical literary texts. Afterwards, pupils progressed to writing 'miscellanies'—collections of practical and literary texts in the current written language—probably for individual pupil masters.[27]

A relatively secular picture of schooling emerges, in which the position of the specialist in knowledge—that is, in traditional texts—is uncertain. Such texts were, however, transmitted for millennia. From the late New Kingdom on, the locus of transmission was probably the 'house of life', a scriptorium attached to temples where traditional texts were both copied and studied (Gardiner 1938; Burkard 1980). This institution became more prominent when written and spoken language had diverged a long way, and its position in society will have narrowed access to elite culture further than previously, contributing to later images of Egypt as a land dominated by priests.

---

[24] For a 19th dynasty text that situates a school at which a high official was educated in the palace, see Wente (1985: 351); new treatment in Frood (in press).

[25] Pointed out to me by Yvonne Harpur, to whom I am most grateful for a mass of documentation; see e.g. Lepsius (n.d.-a: pl. 18).

[26] Cf. Goody and Watt (1968 [1963]: 42). Striking evidence for the universality of reading aloud in antiquity is St Augustine's statement (*Confessions* 6, III, 3) that St Ambrose read in silence because he was never alone, and perhaps in order to discourage bystanders from butting in. The practice is treated as entirely exceptional. In Egyptian the commonest word for 'to read' means 'to recite (šdj)' (Erman and Grapow 1930: 563–4). An Egyptian king is also said in a fictional work to have 'chanted the writings' when young, presumably while learning them in school, with others (Lichtheim 1973: 100–1). On silent reading in classical antiquity, see other evidence cited by Bernard Knox (1968); for the medieval period, see Saenger (1982; 1997).

[27] Lichtheim (1976: 167–78, selection with bibliography). Surprising numbers of these papyri are known, and they may have had a special value for their authors, being buried in their tombs; otherwise the papyri would not have survived. The most important text, the satirical letter of Hori, is a separate composition known from many manuscripts (Gardiner 1911; Fischer-Elfert 1986).

46   *Written culture*

This scarce distribution of high culture was reinforced by language and by the script. Almost no traces of dialect can be identified in texts from before the Graeco-Roman period, even though Egyptian was not a uniform language, as is clear both from stray allusions and from the multiple dialects of its successor, Coptic.[28] The standardized written form aided communication over the country, but must have been for many at best halfway to a foreign language, especially since phonetically, at least, written and spoken forms were far apart by the Middle Kingdom (Fig. 4);[29] such situations are of course common elsewhere. Egyptian is almost unique in its variety of script forms, and different forms are used for different contexts and types of text (Fig. 3; Table 1). The normal literate person was proficient in only one or two forms and types of text written in them. These complex discriminations, which form another parallel to the system of decorum, are ideologically important: hieroglyphs, the monumental but otherwise least widely used form of the script, were called 'god's words' (Erman and Grapow 1928: 180–181.6, esp. 181.2). Such discriminations, however, also limit the impact of writing. Yet the examples of Japan and Korea today show that a complex script with variants is not in itself a bar to widespread literacy. Most forms of the Egyptian script are not particularly difficult to learn.

A typically Egyptian manipulation of the script, in which the symbolism and potentially different values of the signs are exploited, could be used for more exclusive purposes. So long as all forms of the script remained mutually

Table 1. Forms of the script and types of material for which they were used; see also Table 2

hieroglyphic	monumental texts of all periods, including 'monumental' inscriptions on small objects; religious, legal, and historical texts in official and public locations; captions to reliefs and paintings
cursive hieroglyphic	official and major religious texts; scribal training
hieratic	business and administrative texts, c.2700–600 BCE; literary texts; private religious texts from c.2000; official and major religious texts from c.1050; some monumental inscriptions c.1050–700
demotic	business and administrative texts, c.650 BCE – 300 CE; religious and literary texts, primarily in the Graeco-Roman period, as well as some monumental inscriptions (the most important of these being trilingual with Greek and hieroglyphic)

[28] Roccati (1980: 80) proposes that the written language was essentially that of the court; plausible though this is, it is uncertain whether it is true in terms of dialect.

[29] More nuanced discussion, with valuable tabular presentation: Junge (1985). In a number of publications Pascal Vernus (e.g 1996) characterizes post-18th dynasty Classical/Middle Egyptian 'Egyptien de tradition', and this term has become widely accepted. On Late period Egyptian, see also Manuelian (1993).

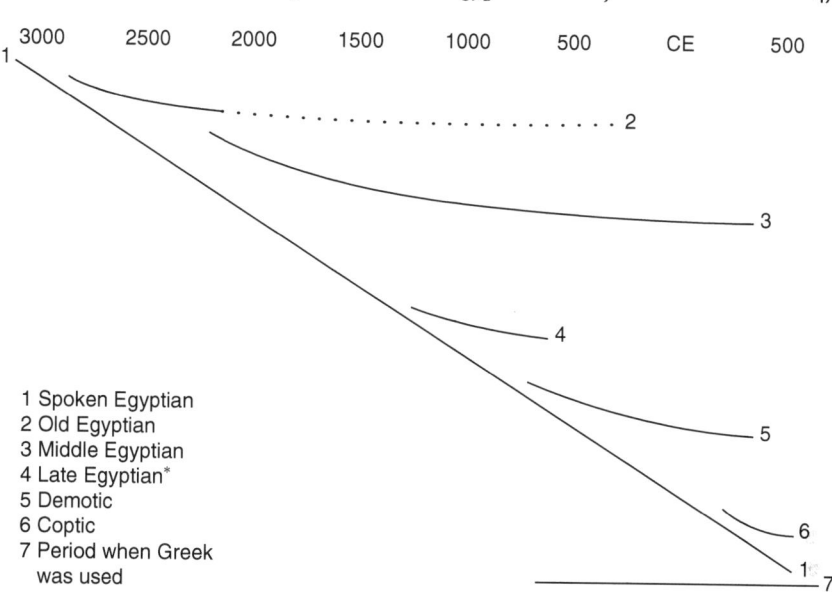

Fig. 4. Spoken and written Egyptian compared; adapted from Stricker (1944: 47 fig. 3).

convertible, these possibilities were realized mainly in cryptography, which occurs in funerary inscriptions from an early date, but is not prominent except on scarabs.[30] Their purpose was mostly to add meaning to short texts or interest to stereotyped formulas. With the invention of the demotic cursive script in the Late period, everyday writing ceased to be convertible into the monumental form, which required extra study. Hieroglyphs evolved from a few hundred signs to several thousand, including widespread cryptography; signs could also provide a simultaneous commentary on the texts they wrote. This system reached its peak in the Graeco-Roman period, when most of the country's writing was in Greek. The indigenous temples had a privileged position because the foreign rulers, themselves unable to read hieroglyphs, responded to a native pressure group and financed their construction and decoration (cf. Crawford (Thompson) 1980: 31–6). Few indigenous Egyptians could gain access to the temples or read the inscriptions, which were effectively answerable in detail only to the gods—an ideal situation for elaborating priestly knowledge.

[30] A related formal device is the 'crossword' inscription, mostly two hymns written vertically and horizontally with the same signs or sign groups; earliest example mid-18th dynasty, c.1360 BCE (Epigraphic Survey 1980: 35–6).

Among these variants, training in writing was mainly in the cursive, 'hieratic' script. Probably as early as the Middle Kingdom initial instruction was in the Book of Kemyt (Barta 1978; Wente 1990: 15–16), a short miscellany written in cursive hieroglyphs, the intermediate script used typically for religious texts. Fully cursive forms existed from the first and were further removed from monumental hieroglyphs than cursive hieroglyphs ever were (see also Ch. 5). Hieratic, which was learned after the Book of Kemyt, diverged more and more from hieroglyphs and tended itself to divide into business and literary forms. The average literate person could probably read little more in hieroglyphs than simple words and a few names; from the Old Kingdom onwards, hieroglyphic inscriptions contain mistranscriptions from hieratic drafts (e.g. Sethe 1933: 123 line 2, 133 line 12), perhaps made by stonemasons who could carve hieroglyphs but not read hieratic for its meaning. Many people probably knew hieroglyphs that were important symbols, and the same could be true of a group such as Menkheperre, the prenomen of Thutmose III ($c.$1479–1425), which became a good-luck charm and occurs on thousands of scarabs (Jaeger 1982). In general, however, knowledge of the monumental script will not have been widespread.

In any period, the range of use of script types and of stages of the language (Fig. 3; Table 1) formed a system; this is set out in Table 2 for the best-known periods, the late New Kingdom and the Graeco-Roman. In the latter, the full range was maintained despite the arrival of the simpler Greek. Five hundred years after Greek became the official language, the transfer of language and culture from script to script was beginning, when it was cut short by Christianity and the consequent irrelevance of the old culture.[31]

These systems are yet another example of the complex structures into which potentially fluid writing was pressed. Changes in script and written language did not occur gradually on their own, but concomitantly with other major change. Although the norm of writing shifted very slightly all the time, inconsistencies in writing and grammar show that it never kept pace with the spoken language, adaptation to which constituted reform (Fig. 4). As with other changes, ease of use and administration were evidently the chief aims of these measures, which were applied to documents before they became current for other purposes, if they ever did.[32] A significant exception here is the slight shift from Old Egyptian to 'classical' Middle Egyptian, which continued as the

---

[31] Some texts were translated into Greek: Roccati (1980: 82–3; add to his list the demotic legal code from Hermopolis: see Rea 1978: 30–8 no. 3285). The only texts known to be translated the other way, or composed for use in both languages, are public decrees of the Graeco-Roman period, such as the Decree of Memphis recorded on the Rosetta Stone (196 BCE; see Simpson 1996).

[32] Akhenaten ($c.$1350) modified the monumental language greatly along with his many other reforms, but probably not in advance of documents of the time.

Literacy and ancient Egyptian society 49

Table 2. *Distribution of Egyptian scripts and text genres in the late New Kingdom (c.1200 BCE) and the Graeco-Roman period*

	Late New Kingdom (c.1200 BCE)		Graeco-Roman[a]	
	script form	language form	script form	language form
monumental inscriptions	hieroglyphic	Classical Egyptian	hieroglyphic; some demotic	Classical Egyptian; Demotic
scribal training	cursive hieroglyphic	Classical Egyptian	demotic[b,c]	Demotic
official religious texts	cursive hieroglyphic	Classical Egyptian	hieroglyphic; hieratic; demotic	Classical Egyptian
literary texts; religious and magical texts for everyday use	hieratic[d]	Classical and Late Egyptian	demotic	Demotic
business and administration	hieratic[d]	Late Egyptian	demotic	Demotic

[a] Indigenous Egyptian literacy only; Greek was the predominant form of writing, but for a small proportion of the population.
[b] There must have been training for writing hieratic and hieroglyphic; these scripts were confined to priestly circles and the uppermost indigenous elite.
[c] Demotic is the name both of a script and of the stage of the Egyptian language which it normally writes. The demotic script was also used to write Classical Egyptian.
[d] Not the same forms. Administrative hieratic forms later developed into abnormal hieratic (known from c.700 BCE) and demotic (attested from c.650 BCE), while traditional hieratic was used for religious texts.

monumental form in most later periods; it was also used for religious and literary texts, new texts being written in it down to the Graeco-Roman period. Thus, although the script could write any sort of text and, I guess, could be written as rapidly as an alphabetic script,[33] its complexity and especially the tying of genre and stage of language to script form restricted its impact. Schooling was limited in extent and duration, and not by itself adequate for reading many types of text or phases of the language.

2.3 Numbers of literate; volume of paperwork; reading public

Various lines of reasoning suggest that in most periods not more than 1 per cent of the population were literate (Ch. 3 §1). If the population rose from one million (Old Kingdom) to 4.5 million (Graeco-Roman period, with Greeks the majority of the literate), the numbers of literate will have been

---

[33] Reading was probably slower, being limited also by reading aloud. It was desirable to know the likely content of a text before reading it, but this is true of handwritten material in much of the world. Classical languages must have been hard to read on account of the general absence of word breaks. See also Ch. 5.

10,000–50,000, but even the lower of these figures may be too high. The rate of literacy, the volume and range of written material, and the loquacity of texts tended to advance, but the increment was not steady. Literacy may have declined between the New Kingdom and the Graeco-Roman period, before rising in different circumstances. The general level of competence is relatively high; only occasionally is writing really deficient, mostly in contexts where the presence of signs is more important than what they say.

Several levels of literacy are possible: reading, of various degrees of competence; reading and the physical ability to write; reading and narrow composing ability, especially in accounting; reading and the full ability to compose texts; and, at the other extreme, the carving of signs with limited reading ability, which was probably the condition of many relief sculptors. There is little place for literate people who did not use their skills or for barely literate scribes, who could not have performed their administrative functions.[34]

Just as the core elite was identified with literacy, both it and the remainder of the scribal sub-elite were identified with administrative office. There is no evidence of scribes with careers separate from office. The Instruction of Khety, a text probably of the Middle Kingdom that glorifies the scribe's career at the expense of manual skills, mentions as his occupation only work in an office at the royal residence (Lichtheim 1973: 184–92; Jäger 2004). This is at least symbolically valid; such scribes were not amanuenses for hire, as a village scribe might be.[35] When someone needed an amanuensis, recourse was not always to a professional scribe, and the scribe did not make his basic living in this way. Ad hoc use of an acquaintance probably provided the normal access to writing for the non-literate; they would go to someone trustworthy. For the dynastic period statistics or generalizations about rates of literacy are devoid of the sense of everyday reality that could come from knowledge of the detail of such practices. Here Deir el-Medina forms an exception (Ch. 3 §4), while for the Roman period the masterly studies of Herbert C. Youtie (1973; 1981) on provincial literacy and its gradations to illiteracy, as seen primarily in official Greek documents, provide a most valuable analogy.[36]

---

[34] The range of objects with inscriptions increases, especially in the New Kingdom, with unquantifiable implications for writing among craftsmen and reading among patrons. This development is paralleled by the diminishing size of signs from the Old Kingdom on. Small scale is economical and rapid, but requires expertise in writer and reader. For the latest periods it is probably indicative of the small numbers who used native Egyptian writing.

[35] The Graeco-Roman period 'village scribe' was compulsorily appointed by the government and had government functions (Criscuolo 1978). He too might be illiterate and have to draw on other scribes to perform his functions (Youtie 1973).

[36] Frank Steinmann (1974) analyses valuable material for Christian Egypt, but his estimates of literacy are unsound in method and exaggerate the reality by an order of magnitude.

Central administration is one privileged area of literacy; religion is another. In these spheres we should expect both the greatest proliferation of documentary writing and the greatest interest in texts. The only large early body of documents comes from mortuary temples of 5th dynasty kings (Posener-Kriéger 1976; 1983; 1986; Verner 1979), and includes examples of minute record keeping that are paralleled in the Middle Kingdom pyramid town of Senwosret II.[37] Both were religious foundations near the royal residence, were relatively wealthy and tightly run, and had the resources for and interest in elaborate documentation. It is uncertain whether such things were typical for the whole country; the bureaucratic grip was probably strongest near the centre.[38]

Literacy was also necessary for the proper performance of ritual in major temples, which involved a lector priest, literally 'he who carries the festal (papyrus) roll'. The archetypal magical practitioner is the lector priest. The position of the higher ranking priests in the elite seems not to have been prominent in early periods—they were not then a professional class—but this changed later, and temples became repositories of written knowledge. For the Middle Kingdom, the high status of chief lector priests in literature may point to priestly involvement in it as an institution, but their prime role was as magicians.[39] Many reputed authors of didactic texts were viziers (highest officials of state); this could be a truer indicator of the focus of written culture, and the chief reading public for high culture was probably in these privileged areas. Finds of texts suggest that the learned had a general education and that interest in traditional texts went beyond the core elite, but probably included only a small proportion of the literate; a number in the hundreds would be enough to keep a tradition alive (the large numbers of garbled school copies are not relevant here). A number of literary texts come from tombs, which implies that their owners kept them for edification or for their role in the next life and attests indirectly to interest in them in this life. Allusions to literature occur in monumental inscriptions, although these were composed by few people. How far they quote and how far they use stock phrases is not clear (Grimal, 1980, is over-optimistic), and such material is not good evidence for a widespread ability to bring literary culture into play.

---

[37] Kaplony-Heckel (1971); Griffith (1898). Only a minority are published (see now Luft 1992; Collier and Quirke 2002). Jan Assmann remarks (personal communication) that in such institutions things were written that one could not easily have guessed, such as a monthly inventory of the entire moveable property of the temple.

[38] At frontiers government interest is again intense; see e.g. Smither (1945); Parkinson (1991b: 93–5 no. 30).

[39] In P Westcar an exceptionally wise magician is a 'free citizen (*nḏs*)' and the prowess of the chief lector priests is doubted (Lichtheim 1973: 217–18). This is surely a deliberate contrast with normal literary stereotypes.

Despite the small size of the body of literate people, there is no evidence that their numbers were deliberately restricted, and in at least one way ideology was expansionist. There was an ideal of efficiency in the form of the best man's being selected for a job irrespective of his origins. This runs counter to the notion that son succeeds father (see above), representing the royal or state view as against that of the individual. Some people claimed that they were of little status until the king advanced them.[40] In fact they were probably literate and well placed to start with, but the texts seek to imply that success is based on merit, and belong with a relatively fluid organization, at least of the elite. The Instruction of Khety may exaggerate in implying that there was a real choice between scribal and craft work, but it too points toward the ideas of mobility and reward for merit. Similarly, New Kingdom 'miscellany' texts contrast the meretricious attractions of the army with the security of a scribal career (e.g. Lichtheim 1976: 171–2). But for the 5th century BCE, Herodotus depicted a very different social order, in which:

The Egyptians are divided into seven classes. These are the priests; the warriors; the cowherds; the swineherds; the tradesmen; the interpreters; and the boatmen.[41]

However much the foreigner may misunderstand, such a society is not likely to encourage the passage into literacy of the non-literate. In earlier periods, both the embedding of conventions of writing in symbolic systems and the centralization of power will have stabilized literacy; the rather less centralized Late period, when writing and administration were focused on temples, may have been positively antagonistic to its spreading.

For the non-literate 99 per cent, a combination of great inequality of wealth and conditions of preservation has robbed us of almost all information about the effects of writing, except that it contributed to their impoverishment by facilitating the centralization of resources. An indication of this impoverishment is the virtual absence of cemeteries of the poor for the central Old Kingdom, in contrast with extensive finds for the predynastic and very early dynastic periods.[42] Less negatively, one might ask how far writing penetrated

---

[40] e.g. Dunham (1938: 4); Kitchen (1980: 283,10–284,4; given as an oracular selection). In the Amarna period far more radical claims for the king's role in advancement were made (cf. Assmann 1980: 9–14), but these need not be closely based on fact (contrast the argument of Rolf Krauss, 1983). An effective route for advance for Egyptians and foreigners was the army; there too only the literate rose far enough to be visible to us. One can imagine non-literate soldiers improving themselves more easily than peasants; this may have sharpened scribal polemics against the military.

[41] 2.164 (less concisely: Diodorus Siculus, 1.73–4, perhaps not of independent value). The Instruction of Khety is organized around Egyptian folk categories of occupational classes which cannot be matched with those of Herodotus; his could be authentic, but are clearly incomplete.

[42] Compare the remarks of William Y. Adams on Egypt and Nubia (1977: 135–41). These claims should be moderated a little; see additional notes to Ch. 4.

Literacy and ancient Egyptian society

beyond the literate in the form of administration, public proclamation of matters of general concern, and perhaps interchange of narrative and myth between elite and popular culture. These questions, difficult enough for early modern societies, are virtually impossible to answer for Egypt. I have suggested above that 'folk' elements in written literature should not necessarily be taken at face value.[43] Even so, some exchange between elite and others must be allowed for; there is little evidence of cultural heterogeneity between classes from before the Late period. In the minority Greek community, Youtie (1981: 198–9) believed that the mutual dependence of literate and non-literate was socially cohesive. For the larger body of Egyptians the matter might be very different. Available written sources cannot provide an answer here.

3 STABILITY AND CHANGE; COGNITIVE ASPECTS

3.1 Texts and their applications

Developments in written forms may help to define potential changes that could be related to writing. During the 3rd dynasty advances in writing, technology, and organization, including the construction of the first pyramids, came together. While these changes are not necessarily related causally, they probably attest to general social and cognitive development. The succeeding Old Kingdom is the first plateau of literate achievement and the earliest period in which extensive cognitive effects of writing could be expected. These could at best be studied only for the literate; even if there were effects in the wider society, they would be strongest among the literate.

The most significant cognitive achievement in connection with writing is the invention and elaboration of the script itself. Its devisers and improvers established principles of derivation (rebus, phonetic association), separated and ordered semantic classes, distinguished morphology and phonology, set up an 'alphabetical' order of initial consonants, and, in extreme cases, employed the highly abstract principle of acrophony. But all of this is deduced from the organization of writing; it was not formulated in such abstract terms.[44] Efficiency in reading and writing any language is enhanced by

---

[43] 'True' folk materials are extremely rare (for a possible source, see Guglielmi 1973). The Old Kingdom herdsman's song, which apparently alludes to a rare myth but is perfectly compatible with other beliefs, could perhaps be an early example (Kaplony 1969; Altenmüller 1973).

[44] I review the level of explicit analysis of language required for developing the script in Baines (2004a: 177–84).

familiarity, not by decomposing groups into constituent elements,[45] so that these insights were the more useful for being concealed from others. The practice of learning to read from whole phrases must have helped their concealment, and the perceptions of the inventors were probably confined to themselves and a few others.[46]

Types of texts that could have broader cognitive significance include astronomical (Neugebauer and Parker 1960–9), mathematical (Robins and Shute 1987), and medical compositions (Grapow 1954–73; Bardinet 1995). These relate to areas of achievement in calendars (e.g. Parker 1950; Spalinger 2001), surveying, mapping, and land measurement,[47] as well as medical practice, in all of which the Egyptians had advanced skills. The precise connection between texts and achievements, however, is not clear. The symbol of perfection in surveying and planning is the Great Pyramid of the 4th dynasty, which belongs near the beginning of the time of written texts; impressively accurate and well-aligned structures were also produced in non-literate Bronze Age western Europe. The Egyptian texts may have come after the practical achievements, perhaps codifying them more than leading to them, while such accomplishments as calendars (also of ritual significance) may be more striking than the texts (in this case astronomical ones). None of this is central to Egyptian ideology, nor does the mode of expression even of the 'scientific' surgical treatise mentioned above seem out of place in Egyptian texts in general. Here, 'science' referring to the relatively non-empirical might be more important than that of the empirical. Significant disharmonies that might point to change should rather be sought in ideologically central contexts. The exact, cognitively demanding tasks reviewed here are easily compartmentalized.

Cognitively interesting exploitation of written form has been seen by Goody (1977: esp. 74–98) in the use of tables and visual presentation, an almost prelinguistic use of writing (see note 9). The impact of these developments will be restricted by the limited character of what can be said in such forms—a list is best sited in a context of continuous text. Such a case is, however, provided by the Amduat, the 'Book of the hidden space', which presents the underworld in mixed text and picture, and is explicitly directed

---

[45] Especially true of demotic, which can only be read in groups; single words are often uninterpretable. It nonetheless constituted an advance in communication for those who mastered it.

[46] With time those who learned to read also learned a second, older language (see also Ch. 6); texts were translated from one stage of the language to another. Such cognitive challenges are available in any multilingual or diglossic context.

[47] Always cited as a great achievement and said to be required by the effects of the Nile inundation. Perhaps as significantly, the dimensions of Egypt and its provinces were measured by the 12th dynasty (Schlott-Schwab 1981).

toward 'knowledge' (Hornung 1984 [1972]: 59; for the dating—Middle or New Kingdom—see Wente 1982: 175–6). The text is also known as an 'abstract (sḥwj)' (with roughly that meaning in Egyptian: Hornung 1967), and there is a catalogue or index of the figures in it, presented in pictorial form with captions (Bucher 1932: pls. 14–22). Such secondary elaboration to extract information from a text looks forward to far later developments, but the material is remote indeed from practical realities. The same applies to the glossing and explication of religious texts, which was highly developed as early as the Middle Kingdom (Faulkner 1973: 262–9). This last example illustrates the authority of old texts, which are worth copying and commenting even if they are not understood (in this case the text cannot have been very old). Ever more texts could be gathered and reused, while few were discarded, although some were lost in breaks between periods or stages of the language. In art and in literature, 'archaism' can be seen repeatedly in different periods, and in the Late period became a comprehensive and eclectic phenomenon. Here writing brings a definite extension of the past, an increase of precision in exploiting it, and an active relationship with it (see Ch. 7). In a non-written culture, most such possibilities are absent, while for the written culture the very common conception of a past 'golden age' may be of the rule of the gods (Luft 1978; Lichtheim 1976: 197–9), of an absolute remote period (attested as early as the 4th dynasty[48]), or be specifically sited. Attitudes of this sort, legitimation mentioning earlier events or texts,[49] as well as cults of deified men or kings, enlarge on the definition of 'history' given above. They do not, however, constitute a discursive or analytic history, which implies a different kind of interest in events and processes and is rare in the world as a whole. Here Egypt was in a common intermediate position, aided by literacy but not transformed by it.

More specifically literate developments that can be imagined would include a more fully historical view of the past, as arose gradually in Greece, or the appearance of canonical sacred writings. In such cases writing and religious development are closely, but at first not causally, related. A religion with a canon and exegesis, such as Judaism, Christianity, or Islam, is a literate phenomenon, especially in its exegesis, which is of a different order from the glossing mentioned above.

Sacred writings are at one extreme of a range of possible modes of transmission of cultural materials that extends to the completely oral and

---

[48] Two royal fragments have formulas with 'since the beginning' (reign of Khufu) and 'antiquity' (perhaps of the same date: Goedicke 1971: nos. 6, 60). See also an early 5th dynasty text '[The like had] not been [done...] any [...] since the antiquity of the land' (Sethe 1933: 43,5). See further Ch. 7.

[49] e.g. Peet (1930: 41 [6,3–5]); Pieper (1929: 8); Epigraphic Survey (1980: 43, 45 n. v).

loosely structured. Here, sharp distinctions between oral (formulaic) and written (free, non-repetitive) are not visible in ancient Near Eastern material. Formulas, which are the basis of the Parry–Lord hypothesis of oral composition (e.g. Haymes 1973; Lord 2000 [1960], with introduction pp. vii–xxix; see also John D. Smith 1977; Finnegan 1981), are nearly as characteristic of written texts as of improvised poetry; in both they ease the process of composition and often the comprehension of the message, especially in letters and documents.

Egypt had neither oral epic nor scriptures, but it did come to have important texts transmitted in copies that were in principle accurate (see e.g. Kahl 1999). Among these, narrative or didactic literary texts have a well-defined structure and a non-'oral' style, although most religious texts are not narrative. Their composition by accumulation of epithets and phrases that do not form sentences looks relatively close to oral form—except that they contain little repetition (see e.g. Assmann 1999 [1975]). Their metrical form is complex, not simple and open-ended. Even so, copies more often have passages omitted or interpolated than is the case with narrowly literary texts; the less obvious thematic organization leads to a looser perception of text structure. Almost all could in principle be declaimed in rituals, so that a theoretical distinction in function from pure literature persisted. These are probably the most prestigious texts of all, so that it is significant for the effects of writing that they did not acquire a canonical form, and yet, despite their function, their form is far from an oral one.

Magical texts have a rather different position. Great emphasis was placed on age and on exact copying and performance,[50] and they could be legitimized by introductory matter or postscripts that emphasized the efficacy of a spell.[51] Writing could also be brought into play in other ways, as when a god issued a written oracle that was then used as an amulet (Edwards 1960), or a statue was covered in inscriptions over which libations were poured, the resulting infusion becoming a magical remedy (e.g. Lacau 1921–2). In such cases the symbolic power of writing is as a vehicle conveying the import of the spells. Similarly, defacing the monuments of those who fell from favour is a symbolic and perhaps magical practice.[52] The wholesale idealization of the monumental written and pictorial record—the two being inseparably linked

---

[50] The search for precision may have stimulated the first writing of Egyptian in Greek letters (2nd century CE). Christian Coptic is only indirectly related to this.

[51] For a cross-cultural collection of relevant usages of writing, see the excellent study of Giorgio Raimondo Cardona (1981).

[52] True also of the mutilating of hieroglyphs depicting living beings so that these could not come to life (Lacau 1913). This practice relates to rites performed on the deceased and dangers of the hereafter, areas that are not accessible to direct experience.

by decorum—is the reverse of the same phenomenon. These areas are vital because symbolically they order and interpret the world. Symbols are therefore manipulated, although the attitude toward them is a general human one, not specifically a literate one. This point is important because special beliefs about writing and pictorial representation, often posited for Egypt (e.g. Iversen 1975: 6), could affect a broader analysis of their position in society. No such special beliefs need be assumed.

Writing is significant in the more open-ended, socially important area of law, which was fundamental in the early extension of literacy and exemplifies the principle of scarcity. Apart from monumental versions of legal documents, Old Kingdom material includes written court proceedings (Sethe 1926; Strudwick 2005: 186–7 no. 103), while in later times one finds the use of documents as overriding evidence (Gaballa 1977: 23, 30), the citation of precedent and of statute (e.g. Janssen and Pestman 1968: 146, 156), and a law manual or code.[53] Elaborate record storage served legal institutions (see text in Lacau 1949). Legal matters could be 'published' in monumental form in a protected but accessible place. These practices mostly respond to needs that can be differently catered for in a non-literate society, but they acquired a notable rigour and generated new modes of intercourse, as in a subject's right to petition the king in writing (Ch. 3 §1). Within the same officially sanctioned context are also wills—technically deeds of delayed transfer—that define inheritance freely, not always according to set social patterns. Where there is no document, a loose rule of inheritance could lead to endless conflict. Wills of women are known, as well as ones that give women the right to decide on an inheritance (Janssen and Pestman 1968: 150–2). There was a high degree of legal autonomy for women in Egypt, hardly a product of literacy, still less a concomitant of it (it was largely ended under the Ptolemies); but at least among the wealthier, written safeguards buttressed it. Most such women were probably not themselves literate (Ch. 3 §3; Janssen 1960: 33), but that point is not relevant here.

3.2 Stability and change

In comparative studies, writing is often claimed to be necessary to the cohesion of large societies and to the promotion of their stability (e.g. Bloch 1968; Gough 1968a; 1968b), to enable them to exist above a certain territorial size (cautious statement of the negative corollary: Beattie 1971: 2–3), and to endure

---

[53] Mattha and Hughes (1975). A second law collection of the Ptolemaic period has since been identified: Lippert (2004).

beyond a certain length of time. While such constraints are flexible and writing may be a contributory factor in these cases, counter-examples can be found for any of them: the long-lived, barely literate civilization of the Indus valley; Teotihuacán and other Mesoamerican states, which used writing surprisingly little in view of its being invented there by the 6th century BCE;[54] the non-literate Inka empire (which had the *khipu*, a system of knotted cords, see Ch. 6); and various African kingdoms. In any case, the cultural stability of such civilizations and others compares ill with that of prehistory. Even if cultures are stable, their politics may not be: Egypt and Mesopotamia, with their similar writing systems and use of them, were also similar in their cultural stability, but politically Egypt was much the more stable. A priori, the case for correlating literacy and change looks more plausible, simply because social structures have changed faster since writing appeared than before, but similar counter-examples can be found for most of the causal correlations that have been proposed between writing and change.

The main points to retain here are the potentially self-sustaining character of writing and its possible role in coercion. In the world as a whole, writing has seldom come to be less used or to disappear completely, although events of that type are well attested. Increase in writing, however, is not automatic; rather, stimuli toward its proliferation come from other developments such as centralization, increased wealth, or attempts to monitor decreasing resources. The proliferation of written and artistic high culture among an elite is characteristically self-sustaining, although it operates in a different way from broader centralization and can come to be insulated from outside pressures. In coercion, writing can serve a symbolic system, as with the Old Kingdom bureaucratic hierarchy which organized the construction of the pyramids and focused on the king. It can also serve military force directly, but an army does not have to rely on written niceties. In the later periods in Egypt, when literacy was probably less widespread than before, the military became more important.

Apart from these possible proclivities of writing, it may be useful to summarize the material reviewed here, in order to present a model of some generality while attempting to avoid extremes of global interpretation. Writing is a symbolic system that passes through stages; its chief development is not progressive. That development can be characterized by the polarity of instrumentality on the one hand and expression or content on the other: as writing develops, its expressive possibilities increase. (Administrative

---

[54] See e.g. Bray (1979: 92). The earliest known Mesoamerican script is now *c.*900 BCE, from the Olmec site of Cascajal (Veracruz, Mexico); see Maria del Carmen Rodríguez Martínez et al., *Science* (15 September 2006) 1610–14.

functions are not specifically mentioned below after Stage I, but remain vital and continue to grow.) For my Stage IV, I continue by considering in more detail how far change may be related usefully to writing. An outline like this one refers to the elite and can hardly incorporate the perspective of the actors:

I. Invention and Early Dynastic period. The principles of instrumentality and scarcity predominate. Writing can assert, but in the absence of written sentences can hardly comment. It is confined to administration and display. The system must be adequate to its needs, for it endures some centuries without great change or loss.

II. 3rd dynasty and Old Kingdom. Writing is reformed so that its potential to record continuous language is realized. Rates of literacy probably rise. The concept of a text appears, but perhaps only for ritual, that is, instrumental matter. The importance of scarcity decreases, and expression and comment are possible, being manifest first in biographies, which become the least instrumental writings. Writing is now prominent in law (where the legal document, another type of text, develops) and religion, which are the points of departure for later developments. There may also be technical texts. Innovation is almost certainly confined to the core elite.

III. Middle Kingdom. Following stimuli of the decentralized First Intermediate period, the expressive aspect proliferates in the form of written literary texts. The formation of literature into a canon is the termination of the expressive development, which is complex, centripetal, and in its implications focused on the core elite. Royal inscriptions appear to follow non-royal stimuli, not to lead. The literary canon has an ideological role comparable to that of the system of decorum, but more complex and less instrumental.

IV. New Kingdom (18th dynasty to c.1350 BCE). Elite culture looks to a broader base, including folklore, while a new centripetal ethos tends to supersede one of more subjective personal achievement (Baines 1986). Writing proliferates further in volume and context, and in a variety of genres, but without decisive change from Stage III.

V. Third Intermediate period and later. This continues the later New Kingdom. Writing becomes more diverse in script forms but literacy is more restricted, specialized, and harder to acquire. Some secular genres in literature and iconography almost vanish. The amount of inscriptions in public places continues to increase until Roman times, which are also a period of great vitality in literature (Quack 2005).

Common to all these phases is the unquestioned maintenance of culture and writing. Changes are within the system and may realize more of its potential, may make it more efficient, or may restrict it, but the system is treated as a given (in myth, language and writing were invented in the beginning by the god Thoth). The only time when this may not be true is the New Kingdom, Stage IV. In summary, development in the 18th dynasty is toward greater cultural plurality. Change of this sort could, I suggest, form part of a 'cognitive revolution' such as occurred in archaic Greece, but in Egypt only its first signs are visible. In Greece, pluralization did not replace central symbols, whereas in Egypt it specifically affected those symbols. The cognitive change that is so striking in Greece is one aspect of more widespread social change. As in Egypt, so in Greece the focus of change was on very few people; in both cases a wider society that tolerated at least the initial stages was a necessary precondition. Egyptian change was within a very old written tradition, which it broadened to some extent. In Greece writing had a less fixed place in society, and textual forms were in process of development—although contemporaries may not have viewed these matters thus.[55]

The first phase of pluralization in Egypt is visible as much as anything in shifting cognitive styles, a potentially fruitful mixture of relativization, scepticism, dogmatism and observation. Relativization can, for example, be seen when a man says 'I was not taught by an old man; in future years I will be praised for my ability by those who will surpass(?) what I did.'[56] Another man describes how he devised a clock (Helck 1983: 110–12), and a third speaks in highly subjective terms of his physical exaltation in performing a dangerous feat and saving the king (Sethe 1907: 894, lines 10–15). Egyptians also cease to consider foreigners not to be 'human' like themselves and accepted them as beings of the created world (e.g. Lichtheim 1976: 98; Assmann 1999 [1975]: 220), a view enshrined visually in the uncertainly dated Book of Gates, a major underworld composition (Hornung 1984 [1972]: 234 fig. 32). These attitudes are more 'open' than 'closed', in the terminology of Robin Horton (1967: 155–6, following Karl Popper). In iconography, rules of decorum become notably looser, implying more individual access to deities than before and a less centripetal general ideology.[57] In art, there are developments toward unified composition and accommodation to the visual image in pictorial schemata (see Ch. 9 §§5–6). Finally, the religious reforms of Akhenaten (c.1350) constitute a drastic simplification of the previous interpretation of experience. In his later years, Akhenaten replaced the toleration of an

---

[55] On the relation between writing and the use of texts in archaic and classical Greece, see the essays collected by Harvey Yunis (2003b, especially the editor's introduction).

[56] Helck (1963: 59 n. 1, with ref.). This has a possible forerunner in the Instruction for Merikare (Lichtheim 1973: 103), but it is unique in a non-royal monumental text.

[57] This could be a matter of decorum and conventions of what could be depicted; see Ch. 1. For access to the god of Akhenaten, see Bickel (2003).

indefinite number of deities with the worship of the sun god alone, knowledge of whom was gained solely through Akhenaten. In his reign, representational art also developed faster and more radically than before, while the written language was brought much closer to the spoken. Some features of these changes continued in the following, Ramessid period (19th–20th dynasties). Other comparable elements occur first then, most notably love poems, the only literary texts to be primarily subjective in focus, and 'harpist's songs', used in conjunction with mortuary ceremonies, which question the value of preparation for death and the certainty of life after death, publicly juxtaposing the affirmation and the doubting of major values (Assmann 1977d; e.g. Lichtheim 1976: 115–16). A more important development, however, is the gradual replacement of the king by gods as the focal symbol of society (kings remained formally significant), and in parallel a new restriction of decorum in which secular themes come to be depicted and celebrated much more rarely. The most radical impulses of Akhenaten were diverted or negated in the ensuing reaction. (See now also Ch. 1, pp. 20–9.)

Comparison with archaic Greece shows clear parallels in the concurrence of new attitudes and artistic development, as in possible stimuli: new influx of wealth; foreign trade and travel; probably social change consequent on the other two. Religious change, however, was very different. What is also missing in Egypt is the abstract form of textual argument that arose in Greece. For Greece, plurality may have helped to formulate a mode of discourse that allowed different areas to be discussed in the same terms without necessary recourse to ultimate values. In Egypt no such mid-level metalanguage appeared; the 'revolution' of Akhenaten was couched in traditional terms and centred on traditional concerns.[58]

Radical reform under Akhenaten involved deliberate reversal of existing convention, which is most noticeable in temple decoration, and iconoclasm. Such shock tactics highlight problems of change and of analysis. The person or group of people who break widespread social forms so drastically may be eccentric or deranged, as Akhenaten could well have been. But the explanation of genius or of madness is at or beyond the limit of what we can do, so that the source of change, even when as clear as Akhenaten, can hardly be analysed; we may say what he built on, but scarcely why he did it. The tiny number who initiated developments would have been drawn from among the literate. One can, however, suggest possible reasons why changes were or were not accepted. Egypt, where change aborted, was monolithic, only partly urban, and had a storage economy. Greece, where it took hold, was scattered,

---

[58] See e.g. Hornung (1982a: 244–50); not necessarily a change of logic, as Hornung presents it (contrast Baines 1984a).

urban, monetized,[59] in comparison a new culture, and the status of writing in it was less well defined. In Egypt, an instant transformation of religion and much of central culture was attempted.

These contrasts do no more than suggest where one might look for an explanation. From the standpoint of an ancient Egyptian, the failure of change would probably not need explaining; its success in Greece would. Oswyn Murray, who has considered the matter for Greece (1980: 90–9), decides as I do that literacy is a necessary factor, but one among many, and Greece was a relatively 'open' society before writing spread widely in it.[60]

The hypothesis of plurality and relativization is compatible with a major role in these changes for writing that can record continuous texts, because of the increased temporal perspective, distance in communication, and diversity that it allows. Involvement with a changing textual tradition, such as the one 18th dynasty Egypt possessed, can encourage individual variation and response. The major part of the change brought by plurality is, however, as likely to affect the individual directly, and to be related to a changing conception of the person and view of the position of humanity in the cosmos. These were the developments that remained in Egypt in later periods, whereas most of the cognitive, or in art the representational, innovations disappeared again.

Literacy is a response more than a stimulus. It may be a necessary precondition for some social and cognitive change, but it does not cause such change. It enhances complex organization and may be necessary to complex societies above a certain large size, but it tends to be introduced after they have come into being. The initial impact of writing is a huge increase in and elaboration of memory. The literate can extend their communication in space and time, and their memory in compass and duration. But although they soon exploit such a skill for status, ritual, and law, they may not see what they do with it as different in kind from the use of similar skills in oral form— or, for administration, in counters, tokens, or knotted cords. As with any invention, full realization of its possibilities comes very slowly, if at all. Only in the modern age of institutionalized invention has this pattern altered markedly. Only late in its evolution in a society is writing likely to provide the reinforcement associated with rapid social and cognitive change.

---

[59] Because of the possibilities it creates in social intercourse and because of its being 'good to think with', money is a likely contributor to both social and cognitive change. These aspects are not discussed by Thomas Crump (1981).

[60] Compare the valuable remarks of F. W. Walbank (1981: 176–97) on the lack of fundamental development in the Hellenistic world.

3

Four notes on literacy

John Baines and Christopher Eyre

PRELIMINARY: CONTEXT AND DEFINITION OF LITERACY

The four studies that follow in this chapter address progressively more detailed questions in an attempt to model a context for literacy in Egypt and to suggest orders of magnitude for the numbers of literate. They are not intended to give any spurious sense of precision as to how many people were literate in ancient Egypt. Some social implications of the figures that we suggest for the percentage of literate are explored in Chapter 2.

Neither there nor in the following studies do we attempt a narrow definition of literacy. Our calculations of the proportion of the population that was literate relate not to all those who ever trained to become literate but to those who completed their training and then exercised a literate function in adult life; implications of this restriction should be apparent from the studies themselves (see also summary: Baines 1984b). Within that context, we define the literate, for the purposes of these studies and not as any absolute measure, as those who had been educated in the practices of reading and writing according to general Egyptian usage and standards of the period in which they lived. In other words, we use a relatively broad measure, but we focus on the professionally literate.

We assume that most of the literate used their literacy in their occupation. People of the highest status would not generally have needed to write themselves, but they partook in the civilization's literate high culture. Some others

---

Göttinger Miszellen 61 (1983) 65–96. This chapter was originally an offshoot of 'Literacy and ancient Egyptian society' (Ch. 2 here). It was published in a purely Egyptological journal, and we assumed considerable background knowledge in the reader, so that much material is more specialized than that presented in the other essays in this volume. For this republication I have added the short opening section and expanded the original text in places. The content, opinions, and evidence cited have hardly been changed, but I have added some more recent references, as well as a couple of qualifying statements in footnotes. Some further updates are offered in the Appendix to Ch. 6.

who had had a training for literacy may not have exercised it during later life because their occupation did not require it. We exclude such people from our calculations in the first of these studies, where we construct models in terms of positions that the literate held, rather than of those who acquired the relevant skills. We believe that the proportion of the literate who were not engaged in literate activity in later life—either practical or more broadly cultural—was small.

The definition of literacy given above is deliberately relative. What a full training taught people to do varied in different periods, as did the uses to which those who were trained applied what they had learned. The accomplishments involved may or may not have had significant cognitive implications; we do not investigate that question here (see briefly Ch. 2 §3). For earlier historical periods, it is not generally useful to make distinctions among the levels of literacy achieved by trained people, even though small amounts of pseudo-writing or incompetent writing are attested from then.

In any period, the applications of literacy varied from routine administrative tasks with little intellectual content to engagement with the most significant products of written high culture, some of which were subject to restrictions of secrecy (see e.g. Baines 1990b). At the lowest end, the literate may have used little of what their training taught them, or the training itself may have been limited. At the highest end, the maintenance of traditions and the creation and adaptation of materials for transmission no doubt engaged leading members of the inner elite. By the later Early Dynastic period, this activity became significant for the culture, but not necessarily for the society as a whole. This continued to be the case, in modest provincial towns in the Fayyum from which evidence survives, as late as the 3rd century CE, as was probably still more the case in at least some major centres.

Different levels of literacy should be related to the social position and occupation of the literate, not to their basic training. As we note below, examples of incompetent writing become more evident in the First Intermediate period and thereafter (late third millennium). From then on, it would be valuable to investigate levels of literacy in more detail.

1 WHAT PROPORTION OF THE POPULATION WAS LITERATE?

In order to ask what proportion of people were literate in ancient Egypt, it is desirable to have some sense of the size of the ancient population. While it might be possible to model a proportion in purely relative terms, by suggesting that a particular percentage of the people attested in our evidence should be considered to have been literate, in practice such an approach has serious drawbacks. No one has suggested that more than a minority of Egyptians could read and write. The literate are generally assumed to have belonged to the elite. Therefore to use only easily accessible evidence in studying the literate group would almost inevitably be to overestimate its size. In order to counter this bias in the ancient evidence, it is desirable to model population size and then to relate that model to a second model of the size of the literate group, approaching the question from at least two points of departure. As with many questions about ancient Egypt, cemeteries are the only source that provides a large enough database for study. Because social inequality is if anything accentuated in burial, this source is by no means neutral. In our analysis we attempt to take account of this bias.

Estimates of population size in antiquity are scarcely more than informed guesses. Since an estimate of the literate involves introducing an additional variable, this is still more true for the proportion of the literate. The following summary of material on population and model of numbers of literate should therefore be treated with all due reserve.

For the chief historical periods, the population estimates of Karl W. Butzer rise from 1.5 million for the central Old Kingdom to 3 million for the later New Kingdom, and 5 million for the 1st century CE (1976: 84–5 with fig. 13). Klaus Baer estimated the Ramessid population at 4.5 million 'with a very sizeable margin of error' (1962: 43–4), but his later figure of 2.4–3.6 million is closer to those of others (cited by Butzer 1976: 84–5 with fig. 13). Diodorus Siculus gave 7 million for times 'of old', continuing down to his own time.[1] The high figure of 7.5 million plus Alexandria, which Josephus put in the mouth of Herod the Great at the turn of the era (*Judaic War* 2.385), may well derive from Diodorus; it has been effectively discredited by Russell, who estimates 4.5 million for the same period.

Butzer's figures for earlier periods are based on the assumption that artificial irrigation, including 'sluice gates', was established by the 1st dynasty (1976: 107). If Wolfgang Schenkel (1978) and Erika Endesfelder (1979) are correct in proposing that artificial irrigation was not introduced until the First Intermediate period, one may need to reduce figures before the early second millennium. Throughout history, however, there may have been more people in the Delta than Butzer would allow (1976: 85 fig. 13): if Delta numbers

---

[1] 1.31.8, perhaps corrupt: Hopkins (1980: 313 n. 34); Josiah C. Russell's 3 million (1966: 70–1) from Diodorus (17.52.6) relates to a different passage, describing the first century BCE, that also gives the figure of 300,000 free men in Alexandria. More recent studies: Bagnall and Frier (1994); Scheidel (2001: 181–250); summary: Manning (2003: 47–9, with references).

need to be raised, this may compensate a little for lowering them elsewhere, because the limited character of irrigation would mean that the land was less productive than would otherwise have been the case. Here we use a minimum population figure of 1 million for the Old Kingdom; for later times even approximate percentages cannot be related to specific material evidence.

The central Old Kingdom—the 4th to 6th dynasties—is perhaps the most suitable period for assessing the proportion of the literate, because the necropoleis of the elite around Memphis have been relatively thoroughly explored and are less built over and destroyed than those of other epochs, so that they can be used, with reserve, for constructing a demographic model. In basing our calculations on these cemeteries, we deliberately give high figures in order to allow for gaps in the record.

Rather more than 1,000 inscribed tombs are known in the literature (figure supplied by Yvonne Harpur). If about a quarter of all the inscribed tombs that existed have been identified, perhaps a larger proportion for Giza and a smaller one for other sites (principally Abusir, Saqqara, and Dahshur), the total for the entire period would be of the order of 4,000 (to add the numbers of decorated provincial tombs would not greatly affect such round figures). Dynasties 4–6, to which almost all these tombs date, lasted about $110 + 140 + 180 = 430$ years (the figures for these dynasties vary in different reconstructions, but not enough to make a significant difference to our argument). On average, therefore, about 10 inscribed tombs would have been begun in a year, perhaps more in the 5th and early 6th dynasties than at other times.

Officials normally began to construct their tombs toward the peak of their careers (as Naguib Kanawati, 1981: 214, also believes). An argument from these figures must therefore proceed in two stages. We propose an average age-span of tomb builders of 30–45; 10 tombs per year should then be multiplied by 15—the number of years in the relevant range—to suggest the size of the tomb owning class, which is therefore around 150. These are, however, only a fraction of potential tomb owners. Although tombs present people at the peak of their careers, their owners vary widely in offices and attainments, so that they are probably representative of the upper elite as a whole, even if heavily weighted toward the highest status. Many more members of the elite, in varying degrees of advancement, would not have had tombs because they died before reaching tomb-building age. These were perhaps two thirds of potential owners; some might have had uninscribed tombs or shafts and burial chambers in the tombs of kinsmen or superiors (a few younger people no doubt had tombs; for more detailed argument, see also Excursus A). The total of the elite emerges as $150 + (150 \times 2) = 450$, which may be rounded to 500. We assume that all men in this class were literate (for women, see §3 below).

In decorated tombs there are pictures of scribes, often in large numbers, performing functions which the tomb-owners 'oversee' (full collection of material from around the capital: Piacentini 2002). The prevalence of scribes in the scenes probably exaggerates the reality for reasons of prestige, and also because this type of scene tends to come in the richer tombs. By contrast, much of reality is not shown at all, and only a limited selection of the contexts in which writing was used is represented. There is little overlap between tomb-owners and scribes depicted in different tombs (e.g. Wehemka as steward in Kaninisut: Junker 1934: 153 fig. 19; Sennuka in Nefer: Reisner 1942: pl. 30b; information provided by Yvonne Harpur). In other words, most scribes depicted in tomb scenes belong to different and inferior social categories to those of tomb owners, forming a literate sub-elite. One can only guess at the number of scribes who did not own inscribed tombs; we suggest ten per tomb owner. If 500 (maximum size of elite) is multiplied by 11 (10 sub-elite scribes each, plus the members of the elite themselves), 5,500 is the resultant figure for the professionally literate; for the sake of caution it may be approximately doubled to 10,000.

All this means that, at the highest estimate of literate administrators (10,000) and lowest population estimate (1 million), one per cent would have been literate in the Old Kingdom. We see no place for a high-ranking literate class of non-office-holders, as a cultured aristocracy might be in some societies (but see §§3–4 below). If the alternative figures of 5,000/1.5 million, suggested above, are used for the calculation, the proportion of literate comes to 0.33 per cent, which is also possible (compare 0.1 percent literati—a more restricted group—for the Hong Kong New Territories in the 19th century, cited by Jack Goody, 1968: 22). These figures are averages: the rate of literacy may have varied considerably during the Old Kingdom, perhaps rising from the 4th dynasty to the 6th.

Development of rates of literacy

The following paragraphs sketch a possible history of literacy rates and of the use of writing from the Old Kingdom onward.

In the Old Kingdom, writing was more parsimoniously used, at least on the monuments, than in later times. Within the period, the amount of writing and the length of texts increased markedly. Illustrations of this growth are the proliferation of Pyramid Texts between Wenis and Pepy II, as well as the steady growth in the length of biographical texts. The size of the hieroglyphic signs themselves tends to decrease, in a complementary development that enabled more text to be fitted into comparable spaces on the monuments (for the range of text types, see Ch. 2 §§2.1, 3.1). Almost all preserved writing is of reasonable calligraphic quality, which suggests that only professionals wrote (contrast the remarks of Oswyn Murray on early Greece, 1980: 95–6). Very few private documents, as against official administrative texts, are preserved, but this lack of material may be in part a matter of chance.

During the First Intermediate period the general competence of writing declined, sometimes to a notable extent (e.g. on some coffins from Nag el-Deir, as Edward Brovarski notes, personal communication), and there was a slight broadening of the social categories of people owning inscriptions (e.g. Gebelein Nubian mercenaries: Fischer 1961). Some of these people may have been socially comparable with dependants in Old Kingdom tombs. This broadening does not seem to have been reversed in the Middle Kingdom, from which one or two inscriptions of artisans, a category missing since the Early Dynastic period, are found (e.g. Ward 1977), as well as stelae that are so vestigial as to be mistakable for ephemeral ostraca (O'Connor 1969: 33; these are forerunners of votive figured ostraca from Deir el-Medina and the Valley of the Kings, e.g. Peterson 1973: 19–20; examples scattered through Andreu 2002). There is a proliferation of the genres of written material preserved and of the numbers of objects bearing inscriptions. It does not necessarily follow from this that more people could read and write than in the Old Kingdom. Although it seems likely that more were literate, the pattern of development also exhibits a more intensive exploitation of the medium of writing that is manifest, for example, in the increased range of genres among written texts.

Patterns of development are difficult to estimate for the New Kingdom. For the 18th dynasty, the same general argument from elite cemetery size to size of elite could be made as for the Old Kingdom, but the period was never quite so centralized, and the archaeological record is much more uncertain. The number of Theban tombs preserved and the extent of the New Kingdom necropolis at Memphis do not, however, suggest a great increase in the size of the elite, whatever other factors may be introduced into the argument. The material also has to be set against a population that could have been significantly larger than that of the Old Kingdom, as is suggested by the greater range of undertakings attested from the period and the denser record of material culture. The amount and range of inscribed material continued to increase; the tendency to use more and more of available surfaces for writing probably reached its peak much later, in the Late or the Graeco-Roman period. (For Deir el-Medina, see §4 below.)

The decentralized Third Intermediate period, from which very few administrative documents are preserved, almost certainly coincided with a decrease in population (Butzer 1976: 85 fig. 13—perhaps not enough of a dip). Literacy may have fallen faster than population, being disfavoured by the close association of administration and high culture with temples, the growing distance between spoken and written language, and the differentiation of script types with the emergence of abnormal hieratic in the south, as well as probably forerunners to demotic in the north. All these tendencies, which made writing ever more specialized, continued in the Late period, although renewed centralization and the wide—but slow—dissemination of demotic countered them. Demotic also brought the final separation of everyday and monumental scripts, the transformation of hieratic into a purely literary and religious form, and a decline in the knowledge of both hieroglyphic and hieratic, because moving from one script to another was no longer a matter of transposition but involved a different mode of writing, as well as a different form of written language (for more detailed arguments, see Houston, Baines, and Cooper 2003).

For the Late period, the concentration of enormous wealth in the hands of a few people, at least in the Theban area as shown by vast tombs such as those of Montuemhat (TT 34) and Petamenope (TT 33), which are larger than non-royal tombs of previous periods, makes it even harder to assess the size of the literate group than earlier (Porter and Moss 1960: 50–61 nos. 33, 34). There are, however, no clear grounds for proposing a higher rate of literacy than in the chief earlier periods. Developments of the Graeco-Roman period kept most of those who wrote demotic at a relatively low social level because Greek was the politically dominant script and language. The estimate of Karl-Theodor Zauzich, that demotic literacy was less widespread than that of earlier times, seems plausible (1968: 1; his standard of comparison is not very clear).

The overall rate of literacy in the Graeco-Roman period was almost certainly higher than before. The vast amount of preserved papyrus speaks in favour of this, especially since none has been found at the capital, Alexandria. Find circumstances in the Fayyum and Middle Egypt are exceptionally favourable, and the quantity of demotic papyri is large, but the overwhelming proportion is in Greek.[2] Greeks and other foreigners will have been a small proportion of the population, perhaps slightly over 0.5 million (more or less evenly divided between Alexandria and elsewhere) out of 4.5 million (Russell 1966: 71), that is, rather over 10 per cent.[3] Even if demotic literacy included less than 0.5 per cent of the indigenous population, there are ample numbers

---

[2] See the old estimate of Claire Préaux of accessible numbers of 30,000 Greek to fewer than 2,000 demotic papyri (1943: 152; cited by Walbank 1981: 25); the figures need updating, but the ratio may be valid.

[3] This statement distinguishes too sharply between the different social groups, several of which would hardly have been 'foreigners' after the 3rd century BCE (see e.g. Baines 2004b, with references). Nonetheless, the ratios given are reasonable.

among the foreigners for a significantly higher total rate of literacy than in the Old, Middle, and New Kingdoms.[4]

Other approaches to modelling the penetration of literacy

We have set out one possible approach to estimating the numbers of literate. It is worth mentioning some others, of which we owe the second (B) to the late Klaus Baer (personal communication); all point in the same general direction.

(A) If the 1 per cent literacy rate (our highest estimate) is modelled at a local level, it implies one scribe per 20–30 active adult males. This might correspond to one or two literate administrators in a village community, which seems a workable number.[5] A relatively high proportion of the literate would, however, be concentrated around the residence and other administrative centres, so that literacy might be still more thinly spread in remote areas, sometimes represented only by sporadic visits of officials from distant places. Illiteracy could also occur among officials: in the Roman period the 'village scribe' Petaus, who administered a relatively large area in the south-east Fayyum, had at least eleven people writing for him, but he was not himself literate (Youtie 1973: 621; for the office, see Criscuolo 1978). For the dynastic period, comparable figures of scribes in local areas would probably have been lower.

(B) Very few documents give the everyday flavour of administration on a personal level, the best being perhaps the late Ramessid letters (Wente 1967; 1990: 171–204). Some of these concern relations between Payankh, the general and high priest of Amun, and one of the most powerful men at the end of the 20th dynasty, and the necropolis scribes Thutmose and Butehamun (list: Wente 1967: 16–17). These do not show much social distance between the various parties—in somewhat shady dealings that might foster a mutual sense of belonging—and thus seem appropriate to a very small ruling group. The point is reinforced by the difference in status between Payankh and the scribes: he involved minor people in his significant affairs. In a more official

---

[4] For detail, see Youtie (1973; 1981). The impression is one of relatively widespread but still 'restricted' literacy in Greek; the distinction between 'indigenous' and 'foreign' tends to break down in the Roman period. For another statistically-based approach, suggesting a generally low rate of literacy in Roman Egypt and in the Roman empire as a whole, see Duncan-Jones (1977; 1979).

[5] Compare the literacy rate of 1.6 per cent in the 13th–14th century in the village of Montaillou (French eastern Pyrenees): Le Roy Ladurie (1975: 358 n. 2; in general 345–76; English edn., 1980: 235, 239 with n. 1).

context, the people of Deir el-Medina were visited personally by the vizier, who read the accession decree of Ramesses V out to them and distributed rations (Černý and Gardiner 1957: pl. 68:1). Since the accession involved beginning the construction of a new royal tomb, this visit is not typical for state institutions in general.

Another way of illustrating the size of the elite is to model the range of acquaintance of its members on the basis of the numbers proposed for the Old Kingdom. Among a group of 500 people, whose composition changed not more than 10 per cent in any year (an assumption that is necessary to our figures, because on average members would have belonged to the elite for 10 or more years), those in the middle ranks could know almost all members, while those at the head of any branch would know all others at the top, as well as the identity of all their own subordinates.

The right of a subject to petition the king or appear before him in person may also be considered. Examples are contained by implication in the Instruction for the Vizier (e.g. Davies 1943: 86; detailed study: van den Boorn 1988), in P Rylands 9, a petition addressed to a leading official of the Persian administration (Griffith 1909; Vittmann 1998), or in the archive of Hor, who drafted a petition to Ptolemy VI Philometor (Ray 1976: 122–3, 126–7; perhaps also a Macedonian custom, see e.g. Tarn 1948: 127). One text from Deir el-Medina states that the officials, or perhaps all employees, swore in their oaths of loyalty to Pharaoh that they would report abuses, presumably to the highest authority (Gardiner 1948: 57, lines 6–10), while in P Salt 124, a late New Kingdom complaint from Deir el-Medina, the author says that he '[reported?]' a theft by the foreman Paneb, as well as denouncing the vizier to 'Mose' (King Amenmesse?) and having him punished (Černý 1929: 244–6). Such statements could be fabrications, and any material of this sort may reflect ideal more than reality. The likely find circumstances and/or the physical nature of all preserved documents of this type show that these particular manuscripts were not sent to their addressees, whether or not other copies did reach them (e.g. Wente 1961; 1980), so that they may record aspirations rather than communication that took place in reality. This is clearly the case with the cuneiform letters of the vassal ruler Rib-Adda of Byblos to the king of Egypt (Liverani 2004 [1974]): although his correspondence did reach the royal offices, he sometimes received replies, which may not have been dictated by the king himself, such as 'you write more than all the other vassals' or 'why did you write?' (Liverani 1979: 10–11). In the much larger context of the Roman empire, communications from subjects to the ruler were again by no means necessarily answered (compare Millar 1977: esp. p. xi).

(C) Appeals to the living, which were inscribed on tombs and tomb stelae from the Old Kingdom onward, include requests to those who saw them to read out offering formulas. The detail of these texts might give some indication of who could be expected to read them. Some are in principle destined for everyone. Thus, one addresses 'all people, all scribes, all wise men, all free citizens (nḏs), all poor men (? twꜣ)' (Sethe 1928a: 88, lines 1–2). The widest category of all, the 'living on earth (ꜥnḫw tpjw tꜣ)' or 'anyone (rmṯw nbw)', occurs already in the Old Kingdom (Sainte Fare Garnot 1938: 24 and passim). More commonly, however, priestly personnel and scribes are singled out, and this may add a touch of realism to the formulas. In most Middle Kingdom cases, the priests are those of Abydos because that site is the source of the majority of surviving inscriptions. One example addresses 'male and female ḥm-nṯr priests, wꜥb priests, chanters and chantresses (ḫnw ḫnwt) of this temple' (Sethe 1928a: 87, lines 21–2). Similar phrases occur in the late 12th dynasty stela of Sehetepibre, which continues with an excerpt from the literary Loyalist Instruction; this also refers to 'all people of Abydos' (Sethe 1928a: 69, lines 4–7) and 'every soldier (ꜥnḫ nb n njwt tn)' (ibid. 70, line 5; for the meaning 'soldier', see Berlev 1971). The formulas in the early 18th dynasty tomb of Paheri at Elkab show a slightly different emphasis on scribes (Sethe 1906: 120, line 16–121, line 4). A noteworthy example at Asyut dating to the First Intermediate period refers to 'every scribe, every wise man who is skilled in his craft, perfect in writing and perfect in knowledge, who has acquired the reputation of a man (of rank), who is in service after having been to school (ꜥq r ꜥt-sbꜣ) …' (reconstruction of Edel 1984: 99, 108–11). The hope that the texts would be read is confirmed by cryptographically inscribed examples that were intended to spur the reader to solve their puzzles and in the process to pronounce the formulas. The possibility that the appeals were in fact read is confirmed by visitors' graffiti in temples and tombs, and by the habit of visiting tombs at festivals (Wildung 1975, with refs.; Schott 1952).

This material suggests that anyone at all might visit the necropolis or a place of pilgrimage.[6] It was naturally hoped that as many as possible would then read the inscriptions; the fact that the task of reading is neither wearisome nor costly is emphasized (Sethe 1928a: 88, line 17; 89, lines 3–4, 12–13, 23–4). It is impossible to know whether those who belonged to most of the categories named in the more restricted lists would really be literate. Moreover, because these categories are often priestly, it would be difficult to correlate such

---

[6] It is perhaps unlikely that the general peasant population would have visited elite tombs, which were the only inscribed ones. In Old Kingdom tombs, secondary captions giving names to subordinate figures show that a wider spread of people had an interest in the decoration, but the implications of this practice are not clear and may not be relevant to the hope that formulas would be read out.

functions with administrative office, even though there was probably considerable overlap in personnel between the two sectors. Documents from temples show an all-pervasive administration (e.g. Posener-Kriéger 1976; Griffith 1898; Sethe 1928a: no. 32; Kaplony-Heckel 1971), and are thus compatible with widespread literacy among the personnel, perhaps also for some female categories (§3 below), but no proof is possible.

In the case of public texts that are addressed to specific people, either these do not give any more detail than is suggested by the recipients specified in papyri, or the addressees named are so general in their tenor as to give no hint of any audience who would in reality read them (e.g. Goedicke 1967; Sethe 1928a: 83–4, 92–5, 98; Helck 1955b: 1238, line 6); propaganda for the elite rather than a broader readership may also be an important element here. The physical accessibility of texts further complicates the issue. Even among those with definite publics, many were set up within inaccessible temples or were physically impossible to read, for example because they were too high on a wall or in a dark location. Texts may often have been read out to assembled groups (compare the vizier's visit to Deir el-Medina cited above), which will have increased greatly the number of people they reached but not the size of the specifically reading public. Find circumstances favour material that comes from inaccessible places, because these were less subject to wear than places that were more visited, while other, more accessible copies of the same texts may be lost. Such evidence is therefore very difficult to evaluate for our purposes.

Because written communication may have been extended significantly by oral practices of the type just suggested, the implications of extremely restricted literacy for government, propaganda, and cultural uniformity are uncertain. There is little evidence for variant non-literate culture or—except in some sources that are themselves written—for failures of contact between king and subjects. The number of those indirectly affected by writings—apart from the general effect of writing on social organization—was probably much greater than that of the literate, but in matters of high culture the non-literate 99 per cent could have been largely indifferent to the interests of the one percent or, rather, of the fraction of that one per cent who were concerned with such matters.

EXCURSUS A: CAREER, LIFE-EXPECTANCY, AND SIZE OF ELITE

An average age for tomb-owners of 30–45 was proposed above. This means that such people had normally passed the life-expectancy of 29.4 years, calculated by Samuel, Hastings, Bowman, and Bagnall for 15-year-olds in Roman Egypt (1971: 25; compare Boyaval 1977, whose conclusions are suggestive despite his denial of their significance). Overall life-expectancy will then have been very much lower than 29. The age of 15 is also a plausible beginning for an official's career, on the assumption that the elite was mostly recruited directly from training, so that officials would begin their careers young or would not become officials. The population as a whole would be halved with every ten years of age (Samuel et al. 1971: 25). If officials conformed to the same pattern of mortality as other people (see also below), about a third of those entering the official classes at 15 would thus be alive at 30, the age we have suggested for beginning tomb construction. All this supposes that conditions affecting mortality did not differ significantly between dynastic and Roman Egypt.

If the elite of dynastic times had a higher life-expectancy than non-officials of the Roman period (Samuel et al. exclude officials for reasons of method), this difference would have two opposing effects on our argument. A smaller proportion of the elite would be invisible in the record, because more lived to a greater age, but the estimated length of the tomb-owning period would need to be increased, so that the figure for years × tombs per year would be higher. Thus, if half the elite died between the ages of 15 and 29 and half constructed tombs between 30 and 50, 10 per year × 20 years would mean that there were 200 tomb owners (150 on the assumptions in 1 above), with an elite of 400 (450 rounded to 500 above). In the very rough estimates that are all we can hope to make, such a difference is not important.

The estimates of mortality just given have further implications for the structure of the elite. Age emerges as a dominating factor in selection for high office, because death eliminates so many contenders. Anyone who survived into his forties would have had a very good chance of high office, because he was among the most senior people available. This pattern could also have something to do with the numerous different offices and titles that people acquired. In such a demographic context, wealth and influence are likely to concentrate among the old, who will form a small, tight-knit group. Such a tendency to gerontocracy is clearly shown by the large number of known monuments of people who reached an advanced age, beyond the average age for tomb-building proposed above. It should not be deduced from such cases that the elite as a whole had a high life-expectancy, but that age increased vastly an official's ability to leave a permanent record of himself. An official aged 50–70 is many times more likely to have left monuments than one of 30–40, because he was in a leading position for so much longer. Compared with those between 15 and 30—officials up to Samuel et al.'s life-expectancy—the chances of our knowing him are immeasurably greater.

Generation counts reinforce this point. These are calculated on attestations of office-holders who survived to adulthood rather than on the basis of births. They exaggerate slightly the average intervals between parents and children and hence average generation length, because the oldest child will very often not succeed to the parent's position. Nevertheless, on any estimate they give an average figure in excess of general life-expectancy.[7] The bias created by the fact that evidence is preserved only for the literate will not distort estimates of their life-expectancy enough to affect this conclusion, which means that the majority of the elite did not live to have children, and only a small proportion lived to see their children grow to be adult office-holders and have viable children of their own. This reality is reflected in a Ptolemaic biography of a widow that celebrates her life, in part as someone who lived to have a son who held high office (Vittmann 1995). What is true for the elite will apply with still greater force to the labouring population.[8]

EXCURSUS B: WITNESSING AND SIGNING OF DOCUMENTS

In a series of studies, Herbert C. Youtie (1973; 1981) analysed brilliantly the evidence provided by different practices in authenticating documents in Greek, or Greek and demotic, for the literacy of those who took part in their production. Here we summarize comparable Egyptian material in hieratic, abnormal hieratic, and demotic.

Egyptian archival practice of earlier periods assumed no literacy in the parties to an agreement or in those witnessing it. The texts were written by anonymous professionals. Witnesses were listed after the text, often in quite large numbers. The witnesses did not themselves write. Important documents were deposited in administrative offices, where they could be consulted for very long periods, as can be seen in the detailed narratives of the 17th dynasty Karnak stela documenting the sale of a high office (Lacau 1949) and the 19th dynasty legal text of Mose (Gaballa 1977).

---

[7] Henige (1981: 183–4), criticizing Bierbrier (1975), suggests a typical range, for generations in dynasties of successive office-holders rather than narrower biological generations, of 25–34.

[8] Subsequent work in demographics (Bagnall and Frier 1994; Scheidel 2001) and on the ageing of skeletons in cemeteries from early periods (several papers at the 'Origines' conference, Toulouse, September 2005) suggests that this discussion may use too low an estimate of life-expectancy. As indicated, a modest shift in such estimates would make only minor differences to the models proposed.

The modest sale records of Deir el-Medina (Janssen 1975a) may have been kept by one of the parties to the sale. These do not rely either on autograph or on witness. Instead, the writer was the primary witness; mostly he was one of the professional scribes. The documents are not highly formulaic and could be drawn up without special training (Janssen 1975c: 295; Donker van Heel and Haring 2003; Haring 2003). Perhaps in part because of the regularity of the practice in the community, the scribes seem nonetheless to have been the chief guarantors of the procedures, for very few such documents are demonstrably in other hands (e.g. Baines and Malek 2000: 201), despite the presence of other literate people in the village (see §4 below).

A most unusual case is provided by a papyrus containing two statements in different hands, one well and the other very poorly written; the subject is the handing-over of a bronze bowl as part of the execution of a will after the death of its owner (Černý 1945: 40, doc. 4). The witnesses were ordinary workmen who belonged to the tomb-building crew, most of them relatives of one another. Two of them were paid 'for the writings they have made concerning the (legal) deposition of their father'. Thus, two literate workmen both earned a little, and saved the cost of having a professional write out the settlement of a family matter, by doing it themselves as well as they could. (See now also Ch. 6, 'Institutionalization'.) Although we know of no record of payments made to the professional scribes for their services, in most cases there was probably some recompense; when documents were on papyrus, the material itself had a value. The use of scribes for this purpose was above all a guarantee of witness and official cachet; it more than compensated for the illiteracy among their customers, which was in any case by no means universal.

After the long Third Intermediate period (*c*.1070–715), from which very few documents are preserved, new archival practices emerge. There is, however, continuity in the position of scribes, who often refer to themselves as 'the witness scribe' (*p3 sẖ mtr*; for Ramessid *mtrw* 'witness document', see Ward 1981: 365–7). Two developments are found from the beginning of the Late period onward: witness copies (see also Ch. 6), and the use of witness signatures. These are mostly alternatives to each other, but they may have had rather different meanings, at least in theory.

In abnormal hieratic documents, witnesses copied out the essential provisions of an agreement, while in demotic documents complete witness copies or signatures were the norm (Vleeming 1981: 39–41); demotic conventions gradually took over with their script. The most extensive example of the abnormal hieratic practice is the Brooklyn oracle papyrus of year 14 of Psammetichus I, which has fifty witness summaries containing varying amounts of text (Parker 1962). This is a ceremonial document beginning with a pictorial vignette, and so may not be typical of general practice. Among demotic documents of the Ptolemaic period, some contain copies of the entire text in four different witness hands (the standard number, e.g. Quirke and Spencer 1992: 144–5 fig. 110). The people who wrote these copies testified to the substance of the document, with which they were necessarily acquainted, in particular those who wrote in demotic. This scrupulous but laborious practice died out during the Ptolemaic period (Smith 1958: 87).

In demotic documents, signatures, of which the standard number is sixteen, are mostly on the back of the papyrus, sometimes one of those that have witness copies on the front. By signing the document or having a representative sign it, the witness attested to his own presence and to the document's authenticity, but not necessarily to its content. This weaker form of certification was carried out by more people. The witness signature is thus the more or less literate descendant of the name of a witness in a list—as in so many other cultures the signatures are often illegible—while the witness copy is perhaps an extension of the role of the witness scribe. In Greek documents, the parties indicated their assent by writing out subscriptions containing the essential content of a text that had been written in full by a scribe. This practice has no precise counterpart in demotic, but abnormal hieratic of the eighth and seventh centuries BCE provides some sort of forerunner. There is a wide range of practices in writing subscriptions, from autograph, through a few words 'slowly' written by a marginally literate person, to complete delegation of the actual writing (Youtie 1973; 1981).

The introduction of signatures and witness copies is not in itself an indicator of rising literacy. Normally the documents come from the literate elite or those near them, but people still commonly employed others as amanuenses to write for them. The value of signatures as indicators of literacy is uncertain in any context (see e.g. Schofield 1968; Youtie 1973; see Blackman 1927: 92 for a modern Egyptian who could read and write his own name but was otherwise illiterate). Some signatures are written very clumsily. The witness may not necessarily have signed himself, and the use of an amanuensis was not signalled formally. Even when someone did sign, he very rarely recorded his rank or title. Detailed study of a corpus of texts defined by date and provenance might provide valuable information about the identities and patterning of the witnesses and personnel involved in legal transactions. Of the witnesses identified so far, most were priests or other temple employees; with one possible exception, women did not sign as witnesses (el-Amir 1959: 98–105, 99 n. A).

By the mid-Ptolemaic period there were officially appointed notaries (*monographoi*) for documents in Egyptian, who charged set fees that were officially displayed (Pierce 1972: 65–6). People who acted as scribes seem all to have held positions as officials, particularly those who had priestly or temple connections (Seidl 1937: 3–5; 1968: 10–13). This pattern probably exemplifies the normal milieu of literacy in Egyptian at the time. It was unusual for a literate man to write his own legal documents and it was never necessary for him to sign himself (Seidl 1968: 13–14), although in the long run the practice of signing became relatively common. In some cases the signature of a contracting party seems to signify that the contract had been fulfilled. More normally, however, it shows assent to the terms, that is, it is a vestigial counterpart of a Greek subscription (e.g. Shore and Smith 1960).

The development sketched here is on the one hand toward a greater involvement of the parties to an agreement in its certification—which would have been technically possible at a much earlier date—and on the other hand toward an increasing formalization and professionalization of the texts themselves. Whatever may have stimulated these trends, both of them constitute steps forward in the institutionalization of writing, more than two thousand years after its introduction, but the second probably also relates to the fact that diffusion of scribal skills was becoming progressively more restricted. Only those who were properly qualified could produce the highly formulaic documents, and much of the preserved demotic legal code or handbook is devoted to stipulating how these should be drafted (Mattha and Hughes 1975). This professional class looked after consistency of text, as well as after its own economic survival; even those who were literate but used their literacy in other milieux elsewhere must have had to turn to these professionals for legal services. Such a mixture of progress and conservatism is characteristic of Late period and Ptolemaic Egypt.

2 KINGS, LITERACY, AND LITERATURE

It is very probable that Egyptian kings could read and write. Evidence relevant to that assertion, however, varies widely in character and reliability.[9]

Several inscriptions state that the king physically wrote their archetypes himself. The earliest of these is the introduction to a letter of the 5th dynasty king Izezi to his vizier Senedjemib Inti (Sethe 1933: 60 line 9; Roccati 1982: 124): 'His Person wrote with his fingers as a favour for me(?) concerning everything I had done [...].' Two other closely comparable texts of the same reign lack this detail (Sethe 1933: 62, 14–63, 11, same tomb as the last;

---

[9] For the Middle Kingdom literary texts cited in this section, see now the renderings of R. B. Parkinson (1998). Revised or new translations of many literary texts from later periods are available in Simpson (2003).

179, 12–180, 10; for translations of the texts, see Wente 1990: nos. 2–5; study: Eichler 1991). The preservation of four texts suggests that they belonged to an established genre, but this does not affect the question of whether the king physically wrote them. What is relevant here is not the literal accuracy of the claim, but the fact that it was made about the king.

In the 12th dynasty Prophecy of Neferti, the 4th dynasty king Snofru 'stretched out his hand to his box of writing materials and took a papyrus roll and a palette (*gstj*). Then he wrote down what the chief lector priest Neferti said' (Helck 1970: 12–13, IIo–q; Parkinson 1998: 135). Neferti was composed about 650 years after the time of Snofru, but the picture it gives would work best if it was credible for a king, at least in the 12th dynasty. The detail that the king himself writes may be a mark of his fictional character as someone who did not insist on rank, which is also visible in the tale of his boating expedition on the palace lake in P Westcar (cf. Blumenthal 1982: 25–6; text: Parkinson 1998: 109–12). Since the action of writing is not essential to the general subject of Neferti, there is no reason why the detail should have been included if it was implausible. The Instruction for Merikare, from the same period, also implies royal literacy. The future king, to whom the text is addressed, is exhorted to surpass the abilities of his ancestors. 'Their words are set down in writing; spread them out so that you may read them and surpass their knowledge' (Volten 1945: 14; Lichtheim 1973: 99). Later he is told 'do not kill a man whose abilities you know, with whom you chanted texts' (Volten 22–3; Lichtheim 100–1). The implication is that a future king would have been taught to read and memorize texts by chanting in a group together with members of the elite, and so should be able to do so himself, but the text does not say explicitly that he would read with his own eyes.[10]

The Old Kingdom evidence of Izezi can be compared with a letter of Amenhotep II to the viceroy of Nubia Usersatet, which is recorded on a stela of the latter found perhaps at Buhen in the Second Cataract. The text is introduced as the 'copy of a command (i.e. royal letter) which his Person made with his own hands to [(the viceroy) ...]' (Helck 1955a: 22/23 line 1, 25), and so claims to reproduce a royal autograph.

Two royal inscriptions emphasize the religious knowledge of kings who, they state, consulted texts themselves. In the Abydos stela of Neferhotep of the 13th dynasty, 'His Person went to the house of writings (*pr-mdȝt*) and His Person spread out texts (*zhw*) together with his companions. Then His Person found the writings of the temple of Osiris ...'; 'His Person [found] these texts

---

[10] Günter Burkard (1977: 321) concludes that the errors found in manuscripts of instruction texts did not derive from dictation. One should therefore hypothesize that there were other modes of transmission, or that dictation was used only in early stages of the instructional process.

[himself?]; no scribe who was in the service of His Person found them' (Helck 1983: 22, 25 lines 6–7; Pieper 1929: §§7, 17 line 21—text uncertain in detail). The introduction to the inscription on the basalt slab bearing the 'Memphite theology' says of the 25th dynasty king Shabaka that 'His Person made this text public (*spẖr*) anew.... His Person found (it) having been made by the ancestors, and it was eaten by worms ...' (Sethe 1928b: 20). Since the authenticity of this monument as a copy of an ancient document is disputed (Junge 1973), the preamble does not have to be taken literally; it is also less explicit than the Neferhotep stela in its statement that the king read the text himself (see Hornung 1982a: 189 with n. 175).

Scribal equipment of palettes and pens, but no papyrus, was found in the tomb of Tutankhamun (Murray and Nuttall 1963: index s.v. palettes—relevant numbers are Carter 271b, 271e(1); Carter 1933: pl. 22). Since such equipment was useful in the hereafter both for kings and for the non-royal (see e.g. Schneider 1977: I, 34–5; Book of the Dead 94, e.g. Hornung 1979: 185–6, 473), well-preserved, intact materials found in tombs are not indicative of whether their owners were able to write. According to Howard Carter, however, one palette inscribed for Tutankhamun bears signs of use (no. 271b: 1933: 80). It is simplest to assume that he had used it himself, having learned to write, and hence also to read.

Other comparable evidence is less persuasive. A palette with the cartouche of Ahmose, the first king of the 18th dynasty, need not have belonged to the king (Glanville 1932: 55 no. 12784), and another with what may be a title 'instructor of His Person' (or possibly 'the one whom His Person taught') need not be taken literally (19th dynasty, temp. Ramesses II, Glanville 1932: 59; see end of this paragraph). There are also fragments of what have been suggested to be two glazed 'ex libris' of the 18th dynasty king Amenhotep III and his queen Teye that bear the titles of texts about different species of tree, but do not indicate specifically that the king or queen would read them (Capart 1935; see now Parkinson 1999: 51–3).

The king's general role was in no way one of reading and writing. Royal iconography does not seem to contain allusions to his writing. As can be seen in non-royal tomb decoration, people of high status transcended the stage of writing, and in most cases reading, for themselves; this will be the more true of kings. These things were done for them. The repertory of scene types includes no context suitable for royal writing; iconography is therefore almost bound to be uninformative. Conversely, scribe statues of non-royal individuals make an ideological point, often about their owners' role in relation to the king, but they do not portray their owners' activities in life: most of these objects belonged to people of much higher status than simple 'scribes' (Scott 1989). The only obvious exception to these rules is where Ramesses II as a prince, not as king, holds the papyri in offering scenes showing ceremonies in the temple of Sety I at Abydos (Mariette 1869: pls. 43, 44, 46); here he is acting as heir and as priest, not simply as a scribe. While we would argue that it is likely Ramesses II could read and write, these reliefs cannot be used as evidence for his literacy.

The education of princes is relevant to the present question. Because of the rate of mortality, no heir could be guaranteed to inherit, so that several royal children were probably raised as potential kings. Kings of non-royal origin—such as Amenemhat I of the 12th dynasty, Aya and Haremhab of the 18th, Ramesses I and Sety I of the 19th, Sethnakhte and Ramesses III of the 20th, and many in the 13th dynasty and Late period—would have been literate in any case, because they rose through the official classes or the higher ranks of the army. By contrast, little that is relevant is known about kings of royal birth before they came to the throne. It is therefore necessary to study princes as a generalized model for heirs to the throne.

Princes of the 4th dynasty held high positions in the state and were presumably literate. They were also represented in scribe statues, claiming literacy in perpetuity (e.g. Smith 1949: pl. 10; Simpson 1978: 7, fig. 17). Some of these princes, such as Kawab, the son of Khufu, were 'eldest' sons of the king and perhaps destined originally for the throne (Simpson 1978: figs. 8, 17). Another son, Hardjedef, was reputed for his wisdom: an instruction text was ascribed to him (Lichtheim 1973: 58–9; Helck 1984), and his role in the fictional Middle Kingdom tales of P Westcar has similar implications (e.g. Lichtheim 1973: 217–20). Perhaps by chance, no king of the 4th dynasty is attested also as a prince, but it is hard to conceive of their having had a very different upbringing from their principal brothers. After the initial three kings of the 5th dynasty (Borchardt et al. 1913: pls. 17, 32–4, 48–9), princes disappear almost entirely from the record until the 18th dynasty, when princes with official titles include an Amenhotep as *sm* priest, probably in the reign of Thutmose III (Glanville 1931: 106, 113, 115, 117–18, 120), and a Thutmose with the same title in the reign of Amenhotep III (Gauthier 1912: 335–6, perhaps the prematurely deceased 'Thutmose V'). These princes were high priests of Ptah like Khaemwese, the son of Ramesses II (Gomaà 1973; Fisher 2001: I, 89–105, II, 89–143). They held a position that would in principle require literacy, although their tenure could have been honorific or have begun while they were minors. No such doubt is possible with Khaemwese, who was fully active in the role as an adult. In the first of the Ptolemaic demotic tales of Setna Khaemwese, whose character derives from the son of Ramesses II Khaemwese, the prince Naneferkaptah walks through the temple reading the (hieroglyphic) texts, about whose nature the narrative seems vague (e.g. Lichtheim 1980: 128).

The subsequent plot revolves around the discovery of a papyrus whose contents he intends to use. Thus, in the period when the tale was written, the royal family of earlier times was presented as being literate.

Princes were educated with non-royal children who entered the bureaucracy or the army (see Feucht 1995: 266–304; see also Ch. 2 §2.2). Although this education probably centred on values and activities as much as technical skills, these too would surely have been learned by all who took part, including the princes. The letter from Amenhotep II to Usersatet cited above refers to relations in youth between the king and his later administrator and viceroy; it is therefore apt that the archetype for the stela should be said to have been in the king's hand.

We have presented this evidence with reserve—royal inscriptions boasting of a king's finding something that a scribe could not belong to a genre and are clearly suspect—but in accumulation it leaves little doubt of royal literacy. Its import is not so much that kings possessed an accomplishment as that it exemplifies the integration of the highest Egyptian elite with administration and affairs of state. In principle, literacy was acquired in the first place for administration, and then for literate culture.[11] Both were diffused from the centre. From early periods there is almost no evidence of separate ideologies that would have centred around values other than those of the leading groups. Later, the force of traditional forms was such that departures from them, for example toward pious, priestly, or purely military concerns, would not have been expressed with full strength. Nonetheless, the focus of traditional elite display on administrative service to king and state lessened from the later New Kingdom onward. Except perhaps for priestly elites, the change in focus may not have favoured a prominent position for literate culture in display, although its very existence presupposes the maintenance of written culture in the Classical (or 'Middle') Egyptian language. Since display materials provide much of our evidence, this change makes it more difficult to assess the position of literacy in later periods.

There may be further cultural implications of the involvement of kings in writing, and specifically in the production of literature discussed above (Neferti; also Instruction for Merikare; Instruction of Amenemhat). For any period before the late New Kingdom, it is scarcely conceivable that written literary works could have gained circulation without central assent, which means essentially royal assent. One may, however, ask whether royal involvement was more for the literary interest of the texts or for their propaganda value. In the Tale of the Eloquent Peasant, the king commissions the high steward Rensi to record the peasant's fine words (Lichtheim 1973: 172–3), and what is produced is not simply propaganda. Kings did use literature as

---

[11] This statement is a little simplistic in relation to the core elite. See further explorations of related issues in Chs. 5 and 6.

propaganda—the Prophecy of Neferti is the outstanding example—if not in the measure often assumed (Baines 1982: 38), but they may also have been the leading patrons of literature, both for its own sake and as a more general vehicle for high culture and for the elaboration of ideology. The complexity of many works is evidence of their being valued as more than utilitarian creations. Such complexity is best appreciated by the literate, among whom a principal figure may have been the king. In representational and architectural arts, where form and craftsmanship are immediately apparent, Egyptologists have willingly seen royal patronage without narrow propaganda intent, and this royal interest is well attested in inscriptions (the Amarna period, with the radical reforms of Akhenaten, is an exception here). The same royal involvement should be allowed for in belles lettres, which offer relatively few easy contexts for taking the credit for munificence.

The integration of the highest elite with literacy in Egypt contrasts with the more narrowly scribal use of writing in less monolithic Mesopotamia, whose rulers did not rise through a bureaucracy and were not normally literate (John A. Brinkman, personal communication). It is claimed in hymns celebrating King Shulgi of the 3rd dynasty of Ur in the late third millennium that he was literate, but comparable texts attribute manifestly impossible exploits to him.[12] This is a very different presentation from the relatively unobtrusive material on Egyptian royal literacy. The principal Mesopotamian king for whom credible evidence of literacy exists is the Assyrian Assurbanipal of the 7th century (e.g. Hunger 1968: 98 no. 319). He did, however, boast of reading tablets 'whose Sumerian is obscure and whose Akkadian is hard to construe', so that his mastery was evidently not complete (Postgate 1977).[13]

3 WOMEN AND LITERACY

So far, we have left the possibility that women might be literate out of consideration. If any women could read and write, they were not significant in administration, and so are not relevant to the kind of model we have used

---

[12] Klein (1981: 15, lines 13–20); Samuel Noah Kramer, in Pritchard (1969: 584–6, lines 148–50). See new editions at: http://etcsl.orinst.ox.ac.uk/.

[13] The exceptional actions of the last king of Babylon, the usurper Nabonidus (556–539 BCE), seem to have arisen in part from his having belonged to the literate priestly group, so that he was able to act differently from other kings in relation to the learned institutions that constrained the monarch's room for manoeuvre. The presence of this case raises by implication the question of what was the social background of the many other usurpers there must have been in Mesopotamian history. Were they generally from non-literate groups? I am grateful to Piotr Michalowski for pointing out this problem to me.

(cf. Fischer 1976b: 69–79; Naguib Kanawati, 1980: 31, proposes that Nebet, the mother of Pepy I's queens in the 6th dynasty, was a genuine vizier, but this remains uncertain). It is unlikely that the numbers of any literate women would affect greatly the total proportion of literate in the society, but the phenomenon itself may have existed. Most of the relevant material has been gathered by Hellmut Brunner (1957: 45–7) and Henry G. Fischer (see below).[14]

Before reviewing the evidence, it is worth outlining a problem of method. There is no iconographic or textual context in which women would normally have been presented as writing (reading being a rare motif in any case), but this gap simply shows that female writing was not part of the official, public life represented by monuments and documents. It leaves open the question of whether female literacy existed in other spheres. If such literacy is held to be possible, indirect confirmation can be seen where direct pointers are absent. We therefore start with possible evidence and continue with indirectly relevant data; the latter may be disallowed by those who consider the initial arguments unconvincing.

The best evidence for female literacy is itself assailable, because it consists of titles, which so often specify roles or functions that are entirely different from what the words which make them up might suggest. From the Middle Kingdom there are a few cases of the feminine $z\underline{h}t$ 'scribe'. These have been discussed in detail by Fischer (1976b: 73, 77–8), who concludes that at least one example on a scarab should mean that its owner was a female scribe; that occurrence must naturally be set against the thousands of known scarabs with male titles (Martin 1971), many of which signify that their holders were literate. Two inscribed elements from the 26th dynasty Theban tomb of the woman Ireteru give many times the title $s\underline{h}$ $s\underline{h}mt$ 'female scribe', in the service of the female divine adoratrice of Amun Nitokris (Graefe 1981: I, 41–2, II, 9, 29 with n. 62, 79–80). This monument seems to have been discounted by some of those who have written on women, but it is worth considering. Nothing in its inscriptions suggests that the title is spurious or present for symbolic reasons only, while the context of serving the divine adoratrice favours its authenticity, as does its form, which is linguistically Late Egyptian or later, not a fossil or archaism. Ireteru may have been rich enough to afford a tomb but, unlike some other personnel, she may not have had any more exalted title that she could display. It is even conceivable that the title of 'female scribe' was itself striking enough to convey an important message of status.

Women's administrative titles in general belong to the service of women for women. Such positions could be real enough, as is suggested, for example, by

---

[14] See the judicious survey of Gay Robins (1993: 111–14).

the female ownership of an appreciable fraction of Old Kingdom and Late period tombs, or it could mimic that of men, while the actual work was done by men. The truth in individual cases may lie between these two possibilities. Among the staff of the first millennium divine adoratrices studied by Erhart Graefe (1981), men appear to have wielded much of the power, but a significant number of women held positions and some of them had their own decorated tombs.[15] The question is therefore how literally one is to take such household and administrative establishments and whether the women holding titles in them would be literate, as men holding comparable titles were. There is no easy way to answer this question, but the example of Ireteru suggests that some of them may have been literate.

Among the late Ramessid letters from Thebes at the end of the 20th dynasty is one in which the scribe of the necropolis Thutmose writes from Nubia: 'and you should look after the daughter of Khonsmose and have her "do" a letter (*jrj.s šꜥt*) and have it brought to me' (Černý 1939: 11, lines 5–6; Wente 1967: 28; for other women in the letters, see below). This wording does not necessarily mean that the girl is physically to write the letter, but there would be no obvious purpose in her dictating a letter to another person who might be writing in any case, since such delegated writing from women is attested in letters that were clearly written down by men (e.g. Barns 1948: 35–8; Wente 1990: no. 132). If that was all Thutmose sought, a passage in a reply from Butehamun would probably have sufficed as a response. That would not be true if some value was attached to the daughter's physically producing the writing herself. Thus, although this sentence is not decisive, it provides possible evidence for aspirations in the necropolis community of the Theban West Bank that a young woman among them become literate. We do not know whether such a letter was in fact written. (On women's literacy at Deir el-Medina, see further Ch. 6 Appendix.)

Among material evidence, a painting palette of the Amarna period princess Mayyati (Meritaten), found in the tomb of Tutankhamun, is worth citing (Carter 1933: pl. 22A, Carter no. 262). Like a palette of Tutankhamun himself, this one shows signs of use, the blue being almost finished. Since blue was not a writing colour, this is not direct evidence for the princess's literacy, and so was dismissed by Brunner (1957: 46). Only miniatures of the scale of a vignette or figured ostracon could be painted with such equipment, however, and writing would form part of the context of such paintings. This object could therefore suggest that some princesses were literate. Although the record for

---

[15] e.g. the subtly designed tomb of the priestess Mutirdis (Assmann 1977b). Separate burials of women in which their own wooden grave stelae were deposited were common from the Third Intermediate period onward.

Amarna princesses is exceptional, the way toward it was prepared during the 18th dynasty as a whole, and the Amarna evidence may be unusual more in term of presentation than in the life of the court. Mayyati was also politically prominent, and her name occurs in the cuneiform Amarna letters, showing that she was known internationally (Moran 1992: 19, no. 11 line 46; 22, no. 11 line rev. 26).

In the Demotic first Setna tale from the Ptolemaic period, which is set fictionally in the time of Ramesses II, Princess Ahwere says that she read a magical papyrus but did not copy it out, leaving that to her capable brother and husband Naneferkaptah (Lichtheim 1980: 130–1, 138 n. 9—in detail the passage is not clear). The tale thus portrays royalty of a millennium earlier as being literate, the women possibly less so than the men.[16]

One early and three New Kingdom letters to the dead are addressed to deceased wives, about a quarter of the known corpus.[17] In general, author and addressee of letters need not be literate, but this might perhaps not be so true of a text destined for the hereafter. Here the social context may be relevant. The Leiden letter (Gardiner and Sethe no. 6) was written by someone who wished to stress his importance and emphasized his wife's former standing in society, while Butehamun, the son of the scribe Thutmose mentioned above, sent a letter to his deceased wife Akhtai (Černý and Gardiner pl. 80). The scribes of Deir el-Medina were highly literate (see §4 below), and they could have shared their accomplishment with their womenfolk to some extent. Akhtai had been 'chantress of Amun', and so in theory had a post in a temple, giving her another possible reason or source for literacy.

Such a possibility may be compared with the addresses to female temple personnel in Middle Kingdom formulas cited in section 1 of this chapter. Similarly, several of the late Ramessid letters were sent by or to women, who seem to have played a full part in the matters discussed (Černý 1939; Wente 1967: 16–17, nos. 37, 36, 42, 44, 35 [see also 21], 38, 39; 5–6 are to men and women; see also Janssen 1990: nos. iv and viii are addressed to women). As just stated, autography or reading by these women cannot be assumed (see further Sweeney 1998), but it is noteworthy that, like Akhtai, all of them bore priestly

---

[16] Graefe (1981, II, 29 n. 62) cites Weber (1969: 91–2 with n. 579), who proposes that the scribal gear in the boat of the 6th dynasty queen Idut implies that she was literate (Macramallah 1935: pl. 7; contra Graefe it is not in the hand). As noted by Brunner (1957: 46 n. 51), the scene is recut, and this detail probably belongs to the earlier male owner Ihi. This scene is evidently the one alluded to by Wenig (1967: 15), whose mention baffled Fischer (1976b: 77 n. 60); it does not constitute evidence for or against female literacy in the Old Kingdom.

[17] Gardiner (1930: nos. 4, 6); Černý and Gardiner (1957: 22, pl. 80; see Wente 1990: no. 353; Frandsen 1992; Goldwasser 1995; McDowell 1999: 106–7); Buchberger (1991)—not published as a letter to the dead but probably belongs to the genre.

titles, whether these were indications of rank or signified functions that they performed.

The remaining arguments relating to women's literacy are extremely indirect.

The existence of a number of love poems composed from the woman's point of view (e.g. Derchain 1975; Lichtheim 1976: 182–93; Mathieu 1996) might suggest that there was a context of use in which composition by a woman was possible, irrespective of whether that was the case with any of the extant poems—on the assumption that composition took place in written form, not in an oral form for later writing down. The positive role of women in love poetry contrasts with their negative presentation as evil seductresses in tales, including the late Middle Kingdom P Westcar (Parkinson 1998: 106–9), the New Kingdom Truth and Falsehood and the Two Brothers (Lichtheim 1976: 203–14), as well as much later in the Demotic first Setna tale (Tabubu: Lichtheim 1980: 133–6). This difference in perspective could be related to different contexts, in one of which women would participate actively in the creation and reception of literature. Since love poetry is known only from the New Kingdom (from which come two of the tales cited above), any such notion should not necessarily be generalized further.

The Late and Graeco-Roman periods are the only ones to have produced biographical inscriptions of women (e.g. Lichtheim 1980: 58–9; Otto 1954: 7; Jansen-Winkeln 1997). Such texts need not have been composed by their protagonists, several of whom had already died unexpectedly, but the point is nonetheless worth citing (on ownership and authorship of inscriptions in the Roman world, compare Duncan-Jones 1977; 1979). Another piece of Graeco-Roman period evidence is the possible signature of a woman in a demotic document (Excursus B above; for female literacy in Greek, see Youtie 1973; 1981). Both for biographical inscriptions and for female ownership of tombs, the phenomena are probably significant more for the position of women than for any specific function or literate accomplishment they may have had.[18]

Of the two deities of writing, Thoth is male and Seshat is female. Seshat is also attested from no later than the 2nd dynasty (Budde 2000: xi, 81, 253 no. 85). The association of Seshat with this domain and activity might seem most logical if women could write (here Brunner is too dismissive, 1957: 46). Yet, although the name *sš3t* is similar to the root for 'to write (*zḫ3*)' and the two were written in the same way in later periods, they are not identical. *sš3t* is probably not an abstract noun derived from the verb but a similar-sounding

---

[18] Janet H. Johnson (1998) comes to an essentially similar conclusion in her study of women's position through documents of the Ptolemaic period; she does not mention the question of literacy specifically.

word that came to be associated with it (see further Budde 2000: 8–13). Therefore one should not explain the presence and sex of Seshat as the goddess of writing on the basis of her being a personification governed by linguistic morphology. Rather, she is likely to be a goddess of independent origin who acquired the role of protector of writing, perhaps favoured by the assonance of her name. The presence of a female deity of writing remains striking in any case. Gods in general appear to be 'preliterate' (Ch. 2, n. 19), so that a literate goddess stands out all the more.[19]

All the possible evidence for female literacy relates to a very narrow social compass. Women who were literate would have been a special class of elite administrators—for whom one might compare in Mesopotamia the theoretically 'cloistered' *naditum* women of Old Babylonian Sippar, among whom were administrators and scribes (Renger 1967: 157–8; Harris 1975: 288, 305; Yoffee 2000; 2005: 116–30)—members of the cultivated elite, or royalty. Much of the material is from the New Kingdom, and all is in texts (as with the king, §2 above). The opposite point can be made about social gatherings in texts and in pictures. In texts, women are seldom active on equal terms with men, but New Kingdom tombs provide many examples of their being present, if mostly seated separately, at the rather special social function of a mortuary banquet, while the queen is shown with the king in a certain number of 'official' scenes in non-royal tombs and in temples (a Deir el-Medina ostracon describes the village's inhabitants of both sexes getting drunk at a festival: Černý 1927: 183–4; McDowell 1999: 96 no. 66B). Different sources treat the role of women in different ways; all must be taken into account.

The context of possible female literacy is significant in other ways. Most women of the highest status had no administrative position. The men in the same circles all had official posts, whether or not such posts involved real work; in theory they had an occupation and the women did not. If any women apart from 'administrators' were literate, they would be the first people one could identify as not being literate in principle for reasons of their profession. For them, the accomplishment would be useful in legal affairs and, perhaps more importantly, as an aid to a cultured life. The cultural side of this point would suggest that slightly larger numbers than the minimum calculated in section 1 of this chapter participated in high culture, which would still be integrated with the leading group in society (§2 above; Ch. 2 §2.2). For the New Kingdom, one may need to reckon with some female influence on high culture, so that the love poetry with women protagonists

---

[19] Amun as 'vizier of the poor' (e.g. Fecht 1965: nos. 1–2) is the model of the highest protector of justice; the context is not relevant to literacy.

could reflect a genuine shift in values (a view found in novels about Egypt). This would be the textual equivalent of Wilhelm Spiegelberg's 'feminine character of the New Empire' (1929). In another perspective, the significant number of powerful political women of the New Kingdom would have delegated the writing they needed to do on business, as any leader does, but several of them occupied positions normally held by men. They might have been most easily acceptable in those positions if they possessed comparable technical and cultural accomplishments. Similarly, when in the later Third Intermediate period princes were replaced as high priests of Amun in Thebes by princesses in the role of divine adoratrices, this shift might have been facilitated if the latter could also exercise some of the former's worldly and cultural functions. As stated above, the partly female institutions surrounding these ladies may in any case have been pockets of female literacy.

4 DEIR EL-MEDINA: THE WORKMEN OF THE NEW KINGDOM ROYAL TOMBS

The best known and documented single group in Egyptian society from before the Roman period, the community of workmen who built the royal tombs of the New Kingdom and lived at Deir el-Medina on the Theban West Bank, is probably the only one whose rate and level of literacy can be investigated directly.[20] Material relating to them is almost all from the second half of the community's life, in the 19th and 20th dynasties ($c.1300$–1070). Extensive though the relevant evidence is, its interpretation is often problematic, while the specialized and untypical character of the setting must be borne constantly in mind. The community is likely to have been one of the most literate of all in relation to its social status, because the men had an unusual amount of contact with writing. Even if few of them were employed on tomb decoration, as against excavation and preparation, their occupation as a whole was to build inscribed and decorated tombs, and they lived near many inscribed tombs and temples. Their daily work, their wages, and the tools and equipment issued to them were recorded in great detail by their scribes. They were paid high craftsmen's wages and were involved in commercial and legal transactions of a value that they considered to be worth recording in receipts and accounts which they retained themselves (Janssen 1975a; 1977;

---

[20] For a critique of this section, proposing a much higher rate of literacy in the village, see Janssen (1992); see also Ch. 6, Appendix.

Allam 1968).²¹ The difference between their situation and that of the ordinary fieldworker, who might come into contact with writing once or twice a year at the visit of a tax or rent collector, is significant also for an investigation of the lowest levels of literacy among them.

The Tomb (pꜣ ḫr), which was the normal name of the institution constituted by the workforce, usually employed between two and four professional scribes (Černý 1973). These men were responsible for most of the administration of the Tomb, not just for writing texts. They also wrote the legal and commercial documents desired by the people of the community (Excursus B above). Only in the position of scribe can literacy be considered a necessary qualification for employment at Deir el-Medina (although note the illiterate 'village scribe' Petaus, §1 above). One should not assume that people were selected for other offices because of their literacy. The two foremen and their 'deputies', who controlled the two 'sides' of the work crew, presumably did not have to read and write for their jobs. Occasional texts stated to be in their hands do, however, indicate that they normally had a professional competence in writing (e.g. Baines and Malek 2000: 201). They must indeed have written a certain amount, because otherwise they would have lost their skills, but even so they may not have written in the course of their work.

It is not clear whether the 'gatekeepers', who supervised access to the institution, and the guardian, who was in charge of its warehouse and the storage and issue of its property, were literate (for the role of the gatekeepers, see Valbelle 1985: 126–7). For them, too, literacy may not have been a necessary condition of employment, since professional scribes were responsible for the records, but most holders of these posts could probably read and perhaps write to some extent. Here, one can cite depictions of gatekeepers carrying scribal palettes in slightly earlier tombs at el-Amarna (Davies 1903–8: VI, pl. 4; 1933: 21), as well as a Ramessid letter addressed to a 'scribe of the offering stand and doorkeeper of the warehouse of "tribute (jnw)"' (Bakir 1970: pl. 22: col. v, 1–2).

The question of who wrote which classes of administrative documents is significant both for assessing literacy and more generally for understanding the organization of the community, but little definite is known about it (for written practice, see Donker van Heel and Haring 2003). Few texts reveal their authorship through internal evidence (Eyre 1979: 85–7), so that progress would come only from a palaeography of individual hands. There is no clear indication that particular types of records were kept by the foremen, gatekeepers, and guardians, rather than by the scribes. It is, however, evident

---

[21] Translated collection and study of written material of all categories from the village: McDowell (1999).

that many of the basic work records were not written by the chief scribe, who together with the two foremen composed the leadership of the institution (see e.g. Černý 1973: 332–3).

At Deir el-Medina, far more people were called scribe than were ever officially employed as scribes. The word may have come to be used simply to mean 'literate' (to whatever degree). In some cases, for example, the context is the address of a letter. If a non-professional sender or recipient is referred to as 'scribe', he may have been addressed thus because he read and/or wrote his correspondence personally. Here there could perhaps be a nuance of pride in the accomplishment (compare the varying attitudes in Roman Egypt: Youtie 1973; 1981). In many other cases author and writer of a text are not the same, even—in the case of model letters used as copying exercises—when a specific scribe is stated to be the writer (see below for the Late Egyptian miscellanies). Unless multiple copies of such texts are preserved, they can be difficult to separate from authentic letters. The presence of the protagonist's name on a letter never guarantees that he (or she) physically wrote it.

The 'title' scribe is often an abbreviation for 'draughtsman', literally 'outline scribe (sh-qd)'; titles do not seem to make a sharp distinction between writing and drawing. 'Draughtsmen' executed the decoration of the royal tombs, both the layout and the painting, as well as carrying out private commissions in the village community. We do not know where their responsibility for planning and laying out the royal tombs began. The overall design and decorative scheme would surely come from a high authority, not from within the village, but the draughtsmen might have elaborated much of the detail on the basis of inherited material. The underworld books, for example, probably reproduce models with rather little creative variation, as against selection to fill available space (see e.g. Hornung 1990). The local chief draughtsman would have laid them out, and in order to do so he must have understood something of their structure and meaning, perhaps under the guidance of the scribes. The men who carved and painted the hieroglyphs, however, would not have needed to be able to read them. Elsewhere, the very finely carved inscriptions of the temple of Sety I at Abydos, which are contemporaneous with the first phase of the Deir el-Medina documentation, show in many places that those who executed the hieroglyphs did not understand them (see material in the introductions to the volumes of Calverley and Broome 1933–59).

In their private work, the draughtsmen and their colleagues made and decorated funerary furniture, and decorated entire tombs in their own necropolis above the village, as well as stelae and statues, many of the last two categories being used in the local shrines of the gods. These activities show that the village community had access to important religious compositions and possessed the ability to design small tombs, to manipulate standard textual material, and to compose some original texts. Here too, the scribes and foremen were probably involved to some extent. More precise attribution of responsibility for execution, if not for design, may be possible after analyses of hands in royal and private tombs are published (interim articles: Bogoslovsky 1980; Keller 1981; 2001). So far, it is uncertain how much of it was done by ordinary 'draughtsmen'.

There were also many contemporaneous users of the title 'draughtsman' at Deir el-Medina, not all of whom will have been employed as such by the Tomb. The competence and knowledge of self-styled 'draughtsmen' would have varied, but all must have been to some degree literate. They probably had at least a basic knowledge of the hieratic script and—especially those officially employed in the capacity—could transcribe it into hieroglyphic. Here, it is significant that many of the professional scribes had earlier been draughtsmen but not holders of other minor administrative posts.

The large number of writing and drawing exercises found at Deir el-Medina shows that draughtsmanship and literacy were taught locally (but for the latter see Ch. 6, Appendix). The general organization of teaching was probably the same as elsewhere (Brunner 1957; Ch. 2 §2.2), under supervision of the scribes of the Tomb. In the first stage, basic reading and writing will have been learned in a group. The scribe Thutmose wrote to Butehamun 'and you must not let the children (ꜥḏḏw šrjw) who are in the school release their hands from writing' (Černý 1939: 10, lines 13–14; Wente 1967: 28; 1990: 180). Because of high mortality, more must have learned to write than went on to take up a post; some of the surplus men may then have become normal workmen and perhaps self-styled 'draughtsmen', while some may have left the community. In the next stage, when pupils copied out, and possibly half-composed, standard formulas of letters of report and literary and didactic passages, they already referred to themselves as ẖrj-ꜥ 'assistant' or 'apprentice'—the status of the writers of the Late Egyptian miscellanies (Gardiner 1937; Caminos 1954; Fischer-Elfert 1986). They received instruction from a superior in a job, whom they attended on and assisted. Many standard administrative texts were no doubt written, and much tomb decoration and painting executed, by such apprentice scribes and draughtsmen who, although already on the lowest rung of officialdom, had no established office; some were perhaps normal members of the crew. It is difficult to see how individuals not selected by the elite literate group as their eventual successors could have acquired more than the most elementary literacy.

The level of literate culture of the scribal elite was strikingly high. The only substantial collection of papyri from the site, of which the Chester Beatty group form about half (Posener in Černý 1978: vi–viii; Pestman 1982)—whether it is the private library of a scribal family assembled over several generations or part of the old archives of the institution itself—contains a notable range of material. As well as letters and administrative documents, it includes school texts, instruction texts, stories, hymns and rituals, magical texts (including a dream book), and medical texts—almost the full range of literary and traditional types. So far as can be told, all of this was written out by members of the community, presumably for their own or their colleagues' use. The writers of the papyri were not, however, only the professional scribes. They may have included an ordinary workman (Černý 1973: 196–7), as well as a draughtsman who acted as 'lector priest of Amun at all his festivals' (Gardiner 1935: 101). The presence of ritual texts suggests that one or two men who acted as ritual performers and physicians (cf. Janssen 1980: 133, 137 with n. 45—otherwise ordinary workmen) may have used the archive and been literate. Elsewhere, too, scribal function is connected with medical titles (Grapow 1956: 92–4). Another reason for the ritualists to be literate would be the need to arrange the written presentation of oracle questions to deities (Černý in Parker 1962: 35–48).

Most of the ordinary workmen were probably not literate to any significant degree. They appear to have used marks, rather than writing, for labelling personal property (Černý 1942: 22; Bruyère 1953: pls. 16–18; interpretation: Haring 2000). The domestic context of such marks may relate also to the non-literacy of the village women, although this might not be a sufficient reason for using marks if their menfolk were fully literate—quite apart from the potentially lesser distinctiveness of marks. Be this as it may, the workmen had writing so often before their eyes that the majority could probably recognize at least their own names (compare Blackman 1927: 92 for modern rural Egypt), and perhaps those of the most revered kings and of the gods whose cults they maintained. Many scrawled their names on the rocks around Deir el-Medina and the Valley of the Kings (Černý 1929: 257–8; Peden 2001: 146–237).

The number of men employed by the Tomb varied between about 30 and 120 (Černý 1973: 103–9). Around half as many again were employed as service staff—fishermen, vegetable growers, water carriers, wood cutters, and so forth. This group, of lower status and living away from the village itself, was surely not literate. Set against an average figure of about 45 full members of the crew and 25 service staff (70 in all), there will have been a highly literate group of about 6 senior officials (an average of 3 scribes, 2 foremen, and 1 draughtsman), and at least twice as many again who were also fully literate—sons and assistants of the first group, including the 'deputies' and other 'draughtsmen', as well as perhaps some lower functionaries—around 20 fully literate people. Other kinsmen of the officials, who were employed as simple workmen, could also be literate to some extent (see e.g. Excursus

B above)—and those who later acquired an office were necessarily so. As many as 25–30 per cent of the adult male personnel of the Tomb would thus have been fully literate. The percentage would be higher when the number employed dropped, lower when more men were taken on, because the institution had a complex and intensive administrative structure and a proportion of literate craftsmen for the work itself, whereas the less skilled labouring force was relatively small. Such a structure also favoured the continuity of the administrative group. The level of literacy for the community as a whole may have compared well with any below the highest social levels in dynastic Egypt.

It remains to relate the proposed percentage of adult male literate at Deir el-Medina to that estimated for the country as a whole in section 1 of this chapter, and expressed there in terms of the total population. For this purpose we exclude the partially literate normal workmen, whose function did not require literacy, as being mostly without counterparts in the wider society. We suggest that the working personnel of the Tomb may have formed a fifth to a quarter of the population of their community, women and children making up the rest. In a society with high mortality, this gives a low figure for family size but allows for overlap in categories, as when a father and his son are both employed. We assume literacy among women to have been statistically insignificant. On this basis the literate percentage in the entire community would be $25\text{--}30 \div 4\text{--}5 = 5\text{--}7.5$ per cent, perhaps five times the rate in the country as a whole. It is thus noteworthy that even in a favoured context, which can be studied in some detail, there is no reason for thinking that levels of literacy were of an entirely different order from those occurring elsewhere. Rather, literacy will have varied—both according to occupation and between capital and province, town and country—from restricted to almost non-existent.

In the case of Deir el-Medina as with female literacy (§3 above), the skill may have been commoner for some sectors of the New Kingdom population than our main hypothesis requires. A very small proportion of people could perhaps have attained the spread of restricted literacy of the Greek speakers in Roman Egypt (Youtie 1973; 1981). This possibility is significant in implying a high level of social and legal documentation and an enhanced spread of literate culture in such contexts. We see no reason to generalize these conclusions to other periods and social settings. If new evidence appears, it may be necessary to increase our suggested percentages of literate slightly. Social groups with 'privileged' literacy in other periods might also be identified.

4

Literacy, social organization, and the archaeological record: the case of early Egypt

INTRODUCTION

The use of writing in ancient civilizations poses problems for archaeology, whose most powerful models and methods of analysis are designed for unwritten materials. The separation of the written and the unwritten is felt to be profound. Elizabeth Carter and Matthew Stolper (1984: vii), an archaeologist and a historian of the ancient Near East, state that 'The creation and preservation of ancient texts and of other artifacts result from—and therefore signify—different intentions, behaviors and processes.' For literate cultures, archaeology has until recently been seen as an adjunct, with social analysis being chiefly the domain of history. The place of writing in society and its effect on society or interaction with it are central to the expanding field of literacy studies, which relies on the written word and on hypotheses or reports about relations between the literate and the non-literate, the written and the unwritten (for the ancient Near East, see Goody 1986). Within the archaeological context, however, written documents are common and important artefacts (see Yoffee 1979; Dunnell and Wenke 1980; Yoffee 1980), and writing has an effect on society—however disputed this may be—which should influence the archaeological record. Interpretive models should therefore take the presence or absence of writing into account.

In John Gledhill, Barbara Bender, and Mogens Trolle Larsen (eds.) (1988), *State and society: the emergence and development of social hierarchy and political centralization*, One World Archaeology (London: Unwin Hyman) 192–214.
   There has been a vast amount of fieldwork and publication on late predynastic and Early Dynastic Egypt since 1988. Where this does not alter the position adopted in this chapter, I mostly do not include additional references. Some necessary updates are given in footnotes; for newer material and supplementary issues, see Chs. 5 and 6.

This theoretical requirement is difficult to meet, because of uncertainties about effects of writing. It is desirable to work in two directions: to analyse potential effects of writing on society together with relevant traces of them that could be recovered in the archaeological record (many 'effects' will leave no archaeological trace); and to examine the record for features additional to writing that may be related to its presence. Such strategies bring archaeology and history together, insofar as both rely on constructing models within which incomplete material can be comprehended and exploited. A single model or pattern should not be set up: literacy is not a unitary, well-defined phenomenon, while societies that use writing vary enormously in structure and in material record.

It is difficult, and not necessarily desirable, to define 'social organization' precisely in this context. I explore characteristics of early Egyptian society in relation to writing, but take a definition of its social type—as a centralized monarchy with a literate, office-holding elite—as a point of departure; refinement is desirable, but is dispensable here. The theoretical sophistication of Norman Yoffee's arguments (1979), relating especially to ancient Mesopotamia, throws into relief problems in formulating general models of state and 'civilization' formation: some of the models he dismisses might serve for Egypt, whose state was very different from those of Mesopotamia. Just as literacy is not a single phenomenon with a single range of effects, so there need be no single trajectory of state formation (see also Yoffee 2005).

Much of this chapter is taken up with presenting early evidence for writing in Egypt (see also Ch. 5). At the end, I review archaeological and theoretical issues. The topic relates more to institutional and administrative aspects of writing than to its properties as a symbolic system, but the latter remain relevant to almost any study. I focus on the first four dynasties (*c*.2950–2465). This is the time of the evolution of the script and its basic uses as well as of intensified centralization of society, and thus exemplifies some key problems; later periods must be omitted.

THE CONTEXT OF WRITING

Writing is an aid to communication (including display) and social organization, and its origin is in complex forms of both. It may be employed primarily to communicate at a distance in space and hence to serve complex networks, as in trade, and it may serve storage and communication in time, so that it enhances administration and control. Often it performs both functions. Its chief focus can be non-material, on symbolic or other-worldly ends. Whatever its long-term effects, its first cause or context is mostly an established and developing complex system in a group of polities or within a polity. The polities or polity mostly share their culture, while scripts, languages, and cultures go together to form integrated wholes. The function of extended communication can be served without great cultural involvement and can cross cultural boundaries. For millennia, forerunners of writing were present in the Near East without apparent major cultural consequences over the region (e.g. Schmandt-Besserat 1977; see also Jasim and Oates 1986), and to this day writing is used with marginal effect in some non-centralized societies (Scribner and Cole 1981), as Oswyn Murray (1980: 98–9) suggests that it was in early Greece, where the drive for innovation may have come from elsewhere. The stimulus to create writing predates the state, and for the periods considered here must be ascribed to social, cognitive, and economic change in prehistory. The combination of writing with central administration and control is culturally more powerful, if seldom more innovative. Although many constraints may restrict writing's absorption and expansion of a cultural repertory, it has great potential for such an expansion, which the elite who use or direct it for administration seldom fail to exploit. It can be integrated with other systems of display to propound and immortalize the dominant ideology.

It is therefore useful to separate centralized uses and origins of writing from non-centralized ones. I am concerned with a centralized example, but the opposite should be mentioned. Ancient Mesopotamia (from the late fourth millennium), early north-west Semitic writing in Syria and Palestine (late second to early first millennium; Hawkins 1979: 157–64; Millard 1985; 1986; Demsky 1985), and Greece (c.7th–5th centuries; opposing views: Murray 1980: 90–9; Havelock 1982) are cases of the invention and spread of scripts through culturally uniform but politically decentralized regions. In all these regions, writing stimulated development and contributed vitally to the definition of the cultural and geographical area that constituted a single civilization (for Mesopotamia, see Oppenheim 1977 [1964]; Machinist 1986), but it did not favour political unification. The social and political structure of the different regions varied in type and complexity, as well as in its relation to writing. Eventual attempted unifications of Mesopotamia, perhaps a millennium after the invention of writing, and of Greece in the 4th century, can hardly be ascribed to writing, although they were influenced by the regional definitions which it encouraged. The effect of writing on the archaeological record varies enormously, from a dominant presence in Mesopotamia (Yoffee 1979), through widespread attestation in Greece, to sparse and variable evidence in Syria and Palestine. Because so much depends on accidents of preservation and the medium used, these patterns tell us little about the use or spread of writing in these societies, but they are not comparable with ancient Egypt, from which the majority of the vast legacy of writing is monumental. The Egyptian record too is skewed by preservation, but it remains clear that the Egyptians produced a unique amount of monumental writing. In the other societies, writing was in varying measures an instrument of communication, social control, and cultural expression, but it was not entirely identified with a centralized political system and a single elite.

EARLY EGYPTIAN WRITING

The first stages

As a context for the independent origin of writing—whether or not this was inspired from outside—Egypt was at an extreme of centralization (see also Ch. 2). Writing came at a late stage in the formation of a centralized state (Ray 1986, which appeared after this chapter was written, offers a rather different account of early Egyptian writing). During perhaps a couple of centuries there was a progression from scattered agricultural settlements with just a few concentrations of population, through the emergence of regional states both in Egypt (Kaiser and Dreyer 1982: 242–5) and possibly in Nubia (Williams 1987), to the earliest 'nation state'. Like its predecessors, the late predynastic Egyptian state was only marginally urban (evidence cited, for example, in Kemp 1977, is not comparable with that from Mesopotamia). The nation state existed for some generations—up to ten rulers—before the 1st dynasty ($c.2950$; Kaiser and Dreyer 1982: 260–9).[1]

Throughout this time, the writing system was evolving; there is no certain trace of writing that might have preceded the centralized state. In the perspective of later times, Egyptian history crystallized with the 1st dynasty, which marks the end of a transformation that separated dynastic Egypt radically from its predynastic forerunners, but that transformation had more to do with the development of ideology and display—including writing—and perhaps with a change of dynasty, than with change in the political structure. The division of history from what went before seems to have been created by the introduction of written annals that were later preserved. This development is the high point of the appropriation of writing

---

[1] This paragraph was composed before the crucial finds of Tomb U-j at Abydos in 1989, which most writers see as coming before the centralized state (see further Ch. 5). The focus of the rest of this chapter on archaeological and theoretical implications of writing is not greatly affected by the more recent finds.

for ideology as well as administration, but advances that can be identified in contemporaneous writing are greater in display than in administrative materials, which were already more highly evolved.

The invention of writing must thus be seen in the context of the political, administrative, and ideological development of a unitary but dispersed state with extended lines of communication. The detail of this context is becoming clearer through continuing excavations, especially of Günter Dreyer at Abydos (Dreyer, Hartung, and Pumpenmeier 1998b) and Michael Hoffman and his successors at Hierakonpolis.[2] Whereas the work at Abydos and at Minshat Abu Omar in the north-eastern delta (Kroeper and Wildung 1994–2000) suggests a high degree of integration of the country from well before the 1st dynasty, at the end of the Naqada II period, the material from Hierakonpolis shows developing regional forms which seem less advanced for the same date but clearly exemplify state formation and the elaboration of a royal ideology. What is uncertain is what precise forerunners writing had. The traditional hypothesis, that its invention was derived from Mesopotamia (examined, for example, by Ray 1986), is based on slender evidence, and even its chronological basis is assailable (see further Ch. 5). The alternative proposed by writers such as William Arnett (1982) and Walter Fairservis (1983), that it developed from traditional signs and emblems used on pottery and in other pictorial representation, is plausible enough in that the context is one of extended communication and the exchange or delivery of goods, but little in their detailed arguments is satisfactory (see also Ray 1986: 309). These questions and linguistic aspects of the invention of writing are considered by John Ray (1986: 309), who does not, however, draw out the implications of the separation of state formation from the origin of writing or consider its role in developing administration; examples of administration that he cites are more ceremonial and ideological than practical.

Dynasty 0 and the Early Dynastic period

The earliest writing preserved, which probably dates to the late 4th millennium, consists of signs on pottery, probably indicating royal ownership (e.g. Kaiser 1964: 113 fig. 7; for material discovered subsequently, see Ch. 5). The signs are either painted or incised; their forms are closer to those of later cursive writing than to the monumental script, hieroglyphs, whose origin may be slightly later than that of the cursive. The most striking of this material may be inscribed pottery of King 'Irihor' (reading uncertain), perhaps the

---

[2] While continuing finds at Hierakonpolis, to which the journal *Nekhen News* is dedicated, are vitally important in many ways, they have produced notably little inscribed material.

fourth predecessor of the 1st dynasty, which exhibits the administrative division of the country into two, as well as a developed system for the notation of deliveries for the royal household or burial (Kaiser and Dreyer 1982: 232–5). This primacy of cursive and administrative uses (cf. Schenkel 1983) is reflected in the invention of the artificial medium of papyrus within a century or two of writing itself (see Ch. 2, n. 4; only an uninscribed papyrus is preserved.) Papyrus was surely not the only administrative writing material but, in part because it offered the possibility of creating large pieces, it was well suited to extensive records and went with an elaborate tabular presentation of documents (Helck 1974a; cf. Posener-Kriéger 1976). It was never very cheap (cf. Janssen 1975a: 447–8), and before Graeco-Roman times it seems not to have fostered the kind of mass use of documents known, for example, from the 3rd dynasty of Ur in Mesopotamia (c.2200–2000; cf. Hallo 1971: 81–3; Van De Mieroop 2004: 72–5). Early administration probably used small records on miscellaneous materials, of which grand examples are the wood and bone tags with year names from royal tombs and related contexts (e.g. Petrie 1900; 1901: *passim*; Emery 1938: pls. 17–18; 1961: 194 fig. 112), with papyrus serving for long-distance transmission and for complex record keeping.

Almost all the contexts from which early writing has been found are royal or close to the rulers. Literacy cannot have been confined to the king and his entourage, but it must have been extremely restricted, perhaps including only them and the not very large number of scribes necessary for administrative purposes. Inscribed objects include seals and seal impressions, the ivory tags, stone vases (e.g. Lacau and Lauer 1959–61; 1965) and other prestige objects with small inscriptions (e.g. Fischer 1972: 5–15; Whitehouse 1987), and rare large-scale monumental inscriptions (see in general Kaplony 1963). The chief administrative purpose of writing appears thus to have been to mark ownership and destination and to tabulate economic activities. It was not used for continuous texts, and hence presumably not for what we would call letters, even though no fundamental change was necessary for it to acquire such functions, which were introduced in the 3rd–4th dynasties (from c.2650; see further Chs. 5 and 6). Until writing encoded continuous language, it was scarcely an autonomous vehicle of administration and would have needed to be accompanied in its transmission by people who supplied a verbal context for the information transmitted; such people were probably often themselves literate.

Rather later than writing is attested on pottery, it occurs on the monuments of the latest predynastic kings (dynasty 0, c.3050–2950).[3] This monumental

---

[3] The subsequent finds in Tomb U-j at Abydos show that cursive and formal, hieroglyphic writing existed together from near the beginning. In Ch. 5 I suggest that they were deliberately introduced together as a complete system.

use is continuous with inscribed luxury objects and sealings and is integral to an important and closely circumscribed system of display and of the presentation of values. Rules of decorum may have limited the currency of this system, whose prime early exemplars are votive objects from temples, such as the Scorpion macehead and Narmer palette (e.g. Smith 1998: 12 figs. 12–14; Lange and Hirmer 1968: pls. 4–5; for decorum, see Chs. 1 and 12 here). Even the most 'public' preserved mortuary object of the time, the early 1st dynasty tomb stela of king Wadj from Abydos, will not have been seen by many (Fig. 17; other royal tombs also had such stelae). But whether or not the system of display, which may have extended to perishable objects, was widespread, it sustained the ruler's and the elite's position, either through the image of a world view and of themselves that it conveyed to others, or through the elite's exclusive access to it, or through both. Its better known Old Kingdom forms, however, focus on royalty and exclude humanity from many concerns, restricting the displayed participation even of the elite in central values. Earlier evidence is too scanty to establish whether the same was always true. If it was, decorum and the scarcity of writing must count as being socially divisive in all periods, and the scribal identity of the elite (see below) would involve some degree of ambivalence.

For centuries, writing was restricted to notation (in administration) and display. This restriction cannot have been found crippling; if it had been, the necessary resources would not have been invested in the institution (cf. Cooper 1989), or the system would have been developed further, as it later was.

Unlike many elites, that of early Egypt displayed no separate power bases, such as local landholding or traditional allegiances of different groups or regions, whether they had them or not. They were literate and had themselves depicted as scribes (see Ch. 2 §2.2). In Egypt, this identification of the elite with writing restricted its members' autonomy, so that in early times there was no opposition between scribes and rulers. The written sign repertory and vocabulary were created for royalty and for a single definition of Egypt. A dissenting presentation was not possible and did not appear until later, when continuous texts, with their less circumscribed context and content, were written; even then, it did not surface for centuries (e.g. Roccati 1982: 288–94: Old Kingdom private letters; Lichtheim 1973: 85–6: display inscription in tomb of Ankhtify, c.2100). This high degree of control conceals much, such as possible ethnic or linguistic diversity; dialects were not recorded until late times, although they certainly existed, while other languages are completely unattested before the second millennium (see also Baines 1996b).

The fruits of central control are visible in just a few monuments: royal tombs and their dependencies at Abydos (Kemp 1966; 1967; Kaiser and Dreyer

1982; O'Connor 1989b); a small number of grand elite tombs at Naqada (Stadelmann 1985: 17–19 [interprets as a royal tomb]) and especially Saqqara (Emery 1938; 1939; 1949–58; Quibell 1923; see also Kaiser 1985a); votive deposits at Hierakonpolis (Barbara Adams 1974) and to a lesser extent Elephantine (Dreyer 1986: 18–19), as well as probably Buto (e.g. von der Way and Schmidt 1985); and wealthy cemeteries, without the massive tombs of Abydos and Saqqara, both around the capital at Tarkhan (Petrie 1913–14), Abu Rawash (Klasens 1975, with refs.), and especially Helwan (Saad 1947; 1951; 1969; Köhler 2000) and in the Delta (Kroeper and Wildung 1985). For the 1st dynasty (c.2950–2800), preserved public inscriptions are confined to Abydos, where all but royal stelae were very crude (see e.g. Petrie 1900: pls. 31–6; late 1st dynasty exception pl. 30), and a single, large-scale but clumsy example from Saqqara (Fig. 18 here; Emery 1961: pl. 30a; Smith 1998: 18 fig. 21; Kemp 1967: 26–8, 27 fig. 2). Some 2nd dynasty stelae are known from Saqqara (e.g. Fig. 12 here; Smith 1998: 22 figs. 31–2; see also Kaplony 1963: III, pls. 138–40) and Helwan (Saad 1957; Haeny 1971). Administration can be studied from texts on sealings and small objects (e.g. Edwards 1971: 35–40), while Egyptian objects with royal names from Palestine, principally of the 1st dynasty, testify to foreign trade or conceivably penetration abroad (e.g. Gophna 1976; 1978; van den Brink and Levy 2002).

It is difficult to estimate the numbers of the literate elite that benefited from this activity. The circle of owners of massive tombs, royal and non-royal, would have been in single figures at any one time, and the dependent tombs at Abydos, which included those of 'retainers' as well as perhaps high officials (cf. Kemp 1966), do not attest to large numbers in the elite, although they do show that the royal entourage numbered hundreds of people. For the core group buried at Abydos and Saqqara, there was the 'official' definition of the order of things in terms that included writing, but writing nonetheless offered rather little of general cultural utility and all connected discourse must have been oral. The slightly less prestigious cemeteries around the capital have yielded few inscribed objects, so that writing did not serve these people in the central focus of display and prestige—their burials—whether or not they were literate. The only references in writing to people below scribal status are in mentions of administrative units to which they may have belonged, and in depictions of defeated 'subjects (*rḫjt*)' symbolized by pinioned lapwings on early monuments (e.g. Smith 1998: 12 fig. 12).

The social organization of the elite—not to speak of the rest of the population—is virtually unknown. The central group was so small that it probably consisted chiefly of royal kinsmen, but important people like Imhotep (see below) and Hezyre (Quibell 1913) in the 3rd dynasty and Metjen (Gödecken 1976; Baines 1999a: 29–34) and Pehernefer (Junker 1939) in the early 4th dynasty were not royal. At the beginning of dynastic times, the 'subjects' mentioned above were the symbolically defeated; later they were contrasted with the p^{c}t 'elite' (cf. Helck 1960: 5–16). jrj-p^{c}t 'member of the p^{c}t', attested from the 1st dynasty onward, was the highest-ranking title in the Early Dynastic period and Old Kingdom, analogous to Tsarist Russian 'Prince'. This usage might imply that in origin the ruling group were distinct in terms of ethnicity or kinship from the rest of the population, but such an assertion need have had little foundation in reality. The notional or real kinship basis of the elite persisted without great change until the end of the 4th dynasty. This basis was contemporaneous with, but had different implications from, the same people's assumed (and probably real) literacy and exercise of administrative office, and this tension surfaced in later times. The fact that it could be kept in control for some centuries is significant for Egyptian state formation (compare Yoffee 1979: 14–17).

This evidence for early state organization contrasts in two respects with that from later periods. First, the capital and a few other centres were dominant. No strong, uniform provincial administration is visible. Such a system could be the creation of the later Early Dynastic period or it could elude recognition for earlier times (compare Helck 1975: 18–44 with Janssen 1978: 225–7). Second, the superstructure of major centres overlays a large number of smaller cemeteries with simple graves (cf. Kessler 1982), which demonstrates that the population was spread over the whole country (cf. Butzer 1976: 57–80), and many could afford to leave behind some memorial for posterity and for the next world. The chief archaeological feature that might point to literacy is the dominance of the capital, Memphis, which is reflected in a number of separate, socially demarcated cemeteries located within a day or so's journey of the centre. The concentration of the elite around the capital probably relates to its prestige and to bureaucratic needs, but these latter must have been served by an effective system of levies and of transport, which will have brought a large non-literate population into the area. A little connected administration can be seen in preserved writing, which must be a minuscule fraction of what was produced. Writing and other modes of administration reinforced each other in the process of centralization.

There is no Early Dynastic evidence for non-elite writing and hardly any from the Old Kingdom (c.2575–2150)—nothing comparable with the quite widespread informal graffiti and inscriptions of early Greece (e.g. Murray 1980: 91–7; Havelock 1982: 185–207). In Egypt, one must look ahead to the First Intermediate period (c.2150–1980) for a slightly broader range of material.

THE 3RD–4TH DYNASTIES: DEVELOPMENT AND ITS CONTROL

The 3rd dynasty (c.2650–2575) is the first stage in a transformation of all aspects of the record. The use of writing expanded significantly. Royal and non-royal monuments include much more writing, and the style and arrangement of the script is near to standard Old Kingdom forms (e.g. Firth et al. 1935: pls. 15–17, 40–3; Wood 1978; Smith 1998: 32 figs. 49–50). Royal reliefs at Heliopolis (Smith 1998: 33 fig. 51) and in Sinai (Gardiner, Peet, and Černý 1952–5: nos. 1, 3, 4; Giveon 1974) may show an expansion of public display, but only the latter were generally visible, and they were addressed as much to foreigners, who were a very tangential public for writing, as to Egyptians; the temple reliefs also have 2nd dynasty forerunners (e.g. Quibell 1900: pl. 2). Developments like these are often related to the statement of the Graeco-Egyptian historian Manetho that in the reign of Djoser, the first king of the dynasty (c.2650–2630) the culture hero '⟨Imuthes⟩'—whose name is supplied by modern editors in the text—'devoted attention to writing' (see Ch. 2, n. 8). More or less 'informal' uses of writing preserved from this time include quarry marks on stone (Lauer 1936: 242–5), an ostracon with calculations for the curve of an arch from Djoser's step pyramid complex (Lauer 1936: 174 fig. 200), and short graffiti on the first enclosure wall of his successor Sekhemkhet's step pyramid complex (Goneim 1957: pls. 11–13, including the name of Imhotep = Imuthes, pl. 13), where quarry marks are also frequent, as they continued to be throughout the Old Kingdom. These, however, were written by people working on the chief projects of the time, and the 'literacy' involved in making quarry marks could be minimal, although those who set up the marking system needed to be more literate. This evidence may suggest that the organization of stone building, on a larger scale than anything attempted before in any medium, generated an appropriate administrative and technical use of writing, but by itself it shows little of how writing was used more generally.

Thus, the proven range and volume of writing increased greatly, and the central elite displayed its scribal status (e.g. Quibell 1913: pls. 29–32; Wood 1978). The most 'advanced' writing, including continuous sentences, is on reliefs from a chapel of Djoser at Heliopolis (Smith 1949: 132–8; Morenz 2002). This pattern shows that central religious material received a privileged treatment; from then on, religious texts could have been written, but it is impossible to establish exactly when they began to be recorded (compare Ch. 6; Baines 2004c). Contemporaneous administrative writing and monumental decoration did not go very far beyond earlier norms, although the tomb of Hezyre shows the potential for change (Quibell 1913: pls. 15–22).

It is difficult to separate 1st and 2nd dynasty material archaeologically from that of the 3rd dynasty; consequently, the impact of the latter's rule in the provinces can hardly be studied. Noteworthy monuments of the period and of the early 4th dynasty are an uncertain number of small, non-sepulchral step pyramids at sites throughout the country (Dreyer and Kaiser 1980; Stadelmann 1985: 79, pls. 20–2; Seidlmayer 1996), and five very large non-royal tombs at Beit Khallaf (Kaplony 1975, with refs.), a little north of Abydos, from which no monument of the period is known apart from one of the small pyramids. Major elite mortuary sites are reduced to Saqqara, Beit Khallaf, and perhaps Helwan and Elkab (Quibell 1898: 3–4), but it is not known whether this concentration applied further down the social scale.[4] Only the step pyramids are at all evenly spread; centralization of wealth seems more pronounced in this period than earlier, as may have been necessary for the very large building projects. Official titles show that the developed structure of the provinces or 'nomes' of later times, which divided the country into 35–40 units of roughly comparable size, existed from early in the dynasty (cf. Helck 1974b: 199–202 [pp. 49–53 tend to place the process earlier]; Fischer 1977a: 408–9). Except near Abydos, provincial administrators must have had no monuments, or they erected them around the capital.

In comparison with the 3rd dynasty, the 4th (c.2575–2450) shows further advances in writing and in decorative display, just as it built upon the former's achievements in stone building to produce architecture of a new order of size and type of design in the vast pyramid complexes of Dahshur and Giza. The earliest long inscriptions on non-royal monuments date to the beginning of the dynasty (Gödecken 1976; Baines 1999a: 29–34, with refs.; Junker 1939). By now, administrative writing could record complete sentences, and so had a much increased potential for action from a distance, and for impersonality, because oral messages no longer had to accompany written communication.

The use of writing in display also expanded. The decoration of the mortuary temples of Snofru at Dahshur (c.2575–2545; Fakhry 1961; Stadelmann 1985: 104) had a number of themes in common with later times, as probably did that of Khufu (c.2545–2520; cf. Goedicke 1971), while non-royal tombs of the beginning of the dynasty at Maidum (Petrie 1892) and Saqqara (Lepsius n.d.-a: pls. 3–7) contain the later scenic repertory in essence. In both cases,

---

[4] See now David O'Connor's discussion (2000: 21–4) of Reqaqna, near Beit Khallaf, as well as its relation with the more modest cemeteries of Nag el-Deir across the river (Reisner 1932). This was the area of the most ancient capital and seems to have had a special salience throughout the Old Kingdom.

however, 3rd dynasty precursors are possible, as is shown by the Djoser material and by the non-royal tomb of Hezyre (Quibell 1913). Among material transmitted on papyrus, certain sacred items, such as a list of gods of the Memphite area, may go back to the 3rd dynasty (Baines 1988a). Ritual texts could also have been recorded, but the discursive use of writing for other traditional matter seems to be much later, except possibly for medical treatises (cf. Westendorf 1966: 27). Here, the royal Pyramid Texts of the late 5th–8th dynasties (c.2350–2125; Faulkner 1969) provide ample evidence of texts of great age, but there is no firm evidence for when they were first written, and they do not demonstrate the existence of a wide written repertory of high culture (see Altenmüller 1972: 76–8, 279, for uncertain arguments on the earliest Pyramid Texts; Baines 2004c). Most of culture continued to be oral, while the socially pluralizing possibilities of writing for private and individual purposes are unknown from before much later times. Scarcity and functionality still dominated the use of writing. A rather different question is whether the technical and architectural achievements of the pyramids required written texts. The surveying and calculation involved in construction, as well as computing the requirement for stone and so forth, are notable achievements, but they are based on simple mathematical procedures (see e.g. Robins and Shute 1982; 1985) and may owe more to tabular and graphic skills than to texts. In accuracy of orientation, the pyramids do not surpass some Neolithic structures in western Europe (although they do surpass them in geometrical execution).

Provincial administration of the 4th dynasty is visible both in titles and in the official presentation of the proper order of things. Series of offering bearers in the mortuary temple of Snofru's southern pyramid (the Bent Pyramid) represent estates located in the various provinces which were to produce mortuary offerings for the temple in perpetuity (Fakhry 1961: 17–58; compare Jacquet-Gordon 1962 for the broader context of these processions). The owners of the chief non-royal tomb inscriptions held land in a number of nomes, either because the king wished to avoid their having a single power base or because men of their status stood above provincial affairs; either way, they were buried at the capital.

The structure of nomes is so regular and logical that it might have been designed by the author of central place theory. Both its overall framework and the titles of provincial administrators show that the system—which must have administered the country efficiently to make the period's achievements possible—existed in reality, but the reality in question is not an archaeological one. The 4th dynasty is the time of greatest concentration on the king and the capital, as is visible in the Dahshur and Giza pyramids, the largest monuments ever constructed in Egypt. In addition to the king, a circle of high officials, many of them his kinsmen (cf. Helck 1968: 50–61), was buried around the pyramids in grandiose but much smaller tombs. There are probably more tombs of high officials at Giza than are known for comparable spans of the Early Dynastic period (for computations of size and significance, see Kanawati 1977), as well as smaller numbers of important ones at Maidum, Dahshur, Giza, and Saqqara, all of which had pyramids. In their stone construction (except at Maidum: Petrie 1892: 11–22), these tombs are sharply offset from any that may have belonged to lower officials.

Against all this, not a single provincial tomb of consequence is dated to the 4th dynasty, and virtually no cemeteries of simple graves have been assigned to the period (for qualifications to this point, see n. 4 here; Ch. 6). In the mortuary record, which is almost all that is available, provincial Egypt is a blank for the period. Vast amounts of labour were brought to the capital to construct a rigidly defined and regimented setting for the afterlife of a small group of people (see e.g. Lehner 1985; for the town under excavation that is associated with pyramid construction at Giza, see e.g. Lehner 2002). Those who provided that labour were so impoverished that they could not bury themselves appropriately for an afterlife of their own, while those who supervised their labours either belonged to the group buried in the monuments, in which case their values were centred on the capital, or they were themselves impoverished. There could have been an ethos according to which the burial of the king and his entourage guaranteed survival for the remainder of the country, as is suggested for the central group by the relationship on the ground between royal and other tombs, but such beliefs could not have been held in earlier times, from which large number of burials are known, and they are not attested from later. However centralization was legitimized in the 4th dynasty, it surely involved deprivation for most of the people. I consider below the role of writing in that deprivation (for numbers of literate, see Ch. 3 §1).

The exclusivity of the ruling group of the central 4th dynasty is apparent in a royal restriction of tomb decoration, that is, of the freedom of anyone but the king to use pictorial representation and writing in mortuary display. The most important non-royal tombs of the period are east of the Great Pyramid at Giza in the East Field (Reisner 1942: 10–19, 27–36). Fragments suggest that the outer chapels of these were decorated with a range of 'scenes of daily life' (e.g. Simpson 1978: pl. 6b–d). Tombs on the west side belonging to people of marginally lesser status (the West Field) were in a less prominent and favourable position and had no visible decoration (their structures were almost as massive). In their offering chapels were set up 'slab stelae' with a single scene of the deceased seated before a table with an enumeration of offerings, but some of these were walled up and rendered invisible, perhaps after the burial had been completed (e.g. Smith 1998: 44 figs. 74–7; study: Manuelian 1998; 2003). These tombs belonged to people of even higher status than the owners of the early 4th dynasty decorated tombs at Saqqara (e.g. Lepsius n.d.-a: pls. 3–7). The obvious explanation for their lack of public decoration is that this form of display was restricted to the king and his closest entourage, all of whom were also both high officials and the administrative or hierarchical superiors of the other tomb owners. In a period when the potential of writing had been much enhanced and was exploited by the ruler and his associates, such a gesture is potent and autocratic; it states in another form the same overweening claims presented by the two great Giza pyramids (the equally massive pair of Dahshur pyramids, which belonged to a single king, does not have quite the same relationship with a surrounding necropolis). In the long term, discipline of this sort could not endure, and by the end of the 4th dynasty decoration of non-royal tombs was often more extensive. In another way, however, the restriction was maintained throughout the Old Kingdom. Even in the privileged tombs of the East Field, the decoration includes no explicitly religious themes. This restriction conforms to general rules of decorum, according to which only the king's monuments, among which were temples to the gods, could have decoration which depicted the gods directly (cf. Baines 1985c: 277–305; Chs. 1 and 12 here).

For the outsider, this socially stratified restriction of writing and decoration is part of central political control, and in seeking to make a scarce resource still scarcer it is repressive. On another level, the strategy of stemming the spread of a 'democratizing' institution is typically conservative, a reaction paralleled for a later period of increasing diffusion of writing by Plato's condemnation of writing and its effects (*Phaedrus* 274c–275b; see Ch. 2, n. 22). The elite's general perception need not have been one of repression, because the inherited scheme could have been accepted for the time being virtually without question. The point of departure is the central creation and control of writing, so that any diffusion may require specific sanction or decision. So long as continuous texts were not written or inscribed on monuments outside a religious context, the limited expressive possibilities of writing might hardly foster interest in such diffusion (irrespective of any possible anti-writing ideology), but once such texts were present, they might bring a self-sustaining development, because it is difficult to control what is said in them—a point that was later exploited by some Egyptians. Since the system of decorum encompasses both writing and pictorial representation, these points apply to decoration too. In this wider context, the restriction of mid-4th dynasty tombs still appears repressive, coming as it did after the brief expansive time of the reign of Snofru (see also Ch. 7), and has the appearance of a vain attempt to stem the diffusion of writing and display. Because of the system of decorum, for many centuries people may not even have considered the possibility of inscribing prayers to the gods or depicting images of them in their tombs;[5] these did not become common until after 1500, around a millennium later.

EXTENSION AND LOOSENING OF THE SYSTEM

The later Old Kingdom (5th–6th dynasties, c.2465–2150) forms the logical conclusion to the development described so far, but for the argument here it is a pendant. During about 300 years, the use of writing and the range of text types extended gradually, as did the amount of decoration on non-royal monuments. There was a slow increase in the number of cemeteries with simple graves. This diffusion and levelling of wealth accompanied a spread of power away from the capital to the provinces, and the two phenomena are probably connected. Some potential developments did not occur: the system of decorum changed only in detail throughout Egyptian history (see Ch. 1), while writing was not used for narrowly literary texts during the Old Kingdom. Decorum was probably so deeply embedded as to be an almost invisible assumption of the order of things, apart from having very detailed applications in particular decorative contexts; more complex considerations relate to the absence of literature (see Assmann 1983b; Baines 1999c). Only very rarely does preserved writing escape from conventional constraints. A piquant example of such a subversive use is a graffito on a vandalized late Old Kingdom non-royal relief which seems to read 'You arrested me and beat my father. Let me be content(?). Who are you (now) to escape from me? May my father rest in peace' (Drioton 1952: 353; Baines 1991c: 141 n. 50). In a divided and socially mobile context—and no doubt elsewhere—writing is well suited to reprisals.

The diffusion of writing and decoration parallels changes in the administrative hierarchy of the 5th and later dynasties. Whereas royal kin were dominant in the 4th dynasty, virtually none of the highest officials of later times were agnatic kin of the king, and for more than a millennium princes seem not to be attested during the reigns of their brothers or nephews (cf. Schmitz 1980). The non-royal elite of this period therefore defined and displayed their status as office-holders and bureaucrats; they appear to have

---

[5] A few 4th dynasty tombs include a vastly enlarged hieroglyph of the god of burial and the necropolis, Anubis, that functions almost as an image of him as a deity (Baines 2004c: 34; Simpson 1978: figs. 24–5). This detail suggests that the limits on the use of such images were perceived as restrictive.

owed allegiance to institutions as well as to a dominant person, the king. Yet this change in institutional patterning came with the new dynasty, after the relaxation in the rules of display in the late 4th dynasty and an implied greater personal independence. It may seem to be a logical concomitant of the increased use of writing, but it was probably initiated by a political act. Nonetheless, the act will have been constrained by the changing environment and requirements of the elite and thus have depended to some extent on writing. The mid-4th dynasty restriction of display and the 5th dynasty institutionalization of the bureaucracy derived meaning from the literate context without being simply determined by it.

DISCUSSION

I now consider the development of writing in society and attempt to relate it to archaeological contexts and to the theoretical problems outlined at the beginning.

The archaeological record

The difference in wealth between the literate elite and the rest of the population was marked throughout the 1st–4th dynasties and reached its highest degree near the end of that period.[6] The elite who possessed inscribed tombs, however, were only a small fraction of the literate elite. For some of the time, many wealthy tombs contained no inscriptions and few or no inscribed small objects, while the administrative use of writing must have required a scribal class of at least a few hundred at any time—more than the class who constructed large tombs—apart from the implausibility of any suggestion that scribes throughout the country were members of the central elite. The archaeological material can thus be divided into that of the wealthy, of whom most were probably literate because they were all in high state service, and the rest of the population, including many of the remaining literate. In the 1st and 2nd dynasties, the less wealthy often had their own proper burials, while in the 3rd and especially the 4th dynasty they did not.[7]

[6] Grave goods seem to have been generally sparse in the Old Kingdom, especially in the region of the capital; see O'Connor (2000: 23–4); Baines and Lacovara (2002: 15 with ref.).

[7] The mixed habitation and cemetery site of Tell el-Farkha in the north-eastern Delta, which is one of the few to preserve evidence from late predynastic times into the 4th dynasty, shows a steady decline in material culture over that period (Ciałowicz in press). This pattern may be an index of administrative and demographic centralization as well as of the impoverishment of non-elite communities.

The record of the centralization of wealth is given extra relief by chances of preservation. Almost no settlement sites are known or excavated for this half millennium because most of them were sited in the alluvium, in which sites have not been preserved or have not been studied. One function of burials is to display status, so that they are likely to exaggerate differences in wealth, which might be less marked in settlements. The most remarkable deficiency of the record was previously the lack of an archaeologically identifiable capital. Geophysical work and borings now show that the area east of the North Saqqara necropolis was probably the urban centre of Memphis (see e.g. Jeffreys and Tavares 1994), but this is a small area in comparison with major urban sites in the Near East. In theory, the royal residence shifted with the site of each new pyramid—over a distance of some 50 kilometres—and some other settlements may also have moved, but even this extra factor does not account entirely for the absence of evidence. The capital was administratively paramount, and in death all the elite wished to be buried near it, but it must have been a dispersed and relatively modest set of settlements. The stereotype that the Egyptians put all their wealth into their burials at the expense of their dwelling places, which is common to classical Greek writers and to many Egyptologists (e.g. Assmann 1991: 17–19), may be exaggerated, but it corresponds to some reality. Egypt appears like an estate focused on the king and his burial, and only marginally like an urban society. The tomb reliefs of the Old Kingdom elite suggest that their ideal life-style too was manorial. Neither king nor elite erected great civic or personal monuments in the world of the living.

This deprivation of the living in favour of the dead (although the living need not have seen the matter in this way), of the poor in favour of the rich, of the rich in favour of the king, and, in theory, ultimately of the king in favour of the gods (see Ch. 7), which reduced the mass of the population to archaeological invisibility, has a parallel outside Egypt that is probably caused by the predatory activities of Egypt. This is Lower Nubia, whose A-Group culture, which was contemporary with later predynastic and very early dynastic Egypt, was obliterated, leaving an archaeological blank of up to 500 years, before the C-Group appears in the 6th dynasty (Nordström 1972: 29–32; William Y. Adams 1977: 132–5; 1985: 188–9; Williams 1987: 16–17). In the narrow Nubian Nile valley, the chances of finding settlements or any archaeological sites are much greater than in Egypt, and the region has been exhaustively surveyed (cf. William Y. Adams 1985: 189). As Hans-Åke Nordström argues (1972: 32), it is unlikely that the region was devoid of people. Rather, Egyptian raids and domination, for which there is good evidence (e.g. Trigger 1976: 40–8; W. Y. Adams 1977: 135–40; Helck 1974c [figures taken too literally]), depressed the inhabitants' material culture below the archaeological 'threshold' for the methods of recovery used up to the 1960s, when the area was lost beneath the waters of Lake Nasser. I suggest that the same may apply to some extent to Egypt itself during the central Old Kingdom. (For Nubia, see addendum, p. 116.)

The question of how far writing affects this development cannot be answered in isolation, but some points can be made about the context. Writing emerged soon after the rapid unification of the Egyptian state and helped to consolidate that unification. The degree of centralization and of regional impoverishment increased as writing became more widespread and could be used for more purposes. Innovations in writing, which came in stages and not through steady development, were probably intended to enhance administrative efficiency.[8] The ultimate degree of centralization was achieved after writing had acquired the potential impersonality of recording messages that were comprehensible without an intermediary—which is not to imply that only 'practical' purposes determined this development. Although writing cannot be proved to be necessary for centralization, its participation in it is clear. It did not contribute very much to creating a discursive ideological context where centralization and the appropriation of resources could be legitimized, but it was used for the ideologically crucial purpose of presenting the world of the gods. By the 4th dynasty, continuous texts were scarcely used in public contexts, while material presented in the system of decorum was too restricted in its contexts to speak to society in general. Public ideology must have continued to be oral; architecture rather than representational art and writing reached out beyond the elite.

Another approach to examining the role of writing is to look at other aspects of material culture. This culture was very uniform throughout the country. The regional cultures of predynastic times were largely displaced by the unifying late Naqada II/Naqada III (see e.g. Kaiser 1990). By the early 1st dynasty, other processes of differentiation emerged. Flint and decorative hard stone vase technology were developed to extraordinary levels, but many of the resulting products were destined for the tomb (e.g. Emery 1939: pl. 11; 1961: pl. 40 [flint], pls. 33, 35–9 [stone vases]; stone vase repertory: el-Khouli 1978). The same applies to copper, in which magnificent vases, jugs, and bowls were made (e.g. Emery 1961: pls. 41, 43), in addition to tools and weapons (Emery 1938: pls. 20–2; 1961: pls. 42, 44–5). Painted or otherwise decorated ceramics, which had been important in Naqada I–II (c.3900–3300), lost almost all significance. A few painted jars occur as late as the 3rd dynasty, but the decoration on these imitates the veining of stone or suspension nets, rather than forming autonomous motifs (e.g. vessels from Egypt Exploration Society excavations at North Saqqara; Bourriau 1981: no. 79). Virtually all production was in plain functional designs that impress by their quantity and

---

[8] For modifications to these points, see Ch. 5.

Literacy and the archaeological record

uniformity (e.g. Emery 1961: pls. 12–13, 20), not through their aesthetic qualities, although some manufacture was of a high standard (e.g. Bourriau 1981: nos. 6–8, 83–8). Decorated pottery is a luxury product that is widespread in many societies and tends to have local traditions; in almost all periods, Nubian pottery exhibited these possibilities (e.g. Bourriau 1981: nos. 193–225). The standardized and centralized culture of dynastic and Graeco-Roman Egypt mostly ignored them, and with them the communicative potential of decoration, perhaps in part because it fell outside the 'official' and more explicit decorative system of decorum. Vessel forms in pottery imitated stone or metal (e.g. Bourriau 1981: nos. 84–5); even some stone vase shapes look as if they were designed for metal (e.g. Emery 1961: pls. 35, 38–9; Saad and Autry 1969: pl. 28; Smith 1998: 16 fig. 20). Stone vases—not to speak of metalware—were primarily an elite product (but see Caton-Thompson and Gardner 1934: 98–9), so that the effect of this tendency is to empty non-elite pottery of symbolic content, except as imitations. These imitations were in turn often relevant chiefly to deposition in the tomb. Most people could not aspire to own a tomb.

The side of this development that can hardly be observed is the development of technology for everyday purposes in agriculture, hunting, fishing, crafts, and so forth. Most discussion of the use of copper relates to prestige applications, such as the cutting of hard stones with copper saws (e.g. Clarke and Engelbach 1930: 203–4) and other techniques developed for large-scale sculpture and stone building (see in general Dieter Arnold 1991). This 'advanced' technology contrasts with modest Old Kingdom sites, including one at Giza, whose material culture is typologically distinct from, but otherwise comparable with, the Predynastic (Caton-Thompson and Gardner 1934: 97–102; Mills 1979: 169–74; Kromer 1978; see also e.g. von der Way and Schmidt 1985: 281–9). The same basic point may also apply to the organizational skills used to construct the pyramids; these contrast with a lack of good evidence for extensive Old Kingdom irrigation works which has led some Egyptologists to question the existence of artificial irrigation before the First Intermediate period (Schenkel 1978; Endesfelder 1979). In this case I believe that an argument from silence has been pressed too far without taking into account decorum, which would disfavour the mention or display of such a 'mundane' activity. There probably was some irrigation, but its possible absence is symptomatic of the direction in which the ruling group directed expertise and innovation.

The social context; theoretical issues

The evidence for centralization of the country and of wealth is supplied by archaeology. The development of writing is contemporaneous with that process: writing records and supplies detail for an ideology which fits well with centralization. The uniformity of the written record also parallels that of archaeology. In the presentation of ideology, the system of decorum excludes humanity from the focal context of relations between the gods and the king that was displayed in temple reliefs and royal statuary. The most it does is to show personified geographical units provisioning the king (Fakhry 1961: 17–58) and, slightly more concretely, 'human' abstractions of agricultural estates bringing produce to the king and to members of the elite (Jacquet-Gordon 1962). This exclusion aptly heightens the material focus on the king and the elite, but because of the system's specialized and 'sacred' character, it would be dangerous to press this point too far, if only because decorum appears to deprive the elite as well as the rest of humanity. For reasons of decorum, elite tombs could not depict the king or the gods. Instead, the gradually increasing decorative repertory shows the tomb owner among his (occasionally her) kin, as well as inferiors or dependants who work in his service on the land, presenting produce, and engaged in subordinate administration. The figures can be named in captions, often inscribed after the rest of the decoration was completed, but they may also be 'genre' figures, lacking a specific identity.

Such a presentation leaves out a great deal of reality and of society, and corresponds at a lower level to the appropriation of Egypt as a royal 'estate'. It omits any concerns that might apply to the rest of society on its own terms and it makes the members of society only slightly more visible than they are in the archaeological record of their activities on their own behalf. Late Old Kingdom biographical inscriptions—from a time when there is far more evidence from provincial sites—exhibit the concern of the elite for the less fortunate (Roccati 1982), probably drawing on traditional oral sentiments of solidarity (for written material, see Assmann 1983b: 74), and thus they soften the divisions of society, but they too cannot speak for the rest. Almost nothing allows a glimpse of the ideology of the non-elite, who could possibly have held different and opposing values, although no period in Egyptian history provides strong evidence for counter-cultures. It is not necessary to believe that all those who built the pyramids, who probably included among them robbers of other tombs, thought they were doing themselves good. To assume that state-imposed burdens were universally accepted (e.g. Stadelmann 1985: 105) is to ignore the fact that this system did not endure and hence that some must have questioned them; but the initial stimulus to change would have come from within the elite who could seize the power to alter it, not from outside. Among the remainder of society, the archaeological record suggests that the acquiescent and the rebellious alike were materially and culturally impoverished by central appropriation, as in a sense were the elite. This degree of centralization and focus on a single person could not last.

Writing affected the non-elite directly through administration, but administrative writing is almost entirely lost, because it was on perishable media (for the earliest such papyri, probably of the late 4th dynasty, see Posener-Kriéger 1975); only the elite could afford to have writing on their monuments. The record of the population's integration into the state cannot be recovered, and it cannot be known what proportion of them was touched by central exactions of labour. Even if this gap were filled to some extent, it would not present the administered on their own terms, and the indications are that the 'texts' would be lists and accounts, not complex records including decisions or ideas and reflections on decisions. The existence of such material would not counterbalance the presentation of subordinates in elite tombs.[9]

CONCLUSION

Writing appeared after state formation in Egypt. From its invention until the notation of texts, its relationship with the state was passive or interactive: it aided centralization and was expanded, through central decision rather than evolution, to contribute more to the same process and perhaps to help in specific aspects of administration. But when texts came to be recorded, writing acquired extra potential that could not be so well controlled, rather as the contemporaneous extremes of centralization could not be maintained. Because of its restricted potential, ultra-limited literacy and a writing system restricted to notations could serve its masters fairly faithfully, while limited literacy poses more problems—if only within the literate elite, since there is no evidence for wider dissemination of its message or for writing-related conflict (which does not mean that the latter did not occur). Limited literacy may have had more political than cognitive implications, but in any case an understanding of its effects must involve many other factors. State formation and structure, which differed so much between Mesopotamia and Egypt, as well as the persistence of the state, remain central to the analysis both of writing and of the archaeological record: the symbolic system of the state provides the context for interpreting both symbolic and material records (which are themselves also symbolic). The exclusive identification of state, kingship, and ideology in Egypt, and the love of monuments, gave a major

---

[9] Norman Yoffee and I have taken the discussion of these issues further (Baines and Yoffee 1998; see also essays in Richards and Van Buren 2000). The record of late Old Kingdom provincial cemeteries can be used to nuance the picture a little more. See Seidlmayer (1990); Baines (2006b).

role to an additional and potent use of writing in permanent display. This writing is an important source in its own right, but insofar as it adds evidence for another field of enquiry, that field is history rather than archaeology.

In other respects, archaeological material and writing, with its distribution and its absences, are parallel sets of evidence. In its interactive relationship with the state, writing intensified the material deprivation of most of society, so that it must be drawn into archaeological models. For archaeology it is also valuable as a stimulus. Preserved writing is a tiny, skewed sample of what there was. Any consideration of its position in society must turn on the analysis of gaps, both in writing and in how writing reports on, and ultimately affects, unwritten communication. Thus, in the construction of hypotheses about the nature of the sample, interpretation of writing shares a basic procedure with archaeology. I have used written and depicted material together with an archaeological analogy (Nubia) and environmental considerations (the alluvium and relations between cemeteries and settlement) to suggest an interpretation in which writing points to gaps in the archaeological record, such as provincial sites, while archaeological material—which includes the pyramids—provides the framework. Archaeology and writing complement each other's silences.

Addendum

Birgit Glück, 'Zur Frage der Datierung der frühen C-Gruppe in Unternubien', *Ägypten und Levante* 15 (2005) 131–53, presents detailed evidence for human burials of the 'proto-C Group' in Lower Nubia, together with interaction between the Nile Valley and the Western Desert, during the Old Kingdom. The material she gathers reduces a little the appearance of a gap in the archaeological record in Nubia for this period. It also throws if anything more strongly into relief the rarity of contemporaneous sites that have been identified in the Egyptian Nile Valley.

5

Writing and society in early Egypt

INTRODUCTION: WRITING AND SOCIETIES

Egyptian writing appeared first in the late fourth millennium BCE, evolving thereafter in stages, until in the later 2nd dynasty the script reached a more or less definitive structure that was applied in some contexts to the notation of continuous language. During this period of perhaps four hundred years, writing was a very limited instrument. It was used both in administration and in artistic display, but there is no reason to suppose that it was intended from the first to record texts in full syntactic form. This restricted form of writing was a vital means of communication for administration and for display within the inner elite, but its impact outside those spheres was probably indirect. Administration, writing, and representational art were three central, interlinked creations of a society that evolved rapidly into a state. The presence of the complex social form of the state—perhaps a regional state rather than a central one—was probably a precondition of the emergence of such institutions (compare Bard 1992; on state origins in Egypt, see now Wengrow 2006). Writing in turn no doubt affected social organization, although the extent and manner in which its earliest forms did so are quite uncertain.

The development of bureaucratic administration, and of art forms of which hieroglyphic writing was an integral and indispensable part, constituted a vast investment in materials and in people and involved a continuing commitment for training and supporting scribal and artistic personnel.

This chapter is based on the underlying English text of an article published in Italian translation as 'Scrittura e società nel più antico Egitto', in Francesco Tiradritti (ed.) (1999), *Sesh: Lingue e scritture nell'antico Egitto—inediti dal Museo Archeologico di Milano*, exhibition catalogue (Milan: Electa 1999) 21–30 (I do not know the name of the translator into Italian). I have revised and extended the article, notably in the discussion of the significance of three script forms for the development of the writing system and in the largely new section 'Oral and written "texts"'.

This commitment can be contrasted with other styles of development in different civilizations of comparable or greater scale and complexity. Thus, in early Mesopotamia writing was highly evolved for administration but not important in art, while the Andean Inka state did not use writing but did administer an enormous polity (see e.g. Boone and Mignolo 1994; Trigger 2004). Among early civilizations, the Egyptian became one of those most focused on creating monuments, and employed 'monumental' writing on 'memorial' objects from the largest to the smallest. The civilization with a usage of writing most closely comparable with Egypt was perhaps the Mayan of Mexico and Guatemala (e.g. Houston 2000; Reents-Budet 1994: inscribed elite ceramics). A highly distinctive feature of Egyptian writing is its separation in all periods into the 'monumental' and the 'cursive', which for the Old Kingdom and later are generally termed 'hieroglyphic' and 'hieratic'. (On the third form, 'cursive hieroglyphic', see 'Further elaboration' below.)

INITIAL DEVELOPMENTS

The precise date of the invention of Egyptian writing is uncertain. The oldest material that clearly constitutes writing and has been recovered from a secure archaeological context is on very small tags (Fig. 5; typically 1.5 × 1.25 cm) originally attached to grave goods in Tomb U-j at Abydos, the burial place of a late predynastic ruler (Naqada IIIa period; Dreyer et al. 1998b). Single and paired signs inscribed in ink on pottery from the same tomb are very different in appearance, and perhaps in usage, from those on the tags (Fig. 6); they may nevertheless be graphic variants from a different sector of a relatively large repertory of signs that belonged to the same overall system and hence also constituted writing. The presence of two repertories of sign forms in different contexts is significant because it suggests that writing was conceived from the first as a resource with different high-cultural and slightly more mundane administrative applications, even though the signs on the pots too probably constituted display of a kind (Baines 2004a: 158–9). The material from Tomb U-j, which may be two centuries earlier than the 1st dynasty, is well formed and is unlikely to have been the very first Egyptian writing (see also Kahl 1994: 156–61). Nonetheless, I would not follow writers such as Ludwig Morenz (2004) in accepting Günter Dreyer's proposal of a sizeable earlier period of development, from late Naqada II onward.

An essential question relating to this earliest writing is the extent to which it was intended to represent language. Dreyer (1998b) and others (e.g. Breyer 2002; Morenz 2004) assume that it does so and hence they seek systematic

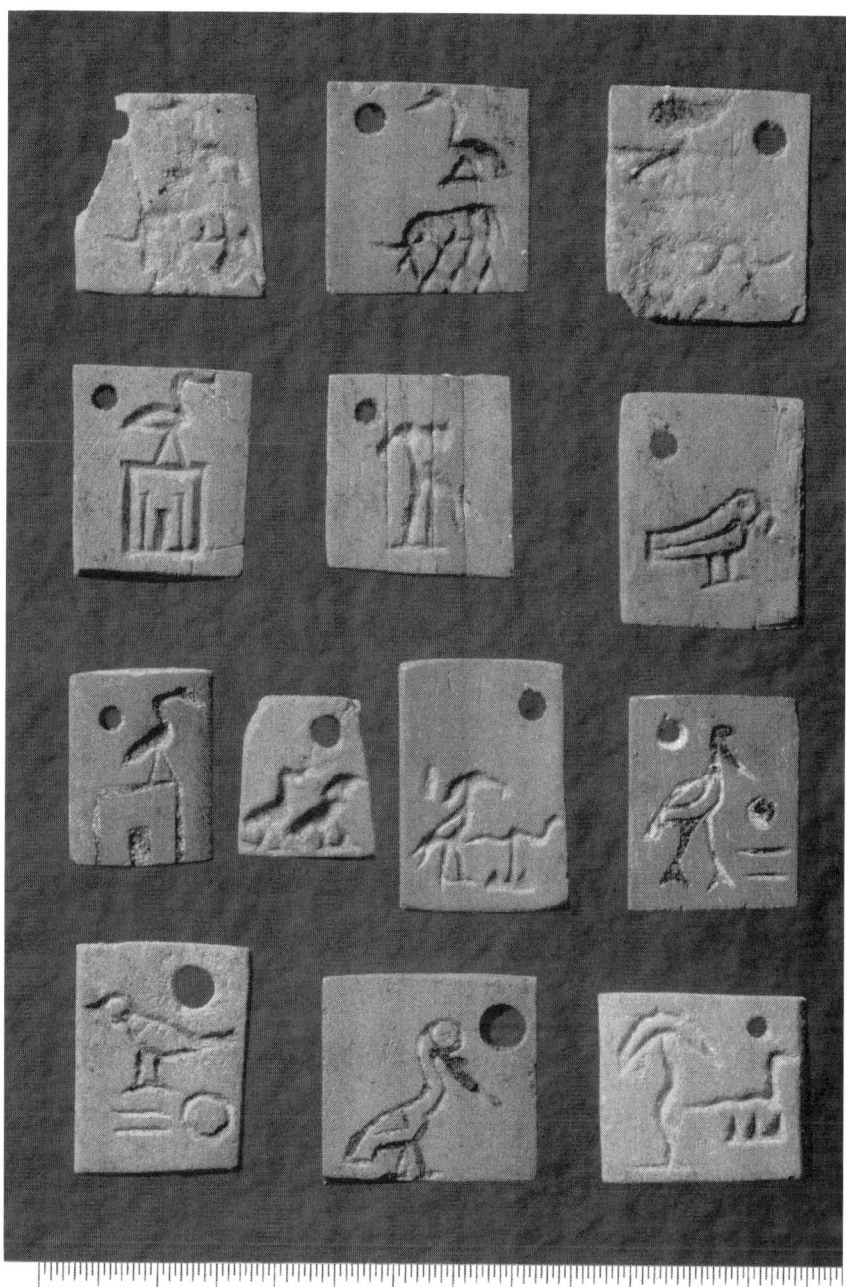

Fig. 5. Selection of bone tags from tomb U-j at Abydos. Naqada IIIa period. Average height c.1.5 cm. Courtesy Deutsches Archäologisches Institut. *Scale is in cm and halves.*

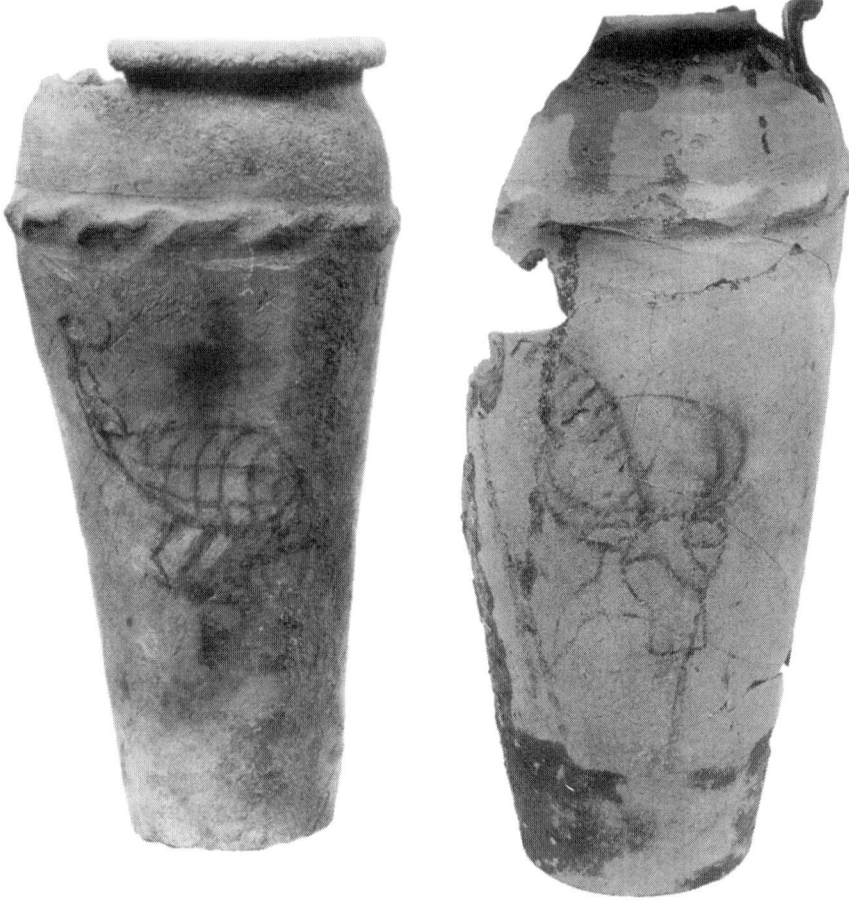

Fig. 6. Two wavy-handled pots with ink inscriptions from tomb U-j at Abydos. The sign on the left pot (height of vessel 25.7 cm) represents a scorpion and that on the right pot (height of vessel 33.5 cm) a bucranium on a pole with a palm frond or similar ornament. Naqada IIIa period. Vessel nos. 5/8 (left), 2/1 (right). Courtesy Deutsches Archäologisches Institut.

decipherments of signs and of the reading of groups. But because the repertory of signs and combinations is limited and the number of entities recorded may be rather small, it is possible that at this stage the writing system was not developed comprehensively so that it could record all aspects of language, even if specific verbal readings of particular groups were envisaged. It seems best to leave this question open (see Baines 2004a; compare Kahl 2001; 2003a).

Somewhat later than these tags are cursive notations of royal names, incised or inscribed in ink on pots and stone vases, and monumental captions to figures and scenes on decorated siltstone palettes, of which the Narmer Palette is the best known (e.g. Fig. 30). These are conventionally assigned to 'dynasty 0', a period of a century or more before the 1st dynasty when the country was already a cultural, and probably a political, unity. The material from dynasty 0 typically consists of the Horus name of kings, that is, a falcon surmounting a rectangle perhaps symbolizing the royal palace compound, mostly with a pattern beneath that represented the niche-panelling of an enclosure; within the rectangle was inscribed a variable element that was the name adopted by a king when he came to the throne. Four or more pre–1st dynasty kings can be identified from Horus names (range of evidence: Kaiser and Dreyer 1982: 263 fig. 14). The content of some inscriptions can be deciphered: examples from Cemetery B, the royal necropolis at Abydos, include such notations as 'produce(?) of Lower Egypt' (Kaiser and Dreyer 1982: 234 fig. 10c–d).

Although the readings of these royal names are uncertain, the script which wrote them was quite developed. Words were encoded both in logographic form—with a single sign writing a whole word—and phonemically, with single signs recording phonemes or pairs of phonemes. Almost all the standard uniconsonantal signs are attested from the early 1st dynasty, as is the use of 'determinatives' that assign words written by phonemic signs to classes. The writing system was thus in essence fully formed.[1] Nonetheless, only a limited range of material was written. Egyptian was the sole language recorded in the script. It is unlikely that it was the only language present in early Egypt, and evidence for a Semitic language is provided by the values of some signs (see Baines 2004a: 186 n. 10). But whatever languages may have been spoken, they were not written down; nor was the script later used more than very occasionally for anything other than Egyptian.

Wolfgang Helck (1985a) proposed an alternative model of the origin of Egyptian writing. A hypothetical more ancient form used in the Delta, perhaps recording a different language, would have provided the immediate stimulus to the invention of the known script. This idea has not been generally accepted. By contrast, contacts between Egypt and Late Uruk period Mesopotamia (late fourth millennium BCE), which probably passed through northern Syria at the time when there were Mesopotamian trading colonies there, may have brought awareness of the existence of writing before it was invented in Egypt. Many scholars believe that writing appeared slightly earlier in Mesopotamia than in Egypt, and for the time being I would share their estimate. Since the Egyptian writing system is quite different from the

---

[1] See Kahl (1994: 156–8), who mentions Günter Dreyer's then unpublished view (Dreyer et al. 1998b) that the considerably earlier material from Tomb U-j exhibits the basic sign categories of phonograms—both consonantal signs and logograms—and 'semograms'. See further Breyer (2002); Kahl (2003a); Baines (2004a); Morenz (2004).

Mesopotamian, any influence would have had the character of transmitting an idea and remains hypothetical.[2]

By late dynasty 0, a further level in the system of writing and representation had been developed. This is an intermediate, 'emblematic' mode, in which symbols, including hieroglyphs, were shown in action (e.g. Baines 1985c: 41–63, 277–305; Ch. 13 here). The emblematic mode is significant because it exploits the distinction between representation and writing to create something that is located between the two in terms of systems of visual communication, that could not have existed without them, and that enriched the potential of representational art by alluding to a few key hieroglyphs whose meaning was evidently well established and symbolically salient. The powerful complex of the three modes of hieroglyphs, emblematic representation, and fully pictorial forms (of which such vital components as the system of register composition crystallized at this time) endured throughout Egyptian civilization.

The distribution of the evidence does not support the hypothesis of authors, such as Siegfried Schott (1950: 50–60), that Egyptian writing was invented in order to record 'history'. Rather, it seems to have been used for administration and for display, both of which are royal in the earliest evidence. If the painted signs on pottery from Tomb U-j belong in the same general category as later cursive writing, the presence of distinct cursive and monumental forms suggests that the inventors envisaged both administrative and ideological purposes for the script and designed distinct sets of forms for them.

Whereas many scholars have sought historical information that would be conveyed by precise linguistic meanings and messages in the hieroglyphs on such monuments as the Narmer Palette, these may not record specific exploits of the rulers who commissioned them, but rather may express general aspirations and conformity to norms of rulership.[3] Nonetheless, an example like the Narmer Macehead (Fig. 7), where precise—if excessively large—figures of

---

[2] This discussion supersedes those of Ch. 2 §2.1 and Ch. 4. For radiocarbon dates of material from Tomb U-j, see Boehmer, Dreyer, and Kromer (1993). Subsequently published radiocarbon dates (Görsdorf, Dreyer, and Hartung 1998) suggest that the U-j material may be older than the Uruk tablets, which bear a fully formed system and are clearly not the earliest writing that existed in Mesopotamia. The differences in the radiocarbon dates from the two regions are slight and inconclusive in themselves, while Egypt does not produce evidence for a prehistory of writing of the sort found in Mesopotamia. That is why I retain the assumption that writing appeared earlier in Mesopotamia, whether or not it influenced its invention in Egypt. The systems in the two regions are so different that they should in any case be studied separately. See also Cooper (2004).

[3] Günter Dreyer (Dreyer et al. 1998a: 138–9 with pl. 5c) suggests that the tag of Narmer discovered at Abydos in 1996 may refer to the same events as the palette. If this were correct, and if new tag forms with names were issued annually as names for each current year, it would be a striking coincidence for the two principal attestations of historical information from a seemingly long reign to refer to the same event.

Writing and society in early Egypt

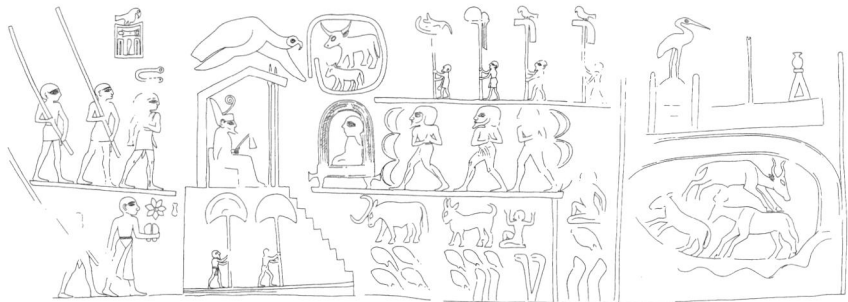

Fig. 7. Narmer Macehead, from the Hierakonpolis Main Deposit, drawing of decoration. Limestone, raised relief. Height 19.8 cm. Dynasty 0, c.3000 BCE. Oxford, Ashmolean Museum E.3631. Drawing by Pat Jacobs; courtesy Ashmolean Museum.

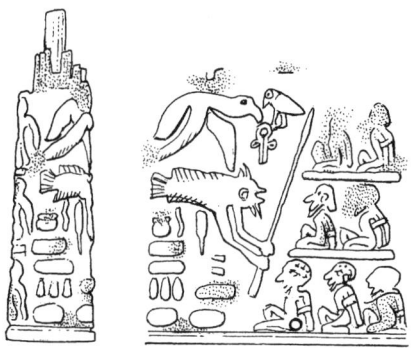

Fig. 8. Cylinder of Narmer with scene of the king as the catfish of his name smiting Libyan enemies, from the Hierakonpolis Main Deposit. Dynasty 0, c.3000 BCE. Ivory, raised relief. Height c.5.7 cm. Dynasty 0, c.3000 BCE. Oxford, Ashmolean Museum E.3915. Drawing courtesy Ashmolean Museum.

captives and booty are inscribed, suggests that these objects could incorporate notionally historical records that were kept elsewhere, perhaps as lists of royal exploits. This was the approach of Nicholas B. Millet (1990), but his specific interpretation of the Narmer Macehead is improbable. The records would have been presented for an exemplary, not a historiographic purpose. These compositions quickly became fossilized, as is shown by an ornamental cylinder of Narmer presenting a defeat of Libyans (Fig. 8) that is essentially similar in design to reliefs of the 5th dynasty king Sahure, more than five hundred years later (Baines 1996b: 370 fig. 8; see also Ch. 13 here).

1ST AND 2ND DYNASTY USAGE

The system that reached maturity around the end of dynasty 0 was stable and changed little for a couple of centuries. Its continuation confirms that it was found effective in its limited range of functions. Many hundreds of inscribed objects are preserved from the 1st and 2nd dynasties, the most numerous categories being sealings and the cylinder seals which produced them, cursive annotations on pottery, and bone or ivory and wood tags originally attached to tomb equipment, especially of 1st dynasty kings (Fig. 9; these are not known from the 2nd dynasty). These tags are different in type from those found in Tomb U-j and much bigger. Larger objects are the tomb stelae of kings from Abydos, as well as the hundreds of crude stelae marking subsidiary burials at Abydos (see below). Continuous language was not written.

The tags attest to a related reform around the beginning of the 1st dynasty, in which year names of kings were used for dating deliveries such as those of grave goods for royal tombs. Many of them are characterized by a year sign ⎫ at the leading edge, bracketing several registers of the content. The oldest such tag known is of the reign of Narmer, who is generally assigned to the end of dynasty 0 but could also belong in the 1st dynasty (see n. 3). Royal titularies grew increasingly elaborate both on the tags and in other contexts where they were written (e.g. Fig. 14). Years were named after salient events and a record kept of

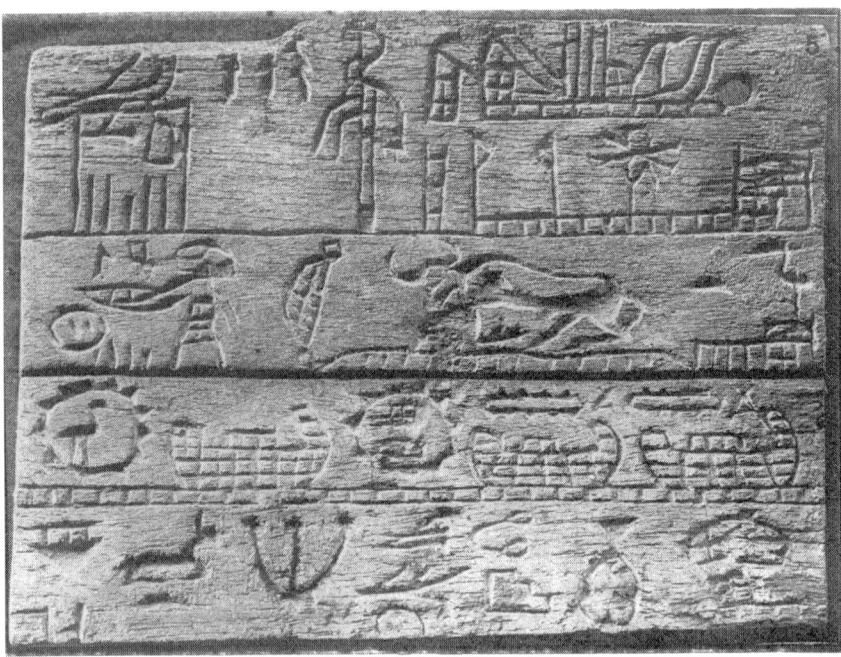

Fig. 9. Tag with the name of Aha from his tomb complex in Cemetery B at Abydos, bearing three registers of pictorial materials and one of information about products. Wood. 1st dynasty. After Petrie (1901: pl. iiia no. 5; dimensions not given).

their order and identification. Many years were named for rituals, probably because these were predictable: they both gave shape to the record and could be anticipated and perhaps proclaimed as a year's name even at its beginning. Repetitions led to the designation of years as 'year of the nth time' of a particular ritual, the most prominent of which was the biennial 'following of Horus', which is believed to have been a royal tour of inspection through the country (e.g. Baines 1995a: 126, 135).

The record of year names, which is often termed the 'annals', survived in increasingly elaborate form at least into the New Kingdom, preserving gradually more information for each year. The 18th dynasty annals of Thutmose III are the latest extensive example, but inscriptions of the Third Intermediate period show that the practice of inscribing annals with royal donations survived, at least for local temples, into much later times (Bickel, Gabolde, and Tallet 1998; Macadam 1949: Texts III, VI). The annals of the first three dynasties were inscribed in a brief form as lines 2–5 of the Palermo Stone, a basalt slab perhaps carved in the mid- to late 5th dynasty on which they were followed by much fuller year-by-year information for the 4th and 5th dynasties (Fig. 10; Clagett 1989: 47–141; Wilkinson 2000: fig. 1); another slab with years of 6th dynasty kings has still more extensive annual information (Baud and Dobrev 1995; 1997). These short year entries can be compared with the seemingly fuller information carved on the tags. It is very difficult to identify year names on tags with those on the stone, but the discovery of large numbers of 1st dynasty tags at Abydos in the 1990s may increase the chances of doing this (preliminary reports: Dreyer et al. 1996: 73–5; 1998a: 162–4). Tags were objects of prestige more than utilitarian value, while the structure of the Palermo Stone, especially the record of inundation levels at the base of each year box, gave its record a general significance. The levels were not included on the tags and so must have formed part of fuller records that were excerpted or worked up in different ways in the two contexts.

The earliest forms of the tags and usages of royal names may underlie in part the division of groups of rulers into dynasties, which is preserved in the fragments of the Graeco-Egyptian historian Manetho (3rd century BCE) and still provides the basic framework for Egyptian history. There was, however, also a mnemonic listing of kings' names only that maintained cultural tradition and awareness, that is, constituted 'history' in the sense of tradition (cf. Loprieno 2003a). The listing of names alone is seen in the 'dynastic seals' recovered from the 1st dynasty royal cemetery of Abydos, which contain enumerations of rulers from Narmer to Den (half way through the 1st dynasty) in one case and Narmer to Qaᶜa (at the end of the dynasty) in the other (Fig. 11); these were presumably the rulers who received a funerary cult in the necropolis. From perhaps five hundred years later, a similar treatment

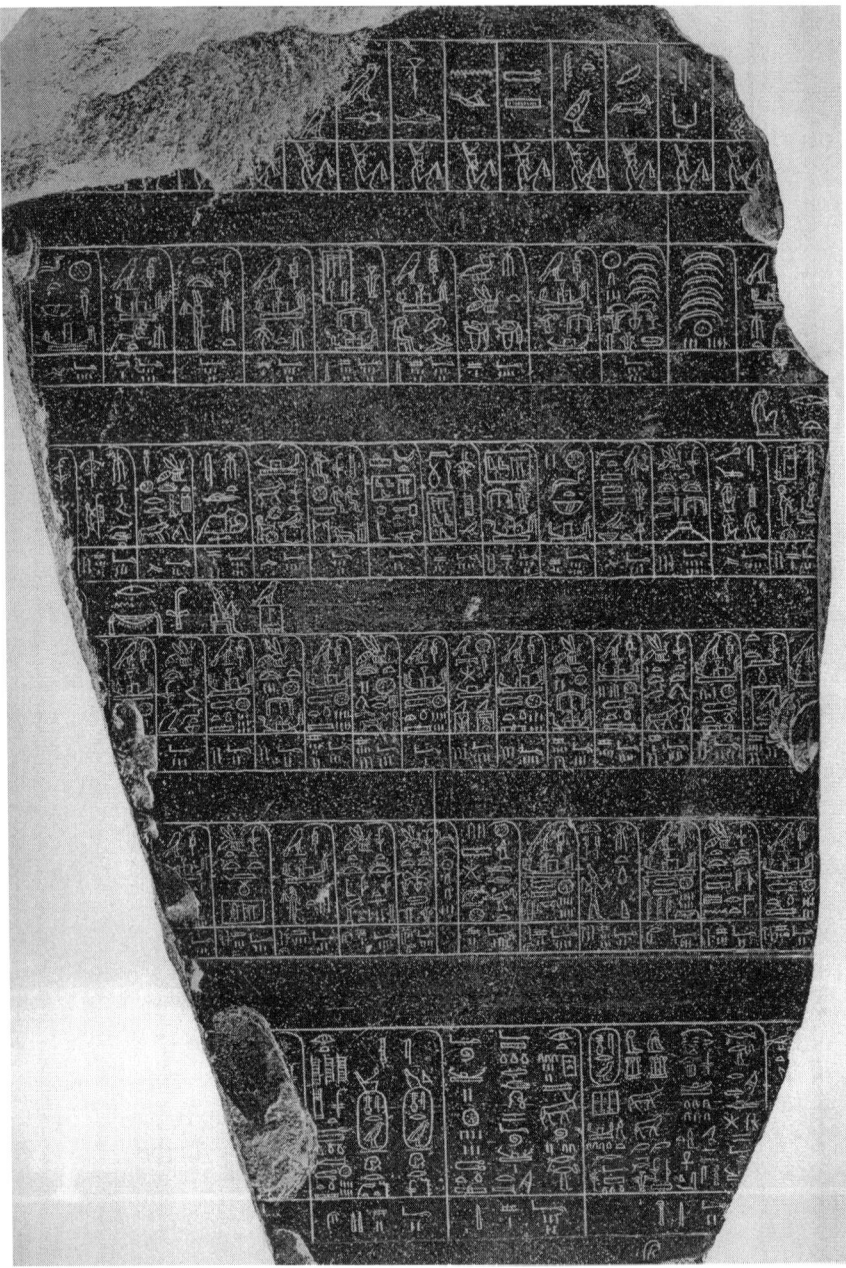

Fig. 10. Old Kingdom annal stone (the Palermo Stone), front, with line of 'predynastic' names of kings (line 1) followed by year boxes for dynasties 1–3 (lines 2–5) and much larger entries for three years of the reign of Snofru (4th dynasty, line 6). Probably inscribed in the 5th dynasty. Museo Archeologico Regionale di Palermo. After Schäfer (1902: pl. 1).

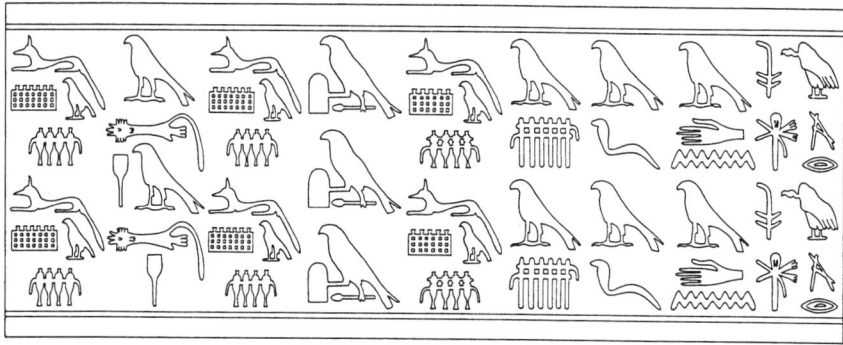

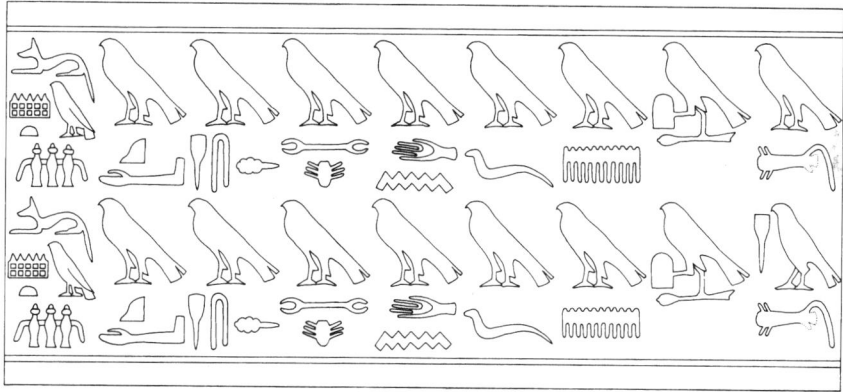

Fig. 11. Seals with names of kings from Narmer to Den and Narmer to Qaʿa. Patterns reconstructed from mud impressions. The upper sequence reads left to right and the lower one right to left. From Abydos, necropolis of 1st dynasty kings at Umm el-Qaʿab. After Dreyer (1987: 36 fig. 3: 12a); Dreyer et al. (1996: 72 fig. 26: 12b). Courtesy Deutsches Archäologisches Institut.

of excerpted Early Dynastic royal names is attested in a 5th dynasty 'onomasticon'—a list of significant beings and categories of the divine, human, and animal worlds (Brovarski 1987).

The tags give fuller year names than the Palermo Stone and exhibit a different principle of organization. Until the Middle Kingdom, when writing in horizontal lines became normal, most writing was arranged either in vertical columns or in tabular form. The tags, however, are laid out in horizontal bands or registers that are basically pictorial in layout, with hieroglyphs often present at a miniature scale like captions to figures, or only partly integrated into the design. This linear organization shows that the tags are elaborate, pictorially organized equivalents for the vertically arranged notations on the stone, not records identical with it. This may be one reason why it has not so far proved possible to correlate them with the years on the stone, but because the vast majority of the years on the latter are lost, the chances of finding a correlation are poor. Coming mainly from royal tombs, the tags are probably ceremonial in intent, and so do not show how year names were used on everyday administrative documents, of which none survive. Dating to the month and the day does not appear to be attested from this period, but the Palermo Stone includes notations accurate to the day, making it probable that such information was recorded.

Writing was probably much used in state administration, the primary sources for which are lost. Papyrus rolls were invented no later than the middle of the 1st dynasty, so that a suitable surface for large documents was available, but the only surviving example is a small uninscribed roll found at Saqqara in the tomb of one of the highest officials of the mid-1st dynasty (Ch. 2 n. 4). The context of this papyrus attests to the prestige of the material, which may or may not yet have been in everyday administrative use (see Baines 2004c: 28–9 for leather as another significant writing material). The oldest attestation of the bookroll hieroglyph ⇌ (Y2 in the sign list of Gardiner, 1957), which is an image of a sealed papyrus, is from the end of the 1st dynasty (Kahl 1994: 833). The earliest preserved inscribed papyri, administrative rolls perhaps of the late 4th dynasty from Gebelein in southern Upper Egypt (Posener-Kriéger 1975), can be seen from their layout and content to belong to a highly developed tradition, the precise age of which cannot be estimated. The invention of papyrus must have been the result of experimentation and will have created a new craft specialization.

Early administrative documents were probably tables, ledgers, and lists accompanying deliveries. Monumental inscriptions with tabular organization, attested by offering lists on tomb stelae, of which the oldest date to the 2nd dynasty (Fig. 12; see also e.g. Kaplony 1963: iii, figs. 833–9, 853), suggest a possible layout for such documents, which would have consolidated the information in notations attached to commodities and would probably also have organized records of work and of deliveries. The documents do not survive because they were used in the inaccessible floodplain. Since continuous language was not written, tabular or other graphically organized form will have been essential for comprehensibility. What we would term letters are unlikely to have been common, and may not have existed at all. In order to be usable, documents will have needed an oral context, either through being possessed by people who understood them or through being delivered to their destinations by someone who presented background information. Writing was therefore an aid to personal contact as much as an impersonal replacement for it; only in places where it was in constant use or conveyed a message in just a sign or two can it have been fully self-explanatory.

Writing and society in early Egypt

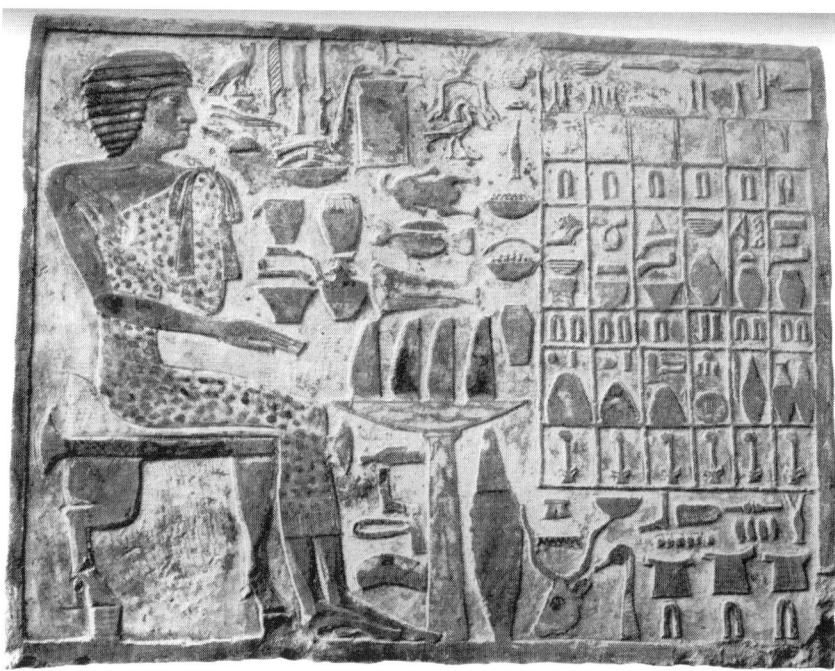

Fig. 12. Stela of the priest Imti with offering list, from excavations of Walter B. Emery at North Saqqara. 2nd or 3rd dynasty. Limestone, painted. Dimensions not known. Location of original and source of photograph unknown. After Smith (1958: pl. 13).

Evidence for the use of writing in administration derives from titles of officials and namings of government institutions on sealings and tags. The administration was quite developed and was divided into separate departments for different products and activities (see e.g. Ch. 4; Wilkinson 1999: 109–49). Sealings were applied to jars (Fig. 13) and probably to other types of container, and thus were guarantees of integrity and ownership, as well as no doubt marking the owner's and the product's prestige. Notations on containers and on tags attached to them or to bundles of goods conveyed ostensibly practical information about quantities, sources, and destinations, but may have been current only among the elite. More of these have been found in the royal cemetery and burials of the royal entourage at Abydos, and in the comparably prestigious Saqqara tombs, than in the rather lower-ranking cemetery of Helwan (e.g. Saad and Autry 1969; renewed excavations of Christiana Köhler, not yet published in detail); this may suggest that the use of such devices was not widespread.

Because this evidence is all from cemeteries and much of it relates to royalty, it is impossible to say how widespread writing was. For early Mesopotamia, the

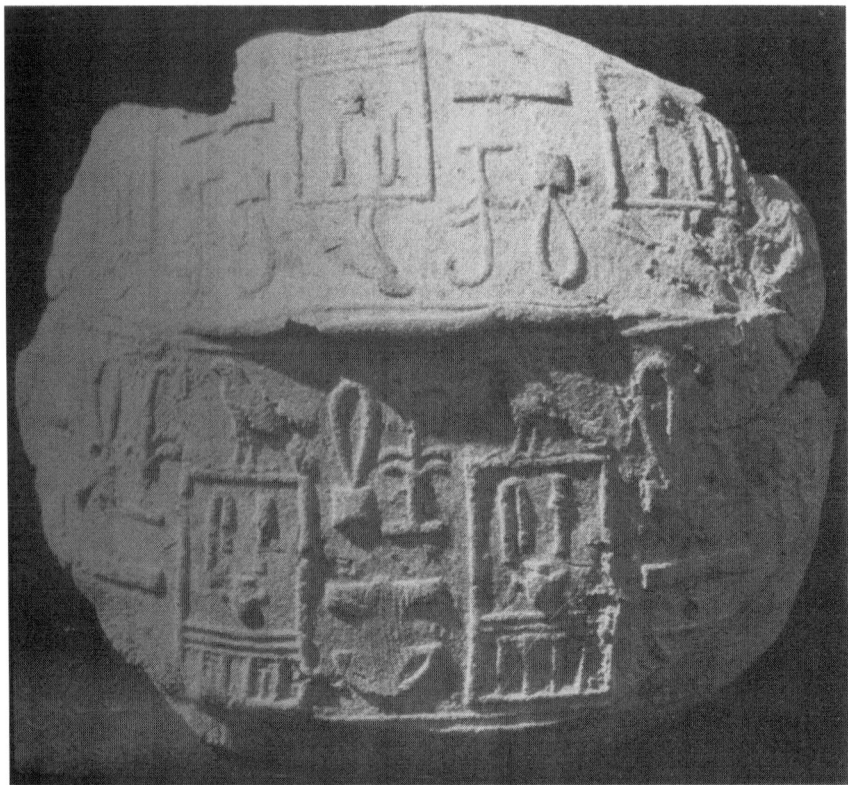

Fig. 13. Mud sealing of Peribsen, probably from the closure of a jar; from Abydos, royal cemetery of Umm el-Qaᶜab. 2nd dynasty. After Petrie (1901: pl. viiia no. 7).

archaic tablets from Uruk appear to extend to quite routine administrative matters (e.g. Nissen et al. 1993), but that was in a society that was very intensively administered in many periods. For Egypt, the altogether more fragmentary, but also much more diverse, evidence does not point unambiguously to such a heavy weight of administration. Writing could have had a less profound impact away from the political and administrative centre in Egypt than it did in Mesopotamia. While this appearance may be due to chances of preservation, it is possible that the state administration exerted less comprehensive control than has often been attributed to it (O'Connor 1995: 320).

The spread of literacy was no doubt very limited (see Ch. 4 for archaeological arguments). Moreover, because the range of uses of writing was so limited, the significance of literacy was different from that of later times. As in later Egypt, and in contrast with the subordinate status of scribes in many societies, the leading members of the elite held administrative office and were literate. Their seals, which disseminated one of the main uses of writing, were important badges of office, marking power delegated from the king, often through royal names inscribed on them (e.g. Donadoni Roveri and Tiradritti 1998: nos. 192–4; sealings collected by Kaplony 1963). Early Dynastic seals often bear personal names, whereas Old Kingdom ones are limited to titles and royal names in a striking arrogation of symbolic privilege to the king (Kaplony 1977–81). By the 3rd dynasty, the connections between administrative power and writing were depicted in the iconography and titularies of such very high officials as Hezyre, the owner of one of the largest tombs at Saqqara, who was shown carrying formalized scribal equipment as a status marker (Quibell 1913; Piacentini 2002: 54–5). A different indication of the status of writing and of seals is the existence of quite large numbers of indecipherable sealings, on which the signs appear to be arranged in more or less random order to form compositions that almost inadvertently mix elements of writing and pictorial representation (Kahl 1994: 16–18; Kaplony 1963: III, figs. 435–720; Baines 2004a: 182–3). This imitation of a prestigious form has a close parallel in the Maya world in the use of 'pseudoglyphs' on high-value ceramics (Reents-Budet 1994: 139–42).

Another usage that points to writing's cultural significance is its occasional presence on small objects, such as metal bowls and decorated pieces of ivory that were deposited in temples as votive offerings or in tombs (e.g. Whitehouse 1987). Stone vases constitute another important category (e.g. Fig. 14); a very fine vessel has the form of two hieroglyphs (Fig. 15; Fischer 1972). Among the thousands of vases from the 1st and 2nd dynasties that were deposited beneath the Step Pyramid of Djoser in the 3rd dynasty, significant numbers were inscribed, some with quite complex information (Lacau and Lauer 1959–61; 1965). Many of these inscriptions relate to the cult of the gods, evidence for which is otherwise largely lacking because few temples survive; in elite circles the cult evidently involved a substantial use of writing. These vases also demonstrate the importance of phyles, groups who served on a rota system in cult and in other contexts (Roth 1991: 145–95). A high proportion of phyle members were probably both members of the inner elite and literate, but their absolute numbers may have been small.

A different sphere of use of 'writing' was in single or paired signs on such materials as quarried stone blocks (e.g. Goneim 1957: 1–4 with figs.), faience tiles (e.g. Spencer 1980: nos. 516–24), and pottery (Helck 1990; van den Brink 1992). Potmarks, many of which have no clear relationship with the signs of the script, are known from the entire Early Dynastic period. Blocks and tiles are attested for the 3rd dynasty at Saqqara, showing that cursive signs were in use among artisans on central royal projects. Since the signs could have served the purpose of distinguishing batches of deliveries and assigning work to groups even if their

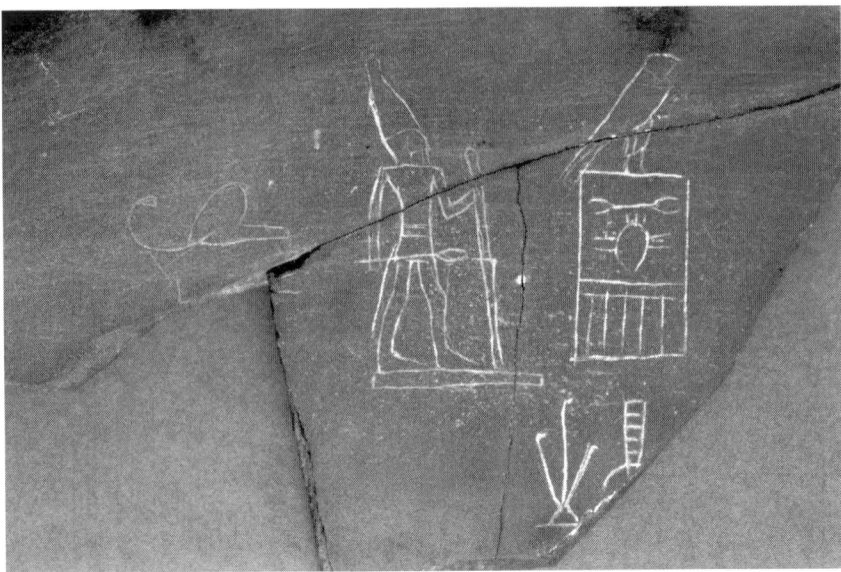

Fig. 14 (a) Fragment of a bowl with inscription of King Anedjib, 'Uniter of the Two Lands', with an image of a royal statue to the left. 1st dynasty. From Abydos, Umm el-Qaᶜab. Siltstone. Width 11.8 cm. Drawing: Baines (1985c: 69 fig. 42). Oxford, Ashmolean Museum E.137. Courtesy Ashmolean Museum.

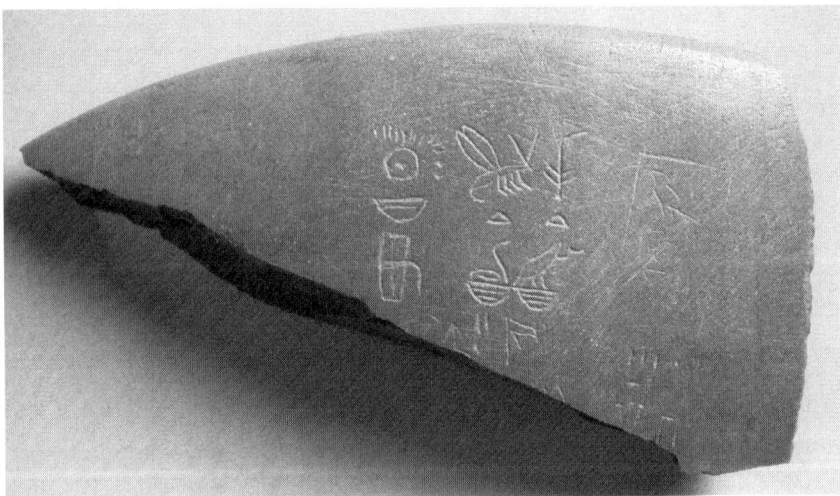

Fig. 14 (b) Fragment of bowl with partly erased inscription including the name of King Reneb, reinscribed for his successor Ninetjer. 2nd dynasty. From Abydos, Umm el-Qaᶜab, tomb of Peribsen (perhaps secondary location). Siltstone. Height 5 cm, width 9.5 cm. London, British Museum EA 35556. Courtesy British Museum.

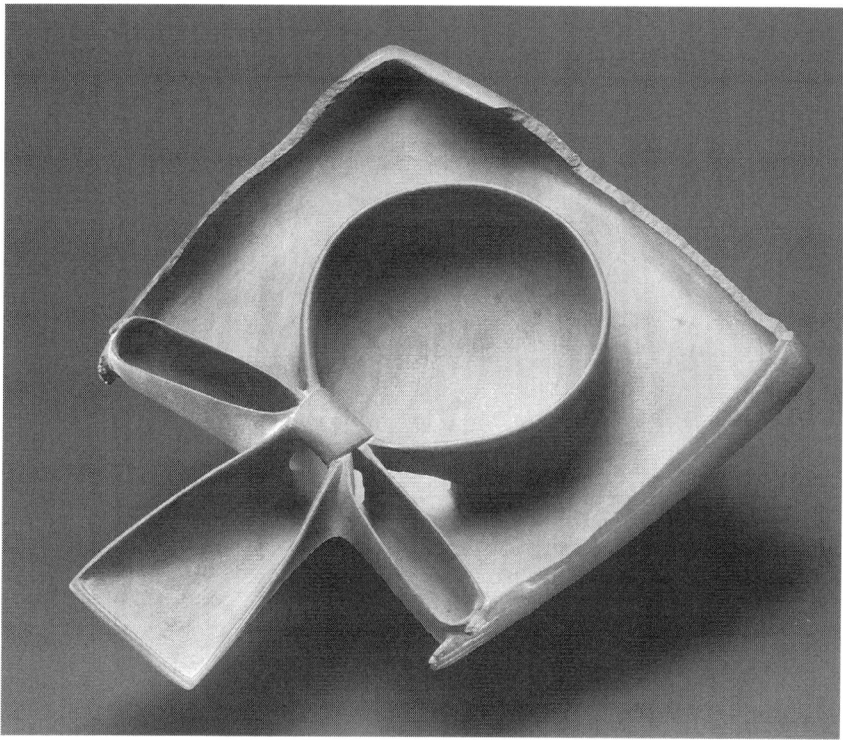

Fig. 15. Vessel for liquid in the form of the hieroglyphs *k3* enveloping *ʿnḫ*. 1st dynasty, perhaps reign of Den. Provenance unknown, perhaps Saqqara. Siltstone. Height 17.5 cm, width 14.5 cm. New York, Metropolitan Museum of Art, Rogers Fund, 1919 (19.2.16). Courtesy Metropolitan Museum of Art.

users could identify only a small range of symbols, they do not demonstrate that literacy, in the sense of reading groups of connected signs and mastering the majority of signs in use, was widespread. The practices involved are even less syntactic than formal inscriptions of the period and thus are on the fringes of writing, although clearly affected by its existence (the Early Dynastic system seems to be distinct from predynastic potmarks). A possible counter-example is a stretch of wall at Saqqara that bears various graffiti including a writing of the name of the later culture hero Imhotep (Goneim 1957: 3–4, pl. xiii); here a full form of writing was used ephemerally and apparently for pleasure (because of a change of plan, the wall was buried shortly after its construction). As is exemplified by potmarks, graffito-like practices using arbitrary marks also occur in nonliterate cultures, so that these poorly understood signs are distinctive only in having been produced in a society that used writing.

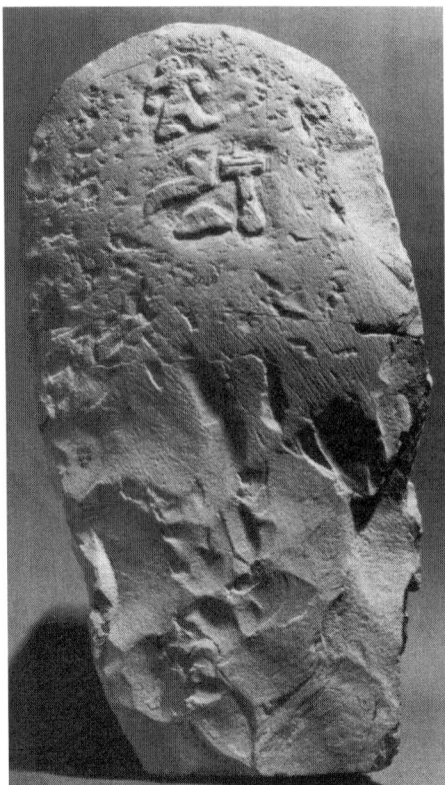 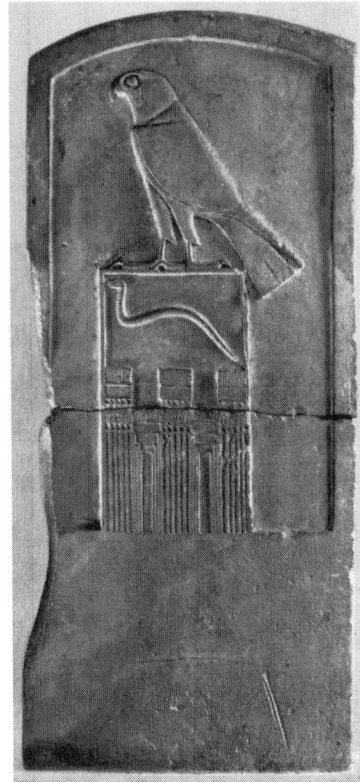

Fig. 16. (*left*) Grave stela of a man named Nefer, seemingly a dwarf. 1st dynasty. From Abydos, Umm el-Qaᶜab, around the tomb of Semerkhet. About half the height was probably a plinth sunk in the ground. Limestone. Height 45 cm, width 24 cm. British Museum EA 35018. After Spencer (1980: no. 12, pl. 6); see also Dasen (1993: 252 no. 8). Courtesy British Museum.

Fig. 17. (*right*) Stela of King Wadj from his tomb at Abydos, Umm el-Qaᶜab. 1st dynasty. Limestone. Height 250 cm (150 cm shown; about 100 cm more sunk as plinth into the ground), width 65 cm. Paris, Musée du Louvre E11007. Photo John Baines.

Despite writing's very high status, inscribed monuments of the 1st and 2nd dynasties are modest in scale and, with exceptions, unimpressive in execution. Non-royal stelae with figures of the deceased are known from Abydos, where those from subsidiary tombs surrounding the royal monuments are notably poorly worked (e.g. Fig. 16; Petrie 1900: pls. xxxiii–xxxvi),[4] and from Helwan

---

[4] These may have been quickly made, temporary objects that were set up during the funeral ceremonies and not further displayed. Because the archaeological context was extremely disturbed, it is not possible to establish how they were used.

(Saad 1957) and Saqqara (Fig. 18—late 1st dyn.; Fig. 12—2nd dyn.). A few have elaborate titularies and a certain number include tabular offering lists. These lists, which became vastly extended in the Old Kingdom, are in a sense the original form of Egyptian 'literature'—that is, a style of written composition that organized culturally significant material in a form that was within the capabilities of the writing of the day (Lichtheim 1973: 3). Contrasting with the non-royal stelae are the more finely worked royal stelae from Abydos and probably Saqqara, whose sole decoration is the king's Horus name. The stela of King Wadj (Djet) in the Louvre is the masterpiece among these (Fig. 17), but it is more a use of a name as an emblem than a normal piece of writing. The most extensive early piece of writing, which is the funerary stela of the high official Merika of the end of the 1st dynasty (Fig. 18), is little better executed than other examples, but it offers a paradigm of the system's potential. Merika is depicted as a seated figure, identified by name, and bears an extensive set of carefully arranged titles. The composition exploits a relatively short-lived convention: the hieroglyphs writing his crucial, highest ranking titles and his name are larger than the rest of the inscription but are not separated formally from it. This highly expressive practice became rare by the 3rd dynasty, with the development of writing for longer passages of text, although the principle of adapting size of writing to context remained in use as long as hieroglyphs were carved.

Limited early writing fostered the development of tabular presentation for the offering list, and probably for lost genres including large administrative documents. Importantly for the relation between writing and language, it also favoured the creation of stylized forms of expression that were distinct from those of spoken language. It probably did not occur to those who devised and first developed the script that it could notate syntactic utterances apart from personal names that happened to constitute sentences (a concept of 'sentences' may not have existed). For other types of record, the verb form of the 'narrative infinitive' appeared by the early 1st dynasty. This form was probably a semi-linguistic construct devised for notation in a limited system—not a spoken form that was recorded in writing—functioning as a kind of heading in such statements as 'following Horus', 'crafting (statues)', or 'appearing by the King', which occur in 1st dynasty year names on line 2 of the Palermo Stone (Fig. 10). In these modes of presentation and expression, which remained prestigious throughout Egyptian history, the constraints of writing were turned to advantage, affecting high culture and the structure of elite written—but probably not spoken—language. Non-syntactic and tabular material was quite remote from speech; people are unlikely to have expected it to be otherwise.

There is no evidence from the 1st and 2nd dynasties for a continuation of the artistic tradition of the palettes and maceheads of dynasty 0 and their

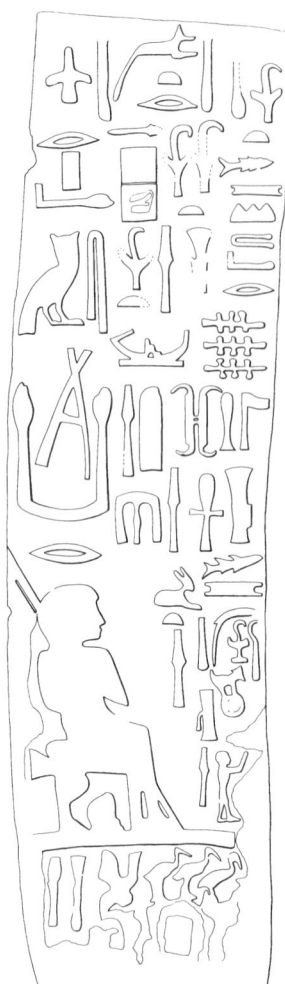 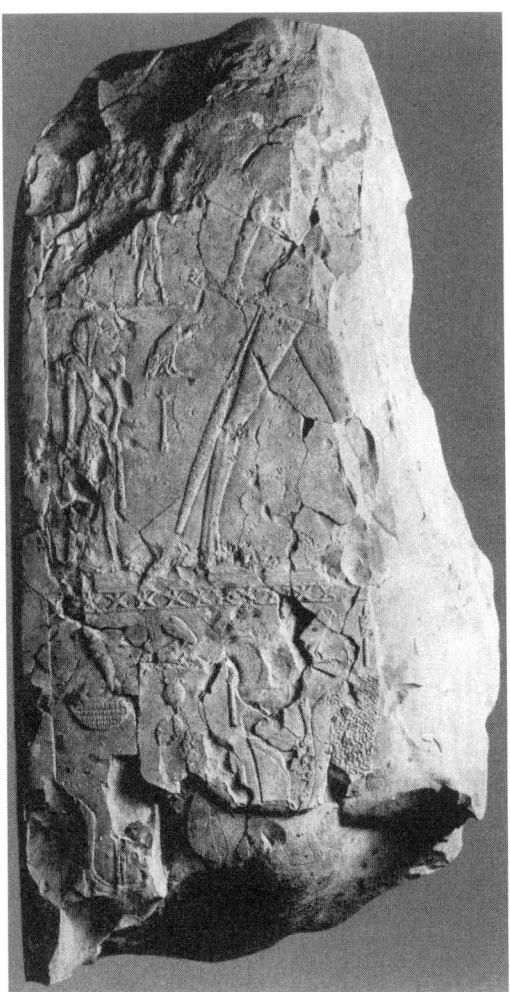

Fig. 18. (*left*) Stela of Merika from Tomb 3505 at North Saqqara. 1st dynasty. Limestone. Height 173 cm, width 54 cm. In storage in Egypt. After Emery (1949–58: iii, pl. 39). Courtesy Egypt Exploration Society.

Fig. 19. (*right*) Early Dynastic royal relief from Gebelein. Limestone. Raised relief. Turin, Museo Egizio S. 12341. Height *c.*85 cm, width *c.*45 cm. After Scamuzzi (n.d.: pl. viii). Copyright Fondazione Museo delle Antichità Egizie di Torino.

associated captions. The conventions established there cannot have disappeared entirely, because the underlying principles reappear in later material. Presumably they were maintained and developed in lost media and contexts. Decoration and inscription were organized in a system of decorum, the core of which was in temple scenes showing the king standing directly before a deity in a semi-abstract setting, with the two of them being captioned and identified, and exchanging actions as well as gifts to and rewards from the deity (see Chs. 1 and 13 here). Scenes like those on the Narmer Macehead are appropriately understood as marginal examples of this system that were suited to mobile objects, and so would have their full meaning in temples that had representational decoration, perhaps on painted plaster, on relief-decorated doorways, or on small freestanding shrines (the latter two of these types are attested). These might have been the finest monuments of their time. Fragments of late 2nd dynasty temple reliefs from Hierakonpolis (Engelbach 1934a; Alexanian 1998) suggest that such decoration was not very rare. An early royal relief from Gebelein, which was probably dedicated in the temple of this provincial centre but may have been made elsewhere, points in the same direction (Fig. 19; Morenz 1994). All these forms include identifying captions to the figures, but their organization is pictorial. In monumental contexts, the pictorial retained primacy over the written (see Baines 1999a: 29–36 for more detailed arguments).

FURTHER ELABORATION

Toward the end of the 2nd dynasty or at the beginning of the 3rd, there was a reform of writing which regularized sign forms, reduced the size of the repertory, and led to an increased use of writing in art, as well as probably in administration. The most important development seems to have been that continuous language was now encoded (compare Kahl 1994: 162–3). The oldest attested fully syntactic narrative clause is on a sealing of the reign of Peribsen of the late 2nd dynasty: 'Sealing of everything of Ombos (Naqada): He of Ombos (i.e. the god Seth) has joined the Two Lands for his son, the Dual King Peribsen' (Fig. 20; see Loprieno 2003a: 126–7). This formulation is especially significant because it is not itself part of a set sequence such as a titulary, but is something more like a generalized statement of royal–divine relations. It suggests that there was a significant development in titularies and associated texts, and can perhaps be compared in that respect with a cylinder seal bearing a cartouche with the name of Peribsen who is stated to be 'beloved of the gods',[5] which may be nearly a century older than the next known cartouche enclosing a king's name, of a probable king Nebka of the 3rd dynasty (Seidlmayer 1996: pl. 23).

---

[5] In the Civiche Raccolte Archeologiche in Milan: Donadoni Roveri and Tiradritti (1998: no. 231); this object is not certainly authentic.

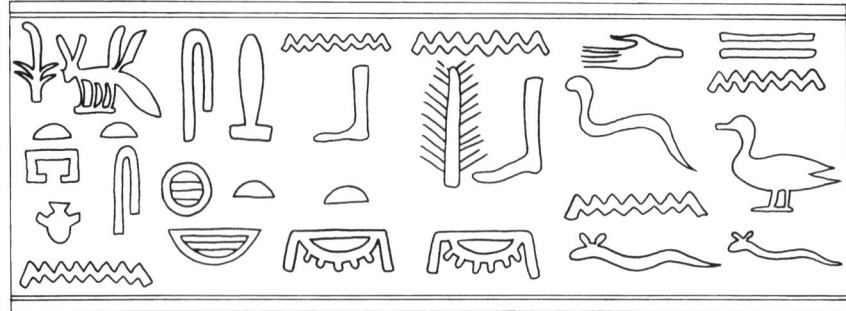

Fig. 20. Seal of Peribsen with text that forms a continuous sentence, pattern reconstructed from several mud impressions excavated at Abydos, Umm el-Qaʿab. 2nd dynasty. Petrie (1901: pl. xxii no. 190); Kaplony (1963: III, pl. 95 fig. 368; II, 1143). Redrawn by Liam McNamara from Petrie.

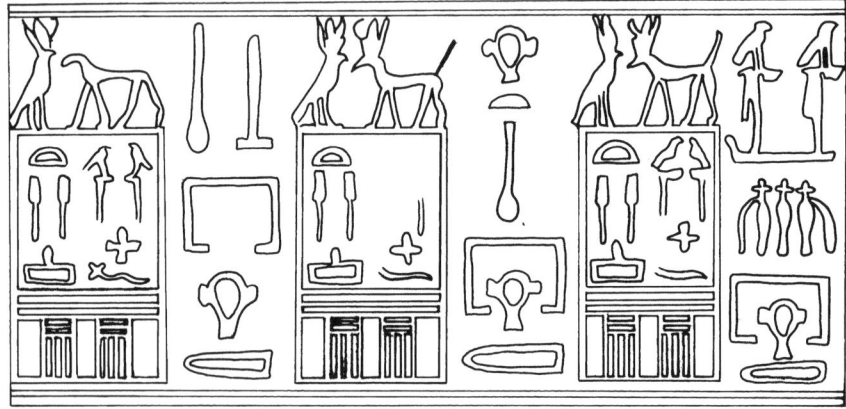

Fig. 21. Final form of the Horus-and-Seth name of Khasekhemwy, on a sealing from his tomb at Abydos. 2nd dynasty. Pattern reconstructed from several mud impressions. Petrie (1901: pl. xxiii no. 197). Redrawn by Liam McNamara from Petrie.

From the following reign comes the Horus-and-Seth name of king Khasekhemwy, which includes an extending clause with a verbal form 'the Two Lords are at peace in him' (Fig. 21). The earliest fully formed temple reliefs, which happen not to include decipherable extensive writing, date to the same reign (from Hierakonpolis, see above). This lack of writing is likely to be a matter of chance. Fragments of a miniature relief chapel from Heliopolis dating to Khasekhemwy's successor Djoser, the founder of the 3rd dynasty, include early versions of the standard speeches of deities to the king vouchsafing to him the gifts of life, long duration on the throne, and power that

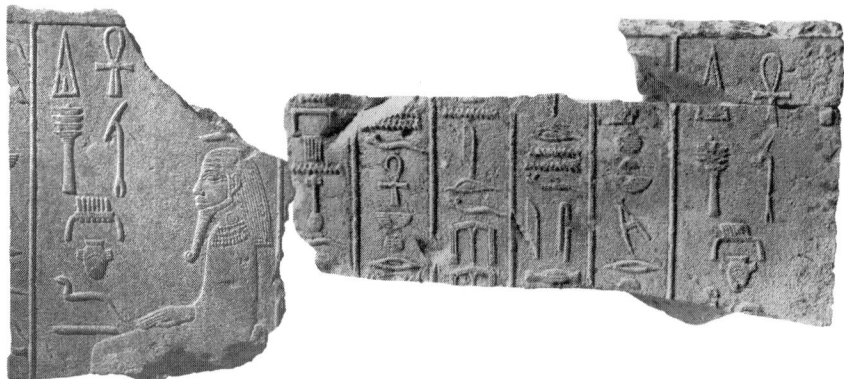

Fig. 22. Relief fragments from shrine of Djoser from Heliopolis. Limestone, raised relief. 3rd dynasty. Reconstructed width c.40 cm. Donadoni Roveri (1998: 55 fig. 2, with nos. 239–41; Morenz 2002). Turin, Museo Egizio. Copyright Fondazione Museo delle Antichità Egizie di Torino.

characterize all later temple reliefs (Fig. 22). The prototypes of these speeches were probably developed by the time the iconography seen in the Khasekhemwy reliefs crystallized; the sealing of Peribsen shows that the potential for them was present at least by the previous reign. Moreover, occurrences of captioned figures of deities on seals of the same reigns and similar material from that of Ninetjer, a generation or two earlier (e.g. Petrie 1901: pls. xxii no. 179, xxiii nos. 192, 199–200; Kaplony 1963: III, fig. 748; Lacau and Lauer 1965: pl. 16 no. 77), may document the same expansion of the system, as well as a concomitant development in decorum that permitted material of this type to be circulated in slightly less restricted contexts, on objects that might move or be used in locations of differing degrees of sanctity, for example temple and palace.

In theory, the expansion of writing's potential during this period could have been implemented progressively or in distinct stages. Parallels, such as the reform of art and writing as part of broader cultural changes at the beginning of the 12th dynasty, suggest however that a specific stimulus is needed if such a significant change is to be disseminated. The presentation of titularies on early 3rd dynasty non-royal monuments approaches the standard and style of Old Kingdom writing and probably marks the conclusion of a phase of change.

The introduction of full syntactic sentence structures in writing opened the way for notating discourse and 'texts' of far greater length than hitherto (see also next section). Now that a relatively full notation of language had been achieved, there was a concomitant lessening of focus on tabular form, but for many centuries the two coexisted; some types of material are in any case better suited to non-syntactic presentation (e.g. Baines 1988a). No very early texts in the new syntactic form survive on papyrus or leather, and it is impossible to date their introduction precisely. Moreover, syntactic language did not instantly spread to many genres or become widely displayed; its adoption outside the sacred texts for which evidence survives seems to have been very gradual.

By the early 4th dynasty, biographical self-presentations that included syntactic discourse began to appear in non-royal tombs (Baines 1999a; Baud and Farout 2001). The point of departure for its employment there had, however, been set by the royal and divine uses just mentioned, from which they perhaps spread to the non-royal elite. The new written forms may also have been applied rather earlier to lost genres that were inscribed on perishable materials. Such a possibility fits with other patterns in the use of writing in mortuary contexts, notably on sarcophagi. I argue in more detail in another article that writing was extended to important religious texts in continuous discourse as soon as that became available (Baines 2004c); such texts could have been the principal original purpose of the extension. Some archaic features of orthography in the Pyramid Texts, of which surviving monumental examples date to the 5th dynasty and later, may preserve Early Dynastic practices. To suggest this is not to imply that the texts were maintained unchanged, but that the evolving tradition which transmitted continuous discourse in religious texts may go back to the later Early Dynastic period.

For about fifteen hundred years, important religious texts were written not in hieratic, the non-sacred cursive script, but in cursive hieroglyphic. This latter form, which may have been introduced at the same time as continuous discourse began to be notated, completed the triad of scripts, which consisted of hieroglyphic, cursive hieroglyphic, and hieratic. In addition to its use for religious texts, cursive hieroglyphic was the medium for instruction in calligraphy for relatively advanced students, as is shown much later by the vast numbers of manuscripts of the cursive hieroglyphic literary composition the Book of Kemyt recovered from late New Kingdom Deir el-Medina (for the status of the students, see McDowell 2000). The restriction of cursive hieroglyphic to religious texts and calligraphy is in keeping with the hypothesis that continuous language was first introduced for material of the former of those types.

The triad of scripts continued largely unchanged in structure, but with evolving sign forms and calligraphic styles, until the end of the New Kingdom. During the Third Intermediate period, hieratic began to separate definitively into a formal variant, which was used for religious texts in place of cursive hieroglyphic from the 21st dynasty onward, and more cursive styles that became standardized as 'abnormal hieratic' in the Theban area and 'demotic' in the north around the 7th century BCE (see Houston et al. 2003: 439–43, with refs.); demotic subsequently replaced abnormal hieratic. In the same period, cursive hieroglyphic began to disappear. This structural shift fits with the view that the triad of scripts was a reality that was perceived as such by the actors.

The most economical explanation of the emergence of the script triad is that it was formulated in the later Early Dynastic period together with the introduction of continuous discourse in writing. The administrative cursive attested from ink notations of dynasty 0 and the Early Dynastic period—which supply indirect pointers to the existence of larger documents on papyrus and writing boards—together with a limited representation of language, was probably found adequate for current administrative purposes. The stimulus for a fuller representation of language would plausibly have come from a different direction.

Distinctions between script varieties are not easy to draw for material from before the Middle Kingdom, because sign forms vary widely with the style of a document—or even within a document—and in different areas of the country. The main reason for positing a distinct script variety for religious texts is that in later periods from which evidence is more abundant, such as the Middle Kingdom, significant religious texts inscribed in ink consistently used the different style of cursive hieroglyphic rather than the less formal, ligatured hieratic (e.g. different manuscripts among the Ramesseum papyri: Gardiner 1955a; Pyramid Text manuscript from the mortuary temple of Pepy I at Saqqara: Berger-El Naggar 2004). It is risky to project this distinction back onto the Old Kingdom and earlier, but parallel distinctions in script forms and the genres of material that they it write are so basic to Egyptian practice that it is logical to seek a point of change when distinct administrative and sacred cursives might have arisen. Since it was a very major step to write down continuous religious texts, the time when that was done could also be when the third script was defined. The scripts may not have been visually very different; what may have been more important was that religious texts be written in a distinct manner. Administrative writing varied from the less to the more formal, the latter being exemplified in some of the major documents among the Old Kingdom Abusir papyri (cf. Posener-Kriéger and de Cenival 1968), and the latter might be more or less identical in appearance with cursive hieroglyphic.

Thus, the writing system was capable of representing fully syntactic language from the beginning of the dynastic period onward, but it probably took a specific stimulus for the practice of doing so to be introduced. Continuous syntax is not attested on a non-royal monument until well over a century after the Peribsen seal mentioned above, a time-lag which suggests that there was a reason for not making the extension more quickly. The most plausible explanation is that syntactic language was originally employed for central and sacred purposes.

If this rather hypothetical argument is acceptable, the triad of Egyptian scripts acquired its initial form in the later Early Dynastic period, after which extensions of genres and usages took place within an existing framework until the early first millennium.

ORAL AND WRITTEN 'TEXTS'

The reconstruction of the development of written forms that I offer has implications for how 'texts' were used and recorded. Here it is necessary to review definitions. Texts may be defined universally or in relation to a specific culture. To define them for Egypt is not to assert anything particular about Egyptian actors' classifications, but rather to model an aspect of cultural transmission. Such issues are widely discussed for many traditions, but have not been significantly debated for pre-Middle Kingdom Egypt, for which Jan Assmann argues that 'cultural texts' became centrally important (1999; for counter-arguments, see Baines 2003c: 9–11).

In the Egyptian case, texts and syntactic discourse are not coextensive: texts need not be formed from continuous language. Continuous syntax, including written forms of it, may not belong to a specific category of text. Extended and universalizing definitions of text have become the hallmark of modern hermeneutic and literary analysis, so that meaningful action, or evidence of action left in some interpretable record, is a 'text' (e.g. Ricœur 1981). While such definitions are not closely relevant to the context of developing writing systems, it is useful to extend the notion of textuality beyond writing and to consider what overlaps there may be between written and oral 'texts', as well as visual forms and performed practices that may have related to both.

An essential feature of texts is that they are significant: they formulate, or at times constitute, important assertions about a cultural repertory in one of a variety of possible modes of language use, including oral and written. Their topics may be fixed even if their wording is not. A fixed topic with a variable realization might be a short, combinable form of words that could be mobilized in a variety of contexts. This is the essential pattern of ritual formulas, and was common in Egypt, where a limited range of topics and motifs applied in a wide range of ritual situations (e.g. Goebs 2002). In a different, perhaps more script-dependent sense, a text may be a set grouping of words and contexts, as in the lists and tables mentioned earlier (see also Baines 1988a); here, the composition as a whole includes the elements which encode distinctions by means of non-pronounceable graphic features. The culturally significant lists and tables may have had oral counterparts, but these could not have been identical with the written forms because the latter depended on graphic features to organized their linguistic or acoustic components.

In this 'textual' perspective, the essential development in the recording of continuous syntax is the potential it offered to go beyond the visual and tabular presentation of central cultural values that had been normative in the first three or four centuries of Egyptian civilization. The formulas preserved in the earliest temple reliefs are integrated into the existing mixed visual and written context, but by presenting speech, they open up a new domain of meaning, perhaps especially since the speeches are those of gods rather than of the king or human beings, and hence are imagined or staged, not simply reported.

While these formulas and their content were of central cultural importance, they are not likely to have been the only context in which continuous syntax was written down. I have suggested elsewhere that crucial ritual compositions could have provided a prime stimulus for the development of syntactic written language (Baines 2004c). These have the culturally portentous, 'textual' character that I am considering here. What seems to be largely absent in early material, and does not become evident before the 5th dynasty, is the presentation of general societal values through writing. Even then, public inscriptions presented an elite perspective, but one that was in principle inclusive, specifically addressing 'everyone' as the moral audience of semi-biographical formulas (e.g. Helck 1972).

The perspective of 'texts' is useful for discussing how matters that had been confined to the oral sphere came to be written down and what was selected for that purpose. Some part of the purpose of extending writing may have been administrative, that is, for a usage that is in principle ephemeral and carried little ideological weight. Letter-writing is an obvious instance of a practice that acquires much potential through syntax. The earliest surviving letters are of the 5th dynasty, during which epistolary form was also appropriated for elite display purposes (Eichler 1991; Baines 1999c: 24–5). One cannot estimate when syntactic letters originated, but there is no clear reason for seeing them as the motor for change. Moreover, the oldest surviving administrative papyri, mentioned above, which are of the late 4th dynasty, appear to be almost devoid of syntax (Posener-Kriéger 1975—not yet fully published: a possibly syntactic formula is cited on p. 213).

Thus, as Ludwig Morenz (2002) argues for temple relief, central high-cultural concerns were probably a driving force in the development of written textual forms. Since much ritual and religious content constituted restricted or secret knowledge (see e.g. Baines 1990b), the decision to write these matters down involved a profound change. Such a shift probably also accentuated divergences in uses of writing, of which some, like the wording of specific rituals, were concealed, while other modes, including such significant forms as instructions in wisdom, gradually became accessible for non-royal display.

This proposed sequence for the expansion of writing to record 'texts' has three principal implications. First, since in the Early Dynastic period all significant linguistic discourse must have taken oral form, the oral domain, together with its probable 'textual' aspects—of ritual recitation, wisdom, instruction, and other genres—was the essential context in which major societal meanings were presented, negotiated, and transmitted. Second, the lists, tables, and other non-syntactic forms in which much vital material was transmitted had a value of their own that was anchored to writing and had visual as well as verbal components. Third, the development of the material culture of architecture and of many types of complex artifacts, together with the use of costly materials in the more ephemeral contexts of elite lives and ceremonial, can be seen, in the spirit of modern approaches alluded to above, to have constituted a domain of 'text' governed to a considerable extent by rules of decorum. Royal and elite action, with its rich context and spatial environment, will have borne a heavier weight of societal meaning and paradigmatic value than is easily comprehended in the modern world.

Written textual form developed slowly, while the oral, the visual, and the performed retained a fundamental primacy. Oral and written linguistic 'texts' can communicate matters that can hardly be realized in other media, but if the long-term development of Egyptian uses of writing, especially its ideological and literary aspects, is to be understood, we must bear in mind that permanent forms for transmitting syntactically organized materials were not introduced until several centuries after writing was invented. In cross-cultural perspective, there is every reason for classifying Egyptian tabular and list presentations as 'texts'. Other linguistic domains were significant, at first in oral form and later also in writing, but they only acquired their standing in writing very gradually.

CONCLUSION

The Egyptian writing system seems to have been extended progressively for purposes of high culture—especially its sacred domains—and for display, at least as much as for administrative utility, and perhaps more so. The introduction of the third script of cursive hieroglyphic completed a stable system that was later extended in the genres it recorded, but did not change in fundamental ways for more than 1,500 years. Until the mid-first millennium BCE, it was possible to transpose hieratic into hieroglyphic; most hieroglyphic inscriptions were first drafted in cursive hieroglyphic or in hieratic.

Because no significant administrative documents survive from before the late 4th dynasty, it is impossible to prove that the key focus of the system of writing and scripts was always on high-cultural rather than practical matters, but such a configuration is in keeping with other aspects of Egyptian elite culture; moreover, these two basic purposes are not necessarily in opposition. Strikingly, the earliest attested complete sentences come in a description of a deity's action and in fictitious divine speeches. The division of Egyptian writing into hieroglyphic/monumental and cursive from when it was invented demonstrates that neither its introduction nor the motivation for its further development can be reduced to a single factor or related to a single sphere of use. The motor of early development seems to have been requirements of the hieroglyphic form as much as of cursive hieroglyphic or hieratic. This symbolic salience of hieroglyphic is a measure of its cultural importance, not evidence for relative frequency of use. In statistical terms, hieratic was probably always overwhelmingly dominant.

This reading of the early development of Egyptian writing helps to set the scene for the range of genres attested in Old Kingdom writing, which include ritual and probably 'technical' texts but not belles lettres. Rare narrative passages in inscriptions appear first in the 4th dynasty and did not become at all widespread for more than a century after that. The forms of display developed in the Early Dynastic period, which hardly used continuous language, were so potent that they discouraged new developments. It is difficult to think our way into patterns of use of writing and pictorial representation that are so different from those of subsequent periods in Egypt, not to speak of the modern world. For the elite of early Egypt, the system was effective, was differentiated into display and administration—attested only indirectly—and carried enormous prestige. Its patterns of use presented and enacted a definition and demarcation of the ordered cosmos.

6

Orality and literacy

INTRODUCTION

Material culture and oral culture in language are indispensable to human existence; the same is not true of writing. People communicate meaning through visual, acoustic, tactile, and material channels, all of which are affected by aesthetic and ethical as well as narrowly instrumental considerations. Speech, music, visual shaping, and finally writing are communicative systems that often overlap in usage, and sometimes in content (compare Michalowski 1990). Communication depends upon memory and socialization. Among other distinctive contributions of writing are temporal extensions of communication and memory, as well as a broadening of spatial impact through the transport of written materials from one place to another, and to a lesser extent through their public display.

Egyptian writing, like all newly invented writing systems, arose from an oral context and had its primary meaning within that context. Writing either was devised to extend existing possibilities of communication and display, or was invented because existing unwritten channels for those functions were perceived as inadequate to current needs so that something completely new was needed, or both. Since writing was a very radical departure from oral modes and had visual forms as its initial models, it is more likely to have been seen as an additional medium than as a way of 'freezing' orality (compare Cooper 2004: esp. 80–4, for Mesopotamia). Writing developed in several stages to a point where it could function as a largely, but not entirely, independent mode of communication. Only from that point onward—whenever it may have been reached—can one ask how far writing was an autonomous institution. If in Egypt, as is now generally assumed for Uruk IV period Mesopotamian writing (c.3200 BCE, see e.g. Nissen et al. 1993), written material, such as lists and tables with simple

---

This essay is hitherto unpublished. A shorter version is to appear in the *Oxford handbook of Egyptology*, ed. James P. Allen and Ian Shaw (Oxford University Press: in preparation). The present version is edited to complement Chapters 2–5 in this volume as far as possible. It also includes fuller discussion and exemplification of some aspects than is possible in the *Handbook*.

indications of operators, was largely separate from a particular language or specific words, it would still have been embedded in social institutions that required language in order to function. If, by contrast, writing was so far developed as to offer an extensive social, cultural, and linguistic system, as was perhaps the case in Egypt from the Middle Kingdom onward, it could make an indispensable contribution to the society's overall configuration. That degree of elaboration requires a heavy investment, which many civilizations have made. It is therefore desirable to explore for Egypt how oral and written institutions interacted. Much in any study in this area is hypothetical, because the spoken word of antiquity is lost, but it is possible to use indirect evidence, including aspects of the embedding of writing in material culture, to approach relevant questions (compare Houston 2004a).

One issue in assessing the position of writing in relation to other modes of communication is whether societies—of a level of complexity that remains to be established—require writing for their functioning (for a range of examples, see Houston 2004b). While today's society is hardly imaginable without writing, the historical existence of large-scale states and empires that did not use it, or only used it marginally, makes any simple correlation between societal type and writing hazardous. Cases in point are the large Mesoamerican state of Teotihuacán in the Valley of Mexico (*fl. c.* 6th century CE) and the Andean pre-Columbian empires (*c.*200–1540 CE). Teotihuacán possessed a writing system, but its use seems to have been very limited (Taube 2000). The imperfectly understood Andean *khipu*, a record-keeping system based on knotted cords, was not equivalent to full writing and does not seem to have encoded purely linguistic data, although it may have extended beyond conventional writing in certain domains (Salomon 2004; Urton 2005). Institutions like these are particularly clearly embedded in their social, material, and visual context, offering valuable comparisons and contrasts with Egyptian writing, as also does Mayan writing of Mexico and Guatemala. The *khipu*, however, also provides a warning about correlations between communication media and societal types, because the earliest comparable object now known appears to be more than 4000 years older than those of the Inka empire, a span of time over which continuity in meaning and function is unlikely (Mann 2005).

DEFINITIONS

In this essay I define orality and literacy broadly (more focused discussion: O'Keeffe 1990: 8–14). Literacy is the general social phenomenon of writing and written communication; I do not use the term here to mean the competence to read and write together with gradations in that competence (compare Chs. 2–5). Orality, which potentially encompasses all communication by voice, is taken here more narrowly as the conduct of significant social institutions, especially those which convey information in a targeted manner, through spoken language. An everyday conversation does not fall within such a definition. By contrast, actions ranging from a messenger's presentation of information in a well-defined context to the narration of a tale or the spoken performance of a ritual are products of orality. Orality and literacy are not in opposition: in the modern world, activities like those just mentioned often have a basis in writing, such as notes, a text, or a script that has been committed to memory. It is a matter for investigation—only partially addressed in this essay—how far ancient practices, in a society where the use and dissemination of writing were restricted, were comparable with modern ones in this area. So far as possible, I take a point of departure in a society without writing or with limited use of it, rather than in a world where it is taken for granted.

SKETCH OF DEVELOPMENT

As discussed in Ch. 5, the earliest surviving Egyptian writing, from Tomb U-j at Abydos (Naqada IIIa period), is in pictorial, 'hieroglyphic' form on small bone tags and in very large cursive ink/paint signs on pots. It is not possible to say whether this material is representative of the range of usage that existed in its period, but it must have depended on its oral setting to have meaning, because the inscriptions themselves consist of just a sign or two. In the context of deposit in a royal tomb, the artefacts and associated inscriptions were no doubt also embedded in ritual. It is not known whether writing was used at that time for a broader range of administration, although ink as a medium was suitable for such purposes.

Writing changed, over about five hundred years (Naqada IIIa to late Early Dynastic period, c.3200–2700 BCE), from a system that may or may not have used language as a model for the entities it recorded but did not notate words fully or syntax at all, to one that could notate language and use syntax as a basic organizing principle. This pattern can be compared with that in Mesopotamia, where the complex tabular arrangements of Uruk IV–III (late fourth millennium), which lack syntactic elements, were succeeded in the Early Dynastic period (c.2800 BCE) by simpler ones that did use them (Cooper 2004: 80–3); Egypt, by contrast, retained elaborate, hierarchically organized layouts for legal documents throughout the third millennium (Helck 1974a: 10–38).

Later significant phases of development include diversification, together with notation of a more current form of language, in the First Intermediate period, followed by reform of orthography and probable first writing of belles lettres in the 12th dynasty. In the New Kingdom, Late Egyptian was notated, perhaps not as the current spoken language but as a standardization relatively close to it that was more easily mastered for writing than Classical/Middle Egyptian, which was henceforth seen as a specialized form used for display and for traditional texts. In the same period the cursive hieratic script became more strongly differentiated into everyday and literary forms, a change that led ultimately to the emergence of abnormal hieratic and demotic in the 7th and 6th centuries BCE; demotic also wrote a hitherto unrecorded phase of the language.

Egyptian language began to be noted in Greek letters during Ptolemaic times, adding a final strand to relations between oral and written that culminated with the emergence of Coptic writing as a prime vehicle of new religions in Egypt—Manicheism, Gnosticism, Christianity—until the last of those came to dominate during the 4th century CE.

The character of connections between spoken and written varied throughout these immense periods. The connections also become more complex, with the appearance of increased numbers of written forms of language and of linguistic phases and registers from which they originated.

EARLY CONTEXTS OF ORALITY AND LITERACY

Relations between orality and literacy must have varied according to historical and linguistic context, not least because the potential and degree of dissemination of writing itself varied. In the earliest phase, complex cultural topics could only be communicated in writing through visual arrangements, notably in tabular forms that organized large bodies of content. Lists and tables are therefore seen as the earliest form of Egyptian 'literature'; examples include tables of offerings to the gods and the dead as well as lists of deities (Lichtheim 1973: 3–4; Baines 1988a). Oral realizations of the content of these compositions, which were essential to the ritual functioning of the offering lists, were necessarily different from written formulations. The form such realizations took is unknown—intermediate written versions are known later in the Pyramid Texts and in New Kingdom temple reliefs—but oral discourse must have surrounded their creation as well as their exploitation. The scarcity of writing will have helped to impart a high prestige to such materials.

By the late 2nd dynasty, syntactic language was notated in the most important surviving contexts, notably in temple relief (Morenz 2002). Indirect evidence from mentions of 'writings (zḫ)' and from linguistic variation suggests that ritual and magical materials in continuous discourse were written by roughly the same date (e.g. Vachala 2004: 42–3; Baines 1988a). The largest surviving body of such texts consists of the mortuary collections of the late Old Kingdom royal Pyramid Texts and non-royal Coffin Texts, the latter mostly attested from a rather later period but probably originating at least as early as the former. Compositions that were drawn upon in these corpora, such as cult offering formulas, were written down no later than the early 5th dynasty, and some of them probably centuries earlier (Kahl 1999, as cited by Morenz 2004: 228, without page reference). Because the Pyramid and Coffin Texts were inscribed in contexts where preservation is uniquely good, they are likely to represent only a fraction of the genres and volume of material written; but because their character is specialized, they do not give strong pointers to what range of other genres of texts was written down in cursive script in the third millennium.

Be that as it may, central religious contexts attest to a partial early transition from orality to the writing of relatively self-sufficient, syntactic language, accompanied by the emergence of various modes of interaction between written and oral forms. For example, in several of the royal burial suites where Pyramid Texts are inscribed, each column begins with *ḏd mdw* 'to be spoken', marking the whole as being for recitation: what is written is an ideal oral form (on the Pyramid Texts as oral compositions, see Reintges forthcoming). Pyramid Text spells were edited for inscription by removing introductory titles as well as postscripts that specified how texts should be performed and declared how effective they were; the latter typically follow after the central sections which were to be recited. The expert knowledge of a priestly performer was therefore presupposed symbolically for realizing what was written on the walls of the burial apartments. In one case where a postscript was retained and incorporated into the inscribed version, its opening runs as follows (Sethe 1908: §855; see Baines 1990b: 11):

> The one who knows it—this spell of Re—
> the one who performs them—these magical spells of Harakhte—
> he will be an Acquaintance (*rḫj*) of Re,
> he will be a Companion (*smr*) of Harakhte.

Such an excerpting of the spoken core of a text implies that oral and written are interdependent. In some contexts to which the material used in the Pyramid Texts related, such as ritual performance in major temples, purely oral transmission was far in the past, but oral retained primacy over written (compare Reintges 2005). In the same period, however, a few more public inscriptions in the accessible areas of elite tombs consisted of strings of titles that might have been voiced as narratives or continuous discourse, the content of which displayed access to ritual and magical 'books' and to restricted knowledge in list form (Baines 1988a). However such inscriptions were realized, the archaic lists to which they alluded were presumably not accessible to possible readers of the inscribed allusions. Thus, the potential of writing to recreate oral performance and to store information was mobilized in statements that exploited the prestige of books and enhanced social differentiation. The Pyramid Texts have a further, performative meaning: in the royal burial apartments, the inscribed texts must have possessed validity by their presence alone (see further Baines 2004c), probably after being brought to life by rituals like the 'opening of the mouth' which was performed on statues and on sacred buildings (Roth 2001). This performative quality of writing is widely known from magical texts and images, as well as having many cross-cultural parallels (see e.g. Cardona 1981). The texts were also oral and performative in another sense, because they were designed for recitation, and at least some of them were used in funerary and other rituals (e.g. Willems 2001). Nonetheless, the inscribed form of many exemplars of the Coffin Texts, as with many mortuary texts, is too corrupt for those particular examples to have been used for performance. Moreover, the location of their inscription on the coffin was destined for the next world, not intended to be used in the funeral.

The religious materials just mentioned are also aesthetic. Much recitation probably had integral musical and visual components, including dance for some genres and for contexts such as festivals. Similar considerations apply to the oral realization of fictional 'literature'. Indirect evidence for 'oral literature' dates to the 5th and 6th dynasties and is thus up to half a millennium older than written examples, attesting to practices that had no doubt existed as long as there was a court society (Eyre and Baines 1989; Baines 1999c). Oral forms were probably as complex as later written ones, perhaps in different ways. When works came to be composed in writing, they were in any case intended for performance; overlap between the two modes was considerable (see e.g. Eyre 1993; 2000; Parkinson in preparation).

A contrary case is where a written document is made the object of a ceremony that may or may not involve reading it out. Ceremonial transfers of pieces of writing are common in the modern world, and comparable practices are depicted in Old Kingdom tombs, where an official or member of the household displays a papyrus before the tomb owner. In two examples in the 4th dynasty tomb of Queen Meresankh III the captions state that the document is 'seen' (partial parallels: Fitzenreiter 2001: 129–34). The more explicit example runs: 'placing the writing (*zẖ*) of the mortuary priests to be seen, by the overseer of mortuary priests Khemteni'. These captions are in the same orientation as the person displaying the document, not as the owner (Dunham and Simpson 1974: 9, 20, pl. IIc, figs. 3b, 12 [perhaps a writing board]; since she was a woman, it is uncertain whether she would be expected to be literate). This focus on the subordinate is unlike that of other 'seeing' captions in tombs, which are oriented with the owner and typically state that he or she is seeing agricultural or estate activity. Since the subordinate sees the papyrus, this may be in order to read out its contents, but the ostentatious unrolling also makes it visible as an object to the owner. The contents would generally be lists or accounts, so that their formal characteristics would derive from writing. They could nonetheless have been voiced aloud, but it might have been enough simply to make them visible. This potentially oral display has a written point of departure, but its formal character is probably its most significant aspect. While it is a potent visual presentation of the importance of writing, it cannot be known how far what is shown corresponded to a real practice.

Another, at first sight unlikely domain of complex relations between written and oral is that of statues, in particular, that were dedicated in temples. These may bear long inscriptions in continuous syntax, but the constraints of space and layout are such that many texts are very short. Yet even the briefest sequences of epithets are well shaped rhetorically and adhere to the same metrical conventions as longer texts (comprehensive collection for the New Kingdom: Rickal 2005; for the conventions, see below). Once the statues were set up in temples, they would have been difficult to read and accessible to rather few people (on mortuary writing and its accessibility in another culture, see Petrucci 1998). In addition to the self-sufficient properties of the inscriptions as commemorations of their owners, they may have been in part tokens of longer performed utterances at the statues' inauguration, when they were completed in the studio or more probably when they were set up on site. Both events would have been accompanied by rituals. The seemingly oral shaping of parts of the inscriptions might then have corresponded to distinct realized oral forms, for example in another stage of the language since most statue texts of all periods are in Classical Egyptian. Despite the very strong integration of these inscriptions into visual, literate forms, they therefore retain elements of orality.

ORAL FORMS AND READING

A vital aspect of written transmission is the way in which writing is physically presented and exploited. While the highly literate no doubt possessed great expertise in reading, ancient scripts—not only Egyptian hieratic and hieroglyphic but also Semitic scripts and classical Greek—were not arranged on their writing surfaces for quick and easy assimilation. It was normal for significant texts to be memorized to some extent and for their written form to be an aide-mémoire as much as something to be read out directly (see e.g. Small 1997—Greek and Latin; Carr 2005—various scripts). In classical antiquity slaves commonly prepared the reading of a text for their masters, who would not decipher the manuscript themselves but would listen to it while it was read out. The controlling elite of Egypt appear to have been literate (see Chs. 2–3), but they may have used subordinates to voice manuscripts for them, so that their normal experience of written texts would be in oral form. A comparable practice is implied for another domain in a letter formula of the Old Kingdom and slightly later, where the recipient to whom a reply is made is addressed as 'your scribe', not 'you', presumably because it was not appropriate to imply that a person of standing would write or read his own letters (this feature is not generally reproduced by translators; see e.g. Wente 1990: 58 no. 67). Rather lower down the social scale, a very brief 20th dynasty letter to the scribe of the necropolis Butehamun instructs him to take another letter to its presumably non-literate addressee, to read it out to him, and to ensure that he has taken note of its contents (Wente 1990: 203 no. 330; Butehamun is to retain the actual letter). The short message, on a separate piece of papyrus from the lost substantive letter, was presumably written to accompany the latter for delivery, and Butehamun was to act both as postal address and as record keeper.

Written texts could be transmitted as high-cultural artefacts, whether or not they were pronounced. Examples occur in Middle Kingdom literature. In the Instruction of Ptahhotep, a sign is split into two in copying from vertical columns to horizontal lines (Žába 1956: 42), while in the Dialogue of Ipuwer and the Lord of All, the 19th dynasty copyist reproduced some hieratic shapes without understanding them, so that they cannot now be deciphered (Enmarch 2005: esp. 3.14, 10.1; for other texts, see Burkard 1977: 68–71). Presumably he did this by visual copying or memorization, not only by oral means. What counted for the owner of the manuscript may have been possessing the text, not whether it could be used to realize all of what it recorded. In its final place of deposit in a tomb, such a realization would have been theoretical, whether or not it had previously been used for performance or reading (Enmarch 2005: 2–5; on the tomb as a place of deposition, see Amenta 2002). Those examples, however, are exceptional. Most reading was probably done by pronouncing the text. Further down the educational scale, the very corrupt New Kingdom ostraca bearing excerpts of the Middle Kingdom Instruction of Khety were probably created through oral memorization and writing down (edition: Jäger 2004). But for the student scribes who wrote the ostraca (see McDowell 2000), this was presumably a required exercise, and they were not concerned about whether what they were voicing and writing made sense: they were transmitting a cultural artefact, not something that was orally alive, although it may have been alive in other contexts in the same period.

It is difficult to analyse this interpenetration of oral and written. Cultures that transmit their text corpora through memorization, as in ancient India, or that have single core groups of texts like the Hebrew Bible in Jewish culture, may value the exact verbal form of a defined corpus, which in India was enormous and over millennia has often been memorized without comprehension of its content (e.g. Gonda 1975). For Egypt, there is no clear evidence for such textual institutions, oral or written. While some texts had a high value, on present evidence only a few religious compositions, and still fewer inscriptional ones, survived for millennia (contrast Baines 2003c: 9–11 with Assmann 1996). What seems more characteristic of Egypt is the constant reuse and reworking of similar textual material in forms that were seldom identical, such as the content of the mortuary offering formula *ḥtp dj njswt* 'an offering which the king gives' (Franke 2003, with refs.) and the biographical phraseology with which it was often associated, as well as the hundreds of hymns to the sun god (Assmann 1999 [1975]). Both formulas and content were relatively constant, but their precise combinations were not.

The framing of mortuary and magical texts, as well as addresses to the living, offering formulas, and some self-presentations, exhibit a noteworthy emphasis on reading out, essentially in order to activate the content of offering formulas. A significant variant is an elaborate address to the living in the late 7th century Theban tomb of Ibi, which encourages readers to view the decoration of a tomb and copy it on papyrus together with the text in order to reuse it and thus to sustain its transmission (Kuhlmann and Schenkel 1983: 71–3; parallel: Schenkel 1975: 136–8):

... May you copy what you wish of it on empty papyrus, so that my name may go forth afterward [...]. There are many who may pronounce it(?) for the sake of one of them, from what you wish in it (= the text?), in order that what you may write (it) on an empty papyrus and pass to the mouth of your (lit. his) fellow—if it is missing on the empty papyrus—so that something may be found in it that will guide those who will come later.

This invitation probably constitutes an archaizing transfer of what was thought of as oral culture to written form, because the decoration of the tomb revived materials and motifs, including the subject matter of scenic compositions, that had not been transmitted directly but had been derived from observation of ancient monuments (see e.g. Kemp 2006: 372–3).

A focus on reading out, or perhaps on performance connected with written texts in an educational context, is visible in a passage of the Middle Kingdom Instruction for Merikare in which a future king is exhorted not to execute anyone with whom he had 'chanted the writings'—evidently while learning them when young (Parkinson 1998: 200, P 50). An analogous phenomenon is the broad distribution of royal decrees, such as that proclaiming the accession of the 18th dynasty king Thutmose I (Sethe 1906: 79–81), and of texts narrating royal deeds that were probably to be inscribed in major temples, often adapted to a local context. Scattered duplicate examples of inscriptions are known from several periods, while the multilingual sacerdotal decrees issued in the Ptolemaic period state specifically that they were to be set up in all main temples (Simpson 1996: 224–71). Such materials had meaning through the dissemination of their content, only parts of which could have had a similar formulation to the written texts.

Readings or proclamations would not have been suitable for the content of every genre of inscription, but there remains the underlying principle that inscribed forms had counterparts in oral institutions, the nature of which is largely unknown. Allusions to 'heralds', for example in the Tale of Sinuhe (Parkinson 1998: 29), where the name of a person who was sought by authority would be called out, exemplify administrative functions that would be exercised orally. Documents from Ramessid Deir el-Medina provide other examples (e.g. McDowell 1999: 205–6). Many magical texts lay emphasis on precise execution, often including the pronouncing of exotic words and sounds or other types of material that would acquire force when rendered out loud (collection: Borghouts 1978). Some fully syntactic texts may appear to be representations of oral counterparts, but they could also be inscribed versions of something that would be differently realized when spoken. Reasons for divergence between the two modes could be, at simplest, that it was not thought that they should be the same, or that what was written had to fit in a small space while a spoken form could be longer, or that discrepancies in language favoured a separation (considered below).

Limitations on length may not have applied so strongly from the New Kingdom onward, when very long narrative texts began to be written down, the salient example being the Tale of Astarte and the Sea, which is reconstructed as having been being at least the equivalent of seventy pages of a modern edition in length (Collombert and Coulon 2000: 199; Schneider 2003b); some Ptolemaic and Roman period Demotic tales were still longer (see below). But even if the potential of written forms expanded, there is no reason to posit that they were identical with oral ones. Moreover, the attested Demotic texts were maintained and transmitted in a high-cultural context in temples (see Quack 2005; Ryholt 2006: introduction); they may have had only a limited function outside.

Thus, the institutions surrounding written and oral compositions were not in opposition, but they did not require uniformity: different categories of material may have intersected, run parallel, or been distinct in the two media. Even for special contexts like that of the Demotic tales, it is unlikely that the written texts had no oral realization: writing was generally voiced in some form when composed, read, or copied.

WRITING AND FORMS OF LANGUAGE

Written notation of syntax involves choosing a particular form of language, far more than is the case when larger compositions are lists and tables, such as continued to be maintained for a few genres. Syntax also requires that a particular language be chosen: while Egyptian is the only indigenous language securely attested from ancient Egypt, it is most unlikely to have been the only one ever spoken. Among other possibilities, some evidence points to the presence of a Semitic language in the country in the formative period (e.g. Baines 2004a: 186 n. 10).

Because the initial period of development of writing was so long, it is impossible to specify a time when written language would have been close to spoken. Written syntactic Egyptian was not unitary, as is shown by differences between the 5th–8th dynasty Pyramid Texts and contemporaneous biographical and other inscriptions in non-royal tombs. While the notated phonology and syntax of Old Kingdom Egyptian evolved significantly, moving very gradually toward the Classical Egyptian of the 12th dynasty, observable changes in it are slight in relation to the timespan of about 800 years from the late 2nd dynasty to around 1900 BCE. Written language was probably always far from spoken and became more so (for Demotic, see Tait forthcoming; Ray 1994a; 1994b; Depauw 1997: 33–9; cross-cultural survey, mainly for modern instances: Chafe and Tannen 1987).

The content of the earliest continuous texts is specialized and rarefied. They are likely to have been composed not in a straightforward vernacular but in a distinct, elevated style. Orality that constituted the spoken counterpart of written texts was probably specialized in register as well as style. Different forms of language may have been employed for different domains of oral performance. The use of written texts in rituals, and for fictional compositions from the Middle Kingdom onward, favoured transmission of several older language forms alongside the changing vernacular. A Roman period papyrus that bears a magical spell written in Greek letters exhibits phonology close to Coptic but language that is essentially the Classical Egyptian of the Middle or the early New Kingdom (Osing 1976; conveniently presented sample: Loprieno 1995a: 2148–9). This example suggests that there was as little attempt to maintain or revive ancient Egyptian pronunciation as there was for Latin in Europe before very recent times, while the full complexity of relations between stages of Egyptian and Greek in the Roman period is most apparent in magical papyri (Dieleman 2005).

Another divergence between oral and written was linguistic standardization. Written Egyptian exhibits hardly any dialectal features, but it is known from Coptic and other evidence that there was significant regional variation in the language. Acquiring literacy therefore involved adapting to a norm that many had to learn—because the spoken form of what was written was in an unfamiliar dialect, because it was obsolete, or both. Those learning to read and write will have expected also to learn the language of their literacy.

From the end of the Second Intermediate period onward, discrepancies between spoken and written seem to have concerned leaders increasingly. Among the earliest relevant major texts, the strongly 'literary' stelae of the 17th dynasty king Kamose, which narrate his campaigns against the Hyksos (e.g. Redford 1997: 13–15) exhibit a number of features close to written Late Egyptian of the post-Amarna period (Kroeber 1970). By contrast, royal inscriptions of a couple of generations after Kamose, such as those of Thutmose I and especially of Hatshepsut, are much closer to Classical Egyptian, in a return to older forms that parallels contemporaneous artistic styles, which looked back to the 12th dynasty. During the 18th dynasty, administrative materials and letters developed toward Late Egyptian. Inscriptional language was reformed under Akhenaten, alongside his other innovations (see e.g. Silverman 1991). The linguistic changes he instituted were reversed, as his other changes were, in the reign of Tutankhamun, but development in inscriptional Egyptian resumed under the latter's second successor Haremhab, leading to its Ramessid form, which is distinct from Classical Egyptian, from the Late Egyptian of documents, and from the Late Egyptian of newly composed literary texts of the period (cf. Baines 1996a). This range of forms was actively exploited and varied within and between compositions (Goldwasser 1991). The complex stratification of the written language, amounting at the least to diglossia, was succeeded in later periods by a variety of patterns, none of them simpler than their predecessors and all of them retaining Classical Egyptian for a range of high-cultural compositions (Junge 1985; Vernus 1996; Loprieno 1996a; detail on one period: Jansen-Winkeln 1994; 1996).

The Classical Egyptian composed in the Graeco-Roman period, which varied considerably in character, was as far distant in time from its primary period as today's Vatican Latin is from classical Latin. The character of this late language varied from forms relatively close to those of more than fifteen hundred years earlier, which are found in some biographical texts, to the rather looser language of many temple inscriptions. This difference may relate to the functions of particular texts and to their social milieux. Most extant temple texts were produced by elites in provincial Upper Egypt; some of them may not have received the same personal and cultural investment as works like the biographical compositions of Petosiris, a conspicuously wealthy chief priest of Hermopolis (c.300 BCE: Lichtheim 1980: 59–65), or of Psherenptah, chief priest of Memphis (41 BCE: Baines 2004b: 45–8, 56–60). The complex rhetoric of these texts probably corresponded to elaborate oral forms. The oral versions could conceivably have been voiced in Classical Egyptian—in contemporary pronunciation but even so accessible only to a very small group—but it is more plausible that they were in the vernacular, perhaps in something like an elevated register of Demotic.

FORMALIZATION OF WRITTEN AND SPOKEN

Inscriptional texts and belles lettres exhibit marked verbal patterning. The most widespread 'literary' device is parallelism, in which essentially the same content is expressed two or more times in differing verbal formulations (Assmann 1982). Wordplay and other sound-based patterns such as alliteration and play on consonantal roots are also common (e.g. Eyre 2000). So far as can be observed in the consonantal script, rhyme was absent or rare.

Repetitive stanzaic forms are found notably in compositions containing refrains or litanies. One song in the cycle in praise of Senwosret III from Illahun has a refrain termed *jnjt*, perhaps etymologically 'that which brings (a stanza back to its point of departure)' (Lichtheim 1973: 199, 200 n. 2). Such patterning, however, is not common among written compositional genres. Most texts exhibit careful wording that exploits numerous stylistic devices, not formalization at a superficially evident level. The scarcity of identifiable strong patterns was no doubt irrelevant to the voicing of texts, which could have been organized, in ways that writing does not capture, by rhythm, prosody, pauses, and other devices.

Several interpretations of the prevalence of organized but not narrowly repetitive language have been offered; so far, no consensus has emerged. Miriam Lichtheim (1971–2) distinguished 'poetry', 'prose', and an 'orational style' that she sited between the other two. John L. Foster (e.g. 1993) characterizes parallelism as operating in 'thought couplets', which he sees working in 'verse', primarily in belles lettres, but also elsewhere (see also the wide-ranging discussion of Günter Burkard, 1993). The most fully worked out, and the most criticized, theory is that of Gerhard Fecht (e.g. 1965; 1982), who proposed that the majority of fully syntactic Egyptian texts, a well as some less syntactic ones, are in a simple form of metre that organizes the flow of discourse into verses (or 'lines'), of two or three (very occasionally one or four) stress units or 'cola', the latter being defined in terms of ordinary prosodic features of the language (critiques: Lichtheim 1971–2; Schenkel 1972; Tacke 2001). Verses are grouped into couplets or triplets that combine to form larger stanzas and ultimately whole compositions. Fecht often analysed stanzas and compositions in terms of numerical patterns of verses and sometimes of stress groups within verses. In his readings, many texts were very elaborately composed, in forms that were devised for a particular composition, not taken from a standard repertory. Egyptian texts exhibit few stanza forms that can be compared with the complex, regular metrical structures of many literatures, but they show similarities with the rhetorical and literary organization of other ancient Near Eastern traditions, such as those of Mesopotamia and the Hebrew Bible (which Fecht, 1990, analysed as having similar metrical structures to Egyptian texts). Bernard Mathieu (1988; 1991; 1994; 1997) has offered a different, more closely focused analysis of metrical forms based on specific small groups of texts, identifying patterns of odd-numbered groups of cola that he distributes in distichs and tristichs; so far, no comparison of his and Fecht's approaches has been published.

How far are features of texts like these 'oral'? How far do they offer analogies to practices in oral contexts? In view of the wide separation of spoken and written language, how far did other practices exist in oral form without having parallels in writing? Implications of these questions can be explored, and they can be set in a hypothetical context of social institutions, but they cannot be answered.

The prevalence of highly formed prosodic organization of texts suggests an oral point of departure for attested written forms, however far removed writing might be from speech and however separate written and spoken compositions were. Only minor influence from writing to oral forms can be detected, but more is not to be expected (see Ch. 2 §2.1). The importance of correct voicing of written texts is evident in 'verse points'. These are large, generally red dots placed above the line, typically in hieratic manuscripts from the late Middle Kingdom onward (Parkinson 2002: 116–17). With exceptions, these points indicate metrical verses as analysed according to the principles of Fecht. Since verse points were a secondary development and were never obligatory, their most likely purpose was as aids to reading aloud by segmenting manuscripts and texts into proper units. R. B. Parkinson's observation (in Parkinson in preparation) that scribes of some literary manuscripts dipped their pens at metrical breaks (in terms of Fecht's rules) provides confirmation of the subjective reality of this segmenting and its embedding in material practice.

Some oral genres had limited representation in writing. The salient case is love poetry, which is known only from the New Kingdom (Mathieu 1996) but is unlikely to have been restricted to that period, not least because depictions of relevant settings are preserved from earlier and later times (Břetislav Vachala,

2003, publishes a possible incipit to a love song in a caption to an Old Kingdom scene of harpists). Harpists' songs, which either celebrate mortuary provision or mock it as futile, have a comparable but slightly broader pattern of attestation (see Ch. 7). Oral forms of such genres of poetry would be highly structured. Institutions of modern societies in which complex verse structures are improvised or transmitted orally suggest that the elaboration of Egyptian works is only apparently characteristic of writing (e.g. Geertz 1983 [1976]: 111–17). The rarity of written layouts that render verbal organization visible can be comprehended if syntactic texts were practised and voiced for reading and use; most non-syntactic ones were laid out in tabular form.

Some compositions, such as the Tale of Sinuhe (Parkinson 1998: 21–53), show themselves to be products of written culture by incorporating 'documentary' types such as dating formulas and letters, as well as numerous instances of the narrative infinitive, a verb form that was probably a product of writing rather than speech (Baines 2004a: 170–1). A few brief passages in the text are also close to standard formulas of self-presentation in tombs. Nonetheless, works like Sinuhe were intended to be spoken and performed aloud (Parkinson 2004). They do not attest to a separation of written and oral, but rather to an enhancement of oral realizations through the support of writing. Sinuhe contrasts strongly with the Tale of the Shipwrecked Sailor, which is also very much a product of high culture but plays artfully with the idea of oral story-telling and affects a simple, formulaic style (Parkinson 2002: 187–92, 298–9, with refs.). This latter type of written narrative is more prominent in Late Egyptian tales, which themselves contrast with two post-New Kingdom narratives, the Tale of Woe (Caminos 1977; Quack 2001) and Wenamun (Lichtheim 1976: 224–30; Schipper 2005). The former is cast in the specifically written form of a letter, while the latter eschews repetition and superficially patterned language. Yet, as noted above, letters were destined for reading out. Similarly, essential sections of Wenamun are conveyed in dialogue and exploit complex plays of register, as well as creating subordinate snatches of reported narrative within the overall tale, which itself is written in the first person and acquires some oral character as it gathers momentum, for example where the protagonist addresses the female ruler of Alasiya, to which his ship has been blown off course by a storm, through an interpreter (Gardiner 1932: 75,6–9; cf. Baines 1999b: 224–5):

I had heard, as far away as Thebes where Amun is, that in every city wrong is done, whereas in the land of Alasiya right is done. And yet wrong is done here all the time.

Thus, in more than one period, oral and written were exploited for literary purposes in ways that at once set the two media apart and brought them together.

Comparable plays with oral and written form are found also in inscriptional texts. A 12th dynasty self-presentation is formulated along the lines of a tale (Allen 2003), as is that of the 18th dynasty soldier Amenemhab, which is presented as something he narrates to his (deceased) king Thutmose III (Baines in preparation-b); a similar strategy appears again in the 'confessional' narrative of the 19th dynasty priest Simut (Frood in press). Another approach is to include part of an 'instruction' in a self-presentation; and this too is known from the 12th dynasty and the 18th (Posener 1976; Helck 1956b: 1408–11; 1961: 82–3). These two styles correspond with narrative and ethical characterization, which are the two most basic types of self-presentation, but they do so by travesty of written or oral genres, not by direct use of the inscriptional type.

An indirect pointer to story-telling as critique has a visual rather than textual form. Quite numerous New Kingdom ostraca and papyri, mainly of the Ramessid period, depict a travesty world of animals that possess parodic human institutions, in which power relations are often inverted, so that mice rule over cats and so forth (Brunner-Traut 1968; there is no detailed study of this material). Such motifs have narrative parallels in many cultures, notably among material created for children. The Egyptian examples, however, do not seem to be child-focused, and the two sections of one papyrus show animal motifs and a seemingly adult set of sexually explicit encounters between one or more balding men and a woman or women (Omlin 1973; unlike the uninscribed animal images, this has brief and cryptic written captions in hieratic). While much in these compositions is almost purely visual, they presumably related to oral story-telling practices, in genres that have clear written parallels only in much later animal fables that were incorporated in Demotic tales, notably the Myth of the Sun's Eye (Quack 2005: 128–40; Robert K. Ritner, in Simpson 2003: 494–6; partial visual parallel: Daumas 1968). Such materials no doubt belonged in oral contexts of transmission, presentation, and interaction. How serious a social critique they made can hardly be assessed (some of Lynn Meskell's arguments are problematic: 2004: 147–76); what is more significant here is they display a visual transformation of an oral practice. Most of the relevant material is from the later New Kingdom, when genres that are not known from other periods, such as love poetry, were written down, suggesting that the decorum of the stream of tradition altered in that period, later shifting back in some ways closer to an older configuration.

Practices of orality and its setting, including the use of music in performance, set compositions off against their lived contexts in further ways. The aesthetic frame creates a space in which problematic things can be said and licenses content that would not otherwise fit within rules of decorum. Literacy, then, is significant for the lasting formulation of social meaning in texts that address disturbing matters; it may broaden the range of what is transmitted in writing, even if the oral range is almost always more extensive. There is no simple congruity between written tradition and oral performance.

RELATED QUESTIONS

For the Graeco-Roman period, the highly specialized character of indigenous written culture could point to a decline in oral realization or to a bifurcation in narrative traditions between oral and written. Among the most distinctive works of the time are the Demotic tales, which are preserved notably in Roman period manuscripts from the provincial towns of Tebtunis and Dime in the Fayyum, but are also known hundreds of years earlier in 4th century BCE manuscripts from Saqqara (Smith and Tait 1984; on the dating of Demotic tales, see also Quack 2005: 22–3). These compositions are often much longer than those written earlier in hieratic. Papyrus rolls could be well over a hundred 'pages' long, some bearing indications for the user both of pages counted from the beginning and of ones remaining to the end (see Ryholt 2005, who also discusses the cultural setting of the tales). Despite this great length, the texts retain features that relate to performance or oral realization, such as division into many sub-stories, some of which are set within an overall narrative, in structures comparable with collections belonging to other traditions such as the *Thousand and One Nights* or the *Decameron*. It is possible that these works, which date to the first couple of centuries CE, were part of a purely scholastic culture, but even if they were, they would have been composed, used, and copied with oral accompaniment. They do not point to a significant split between written and oral.

The most difficult written compositions to interpret in relation to orality and literacy are 'scientific' texts that do not have a syntactic organization, such as the onomastica, which are lists of words without an explicit visual ordering (Gardiner 1947), or treatises like the Demotic herbal (Tait 1991), which is arranged by names of plants. Yet even these were written down with oral realization in mind, as is clear from the Roman period hieratic onomasticon from Tebtunis, which bears glosses in Demotic and Old Coptic (pre-Christian Egyptian written in Greek letters) that were presumably intended as aids to pronunciation (Osing 1998).

A final relevant category here is that of mixed pictorial–verbal written compositions, notably the underworld books attested from the New Kingdom and later, in which the pictorial element seems as important as the verbal. These works include many captions and some longer passages, including speeches, and are stated to be beneficial to those who 'know' them (Wente 1982; in general: Hornung 1984 [1972]; 1999). They too must have had an oral context of learning and transmission, but this might have been a social institution, in which the physical manuscript was displayed and consulted, rather than a performance. As with the 'writings' that are evoked in Old Kingdom biographical inscriptions (mentioned above), for long periods the underworld books appear to have been secret knowledge. Any transmission and voicing of their content would therefore have constituted significant occasions, presumably restricted to initiates. The probable imitation of a papyrus in early examples in the tombs of Thutmose III and Amenhotep II in the Valley of the Kings (c.1440–1410 BCE) makes it likely that their physical form was valued (Fig. 23; Bucher 1932; Hornung 1990). Sections of papyrus that bore images of whole 'hours' of the night might have been too long to consult across the lap in the normal manner of using papyrus, although this is difficult to assess because the size of inscription on the papyrus originals is unknown. Such works might have been displayed in a ceremony for initiates, the oral components of which are unknown.

Whereas orality could relate to secrecy in contexts like that just suggested, an opposite point can be made about a couple of classes of demotic documents of the Ptolemaic period (with forerunners), which are described by Mark Depauw as 'highly aesthetic'. Contracts with witness copies (Fig. 24; Depauw 1999) and marriage agreements are often inscribed in just a few very long lines, on papyri sometimes more than two metres wide (dimensions of marriage documents are not given in the standard studies of this type of text: Lüddeckens 1960; Pestman 1961). The former type are papyri bearing important contracts on which several additional copies of the text are written around the principal inscription that runs across the middle. Marriage agreements are property settlements that are associated with a marriage but do not ratify it through their content. Neither document type could easily have been written or copied on the lap; they were probably spread out on a large surface (contra Depauw). Since, as indicated, writing was generally accompanied by voicing of the text, one might envisage a ceremony in which a marriage agreement was laid out for a group of people, either ready-written or in process of writing, and simultaneously spoken. Witness-copy documents would have been voiced by the witnesses—some of them people of higher standing than the parties to the contract—as each of them wrote in turn around the central inscription, imparting added authority to the agreement. Thus, the physical form of these papyri points to oral and written practices that are not mentioned in other known sources and are likely to have oral antecedents in formal gatherings around significant transactions. Scholars have sought largely in vain for traces of ancient marriage ceremonies; in doing so, at least for the Ptolemaic period, they seem to have overlooked relevant evidence in the form of the documents themselves (for similar implications of a will, see below).

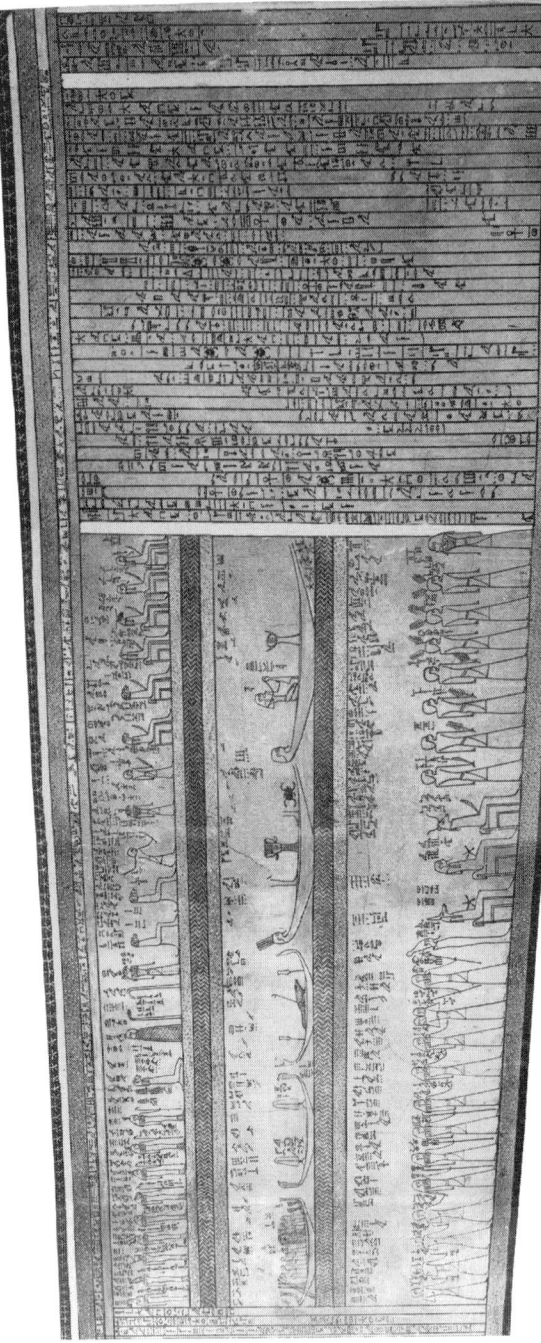

Fig. 23. Second hour and opening four columns of the third hour of the Amduat as painted on the wall of the burial chamber in the tomb of Amenhotep II in the Valley of the Kings at Thebes. The headline running along the top reads continuously in retrograde writing from left to right. Mid-18th dynasty. Perspective montage by Liam McNamara after Bucher (1932: pls. xxvii–xxviii).

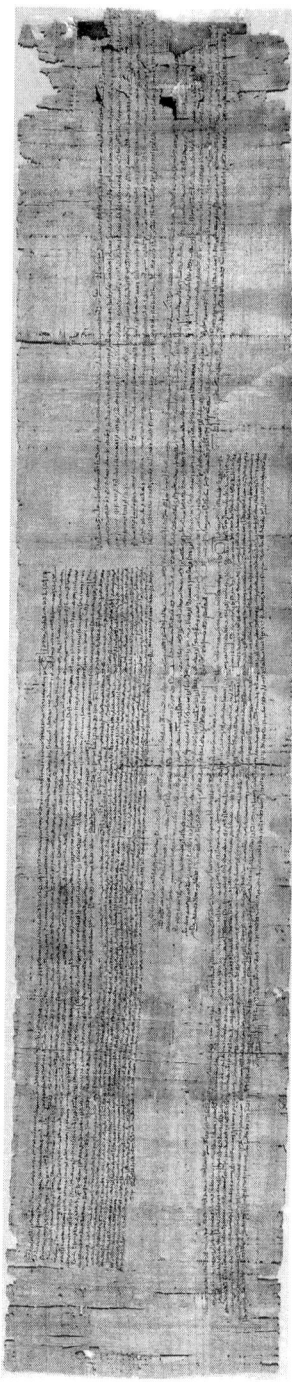

Fig. 24. Transfer document of Neskhons in favour of her son, in which she willed her property to him in return for his care of her until she died. Four witness copies are written below and to the left of the main text, which is the upper block on the right (sixteen witness signatures are on the back). Papyrus, length of preserved part 191.5 cm, height 39.5 cm; about 100 cm estimated missing from a total length of c.3 metres (Andrews 1990: 16). From Thebes, 265 BCE. British Museum EA 10026. Photograph courtesy British Museum.

The most striking instance of ceremonial inscription of a papyrus as a record of an important transaction is an early 26th dynasty papyrus in hieratic and abnormal hieratic that records the oracular confirmation of appointment to a priestly office in Thebes (Parker 1962). In addition to bearing more than fifty notations of the basic terms of the oracle in as many different hands, the written part of the papyrus is faced by a beautifully executed coloured vignette depicting the emergence in procession of the cult image of Amon-Re inside a shrine, preceded by high-ranking priests, whose figures are captioned in hieroglyphs. One of the priests is coloured distinctively darker, depicting someone of Kushite origin. This visual element, in which the figures and the writing face in the opposite direction to the cursive texts, shows the god coming out from the temple, and thus provides a 'living', enacted, and also oral context to balance the multiple written record of the oracle. The fact that such a document survives suggests that it was deposited in its beneficiary's grave. Because well-preserved burials are extremely rare, it is possible that pieces like this were commonly created to mark appointment to high-ranking offices.

CONTEXTS OF PERFORMANCE

The concept of orality used here relates to performance and implies both audience and defined institutions of transmission and reception that are often specific to particular types of utterance (R. B. Parkinson discusses many associated issues: in preparation). Some Egyptian texts and pictorial forms comment reflexively on such institutions, while for others this feature is not evident. In many cases relevant meanings may have been obvious to the actors but escape identification. I mention a couple of indicative domains. I do not discuss contexts where tales were told, instructions delivered, and poems performed; these must have existed, but evidence for them is sparse.

One pointer to the importance of oral forms is in iconographic conventions. In Egyptian art as in many traditions, very few figures are shown with their mouths open to indicate speech. Some gestures often signify speech together with accompanying ritual action, notably figures dedicating offerings, who hold their forward arm out with bent elbow and the open hand a little below shoulder height, but also tomb owners who gesture to the inscriptions around them and implicitly draw the viewer into the textual setting (textual also in the sense of Ch. 5); some examples have 'he says' inscribed in a prominent position next to the figure (Kanawati 1999: 284–90 with figs.). These gesturing figures, which are common in core offering scenes in tombs, on stelae, and in temple relief, seldom if ever have their mouths open; the same applies to various types in 'scenes of daily life' (Dominicus 1994: 77–130). A comparable reticence in expression is visible in hand details: in several periods the open hand does not show the palm with its lines (summary Baines 1992b). More pronounced and varied gestures are typical in particular of mourning scenes, where they represent actions that would probably be accompanied by patterned cries as much as by speech. Strong gestures and open mouths seem otherwise not to be compatible with the dignity of depicted settings. Figures whose mouths are open therefore give a marked signal either of their oral action's importance or of their departure from conventions of dignified comportment. Salient examples are harpists, attested in tomb scenes and on their own funerary stelae, whose songs are either the purpose of their presence or the salient element in their social role (stela: e.g. Malek 2003: 267). A revealing case is where a tomb owner is shown as an emblematically blind harpist in one relief in his tomb while he is sighted elsewhere (Martin 1985: pls. 21–2, with blindness extended also to mourners; contrast pls. 17–19 for sighted examples). The importance of orality is also evident in a scene from the Saqqara tomb of the general and later king Haremhab (c.1330 BCE), where the tomb owner, who is shown twice, mediates indirectly between petitioning captives and the king (Martin 1989: pls. 110–15; in the convention of the period, his open palm is shown). Several of the captives, who are represented in disarray, gesticulate wildly and have their mouths open. In another case, enemies in the sway of the oppressing king bare their teeth, presumably in pain (Andreu 2002: nos. 168a, b). The harpists might sing specific literary compositions—for example the cynical Harpist's Song from the Tomb of King Inyotef, one example of which is inscribed around the scene of a group of musicians (Lange and Hirmer 1968: pl. 210). Other occurrences are more likely to depict unscripted but formally organized speech. In the case of the enemies, perhaps a specific noise or anguished silence is depicted.

Another relevant context here is the funerary lament (Lüddeckens 1943; Rössler-Köhler 1986), the form of which may have influenced a Middle Kingdom literary text, the Dialogue of Ipuwer and the Lord of All (Parkinson 1998: 166–99; Enmarch 2005). Funeral processions are represented in tombs of several periods. Only a minority of examples include lament texts in captions above the figures, but related oral practices, together with elaborate rituals and customary performances of various kinds (e.g. Gardiner 1955b), were a major expressive domain. Like the oral realizations suggested above for marriage agreements, performances such as these can be posited only from indirect, mainly pictorial evidence. Laments are not attested in the literary stream of tradition, but this does not make them any less a major oral genre. Another reflection of a poorly attested, presumably oral genre is the dirge of the deceased Taimhotep addressed to her surviving husband on her funerary stela of 42 BCE, which is also likely to belong with funeral performances (Lichtheim 1980: 62–3; Baines 2004b: 56–9 with refs.).

In a more limited way, the Old Kingdom Herdsman's Song (G. Meyer 1990), which is inscribed in several tombs and is presented as what the herdsmen sing as they ford a watercourse, exemplifies some sort of written 'literary' transmission, and yet points more toward oral performance; again, no comparable text is known from the later stream of tradition. This text is attested from a period when belles lettres seem not to have been written, but a couple of tombs contain moralizing addresses inscribed next to figures of their owners that offer analogies for later teachings (e.g. Edel 1953: 213; Kaplony 1968). The fairly consistent form of the Herdsman's Song in different tombs suggests that there was some transmission of texts that fell outside later written genres, while the addresses point more toward variable oral institutions. Snatches of subordinates' songs are attested from other contexts; some of these exist in multiple copies (Altenmüller 1984–5).

The protagonists of laments and of musical performances depicted as part of banquet scenes include, or consist principally of, women. Women are also attested by titles and roles as singers in cults, in that of Hathor from the Old and Middle Kingdoms (Gillam 1995), and of other deities including Amun from the New Kingdom and later (Robins 1993: 142–56; Graefe 1981; Naguib 1990). This pattern exemplifies the gendered character of oral performance. Most evidence from the tradition as a whole relates to men, while women seem to be associated with particular vocal and sonic qualities and with the expression of strong emotion: in funeral processions men are generally depicted as dignified and unexpressive, while women exhibit feeling far more visibly, no doubt in cries and ululations as well as song. The presence of women in New Kingdom banquet scenes may also have mortuary meanings. These distinctions between female and male roles probably relate also to the bracketing of aesthetic performance within its social context, which enabled it to include subject matter that was otherwise not part of transmitted high culture. Those who, like women, mostly had limited opportunities to act out a personal role, could have such a possibility in performance. This point is mobilized in the Tale of Sinuhe, in which the queen and royal daughters have a major part in the culminating episode where the protagonist is reintegrated into court society: after Sinuhe is overawed by appearing before the king, they enter bearing symbols of Hathor and perform a song of royal propitiation (Parkinson 1998: 40–1). Such roles for women did not, however, form a distinct domain of written literary tradition. Women seem to have been largely excluded from the written practice of high culture, but they may have participated a little more in its oral aspects.

INSTITUTIONALIZATION

A question that is often at the heart of cross-cultural studies of literacy, but has been left aside here, is how far writing changes social practice. In interdisciplinary discussions, such issues have been associated closely with studies of possible related cognitive change or development (compare Ch. 2 §3.2). The key place in Egypt for which such matters can be investigated is late New Kingdom Deir el-Medina, where documentation for the 19th and 20th dynasties is uniquely rich. This community was one of the most literate in Egypt; in a number of domains its practices moved from oral to written during that period (Haring 2003; Donker van Heel and Haring 2003). This change, which is visible in both official and personal documents, may have been due in part to social aspiration, in which the village's 'middle class' inhabitants adopted conventions of their social superiors. There is no good reason to suppose that the increased pervasiveness of written practice among them during this period had significant cognitive implications.

Comparable developments are visible on a wider basis in legal provisions in such domains as inheritance, where the binding force of enactments, which was originally vested in oral and ceremonial forms, came over centuries to be entrusted to writing—perhaps with attendant ceremonies like the one posited above for witness-copy contracts. Such processes of change were not irreversible and may have been repeated in different periods and contexts. The use of writing probably favoured variety in testamentary provision, which might have been a breeding ground for dispute in the absence of a document. Relevant examples are attested from the Old Kingdom onward (Goedicke 1970; Helck 1974a). The Old and New Kingdom uses of writing and phases of change just mentioned can be usefully compared with those reported in Michael Clanchy's classic study of developing uses of writing in medieval England (1993 [1979]).

An excellent example of such developments is the group of 20th dynasty documents recording the testamentary arrangements of Naunakhte, a woman of Deir el-Medina (Černý 1945). Her core will was written by a scribe of the necropolis, but two other documents were written by ordinary workmen. In another essay (Ch. 3, Excursus B), Christopher Eyre and I note this as an instance of people being paid to witness a juridical transaction and thus saving some expense. While this interpretation may be valid in itself, the context suggests that more was at stake. Naunakhte, who left only a small amount of property, distributed it unevenly among her children, excluding those who she stated had not supported her as they should have done. The men who wrote two subsidiary documents were two of her sons. I suggest that while they earned a little by doing so, it was at least as important that they participated actively in the process of creating the will and ratifying its contents. Some statements in the will contain moralizing by Naunakhte that would hardly have had binding force and might reflect the oral, ceremonial setting of the juridical act.

Phases of change and intensified use of writing analogous with late New Kingdom Deir el-Medina could perhaps be studied for other periods and contexts, but no consistent long-term analysis is possible, because evidence is scattered and often not comparable between different bodies of material. The distinctive character of the evidence from Graeco-Roman period Tebtunis and Dime, mentioned above, exemplifies such problems. The temples in these relatively small places exhibit a more intense high-cultural engagement than is attested from Deir el-Medina, while recent archaeological and textual work at Tebtunis shows that there was a marked increase in prosperity there between the Ptolemaic and the Roman period (Ivan Guermeur, personal communication). Outside the temple environment in the Fayyum, much literate practice may have been in Greek and subject to different conventions and constraints from those affecting Egyptian writing practice. The Fayyum is striking in any case for the large number of literary texts in both Greek and Egyptian that have been discovered there (van Minnen 1998). One suspects that the urban–rural dichotomy often used in analyses of this material may be misleading in various ways, including the high level of prosperity of much of the Fayyum in Graeco-Roman times, the significance of local centres there, and specific patterns of urban–rural interchange both within the area and between the Fayyum and major urban centres, for example through the channel of major elite landholdings. In cultural terms, Tebtunis and Dime may not have been 'remote' or 'rural'.

CONCLUSION

Scholars realize increasingly that written tradition cannot be comprehended satisfactorily without being set in its living oral context (see e.g. Olson and Torrance 1991). Egyptian writing transmitted a subset of cultural materials that was sustained through, or realized in terms of, orality. Some written practices had little direct relation to oral forms, but they too were sustained by the wider oral environment (compare Goody 1977; 1986). Writing could effect communication across spaces and expanses of time that were otherwise difficult or impossible to bridge, and it was particularly important in maintaining traditions of forms of language, textual formulas, and complete texts. There is, however, no strong evidence that writing acquired any of the 'autonomy' in instituting change that was commonly attributed to it in mid-20th century studies of literacy (see Ch. 2 §§1, 3.2). Here one might compare the variety of approaches that have been applied to European developments in particular, on a wide basis by Walter F. Ong (1982) and with a focus on medieval Europe and intellectual developments by Brian Stock (1983; 1990; for social aspects, compare Clanchy 1993 [1979]). Scholars such as these have been criticized for recent historical periods, notably if tendentiously by Brian Street (1984), who argues that the social context of writing has hardly been taken into account. While this criticism has some force, and discussions have often tended to focus on literacy at the expense of orality, it does not do justice to the problems involved in addressing long past societies. In Egypt as elsewhere, orality was both the setting for the realization of literacy and a vital institution, for which analyses of rather better understood societies like those mentioned offer valuable parallels. The Egyptian case is distinctive in belonging to a culture that was independent in its development of writing and, for example, only gradually constructed written genres that included compositions of great extent, whatever expansive oral institutions may or may not have existed alongside them. Access to orality in premodern cultures is difficult or impossible; modelling of its role is essential.

APPENDIX: UPDATES TO CHAPTERS 2–5; COMPARATIVE STUDIES

I note here some published criticisms and revisions for Chapters 2 and 3, as well as surveying cross-cultural and comparative writing on literacy, and to a lesser extent orality, that has appeared since those chapters were written, together with case studies. Although the range of material I cite is limited, it may help to give a path into the literature. A focus that has grown in the last two decades, notably in work on post-antique European civilization, is the study by historians of inscribed artefacts as material objects, either public and inscriptional, or portable like individual inscribed items, manuscripts, or books. This tendency is valuable for archaeologically recovered civilizations, and it balances the opposing point that while writing forms a domain of its own, the proportion of language-based behaviour that relates to writing is generally small. Writing is a practice of material culture that has a complex, organizationally and aesthetically tempered connection with language.

The secondary literature is given below in several categories, omitting work on the post-medieval world that is not included in collected volumes. Some relevant major discussions on more recent periods, notably on writing as material culture, centre around changes subsequent to the advent of printing with movable type in Europe. The best known work in this area is that of

Elizabeth Eisenstein (1993 [1979]; 1993 [1983]), which has stimulated much further research (e.g. Wood 1985, for Kerala in south India). For altogether later times, Jean Hébrard (2002) offers a striking analysis of a man's hesitant writings about World War I in terms of his education and general literacy. I give very few references for studies on Asian traditions, with which I am not familiar.

Chapter 2: Literacy and ancient Egyptian society

Revisions to the views expressed in Chapter 2 appear in other chapters of this book.

The discussion of the display of roles, including that of scribal status (§2.2 with n. 18), in the Early Dynastic period and Old Kingdom does not take into account that many of these are travesties (compare also Roth 2002). Someone who shows himself as a 'scribe' has that position in relation to the king, but it does not follow that he exercised the role of scribe. The example cited of a shipwright points in the same direction: the man did not necessarily work with the adze which was the symbol of his profession, but he may have been responsible to the king for work on ships.

Chapter 3: Four notes on literacy

The treatment of rates of literacy by myself and Christopher Eyre has been criticized by Leonard Lesko as underestimating the worth of Egyptian civilized culture (1990: 655–9; Lesko 1994 goes over similar issues for Deir el-Medina, see below). Lesko does not produce specific arguments for the very much higher rates he favours, which might be comparable with those of some early modern societies with very different styles of economy and social organization from ancient Egypt (he does not give figures). Our estimates do not imply any evaluation of the worth or otherwise of Egyptian civilization, nor do we think that such worth would relate in any meaningful way to levels of literacy. The aim of our study is to suggest orders of magnitude for the literate as a contribution to modelling the role of writing in the society.

A more specific criticism on rates of literacy is Jac J. Janssen's (1992) of our estimates for Deir el-Medina. His study can be read alongside ours. Janssen argues for a significantly higher rate on the basis of his comprehensive knowledge of the village's inhabitants, seeking to establish which individuals were literate, whereas we are concerned more with which roles required literacy institutionally or were likely to be occupied by literate people. His higher estimates are therefore to some extent compatible with our lower ones. Were the Deir el-Medina community not so exceptional in occupational and social terms, one might see a 'cultural literacy' as pervading more of New Kingdom society below the level of the administrative, priestly, and military elite, but to us it seems more likely that Deir el-Medina was the exception, even if it may show what aspirations a wider group might have. Here, we would comment that Janssen may underestimate the social prestige of writing, both generally and in the community, and hence the extent to which people would normally use others to write for them, in a society in which the use of serving personnel, subordinates, and other forms of assistance were pervasive.

That point is relevant also to letters written on behalf of, or by, women: it is not easy to tell whether they read or wrote these pieces themselves, even if their content is seemingly personal and intimate. In a group of letters from Memphis from the reign of Ramesses II, Janssen (1960: 33) has argued on the basis of a relatively less cursive hand that one addressed to a high-ranking woman was intended to be read by her. This is a possible explanation, but not the only one.

Betsy Bryan (1985) argues that depictions of boxes of scribal equipment under the chairs of women in New Kingdom tombs display their literacy. This conclusion is problematic, because the women are seated on a single wide chair with their husbands. It would not have been possible to show the box beneath the man, because the woman's legs occupy that space, so that the equipment is as likely to relate to him as to her (as Gay Robins pointed out to me).

Bryan's article exemplifies difficulties in establishing whether there was significant female literacy. Our review in Ch. 3 §3 leaves the question open; unless evidence of a different character from what has so far been identified becomes available, it may not be possible to resolve the matter. Material as clear as some of that cited by Youtie (1973; 1981) for Greek literacy in Roman period provincial Egypt remains elusive.

One aspect of the argument on women's literacy has been rendered problematic by work of Andrea McDowell (1996; 2000) on scribal training, primarily at Deir el-Medina. She shows that the scribal exercises from the site were done by advanced students, who presumably learned basic literacy in a different location and at an earlier age. If no significant basic schooling was done at Deir el-Medina, for which scholars had generally posited the existence of a school, any teaching of girls could not have been integrated with what was done for boys. If girls were taught to read and write by leading families of the village, this would show a strong commitment to education and to cultural values for their own sake. Such a possibility is compatible with other aspects of the community's life, such as its high-cultural aspirations, but it remains hypothetical.

In two articles, Annie Gasse (1992; 2000) has collected statistics of numbers of ostraca discovered at Deir el-Medina and the ratio of non-literary to literary. The striking conclusion is that literary ones are the majority (7,400 out of 13,000); a third category, not covered in her statistics, is figured or pictorial ostraca, probably about half the size of the literary group and raising further the proportion with an aesthetic more than an everyday purpose. This ratio shows that advanced scribal training (on the lines suggested by McDowell) was a major activity of writing in the village, but it does not situate that activity at a particular point in the educational process. Her second article (2000) identifies a location on the site that could have been used for instruction or for practice. The material identified as coming from there fits with McDowell's analysis, because it does not include truly elementary exercises, while the hands are more hesitant in Classical Egyptian than in Late Egyptian, which the writers may have learned previously elsewhere. If so, the general assumption that initial learning of writing was on classical literary texts may need revision. Perhaps these formed part of a subsequent, more highly cultured phase of education at Deir el-Medina. It would be risky to generalize that point to practice in the core areas of court institutions and temples, where the literary tradition was presumably created and maintained.

Ben Haring and Koen Donker van Heel (2003) have published the most detailed study of the use of writing at Deir el-Medina, while Haring (2003) has presented a model of change in the 19th and 20th dynasties that builds upon their results. This work is discussed briefly above in the present chapter (Institutionalization).

Publications on literacy and related topics

General and comparative.   Work on the origin and character of writing systems provides essential background to research on literacy, while the increasing body of studies of orality throws into relief the complexity of interplay between oral and written domains. In the text of this chapter I attempt to take the latter aspect into account. Studies not mentioned there include Finnegan (1988; 1992) and Olson and Torrance (1991); the essays of R. Narasimhan (1991) and D. P. Pattanayak (1991) in the latter volume are valuable, that of Pattanayak for its strongly politicized critique of unreflecting western valuations of literacy. Other general collections are Street (1993), which again has a political aspect, and Taylor and Olson (1995). The review article of James Collins (1995) provides an entree to much further literature.

Two works that develop older lines of research are John DeFrancis's study (1989), which champions the relationship of writing, language, and phonetics from the perspective of a Sinologist, and Jack Goody's most recent book on literacy (2000), which extends some of his earlier arguments. While DeFrancis presents a distinctive view, I do not find his approach illuminating for ancient Near Eastern inventions of writing; even for China, the notions that writing was invented to record language phonologically, and that a system should not be characterized by the term if it does not do that, do not address early material well and have a teleological cast.

Here, the volume on the Precolumbian Americas edited by Elizabeth Boone and Walter D. Mignolo (1994) opens new perspectives by including a wider range of phenomena within its definition of writing than is generally done for the Old World. Stephen Houston's essay (1994) offers a comparative assessment of aspects and rates of Maya literacy, providing a rare analysis of writing in a civilization where it is not known to have been used for administration and counterbalancing the often excessive scholarly emphasis on the pragmatic worth of early writing.

Houston has developed a set of studies, including edited volumes on origins of writing (2004b) and on the disappearance of writing systems (Houston, Baines, and Bennet in preparation; see initial article: Houston et al. 2003), as well as a survey of the archaeology of communication technologies (2004a), in which he sets writing among a broader range of practices. This body of work opens out research on archaeologically recovered societies to a variety of new approaches, as well as addressing issues that had often been ignored.

Ancient Egypt. Herman te Velde (1986) has analysed Egyptian literacy in a short article that is very close to Chapters 2 and 3 in its conclusions. By contrast, the study of Donald Redford (2000) is very dismissive of my work and that of Christopher Eyre, although it does not address our arguments directly; his main sections focus on the Near East rather than Egypt and include useful discussions of orality. Laure Pantalacci (1996a) discusses writing practices in Dakhla Oasis in the late Old Kingdom and their implications for literacy. Clay tablets were used there for writing in hieratic both in the Old Kingdom and in the Late period, extending the range of media known from Egyptian civilization. While papyrus or writing boards might have been scarce in the oases, it is also possible that tablets have been overlooked in excavations in the Nile Valley.

John Ray (1994b) and Dorothy Thompson (1994) have published discussions of relations between literacy and power in Late period and Ptolemaic Egypt. An imaginative contribution for the latter period is Philippe Derchain's succinct analysis (1997) of an inscription in the temple of Edfu that evokes writing.

In a wide-ranging book on early Egypt, David Wengrow (2006) sets writing practice in relation to changing social institutions, focusing on the funerary domain from which most of the earliest writing has been recovered, interpreting its presence meaningfully in terms of funerary ritual and making minimal assumptions about its role in administration. This approach, which has some affinities with that of John Bennet for Aegean Linear B (see below), helps to overcome the bias toward the modern sense of writing's indispensability that almost inevitably informs much work on its invention and early use. It remains an open question how widespread the ceremonial or pragmatic use of writing may have been in early non-funerary contexts.

Three works on writing and education in Greek in Graeco-Roman Egypt complement the picture that can be drawn for earlier times: Cribiore (1996; 2001); Legras (2002, poorly informed on indigenous Egyptian writing).

Mesopotamia and ancient Near East. The invention of writing in Mesop-otamia is the example most closely parallel to Egypt, while the very different social setting and patterns of development there shows that such institutions may be weakly constrained. A notable theoretical study is that of Peter Damerow (1999, not printed but available online). Jean-Jacques Glassner (2003) has published the fullest work on early Mesopotamian writing, with a distinctive and controversial interpretation. Important essays on literacy in Mesopotamia are those of Mogens Trolle Larsen (1987) and Piotr Michalowski (1994). Peter Machinist (2003) includes themes of literacy in a highly stimulating discussion of the theme of history for Mesopotamia and the Hebrew Bible. A short academy publication by Claus Wilcke (2000) is the most direct treatment of the question of levels of literacy and of the identity of the literate group in Mesopotamia. The edited volume of Michael Hudson and Cornelia Wunsch (2004) on accounting in Mesopotamia addresses the domain that is generally thought to have led to the invention of writing there, as well as remaining at its core in later times. For the biblical world, the study of William M. Schniedewind (2004) addresses the creation of texts in a later period and a different perspective from my discussion in Chapter 5.

Bronze Age Aegean and classical antiquity. In an article that arises from continuing research, John Bennet (2001) models a social and institutional context for the Linear B clay tablets of the Late Bronze Aegean. His study shows how it is not necessary to see archaeologically attested practices as part of a much larger whole. This case offers ways of thinking about highly restricted uses of writing, notably where it was not used in aesthetic contexts, either literary or monumental, for which one might see parallels in contemporaneous societies in much of Anatolia, where writing was known but has left little archaeological trace. For early alphabetic usage in Greece, the article of James Whitley (1997) focusing around the public inscription of Cretan laws is valuable in showing how assumptions of many Classicists about the spread of literacy and the social impact of writing are unrealistic. As in many societies, such an inscription was not necessarily intended to be read, and its setting up did not presuppose the existence of a large literate group.

The study of literacy in the classical world was given a major stimulus by the work of William V. Harris (1989), which covers Greece and Rome over almost a millennium. Harris offers a rather sceptical analysis, seeing levels of literacy as in general relatively low and arguing against the idealized standing of writing that had been assumed by many writers (see already Harris 1983, with valuable history of modern attitudes). An edited volume was devoted to reviews of Harris's book by Romanists, all of whom argue for higher levels of literacy and a greater penetration of writing in Roman society than he had proposed (Beard 1991). Bowman and Woolf (1994), on literacy and power, also originated in the wake of Harris. Publishing independently at the same time as Harris, Rosalind Thomas (1989) presented first a detailed work on classical Athens and then one on classical Greece as a whole (1992, with bibliographical essay and discussion of Harris), going beyond assessing levels of literacy to analyse the social impact of writing and discuss such themes as oral poetry.

The studies in the volume edited by Harvey Yunis (2003b), which has an excellent introduction (Yunis 2003a), attend more than much other research to the precise context of written genres, but their chronological location of the emergence of 'literate culture' in Greece in the 5th century BCE is late in some respects. Some contributors attribute too much influence to specific genres, for example in changes in medical practice (Dean-Jones 2003). Detailed studies of Teresa Morgan (1998; 1999) on education in the Greek world complement that of Raffaella Cribiore for Graeco-Roman Egypt (cited above).

Works with a rather more archaeological focus include that of Elizabeth Meyer (1990) on epitaphs in the Roman world, contributing to an ongoing discussion of the status and significance of public inscriptions that is associated particularly with Ramsey McMullen (1982). Jocelyn Penny Small (1997) analyses the use of writing implements, equipment, and inscribed materials such as scrolls, in order to gain a sense of how written works were consulted and composed. This is one of very few works that convey a strong sense of elite practice in action. In a different direction, Deborah Tarn Steiner (1994) examines the pictorial and mythical image of writing in the Greek world, suggesting a dimension that has parallels in Egypt in the position of the deities of writing, Thoth and Seshat (Budde 2000), but is relatively little explored.

Medieval Europe. The book of Rosamond McKitterick on writing in the Carolingian world (1989) may overestimate its role there, in comparison with what is known or suggested for its prevalence in other areas of medieval Europe, notably in the succeeding centuries; part of its argument, however, is that there was a falling-off in literacy after Carolingian times. While writing evidently had great prestige in the Carolingian revival, that prestige it likely to have been due in part to its being a scarce resource. McKitterick (1990) has also edited a volume on literacy in early medieval western Europe, most of the contributors to which again take maximalist positions. The book includes a case study of inscriptional literacy in an Italian monastery where writing must have stood out in its proliferation in comparison with the wider society (Mitchell 1990); such an example offers a valuable comparison and contrast with Egypt. In a different direction, Katherine O'Brien O'Keeffe (1990) presents a theoretically informed study of orality and literacy based on Old English verse, its text traditions, and the differential treatment of Latin and Old English in manuscripts, in terms of layout, punctuation, and other features, arguing that the Old English exhibits 'transitional literacy'.

Among scholars who explore the physical presence of writing in the medieval and Renaissance world, Armando Petrucci is the best known (1993; 1995; 1998). His studies range from detailed analyses of manuscripts to work on public and mortuary inscriptions. In a different direction, Paul Saenger (1997; preparatory article Saenger 1982) analyses in great detail cognitive and other implications of the introduction of space between words in manuscripts, which spread from the British Isles to continental Europe toward the end of the first millennium CE. His work, which is informed by experimental psychology and related disciplines, studies ways in which manuscripts became increasingly suitable for quick reading and scanning as their physical design developed during the Middle Ages. While such changes probably outstrip any ease of reading that might have been achieved with Egyptian cursive or monumental writing, studies like his raise the question of how far it is possible to allow for familiarity and expertise in consultation that might counteract what a modern user may see as difficulties in using old formats. Despite this reservation, his work has the same advantage as that of Small (cited above), that it approaches the reality of literate practice before the conventions of the printed page developed. It may be impossible to model effectively the use of written materials by expert readers and writers of the pre-printing era, whether in ancient Egypt or in the Middle Ages. Works like these offer an illuminating way of thinking about relevant issues, but it should be borne in mind that the material they analyse belonged to, and was read by, small elites, and cannot easily provide evidence for broader social implications of writing.

7

Ancient Egyptian concepts and uses of the past: third to second millennium evidence

INTRODUCTION

In the words of a medieval Arabic poem, the Great Pyramid, the archetypal ancient Egyptian monument, is 'feared by time, yet everything else in our present world fears time' (ʿUmāra al-Yamanī, cited by Schäfer 1986 [1974]: 24 with n. 43). At any moment, the chief actors in such a culture are defying the future to erode their achievements and they may appear to be set against change. Yet their successors must be aware of change, and they have the monuments of the past almost ineradicably before them; they too seek to construct enduring monuments; in looking to the future they emulate the past and extend its traditions.

Paradoxes like these are apparent to the outsider and could hardly be suppressed completely by the actors. They supply some kind of context for people's involvement with past, present, and future in a complex society or civilization. Here I add 'complex' because the presence of large monuments is characteristic of complex societies and archaeologically relevant, but this does not imply that tension between the transient and the enduring is lacking elsewhere. A literate complex society such as Egypt can additionally supply

---

In Robert Layton (ed.) 1989, *Who needs the past? Indigenous values and archaeology*, One World Archaeology (London: Unwin Hyman) 131–49.

Except for a few references, notes to this chapter are additions to the previously published text, to which some material that had been cut has been restored. Recent bibliography in the areas covered by the essay is abundant; see especially the excellent micro-study of Deir el-Medina by Andrea McDowell (1992) and the collection edited by John Tait (2003a), notably the contribution by Antonio Loprieno (2003b: 139–54). I give some general and some detailed references in the notes, as well as comments on a couple of points where both the consensus and my own opinion have changed, because either new evidence has appeared or interpretations have developed.

a continuing, precisely formulated record of an ideological context within which these very widespread reactions to the past can be sited; in this chapter I consider these and some other implications of literacy for uses of the past. Very restricted literacy, as there was in ancient Egypt, brings other limitations: the chief evidence, which consists of texts and works of art, provides information only about the elite, mainly those near the rulers. I do not study the cult of the dead and of ancestors—a limited phenomenon in Egypt—which might give evidence for uses of the past in slightly wider sectors of the society. Only a small part of a vast topic can be approached, and I omit the first millennium BCE, the period that is richest and most diverse in its uses of the past, because it requires a separate study.[1]

Egyptian texts are often thought to be homogeneous and ideologically consistent: Egyptians seldom allowed dissent to surface and presented a bland exterior. The past is, however, an area where diversity is apparent, between the most narrowly defined official ideology or mythology and works of literature with more general themes, between different literary texts, and to some extent between literary texts and non-royal inscriptions. The past legitimizes the present order of things, but if that order needs legitimizing it is not perfect. This imperfection can be set against the perfection of the past, which may be used as a model or as something more subversive: criticism of the present is in terms of the past. I review where and why Egyptians exploited different pasts. Like any other society, they constructed their present and projected their future out of their past, but the character of Egyptian evidence, its time depth, and the type of society which created it, are all distinctive. Here, one can usefully contrast treatments of the past that can be identified for Neolithic monuments in western Europe, no doubt among many other traditions (Bradley 2002).

First, the past must be related to Egyptian time concepts in their broadest extension.

TIME AND ETERNITY; FUTURE-ORIENTED ROYAL 'HISTORY'

In Egypt, creation was seen as involving the setting-up and demarcation of an ordered cosmos surrounded by, and shot through with, the disordered and

---

[1] See further Redford (1986); and especially the essays collected in Tait (2003a). The study of Sabine Neureiter on first millennium archaism (1994) does not contribute to the discussion because its grasp of the primary materials is insufficient.

the 'nonexistent' (Sauneron and Yoyotte 1959; Hornung 1982a: 172–85). Time is part of the ordered world, whereas 'eternity' as construed in western terms—a complete transcendence of time—is not. As a positive concept, however, eternity has its counterpart in two much discussed Egyptian terms, *nḥḥ* and *ḏt*, which are mostly used synonymously, but when distinguished appear to refer to cyclical and linear time respectively (see e.g. Assmann 1975: 41–8; Iversen 1963; Hornung 1982b: 102–5, with refs.). Although *nḥḥ* and *ḏt* are neither infinite nor non-time, they are words for indefinitely extended and positively evaluated time. In Chapter 175 of the Book of the Dead (manuscript *c.*1250), the creator says that the 'lifetime in life' of Osiris, the god who is archetypally subject to linear time, will be 'for millions of millions, a lifetime of millions (of years or people?)', and then the creator 'will destroy all that (he) created, and this earth will come to the primeval water and the flood, as in its first state' (Budge 1910: 73–4; Allen 1974: 184; the word for 'million' is etymologically related to *nḥḥ*). The created world will endure for an indefinitely long time—the word for 'million' soon lost any mathematical precision it may have possessed—and will finally be destroyed, when, to quote a comparable text, there will be a social reversal, and 'mounds will be cities and vice versa. Dynasty(?, or "estate") will expunge dynasty' (de Buck 1961: 468a–b; Otto 1977; Lichtheim 1973: 132 is inaccurate). Both human societies and the gods inhabit the same bounded cosmos. Within that cosmos, there is a vast extension of time that is worth aspiring to.

These global time concepts coexisted with complex calendars (e.g. Krauss 1985). There were two lunar calendars used for religious purposes and a schematic solar civil calendar of 365 days, introduced in the early third millennium, by which documents were dated. Despite the existence of lunar and Sothic cycles, the latter of about 1,456 years and defined by the interaction of the civil calendar and the star Sirius/Sothis, no epoch longer than a year or a king's ideologically evaluated reign was thematized. From the 4th dynasty onward, longer periods were dated by biennial cattle censuses, and from the Middle Kingdom by regnal years (compare Assmann 1983a: 193; for 'periods', see below). There was thus a sharp division between the limited yearly cycles of the present, which were important in religion and cosmology, and the distant past; remote dates had to be computed from annals or kinglists.

Official ideology presents human action as royal; humanity is almost excluded from consideration. The position of humanity in the official scheme of things is seldom formulated. The king's function, however, is well known. With an authority delegated from the creator god, he establishes and maintains 'order', or the created world. In a 'treatise' on his role in the solar cult, perhaps of the Middle Kingdom (*c.*1975–1700), there is a wonderfully succinct definition of what he does. The creator placed him on earth 'for ever and ever (*nḥḥ ḏt*), judging humanity and propitiating the gods, and setting order (*mꜣꜥt*) in place of disorder (*jzft*). He gives offerings to the gods and mortuary offerings to the spirits (the blessed dead)' (Assmann 1970: 22). Despite the king's dependence on the gods, his role minimizes the creator's and is 'everlasting (*nḥḥ*)', while it also stands between this world and other worlds—the gods and the spirits—and between the present and the past. Yet concern for the past is directed away from the ideological core of this world: since the king's position is everlasting, the definition of his role is oriented primarily toward the future (the text does not descend to saying what happens when one king succeeds another).

This orientation toward the future is more generally characteristic of the king's role in 'history', as recorded in royal 'historical' inscriptions (see also below); indeed, Egyptian has no single word for 'prehistory' or for 'history'. At the beginning of his reign, the king sets order in place of disorder, and later, whenever there is a threat to the established order, he instantly counters it (see Hornung 1966; 1971; Otto 1964–6). He may also act positively to enlarge the order of the world, notably by extending the frontiers of Egypt. These actions imply taking the past into account, but only the most immediate past is relevant, and achievement of that time may be exceeded. The king's entire role is ritualized, so that there is no sharp distinction between his performance of the cult, which is presented in the treatise cited, and his actions toward the outside world; the significant difference is in the location and the sanctity of what is done. 'Historical' actions have a more evident meaning for humanity, but there is little emphasis on human participation in most accounts of royal deeds, which were set up in temples and not accessible to many. There is therefore much room for human ideology on levels different from the royal, although non-royal inscriptions that recount their owners' achievements mostly relate them to the king. By relating the actions of kings to the gods and to the future, royal inscriptions exempt them from conventional ethical norms and have a significant legitimizing function.

The treatise is at such a high level of 'theory' and generality that its definition of society and royal action is not necessarily paralleled even in official sources, such as royal inscriptions, that have more pragmatic purposes. In stating that the king judges humanity, the text relates the king's moral role more to the gods, and this is no accident. Concern with what is less than everlasting and with the past is an explicitly moral dimension of thought and occupies a position a little below the grandest statements about the cosmos, which lack a human scale. Thus, despite the—to western eyes—alien context in which Egyptian concepts of time are cited, ideas of the past can be relatively small-scale and unsystematic; when they are presented specifically, they still have a this-worldly dimension. The focus on this world and on its moral status affects the king too: his position is relativized by his mythical and royal predecessors.

EARLY POSITIVE EVALUATION OF THE PAST

The most decisive period for the definition of an absolute past in relation to the later Egyptian present must have been the centuries around 3000 BCE, when the Egyptian state was unified, writing was introduced, and the ideological presentation of the cosmos on the monuments was formulated. From then on, 'history' could be separated from the indefinite, or less definite, past. Even in those early times, the past was a significant dynastic factor. In the 1st dynasty, the capital of the country was moved from Abydos, the capital of the earlier united but not historic state of Egypt (Kaiser 1964), to Memphis, where high officials had grand tombs on the edge of the desert escarpment at Saqqara. The kings, meanwhile, continued to be buried at Abydos in remote, architecturally more modest tombs next to the cemeteries of their predecessors (see e.g. Kemp 1967; Kaiser and Dreyer 1982). Tradition and lineage appear more powerful legitimations than scale or proximity to the centre of power. This physical disproportion between the tombs of officials and kings has led to a long-running controversy over which group contained the true royal tombs (see now references cited in Ch. 14 n. 14).

Dynastic history began with the serial recording of year names used for administrative purposes. These year names were gathered into a single listing, or set of 'annals' (cf. Redford 1984; 1986: 65–96), of which a fragmentary version made about 500 years later survives (Fig. 10); this included more extensive records from the 4th–5th dynasties, when the system had been superseded by a partial numbering of years of reign.[2] In the present context, the most relevant feature of the monument is that it has a top line giving the names of 'predynastic' kings (without any details of reigns), who provided a transition between 'prehistory' and 'history'.

Nothing mythical seems to have been recorded in the list of kings and years of reign. Perhaps the time before the existence of the Egyptian state was treated as uncreated, since it was not within the established order of things.

---

[2] The surviving inscription was considered for some years to be a first millennium copy (e.g. Helck 1974d; contra: Fischer 1976a: 48). Parallels discovered subsequently, notably the late Old Kingdom annal stone published by Michel Baud and Vassil Dobrev (1995; 1997), show that this is unlikely.

Nonetheless, sources that were compiled in later periods place before the first dynasty of kings, which we now term the 1st dynasty, not earlier human rulers but a sequence of groups including gods, who had precise but very long reigns, and 'spirits, followers of (the god) Horus', a kind of category of demigods (Gardiner 1959: pl. 1 col. 1; Waddell 1940: 3–27; Helck 1956a: 1–8). This material is very fragmentary, but it seems to be irreconcilable with the earlier annalistic listing: at some time between the mid-third millennium and the 18th dynasty (c.1500–1300), prehistory as a mythical and better time was integrated into the official chronology of rule (Kákosy 1964a; 1964b; Otto 1969). Later full kinglists included rival lines of kings and usurpers, so that annals must have been relatively 'value-free'. The annals may, however, not have been abreast with thinking of their time or even that of a rather earlier period. Two types of evidence, archaeological and written, can be cited for different views that are less pragmatic than those of the annals.

The archaeological material comes from the Step Pyramid of Djoser at Saqqara (c.2650), the earliest large stone monument and the earliest pyramidal structure (see e.g. Edwards 1985: 34–57, bibl. 289–91; Lehner 1997: 84–93). This highly innovative complex has the appearance of a vast commemoration of the past. It is sited at the capital, not at Abydos, but includes a symbolic 'south tomb' that probably alludes to the traditional burial of kings in Upper Egypt. In the surrounding complex, the conservatism of design of the buildings, which are solid dummy reproductions of structures perhaps once made in flimsy materials and later reproduced in mud brick, together with the more direct mimicking of mud brick in the enclosure wall, have generally been attributed to the architect's caution in using the new medium (e.g. Smith 1998: 26–7; Edwards 1985: 51–2), but this need not have been the only motivation. Moreover, this explanation cannot account for the stylistic, as against technical, transformation of stone architecture in the succeeding century. Apart from the obvious point that some model was needed in the new medium, stone could also have been an everlasting celebration of the building media and styles of the past. Among the finds from the entrance area is a statue base that has been dated much earlier on stylistic grounds and may be an old piece reused for antiquarian reasons (Schäfer 1986 [1974]: 15; there was also much statuary in the style of the day).

The most striking commemoration, however, was in a labyrinth of underground galleries beneath the pyramid itself. Here tens of thousands of stone vases were deposited, many inscribed under kings of the previous two dynasties. Most of these bore single rulers' names, often with additional elements, but some were inscribed with sequences of up to three kings (e.g. Lacau and Lauer 1959–61: pls. 8–17). Such objects, in particular, had probably not been buried in the tombs of the last king named on them, but might have been used in cult or have formed part of the inherited equipment of the palace (see Roth 1991: 145–95). There is no means of assessing what proportion of the accumulated material was buried, so that the action cannot be seen in context. The reason for the deposition can, however, hardly have been a desire for tidiness, so that the best explanation is that it constituted some sort of *pietas*, whatever other factors, such as a symbolic provision for the mortuary cult (perhaps of Djoser's predecessors as well as himself), were involved. In the eyes of the hereafter and of contemporaries who witnessed and partook in the deposition, the presence of so much ancestral material in the king's tomb complex may have helped to legitimize his position and his exploitation of labour in constructing the monument. Whether or not this explanation is correct, Djoser's complex mobilized the past for the present on the most grandiose scale, in both accessible and inaccessible areas. Such a mobilization is most likely to occur if the past is positively evaluated, however much the present might subsequently transcend it. By then, the Egyptian state was at least 300 years old. It is not surprising to find respect for 'ancient' kings being shown, perhaps especially in a period of rapid change.

During the time of Djoser or a little earlier there was also great development in the writing system (Chs. 2, 4, and 5), which was used within two generations for extensive monumental texts, although not yet for continuous metrical writing or for 'prose'. Once 'texts'—that is, relatively long compositions in continuous syntax—are recorded, a context is available for explicit comments on the significance of the past (see also Ch. 5). One of the earliest preserved complete sentences probably comes from the mortuary temple of Khufu, for whom the Great Pyramid was built (*c*.2550), and is directly relevant here because it says, apparently as a caption to the image of a boat shown in the adjacent relief: 'never [had] the like [happened] under [any king] since ant[iquity ...]' (Goedicke 1971: 20–3 no. 6; see also fragment of longer text mentioning 'antiquity': 105–6 no. 60). This is a standard formula found in better preserved texts of the next dynasty and in later sources (Luft 1976; 1978: 155–66).[3]

Thus, from the time when longer texts were written, their commemorative potential was exploited and their content was measured against 'antiquity': for the members of the elite who could read them and had access to them, they displayed status for the present, recorded the past, and created an absolute, mythical past that the present aimed to emulate or to surpass. Because the Khufu text uses a standard formula, it may not have been the

---

[3] See also Ch. 2 §3.1. It is possible that the text and picture relate to the very large boats buried around the pyramid, but if they do, the picture is not close to the form of the known and reconstructed boat (Jenkins 1980).

earliest instance to be inscribed, but predecessors would have been few unless it went back to oral forms, which is intrinsically likely. If the formula is ultimately oral, it implies a continuity in evaluating the past that extends at least into the Early Dynastic period, the time of Djoser's Step Pyramid. The evaluation is positive: achievements of the present—seemingly unremarkable in the case of the boat—are set against those of the past, but are not said to surpass them. Since the Great Pyramid visibly and probably explicitly surpassed earlier achievements in architecture, such a modest estimate belongs in a different, non-realistic dimension. A mythical, absolute past therefore exists. If this past was the rule of the gods or the spirits on earth, it is not reflected in the 'historical' annals of the period, but such a conception could have been parallel to the annals and have operated on a different plane, just as the ascription of values to it does not relate directly to this-worldly achievements but sets a standard outside and, it seems, above this world.

I present this evidence at length because it has often been denied that in early periods the Egyptians had a complex attitude to the past, being instead wholly absorbed in the present and its achievements (e.g. Wilson 1951: esp. 69, 78–9; more nuanced statement: Helck 1968: 88–90; explicit religious correlation: Hornung 1982b: 90–1). It is said that the collapse of the Old Kingdom around 2150, amid famine and the questioning of values, created a sense of the imperfection of human institutions and hence of the superiority of antiquity, with its rule of the gods on earth.[4] This general line of interpretation, which assumes a remarkable naivety in the Egyptians, is followed even in a recent treatment of the topic (Luft 1976: 75), despite the author's citation of an example of the formula quoted above from the early 5th dynasty (c.2450), more than two hundred years before the Old Kingdom's collapse (the earlier examples were not known to Luft). As Luft notes (1976: 74), the formula 'since antiquity' is closely related to 'since the reign (rk) of the god (or: name of a particular god)'. The word rk refers to a period of rule or reign, so that a belief in the rule of the gods on earth was probably present in all periods that are accessible for study, even if it did not form part of the official listings or narratives of kings until the Middle or the New Kingdom.

WAYS OF MOBILIZING THE PAST

The use of these phrases mobilizes the past for the present and for anyone who may read them, creating a secondary past, or level of the past, as monuments

---

[4] This vision of the Old Kingdom is apparent in many writings of Jan Assmann (e.g. 1977c); for a critique, see Baines (1991a: 89–92).

are seen to endure for long periods.[5] As I have suggested above, the likely oral counterparts of inscribed texts would reach more of the society and would relate to otherwise inaccessible folk uses of the past. Texts may project the past: as a 'golden age' of the rule of the gods; as a mythical 'antiquity'—both those approaches are implied by the Khufu material cited; or as a specific earlier time when some deed occurred or situation obtained.

Of those three approaches, the last is attested in a late Old Kingdom inscription (c.2250) in which a dwarf brought back from abroad is said to be 'the like of the dwarf whom Werdjededba brought from Punt in the time (rk) of (King) Izezy (about a century earlier)' (Sethe 1933: 128,17–129,1, also 131,1–3; translation Lichtheim 1973: 26–7). A negative counterpart is a formula in which people say that they could not 'find' that others had achieved what they themselves had (e.g. Vandier 1950: 196), and thus imply that they searched the records before stating this (those records could have been in writing or in oral tradition). The second approach is not known before belles lettres begin to be found in the Middle Kingdom (c.1975–1700), but might have occurred in their oral precursors. The model earlier time is provided by specific historical periods before the present, the chief among which is the Old Kingdom, which could hardly have been a global model for itself before it came to an end. At a more detailed level, the reign of Snofru of the 4th dynasty (c.2600) is the most prominent good time in Middle Kingdom texts.[6] Apart from the singling-out of this ruler through his deification, which is attested from the Old and Middle Kingdoms (Wildung 1969: 117–40), this literary treatment must be based on an earlier tradition that was probably formulated by contrast with Snofru's immediate successors who built the Giza pyramids and had a bad reputation as late as the Greek writer Herodotus (2. 124–8; 5th century). The obvious time for such a tradition to have arisen is the 5th dynasty.

Other Middle Kingdom literary traditions, as well as later religious sources, refer to various rulers of the 5th–6th dynasties (e.g. P Westcar, Instruction of Ptahhotep: Lichtheim 1973: 62; Neferkare and Sisene: Posener 1957: 124–5). Such allusions could have created the stimulus to 'historicize' the rule of the gods on earth, so that literary texts based on human or on divine events would have their point of reference in the same complete listing of divine reigns, including even their precise durations. The text containing this list will have been 'literary', because all transmitted high-cultural traditions, including

---

[5] For the literary texts cited in this section, see the translated collection of R. B. Parkinson (1998) and his interpretive study with full bibliography (2002).

[6] Instruction for Kagemni, Prophecy of Neferti, P Westcar: Lichtheim (1973: 60, 140, 216–17). Erhart Graefe (1990) suggests that one reason for Snofru's reputation was his name, which is derived from the word *nfr* 'perfect'.

such materials as medical and mathematical treatises, were part of the same complex stream of tradition.[7] Thus, the kinglists that include the rule of the gods could be literary creations of the Middle Kingdom or later. The listing could still separate the gods from 'human' kings (who had a semi-divine status), as is shown by the epigraphic cult version from the New Kingdom at Abydos, where they are omitted (Mariette 1869: pl. 43). Their new status would be evidence for uses of literature rather than for new conceptions of the past. Records of kings' names, reign lengths, and dynasties must have existed in any case, because theoretically accurate versions survived to form the basis of later lists.

Egyptian literary texts are almost never sited in the present—as is widely the case in premodern literature. The nearest approach to a use of the present is in royal inscriptions that record a king's deeds of the immediate past. On available evidence, these originated as a genre after written literary texts and may thus form a special category of them. The king controlled these texts, which were central to the later official presentation of the state and seldom related anything untoward. Even in them, critical discourse is mostly conducted in terms of the failings of people in the past, often those of the king's immediate predecessors. The king's role to establish order in the world necessitates a response to immediate threats, but these are almost all from abroad or are natural disasters, rather than social or political issues. One notable exception is in a text of Senwosret I (c.1935–1890: Helck 1985b),[8] among the earliest preserved royal narrative inscriptions; this example may suggest that the rules of the genre were not completely formulated by the time of its composition. The world abroad of the majority of texts is almost a spatial past, a dimension outside the present order, like the temporal past. This parallel can be related more globally to texts in which the normal categories of space and time are progressively abrogated as the edge of the cosmos is approached, notably in the Tale of the Shipwrecked Sailor (Lichtheim 1973: 211–15; see e.g. Derchain-Urtel 1974; Baines 1990a).

The ascription of literary texts to particular past figures must carry implications for the discourse that is conducted in them, but these are difficult to catch. Several of the Middle Kingdom instruction texts that contain general advice for the conduct of elite life are sited in the Old Kingdom and were formerly assumed to have been composed then (for the later date, see Ch. 2, n. 10; Assmann 1983b: 80–8). The Instruction for Merikare and the Eloquent Peasant, which have more pointed discussions of justice,

---

[7] See Ch. 2 § 2.1; for a major collection of studies, see Loprieno (1996b).
[8] Much discussed since 1989; final publication Barbotin and Clère (1991). Cited in many places by Parkinson (2002).

injustice, and rulership, are placed in the following First Intermediate period (c.2150–1980).[9] This temporal setting could give the discussion added urgency by locating it in a period of conflict a little nearer to the present, but if, as is likely, the texts date from a later time of superficial peace, such an effect might be minimized by historical distancing. Texts with a more immediate message for the political life of the day, or which constituted a more complex literary presentation of a novel type, came still closer to the present: the Instruction of King Amenemhat was probably composed in the reign of his successor Senwosret I, while the Tale of Sinuhe, the most elaborate of all literary texts, depicts events of the same reign and may date near its end or a generation or two later (Lichtheim 1973: 135–9, 222–35; cf. Baines 1982). These texts contrast with the pseudo-apocalyptic Prophecy of Neferti, which was probably written in the reign of Amenemhat I, and whose coming it purports allusively to predict from the perspective of the time of Snofru, the founder of the Old Kingdom (Lichtheim 1973: 139–45). Here, the timeless golden age of the archetypal good king relativizes the period between him and Amenemhat I, no doubt attacking in particular the latter's immediate predecessors.

The Instruction for Merikare is—among other things—almost a paradigm for the uses of the past in a literary text (see n. 9). This treatment is significant because of the text's position near the beginning of written literary tradition: it is as if the issue of the exploitation of the past was especially pressing when the potential of written texts without direct utility was first explored. The discussion constitutes a reformulation of oral discourse more than the continuation of the written biographical tradition, although that could have been the stimulus to creating belles lettres.[10] The text refers to a number of legitimizing forces, such as the 'ancestors', as well as citing a 'prophecy of the Residence' and a 'teaching' of Khety (a royal predecessor of the author to whom the text is ascribed). Thus, within the hitherto short tradition of written literary texts it makes play with literary antecedents, although these appear to be pieces very similar to the one we have, and they could have been fictitious or not have belonged to a comparable genre.

Merikare exhibits a range of attitudes both to the past and to the future. The importance of the latter is presupposed by the context, in which a ruler gives advice to his designated successor. This point is given extra significance by abstract references to 'acting for the future' (line 75) and to surpassing earlier achievements (e.g. line 35). The past itself is alternately idealized and

---

[9] Merikare: Lichtheim (1973: 97–109, 169–84); Helck (1977); cited here by line number. Eloquent Peasant: Parkinson (1991a).
[10] Assmann (1983b); for an alternative approach, see Baines (1999a; 1999c).

problematized, as when the author says that he captured a town which an earlier king, probably the founder of the dynasty, had not taken (lines 73–4); such a statement would be unusual in royal inscriptions. The ancestors, in whose sayings 'order (*mꜣꜥt*)' was 'strained clear' (line 35), are both authors of texts that should be read (lines 35–7) and prophets of perpetual unrest (lines 68–9); their nearest horizon is not necessarily very distant, since the author himself had dealings with them (lines 75–6; here they are earlier rulers of the other half of the country). There are also references to the 'time (*rk*)' of Horus (line 93) and of 'the Residence' (line 102), the latter perhaps an allusion to the Old Kingdom. In any case, nomads have fought Egypt since the time of Horus and cannot win or be defeated (lines 93–4). This texture of past, present, and future is so complex that, in the text's words, 'a blow is repaid with its like, that is, everything that is done is intertwined' (line 123), a statement that concludes a passage acknowledging the protagonist's ultimate responsibility for the recent destruction of the sacred necropolis of the early kings—as was probably known at the time, although not stated in so many words.[11] The present is devalued against the conflict-laden past in many statements, while the future may also aspire to emulate or even surpass the past. Yet little reason is given for high expectations, while the general tone is harsh and often opportunistic. The text ends with an evocation of an ethical judgment after death (lines 128–9, also described in lines 53–7) and of the deity's role in creation. This latter minimizes even the splendour of the past by saying that the world was created for humanity, the 'likenesses' of the god, who repelled the disorderly waters (of the nonexistent world?), 'killed his enemies, and destroyed his children (probably again humanity), because they plotted rebellion' (lines 131, 133–4). This statement, which has a parallel in a roughly contemporaneous text where humanity and not the creator is said to have brought evil into being (de Buck 1961: 464a–b; Lichtheim 1973: 132), provides early allusions to myths of the rule of the gods on earth, as well as giving the present world its bleakest possible status—even though the end of the text superficially reverses this bleakness.

The other texts cited above, which present the Old Kingdom as a glorious past, read more like romances in comparison with the Instruction for Merikare (see Luft 1976: 75, who also compares inscriptional evidence). Another pessimistic work, the Dialogue of Ipuwer and the Lord of All (e.g. Lichtheim 1973: 149–63; Fecht 1972; Enmarch 2005), takes almost the opposite line in relation to the past by using the structure of a funerary lamentation to

---

[11] Archaeological work since the 1990s has shown that there was a substantial Middle Kingdom programme of restoration on the site (Dreyer et al. 1998a: 141–2, with ref.). The passage in Merikare probably relates in some way to this programme.

say that the present is a travesty of the proper order of the past (cf. Junge 1977). This wide range of literary uses of the past in a single text and between different texts of the same period is potentially paradigmatic for later periods, during which these works continued to be known. The allusion to the destruction of humanity in the Instruction for Merikare suggests that narrative myths of the gods' rule on earth could have been current in the Middle Kingdom but, with uncertain exceptions (the Herdsman's Story: Lefebvre 1949: 26–28; a Horus and Seth fragment: Griffith 1898: 4, pl. 3), none is preserved before the New Kingdom; even then, two important examples (Destruction of Humanity: Hornung 1982b; Isis and Re: Borghouts 1978: 51–5) are known only from contexts other than belles lettres.[12] Be this as it may, there would have been oral antecedents for these narratives, so that the full range of treatments of the past, including the narrowly mythical, should be posited for the Middle Kingdom. I suggest that the reason for our not possessing evidence from any earlier period lies in genre, and in rules of decorum governing the inscription of texts (Baines 1985c: 277–305; Ch. 1 here), as much as it does in changing attitudes to the past. But this does not imply that written literary works simply reproduce oral forms or concepts, or that the formulation of a written tradition is necessarily rapid. Apart from the fragmentary Old Kingdom textual evidence I have cited, material in the visual arts points in the same direction.

USES OF THE PAST IN VISUAL ARTS

Old Kingdom representational art supplies copious evidence for the use of the past in non-textual contexts. This is a later parallel for the architectural *pietas* of Djoser, but needs also to be seen in more specifically artistic terms. This material should be set in a global context, just as textually attested concepts of the past relate to general time concepts. Egyptian representation integrates picture and text captions. Its hierarchies and organization set out the ordered world and fuse narrowly representational conventions with ideological statement (cf. Baines 1985c: 70–5, 277–305). These features were defined during the period when the monumental writing system was devised, at the beginning of the dynastic period, and almost all later art operates within them (a notable exception is the Amarna period, c.1350–1335). Stylistic

---

[12] For arguments for a late origin of myths, see Assmann (1977c). Several authors have argued against Assmann's position; see e.g. Baines (1991a; 1996c); Zeidler (1993); Goebs (2002). For Middle Kingdom mythological tales, see Parkinson (2002: 294–5).

development took place within this framework, and so does not appear superficially as radical as it does in western art. There remained, however, plentiful opportunities for artistic choice and for meaningful recourse to different periods in the past.

The classic style of the Old Kingdom was not completely formulated until the 4th dynasty, which is—hardly coincidentally—the time of the great pyramids. The dynasty initiated about 400 years of consistent development, during which artistic styles could either evolve on the basis of their immediate predecessors, a process that reflects normal methods of artistic training in workshops, or they could look to more distant models; the latter should constitute an explicit, and perhaps ideologically pointed, exploitation of the past. Artistic styles of the 4th to early 6th dynasties developed by enrichment of detail and elaboration of composition. In the late 6th dynasty (c.2200), this enrichment ceased and development was no longer uniform. Some non-royal tombs look back to the sparer style of the 4th dynasty, over 300 years earlier, a change that is made more specific by the revival of details such as a treatment of wigs in which a small piece of natural hair or a skull cap is visible under the wig itself (e.g. Junker 1941: pl. 9 [6th dyn.]; compare Dunham and Simpson 1974: pls. 17, 19 [4th dyn.]), or where the same skull cap is worn by itself (e.g. Junker, 91 fig. 23 = p. 5b, compare Dunham and Simpson, pls. 7, 20). This archaism is so convincing that it has led to an implausible earlier dating of one of these tombs (Cherpion 1984).[13] Another tendency visible in different tombs is the use of a few great monuments of the relatively recent past as models. Here, assessment of the material is complicated by the loss of many of the finest tombs, but an extant example is the adoption of compositions attested in the tombs of Ti (late 5th dynasty: Epron, Daumas (senior), and Wild 1939–66) and Mereruka (early 6th dynasty: Sakkarah Expedition 1938). A striking case is a relief of the tomb owner with two sons in Mereruka (Sakkarah Expedition 1938: pl. 1), taken up for a different purpose by Pepyankh Heny the Black at Meir (late 6th dynasty: Blackman 1914–53: V pl. 16).

Reasons for this diversification can be suggested but not verified. The recourse to classic 4th dynasty style is accompanied by general impoverishment and may combine a search for models for sparse and concentrated decoration, in which pictorial elements had focused on the false door as was now once more the practice, with detailed emulation of the ideal time in which those models were produced. Some of the revived features of dress and ornament are more likely to be strictly artistic than to reflect current fashion, so that they argue for pure archaism. By contrast, the use of a few great

---

[13] The approach of Cherpion and her conclusions have subsequently been accepted widely. For her full treatment, see Cherpion (1989); for a more recent dating study, see Baud (1999).

monuments shows a highly developed style that is marking time and being imitated in works that are inferior and mainly provincial; it looks more like stasis than a movement with a specific meaning. The case of Meir is notable, because a major tomb of the 12th dynasty at the site (c.1750) contains a number of Old Kingdom revivals, one of them again drawn from the tomb of Mereruka (Sakkarah Expedition 1938: I, pls. 6–7; Blackman 1914–53: VI, 30–1, pl. 13); here, artistic revival is eclectic, deliberate, and focused on distant times.

These developments are part of more general artistic strategies: artists may build on the work of their teachers, seeking to perpetuate a style or to carry it forward; or they may react against their immediate mentors and look to more remote models. The latter principle can be adopted in superficially surprising cases, as in the training of Gianlorenzo Bernini (1598–1680), whom one might consider to belong within a continuing Baroque tradition, as a sculptor, but who schooled himself by going back to works of classical antiquity (Hibbard 1966: 25–9). It is impossible to trace such subtle occurrences without documentary evidence; in its absence, identifiable examples of archaism are cases where the borrowing is clearly visible, or where there is physical evidence on a monument that it was copied (e.g. Baines 1973). Rejection of the immediate past may be more narrowly artistic than broadly ideological, in which case it can hardly be termed archaism. The term 'archaism' thus describes instances where some extra meaning can be seen in these practices, and is thus aptly applied to the late 6th dynasty tombs that look back to the 4th dynasty, but perhaps not to the imitation of late 5th dynasty tombs in lesser work of the 6th. It is significant that, just as the concept of an absolute 'antiquity' is found within the Old Kingdom, programmatic archaism also occurs both under Djoser before it began—although no stylistic archaism is visible there—and near its end.

In complex literate societies, an ancient model can be sited precisely within a historical period. If they were able to read—as patrons surely could—the late 6th dynasty artists at Giza could know from inscriptions in what reigns the monuments they used as inspiration were constructed; even where there was no royal name preserved, the proximity of tombs to major monuments guaranteed a general identification. For later times, the overpowering monumentality of the pyramids could have made them and the surrounding burial grounds an inevitable focus of respect and inspiration, but in fact it did not do so, for Giza is archaeologically blank from the end of the Old Kingdom to the New Kingdom. I cite the only known—destructive—reuse of its monuments in the next paragraph but one (see also Wildung 1969: 162–4).

A corollary exists for this absence of archaism. The Middle Kingdom, the next major centralized period of history, inherited a wide range of artistic uses of the past. The styles of the Old Kingdom capital were imitated in a few details in the reign of the reuniter of the country and founder of the Middle Kingdom, Nebhepetre Mentuhotep (c.2025–1975; Fischer 1959), and there was a revival of relief carving in his reign and the next (e.g. Bisson de la Roque 1937: pls. 18–28), but essentially the dynasty's art built on Theban traditions of the divided First Intermediate period. In the following 12th dynasty, the capital was moved back to its old location of Memphis, and Old Kingdom capital styles were revived, notably in the pyramid temples of Amenemhat I (c.1955–1925) and Senwosret I (c.1935–1890) at el-Lisht, just south of Memphis.[14]

This is the time discussed above, when literature used the Old Kingdom as its golden age and texts often referred to 'antiquity' and the 'time of the god'. The pyramid of Amenemhat I reused a great deal of stone from the mortuary monuments of Old Kingdom kings. This reuse intensifies normal Egyptian constructional practice, in which ready-cut stone was preferred to new and more laborious quarrying, while any structure that stood in the way of new building, or was no longer in use, was incorporated in the foundations of its successor, but the specific reference to earlier kings is probably programmatic in some sense, if not in the sweeping way suggested by Hans Goedicke (1971: 4–7). It runs counter to the recommendation of the roughly contemporaneous Instruction for Merikare, that a king should 'not build (his) tomb from ruins (or) from what was made for [another purpose]' (lines 78–9). Despite this reuse, in which Giza material is prominent, the style of the reliefs from these complexes owes little to the early Old Kingdom; its clearest antecedent is the mortuary complex of Pepy II (c.2240–2175) at South Saqqara (Jéquier 1936–40; for the el-Lisht reliefs see Hayes 1953: 171–95; Smith 1998: 91, 96–7). The archaism of these kings' artists is thus their reference to Memphite models in opposition to the provincial continuity of the 11th dynasty. In another sense, the use of Pepy's complex, the latest significant one of the Old Kingdom, asserts continuity with the previous great period as much as renewal, and is not archaism as it is normally understood. The Theban monuments of the early 12th dynasty (e.g. Lacau and Chevrier 1956–69) continue the style of the local 11th dynasty without a marked break. Here, perhaps, a different form of legitimation—or of artistic model—was appropriate.

After the early 12th dynasty, royal works of art continued the trends of their predecessors or struck out in new directions, while non-royal monuments,

---

[14] The material is largely unpublished; many reliefs are in the Metropolitan Museum of Art, New York. Dorothea Arnold (1991) dates the move to the Memphite area in the second half of the reign of Amenemhat I.

especially statuary, looked back strikingly little to the Old Kingdom; these general tendencies apply also to the succeeding Second Intermediate period (c.1640–1530).[15] This continuity and lack of focus on the more distant past suggests that the artists, at least, considered themselves to be living in a time that was a unity or period, as do modern scholars.

PERIODS AND 'HISTORY': THE MIDDLE AND NEW KINGDOMS

Thus, in its public display the Middle Kingdom, which was considered the classical period in later times (although this is never stated in such terms), appears to have been notably absorbed in the present and to have put itself forward as a cultural and historical unity. Here, art and architecture were in marked contrast with texts, various aspects of which have been considered above. Even a text whose prime purpose is to convey the rhetoric of present and future may continually exploit concepts of the past.

A striking example of this strategy is a building inscription of Senwosret I preserved in a New Kingdom copy, which mobilizes all the possibilities of myth and of association of the king with the primeval creator god (Lichtheim 1973: 115–18). The more expansive stela of Neferhotep I from Abydos (c.1700) is perhaps the earliest to use past written texts as a legitimation, although this general potential of writing is visible as early as the royal Pyramid Texts, where a deed of transfer or will that might have written form is referred to (c.2350; Faulkner 1969: 129 spell 391). On the stela, the king wishes to 'see the writings of the antiquity of Atum (the creator god); spread out the great inventory for me!'—and this is then done (Pieper 1929: 8–17; Helck 1983: 21–3). The texts in question appear to specify the proper form of a statue of Osiris, and they have generalized parallels in Graeco-Roman period temple inscriptions; in both contexts, recourse is made to them because of their great age (see e.g. Daumas 1973; compare Osing 1975, with references to many other examples). Middle Kingdom non-royal inscription owners similarly used their lineage to assert their status (see e.g. Luft 1976: no. 3; Sethe and Erichsen 1935: 26–8), a way of

---

[15] Marianne Eaton-Krauss (2003) proposes plausibly that the statuary of late 12th dynasty kings sought inspiration in that of the 3rd dynasty. Her position is supported by architectural parallels she cites between the Step Pyramid complex and those of Senwosret III and Amenemhat III, as well as the reconsecration of sarcophagi from the Step Pyramid in the complex of Senwosret III (Dodson 1988). This material suggests that recourse to the past was a significant element in new directions throughout the 12th dynasty and not just near its beginning.

proceeding that appears to be absent from the more centripetal Old Kingdom texts, where royal favour is the key motif. Despite the Middle Kingdom textual recourse to earlier times, a sense of continuity within literature can be seen there too. One literary text that probably dates to the late 12th dynasty even complains that everything has been said, so that the author has no new way to express his complaints—almost a parody of belonging in a stream of tradition (the Complaints of Khakheperresonbe: Kadish 1973; Simpson 1973: 230–3; Parkinson 1996). But while this generalized evidence can be identified, texts do not show how periods were viewed in the Middle Kingdom; the New Kingdom supplies better information here.

Although there may have been literary lists of dynasties of gods and kings in the Middle Kingdom, the first clear evidence for major 'periods' dates to the New Kingdom (c.1530–1070). New Kingdom reliefs and texts contain explicit formulations of the sense of period and of respect for antiquity, and present diverse views in different contexts, in some cases creating a feeling of a debate that is more widespread than the internal one of the Instruction for Merikare. This historical sense is applied to the performance of ancient rites according to ancient prescriptions (e.g. Epigraphic Survey 1980: 43, pl. 28—also said to surpass previous performances), the revival of classical—in this case Middle Kingdom—statue forms specifically for the learned (Lange and Hirmer 1968: pls. 158–9), the visiting of ancient monuments (principally of the Old Kingdom) by princes (Helck 1961: 140–3) and others including schoolchildren (Helck 1952; unpublished study by Allan K. Philips), and the wholesale restoration of ancient monuments by Khaemwese, a son of Ramesses II (1279–1213; Gomaà 1973). Perhaps the most vivid of all allusions to the past occurs in a late 20th dynasty (c.1100) record of an inspection of looted royal tombs. In emphasizing the seriousness of the crime under investigation, one of the chief officials was reported as saying of the king whose burial had been violated—an otherwise almost unknown and ephemeral ruler of the Second Intermediate period (c.1600)—that he was 'a great ruler who performed ten significant tasks for Amon-Re king of the gods, the great god; his monuments endure in (the god's) courtyard to this very day' (Peet 1930: II, pl. 3, 6: 2–3). The point here is not whether what is said is true or whether the speaker really knew anything about the king, which is unlikely; the passage shows how the past could be drawn almost automatically into discussion focused on the present, in this case on disputes between different factions among officials.

None of these usages implies a critical or disinterested interest in the past, or a detailed knowledge of it. The deeds of Egyptian kings, recorded most notably by the Greek Herodotus in the 5th century BCE, are exploits, not part of a historical process, while their self-presentation in their inscriptions is not meant to be objective; in neither case is there a modern-style history.

Rather, a substantial awareness of the past is mobilized and articulated for various, often moral purposes, in a wide range of contexts and directions. If in earlier times the past was a very 'scarce resource' of the type discussed by Arjun Appadurai (1981), in the New Kingdom that scarcity was moderated. This development is part of a pluralization of written culture; it is not confined to the uses of the past. I consider four developments a little further.

Artistic periods

The dynastic temple of Amon-Re at Karnak goes back to the early Middle Kingdom, but some much more ancient objects have been found there (Romano 1979: 3 fig. 5; nos. 4, 10), one, of uncertain date, heavily worn by visitors (Romano 1979: no. 10; Goyon and Traunecker 1980: 132–5). These objects show that people exploited antiquity to honour the deity. New Kingdom structures, among which these objects may have been deposited, look back to specific times. Reliefs of the reign of Ahmose (c.1540–1514; e.g. Vandersleyen 1971: pl. 1), the founder of the 18th dynasty and of the New Kingdom, look to the early 12th dynasty, and this is more explicit under his successor Amenhotep I, who built a shrine that was a copy of the 'White Chapel' of Senwosret I (Björkman 1971: 58–9; 134, J; Lacau and Chevrier 1956–69). In modelling itself on the 12th dynasty, the early 18th avoided artistic reference to the 11th, the previous reuniters of the country whose rule did not last. Early New Kingdom non-royal statuary also uses 12th dynasty models (e.g. Bothmer 1966–7: 155–9). In both cases, the source of inspiration is the earlier part of the first period, marking a conscious break from the immediately preceding style and referring to what was now classical visual art, language, and literature. The same reference is given an individual point in the mortuary temple of Hatshepsut (c.1472–1468) at Deir el-Bahri, which is inspired by the adjacent one of the founder of the Middle Kingdom, Nebhepetre Mentuhotep, and contains many texts in remarkably pure Classical Egyptian (Naville n.d.: *passim*), some of them probably compositions of great age (compare Assmann 1969: 113–64; 1970). Hatshepsut also set up an inscription attacking the Hyksos rulers of the Second Intermediate period (Gardiner 1946). This action may appear bizarre, since they had been expelled from the country some decades earlier, but it fits well with her evocation of earlier times in her temple at Deir el-Bahri. Similarly, monuments of the Nubian 25th dynasty were mutilated more than sixty years after its expulsion from Egypt by the 26th dynasty (Yoyotte 1951). These fine distinctions in the use of earlier models show that, both in the early New Kingdom and in the

Late period, artists or their patrons were well aware of precise periods, their monuments, and their associations.

Historical periods

The 18th dynasty is incorporated into a formulation of major periods that is known from the 19th dynasty. This occurs in the form of excerpted sets of kings, in written or pictorial form, and in the greatest detail in the theoretically complete listing of the Turin kinglist, often called the 'Turin Canon' (Gardiner 1959), whose tradition is preserved to some extent in the Graeco-Egyptian historian Manetho of the early 3rd century BCE (Waddell 1940; Helck 1956a). The Turin kinglist gives a special status to Djoser, whose name is written in red, and provides totals for individual dynasties (6, 12, and 15 are preserved) and for the 1st–8th—what are now termed the Early Dynastic period and Old Kingdom (I do not accept Malek's dismissal of these features as arising from the physical format of the documents: 1982: 105–6; compare Beckerath 1984). Comparison of the Turin and Abydos lists, in particular, shows that the intermediate periods were treated separately: the Second Intermediate period as a whole is absent at Abydos (Mariette 1869: pl. 43). Periodization of this sort could contribute to the prominence of Snofru, the first ruler of the 4th dynasty and effectively the founder of the Old Kingdom, from whose reign fuller annals begin to be attested, but other factors relating to his posthumous reputation have been cited above. The Late period cult of Menes, the semi-mythical founder of Egypt, and of other very early kings (Wildung 1969: 15–20, 26–31; Otto 1957: 196–204), can hardly be understood except as displaying knowledge of periods, their founders, and kinglists.

The most significant documents here are some that juxtapose Nebhepetre Mentuhotep, the reuniter of Egypt and founder of the Middle Kingdom, with Ahmose, the founder of the New Kingdom. Mentuhotep was the fourth king of his dynasty, so that he cannot have been cited mechanically from a list; some historical tradition is implied. Ahmose's status at the beginning of a dynasty is probably in part a historicizing fiction, because he ruled from the same capital as his predecessor and was his son or nephew. This same process of dividing history and acknowledging significant figures is visible in a list from Deir el-Medina in western Thebes that includes an extra pair of names placing Haremhab (c.1320–1293), the last king of the 18th dynasty, in a similar position to Mentuhotep and Ahmose (Philips 1977). Manetho makes Ramesses I the founder of the 19th dynasty, but the Theban tradition of only a few decades after the latter's reign seems to have given preference and prominence to his predecessor. Because no ties of kinship were involved in the succession of kings in this period, either division is meaningful, but Haremhab is a far more prominent historical figure than Ramesses I. This veneration for selected past rulers is visible in the 19th–20th dynasties, when several of the royal family of the early 18th dynasty were venerated by the workers on the royal tombs, partly in acknowledgment of the founder of their institution, Amenhotep I (c.1514–1493), but also perhaps because of the status of the whole group of the royal family as inaugurating the current period of history (e.g. Lepsius n.d.-b: pl. 2). The position of Haremhab marks a more recent break in period, which has a linguistic correlate in the introduction of Late Egyptian as a written language (cf. Assmann 1985: 46).

Discussion in texts

The Ramessid period (c.1290–1070) produces examples of veneration and of cynicism in relation to the most important display and expense of non-royal Egyptians—provision for the tomb. Tomb construction is future-oriented, but lessons of the past are very relevant to it. In literary texts and in songs inscribed in tombs, the motif of denying the value of mortuary provision appears (offerings to the gods could also be questioned: Fecht 1973). The Harpist's Song from the Tomb of King Inyotef is an ostensibly Middle Kingdom text, with a probably fictitious ascription, asserting the futility of mortuary provision in the face of certain death, from which none return to tell of their experiences: one should live for the day (Lichtheim 1945: 192–5; Assmann 1977d: 55–6). This text has a partial parallel in the Middle Kingdom literary Dispute of a Man with His Ba (Lichtheim 1973: 163–9) and could be genuinely of the same period. A Ramessid instruction text preserved only as an excerpt goes further and states that the tombs of the past are gone, including those of the sages, of whose names a list is given, but the sages and their wisdom live on in their works, which can be read by the well-versed scribe (P Chester Beatty IV verso; Lichtheim 1976: 175–8; cf. Assmann 1985). This last text proclaims to show that all but writing decays—but then it does form part of an exhortation to be a scribe.

An additional irony is visible in a Ramessid tomb relief, whose original location is lost, where a selection of the same sages is depicted with various notable deceased officials and probably a group of kings; the complete set may be co-recipients of some kind of commemorative cult (Simpson 1973: pl. 6; Assmann 1985: 42–3). The owner of this tomb must have known the cynical attitude of the works of literature, which is also attested in harpists' songs in some other Ramessid tombs (with one 18th dynasty forerunner). He may have reacted against the attitude, or he may have had a cynical harpist's song on the opposite wall of the tomb chapel. The songs display a private discourse about central values and cast it in the form of high culture that sees the past as a source of both fame and decay—which often came through the mutilation of monuments of disgraced or dead enemies. While the songs deny permanence, in their attitudes they look forward to the Late period revival, or creation, of cults of ancient figures, including sages (Wildung 1977). Such a discourse may use the past to legitimize the expression of almost heretical doubts—although these probably surfaced in all periods—and they are set up in future-oriented tombs decorated mainly with religious scenes, dramatizing human uncertainty in the face of death. As Jan Assmann notes (1985: 47–52), this complex view of the past coexisted with significant Ramessid innovation in a variety of cultural spheres.

Depth of perspective

While the restoration and reinscription of monuments is a pervasive Ramessid practice relating to many earlier periods and symptomatic of a great time depth that is also visible in the inscription of kinglists in several temples, other indications point to a shrinking of perspectives. The text, cited above, which presents Haremhab as the founder of a period, was written within a century of his death. A couple of decades later, Ramesses III based his royal titulary on that of Ramesses II (e.g. Helck 1968: 193) and followed closely the design of the latter's mortuary temple (see e.g. Badawy 1968: 354–60). He in turn was succeeded by eight more kings, all of whom took Ramesses as something like a dynastic name in addition to their birth names, in a practice that was hitherto unknown in Egypt. In this period, legitimation could be presented in traditional terms, in which a king overcame the disorder of the time before his accession and then assumed the regalia of the most ancient gods (e.g. Breasted 1906: 198–200; Grandet 1994–9: I, 335–41; Erichsen 1933: 91–3). Political credibility, however, was generally sought nearer at hand. Modern scholars have tended to see the Ramessid period as a time of decline, over which the immense reign of Ramesses II cast a long shadow (e.g. Helck 1968: 179–205). In the long term, the maximum depth of perspective was regained in the mid-first millennium, which is not treated here.

CONCLUSION

Of the periods reviewed here, the Ramessid was the time of maximum diversity and explicitness in the use of the past, and thus fittingly concludes a survey. The past came to be both integral to many aspects of high culture and the subject of active discussion, in contrast with the Old Kingdom, from which the sparse evidence has often been overlooked. The development of attitudes relates to the gradual expansion of writing, which opens up many possibilities, but writing should not be held to account for the cultural stability and long duration of the material and for views of the past. Here, decorum is a more useful concept: stability was favoured by normative definitions of cultural forms that had a cosmological dimension; this meant that only some of what was said and thought could be expressed in public contexts. What is difficult to establish is the degree to which writing and the consequent increase in scope and precision of social memory creates attitudes, merely allows them to be recorded, or, more plausibly, interacts with oral modes of discourse to foster possibilities that are neither oral nor exclusively literate. Many theoretically possible developments did not occur. Egyptian records allow Egyptologists to write some sort of history of ancient Egypt, but it never occurred to an ancient Egyptian to undertake such an enterprise, which is alien to the material itself and is embedded in quite different cultures. For the exploration of this diversity, the parallel testimony of non-literate cultures, archaeologically studied, observed in the field, and presented by the actors, is very desirable.

Visual culture

8

Introductory note

The studies assembled in this part address two different styles of question. 'Theories and universals of representation' (Ch. 9) and 'Colour terminology and colour classification' (Ch. 11) review issues raised by salient features of Egyptian material high culture that are also significant for cross-cultural analysis. 'Schäfer's mottoes and the understanding of representation' (Ch. 10) is a note on the history of scholarship that grew out of my work on Heinrich Schäfer and exemplifies the difficulties that western art historians—in this case including Schäfer himself—have had in approaching a tradition, like that of Egypt, that has different representational conventions.

The conclusions of Chapters 9 and 11, both of which were first published in 1985, are formulated in terms of classificatory and cognitive universals, contributing to debates that had a partly evolutionary cast but are, I hope, not unduly prey to occidental triumphalism. In Chapter 11 I argue that the universals are not primarily based on language but on patterns of human thought that analysts generally approach through language but that operate in other ways. One aim of the discussion, therefore, is to argue that the rich record of material culture from Egypt, and no doubt of other premodern civilizations, provides a mode of entry into such questions through material and linguistic cultural domains that were self-consciously developed by the ancient actors, but without reference to these particular research questions. The theoretical study of pictorial representation (Ch. 9) addresses something that was surely the subject of discussion in antiquity, although nothing is preserved from such debates. By contrast, colour classification (Ch. 11), while well attested from texts as an organizing principle, is unlikely to have been theorized explicitly in terms comparable to those now used; nonetheless, the development of colours in paint demonstrates an enormous and prestigious investment and must have had very strong cultural motivations. The two studies therefore exemplify different methodologies that I selected for the different types of material covered. They also contribute background topics to the more intrinsically social issues addressed in the last three chapters.

The rest of the studies have a more specifically Egyptian and historical focus. 'Communication and display' (Ch. 13) approaches the same period as 'Writing and society in early Egypt' (Ch. 5) but from the opposite thematic direction, addressing the interplay of visual and written in the crucial formative period of the state. A major consideration here is the development of compositional and iconographic norms that also had cosmological meaning (compare also Baines 2003a). Such meanings are present in many artistic traditions; Egypt offers clear evidence for them that can be traced in changing forms from the end of predynastic times to the Graeco-Roman period. 'Stone and other materials: usages and values' (Ch. 12) analyses the role of stone, together with some artificial materials, as a single complex in the elaboration and display of Egyptian high culture.

The final study, 'On the status and purposes of ancient Egyptian art' (Ch. 14), has as its main topic the social significance of aesthetic display. One of its aims is to argue against the view, which is widespread especially among historians of western art, that the position of 'art' in western society, particularly since the 18th century and the writings of Immanuel Kant, is different in kind from those of aesthetic products in other societies. In what way this is thought to be the case is often not clearly formulated, but the twin requirements of an explicit concept of 'art' and a lack of specific function for artworks are generally prominent in the argument. While the context of Egyptian art in elite discourse can never be reconstructed fully, phenomena like use of the past in visual aesthetics (also addressed briefly in Ch. 7 and alluded to several times elsewhere in this book), as well as the simple level of investment in aesthetic production, bespeak the centrality of these institutions. Almost the only phenomenon that seems specifically modern in the position of art and artists is the existence of the art gallery; even for that some analogies can be found in ancient civilizations. Here too, I argue that the Egyptian case can contribute distinctively to wider discussions, especially to breaking down the 'exceptionalism' that characterizes so much western writing, both about the West and about different periods and places as its 'other', and on art as on so many other subjects.

9

Theories and universals of representation: Heinrich Schäfer and Egyptian art

1 INTRODUCTION; DIFFICULTIES IN SCHÄFER'S APPROACH

The fundamental work on representation in Egyptian art is Heinrich Schäfer's *Von ägyptischer Kunst* (English edition, *Principles of Egyptian art*).[1] This solves, with outstanding success, many problems in the analysis of non-perspective pictorial representation. The book provides insights that affect the understanding of an enormous range of representational art, Egyptian or other; and this was the author's intention, for he argued that his discoveries had important implications for the study of pictorial representation as such (xiii = xxviii). These broader implications are significant for more general debates among art historians, of which many are reviewed by E. H. Gombrich in *Art and illusion* (1977 [1960]); in comparison with some writers, however, Schäfer's work has been neglected. In this chapter, I argue that Schäfer's issues remain vital for the reading of non-perspective art and have 'evolutionary' and cognitive

---

Art History 8 (1985) 1–25. I have updated some points in the references and notes in this chapter, particularly where previously current approaches on specific topics have been superseded. The argument is unchanged, and all references cited in the original publication are retained.

I have found relatively little later work that relates to the overall theme of the chapter. Two works that take forward the positions of authors who contributed to Freeman and Cox (1985), frequently cited here, are Hagen (1986; see earlier Hagen 1985, in Freeman and Cox) and Willats (1997). These are useful treatments and valuably different from each other, but they do not seem to me to take fundamental questions of representation further.

[1] First edn. 1919; 4th (posthumous) edn. 1963; English 1974, revised reprint 1986, 2002 (cited here by page numbers only, in the form German = English). Citations of Schäfer are to the 1963 German edition and the 1986/2002 English printing (numbers after '='), without indication of name and date. For a treatment of questions similar to those addressed in this chapter, see Martin Kemp's valuable discussion (1984). My arguments are generally complementary to his, rather than competing with them, and take different materials as a point of departure; the focus of his study is also much broader.

implications for the understanding and classification of representational systems. For convenience, I review some difficulties in Schäfer's approach before summarizing his position and considering possible improvements to it, as well as a broader theoretical framework within which it might be sited.

There are two major questions for which Schäfer's solutions are not adequate. The first is the nature of the mental basis of Egyptian two-dimensional representation, a problem which he related closely to the absence of foreshortening and perspective in many cultures. The second is the relationship between two-dimensional representation and rigidities in the rendering of nature in sculpture in the round, whose distribution around the world is rather more uneven than that of the two-dimensional principles he described. A third, rather different issue should be added here. This is the problem of what may loosely be termed 'realism' or 'literalism'. A 'realistic' art style may contribute to the breakdown of a non-perspective system of representation. The problematic status of realism in such contexts parallels its impact on those who study artistic traditions: the relatively realistic character of Egyptian art has been the source of many difficulties, because it has led people to underestimate how far the principles of Egyptian representation differ from those of western art. What is the significance of this realistic character, and how does it relate to developments in representational conventions, or more broadly to the society which produced the art?

None of these questions has a simple solution. The first—the mental basis of representation—is difficult of access and perhaps best studied by experimental psychology. The second—the relationship between two-dimensional rendering and sculpture—can be related to artistic techniques and procedures about which little is known in the ancient material, but otherwise requires similar approaches to the first. The last problem—realism—seems scarcely to have been discussed. Any attempt to go beyond or replace Schäfer's interpretations is therefore hazardous, but it ought to be possible to produce a descriptive model that is more comprehensive and more empirical than his. I believe that such a model should include an extra factor that he placed in the background. This is the influence of artistic tradition, and in some contexts of technique, on conventions of representation. Most of the available evidence on these questions was meticulously presented by Schäfer, but he did not examine it in relation to specific conventions, or to the conventions as a system. Schäfer should not be criticized for not focusing on this area, for his main interest lay elsewhere. Nonetheless, this and other social factors have implications for his whole analysis. These additional approaches do not, however, lead easily toward a replacement for Schäfer's explanation. After considering realism (§5), I suggest why they do not assist in this respect, and in what more general context the enigma of representation could be sited.

2 SCHÄFER'S HYPOTHESES

Schäfer's position is difficult to summarize; here I outline his most important conclusions and quote some significant passages. In his chapter 4 he outlined what he termed 'pre-Greek' representation. By 'pre-Greek' he meant representation anywhere and at any time that is not influenced by the Greek development—which he believed to be unique—of the regular incorporation of foreshortening and subsequent elaboration of perspective. In a word, for Schäfer 'pre-Greek' representation is *geradvorstellig*, a neologism that I render 'based on frontal images', where 'frontal' means 'unaffected by foreshortening' and the images are mental or memory images. The word *Vorstellung*, from which the new term was coined, implies both 'image' and 'conception'. Schäfer wrote:

The user of the 'pre-Greek' method of representation ... aims to show things objectively as they are, or as they live in his imagination ... he creates order ... by eliminating foreshortening, shadows, and other distracting features. (97 = 89)

Any draughtsman's senses give him a host of perceptions of different objects, and of one and the same object. The 'pre-Greek' rejects from these the ones with a perspective character, because of his experience that the 'foreshortened' view deprives the original of its rights, cheats it of what belongs to it. (97–8 = 89)

The great majority of the non-foreshortened views which dominate Egyptian drawings are based on images which the eye at some time provided. In addition, however, the sense of touch unquestionably contributes to those images. One can even say that in any representation, whether perspective or based on frontal images, the hand seeks out the images in the material ... (98 = 90, amplified in the next citation but one)

... the rendering of a pre-Greek does not correspond to a visual impression of a seemingly foreshortened object, that is, to a defined view of it, but to a mental image which alone is relevant to the rendering, and is not foreshortened as a whole or in its parts. The work of art embodies this image. So it is not faithful to a perceived visual impression but *image-based* (*vorstellig*). (99 = 91, Schäfer's italics)

We can ... formulate the procedure of a pre-Greek painter when he draws a flat model thus: the hand which does the drawing feels its way over the picture surface in accordance with the painter's frontal image of the object. If the drawing surface is parallel to that of the model, the drawing implement follows the direction of all the lines in it. But if the drawing surface is at an oblique angle to that of the original, the hand allows its course to be modified in the case of receding or advancing lines, either because of resistance by the drawing surface or because it has to maintain contact with it, and instead of following the lines of the original it performs corresponding non-foreshortened movements. (103 = 94)

[That last formulation is limited, but can be extended to cover the more complicated and conventionalized treatment of three-dimensional objects. Schäfer did not present his views on the depiction of these in a few quotable sentences; see further §4.]

These points are formulated in general terms and relate to more than just Egyptian art; discussion should therefore be similarly general. After this introduction, Schäfer studied the methods of rendering objects from the simplest—pure two-dimensional outlines, as cited above—to the grouping of complex objects and the rendering of spatial distribution (ch. 4.2–4). There follow an excursus on perspective (ch. 5), an analysis of the rendering of the human figure (ch. 6), and a study of sculpture in the round (ch. 7). His conclusion (ch. 8) attempts a synthesis of his results in two dimensions (chs. 4–6) and in three (ch. 7).

The basis of representation in mental activity, which is spelled out in the passages quoted, is indisputable: representation is not reproduction of what the eye sees; visual material is in any case processed, in a highly complex fashion, through the brain. Representation is therefore doubly processed, in the input of visual information and in its transformation into depiction; where representation is on the basis of tradition, as it mostly is, it is a double processing of doubly processed material. The question is not whether the brain plays a part, but how it stores and processes visual information, and at what stage it operates its final selection, transformation, and definition. The transformation between the foreshortened sensations received by the eye and the unforeshortened representation is also unquestionable. Unforeshortened representation is a cultural near-universal, whose presence is innate in untrained modern subjects, so that the transformation is in principle unproblematic—or at least the natural thing to do—for the person who performs it (which is not to say that it is easy).

Schäfer seems to have believed that human memory stores unforeshortened images, irrespective of whether they are used for representation; only an infinitesimal proportion will be so used. If he did not mean this, he must have assumed that artists have a special type of memory image, which is true insofar as they remember works of art and their constituents as a distinct category, but is unlikely to hold for their memory in general. A summary in these terms may simplify Schäfer's position, but it is useful in bringing out the issue. He gave examples, mainly from children's drawings, where in the physical production of a work the two-dimensional format is felt to be an obstacle to a correct, that is, an unforeshortened rendering (p. 111 = 103). However, no contradiction between the dimensional characteristics of subject and representation need be perceived until the depiction comes to be made. This does not imply that there is no awareness of the three-dimensionality of reality, but that the memory image—the stored information—takes account of the third dimension, probably in a processual as opposed to a static form. As attention is focused on a remembered object, one casts one's eye over it or walks around it, so to speak. Schäfer's memory image hypothesis is thus dispensable on the assumption that the transformation of two-dimensional form takes place at a late stage in representation. As he himself said, it need not occur to artists that there should be a substantial correspondence between the visual impression produced by objects and by representations of them. The irreducible component of a representation is then more symbolic— the idea that something may be depicted—than iconic—requiring visual resemblance—although both aspects are always present.[2] Vision, as used by an artist in depiction, must in any case be memory—that is, visual matter must be processed and stored before being applied to representation, so that neither vision nor memory need correspond with depictions.

Since Schäfer's argument relies on memory images, these should be considered further, particularly if it is posited that they are transformed only at a late stage in depiction. The 'processual' form I suggest for images implies that memory, like vision, works by movement. Perhaps movement combines with the correction produced by previous knowledge to include information about the third dimension in memory. In this sense, memory 'images' will be as much complexes of information as visual entities. If we think we have static, perspective, and three-dimensional memory images, this may be in part because we are so used to looking at perspective pictures (even though our eyes are never still when we do that). The characterization I give of the memory image largely dissolves any special features it may have and assimilates it to visual perception (compare Gombrich 1983: 193). This approach brings gains for the economy of explanation, because one can posit that the visual aspects of perception and memory are processed mentally in the same fashion. If visual memory is a weakened form of vision—with vital associative advantages—it cannot by itself crystallize a representational form, although it will offer schemata that may serve as the basis of representational forms. Such semi-representational schemata must exist, because they occur in natural phenomena like zoological mimicry, where they do not form the basis of active depictions (e.g. Hinton 1973). It is virtually meaningless to ask in detail how representations resemble schemata, because the visual form of the latter is probably not fixed.

---

[2] Schäfer made these points, if in a somewhat different form, but he did not bring them to bear in connection with the origins and production of representational images (instead, he used them to analyse specific examples). In Egyptian art, the symbolic side is especially highly developed because writing and pictorial representation are almost inextricably associated with each other. See e.g. Tefnin (1984); Fischer (1986).

This hypothesis about the character of schemata cannot easily be established for the creation of representations, but it is surely valid for their identification, as is illustrated in an extreme case by an experiment. Subjects are presented with images in rapid succession and asked to identify one belonging to a particular class, such as boats. In a second test they are not given the name of a class but shown the image to be found. Performance is not notably different for the two tasks. This suggests that the category as much as the shape is stored and matched, with the strategic advantage that few failures will be due to the rejection of objects that are far from a stored shape but still belong in the same category: a perceived shape will often be remote from any stored shape.[3]

This psychological parallel relates to the optimum performance of perception in difficult conditions. Such conditions apply to the creation of representational forms insofar as the initial devising of a suitable form is difficult. The parallel may also suggest a model for the communicative aspect of representation, one of whose principal purposes—apart from any aesthetic or other considerations—is to stimulate in the viewer a recognition that is often far from automatic. Recognition may be triggered by a minimal 'likeness', which is primarily the likeness of a class or concept. Both perception and representation can be refined to any degree and, for representation, in any stylistic direction, after the initial recognition or devising of a form.

The model of memory and vision that I have presented so far relates to a large body of work in experimental psychology, of which one example has been cited. This work is revealing in its emphasis on conceptual factors and on the centrality for vision of object-centred 'descriptions'—non-perspective descriptions that do not take the viewer's position into account.[4] Both the processed input of information in perception and the use of visual memory to encounter and predict the environment are object-centred. It requires the battery of special techniques of the academic art school (or in earlier centuries studio training) to counteract this basic predisposition (cogently stated by Francis Pratt, 1985). The development of skills in depiction allows an increasing amount of information to be given about what is shown, but it may take rather special conditions for the viewer's position to become important for

---

[3] Potter (1975); Rabbitt (1984). Experiments like this one are a striking analogy for Schäfer's basic procedure of analysing compositions in terms of hypothetical 'conceptions' of artists. Here, the criticisms of Walther Wolf (1957: 687–8 n. 79 [1]), who argued that an analysis should not take into account the point of departure of pictorial representation but rather focus on the end product of the works, point to limitations in Schäfer's approach and bring out its chief focus, but do not thereby invalidate it.

[4] Much valuable material is presented in Freeman and Cox (1985). These studies include important discussions of the meaning of contours and the areas enclosed within them, a topic that I do not consider here (but see n. 10). See also Marr (1982).

such information (see Light 1985; Davis 1985). Because of this primacy of object-centring, representation should not be presumed to imply a viewpoint unless specific evidence suggests one. In this respect, the presentations of M. A. Hagen (1985), John Willats (1985), R. K. Duthie (1985), and Fred Dubery and John Willats (1983) omit a vital initial stage. It is doubtful whether either the creator or the recipient of a simple pictorial representation need necessarily ask themselves from what viewpoint an object is depicted. Here, Schäfer's approach, in which he systematically considered alternative assumptions to that of a viewpoint, is in advance of much subsequent work.

If forms are not created initially on the basis of fixed visual schemata or memory images, they need not have any well-defined visual antecedents, but can be the products of the artist's depiction, bringing into play a mental model rather than a visual form, with the picture surface acting, like the blank page for Mallarmé, as part stimulus and part hurdle. New forms will exploit analogies with existing schemata and must respect to some extent the appearance of the original—which is very difficult to define precisely. (There are notable natural biases here, such as children's preponderant focus on heads and eyes at the expense of bodies.) Typically, new forms are further defined by opposition to existing ones, and are then taken over into the general repertory; insofar as representation is a system of signs, there can be a tension between the visual criterion of appearance, or resemblance, and the system's requirement of intelligibility. Such a tension also characterizes visual perception.

The artistic conception of what is to be depicted—the schema of an object or a figure—was Schäfer's main concern. In analysis one may alternatively focus on the artist's involvement in the process of depiction—the difficulty of producing a depiction in two dimensions. Both factors must play a part. For the latter, the question of artistic tradition is particularly significant. Cases where problems of depiction are solved without reference to tradition are few, however important they may be. In exploiting tradition for representation, the average artist makes a use of memory that may be different from that of the innovator, but is common to non-perspective and perspective artists. Artists' training teaches them techniques of representation and how to improve their memory in particular directions, both for individual schemata and for whole compositions.[5] In an art like that of Egypt, where styles and schemata change slowly and artists work in groups, almost all their attention in training must be focused on reproducing existing schemata and absorbing the influence of existing works. In Egypt there was innovation and change,

---

[5] Compare Schäfer's comments on memory, 86 = 93, with a citation from Hermann von Helmholtz, the inventor of the ophthalmoscope; see also e.g. Scoditti (1982).

but periods of rapid change were few, while novelty was not at a premium even if artistic change was valued.

In most respects Schäfer's memory-image hypothesis is well suited to continuing artistic traditions. To a lesser extent it also applies to the viewer, who recalls schemata in order to 'read' new works. The prime viewers, however, are other artists, who use inherited schemata in preference to elaborating new ones. In many, perhaps most, artistic traditions a full understanding of works of art is spread to few beyond the community of artists. This can be true of representational aspects, so that in Egypt it is possible to discover cases where later artists misunderstood representational features of earlier works in their own artistic tradition (e.g. 118–19, 145–6 = 110–11, 139–40).

All these points situate representational matters within artistic traditions, but the initial stages of such traditions need special attention. It may seem perverse to insist on origins, but the existence of representation, particularly in two dimensions, should not be taken for granted. In premodern times a high proportion of people never saw a representational image; even in Egypt, with its well-established traditions, images were probably widespread only among the elite. In the period of origin, a resource that remained scarce was still more restricted than later and may have been at its most prestigious. The beginnings of this elite artistic tradition, which lasted for more than 10 per cent of the securely established human history of representation (*c*.3500 BCE–early CE), can be glimpsed.

I now summarize the discussion so far and apply the resulting model to the formative stages of Egyptian art at the end of the fourth millennium BCE and its elaboration in the Old Kingdom (third millennium).

3   AN ALTERNATIVE HYPOTHESIS

Two-dimensional pictorial representation symbolizes three-dimensional entities on a flat surface, normally at a vastly reduced scale from what it represents. The depicted entities, most typically living beings, very often interact on the flat surface. Both the scale, which need not be applied consistently through a composition, and the flat surface mean that there is no simple, direct correlation between representation and reality. The representational form symbolizes what it depicts almost as much as it reproduces it, but it can be developed until it approximates to the character of a more or less literal reproduction. Its origin is presumably in the insight that a schema (of whatever type) that is used in processing visual information and in memory can be given an external, communicable visual form.

An initial representation is a special type of symbol, whose referent is a concept or class. Symbols are comprehended because they are used regularly and because they form part of systems of symbols. Unless there is an overriding and easily assimilated system of representation, such as advanced perspective or photography, representational conventions are necessary wherever things are depicted with any regularity, even if the simplest ones, such as depictions of people as 'stick men', are fairly transparent. The further development of these conventions takes place within a system more than through observation of models in nature. In many cultures the direction of development is toward conformity with the visual image; such development marks, among other things, advances in skill and experience. The more conventions approach the visual image, the greater is the possibility that the lack of foreshortening may be felt as an absence, because depictions will come to resemble less highly processed visual input, in which foreshortening is more prominent. In the most rudimentary representations, the issue of foreshortening does not arise, and it is in part a matter of style whether it will arise later.

Such a development can be compared with that of children, for whom the picture surface is at first completely dominant. At an early stage, it does not occur to them that depth is a problem, although older children become aware of it (convenient summary: Arnheim 1974: 162–217). Representation on a flat surface is elaborated on the basis of symbolic schemata that come slowly to relate more closely to the visual image. By that time, modern art education and the image conventions of our culture complicate the use of parallels from children for adult art such as Egyptian (cf. Gombrich 1977 [1960]: 101–7) or for any radically different tradition. Egyptian pictorial representation could nonetheless be characterized as an immense adult elaboration of principles similar to those of children's drawings. Explanations of the non-incorporation of depth in children's drawings are therefore potentially relevant to it.

The case against foreshortening is in part a concomitant of the status of representational schemata as symbols. A symbol generalizes, which is not normally true of a particular, foreshortened image.[6] It is also difficult to create symbols for complex visual matters, while the visual form of the symbol itself may at times impede its representational function, for example if it is not easily decoded. Compositions that organize visual groups can be transmitted as wholes. This codification of compositions generally requires a stable artistic tradition and transcends the development of representational forms for individual figures or elements. Whatever the role of the individual figure

---

[6] The conception of 'perspective as a symbolic form' (Panofsky 1991 [1927]; an idea adopted in Egyptology by Walter Wolf, 1957: 276–8) is irrelevant here; see Pirenne (1970: 93 with n. 1).

may be, as against that of the group, representation remains a difficult undertaking. Its difficulty fosters reliance on tradition. Because works of art are less complex and changeable than reality, it is easier to copy or adapt them than to work from nature. An artist whose prime activity is to manipulate visual symbols need not feel the need to observe nature in order to enhance his rendering of it. If the idea of observing nature for its specific—as opposed to generalizing—character is absent, tradition will be still more dominant. Furthermore, representational systems are rarely 'value-free'; they are integrated with other important symbolic systems. They are not lightly discarded or modified, and they are thoroughly permeated by values; neither artist nor viewer need separate representational elements from ideological.

Egyptian pictorial representation of the dynastic period (from c.2950) is central to the definition of Egyptian culture and embodies, depicts, and defines the order of the world (e.g. Baines 1985c: 277–305; Ch. 1 here). Developments in representation or in composition take place within the system and are primarily in matters of detail. Their existence shows that artists had considerable autonomy and prestige. Such developments exhibit a concern with the visual image, but they are subordinate to the socially important purpose which representation serves.[7]

This force of tradition was established quickly. Egyptian predynastic representation (before c.3200) shows little kinship with dynastic forms, which were devised within a couple of centuries, during which there were crucial changes both in composition and in the rendering of individual figures, especially the human figure.[8] Predynastic compositions are organized for the spaces they occupy, such as pots of the Naqada II period or cosmetic palettes of Naqada II–III, and few general principles of composition can be discerned (for illustrations, see e.g. Asselberghs 1961). Yet all this changes already with one of the first probably 'royal' monuments, the 'decorated tomb' at Hierakonpolis, where some features of composition in horizontal registers can be discerned, as well as the use of three figures to signify a general 'plurality', as in the Egyptian script.[9] At the end of the predynastic period, the

---

[7] Here, Egyptologists have often invoked the supposed 'recreative' power of Egyptian representation (e.g. Iversen 1975: 5–13). This is, however, much less important—and less well established—than is often maintained, and is almost certainly irrelevant here; see Baines (1978: 189–90; Ch. 2 §3.1 here).

[8] This formulation may overstate the extent of the transformation and understate the importance of the period of transition, which lasted a number of generations. Nonetheless, works from the Early Dynastic period generally resemble those of the Naqada II period rather little.

[9] Quibell (1902: pls. 75–9); line: Schäfer, fig. 144. This tomb dates to Naqada IIc, relatively early in the process of development and contemporaneous with the tradition of decorated pottery; see e.g. Baines (1995a: 97–8).

characteristic 'Egyptian' form of the human figure emerged, remaining very similar thereafter throughout Egyptian history. For present purposes, the most noteworthy features of the standard human figure are its representational literalism and exactness and its lack of 'unity'. Within the enveloping outline, several of its parts are treated as discrete elements, presented in object-centred terms. Human figures of the Old Kingdom (c.2600–2150) and later are depicted with very good proportional accuracy (see Robins 1983; 1994). This advance in accuracy, which can also be seen in the depiction of animals, is accompanied by great consistency in the application of representational schemata and a notable anonymity of style. Much of what one might consider characteristic of Egyptian style is almost more an aggregate of representational and compositional conventions; there is remarkably little adjustment of physical features for stylistic effect.

The development of Egyptian representation before the 1st dynasty (c.2950) almost certainly took forms like those of the Hierakonpolis wall painting as its point of departure. These consist mainly of outlines and solid patches of at most four colours, with virtually no internal detail (see also 75–80 = 69–74). Their crudity contrasts with the sophistication of some of the design and may be related in part to the medium, because roughly contemporaneous carved relief, which runs in parallel with a fine tradition of hard stone vases, is greatly superior in execution. Relief shows varied conventions and developments in representational forms, such as the presentation of a full-view, narrow-shouldered chest (e.g. Schäfer pl. 3 = 2:3), which is eliminated in the standard form in favour of broad shoulders with a 'profile' forward outline and no internal detail on the chest (e.g. Narmer Palette of the end of the predynastic period: Fig. 30 here). In the single figure, these changes tend to emphasize the primacy of the outline,[10] within which much of the body surface is representationally mute; the outline supplies the holistic image that is lacking in the treatment of its individual parts. The outline in the standard form also approximates rather more than earlier to a geometrical projection of the human figure, a feature that may be important for later developments. In compositional terms, register lines—already present in one group in the Hierakonpolis painting—and the manipulation of scale contribute to the

---

[10] See in general the work of David Marr (1982). This emphasis on the outline does not exclude internal detail, but, with the salient exception of the eye, little that is vital to the human body, as opposed to its dress and ornament, is shown within the surface of a figure. The attempt of Erik Iversen (1975: 34–7) to make a general principle or law out of this practice is unconvincing (for a psychological parallel, see n. 4 here). In the relief styles of certain periods internal bones, such as collarbones, and some muscles are emphasized, but they are almost never present in pure drawing.

dominance of principal figures, as is appropriate to conventions produced in the service of royal ideology. Taken together, these conventions emphasize the 'heroic' status of individual figures. They are anti-realistic in their treatment of the picture surface, which is organized for the most effective ideological statement, not for spatial or topographical information.[11] This is true both of the precursor at Hierakonpolis and of Early Dynastic works. When large-scale compositions appear in the 4th–6th dynasties, they follow the same general principles, and are mostly extended in terms of the schemata devised for particular scenes or groups rather than through observation of nature independent of works of art. In addition to ideological statement, composition is elaborated both for stylistic reasons and in order to enhance the information conveyed by representations.

Development of compositions is in the form of sequences that can be read along registers or sets of registers. The design of an entire picture surface is not centralized except by the presence of a colossal figure of the king or tomb owner bracketing all the smaller scenes. Narrative, so far as anything of the sort is present, and the interaction of figures are presented episodically rather than focused round a climax. Among the major figures, tomb owners are mostly shown inactive, being related to their context by juxtaposition (see in general Groenewegen-Frankfort 1951; critique: Baines 1974), so that no spatial information is given except in sub-scenes; nor is what is shown temporally unified. The major stimulus to changes in overall composition seems to have been the need to organize numerous motifs on the surface, rather as the designer of an illustrated book organizes text and pictures in order to fill and exploit the space on a page. Compositions vary in the degree of crowding they exhibit, but there is almost no potentially innovative use of voids or empty areas: in principle the entire picture surface is evenly filled to a greater or lesser degree of density.

The features just described exemplify how the tradition could evolve with little reference to outside reality and much to the elaboration of the system. The remarkable literalness of Egyptian representation also requires comment, and it is this literalness which can seem to western eyes to ask for the western-style perspective development it did not receive.

The Egyptian canon of proportions, alluded to above, is a method of depicting the human figure consistently, using measurements derived—with a little licence—from the observation of real bodies and related to Egyptian

---

[11] Realistically plastic details, such as the imprint of the bull's foot on the calf of the captive's leg on the Bull Palette (e.g. Schäfer, pl. 2.1 = 2), are almost always minor, and tend to disappear, although comparable features occur as separate developments in fine works of later periods, especially in statuary.

metrology (itself anthropometric).[12] Because the conventions of representing a figure on a flat surface are not governed by rigid laws, the way in which canonical figures record 'true' dimensions is not straightforward. For artists they would contain much that had to be learned, but they certainly do record such dimensions, and a central purpose of the procedure must be to ensure a generalized accuracy in representation—a precise typification rather than a specification; in other words, what is sought is not necessarily the depiction of a particular individual's appearance (see further §4 with n. 21). The same concern with accuracy is found in representations of animals, birds, and fish. This concern extends, for example, to the complex details of birds' plumage (cf. 50–1 = 47), and must have required vast amounts of minute observation, probably with captive and dead specimens.[13] Interest in precise details of nature is also seen in a different form, in a cycle of captioned pictures of the seasons (Edel 1961–4; Edel and Wenig 1974), which includes 'zoological' information about the migratory patterns of birds and fish, although the context is a solar temple, where they document the god's benevolent creation of the order of things. Because much Egyptian art praises established order in one way or another, accuracy is part of a similar celebration in many contexts, but this is hardly a sufficient explanation of the level of concern for accuracy. What is relevant here is not so much the motivation of this focus as its existence, its scope, and the context within which it applies: it does not go beyond the single figure to entire compositions, in which scale, in particular, is treated in a notably non-'realistic' fashion. To return to the analogy of the book-designer's page, birds and fish are arranged in clear, space-filling patterns, but more often as specimens than as integrated, active groups. Concern for accuracy is less strong in the representation of inanimate objects. This difference probably implies a classificatory hierarchy, in which less information is given about what is culturally less important. In later periods the hierarchy was not necessarily the same: New Kingdom temples and tombs, for example, include highly elaborate pictures of cult and other equipment.

Despite the significance of accuracy as a value, it did not lead to any general transformation of Egyptian representation toward a more literal notation

---

[12] The work of Iversen in this area (1975) needs extensive revision. It is now essentially superseded by that of Gay Robins (e.g. 1982; 1983; 1994). The canon of proportion is not the same as what Whitney Davis rather confusingly terms 'canonical' Egyptian art (e.g. 1989; cf. Baines 1991b).

[13] This interest in accuracy is not found in the stylizations of the animal forms of several important deities and related protective figures. Notable examples are hawks, protective vultures, the jackal of Anubis, and in some cases the cow of Hathor. Most of these originated very early, while for some the context in the highly abstract setting of temple relief and religious scenes may have favoured such non-realistic forms. I am grateful to Gay Robins for this observation.

of the visual image, perhaps in part because of the non-realistic design of compositions as a whole. Accuracy must be seen in the context both of style—because stylistic variation may predominate over precision—and of the concern for conveying information. The reliefs of the seasons mentioned above impart a wealth of information in mixed textual and pictorial form, but in style they are more 'impressionistic' than some contemporaneous works. Accuracy of information might be served by the proliferation of figures in 'scenes of daily life' in 5th–6th dynasty tombs (c.2450–2200; detailed analysis of some groups: Spiegel 1957). Here too, however, style is significant, because the proliferation goes beyond the 'realistic' and becomes an almost baroque feature, part of whose raison d'être is the display of artistic virtuosity and of the patron's prestige. In works of poor quality, information and style predominate clearly over precision, so that figures and scenes are virtually reduced to the informative symbols they had been at the beginning of the process of evolution. All these points amount to saying that, with some modification, conventional explanations of stylistic development apply almost as well to the rather different conditions of Egyptian art as to western art. Here, Schäfer's consciousness of the differences between Egyptian and western artistic traditions and his specific concern with representation led him to play down factors, such as narrowly aesthetic tradition and innovation, that are vital in any tradition and can also affect pictorial representation itself.

Style, information, and values are related in the development of the single figure. The principal figure is mostly shown at rest, with full shoulder width, while subordinates appear in many poses. Thus, in a common Old Kingdom rendering of the torso, the back line is something like a profile from the neck down, while the 'nearer' or rear shoulder is abbreviated beneath the neck and head. For figures using both hands together, this is an alternative to true profile (almost unknown until later times),[14] depicting the body atomistically and placing information first. Principal figures are relatively rarely shown in this visually ungainly form; for them, perhaps, style and dignity came before information.

So far, I have discussed representational implications of an ideologically central system of signs in Egypt, whose realization is strikingly accurate in the individual figure, but schematic in the design of whole scenes and compositions, which are organized in order to convey information and values

---

[14] The 'abbreviated shoulder' form is common in Old Kingdom pictures of statues, some of which are shown in an approximation to true profile. This treatment provides additional evidence for the hypothesis that the two have the same meaning (in later periods the 'true profile' depiction of statues is standard). See Eaton-Krauss (1984: 1–5).

rather than the appearance of groups of things. The system shows little concern with how individuals look and a striking indifference to temporal unity. There are hardly any examples of foreshortening, which is the most important feature that might undermine the system, although comparable systems that incorporate a certain amount of it are known from other cultures. Before returning to 'realism' and possible changes in the two-dimensional system, such as incorporation of some foreshortening and a tendency to viewer-centred presentation, I consider three-dimensional representation.

4   THREE-DIMENSIONAL REPRESENTATION

Schäfer believed that one of the principal advances in his work was the correlation of two- and three-dimensional representation. He accounted for the evident stylistic analogies between relief and sculpture in the round by saying that both were produced on the basis of the same type of mental images. He stated that:

The creator of a piece of true sculpture based on frontal images can attack his work from all sides, as he also exploits the dimension of depth, and so is able, unlike a two-dimensional artist, physically to feel his way along the directions of the surfaces and lines of the original by removing and adding material. (324 = 315)

Three-dimensional representations of human beings, animals, and other objects that are symmetrical round an axis, which are produced by all peoples and individuals who have not been influenced directly or indirectly by Greek fifth-century art, conform to the 'rule of directional straightness'. This rule results from the opposition between the method of representation based on frontal images and the structure of the objects serving as originals: a plane is imagined as a starting-point, and the other principal planes of the torso and limbs adapt to it to form an intersection of planes at right angles. (325 = 316; in italics in the original)

Schäfer's 'rule of directional straightness' was formulated in response to Julius Lange's 'law of frontality' (1899), which described the characteristic stance of archaic Greek sculpture, in contrast with the freedom of classical and later work.[15] Both hypotheses aim to account for the rigid geometric axes of sculpture in much of the world (all of it, according to Schäfer), but 'Lange's law' is more descriptive than explanatory, and Schäfer aimed additionally to relate two and three dimensions. The rigidity to be explained is remarkable,

---

[15] Iversen (1975: 37) sought to reinforce Lange's position against that of Schäfer, but his arguments are questionable.

but it does not seem to be universal in the way Schäfer suggested. He pointed to exceptions to it in Egypt, but discounted their significance.

Like his theory of two-dimensional representation, Schäfer's 'directional straightness' is a general hypothesis about cognitive processes. It also relates to technical procedures for producing sculpture, which in Egypt were closely comparable with those used in two dimensions (335–42 = 326–33). These procedures were well suited to the style of Egyptian sculpture and difficult or impossible to adopt for some other styles. From the New Kingdom on (c.1530; evidence for earlier periods is sparse), the sides of a squared block were marked out with drawings prepared on grids according to the canon of proportions; the carving was then done on the basis of these drawings, which were renewed, essentially as aids to cutting and without grids, again and again as work proceeded.[16] The initial drawings were not identical with normal Egyptian pictures, but were closely similar to contemporaneous pictures of statues. Like all Egyptian drawing, they did not incorporate foreshortening, so that they could not be used, except very approximately, as models for works that departed from more than one major axis. Full-face drawings of the human head, which were needed for the front of most statues, were crude in comparison with normal Egyptian two-dimensional rendering, perhaps because they were never of much artistic, as against technical, interest; they cannot have suggested the character of the work that would eventually emerge as they were cut away. These procedures were thus limited in what they could depict but they were ideal for directionally straight Egyptian sculpture, whereas they could hardly be used for directionally free work. They would have acted as a powerful constraint on different methods of representation, but they were devised to serve an already existing style and rendering of nature,[17] so that they cannot be used to explain that style and rendering of nature.

There are numerous arguments in favour of Schäfer's 'directional straightness'. However, his further point that important people are shown in 'dignified' poses (326 = 317), which favours rigidity in all major sculpture, has precisely the opposite implication to that which he would give to it. If such a significant ideological factor is present in the definition of the style, which was elaborated for these elite works, the exceptions should be accorded more

---

[16] See 335–42 = 326–33. See also Anthes (1941); Robins (1994: 177–81); Seipel (1992: 453–503: examples of unfinished works and practice pieces); Aston, Harrell, and Shaw (2000: general study of stones and stone use, including brief treatment of statuary).

[17] The style is visible in two- and three-dimensional works of the 1st dynasty (c.2950–2800), but a large group of unfinished works of the 4th dynasty (c.2500) does not appear to use the drafting system of later periods, of which a fundamental feature is a vertical dividing line drawn down the central axis of the body; see Reisner (1931: 112–16, pl. 62); see also previous note.

weight rather than less, because they were produced despite a strong tendency to follow the normal code. As Schäfer noted (326–7 with 392–3 n. 379 = 318 with n. 15), the exceptions are mainly in later periods and in small-scale works, but some are in more 'major' pieces, in stone and on a large scale. These deviations both dissolve the 'timeless' character of the works, by implying that a pose is temporary, as for example with kneeling statues of men with tensed muscles presenting offerings (e.g. Russmann 1973: 34–5, 40–6), and introduce some loosening into their structure, so that, for example, a hint is given of the organic interplay of a figure with one leg advanced.[18] The depiction is so subtle that it is easily missed, but it does imply that the geometric requirement to view a statue in one plane at a time, as it were, which Schäfer saw as fundamental (332–3 = 323–4), was transcended—if it ever existed. Taken together with the more radical departures in smaller works,[19] this feature casts doubts on his basic position. Whatever the nature of the 'mental images' or models on the basis of which two-dimensional representation may be produced, so far no clear reason has been identified for why artists should not observe the liberation of three-dimensional objects from their defining axes and at least occasionally record it.[20] If no immediate reason can be found, is it possible to suggest a more general context in which this evidence might be placed?

The problem which was correctly seen but not, I think, solved by Schäfer may be formulated as follows. In much of the world, including Egypt, most sculpture is axially fixed. Axial freedom correlates quite closely with foreshortening in its position in the development of western and other art. There are sufficient numbers of exceptions to this pattern for it to be clear that the absence of axial freedom is neither a matter of incapacity nor a rigid 'law', yet its ubiquity goes beyond stylistic predilection or simple adherence to tradition and must be explained in broader terms.

---

[18] For examples of the Middle and New Kingdoms, see e.g. Vandersleyen (1975: pls. 169, 175, 187b, 198). See also the comments of Bernard V. Bothmer (1969 [1960]: xxxiv–xxxv); he noted that there was no study of this phenomenon; none has appeared since he wrote.

[19] The most striking examples are statuettes of offering bearers, principally of the late eighteenth dynasty (c.1370–1300); in addition to material cited by Schäfer, see e.g. Vandersleyen (1975: pl. 374, 18th dyn.); Koefoed-Petersen (1950: pls. 144–5, Æln 1597: sleeping boy, date uncertain; see further Feucht 1984). Old Kingdom scribe statues sometimes have asymmetrical poses, e.g. Vandier (1958: pls. 21, 57: 2). The greatest freedom is perhaps in figures of suckling women, e.g. Vandier (1958: pl. 20: 6—very crude); Kaiser (1967: no. 316: copper group, Middle Kingdom). For a photograph of Schäfer's group fig. 321 and partial parallels, see Vandier (1958: pl. 40).

[20] Schäfer's position is not affected by the varying degree of 'cubism' in the sculptural styles of different cultures, because rotund forms may imply axes as rigid as those of the more angular Egyptian works. The sculpture of the parallel civilization of ancient Mesopotamia is much more 'rotund' than Egyptian works, but has essentially the same representational characteristics; see e.g. Collon (1995); Frankfort (1996).

Even if the question is stated thus, training, tradition, and ideology remain important for the context. Depiction according to fixed axes involves simplification, as was recognized in classical and Hellenistic antiquity, when the freest works were considered pinnacles of virtuosity. With axial fixity, representation is primarily the accommodation of forms to an implicit, predefined structure, and the artist does not need so much to observe the precise appearance of a figure as when choices are freer. Such schemata may be elaborated or refined, and ultimately loosened as indicated above, but so long as there is no great stress on innovation, there need be no radical departure from them. In addition, values such as dignity and repose, which are easily read into such forms, are fundamental, because of the high prestige and serious purpose of the works. This ideological aspect parallels the integration of values into the symbolic system of two-dimensional representation. Despite this importance of ideology, the visual character of the works may generate 'realistic' developments, a possibility with obvious relevance to as 'realistic' an art as Egyptian art.

One development, of great potential importance in sculpture, that is relevant here is the incidence of 'portraiture'. If this occurs, it marks a reversal in which individuals are displayed not just in a social role but also in their own—by implication highly valued—identities, instead of emphasizing the social side and making themselves almost anonymous.[21] Although the facial features of specific people, principally of royalty, are probably reflected in Egyptian sculpture, only in a few periods do statues seem to ascribe any special value to those features. Such a value can be seen most clearly where faces have non-ideal elements, marks of age, lines, and so forth. Periods when these are relatively common in Egypt are the later 12th dynasty (c.1850–1800; see e.g. Aldred 1970: 15–24), the late 18th dynasty (c.1380–1300),[22] and the Late and Ptolemaic periods (c.700–30; Bothmer 1969 [1960]: e.g. figs. 250–5, 259–60, 264–9); for the last, the most striking 'portraits' are Ptolemaic in date

---

[21] This formulation leaves aside the possibility that the features of particular people may be shown in highly idealized or generalized forms. This question has been much debated, as part of the general problem of how far there is 'portraiture' in Egyptian art, and cannot well be solved. Whenever features are idealized, a statue of a person is not simply a portrait, since it presents the person as an example of a type, so that this question need not affect the discussion here. In several periods the source of facial types in sculpture was the king, but this fact does not help to establish how closely his features were recorded. For studies of portraiture, see e.g. Vandersleyen (1982, with references); see also Tefnin (1983: 106–7); Weeks (1970: ch. ix). For a judicious review of the question, see Spanel (1988: 1–37).

[22] Here it is best to leave aside the aberrant and poorly understood Amarna period itself. For other material of the surrounding period, see e.g. Riefstahl (1951); Charbonneaux (1958: pls. 62–3, probably late 18th dyn.); highly individual bodies of Amenhotep III, heads missing: Kozloff and Bryan (1992: 146 fig. V.28); Hayes (1959: 237 fig. 142 = Kozloff and Bryan no. 23, pp. 204–6).

and to a greater or lesser degree influenced by Hellenistic art.[23] Portraiture of this sort can bring with it asymmetry and axial freedom, but it does not have to do so. Its most significant aspect is perhaps its move away from schemata toward the observation and recording of specific appearances, that is, its interest in the changeable and temporary. It is, as it were, a more highly wrought and detailed analogy for the temporary poses and organic asymmetries mentioned above. The chief periods of portraiture were times of more general cultural change, in which different renderings of human features could relate to cognitive developments or to an altered concept of the person. Despite the significance of such tendencies, especially in relation to portraiture in the Graeco-Roman world, their impact in Egypt was nearly as limited as that of directionally free sculpture in three dimensions and of foreshortening in two.

Portraiture is a case of how axial fixity might change into freedom through detailed concentration on individuals rather than types. The examples of offering bearers and other groups, and of unusual poses, suggest a slightly different alternative, in which the depiction of processes and movement stimulated some subtle changes and could have led to a more radical breakthrough. Neither development can explain why fixity came to be the norm in the first place. Schäfer's belief that it correlates with absence of foreshortening seems correct, and some of the same arguments apply to both.

If one starts from the assumption presented above, that no fixed visual model necessarily precedes representation, three-dimensional forms should in the first instance be elaborated directly in confrontation with their material, which is the counterpart of the picture surface in two dimensions. Some characteristics of the material may be significant, the chief division being between harder substances that have to be carved subtractively and the additive modelling of clay for terracotta, or wax for metal casting.[24] The latter, especially clay, encourage a freer treatment than the former, and it is symptomatic of Egyptian art that terracotta was very rare until Hellenistic

---

[23] In relief, this development had a short-lived native Egyptian counterpart in the mixed style of the tomb of Petosiris at Tuna el-Gebel (*c.*320–290: Lefebvre 1923–4; e.g. Vandersleyen 1975: pls. xxxviii–xxxix). This style has some fragmentary parallels and should not be seen as unique. For related arguments and bibliography, see also Baines (2004b). Striking cases of individualization are two heads with a wart and a scar on the face (Bothmer 1969 [1960]: nos. 108, 131). These parallel descriptions of markers of personal appearance that are common in Greek documents, but they may still have a schematic character; see Dasen (in press).

For a valuable treatment of portraiture in the Byzantine world, with stimulating parallels to and differences from the Egyptian material, see Maguire (1996).

[24] Egyptian faience was used mainly for small objects and normally cast in pottery or stone moulds. Most work in faience derives from stylistic models in stone or metal. On ceramic statuary, see Dorman (2002). Rudolf Wittkower (1977) engagingly presented relevant implications of sculptural materials for the western tradition.

times, while metal did not become widespread until the first millennium BCE and adopted most of its formal and stylistic characteristics from stone, wood, and for small works, ivory.[25] Thus, in sculpture the more difficult materials were generally preferred; the artist's aim was to master the material, but its rigidity evidently had an intrinsic value. The more prestigious the work, the harder was the material used. Prestigious sculpture in hard stone was not an important locus of innovation until the Late period (c.700–30).

The difficulty of producing three-dimensional representations may be accentuated by the ambitious choice of medium, but it is also worthy of note on its own account. Representational problems in three dimensions may not seem so great as those of condensing three dimensions into two, but such a formulation implies that the subject can be reproduced directly, which is not the case. Rather, sculpture, like two-dimensional work, is a realization of a symbol that is created or repeated by artists in their encounter with their material. There may be a tendency to use the simplest approach for recalcitrant material, and the organization of figures around axes limits the task artists set themselves. Sculptors' creations may be easier to compare with reality than is the case with two-dimensional representation, and observation of their intrinsic characteristics may more easily lead to refinements and developments that loosen traditional forms. Sculpture inhabits the same spatial world as our own, and cannot depict the spatially impossible, whereas in the separate world of two dimensions the impossible may be realized, and it is in part a matter of conventions of representation whether what is depicted in a particular instance is understood as being possible or not. This greater freedom in two dimensions lies primarily within the symbolic realm. It means that the significance and autonomy of two dimensions is of a different order from that of three.[26] But, despite these differences in potential, the difficulties posed by two- and three-dimensional rendering have strong

---

[25] This probably understates the significance of metal statuary in earlier periods, despite the small amount that survives. Such works are attested in texts from the Early Dynastic period on, and particularly fine examples date to the 6th and 12th dynasties, the quality or existence of which was not suspected until the 1980s and 1990s. This material is not yet available in a synthesizing publication, but see Eckmann and Shafik (2005).

[26] This does not imply that the Egyptians created physically impossible scenes of the kind familiar from the works of the 20th century Belgian artist M. C. Escher and of others. Such fabrications often rely on ambiguities of foreshortening and perspective, and for that reason alone are not compatible with Egyptian art. The point is rather that the literal possibility of what is shown in two dimensions may be irrelevant or not considered; a scene may also belong to a mythical realm. Very often the yardstick for interpreting difficult representational forms is what is physically possible in three dimensions (much of Schäfer's analysis works on these lines), but it is also assumed in such cases that the intention was to depict a real object that it was difficult to show in Egyptian conventions. (The Egyptians often depicted impossible figures in images of the underworld, but the representational character of such images is not at issue here.)

analogies independent of technical considerations. Both also share the relative scarcity of representation of any sort until fairly modern times. In a context in which innovation is not at a premium, something that is difficult, scarce, and value-laden needs a special stimulus if it is to change radically. When change occurs, it is likely to form part of wider changes in society, in ideology, or in both.

5 'REALISM' AND ITS IMPLICATIONS

Both two- and three-dimensional representation may be more or less 'realistic'. I suggest that realism has its own dynamic that can relate to radical change toward foreshortening (and ultimately perspective) and axial freedom in the two different contexts, but does not presuppose it or necessarily prepare the way for it. By 'realism' I mean no more than that an art style reproduces single features—and often groups of features—without great distortion, as is amply shown for Egyptian art by the canon of proportions. Such a formulation does not define realism according to western criteria—western perspective is only one among a number of projective systems—but it does imply that representation can be closely described in terms of one or more projective systems, which is hardly true of the most highly stylized art. Because Egyptian representation is object-centred, projective systems are of limited use in understanding its principles, even though they can usefully describe some of its procedures.

In Egypt, realism is characteristic of the finest works, particularly those of earlier times. Periods when artistic standards fell were also those when representation was much less literally accurate—although there is no close correlation between realism and major artistic periods. What is significant in the development of realism, however, is what happens in times of positive development rather than of decline. The criterion mentioned above, that new forms may contain more information than those they replace, needs the rider that those forms are also more like projections based on a single projective system, so that they appear more viewer-centred than their forerunners.[27] Erik Iversen, following Aladár Dobrovits, wished additionally to specify that Egyptian art followed a 'law of the broadest surfaces (*Gesetz der grössten Flächen*)', according to which such surfaces were presented in full view

---

[27] Schäfer was rightly wary of the concept of a 'viewpoint', some of his objections to which are met by the more cautious formulation 'viewer-centred'. The problem of viewpoints and the general lack of them in Egyptian art remains central to his treatment; his detailed exposition shows how they are largely dispensable in the analysis of representations. See esp. 92 = 85; see also §1 of this chapter.

where possible.[28] Iversen's formulation covers much of the same ground as the notion of information, but it is contradicted by certain features, such as the treatment of the human chest as a semi-profile in dynastic art, in contrast with late predynastic art, which allowed a theoretically broader full view (e.g. pl. 2:3 = 3). Constructs like this one would allow many features of Egyptian representation to be integrated under a single theoretical heading, but they ignore the fact that the system is a more pragmatic, conventional set of symbols. It cannot be neatly circumscribed, whereas a system that derived from a single law should be amenable to concise exposition (compare Schäfer's wide range of types and exceptions).

Realism is thus a general tendency that can be manifest in any number of specific ways and that may complement the purpose of representation to convey information. It cannot be rigorously or neatly defined. Although this lack of neat definition makes it difficult to discuss realism, it does not mean that it is any less present or significant as a phenomenon. In part it may be a self-sustaining elaboration on the forms inherited from earlier generations. Insofar as this is so, realism need not depend on the stimulus of much extra observation of nature, but rather reflects a desire to simplify or unify schemata and elaborate on possibilities that are implicit in the inherited system. Its importance lies in two directions: more realistic forms may emphasize implicit inconsistencies in the system and in this way serve as a stimulus for more radical changes in the depiction of single figures or in whole compositions; and it may correlate with developments in society and thus have an 'evolutionary' significance.

The first of these points is relatively obvious: the more a representation resembles its visual counterpart, the more salient and potentially discordant are any marked differences between them, although such discordances can be isolated and minimized.[29] The most innovative treatments of single figures in Egyptian art, which seem to come near to negating the normal system, are still minor in their overall context. They are mostly in small groups of human figures, such as female musicians, or serving girls and the ladies whom they attend, in 18th dynasty painted tombs (e.g. Russmann 1980; collections of material: Davies and Gardiner 1936; Mekhitarian 1954). The physical attractions of these people were important and probably contributed to the careful observation. New features include full-face heads, the depiction of a woman's second breast, and a 'back' rendering of the human form which is

[28] Iversen (1975: 34–7), citing Dobrovits (1937; 1959). This proposal relates also to 'Lange's law', discussed above.
[29] Compare Gombrich (1977 [1960]: 122–3), who remarked, following Schäfer (e.g. 87 = 81, 269–72 = 265–9), that what is significant about exceptions is not their existence but their lack of influence and the relatively tiny number of them.

the reverse of the normal 'front' version;[30] later, the depiction of all the toes of the nearer foot was introduced, at first on figures of women (302–3 = 295–6, with addenda 367; Russmann 1980). Some of these developments were adopted in reliefs of the Amarna period (e.g. a figure with two breasts in full view, fig. 316 = English edn. pl. 107; English edn. 368, addenda to 306). As noted by Edna R. Russmann (1980), for such details relief is a more problematic medium than painting, because of the depth it implies and the extreme compression of layers that the details require. Thus, in relief they more clearly subvert the general system. The fact that the figures are normally in groups is also significant. Artists seem to have asked themselves how the group might appear from outside, instead of placing the figures in suitable series and relating them chiefly in terms of overlaps and thematic association. In Archaic Greek art too, the single figure is the point of departure for the introduction of foreshortening or allied changes, but again such single figures almost always form part of groups. It is possible to see developments from these beginnings in terms of function, of interest in how something is done, or as specifying the relative positions of the figures.[31]

I suggest that such concerns will arise most easily on the basis of literalistic representation such as was traditional in Egypt, although the stimulus provided by literalism was not strong and never led to truly radical change. The developments just described do, however, have a parallel in compositional changes, and these too point to the potential dissolution of the traditional system. The traditional rendering of topography spread over the surface like a map (cf. Gombrich 1975) becomes fused with other techniques. In 18th dynasty compositions, register lines begin to meander over the picture surface or to disappear. The same new treatment is found in battle scenes of Tutankhamun and their 19th–20th dynasty successors.[32] Neither the hunting

---

[30] Some of these features occur earlier or more frequently on figures of enemies than on Egyptians; this distribution implicitly classifies them as aberrant. See Baines (in Schäfer 1986 [1974]: 362 to 214 n. 178).

[31] There are examples of foreshortening in Precolumbian Mesoamerican art. See e.g. Schäfer (1986 [1974]: 365 to 372–3); Robertson (1983: pls. 98–9, 140, 144, 155, 158, 166, 168, 181, 185 etc.). The man shown in Robertson's pls. 98–9 was probably club-footed (see her pls. 140–1), but the figure still implies foreshortening. For the presentation of fingers and toes in pls. 155 ff., compare perhaps the Mesopotamian relief illustrated by Russmann (1980: 62–3 with fig. 1).

[32] For Tutankhamun, see e.g. Davies and Gardiner (1962); Lange and Hirmer (1968: pl. xxxiv). In this case the medium of a painted box may be relevant to the 'advanced' composition, but royal forerunners in other media and contexts may be lost, or such compositions may have been more frequent in less formal contexts. For New Kingdom battle reliefs see e.g. Wreszinski (1923–35). The recently discovered fragments of battle reliefs with chariots from the reign of Ahmose, the founder of the New Kingdom, show that this tradition began earlier than had been realized; see e.g. Harvey (1994); Spalinger (2005: 20–2).

scenes nor the battle scenes have unified viewpoints, but their large-scale, open organization of quasi-narrative offers a significant analogy to the treatment of single figures. A parallel development of the Amarna period is the fusion of more than one register into a single overall scene, accompanied by the meaningful use of blank spaces.[33] The 'open' character of Amarna compositions has a close parallel in first millennium Assyrian palace reliefs, particularly those of Assurbanipal (668–627; see e.g. Barnett 1976; more generally Winter 1981). In a crucial phase of Archaic Greek painting something similar can be seen, with many figures possessing the added quality of repose or 'silence' (e.g. Robertson 1959: 122–9; 1975: I, 242–59; II, pls. 88–9). The opening-out of compositions relativizes the human figure in context and shows new possibilities of creating focus or 'drama' that are less artificial than the traditional close grouping.[34] The melee of a battle scene is a wholesale variation of a traditional type, whereas the open compositions offer more potential. The traditional regular distribution of content takes the picture surface for granted, whereas a more irregular treatment calls attention to the surface and problematizes it.

In figures and in composition, different aspects of realism provide the context in which the breakthrough to foreshortening, and ultimately to the unified use of pictorial space, could occur. It seems likely that realism is a necessary, but not a sufficient, condition for such developments, which may perhaps occur more easily in the stylistically freer medium of painting than in purely linear representation or in relief. In styles that evolve after the transition to foreshortening, many elements of non-perspective representation often continue to be present. Such styles vary greatly in their realism, which is a separate factor but converges with foreshortening in the crucial transition between the two methods of rendering nature.

Edna R. Russmann (1980) draws an elegant postscript to 'realistic' changes in Egyptian representation. The depiction of all the toes on the near foot was rapidly annexed for figures of the highest status, primarily kings. A seemingly insignificant, viewer-centred detail, which could have contributed with others to the formation of a new system, became instead one more element in the pervasive Egyptian notation of hierarchy—something that was more central

---

[33] See in general Groenewegen-Frankfort (1951: 96–110). The most striking use of a blank space is perhaps a trumpeter who has the entire central sub-register of a composition to himself: Groenewegen-Frankfort (1951: fig. 22; Davies 1903–8, III, pl. xxxi). One suspects that this treatment may evoke the sound of a trumpet and its carrying over distance. An additional factor is that the trumpeter faces toward the major figure of the king and in the opposite direction to the bodyguard soldiers in the four flanking sub-registers.

[34] Openness or crowding of compositions are independent stylistic variables (cf. 46–8 = 43–5), but they remain potentially significant for the changes under discussion.

than realism to Egyptian concerns. The other developments I have described were equally short-lived.

6   CONCLUSION: UNIVERSALS

The simplest formulation of Schäfer's conclusions is that non-perspective representation and analogous features of sculpture in the round are a human universal. The conclusions themselves can hardly be questioned, while the formulation as a universal is essentially a stronger statement of E. H. Gombrich's position that:

> all representations can be ... arranged along a scale ... from the schematic to the impressionist ... there exists a natural pull toward the schematic which artists such as Giotto or Constable succeeded in overcoming. Because of this gravitation toward the schematic or 'conceptual', we have a right to speak of 'primitive' modes of representation, modes, that is, which assert themselves unless they are deliberately counteracted.   (Gombrich 1977 [1960]: 247)

Gombrich's 'pull' is in part technical: the schematic is more easily executed than the variability of foreshortening. This aspect relates in turn to the status of representation as a system of signs at a greatly reduced scale from reality. Any particular system of non-perspective representation is one culture's set of signs that constitutes its version of this universal. Schäfer's suggested explanation of the universal is faulty, but his identification of it is correct. It remains briefly to evaluate alternative explanations and consider implications of the universal.

The analysis of representation offered above assumes that the universal emerges in the process of depiction and should be seen as a feature of communication, and of the construction of symbolic systems, as much as of memory, which was the focus of Schäfer's explanation.[35] Representational systems are integrated with their cultures, and are very often scarce and prestigious. As soon as a norm of representation has been set or a tradition initiated, instances of it are based not so much on observation of reality as on inherited two-dimensional schemata. If they are to be readily understood, they must be integrated within

---

[35] David Marr's theory of vision (1982) implies that some of the symbolizing may belong to an earlier stage in vision itself. A comparable approach is followed for representation by Phillips, Inall, and Lauder (1985). I am not completely persuaded by their arguments and, at least for adult art, would prefer to place the construction of symbols later in the process of representation. The evidence from the modern world that they use for adults is probably too much contaminated by training and the sight of perspective images to be informative about general human propensities in visual description.

the system, so that, in the absence of revolutionary intent,[36] there will be a strong bias to continue with the same technique, which need not unduly constrict artistic freedom in style or detailed composition. It must be borne in mind that a visual system of signs is not sharply defined, so that small-scale variations need not compromise it. This looseness of definition makes precise discussion difficult, and also means that the transition through the notation of foreshortening to full perspective—so far as that is a meaningful concept—can be very gradual, as it was in classical Greece and again in late medieval and early Renaissance Italy.

These and other points may explicate Gombrich's 'natural pull', but they do not explain the universal. For the sake of economy, an explanation might ideally name a single compelling factor, but it may be better to reverse the argument and suggest that perspective is what needs an overriding explanation of this sort. Perspective is a 'natural' universal in the sense that it obeys laws of optics and of geometry, but its rigid application has difficulties of its own, because visual perception is not a matter only of optics and allowance must be made for the viewer's knowledge and expectations (as is true of all representation). Because perspective is in some sense natural, the development of representation is virtually unilinear in tending potentially toward it.[37] By contrast, non-perspective representation is a 'cultural' universal of the sort indicated above. Fred Dubery and John Willats (1983: esp. 7) have formulated the position of perspective more rigorously, as the most comprehensive of all projection systems, in which—with important limitations—a view from a particular point can be shown with full consistency. They present their material from 'the simplest and most special projection systems' to the 'more general and more complex', continuing 'it seems that this is the order in which various systems develop historically, within a particular culture ..., and also the order in which these various systems are acquired by children ...'. To this should be added the rider mentioned above, that projections may be used to describe representations, but an object-centred, symbolic mode of representation need not take any projection as its point of departure. Moreover, such modes are unlikely to conform to a single projective system. In the subsequent development of representation in any culture,

---

[36] Both in classical Greece and in the early Renaissance, such ideas did exist and were applied explicitly to the representation of foreshortening or perspective. For Greece, see White (1987: 242 with n. 9); for the Renaissance, see e.g. Gombrich (1966).

[37] The comprehension of perspective in two-dimensional representations is not unproblematic. See e.g. Jahoda (1981a; 1981b). Dubery and Willats (1983) and Pirenne (1970) illustrate in detail problems with perspective in wide-angled views. Leonardo da Vinci recommended creating compositions within an angle of no more than 20 degrees in order to avoid the appearance of distortion. None of these authors emphasizes the importance of small scale in generating these problems: at a large scale and with a restricted viewpoint, similar devices are used in trompe l'œil.

any stage is optional, and some alternatives to linear perspective have remained in use throughout cultural traditions, as in East Asia.

The suggestion that perspective is the goal of a unilinear development implies that methods of representation are subject to an 'evolutionary' universal. Reduced to its simplest form, such a universal might run: (i) schematic; (ii) realistic; (iii) incorporation of foreshortening and use of oblique projective systems; (iv) perspective. Those four stages also map the complete transition from object-centred to viewer-centred representation. It is clear from some Palaeolithic art that the shift from (i) to (ii) is possible in any context,[38] but (ii) to (iii) might depend on extra factors, such as the extent of coverage of the representational system: however realistic a system might be, if it were used only rarely, without complex compositions, it might not provide enough of a basis for the next stage. Stages (iii) and (iv) must be separated because of the wide gulf between full perspective and the many systems in which foreshortening is incorporated or oblique projections are used but there is no overall perspective system. Linear perspective is characteristic of a few centuries of western art and quite exceptional in the more general history of representation.

A parallel in classification, with a more precise realization than the stages I put forward, is the 'evolutionary encoding sequence' for colour terms proposed by Brent Berlin and Paul Kay (1991 [1969]) and refined by numerous writers (for detailed arguments and revisions to them, see Ch. 11); the method has also been extended to ethnobiological classification (comprehensive study: Brown 1984, with discussion of the colour universal). According to this hypothesis, languages acquire colour terms in a limited range of orders and combinations that can be summarized in seven stages, containing between two (stage I) and eleven (stage VII) 'basic colour terms' (with some variants, for example IIIa and IIIb). The sequence, which like pictorial representation orders visual matters, is not determined by language itself but by more general constraints of classification, and perhaps ultimately of perception. The simplest colour terminologies are in simple societies, while most modern complex societies have the most highly developed set. It is difficult to identify a stimulus for enlarging colour terminologies, but this rather vague correlation remains significant.

By analogy with the colour sequence, stage (i) of the representational sequence might correlate with simple societies and stage (ii) with simple or with complex ones. Stage (iii) would mark a further degree of evolution, but its

---

[38] See e.g. Ucko and Rosenfeld (1967). The frequent use of the designation 'twisted perspective' in descriptions of Palaeolithic art (e.g. ibid. 61, 67 ff., with references), should not mislead one into thinking that it contains perspective, which it does not seem to do.

wide diffusion from one or a few points of origin allows it to occur almost anywhere. Stage (iv) is characteristic of some civilizations. Traditions need not pass through all the stages to reach the last. In the evolutionary process, stage (iv) is the exception, because it is the only one in which rules of representation and composition override symbolic content, which must be expressed within them. Both as depiction and as symbolism, stages (i)–(iii) are culture-specific, although such features as the correlation of size and importance are themselves nearly universal. As a system of representation, perspective is culturally neutral, even if it has ideological and cognitive implications, for example in terms of the relationship between viewer and depiction.

The evolutionary changes in colour and in representation seem to be ultimately cognitive in character, but, since they occur in whole societies or sectors of them, they are social and not only individual. They belong with more general human approaches to classifying, interpreting, and naming the world. In detail, both Egypt and ancient Greece provide important evidence for the colour universal, supporting Berlin and Kay's conclusion that it is a more than merely linguistic phenomenon (this aspect is hardly explored in their later work on the topic). In the case of Egypt, there is a four-term set of 'basic colour terms', black, white, red, and GRUE (that is, green and/or blue), corresponding to Stage IIIa of Berlin and Kay's sequence. In pre-classical Greece and in Egypt, painting was polychrome (cf. Bruno 1977), distinguishing clearly between colours and implying a classification of them. Egyptian polychromy of the Old Kingdom used seven basic colours: black, white, red, yellow, green, blue, and grey. In subsequent periods this repertory was increased by the addition of brown and later pink, and by the subdivision of blue. This expanded set, attested around 1400–1250, corresponds approximately to Berlin and Kay's Stage VII for language (presence of all eleven basic colour terms); significantly, this was the time when there was also greatest change in representational conventions. The use of colour also began to depart from polychromy, for example in the very occasional use of shading and in complex effects of drapery. Both in colour and in general representation, the traditional system was developed as far as it could go without losing coherence, but not further. In Greece, the development of colour use and of representation crossed the boundary into other modes between the Archaic and Classical periods. Classical and Hellenistic art became viewer-centred, directionally free in three dimensions, and ultimately 'painterly' in its use of colour.[39]

These parallels in development between Egypt and Greece are unlikely to be coincidental. In Greece, they formed part of the more general social,

[39] For painting, see Bruno (1977); for perspective in the Hellenistic world, see White (1967: 236–73).

intellectual, and artistic 'Greek revolution'. Texts from classical antiquity say much about the changes, but it is not easy to interpret. Both in Egypt and in Greece, the representational and coloured record is clearer than language as an indicator of some sorts of cognitive change.

Neither the colour universal nor that of representation is easily accounted for. All the factors adduced above that favour non-perspective representation and counteract stimuli to record perspective are partial. Even taken together, they cannot explain why full perspective is rare. The case of colour is simpler. There is no evident bias toward any more 'evolved' form of colour classification or of its notation in language, so that the universal is reasonably comprehensible. Extended colour terminologies are a convenience but hardly a necessity, and they can never master the variability of the phenomenon. In the case of representation, it must be accepted that non-perspective is the natural and universal form.

A replacement for Schäfer's memory-image explanation of this fact should ultimately be sought in terms of cognitive processes, but such an enterprise will not be easy. Similarly, partial explanations of the change to foreshortening and perspective, like those given by Gombrich (1977 [1960]: esp. ch. iv; foreword to Schäfer 1986 [1974]), or suggested above, may be supplementary to a possible understanding in terms of general social and cognitive change. Whereas in some senses the comprehension of non-perspective representation offers a challenge only to modern westerners, the move away from it more genuinely needs explanation, because it is so exceptional in the global history of art. In its basic strategy of blocking or re-examining natural perceptual responses and methods of communication, it has clear parallels in the development of thought in other areas. Such developments are universally possible, but are documented in relatively few cases.

10

Schäfer's mottoes and the understanding of representation

Heinrich Schäfer used as his principal motto ('A') for *Von ägyptischer Kunst* (*Principles of Egyptian art*) a sentence at the beginning of the 1764 edition of J. J. Winckelmann's *Geschichte der Kunst des Alterthums*:

> The oldest sources show that the earliest pictures represented what a man is, not how he appears to be, his outline, not a view of him.

He gave as a successor to the same idea a rather tortuous statement of Goethe (motto 'B') in a commentary on an exhibition of reconstructions of paintings by Polygnotus (*c.*480 BCE) held in Weimar in winter 1803–4:

> To look back to the first beginnings of painting from the pinnacles of achievement it has reached in modern times, to gain an awareness of the admirable qualities of the founders of that art, and to pay homage to the artists, who were ignorant of some methods of representation with which even novices are familiar today; all this demands firmness of purpose, calm detachment [*Entäusserung*], and an appreciation of the great value of the style which has with reason been termed 'essential' [*wesentlich*], since it is concerned more with the essential character of objects than with their appearance.[1]

As a source for Winckelmann Schäfer pointed, with a query, to Plato. In his commentary on Plato, *Sophist* 235a–236c, in his Appendix 4 (pp. 351–2), Schäfer went further and stated that 'Winckelmann's inspiration ... certainly came from Plato.' The closest approximation to Winckelmann's formulation in the Plato passage is where the Stranger says that artists of his time 'incorporate into their images not proportions that are really beautiful, but

---

Journal of Egyptian Archaeology 71 (1985) 194–6.

[1] Schäfer (1986 [1974]: [viii]; 1963: [vi], Schäfer's italics); detailed sources are given in the English edition. Winckelmann's opening paragraph, which immediately precedes the motto sentence, shows that, contrary to what one might expect (see below), he had both two- and three-dimensional art in mind. For a modern edition of Goethe's 'Polygnots Gemälde in der Lesche zu Delphi', see e.g. Goethe (1962 [1804]).

those that appear to be so',[2] but proportions, not the nature of things, are at issue in the discussion, and the general context shows that Plato had large-scale sculpture in mind, later moving to something like trompe-l'œil effects. (For other points in Schäfer's discussion, see below.)

Schäfer's assumption that this vital sentence in Winckelmann had a classical authority was correct, but the source is not in Plato. Since the ascription of the passage affects its meaning, turning the motto from a declaration of faith into a statement about the limits to a period's interpretations, it is worth correcting and commenting on the point. The source is a passage in Pliny's *Natural History*, where it is said of Lysippus:

He is said to have contributed much to the art of casting statues ... by making the head smaller ... the bodies slenderer and more tightly knit, as a result of which the height of the statues seems greater. There is no Latin term for the [Greek word] *symmetria* which he observed with the utmost precision by a new and previously unattempted system which involved altering the 'square' figures of the older sculptors; and he used commonly to say that by them [that is, the earlier sculptors] men were represented as they really were, but by him they were represented as they appeared.[3]

Pliny in his turn depended on earlier writers, and it is generally believed that his chief source was Varro, through whom many Greek writers on art were transmitted to the Roman world (see e.g. Pollitt 1974: 73–81, esp. 80–1). One such author cited earlier in the same passage about Lysippus was Duris of Samos, but it is uncertain from whom the crucial quoted sentence derived.

The putative context to which the quotation refers is thus the later 4th century BCE, the period of transition from Classical to Hellenistic Greek art. From the point of view of Lysippus, Classical Greek art showed people as they were; there is no reason to assume that he, or those who quoted the anecdote about him or reported it, had in mind earlier art whose representational techniques were similar to those of Egyptian art. There is also no reason for thinking that Winckelmann had anything else in mind, because he knew the historical context of the passage. Thus, for Lysippus, Greek critics, Varro or another intermediary writer, Pliny, and Winckelmann, the reference should

---

[2] Translation by John Tait, quoted from Schäfer (1986 [1974]: 350).

[3] *Hist. Nat.* 34. 65; translation quoted from Pollitt (1990: 98–9); for commentary on the reference to Lysippus, see, e.g., Robertson (1975: I, 464), who remarked that 'He aimed, in fact, not to reproduce nature (which can never be the aim of art) but to create a new and more natural ideal'. According to Carl Justi (1923: II, 74), Winckelmann's reading of Pliny and Pausanias stimulated his plan for a history of art, formed in 1756. The allusion to Pliny was, therefore, natural at the beginning of the resulting work. On Winckelmann, Pliny, and this passage, see Potts (1994: 72–4). Winckelmann related different stages in Greek art to different modes of representation.

be seen as lying within Graeco-Roman artistic traditions. So far as classical antiquity was concerned, the rendering of nature in classical art was subject to variation and development, but was not questioned at a fundamental level, just as Egyptian artists scarcely considered alternatives to non-perspective rendering. The contrast between the two is graphically brought out by Egyptianizing Roman statues, which mostly fail to comprehend the Egyptian rendering of the human form and structural principles of sculpture (see e.g. Roullet 1972: *passim*).

Both Pliny and Plato focused on the question of proportions, which is secondary to the rendering of nature but has much to do with how a work is perceived. Proportions are manipulated in almost any artistic tradition, and are only marginally relevant from the point of view of Schäfer's interests.[4]

Schäfer untypically denied any great importance to Goethe's text, which, he said, 'does no more than repeat [Winckelmann] at greater length' (1986 [1974]: 351–2); this is not entirely fair. Goethe stated that Polygnotus' groups of figures should be imagined as 'in no way' in perspective, but 'in the manner of the art of the period, juxtaposed or set above or beneath one another'. Later he stated that painting of the time of Polygnotus, and probably of the master himself, lacked 'correct perspective, unity in complex compositions, the massing of light and shade, attractive alternation of chiaroscuro, and harmony in colouring'. He cited vase painting, 'especially in the earlier style', as an indication of how such paintings would have looked, and named a number of compositional characteristics that could as well describe Egyptian art, such as where a window is indicated as a rectangle or furniture is 'simply added' to a scene.[5] He did not, however, comment on single figures and whether they exhibited foreshortening. Since the chief representational changes in Greek art begin with foreshortening and single figures, his statement is incomplete; the works of Polygnotus evidently contained foreshortening, but the parallel of vase painting suggests that they did not contain compositional perspective (see e.g. Robertson 1975: I, 240–60). Thus, although Goethe had penetrated further back in the transformation of representation than Winckelmann, he may not have realized that a radically different rendering of nature was possible; much in his comments could as well apply to medieval western as to classical Greek art. What characterizes the forty years between the two statements Schäfer used as mottoes is a general improvement in the comprehension of remote artistic traditions, to which Winckelmann himself contributed.

[4] For unusual proportions in the relatively eccentric style of the 11th dynasty, see Hanke (1959: 117–19 with fig. 2). For the elongation of natural proportions in the normal Egyptian canon, see Robins (1983).
[5] For these points see Goethe (1962 [1804]: 80, 91–2).

Goethe's treatment has an additional relevance to Schäfer, because his discussion focuses on two-dimensional representation. In considering two- and three-dimensional works together, Winckelmann fused issues that need to be kept separate in the analysis of representation—although Schäfer believed that his own achievement was to reach a unified understanding of them after separate consideration (see Ch. 9). Despite Schäfer's justification of his mottoes in his Appendix 4, they show something quite different from what he believed. They document the gradual dawning of awareness of the problem of representation in the late 18th and the beginning of the 19th century. Winckelmann had no conception of the questions tackled by Schäfer, and Goethe only the glimmerings of one. It was, indeed, very difficult to grasp these issues until reliable and stylistically self-effacing reproductions of Egyptian works of art and of works from other non-western traditions became available in the mid-19th century. Writers of the two generations before Schäfer were the first to appreciate the extent of the problem, while he himself retains much of the credit for comprehending its nature.

11

Colour terminology and colour classification: ancient Egyptian colour terminology and polychromy

INTRODUCTION

In *Basic color terms*, Brent Berlin and Paul Kay propose that 'there exist universally for humans eleven basic perceptual color categories, which serve as the psychophysical referents of the eleven or fewer basic color terms in any language' (1991 [1969]: 104). Later research has not invalidated this claim, although their evolutionary 'encoding sequence' has subsequently been modified (Fig. 25).[1] The 'perceptual' and 'psychophysical' component of their theory has been investigated in relation to ethnographic and other materials, and synthesized by Kay and Chad McDaniel (1978: esp. 617 n. 4, 620 n. 5; see further Cole and Scribner 1974: 43–50; Tornay 1978; von Wattenwyl 1979). These studies have confirmed that the common human perceptual response to some wavelengths of light coincides with some category foci for colours, and that in essence the Berlin and Kay colour encoding sequence maps the progressive naming of potential colour categories in a set of alternative orders. Language is an index of the discrimination of these categories, but not the

American Anthropologist 87 (1985) 282–97. Some arguments at the end of this chapter resume ones presented in Ch. 9, which was sent to press around the same time. For updates, see 'Postscript' at the end of the chapter; some minor revisions of bibliography are made within the main text and notes. I have not altered the argument.

[1] Stanley R. Witkowski and Cecil H. Brown (1977) have proposed a 'weaker' version of the encoding sequence (repeated in Witkowski and Brown 1981; see also Sun 1983). As David Turton remarks (1980: 333), this may go too far in accommodating particular languages within the general scheme when other arguments could be used to explain exceptions. Here I use the 1975 reformulation of the Berlin and Kay sequence (as presented schematically by Turton), which is in harmony with the Egyptian data and differs less from their original proposal than does that of Witkowski and Brown. Except in the use of grey, the Egyptian material is also compatible with the 1969 sequence. The 1969 discussion remains fundamental.

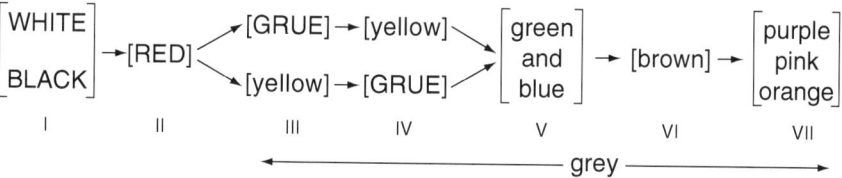

Fig. 25. Colour encoding sequence (after Turton 1980: 313 fig. 2); schematic version of data in, for example, Kay (1975: 260–1); Kay and McDaniel (1978: 639 fig. 13).

only one. If the categories have any meaning, they should exist outside language, because there is no constraint in language that would require precisely this set or 'evolutionary' order to obtain (see also Sun 1983). So far, studies in this area have used primarily physiological and psychological data. It is therefore desirable to investigate suitable non-linguistic but specifically cultural material in relation to the linguistically based theory of Berlin and Kay.

Here, unusual ancient Egyptian evidence is valuable, for it shows colour being used as well as spoken about. This material fits neatly with Berlin and Kay's linguistic hypothesis, placing it in a different light and suggesting some alternative reasons for its organization and 'evolution'. In this article I explore 'perceptual' and 'evolutionary' implications of Egyptian colour terminology and of colour classification as it can be seen in coloured decoration and in pictorial representation, concentrating on the latter material. Whereas Berlin and Kay treat the use of colour terms as a 'response', this can scarcely hold for pictorial representation (e.g. Gombrich 1977 [1960]; Schäfer 1986 [1974]), of which colouring is a part; evidence in paint may therefore reveal different aspects of the issues. At the end of the chapter I return to these questions and consider whether Berlin and Kay's model for explaining the progress of languages along the encoding sequence is adequate, or whether an 'active' model, in which the ordering of experience is central, would be more appropriate.

EGYPTIAN COLOUR TERMINOLOGY

Egyptian colour words are attested from the mid-third millennium BCE to the Middle Ages, and appear not to have changed greatly during that immense period. Partial extensions of the set of basic terms may have occurred in restricted social contexts and periods, but they did not leave an enduring legacy.

Egyptologists have studied this terminology more or less independently of other work in the area, have entertained hypotheses similar to those of other scholars, and in one respect have arrived at conclusions in advance of more widely known disciplines. In an important study, Wolfgang Schenkel (1963) anticipated some features of the work of Berlin and Kay, dividing Egyptian colour terminology into 'basic' and 'secondary' and arranging the basic terms on a biconical rather than a 'Mercator' diagram (1963: 145 fig. 4; compare Kay and McDaniel 1978: 628 fig. 8). Schenkel concluded that there are four basic colour terms (not his way of putting it) in Egyptian: BLACK ($km(m)$), WHITE ($ḥḏ$), RED ($dšr$), and GRUE ($wȝḏ$). Schenkel formulated his conclusions in terms of 'warm' and 'cool' colours rather than the foci of red and green/blue, anticipating much discussion that followed in the wake of Berlin and Kay (and unnoticed in that discussion). To the four terms of Schenkel should perhaps be added $sȝb$, a texture term meaning 'variegated' or 'multicoloured', used for animals' skins, birds' plumage, and snakes' skins, but apparently not for anything else (Erman and Grapow 1930: 15 ref. 13; 16 ref. 3). This terminology corresponds to Berlin and Kay's Stage IIIa. The only subsequent discussions of the terms are those of Alfred Hermann (1969), who wished to reinstate a basic term for 'blue', the existence of which was denied by Schenkel (1963: 142), and of Emma Brunner-Traut (1977), who does not address the same issues directly (see also Weeks 1979: 66–8; see further n. 3 here). The proposal of Hermann is effectively excluded by the Berlin and Kay theory (which he could not have known), because the term Egyptian should have acquired after GRUE is not blue but yellow. Other evidence, such as the fact that blue plays no part in colour symbolism in texts (Kees 1943), also speaks against Hermann's view. Schenkel's analysis still stands, and words for blue, of which there are at least two, $ḥsbḏ$ and $jrtjw$ (also sometimes applied to red objects), are secondary.

In distributing the chromatic terms $dšr$ and $wȝḏ$ on his biconical diagram, Schenkel assumed that they designated sectors of the colour solid. Since the work of Berlin and Kay this is known to be improbable, because colour terms have a focus, rather than delineating an area. Instead of saying that $dšr$ covers both red and yellow, we should say that it describes 'warm' colours (as Schenkel also put it) and focalizes in red; similarly, $wȝḏ$ almost certainly has its focus in green. The work of Berlin and Kay allows a better understanding of how colours, and, in Egypt, the use of colours on the monuments, can be related to colour terms, but it does not affect the basic findings of Schenkel.

According to the analysis of Benno Landsberger (1967), Sumerian and Akkadian, the languages of ancient Mesopotamia, also possess four basic colour terms: BLACK (Sum.: gi_6/gig_2/Akk.: $ṣalmu$), WHITE (babbar/$peṣû$), RED ($su_4/sa_5/sāmu$), and GRUE ($si_{12}/sig_7/(w)arqu$), as well as a word, gunu₃/*burrumu*, for 'variegated'.² These are given in the canonical bilingual lexical list ur₅-ra—*hubullu*, in the order just used, except that 'variegated' comes between RED and GRUE—possibly pointing to a later incorporation of GRUE in the set. Sumerian and Akkadian are unrelated languages, although there was mutual influence, especially from the former to the latter; the constancy in colour terms across a change in language and language family emphasizes the primacy of non-linguistic factors in the formation of the set. In their basic colour terms, the two most important civilizations of the ancient Near East are thus identical.

It might be possible to reduce the Egyptian terminology further and reconstruct an original three-term set in which *w3d* (GRUE) was absent or secondary (Berlin and Kay's Stage II); such a set could have existed before the Old Kingdom (*c*.2600; for comparable reconstructions, see Witkowski and Brown 1981). *w3d* is the least 'stable' of the terms, also meaning 'fresh' and 'papyrus stem', both of which senses have strong symbolic associations. It can even describe an archetypally red object, the king's 'red crown', but this can be explained without assuming a reduced terminology (Schenkel 1963: 146; but compare Harris 1961: 226; see also Goebs 2007). The best interpretation is that red, whose symbolism can be negative, is being avoided, and such an avoidance is most neatly accomplished if the word substituted can be a colour term, so that the 'fresh' crown also implies the 'non-red' one.³ The other basic terms also have strong non-colour associations: *km(m)* (BLACK) with 'Egypt (*kmt*)' or the colour of the soil, *hd* (WHITE) with 'silver' (also *hd*; reduced to that meaning in Coptic), and *dšr* (RED) with 'desert (*dšrt*)'. It is not, therefore, possible to argue that, unlike the others, *w3d* is not 'abstract' enough to be a basic colour term. Despite its ambiguous status, the evidence

---

² Landsberger did not use any particular theory of colour terminology; the revised readings of the Sumerian terms given here were provided by Norman Yoffee and Graham Cunningham. For Old Testament Hebrew, also a Stage III system, see Brenner (1982).

³ For a comparable 'anomalous' use of 'green', see M. Lionel Bender on Sudanese Arabic (1983). Helen Whitehouse remarks (personal communication) that some alternations of green and blue stones in Egyptian inlay work imply a basic colour term under which they would be grouped; the only candidate for such a term is *w3d* (see also below). Schenkel (1963: 146–7) analyses Old Kingdom painted colours with the same general point in mind and concludes that basic colour terms influenced alternations of blue and green and of red and yellow (he now believes that the statistical aspect of his presentation was not valid [personal communication]). As he states, there is also a certain visual logic in the alternations. The relevance of this evidence to the status of *w3d* remains uncertain; compare the approach of John A. Lucy and Richard A. Shweder (1979). Lise Manniche (1982; a promised sequel seems not to have appeared), who does not consider *w3d* a 'genuine' colour term, relates coloured inlays to colour classification. Her argumentation, however, is not theoretically informed and several of her conclusions are implausible.

for excluding it from an original set is insufficient. In all known stages, Egyptian possessed a set of four basic colour terms.[4]

Coptic, the post-antique successor of Egyptian, has a set of terms derived etymologically from Egyptian, with one or two changes (Schenkel 1963: 144–5; see in general Černý 1976; Westendorf 1965–77; Vycichl 1984). The repertory is *kmom* (BLACK), *ubaš* or *alaw* (WHITE), *tōrš* (RED), and *wōt* (GRUE). In addition, there is a term, *mroš*, of uncertain focus in the red area. If this is a basic colour term, there are two with apparently similar meaning, and one of them might turn out to be 'yellow'. If so, some stage or dialect of Coptic may have had a terminology corresponding to Stage IV of Berlin and Kay. Both *tōrš* and *mroš* derive from Egyptian roots with red associations, so that etymology does not offer a solution.[5]

Colour symbolism in Egyptian religious texts supports Schenkel's interpretation (Kees 1943). The only symbolically important colours are the basic four, together with *s3b* 'variegated'. This symbolism is to a great extent independent of the equally religious symbolism visible on coloured monuments, where a larger number of basic colours is employed (discussed below). There are points of contact between texts and colour on the monuments in such contexts as descriptions of the bodily forms of gods in terms of coloured minerals, including gold, silver, lapis lazuli, turquoise, Egyptian faience (an artificial substance), jasper, and carnelian. Although these descriptions, which correspond with the use of precious substances in the manufacture and inlay of statues and reliefs, enable additional colour values to appear in texts, they are specialized and in many instances metaphorical (e.g. Lichtheim 1973: 220; 1976: 198; Fecht 1965: 52–5; Harris 1961: 222–3; see also n. 3 here).

As well as basic colour terms, Egyptian possesses a word for 'colour', *jwn* or *jnm* (Harris 1961: 225–6; on words for 'colour', see Conklin 1973: 934). There are sufficient examples of *jwn/jnm* meaning the 'colour' of a material for it to be clear that this is an autonomous usage. These roots also have the meanings 'skin' and 'character'; in Egyptian terms, colour is an indissociable part of anything (Kees 1943: 414–15). The presence of a word for 'colour' shows that

[4] Another pointer to a three-term set might be the black, white, red, and variegated calves in the ritual of 'striking the calves' (Blackman and Fairman 1949–50; see also Egberts 1995: 256, 337; the scene type is known from the Old Kingdom on: Borchardt et al. 1913: 115–16, pl. 47). Cattle do not, however, provide a good 'model' for green (compare Turton 1980: 333–4), and there could be other reasons for this choice of colours. In one commentary from the Ptolemaic period (305–30), the 'red' and 'variegated' are glossed as 'green' and 'blue' (?—*jrtjw*; Blackman and Fairman's [1949] no. 4), which shows that there was no simple understanding of the colours.

[5] *mroš* may derive through Graeco-Roman Egyptian *mrš* from earlier *mnš(t)*, possibly a word for red ochre (Harris 1961: 146–7; Schenkel 1963: 145; Westendorf 1965–77: 100; Černý 1976: 89). There are various words for ochre pigments (Harris 1961: 141–62), one of which could have become specialized for yellow ochre, but this would have to have been a development from the period after Egyptian civilization had disappeared.

colour was perceived as a distinct domain, but it is uncertain how much general significance can be attributed to this fact. The prominence of colour symbolism and classification in a culture may be in inverse ratio to the complexity of colour terminology and to the use of abstractions for ordering phenomena. Here one might compare the Stage II language of the Ndembu of Zambia with the role of colour classification in their rituals (Turner 1966). In psychological testing, colour is preferred to form or function as a criterion of classification precisely by those who will have a relatively restricted vocabulary of basic colour terms (cf. Cole and Scribner 1974: 90–4).

POLYCHROMY: NATURE AND STATUS OF THE EVIDENCE

In strong contrast with Egyptian colour terminology, the evidence for the *use* of colour in Egypt is unique. All representations in sculpture in the round, relief sculpture, and painting were ideally completed in full colour, and much colour is preserved on monuments and objects from earlier periods (c.2600–1000; cf. Reuterswärd 1958). Little of what is preserved and now vanishing is published, but it is still possible to make a better comparison between linguistic and artistic colour classification in Egypt than almost anywhere else. Except in the work of Schenkel, one bar to progress has been a tacit assumption that colour use and colour terminology should coincide.[6]

Egyptian painting is basically polychrome, that is, it uses colours in solid patches or, more rarely, in textures and patterns.[7] Shading (e.g. Davies and Gardiner 1936, II, pl. 91) is extremely rare, and colour perspective and other similar modifications almost unknown. Each colour indicates in schematic fashion that the class of object shown is 'red', 'green', and so forth; it does not show the colour of a particular object or of that object as seen on a particular occasion. The same is generally true of Egyptian representation, which shows objects and scenes in the first place as examples of categories or types and secondarily—if at all—in their specific appearance (Schäfer 1986 [1974]; Ch. 9 here). In the present context, what is at issue is not so much the representational role of colour as the number of colours used and how far they form a set. If the number is stable and the usage consistent, the set of colours in pictorial representation and decoration should reflect a classification of colours—within the technical limitations of pigment production—irrespective

---

[6] In the description, I mention few works earlier than Schenkel (1963). Where possible, I quote well-published monuments in order to ease verification.

[7] Ransom Williams (1932); Davies and Gardiner (1936: III, xxxvii–xli); Smith (1949: 255–72); Lucas and Harris (1962: 338–46); Schenkel (1963: 131–2).

of how precisely it is used (compare Vincent J. Bruno's comments, 1977: 50, on classical Greece). The colour categories that are reflected in representation exist outside it, just as the set of colour terms in a language attests to, but does not itself constitute, a colour classification.

In theory, it would be possible to have wholly arbitrary colour conventions, but in fact the choice of colours in Egyptian painting seems relatively natural and its motivation straightforward. There is, in addition, a non-realistic, symbolic use of colour, in which, for example, figures of deities may have a blue or green skin. Because of the association skin–colour–nature, these colours may in part display the 'nature' of the being who is depicted, but colours are also used in more arbitrary fashion, so that sets of figures are coloured according to numerical schemes, and different parts of a figure may have distinct, non-realistic colours for reasons of pattern (Baines 1985c: appendix). Such examples demonstrate that colours are not always believed to be inherent in the figures that receive them and may convey meaning as a set. Since blue is very prominent in patterning, the set must be excerpted from the range of colours used in paint, not one defined by basic colour terms in language.

The precise shade of painted colours is in part technically determined. Pigments are not completely stable and have suffered loss and occasional discolouration since antiquity (cf. Green 2001); the original character of painting often has to be reconstructed (compare Ransom Williams 1932: pl. 13 with pl. 12). In any case, the Egyptians seem not to have been concerned with reproducing identical shades in paint, so it is not relevant to define the shades of the different colours on a chart (for values, see Schenkel 1963: 136–8). An obvious illustration of this is where figures of men in a layered row are painted in alternating lighter and darker shades of red (e.g. Davies and Gardiner 1936: I, pls. 28 mid, 45, 48; II, pls. 60, 61 [men and women], 63, 71, 73, 81 [Nubians], 98). The colour is mostly the conventional male red, and the alternation is there for the visual purposes of making the picture more attractive and easily decodable. Men are red and women yellow (with many exceptions).[8] Here, different colours were used to keep categories apart and to say something about ideals of beauty, in which women were paler, probably because they led a more indoor life (cf. Fischer 1963: 17–22).

Colours in the polychrome repertory are not restricted to single shades. From as early as the beginning of the Old Kingdom (c.2550), different shades

---

[8] Both the differentiation of red and the complex question of skin colour would repay further study (cf. Staehelin 1977). The same basic convention occurs in painting of classical antiquity, from as early as the 7th century BCE (Pfuhl 1923, I: 498).

of a single colour, especially of red, occur side by side.[9] The colours—red, yellow, etc.—remain distinct, however, and gradations of colour within one patch of paint are rare in all periods.

Another significant feature of colouring is that coloured textures such as brindled animal skins, unlike other types of shading, occur alongside plain colours. This may relate to the importance of the texture term *ssb* 'variegated', which is paralleled in Mesopotamia (see above). This prominence has parallels elsewhere, as in Mursi, in which all colour terms are ultimately terms for cattle colour or pattern and texture on cattle hides (Turton 1980: 320). Texture terminology, which can be far more specific than colour terms, appears to have received little attention (see also Turton 1980: 328–9).

The schematic character of Egyptian colour use justifies an attempt to analyse the colour classification it implies, as well as the development of that classification, in relation to the Berlin and Kay theory.

THE CHANGING SET OF COLOURS IN PAINT

Painted colours changed significantly between the Old Kingdom (*c.*2550) and the later New Kingdom (*c.*1540–1070), and evolved further by the Graeco-Roman period (332 BCE–*c.*250 CE). The sparsely recorded but relatively abundant Graeco-Roman evidence shows that colour use in that period was different from, and more heavily symbolic than, that of earlier times.

The Old Kingdom repertory of painted colours consists of black, white, red, green, yellow, blue, grey.[10] Red tends, as in all periods, toward brown, and yellow tends to be an ochre shade. These characteristics might relate to the objects for which the colours are used—because bright red or yellow men and women would not look natural—but they could also be the result of the technical origin of the pigments, or of a compromise between the two factors. In any case, they are far from the foci of these colours as defined by Berlin and Kay.

The first four of these colours are covered in an obvious way by colour terms in the Egyptian language. In normal usage, yellow would probably be described by the same word as red, and blue by the same as green; how grey would be designated is uncertain.

---

[9] A slab stela of the 4th dynasty (Junker 1929: pl. 27, Hildesheim, Pelizaeus-Museum 2145, checked on original; see now Manuelian 2003: 26–7 pls. 25–6, 98–103) has three different reds, on the human figure, bread (darker), and standards. See also, e.g., Moussa and Altenmüller (1977: frontispiece, top left: men and desert animals; top right: men and boat).

[10] The colour brown, mentioned by William Stevenson Smith (1949: 255–6) among other authors, is of uncertain status and much too rare to be included among standard colours.

Blue is not found in the earliest material, but from its introduction in the form of an artificial frit around 2550 it was used as a normal colour along with the others. Many features of its usage show that it was the most prestigious colour in paint, and in later periods it came to be the commonest, but in the Old Kingdom it was sufficiently rare to be worthy of note. In the 5th dynasty biographical text of Niankhsakhmet (c.2450), the protagonist states that the king 'caused pigment (?) to be placed in' the hieroglyphs on the false door destined for his tomb, and they were 'inscribed' in 'blue (ḫsbd)', an implied contrast with the more widespread and less prestigious green paint used for inscriptions (Sethe 1933: 39 lines 2–3; Posener-Kriéger, 1983: 52, reported another occurrence of 'inscribed in blue' in an unpublished text). ḫsbd is also the word for lapis lazuli, which was not used as a pigment (it was so used in the European Middle Ages), so that here it should have the transferred sense of blue, either the pigment or the colour (the object the text describes, which is preserved, shows no abnormal treatment).[11] As a term ḫsbd is secondary (Schenkel 1963); in context here it describes a significant favour bestowed on Niankhsakhmet. In normal speech, he might have used w3ḏ for both blue and green, but here it was necessary to be more specific.

Whereas blue is a latecomer in paint, yellow is not. It is derived from an easily available mineral and was used in all periods (Lucas 1962: 349–51). It is therefore especially significant that there is no basic colour term for yellow in Egyptian.

Grey is seldom a specific colour in Old Kingdom depictions of objects, but it was used, often as a blue-grey, as an overall background to scenes (Ransom Williams 1932: 70). It also occurs in the texture of goose plumage in an early 4th dynasty painting (c.2550)[12] and extensively on slab stelae dating from a few decades later (Manuelian 2003). On these, grey appears to substitute for both green (present, but sparingly used) and blue, the chief colours employed being black (also used for more objects than normal), white, red, yellow, and grey.[13] The reasons for the near-absence of green are not clear, but the distribution of colours can be understood as the result of scarcity or restriction, not of unusual terminology or classification. Among the earliest uses of grey for large areas of figures are grey donkeys of the First Intermediate period (c.2150–2040; e.g. Baines and Malek 2000: 82; Stadelmann 1962: 57 with n. 1;

---

[11] J. R. Harris (1961: 149) suggests that this does not refer to the normal pigment but to the very rare azurite; I assume a contrast with green.

[12] Mekhitarian (1954: 9). The colour in the original publication (Petrie 1892) is unreliable.

[13] Iunu (Junker 1929: pl. 27); Wepemnofret (colour: Arnold and Ziegler 1999 no. 52); Louvre, stela of Nofretiabet (ibid. no. 51). On the last of these, green seems to be entirely absent; a special pale yellow/cream is used for the woman owner's skin. Nefer (ibid. no. 53) bears faint traces of colour. Full treatment of the stelae as a whole: Manuelian (2003).

New Kingdom example: Mekhitarian 1954: 26). In contrast with the earlier cases, the representational purpose of grey here is straightforward, because donkeys are distinctively grey.

The Old Kingdom repertory of painted colours thus corresponds neatly with Stage V of the Berlin and Kay encoding sequence for language (Fig. 25).[14]

Little suitable coloured material from the Middle Kingdom (c.2040–1140) has been published adequately. In this period the general character of colouring was not very different from that of the Old Kingdom, but there may be one significant development. Red is differentiated more frequently and in an increasing number of shades. On the elaborately painted coffin published by Edward L. B. Terrace (1968), several reds occur, including a dark one used for copper, which might better be described as a brown (e.g. pls. 15, 16, 19, 20), and in at least one case there is a very pale tone that looks like a distinct pink.[15] Possible browns are found in other paintings of the period (e.g. Davies and Gardiner 1936: I, pl. 5 [copper, as on Terrace's coffin], pl. 6, mid-right and lower, pl. 9 [tree]). This sparse evidence for the division of red into distinct colours—as opposed to shades of the same colour—is suggestive, because it fits with the sequence of Berlin and Kay, in which the four 'primaries', red, yellow, green, and blue, are distinguished before 'secondary' colours, and the first 'secondary' division is in the most salient primary colour, red (see also Turton 1980: 331–2; Sahlins 1977: 168, 175). If brown is a distinct colour, it enlarges the previous repertory without changing the basic approach to colouring.

In New Kingdom material (c.1530–1070), the use of colour becomes richer and more diverse and develops within the period, especially from 1400 to 1250. Restricted and specialized colour repertories occur.[16] Pink is found in this period[17] and is not always a lighter red, which would often be a beige because of the basic shade of Egyptian red (Lucas 1962: 346; see also examples cited in n. 9 here). Brown becomes rather more frequent.[18] The extended range is black, white, red, green, yellow, strong blue, light blue, grey, brown, pink.

---

[14] The restricted 4th dynasty repertory resembles Berlin and Kay's stage IIIb (yellow acquired before GRUE), but this is probably coincidence.

[15] Terrace (1968: 41) stated that pink occurs 'throughout', but neither his plates nor his comments on them support this assertion. Only on plate 19 does there seem to be a clear pink, and even this is uncertain.

[16] e.g. Davies and Gardiner (1936, I, pl. 39: black, white, and red only; also southerly extension of the temple of Sety I at Abydos; see further Baines 2001). There are entire 'monochrome' 19th dynasty tombs that use black, white, yellow, some red, and, very occasionally, blue (Bruyère 1952, with the plausible suggestion on pp. 9–10 that the yellow was in substitution for gold).

[17] e.g. Davies and Gardiner (1936: I, pl. 44: shirts over torsos; II, pl. 70: jars on right; pl. 102: human body in contrast with desert).

[18] e.g. Davies and Gardiner (1936: II, pl. 76: papyrus umbel bases; pl. 78: Nubians and horses).

Of the eleven basic colours of Berlin and Kay, only orange and purple are absent. Thus, in more elaborate works, New Kingdom paint usage is a partial parallel for their Stage VII in language (Fig. 25).[19]

According to Berlin and Kay (1991 [1969]: 20), languages that have progressed beyond Stage VI (addition of brown) and include any of the Stage VII colours, purple, pink, and orange, normally acquire all three rapidly. Both the division of blue noted above and the absence of purple and orange should therefore be considered, but for purple I can offer no specific explanation. The New Kingdom painted set is not among those attested in Berlin and Kay's tables (1991 [1969]: 3 table 1, 21 table 3). However, this point does not seem to have any theoretical significance. As Berlin and Kay note (1991 [1969]: 3), only 22 out of 2,048 logically possible patterns were known at the time of composition of their monograph; whereas some new patterns would speak against their hypothesis, this one does not.

I have included the division of blue in the list of New Kingdom colours because it is very noticeable[20] and because blue divides into two, and not, like red, in a variety of ways. The different blues are not, however, normally used to differentiate between classes of objects, and there is no reason for thinking that the second blue is an important extra category as it is, for example, in modern Russian. Rather, it is a mark of the prestige of blue in Egyptian polychromy. It occurs so much and is the object of so much attention that it is subdivided. Coloured inlays, in which the use of colour is more varied and more arbitrary than it is in paint, can also have two blues (Manniche 1982).

Orange is not a distinct colour, but Egyptian yellow is often half way to orange, and so might not easily have been divided; pigment production could also have been difficult. There are, however, notable subdivisions of yellow that show how orange could develop, and costly new pigments were used as well as the traditional yellow ochre (Erika Feucht, personal communication;

---

[19] Painting palettes add an ambiguity (Glanville 1932; Carter 1933: pl. 23A; Hayes 1959: 256, fig. 154; Grand Palais 1982: 315, no. 293; Helck 1982). They are intended for painting miniature vignettes, and have holes for blocks of ink and painting pigments. Two of those cited have 6 holes, for the 6 canonical colours (grey being made by mixing black or black and blue with white), one has 7 (6 plus 1 for black ink?), one has 14 (two rows of 6, with a larger pair for ink), and one 11 (2 for ink and 9 for colours). The ones with 7 and 11 holes have inscriptions for craftsmen. Only the latter (Glanville 1932: pl. 8, no. 3) has a suitable number of holes for the enlarged colour repertory. This suggests that the new usage of colours was not widespread, or that it did not much influence the design of traditional equipment (see also Schenkel 1963: 147). It is possible that the range of colours used in small vignettes was smaller than in wall paintings.

[20] e.g. Davies and Gardiner (1936: II, pls. 87–9, 104; also temple of Ramesses II at Abydos, offering series in first hypostyle hall).

McCarthy 2001; Colinart 2001). Where objects of gold are depicted, their colour is often different from, and more orange than, other yellow in the same composition (e.g. Davies and Gardiner 1936: II, pl. 53). Such objects are outlined in a darker colour that is not otherwise used and could be seen as a dark orange or brown. Thus, in this area, differentiations comparable with yellow/orange/brown can be observed, but they do not correspond with the normal foci of these colours and are too closely tied to the depiction of particular objects and materials to be generalized. They are comparable with secondary colour terms in language, but they demonstrate the potential, as it were, for the introduction of orange in painting. The question remains, whether there could be a classification including orange (and purple) that was not realized in paint or in language.[21] It may well prove impossible to address such a question for a non-contemporary society.

As is clear from blue and 'orange', late 18th–19th dynasty colouring is at the limit of polychromy. Further elaboration would take the system, which is already far outside Egyptian basic colour terms, beyond 'basic colours' altogether. Polychrome colour operates like a conceptual classification, in keeping with the 'conceptual' character of Egyptian pictorial representation. There is a fundamental kinship between polychromy and non-perspective representation, and, conversely, between perspective and what would in western art be called 'painterly' colouring. If there is a painterly accommodation to the visual image, in which shading is used and the incidental effects of light may be recorded, this will render inappropriate any attempt to see colour classification in painting as being related to discrete colour concepts. For this reason, an investigation of the colour terminology of classical antiquity in parallel with preserved wall paintings, for example, would not show whether classical colour classification went beyond the rather restricted colour terminologies of the time (for Homeric Greek, see Berlin and Kay 1991 [1969]: 70–1; P. G. Maxwell-Stuart, 1981, does not consider theoretical issues). As colour use moves away from a few clearly demarcated categories, its role in symbolism may decline. In realistic representation, the classificatory and symbolic use of colour can become anomalous.

In later 18th dynasty material (c.1400), in which the most striking developments occur, colouring in narrowly religious contexts—principally temple relief—diverges from that of the most sophisticated works in other areas. In one case the non-temple style even occurs in another part of the same wall as 'religious' temple painting (temple of Amenhotep III at Wadi el-Sebua:

---

[21] For orange and yellow among representational glass inlays of the 4th century BCE, see e.g. Scamuzzi (n.d.: pl. 109); Malek (2003: 318–19).

Baines 1985c: 361–2, with refs.). Among the extant evidence, the non-temple colouring scarcely survived the general decline in non-religious art in the 19th–20th dynasties—a decline that forms part of a tendency visible in many cultural spheres. At least in their artistic context, the new colours and treatments seem to have acquired secular associations that contributed to their later rarity.

In consequence, New Kingdom innovations do not seem to have been built upon in later periods, except in a tendency to use special ranges of shades. Colouring differs in secular and religious works, but the basic colours are the same in both. The general colour effect of Graeco-Roman period reliefs (332 BCE–c.250 CE) is much more pastel than that of the New Kingdom, but there is still no shading, so that it should be possible to analyse its repertory in terms similar to those employed above; the transition to a painterly treatment is not made.[22]

As noted above, in all periods painted colour could be applied in a symbolic rather than realistic or narrowly classificatory fashion. Because of the divergence between terminology and paint, this symbolic use is necessarily different from colour symbolism in texts, but there are many correspondences. Blue is the most prestigious painted colour; it is also employed in the most obviously non-realistic way. Among symbolic references that can be discovered for blue are water, as when the body of a figure is in one example covered with water lines and in another blue (Baines 1985c: appendix z), and air and sky, which are probably the referents of the blue body colour of the god Amun. The ceilings of New Kingdom royal tombs are dark blue, symbolizing primarily the night sky. In the Graeco-Roman period, blue abrogates distinctions hallowed in texts and on the monuments: there are blue painted examples of the very ancient white and red crowns of Egyptian kings, the colours of which were also their principal names. Here blue appears to be used for its own prestige and perhaps for a general association with the premier semi-precious stone, lapis lazuli.[23] Such cases are valuable in showing that blue acquired a discrete symbolism as well as pictorial functions, even though

---

[22] There is probably enough surviving colour for a study of the native temples of this period, but no painting is adequately published. These temples are fully Egyptian and a good source of evidence. Much non-temple painted material from the period fuses Egyptian, Greek, and sometimes other elements and so would pose additional challenges for interpretation.

[23] Blue examples of the crowns: Edfu birth house, south exterior wall; Esna, column south of axis; Kom Ombo, column in forecourt. Katja Goebs points me to identifications of the white crown in the Middle Kingdom Coffin Texts as being 'fresh (w3d)', which can also mean 'green', and one where it is stated to be of lapis lazuli. The potential for such symbolic uses of the colour blue was thus embedded in metaphorical usage in language from an altogether earlier date. See Goebs (2007: discussions of Coffin Text spells 398, 473).

there is no basic colour term for blue.²⁴ This pattern of attestation contradicts statements like Landsberger's that although the Babylonians perceived colours as we do, 'they could not see [lapis lazuli] as blue, because they simply did not know what blue is' (1967: 140, n. 7 from p. 139; translation John Baines). Like Egyptians, Babylonians knew 'what blue is', but 'simply' did not say so.

This use of blue suggests that experiments such as those of Eleanor Rosch Heider (1972; see also von Wattenwyl 1979; Jernudd 1983), in which people whose mother tongues had restricted colour terminologies learned to 'activate' additional Berlin and Kay categories and showed greater aptitude for 'focal' than for 'intermediate' tones, essentially replicate processes that can take place without external stimulus or change in the basic colour terms in a language. (Here, the attempt of John Lucy and Richard Shweder [1979] to controvert Rosch Heider's and Berlin and Kay's results is unconvincing.)

DISCUSSION; COGNITIVE IMPLICATIONS

If the Egyptian language is at Stage IIIa of the Berlin and Kay sequence, while painting in the Old Kingdom is at Stage V, in the Middle Kingdom perhaps at Stage VI, and in the New Kingdom at a partial Stage VII, language will be ill-adapted to describing some of the different, for the most part clearly demarcated, colours used in paint—although descriptive phrases or terms for pigments could no doubt be employed.²⁵ Here, the main point is the demarcation of the colours: if they shaded gradually into one another, no terminology would be adequate, as the compilers of colour charts know only too well. The Egyptian basic colour terms cannot be the stimuli to increase the range of colours in paint. Still less can they provoke the movement from the narrower Old Kingdom repertoire to the wider one of the New Kingdom. In the Old Kingdom, yellow, blue, and grey were produced in response to non-linguistic requirements, the case of blue being noteworthy because an

---

[24] Waltraud Guglielmi remarks (personal communication) on the common occurrence of words for blue in Graeco-Roman temple texts. In some cases, this seems to be an arbitrary extension, as when the sun god is said to 'make the fields blue (ḥsbd)' (Rochemonteix 1892: 71, line 11; 106, lines 2–3; see also Wilson 1997: 750–1). Such usages in texts may parallel the vast expansion of the use of blue paint in temple reliefs. They did not produce a general basic colour term for blue. The dead language in which these texts were written (Classical Egyptian of some 1500 years earlier) may have come to use ḥsbd/ḥsdb and/or jrtjw as a basic term for blue, but the context is highly specialized.

[25] Words for pigments are attested for yellow and blue, which lack basic colour terms (Harris 1961: 160–2). The evidence for pigment names appears to be incomplete. The discussion of Ingrid Blom-Böer (1994), in which she compares pigment use and colour terminology, does not go beyond what was already known for the latter.

artificial pigment was invented.[26] The polychrome evidence therefore suggests that the seven-colour 'Stage V' set existed before any verbal representation of it, and that it formed a set of foci corresponding approximately to those of Berlin and Kay.[27] Its visual elaboration must be in response to stimulus from patrons or artists, so that logically it will have existed in some other form, if not in an explicitly recognized set, before it was painted. Art was central to Egyptian high culture, and it is not surprising that resources and creativity were exploited for the production of new pigments. It remains significant that those pigments had no major linguistic correlates except words for minerals and their names as pigments (n. 25 here).

The date of origin of the classification of seven (or more) colours cannot be investigated; it can only be said that it coexisted with a Stage III four-colour terminology for a very long period. I add 'or more' to allow for the possibility that the seven-colour 'Stage V' set was excerpted from a larger acknowledged number of foci—up to the 'universal' eleven of Berlin and Kay. This is, however, improbable, because the seven correspond with a stage in the Berlin and Kay encoding sequence, which is unlikely to be coincidence. A better hypothesis would be that, within the constraints of pigment production, interest in expanding the colour repertory follows roughly the same line as the encoding sequence—evidence is insufficient for a stronger formulation. Where possible, then, distinctions in paint emerge in the same order as in language. But whereas language is generally ahead of pictorial representation in recording explicitly visual phenomena such as the diminution of scale with distance (cf. Schäfer 1986 [1974]: 82–3), in the case of colour, language lags behind, at least in Egypt.[28] As is the case with music, colour is more easily seen and painted than talked about. Simple considerations of representation and recognition must play some part here, and they probably also relate to the encoding sequence. At a minimum, representation in black—or another colour—and white ('Stage I'), which produces figures in line or in solid colour, is comprehensible and very efficient, and has been the point of

---

[26] Although Lucas and Harris are cautious (1962: 342), there seems to be no good reason for doubting the 4th dynasty examples of Smith (1949: 256). The 5th dynasty text of Niankhsakhmet quoted earlier is an instance of blue colouring for prestige and symbolism, but Smith's material includes earlier conventionally representational cases. For a 4th dynasty painting in which blue is already used more widely than demanded by the logic of depiction, see Dunham and Simpson (1974: frontispiece; note that this is in a queen's tomb).

[27] Here, the status of grey is uncertain. Before the First Intermediate period it appears to signify simply 'coloured' (as discussed earlier). In view of the problematic status of grey both in the Berlin and Kay scheme and in the general organization of colour, this uncertainty is not surprising.

[28] This is true in a different sense of Hellenistic antiquity, when a full range of colours was used in a different mode of representation (partial perspective); no classification can be derived from this (see also n. 31).

departure for pictorial representation in most of the world.²⁹ At the other extreme, a system that concentrates on the Stage VII colours, pink, purple, and orange, will be affected, to say the least. Egyptian Old Kingdom works seem so natural that one does not miss the Stage VI and VII colours.

Like the Old Kingdom set, the slightly richer New Kingdom set should be seen as embodying a pre-existing larger visual repertory of colour foci. The question is whether the new colours were devised in response to a long-felt need for them, or more directly as a result of artistic developments that we can see were taking place. This issue is similar to, but narrower than, that of the stimulus to increase the number of basic colour terms, which Berlin and Kay relate tentatively to increasing 'cultural complexity' (1969: 16; see also Kay 1975; Friedl 1979; Turton 1980: 331–2; Witkowski and Brown 1981: 15). Such an explanation could apply to Egyptian New Kingdom culture, which was probably more plural, sophisticated, and technologically advanced than that of the Old Kingdom, with wider horizons of knowledge and experience. It is, however, initially more cautious to view the development within its context and assume that artistic and partly representational goals were being pursued. The new colours are not an isolated phenomenon, and in combination with other considerations this approach has suggestive, if speculative, implications.³⁰

The increase in the number of colours coincided with a proliferation of special pictorial techniques and unusual colour effects. This diversification may have been favoured by a concentration on the medium of painting rather than painted relief, and by the existence of much painting for secular contexts such as palaces and private houses (the latter poorly attested); a great deal of the finest work at this point was painting. This pattern contrasts with the Old Kingdom, when the normal medium was painted relief, of which colouring was the final stage and was often not reached. Painting encourages a freer treatment, and may have influenced other contemporaneous developments in conventions of representation. Examples of these are the occurrence of some full-face figures, occasional indication of the second breast on women, and the depiction of all the toes on the backward foot (cf. Schäfer 1986 [1974]; Ch. 9 §5 here). The most characteristic is perhaps a new treatment of drapery, in which the underlying colour of a figure is partly seen through cloth in a

---

[29] Here it might be worth investigating Palaeolithic painting, which also uses a very restricted set of colours. It could be argued that the availability of pigments was what determined their choice, but other approaches need not be ruled out.

[30] The argument of this chapter relates here to the conclusions on universals in pictorial representation, presented here in Ch. 9 §6, that are comparable with those in colour terminology and, I argue, in polychromy. Ancient Egypt provides particularly good evidence in this area (see Schäfer 1986 [1974]). This parallel, which I developed after composing the present chapter, gives added significance to the New Kingdom developments in colouring discussed here.

paler form, in some cases forming the distinct colour pink. Where this technique is combined with elaborate folding or pleating, there may be an approach to shading. Taken together, changes such as these show a slight but definite tendency away from conceptual representation toward realism, or accommodation to the visual image; in the case of drapery, the development is a fusion of the representational and the painterly, and is especially noteworthy because of parallels with drapery in the art of classical antiquity.

I argue in other chapters (Chs. 2 and 9) that in the 18th dynasty, detailed changes in non-royal inscriptions and elsewhere attest to a relativization of viewpoints, which suggests that the Egyptian elite approached the brink of a cognitive transformation comparable to that of archaic Greece, but that the breakthrough did not occur, while later periods show little sign of the approach to it. Here, the approximation to a Stage VII colour classification in paint is significant in offering a parallel, albeit remote, for the assumption that such systems in language are typical of 'highly industrialized ... peoples', and that 'the sequence of elaboration of colour lexicon is an evolutionary one accompanying, and perhaps a reflex of, increasing technological and cultural development' (Berlin and Kay 1991 [1969]: 16). If this parallel has any merit, it suggests that development toward more detailed classification of basic colours should be related as much to cognitive or intellectual change—in Egypt attested only for a tiny elite—as to broader social evolution. This need not always be the case; if and when colour terminology reflects colour classification accurately and is common to the speakers of a language (but see Kay 1975; Friedl 1979), in complex societies it will be used by people and sectors who vary in their intellectual attainments. In Egypt, the extended colour classification could have been confined to the elite (including artists and craftsmen), while the rest of society had the simpler set known from the language, but here it should be remembered that other methods of organizing colour and secondary colour terms may complicate the picture. Changes in colour classification are also more easily diffused, and relevant to more people, than—for example—the law of the excluded middle. Whatever the colour terminology and classification of classical Greece, where that law was formulated, the cautious statement of Berlin and Kay (1991 [1969]: 16) that their Stages I–III are found in languages 'spoken by peoples with small populations and limited technology' can be pursued a little further, because, at least in the material they collected in their original study, few large, complex societies have languages at Stages IV–VI either. I therefore doubt whether the distinction of societal complexity that Witkowski and Brown (1981) use for Stages II–VI is fundamental. Rather, I suggest that Stage VII, and in some cases perhaps Stages VI (Javanese and Malayalam in Berlin and Kay 1991 [1969]) and V (Hausa; Chinese Mandarin; Plains Tamil) show a more important change, but that such a change is not obligatory. The Egyptian material shows how uncertain such correlations are, because they use language, which is only one indicator of colour classification.

No society closely comparable with ancient Egypt exists today, and the development of Egypt cannot easily be matched with that of other societies, so the parallel I propose between changes in colour classification as evidenced in paint and other changes is uncertain. The model implied by the parallel is a multilayered one in which paint may reach its terminus in polychromy long before language attains a comparable stage. It follows that the process of enlargement of colour vocabularies described by Kay (1975) and Erika Friedl (1979) need not necessarily reflect change in colour classification. In Egypt, colour classification appears to have been refined without any change in colour vocabulary (except words for pigments). Its society, in which this transition occurred, was far removed from modern complex societies. Despite the indications of a possible transformation mentioned above, it was also far from the societies of the Greek Classical and Hellenistic periods, in which the next transition, to a painterly use of colour, took place.[31] These societies in their turn did not possess Stage VII colour terminologies and were very different from Berlin and Kay's 'highly industrialized ... peoples'. It is unlikely that any societies with Stage VII colour terminologies in language have a homogeneous polychrome painting system; thus it may be impossible to investigate parallels there. Be that as it may, the transition to a Stage VII set is probably an indicator of linguistic or, conceivably, cognitive change rather than of basic colour classification, which may reach an analogous point at a much earlier juncture in a process of development. There will be a number of stages on the way to the Stage VII set, not all of them detectable in language.

Since colour classification may expand and be used for pictorial representation independently of language, its evolution should reflect the active dissection of the environment and the elaboration of mid-range abstract categories rather than a 'response to an informationally richer visual environment' (Berlin and Kay 1991 [1969]: 16)—itself the product of a complex, active process of change and not a simple 'response' (compare also Sahlins 1977). It is not so much that the environment is informationally richer as that an informationally richer model of it is constructed, whether in language or in some other medium. If, as in Egypt, partly incommensurable sets are used in

---

[31] 'Four-colour' Greek painting of the Classical period used a restricted range of colours—black, white, red, and yellow—but not always so few pigments (Pfuhl 1923: I, viii, x; Robertson 1959: 13; Bruno 1977). This restriction came after a time when at least blue and green were used in addition. Bruno suggests that this style was the first stage in the notation of shading and perspective. It would then have led to the more fully 'painterly' colouring of the Hellenistic age.

different media, the selection and manipulation of them must be complex. The coexistence of such sets is evidently a routine matter for their users, but the choice between them should again be 'active'; the nature and significance of this routine would repay investigation.

Growth of mid-range abstractions of this sort seems fundamental to cognitive change. Abstractions of the highest order are found in societies of almost any type; as abstractions proliferate, their range lessens and their cognitive utility is enhanced. Dynamic evolutions such as these are more difficult to account for than 'responses'.

All this leaves open the original question of how universal the 'eleven basic perceptual colour categories' are and whether they are all put to non-linguistic use. The Egyptian polychrome evidence shows that the finding that more colour categories than are used in language are available to those who have a restricted terminology can be valid for very long periods of time, as well as demonstrating that the larger range can be employed actively and expanded in order to represent and classify the world. Such a characterization is bound to apply also to other societies. The Egyptian material includes most of the eleven colour categories, but because they undergo much the same 'evolutionary' development as language, they may not exist beforehand ready to be made visible in an expanding system. The simultaneous occurrence of diverging systems in language and in paint supports the hypothesis of a fairly full range of categories. If the colour solid were not focalized, the discrepancy between the systems would surely be awkward. The solid is therefore probably focalized, but areas of it are not closely mapped in language or in paint. If these, too, are always 'perceptual colour categories', they may not be easily available to their possessors, but could become available through progressive differentiation (see also Kay and McDaniel 1978: 638–44). In other words, a sudden large increment of explicit colour categories is unlikely except, possibly, with the change to a painterly use of colour. There, however, the correlation between paint colours and categories breaks down, and the two may develop in different directions.

CONCLUSION

The evolution of colour classification and colour use is an active process. The Berlin and Kay theory need not imply any simple 'determinism', as asserted, for example, by Paul Wald (1978). The Egyptian evidence supports the culturally-focused analysis of Marshall Sahlins (1977) and implies some revisions in the original theory. In exploring and ordering colour, people discriminate progressively between foci and construct increasingly complex models, which may differ in different media. These developments are strongly constrained by physiology and by the 'logic' of the colour solid, but they are motivated by social and cognitive factors, rather than determined by laws.

Egyptian material confirms that the Berlin and Kay encoding sequence pertains to other areas beyond language, supporting the general hypothesis of 'perceptual colour categories' and extending it beyond the 'primaries' discussed, for example, by Sahlins (1977) and Kay and McDaniel (1978). It also highlights other questions that must be tackled before a comprehensive theory of colour categories can be formulated.

POSTSCRIPT (2005)

Discussion

In retrospect, my 1985 treatment of colour classification was too straightforwardly accepting of the 'psychophysical' basis and 'basic perceptual color categories' proposed by Berlin and Kay in 1969; much subsequent work has questioned, modified, and weakened the points made at the beginning of this chapter. The existence of the 'Hering primaries' of black, white, red, yellow, green, and blue, which have some psychophysical basis and are often cited in later discussion of Berlin and Kay, also cannot account for processes of change or for divergences between categories in language and other modes of classification (for a convenient collection of studies, see Backhaus, Kliegl, and Werner 1998; notable among these is Hardin 1998). Nevertheless, with exceptions such as Barbara Saunders (e.g. 2000), work since 1969 has not led to a concerted rejection of the Berlin and Kay approach. Saunders argues for more locally based methods in recording and interpreting attitudes to colour—something few would argue against—although she seems additionally to doubt whether colour itself is a valid category (2000: 92; see also below). She does not provide any example of suitable data or of what she would accept as a proper analysis. Without any such pointers, her approach does not appear useful, while the Berlin and Kay hypothesis retains much of its attraction.

In this context, I would reiterate the arguments presented above, that ancient Egypt offers indigenous datasets that are simultaneously linguistic and non-linguistic and that can be investigated in relation to the Berlin and Kay hypothesis. This possibility may exist for other societies but appears not to have been investigated. The use of colour terms and of a word for 'colour' in Egyptian texts shows that we are dealing with an actors' and not only an observers' category (a point that is questioned, for example, by John Lyons, 1995). The long timespan of the Egyptian material makes it possible to offer a diachronic study of a type that has not been much pursued in work on colour terms. In my opinion, the lack of fit between the Egyptian linguistic and non-linguistic material in essence supports the Berlin and Kay approach, because the two groups of evidence and differences between them can be related to their hypothesis. My approach entails giving more attention to Berlin and Kay's original point that the hypothesis is not intrinsically about language but about human categorization, as evidenced in a particular domain. Most subsequent research in the area has been in linguistics or linguistic anthropology, on the one hand, or in neuroscience (broadly categorized) on the other hand, while the domain of the meaning of colour and its social use has seldom been a focus of relevant attention, no doubt in part because it is difficult to formalize (Kay's work in particular relies strongly on formalization and statistics; see references below). It may be worthwhile to see features of the colour solid and of human perception as providing predispositions that different societies exploit in different ways.

Berlin and Kay's correlation between the largest numbers of basic terms and 'highly industrial' societies could perhaps be taken in other ways, for example as suggesting that colour is good to discriminate with as social complexity renders such discrimination and context-free discussion more prevalent, whether for functional purposes or more simply as discrimination becomes easier to apply. Problems with any simple 'evolutionism' or 'behaviouristic' correlations of societal type and colour terminology are highlighted by Don Dedrick (1998: 91–4). Kay and Luisa Maffi (1999: 746) argue that 'cultural salience' of colour and number of colour terms may be correlated. They also reiterate earlier arguments that increases in colour terminology may correlate with technological complexity. A difficulty with both of these points is that they rather neglect the human actor; in this respect the approach of Sahlins (1977) is valuable because it highlights the contribution of culture to the meaning of colour. Since the deliberate use of pigment is among the oldest symbolic cultural traits plausibly attested for humans (Barham 1998), there is every reason to think that cultural salience for colour is a social given rather than something that has emerged with complex societies and civilizations. The drive to develop pigments and to discriminate increased numbers of (basic) colours is similarly cultural in focus and for millennia has been the object of intense effort and expenditure. The medieval and Renaissance use in Europe of ultramarine (ground lapis lazuli) as a pigment is a well-known example of the vast amounts invested in a desired colour. The symbolic and material use of colours is thus at least as much a motor of development as a response to technological change, while the fact that much material culture in the modern world is made easily identifiable by colour-coding (normally using simple and restricted colour sets) exemplifies colour's properties as a visual and classificatory resource and a medium for mapping distinctions, not necessarily its greater salience in the modern world. The intense and vivid use of colour on Egyptian monuments (e.g. Baines 2001) is another relevant example of its cultural salience in a premodern society. A comparable salience can be seen, for example, in ancient Greece (e.g. Brinkmann and Wünsche 2004). In this area, western culture since early modern times has been at a disadvantage in appreciating the full significance of colour because of its stress on published reproductions, which like photography were largely in monochrome until very recent years. Archaeologists have noted the same point, on the level both of colour symbolism (e.g. DeBoer 2005) and of colour use (e.g. Gage et al. 1999). An example of a study that is intended to address this gap is Stephen Houston's collaborative volume on Maya colour (in preparation).

A further aspect of the cultural significance of pigment and colour may be seen in fact that in both Egyptian and Mesopotamian languages texture terms seem to form part of basic sets alongside hue terms (evidence is cited in the chapter above). Although words for texture or surface are sources for basic colour terms in many languages, so far as I know this related domain has hardly been addressed for its own sake, no doubt in part because research on colour terms and classification has focused on language and specifically on hues; texture terms are also probably more difficult to study. If the cultural embedding of colour is to be comprehended, these wider relations will need to be addressed. Such an undertaking would amount to an ethnography of colour, which would be major undertaking for a single society, not to speak of several societies, and would be particularly difficult for societies of the past, in the record of which colour is almost always lost or very fragmentary. Perhaps that complicating aspect of research is one reason why my 1985 article, which is explicitly addressed to other domains in addition to language, is seldom cited in later anthropological literature, although it has a little more currency in archaeology (e.g. Gage et al. 1999; DeBoer 2005, cited only to exemplify difficulties).

Later bibliography and Egyptological discussion

A vast amount of further work on colour classification and on the Berlin and Kay hypothesis has been published since this chapter first appeared in 1985; a few items are cited in the update immediately above. Publications down to 1991 are listed in the reprint of *Basic color terms* (Berlin and Kay 1991 [1969]). Several collected volumes gather relevant research; examples are Lamb and Bourriau (1995), Hardin and Maffi (1997), and Borg (1999). A major contributor was the recently deceased Robert E. MacLaury (e.g. 1997; 1999). A wide-ranging hostile critique of the Berlin and Kay approach by Barbara Saunders and J. van Brakel (1997), with feedback from many writers, assembles a large bibliography. A more recent article of Kay and Maffi (1999) includes additional references and continues existing lines of research, which are further developed in later articles such as Kay and Regier (2003) and Regier, Kay, and Cook (2005); see also http://www.icsi.berkeley.edu/~kay/. Saunders (2000, also cited above) is an example of an attack on Berlin and Kay, and more broadly on colour science as a whole (extending Saunders and van Brakel 1997). A useful bibliography of colour studies is available at http://www.coloria.net/lahteet/artikkelit.htm, revised 30 August 2005. Three edited volumes on various aspects of colour appearing in 2006–7 are: Biggam and Kay (2006); Pitchford and Biggam (2006); Dedrick, MacLaury, and Paramei (2007).

On the Egyptological side, Davies (2001) contains a range of studies, only some of them relevant to the Berlin and Kay hypothesis. In that volume, Stephen Quirke (2001) presents some specific arguments against Berlin and Kay on the basis of a Late period Egyptian text that includes blue among symbolically important referents; he also summarizes related arguments of John Gage (1995) and John Lyons (1995). The set of terms that Quirke posits for Egypt would not fit the original formulation of the Berlin and Kay hypothesis, which would require Egyptian to acquire a basic term for yellow before one for blue. My article in the same volume (Baines 2001: esp. 155–6 n. 2) is not primarily concerned with Berlin and Kay but includes some bibliography as well as a brief discussion of Quirke's objections, based on the conference paper because I had not seen the article. I argue that this particular example is not very significant for the Berlin and Kay hypothesis and that Quirke's argument does not address the wider, non-linguistic context of attested Egyptian colour use. In this specific case the repertory of colours in paint is a better guide to classification than are colour terms; there is clear evidence for a painted colour yellow long before any word for it is attested, while blue as a pigment was a relative latecomer.

A more recent article on Egypt by David Warburton (2004) contains potentially useful bibliography, including references to a couple of studies of his own, but a number of the works he cites are not yet published and so cannot be considered here. I am not convinced by his approach, which mixes a variety of styles of evidence and analytical methods. I am very grateful to Wolfgang Schenkel for giving me access to his own new contribution on the subject (2007), which contains a most valuable review and documentation, as well as the important proposal that Coptic divides RED with two terms, focused in the darker and paler areas of the colour. If this idea finds favour, it will be a significant development that should be taken into account in future work.

12

Stone and other materials: usages and values

INTRODUCTION

Stone is fundamental to ancient Egyptian monumental buildings, statuary, and objects of all sizes down to amulets and beads. It played a leading role in the Egyptian elite's display of high culture through its main actor, the king, to its eternal participants, the gods and the dead. The Egyptians used some stones to give structural strength as well as aesthetic and symbolic value to their most important buildings; they exploited an overlapping, wider range of stones for statuary and other monuments such as stelae; and they employed yet other varieties as inlays and display elements in such contexts as jewellery. Egypt was also among the earliest civilizations to exploit artificial stone-like substances on a large scale, principally 'Egyptian faience' and glass—both invented in Western Asia—and blue frit or 'Egyptian blue', which was probably an Egyptian invention. Even though deposits of some gemstones, such as emerald, are found in the Eastern Desert, before the Graeco-Roman period the Egyptians did not use them, abstaining from what have been—alongside precious metals—the most highly valued display substances of later civilizations. The reasons for this non-use are not known; while they could be due to the difficulty of working the stones, other explanations are possible. (In this chapter, I use 'precious stones' to refer to the stones the Egyptians valued most highly, notably turquoise and lapis lazuli, not for modern-style gemstones.)

Except for tools, most of the usage of stone known from Egypt is in prestige forms: rough stone housing is found in the deserts and crude stone domestic and industrial bowls appear on sites within Egypt, but such examples form a small minority of the evidence.

While vast quantities of stone are preserved in many uses, texts relating to stones, which might give a formalized Egyptian view of their meaning, are sparse. Series of offering bearers carrying minerals depicted in temples of the

---

In Christina Karlshausen and Thierry De Putter (eds.) (2000), *Pierres égyptiennes ... Chefs-d'œuvre pour l'Eternité*, Exhibition catalogue, Faculté Polytechnique de Mons, February–May 2000 (Mons) 29–41. The current text includes some minor revisions, as well as clarifications suggested to me by Gay Robins.

Graeco-Roman period are accompanied by explanatory inscriptions, but these are closely adapted to their context and are eulogistic more than informative. It is likely that there were treatises on stone types and their meanings, comparable with texts that describe such domains as plants (Tait 1977: 67–9 no. 20; 1991: 47–92) and snakes (Sauneron 1989), but these are not preserved. Although texts pose at least as many questions as they answer, their absence means that any reconstruction of an Egyptian perspective on stone is based in part on indirect evidence. In this chapter I attempt to supply something of such a perspective by setting stone in relation to other materials and discussing a little textual evidence, on an altogether smaller scale than the work of Sydney Aufrère (1991).

STONE AND OTHER MATERIALS

Our image of Egypt is probably over-dominated by stone, which survives well in an archaeological record from which much else disappears or is recycled. In high-cultural usages, particularly in statuary and smaller objects, stone needs to be seen in relation to such materials as ivory and bone, wood, and metal. It also had vital part-prestige and non-prestige uses in tools and weapons. Ceremonial knives were made of flint (Midant-Reynes 1987), or had forms that evoked older ones in flint; many tools continued to be of flint at least until the mid-second millennium BCE, and throughout Egyptian history for the working of very hard stones (e.g. Dieter Arnold 1991). Flint had powerful symbolic associations that were exploited especially in magic (Ritner 1993: 163 with n. 768).

Metal—copper in the first instance—which might be thought a more effective material than stone for tools and weapons, was initially at least as important for display purposes. High-value metal containers of great technical mastery were widespread in the Early Dynastic period (e.g. Emery 1949–58: I, 20–57, pls. 4–10, together with many prestigious tools), which was also the greatest time of manufacture of stone vases (Aston 1994). The creation of a copper statue was celebrated in a year name of the 2nd dynasty king Khasekhemwy (Clagett 1989: 80, no. 4 with n. 71; Wilkinson 2000: 133, fig. 1), and the earliest copper statues preserved, of Pepy I of the 6th dynasty, are among the finest of all Egyptian statuary and vastly superior to contemporaneous stone works (Smith 1998: 77 fig. 144; Eckmann and Shafik 2005). In addition to copper, gold was used in increasing quantities from the late fourth millennium onward and remained, alongside lapis lazuli, the most highly valued and symbolically laden material until the end of Egyptian civilization (e.g. Daumas 1956).

Wood was another vital artistic material that may have been at least as widespread as stone in statuary. Wooden statues were made at all scales up to the colossal (e.g. Loeben 1997). Wood gave the sculptor more freedom than stone and encouraged subtle treatments; masterpieces are not uncommon among the relatively small numbers of extant wooden works of statuary and relief. Many types of statuary are likely to have originated in wood, being later adapted or developed in stone. The most central and to us the least known statues, which were temple cult statues of deities, appear to have been made largely of wood, with bronze elements, precious stone inlays, paint, gilding, and clothing that enhanced an appearance perhaps comparable with that of images of the Virgin Mary in many Catholic churches.

Stone, metal, and high-quality wood had to be obtained from outside the Nile Valley. Much stone could be quarried in the escarpment next to the low desert, or for example near the Nile in the Aswan area, but other stones were gathered, quarried, or traded from much farther afield, including northeastern Ethiopia for obsidian and Afghanistan for lapis lazuli (Bavay 1997; Bavay et al. 2000). These materials were motors of international relations and were vital to central elements in the civilization. In the diplomatic correspondence between Egypt and Western Asiatic states of the 14th and 13th centuries BCE, exchanges of gold, prestigious stones, and woods are crucial topics of discussion (Moran 1992). Rulers seem to have been more interested in the materials than in the forms into which they were worked: objects that we might consider 'works of art' were evaluated according to the weight of their precious materials rather than for their workmanship, and one suspects that gold, for example, might have been melted down for reuse on receipt. Such attitudes reinforced the status of the materials in the eyes of the ancient elites, who went to enormous lengths to acquire what they valued most highly.

DOMAINS OF USE AND SYMBOLISM OF STONE IN ARCHITECTURE AND STATUARY

The vast majority of Egyptian buildings were constructed of mud-brick or of more perishable materials. Stone reinforced and added accents to mud-brick buildings, including the royal palace compounds that were politically vital this-worldly structures, and provided the complete fabric of major temples and funerary structures (the less important of those too were built in mud-brick). In significant buildings, both mud-brick and stone were meant to be decorated with scenes and painted, so that in final execution they could look rather similar. Patron and viewer would know what the underlying material was, so that it did not need to be visible to have its effect. Very often, however, the final decoration was not completed and the stone remained completely visible, while borders and undecorated areas of walls would often retain their natural colours. While it is frequently uncertain whether stones in architecture or statuary were chosen for their appearance—this seems unlikely in such cases as statues of petrified wood (e.g. late 18th dynasty king: Vandier 1958: 625, pl. cxx, 1, 3)—the value of the stone itself is evident where one stone was painted to imitate another, notably limestone false door stelae speckled to appear like pink granite or painted red in imitation of granite or quartzite (more precisely 'silicified sandstone'); these are known from as early as the Old Kingdom (e.g. Fig. 26; red: Altenmüller 1998: pl. 75, 6th dyn.; Davies and Friedman 1998: 81; speckled: Shedid and Seidel 1991: 42, 18th dyn.).

The period of the greatest funerary use of stone was the Old Kingdom. The majority of significant stone tombs of later times are rock-cut, using the material in a different way. In prosperous periods, such as the New Kingdom and Graeco-Roman times, large numbers of temples were built of stone. This reservation of stone to high-cultural and sacred domains gave it an enormous prestige, which is most clearly expressed in descriptions that emphasize its hardness and colour. Other appreciated properties, such as fine grain or load-bearing strength, can be seen in the choices made by architects and sculptors, but happen not to be known from texts. An order of value from coarse limestone to granite, the hardest stone that was used at all frequently in construction, is visible in buildings rather than known from texts. Special stones were employed for the most highly valued elements in a building complex and might survive longer than the structures to which they related. Thus, the monolithic granite naos for the lost principal cult statue in the Ptolemaic temple of Horus at Edfu (Fig. 27) dates to Nectanebo I (380–362 BCE) but was transferred from an older structure (Cauville 1984: 37). An element such as a naos is on the margin between architecture and sculpture. Granite is not otherwise used in the temple, and this piece was polished to a finish that is more sculptural than architectural, emphasizing the special character of this usage.

Elements that were emphasized by contrasting stones could also be highlighted in paint. The reliefs on a granodiorite doorway in a sandstone building might be painted yellow in evocation of gilding; some significant parts of buildings also had gold foil or leaf applied to them, giving literal and extravagant form to the same basic meaning. In either case the work of architecture became in a sense a representation of itself: the treatment of its decoration declared its value in addition to expressing that value directly.

These practices, which mix stone and metal through the use of gilding, were one aspect of how prestigious buildings constituted total works of art. Very little in the Egyptian record can count as artistic 'criticism' or secondary discourse on works of art, but praise and judgment could be articulated

Stone and other materials: usages and values 267

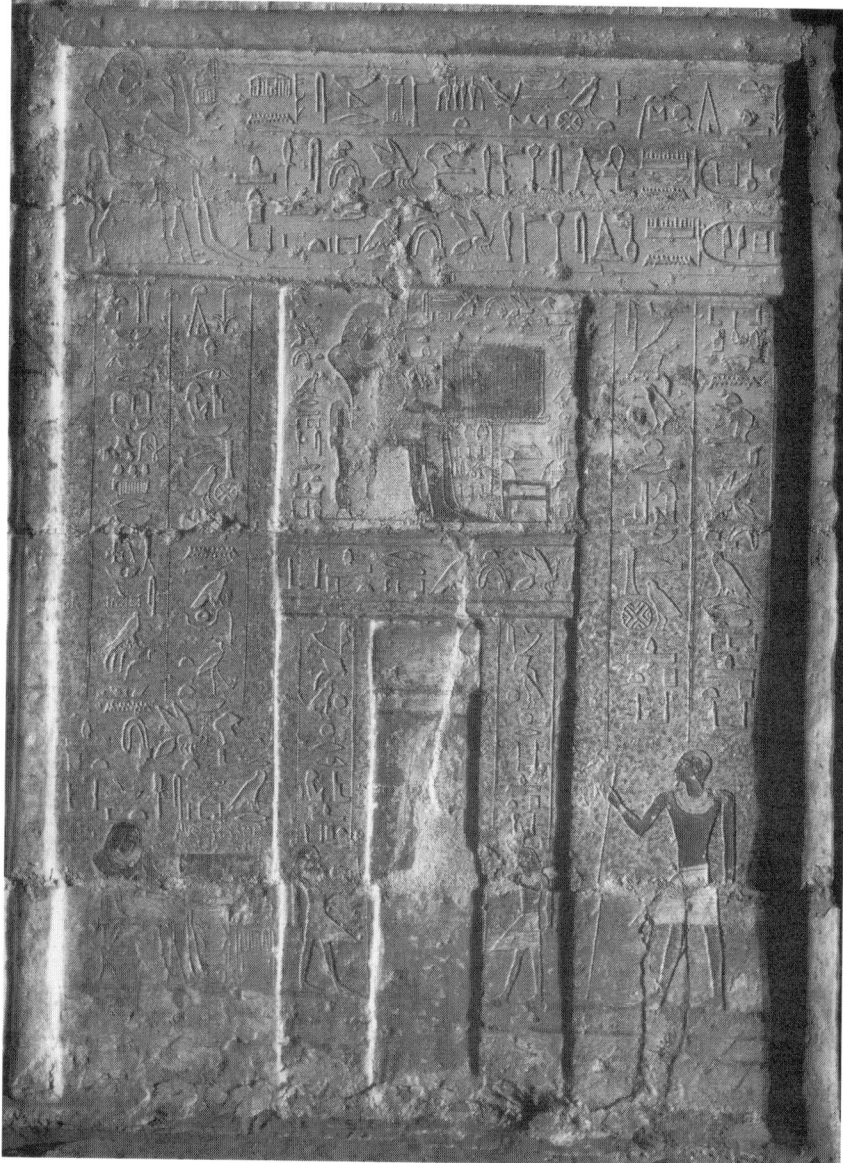

Fig. 26. False door in the tomb of Mehu at Saqqara, painted with a speckled pattern in imitation of granite. 6th dynasty. After Altenmüller (1998: pl. 96). Courtesy Deutsches Archäologisches Institut.

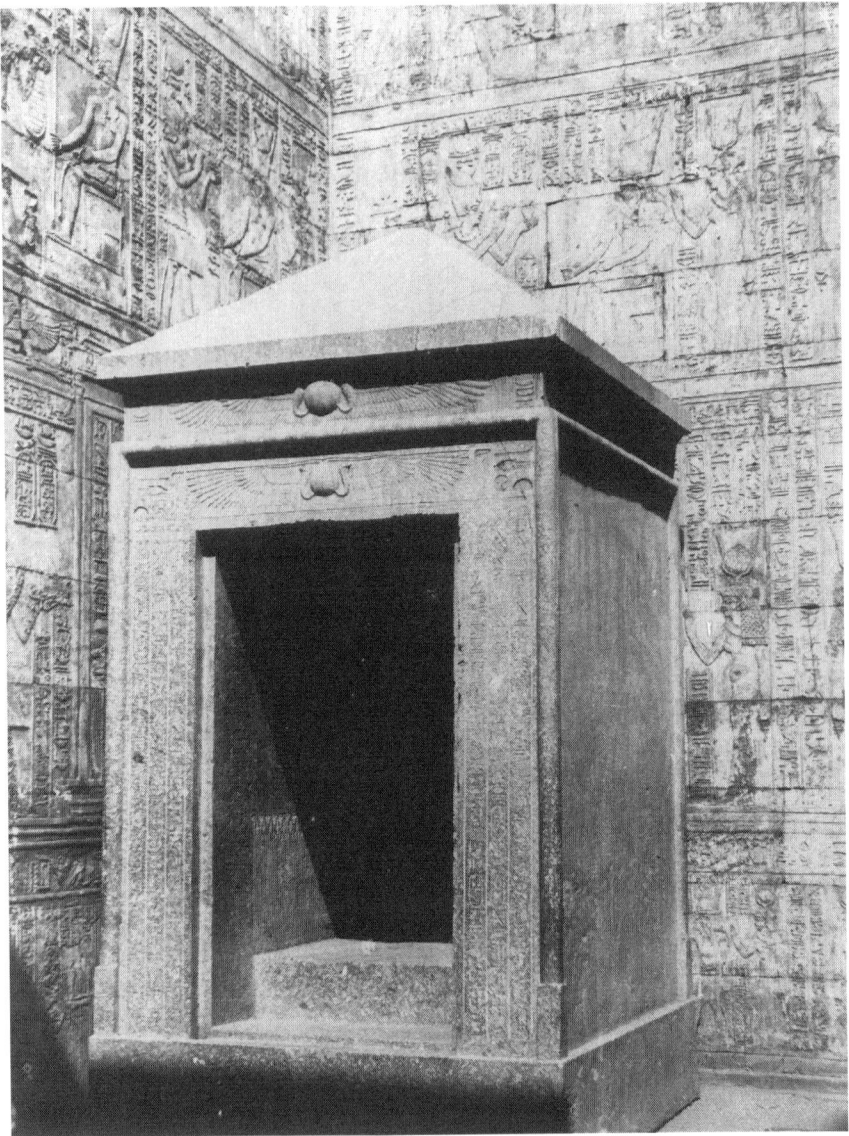

Fig. 27. Monolithic granitoid naos in the sanctuary of the temple of Edfu. Reign of Nectanebo I (380–362 BCE). Photograph from the 1890s, showing the naos in its original location in the north-west corner. Griffith Institute archive nos. 759/6276. Reproduced with permission of the Griffith Institute, Oxford.

Stone and other materials: usages and values 269

through mention of the materials of which monuments were made. A good example is a colossal stela from the mortuary temple of Amenhotep III (*c*.1390–1350 BCE) that describes this and other structures constructed by the king in Thebes. This is an official statement of the temple's beauty that publicized the building perhaps to the gods as much as to humanity, but the terms in which it praises the structure and its furnishing must have had some relation to its actual appearance. The phraseology was rather standardized, both in this stela's description of several temples and in comparable texts of other kings.

The temple is said to be:

> a fortress for ever and for all time
> in fine white sandstone;
> worked in gold throughout its length,
> its ground purified with silver,
> its doorways in electrum;
> made broad and large, greatly,
> enhanced for all time;
> made festive with this very great monument (= the stela?);
> made numerous with statues of the Lord (= the king),
> of granite, quartzite, all sorts of precious stones[1]
> (that were) enhanced with everlasting work,
> their height rising up to the sky,
> and their rays being in (people's) faces
> like the sun-disk when it shines at dawn;
> equipped with stela(e) of the Lord
> worked in gold and numerous precious stones;
> flagpoles set up before it
> worked in gold;
> made to resemble the horizon that is in the sky,
> Re shining in it;
> ...
>
> [The text goes on to enumerate natural features of the temple such as plants and the sacred lake, as well as its endowment with personnel.][2]

---

[1] ꜥꜣt nbt špst. Some of the stones characterized by this phrase are approximately 'semi-precious' in modern terms, but they encompassed the most precious ones used in ancient Egypt, including lapis lazuli and turquoise (see also discussion of ꜥꜣt below). The rendering 'precious' is therefore more appropriate. I thank Gay Robins for emphasizing this point to me.

[2] Cairo Museum CG 34025, granodiorite (?), height 3.18 m; Helck (1957: 1648,8–1649,5); translation: Lichtheim (1976: 44); discussion: Müller (1990: 45–8). Metrical transliteration of the translated passage: *mnnw n-nḥḥ ḏt* | *m-jnr-ḥḏ nfr n-rwḏt* | *bꜣk.tj m-nbw r-ꜣw.s* | *swꜥb-sꜣtw.s m-ḥḏ* | *sbꜣw.s-nbw m-ḏꜥm* | *swsḫ.tj sꜥꜣ.tj wrt* | *smnḫ.tj ḏt* | *šḥb.tj m-mnw-pn-ꜥꜣ wrt* | *sꜥšꜣ.tj m-twtw n-nb* | *m-mꜣt-ꜣbw ꜥꜣt-bjꜣt ꜥꜣt-nbt-špst* | *smnḫw m-kꜣt-ḏt* | *qꜣ.sn ḥr-wbn r-pt* | *stwt.sn m-ḥrw* | *mj-jtn psḏ.f*

The description is formulated in hyperbolic and poetic terms. The words for stones are metaphorical and carry a load of meaning that could either be purely routine or could be mobilized to the full. Literally, 'sandstone' is 'perfect white stone of hardstone (*jnr ḥḏ nfr n rwḏt*)', whereas limestone is simply '(perfect) white stone'; this distinction praises the structural qualities of sandstone and its colour while passing over its relative coarseness for relief carving. The description's use of terms for metals could relate, in the case of gold, to gilding or simply to the use of yellow paint. The 'silver' of the floor must be seen in relation to the 'gold' and no doubt signifies that it was pure and bright. In practice, it might have been of rough limestone covered with gypsum plaster, giving a white appearance: the words for 'silver' and 'white' derive from the same root *ḥḏ* The 'electrum' of the doorways evokes a naturally occurring alloy of the other two metals half way between them in colour, and gives extra value to doorways as against the floors. In practice, the decoration of doorways more often symbolized gold than a white metal.

The text evokes stones more specifically for the statuary, of which this temple possessed unprecedented quantities (Bryan 1997). The word for 'quartzite/silicified sandstone (*bjзt*)' also means 'marvellous stone', elevating it to a special position; it was also the hardest stone used at all frequently in statuary. Among finds from this temple are significant numbers of quartzite statues, showing that the description is not completely fanciful. Granodiorite/quartzdiorite is the material of the majority of the statues, notably the hundreds of Sakhmets transferred in the following century or two to the temple of Mut at Karnak, many of which are now dispersed through the world's museums. In referring to the stones under the general term *mзt*, which certainly encompasses the normal pink granite, the Egyptian text brings together minerals from the same area, as did the earlier Egyptologists who termed granodiorite 'black granite'. Painted imitations of granite, which use a speckled pink to represent the stone, show that this was what the Egyptians considered the normal form of *mзt*. This text shows that *jnr km* 'black stone', which is the more precise term for granodiorite (Harris 1961: 72–4), was seen as a subcategory of *mзt* 'granite'. Thus, together with the finds in the temple this passage shows something of an Egyptian classification of stones, as well as a related scale of values. On another level, the root of *mзt* 'granite' is also a verb meaning to 'imagine' and to 'mark' with a name (Erman and Grapow 1928: 34). The significance of this parallel is not clear, but granite's massiveness and hardness may not always have been its most important associations, which could have been with the world of the divine, and with the imagination and the desire to create memorials that pointed toward that world.

tp-dwзjt | ʿ*pr.tj m-ʿḥʿw n-nb* | *bзk m-nbw ʿзt-ʿšзt* | *smnw-snwt.f ḥft-ḥr.s* | *bзk m-dʿm* | *stwt.tj r-зḫt jmj(t)-pt* | *rʿw ḥr-wbn-jm.s* . . .

The other main term in the passage translated is ꜥꜣt, which is qualified by the adjective špst 'noble' and rendered above 'precious stone'. jnr is the most general word for 'stone', encompassing all varieties and seemingly not excluding what we would not consider to be stone, such as artificial substances.[3] ꜥꜣt has a very broad range of meaning, but in texts like this one seems mainly to designate 'other' categories of stone—those that are neither the basic limestone or sandstone nor the other stones the text names individually. It thus includes both such materials as calcite (Egyptian alabaster, now generally termed 'travertine'), from which whole statues, occasional stelae, and some small buildings could be made, and whatever may have been inlaid into statues, for example in their eyes or eyelids. Since the substances used for inlay included both what we would term semi-precious stones and artificial materials such as faience and glass, ꜥꜣt is likely to have covered those too. Here, the statues and their detailing were praised under a designation for all the materials that might be applied to them. (In the following reign of Akhenaten these techniques were taken further with the widespread creation of composite statues made of a number of stones and other materials: Phillips 1994.)

The key property of these materials was their colour, texture, or other visual quality. An example would be the translucence of the rock crystal used as eye inlay in statues and sometimes in stone reliefs. Much value was attached to luminosity and radiance, as is evident from this text and from its emphasis on gilding, for example of flagpoles that would glint in the sun (on luminosity, see Goebs 2007). The artificial materials were also radiant—that is, shiny rather than necessarily very bright—and they paralleled the most valuable precious stones, turquoise (a model for faience) and lapis lazuli (a model for glass), but were shinier than what they imitated (see essays in Friedman 1998). The Egyptians treated materials and imitations of them together. Thus, ḫsbḏ 'lapis lazuli' also meant 'blue frit pigment' (Sethe 1933: 39, 2–3; Posener-Kriéger 1983; see Ch. 11, at n. 23). Although blue was of the greatest symbolic importance, there was no basic colour term for it; 'lapis lazuli' was the nearest equivalent. We should not seek to match Egyptian classifications across different categories of materials to our own. The Egyptians seem to have had different attitudes to artificial materials from ours, perhaps in part because of the high prestige of the effects aimed at, as well as of the artificial materials themselves.

Any of the features the text evokes could be imitated in such paints as yellow ochre for gold and blue frit for lapis lazuli and would then make an equivalent statement. The effect of Egyptian monuments with their originally white stone surfaces, covered in white gypsum plaster and painted in a range

---

[3] For jnr and ꜥꜣt, see Harris (1961: 19–23); while his classification of the two terms is sound, it does not take enough account of overlaps in their meanings with each other and with other words.

of strong, generally bright colours, and containing statuary and other objects of rich stones, much of it also painted, must have been overwhelmingly brilliant, especially in comparison with the drab mud brick and mud plaster of most structures. Only occasional fragments of relief, as well as some modern coloured reconstructions, give any sense of that appearance. In temples and palaces, these colours were integral to a world that aspired toward and in part recreated the divine, as temple texts make clear.

SYMBOLIC AND STRUCTURAL ASPECTS OF STONES

Stones had meanings that may or may not have been recorded in texts but are evident in statuary and architecture. The stone might be invisible in the finished work, which was often painted, obscuring the underlying material, while limestone was treated essentially as a neutral surface that could receive paint of any colour (Reuterswärd 1958). The appearance of the stone was then in a sense irrelevant, but the value attached to it is clear, for example in the extraordinary range of Early Dynastic stone vases of all types and materials and in the continued use of calcite for such vases in later times: in both cases the stone was not painted and was appreciated for what it was. Where a statue's coloured stone was obscured by paint, the patron no doubt specified that stone because of its meaning and/or prestige; his knowledge that it had been used sufficed for him, while the ideal of some degree of representational 'realism' favoured colouring with paint. Some statues were coloured partially; the king's flesh areas, for example, might be left in unpainted granite, while the crown, garment, and other attributes were painted.[4]

Any stone, other than the most frequently used fine limestone, that was chosen for a statue probably had some special value, symbolism, or both. Thus, anorthosite gneiss, the material of the celebrated 4th dynasty statue of Rekhaef (Khephren) from his valley temple, seems to have been confined largely to royalty and deities. This stone came from southern Lower Nubia, about 80 kilometres west of the Nile, now far from a water source but seemingly not so in the third millennium (Engelbach 1934b; Shaw and Heldal 2003). Apart from its hardness and appearance—perhaps painted over in the

---

[4] e.g. granodiorite statue of Thutmose III found at Deir el-Bahri: Michalowski (1994: pl. 102); pink granite colossus of Ramesses II found at Mit Rahina: Freed (1987: 1–7). For the painting of Old Kingdom hard stone statues, see Reisner (1931: 100–27, esp. 127). For a statue of Haremhab with traces of gilding, see el-Saghir (1991: 35 fig. 76). Gilding was common on Kushite statues, see Bonnet, Honegger, and Valbelle (2003); Bonnet and Valbelle (2005).

finished statue[5]—it was difficult to obtain and highly prestigious. Granite was common in comparison, but in that period it too was restricted to royalty and a few officials who were mostly members of the royal family. In the Late period there was a strong preference for hard and dark coloured stones in statuary, the visual effect of which influenced later perceptions of Egyptian art. The reason for this preference is unknown, and how the statues looked at the time of their creation is uncertain. Since most of them were in temples where the environment is humid, any paint would now be lost, so that it cannot be known to what extent they were painted.

The meanings of some usages of stones in architecture cannot now be reconstructed. Occasional whole buildings were made of a special material, the most striking case being the 30th dynasty and early Ptolemaic temple of Isis at Behbeit el-Hagar in the Delta, which was built entirely in granite and granodiorite (Meeks-Favard 1991). Barque shrines of Amenhotep I, Thutmose III, and Thutmose IV at Karnak were constructed in calcite, but these may have been seen as non-monolithic, quasi-sculptural elements comparable with the granite naos at Edfu—essentially enlarged 'boxes'.[6] The central barque shrine erected at Karnak under Hatshepsut and now reconstructed elsewhere on the site was in quartzite—the largest-scale known architectural usage of that stone (Carlotti 1995: esp. 152)—with granodiorite base courses and doorways (Fig. 28). Its successors were built of slightly less prestigious pink granite.

In the late Ptolemaic temple of Dendara, the lower parts of the columns in the inner hypostyle hall were made of pink granite, in contrast with the sandstone used for the rest of the structure, except for the later entrance doorway, which was partly in granodiorite, as was normal (Daumas 1969: 35–6). The significance of these granite elements cannot well have been structural, unless it was thought that the lower parts of columns would be subject to exceptional wear from the passage of priests carrying processional equipment—but there is no good parallel for such a usage. More probably the stone had some symbolism, if only that the columns were 'virtually' of the prestigious granite but in fact only partly so, either because it was in short supply or because a uniform sandstone was desired for the upper areas.

The patterning of stones in buildings shows that their assumed structural properties were taken into account in constructional practice. In part, that

---

[5] Some areas of the statue, for example along the line of the jaw and beard support, as well as the plumage of the protective falcon's right wing, look as if they may have been painted (see e.g. Saleh and Sourouzian 1987: no. 31; it is almost impossible to assess such questions from photographs). More generally with hard and polished stones, the question arises of whether pigments could have been made to adhere to the surface. This is difficult to answer; paint may often have been applied to a thin intervening layer of plaster. See also Reuterswärd (1958).

[6] Shrine of Amenhotep I: Porter and Moss (1972: 63–4); shrines of Thutmose III and IV: Larché (1998). The Thutmose IV blocks were remarkably large, two weighing 35 tonnes each.

Fig. 28. Barque shrine of Hatshepsut at Karnak: granodiorite base course, with yellow paint on the sunk relief figures to signify gilding. 18th dynasty, 15th century BCE. Karnak, Open-air Museum. Photograph John Baines.

practice went back to the early phases of stone building in the Old and Middle Kingdoms, when the largest internal spaces spanned by horizontal architraves were about 3 m wide. From the New Kingdom on, such spaces were much larger and were generally spanned in sandstone, which was used for architraves of up to about 9 m.[7] The Egyptians evidently believed that sandstone had greater spanning strength than limestone, as is illustrated by the temple of Sety I at Abydos, which has limestone walls that provided an excellent surface for fine reliefs, but its doorways, columns, architraves, and roofing slabs are in sandstone, with granite and granodiorite for the most important entrances. When complete, this usage of limestone and sandstone would have been scarcely visible, because the slightly darker sandstone received a fine gypsum plaster wash and was painted like the main wall areas (Baines, Henderson, and Jaeschke 1989; there is no detailed architectural publication). This is the most northerly well-preserved temple in Egypt and was nearer to sources of fine limestone than Thebes, as well as further from the sandstone quarries of Gebel el-Silsila. The use of sandstone was thus focused on the areas that bore the greatest structural load. Recent research has shown that the Egyptians were mistaken in their understanding of the stones' structural potential and that limestone has greater spanning strength than sandstone (Thierry De Putter, personal communication). A likely explanation for this misapprehension is that styles of building with larger open spaces evolved near good sources of

---

[7] See Clarke and Engelbach (1930: 136, 151–2); their argumentation is now largely superseded; more generally, their approach was marred by a disdain for the Egyptians' constructional standards, which have nonetheless stood the test of time better than buildings in most civilizations.

sandstone. Because major temples of later periods in the limestone-rich north of the country are all lost, their stone having been turned into lime or reused in later buildings, it is impossible to say whether other practices in the use of architraves were adopted there.

The proportions of obelisks demonstrate a striking knowledge of stone properties. Granite can withstand the strain of unsupported rotation around a fulcrum up to a proportion of about twelve times as long as thick. This is the ratio attested in surviving obelisks, which were probably raised by dragging them up a ramp just over half their height and tipping them over into position, at which moment they were subjected to a breaking strain (modern resitings have used different methods; see e.g. Dieter Arnold 1991: 67–70). The Egyptians would have had no means of investigating structural properties or calculating this ratio; its occurrence in obelisks is presumably evidence for a process of trial and error. Here, they reached a finer limit of tolerance than did Gothic architects, for whom discussion about what was feasible is documented for Milan Cathedral (White 1993: 517–28; compare plans in Siena that proved unrealizable: 234–40). In both the Egyptian and the Italian cases, however, symbolic or aesthetic aims were as important as structural ones. The Egyptians were familiar with structural vaults and domes, which could have enabled them to span vastly greater open internal spaces than they ever attempted, but such techniques were used only in brick, presumably being deemed inappropriate for stone. Milan, similarly, was a cautious design in comparison with many French structures; even though German and French master builders were employed, their work was in practice tempered to local tastes.

SYMBOLISM OF PARTICULAR STONES

For stones like granite and gneiss the sparse evidence does not point to any particular symbolism, beyond hardness and prestige. For quartzite and turquoise the matter is different. In addition to the verbal associations mentioned above, quartzite was used especially in a few periods when the sun god was very salient. At Abusir, the columns of the 5th dynasty funerary temple of Sahure, a king who built a solar temple associated with his funerary cult in addition to a pyramid complex, were of quartzite. The same stone was used for the 'Memnon Colossi' in front of the mortuary temple of Amenhotep III, the subject of the passage discussed above. These statues, which come from another strongly solar period, were among the largest ever set up in Egypt; their carving and transport, which were celebrated in inscriptions of the official Amenhotep Son of Hapu, expended enormous resources (Helck

1958: 1822–3, lines 16–17 of edition; 1961: 272–3). Both yellow–red and the rarer purple quartzite were very widely used at el-Amarna, the capital of Amenhotep's successor, the solar revolutionary Akhenaten.[8] Quartzite was quarried principally at Gebel Ahmar, at the extreme north-east of the Nile valley and very close to Heliopolis, the traditional centre of solar worship. Another source, exploited particularly in the New Kingdom, was on the West Bank near Aswan. This stone was probably valued for its provenance, hardness, and colour. Akhenaten's use of purple quartzite, which is not exclusive to his reign, is not easy to interpret because that colour is not obviously superior in solar associations; perhaps its selection was part of the general tendency at el-Amarna to intensify tendencies of the preceding reigns, departing from tradition and seeking alternative canons of beauty, as well as valuing strongly coloured stones.

Turquoise is the stone best known for its symbolism. It was mined in western Sinai at Maghara and near Serabit el-Khadim, where there was a temple of the goddess Hathor, the 'Mistress of Turquoise'. Expedition leaders and other personnel set up hundreds of inscriptions in the names of kings or on their own account.[9] Turquoise was a divine stone used in jewellery and adornment for deities and members of the elite and often imitated in other materials, especially the artificial faience (Aufrère 1991: II, 491–517; Valbelle and Bonnet 1996: 118–25). Perhaps because of these associations, the Sinai inscriptions refer explicitly to the material. Other stones commemorated in quarrying inscriptions include calcite at Hatnub in Middle Egypt, granite near Aswan, and schist in the Wadi Hammamat, the extraction of which was accompanied by marvellous portents on one occasion (Schenkel 1965: 263–4; Lichtheim 1973: 113–15). Inscriptions, both at the quarry sites and at the destinations to which objects from them were brought, tend to emphasize the feats involved in transporting colossal objects, as well as the speed with which it was done, more than dwelling on the materials themselves. Such could not be the case with turquoise, which was mined in quantities that were comparatively minute. A single, much studied inscription, in a style that probably exhibits the author's unfamiliarity with presenting such a theme in a formal inscription, deals with the difficulty of extracting turquoise in the heat of summer and the problem of finding the right stone colour (see e.g. Pantalacci 1996b; no. 90 in Gardiner et al. 1952–5); but most other texts from the site have different concerns.

---

[8] There seems to be no study of this material. Purple quartzite is common, for example, among the sculptural fragments from el-Amarna in the Ashmolean Museum, Oxford. His predecessor Amenhotep III also used the stone for statuary: el-Saghir (1991: 21–7).

[9] Gardiner, Peet, and Černý (1952–5). For a divine oracle solicited before an expedition to Maghara, see Baines and Parkinson (1997); alternative interpretation: Kammerzell (2001).

Inscriptions in mineral-rich areas such as the Eastern Desert often give little or no indication of the reason for their authors' presence in the region. A modern survey that searched for and identified sources of tin south of the Wadi Hammamat discovered a late Old Kingdom inscription that uses some formulas of standard 'ideal biographies' and mentions the benefits of digging wells, but does not state whether tin or any other mineral was the goal of the ancient expedition, as is likely to have been the case (Rothe, Rapp Jr., and Miller 1996: 97–8, inscription M1 at Bir Mueilha). The Middle–New Kingdom galena (lead ore) mines at Gebel el-Zeit in the Eastern Desert have produced evidence for a cult of Hathor (e.g. Pinch 1993: 71–7), but this worship probably relates to the ore's use as eye paint, which was a prestige purpose with religious associations, not as a utilitarian metal either by itself or alloyed. The most prestigious metal, gold, was extensively mined in the Egyptian and Nubian Eastern Desert, but inscriptions generally do not celebrate its mining, even though several describe improving roads and wells in the region[10]—something that is also a topic of a stela of Ramesses II probably set up in a temple in Heliopolis[11]—and thus was part of the king's general provision for those who worked for him rather than specific to goldmining. The chief exception is in the inscriptions of Sety I in the temple at Kanais, near a well on the way to a group of mines that the texts say were a source of electrum as well as gold. The texts both emphasize that gold is not the affair of normal mortals and celebrate provision for water sources and for the safeguarding of the gold-washing teams. A comparable area of endeavour that was seldom if ever recorded in inscriptions was the creation of artificial materials such as faience and glass. The latter was very significant in New Kingdom art, for small objects, statuary (Cooney 1960), and inlay (e.g. Fig. 29), but is known only from its material remains (Shortland 2000).

These patterns in the content of inscriptions exemplify values that attached not so much to materials as to the domains of action and display to which they related and the prestige or otherwise of their extraction. Despite the great value of metals, they were extracted by means that carried no prestige, at least in part because they used forced and often convict labour under the harshest conditions (e.g. Gundlach 1977: 737). This evidence is indirect, but it is supported by oaths in which witnesses swore that they were telling the truth on pain of exile

---

[10] Inscriptions of Sety I at Kanais: Kitchen (1975: 65–80; 1993a: 56–60; 1993b: 60–2, with refs.); Quban stela of Ramesses II: Kitchen (1979: 353–60; 1996: 188–93).

[11] Stela from Manshiyet el-Sadr: Kitchen (1979: 360–2; 1996: 193–5); Hamada (1938); De Putter (1997). The initial occasion for the creation of the stela is given as the king's discovery of a quartzite block of exceptional dimensions; this is a style of royal inspiration known, for example, from a naos of Thutmose IV: Helck (1957: 1565 no. 506; 1961: 153).

278   *Visual culture*

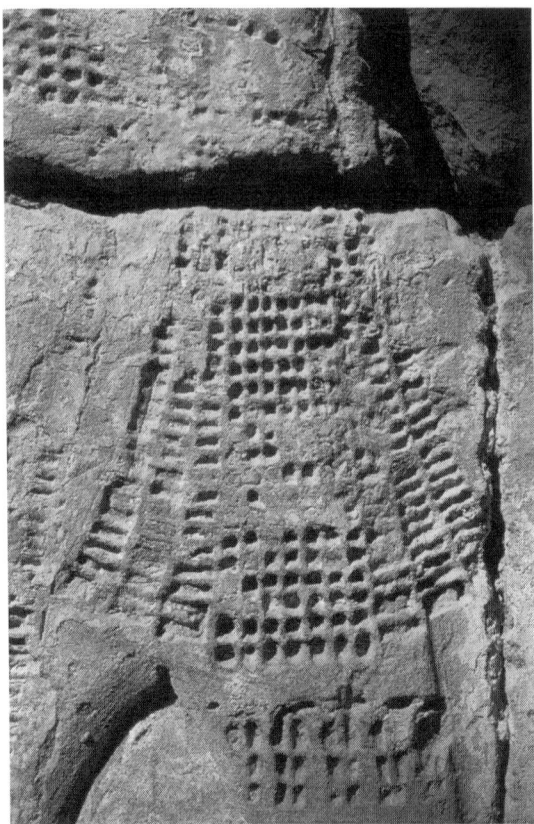

Fig. 29. Relief of Ramesses III in the temple of Medinet Habu on the West Bank at Thebes, showing the king's kilt depicted in inlay. Sandstone with fragments of blue glass paste. 20th dynasty. Courtesy Thierry De Putter and Christina Karlshausen.

to Nubia (Wilson 1948: 135–6 nos. 46, 50–1). The extreme instance of such discrimination is in Sinai, where inscriptions mention turquoise but never copper, even though large mounds of copper slag show that the metal was mined and processed there (e.g. Helck 1971: 15; Lucas 1962: 202–5).

CONCLUSION

This absence of reference to technical processes shows a focus on the public aspects of the transport of works of art and their final display—activities that were organized by the elite. Such a focus is found in many cultures and tends to privilege the artisanal exploitation of natural materials above complex manufactures, for which the possibility of displaying the end products may be more important. A great premium is placed on the remoteness of stone sources. Imported stones may be valued in part for diplomatic connections or other activities, such as warfare, that lead to their acquisition, while those that are extracted under the protagonists' direction are cited for what they contribute to their own biographies. In their public record the Egyptians hardly showed a concern with stones for their own sake, focusing rather on their ideological and religious exploitation. As indicated, more 'scientific' or encyclopaedic treatments may have existed but are not extant.

To say that Egyptian exploitation of stones was not disinterested is not to belittle it. Geologists who surveyed the Eastern Desert reported that almost any mineral deposit they identified showed signs of having been worked in antiquity (e.g. Gundlach 1977: 735). Some inscriptions refer to a particular stone in a place where that stone is no longer to be found: extraction was so efficient as to leave no trace of the material. This intensity of exploration, as well as the vast number and size of quarries near the Nile and the relatively frequent presence among them of small temples or shrines, attest to stone's fundamental importance for both divine and human society.

Whereas in the earlier predynastic Badarian and Naqada I periods the range and number of stones used was relatively limited, the complex societies of later Naqada II and Naqada III and the civilization of the dynastic and Graeco-Roman periods—whose basic technology continued to rely on hard stones as much as on metals, notably for stone extraction and working—gloried in the vast range of stones that could be obtained in the escarpments adjacent to the Nile Valley and in the deserts, with their colours and other properties. Except for tools made of flint, chert, and dolerite, these stones are known in elite usages in architecture and in a vast range of artefacts; they were essential to the web of high-cultural meanings that were monumentalized in forms recovered by archaeology. The drive to exploit all these materials came from the elite, and its intensity is a function of the complex society—in a rather different pattern from the similarly strong interest in such materials known from non-hierarchical societies. Among the many known ancient uses of stone, only some of which I have touched upon, aspects and meanings that are in a broad sense artistic are dominant. But while stone was the most widespread material in elite display, because so much else is lost its uses may have been less salient than they now appear to be. Thus, temples, which with tombs contained most examples of stones intended for perpetual display, were surrounded by mud-brick enclosure walls within which relatively few people were permitted to enter (minor temples, too, were often of mud brick). Only the pyramids, and to a lesser extent Old Kingdom mastaba tombs, were large stone monuments that were created for all to see. The stones within tombs were deposited on a single occasion at the burial; thereafter, only the public areas of tombs were accessible to anyone except robbers.

The use of stones for display purposes in everyday and ceremonial life, either by the elite or by the rest of the population, is largely unknown and is likely to remain so. Bodily adornment and protection—including, for example, the wearing of jewellery and amulets and the use of stone seals—were very important and are likely to have tempered the sharp distinctions we now see between the perpetual and the temporary, the high-cultural and the 'popular'. Here, Jan Assmann's characterization (1991: 17–24) of Egyptian high culture as focusing uniquely on stone and perpetual values may be too sharply drawn. The vast range of known Egyptian usage of stone and related substances, including some forms that are among the most compelling and intuitively fitting to the materials' character that have been created anywhere, should be seen in their broader civilizational setting. The civilization created meaning in stones and exploited their properties. It was the civilization, with technology as its often sacralized instrument, that realized these extraordinary achievements.

13

Communication and display: the integration of early Egyptian art and writing

INTRODUCTION

Among systems of writing and pictorial representation, the ancient Egyptian is the most closely fused, with the possible exception of those of Mesoamerica (e.g. Marcus 1976; Schele and Miller 1986; Houston 2000). Whereas most scripts have moved away more or less quickly from being clearly representational, Egyptian hieroglyphs continued to depict identifiable objects until they ceased to be used in the 4th century CE (te Velde 1988). Egyptian art should also be distinguished from East Asian systems, where an awareness of the representational origins of characters is retained even though their calligraphic form is not immediately representational. There too, writing is very common in pictures, but, if anything, the influence is from writing to pictorial style and convention rather than the other way around. Nearer to Egypt, there is a strong contrast with Mesopotamia, where cuneiform writing very soon lost its representational character and there is little interplay between writing and representation, even though many pictures bear inscriptions; there, the public and monumental use of writing seems to be a rather later development (e.g. Larsen 1988).

The principal reason why Egyptian writing was able to stay so close to representation is probably that the script existed from the beginning in two forms; the cursive signs used for administrative purposes, which developed into the 'hieratic' script; and hieroglyphs, which were the vehicle of public writing, and more generally of written display (which mostly had a pictorial element). Although the two remained closely linked for two thousand or

Antiquity 63 (1989) 471–82. For some modifications to the position outlined at the beginning of this chapter, see the analysis of more recently discovered evidence in Chapter 5; for renewed interpretation of some crucial pieces, see Baines (2003a). I have made some factual updatings within the text of the present chapter.

more years, hieroglyphs, which were not used in everyday contexts, were able to retain their original organization and sign forms fundamentally unchanged. Because of the close links between the scripts, hieroglyphs probably moderated the development of hieratic. The connection between hieroglyphic and cursive was maintained until the appearance of demotic cursive in the 7th century. (On early Near Eastern writing, see e.g. Grand Palais 1982; brief introduction to Egyptian writing: Davies 1987.)

This integration of writing and representation, together with the separation of forms of writing, relates to issues of literacy, which I have explored partially for the third millennium (Ch. 4). Here, I discuss the integration itself for the beginning of that period and relate the system to its creators, the elite of a large, monarchically organized state, and their use of media of what is generally called display (cf. Baines 1995a).

THE SETTING

The political context

Egypt was politically centralized in most periods, as was its artistic production and style. The system of writing and representation originated in late predynastic times, at the end of the fourth millennium. On present evidence, writing may have been invented and used for extended marks of ownership, especially royal names, slightly earlier than representational and iconographic conventions stabilized (e.g. Kaiser and Dreyer 1982). This distinction is suggested particularly by brief but detailed annotations of the delivery of goods that date several reigns before the beginning of the 1st dynasty (Kaiser and Dreyer 1982: 235), as well as being earlier than the principal monuments considered in the past to belong to the 'unification' of Egypt. This period of definition of representation and invention of writing postdates slightly the creation of a large, centralized state with borders similar to those of later Egypt.

The system was thus probably created by the new regional or central state as an instrument of control, directed in the cursive forms of writing toward administration—about which little is known—and in the monumental, hieroglyphic and representational form toward display (a problematic category), prestige, and the articulation and affirmation of values. Egyptologists have mostly, and perhaps correctly, assumed that writing was invented for administration, which was its predominant use in later times. In such a view hieroglyphs are secondary, but for the early elite they should be considered as important as cursive, administrative uses of writing. The inner elite were literate, probably in both cursive and hieroglyphs; their artistic monuments, which included hieroglyphic writing, were central preoccupations. In addition, writing and representation were crucial for the formulation and presentation of royal and religious ideology. Egypt is thus a mixed case, whereas on present evidence Mesoamerica used writing exclusively for monumental purposes for many centuries.[1]

Representation and style

The instantly recognizable Egyptian rendering of nature and artistic style, which was analysed in the classic work of Heinrich Schäfer (1986 [1974]; Ch. 9 here), is oriented toward the 'accurate' representation of figures and objects and lacks the stylistic exuberance of many artistic traditions. What is true of the rendering of nature by itself applies also to the fusion of the pictorial and linguistically-based representational systems—the latter being hieroglyphs—which come together in an artistic complex that was organized to a great extent for clarity and 'semantic' expression, rather than for emotional or sensuous impact, or for technical and compositional virtuosity. It is as if the originators of the mixed Egyptian system were the first semioticians: the system seems to be designed with the maximum emphasis on differentiation and meaning. Among other issues, this emphasis raises the question of why such clarity was sought, that is, in part, of whom it addressed. It is possible to speak of the system's being designed, because of its contemporaneous integration of representation and writing, and because it was the product of a ruling group in a centralized state and was created in quite a short span of time, probably no more than a century leading up to the Narmer Palette (Fig. 30), which exhibits all its features completely formed.

A vital feature of Egyptian representation is its use of the human figure as the organizing principle of scale and composition. This focus emerges in late predynastic monuments, of which the earlier ones show more animals than humans (e.g. Asselberghs 1961: pls. 65–7, 70–4, 76–9), and continues throughout dynastic times. Its definitive form is the 'canon of proportion',

---

[1] Subsequent research generally suggests that the integration of representation and writing existed from when the latter was first invented, while many scholars now see political unification as having occurred late, perhaps no more than a few reigns before the beginning of the 1st dynasty (see also Ch. 5). Postgate, Wang, and Wilkinson (1995) argue that Mesoamerican writing too should be seen as administrative in origin, but without specific evidence; this interpretation has not been generally accepted by Mesoamericanists. For the origins of Chinese writing, see Bagley (2004); Bottéro (2004).

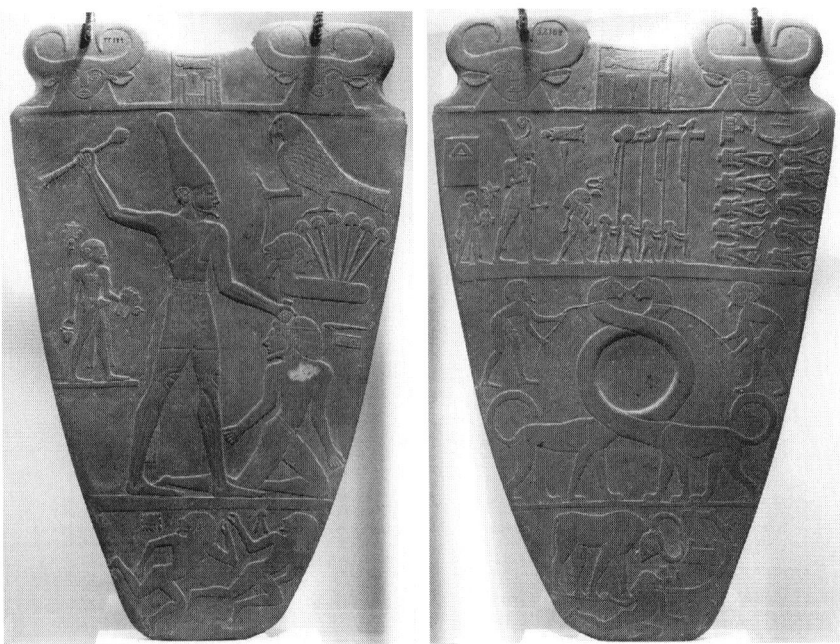

Fig. 30. Narmer Palette, from the Hierakonpolis Main Deposit. Dynasty 0, c.3000 BCE. (*left*) Side with smiting scene; (*right*) side with grinding depression. Height 64 cm. Cairo Museum CG 14716. Courtesy Hirmer Fotoarchiv München.

a set of rules for the ideal and proper proportioning of the human figure which can be extended to the design of whole compositions (see e.g. Robins 1986; 1994; to be distinguished from 'canonical' representation, often confusingly so termed by Whitney Davis, e.g. 1984; 1989). It is uncertain when the canon was introduced. Attempts to see its application in major early monuments have been methodologically circular (e.g. Iversen 1975: 60–6; Meyer 1974), but the compositional principles of these pieces are nonetheless comparable to later ones. Other evidence is restricted to an empty, possibly canonical grid on a practice piece from a probable Early Dynastic context (Emery 1949–58: III, 84 no. 1, pl. 97; Spencer 1980: 16 no. 16).

This central significance of the human figure is a powerful cultural statement, which has been variously interpreted, often as showing that whereas earlier Egyptians had conceived of divinity in animal form and felt that their own power was inferior to that of animals, those of the early state viewed human form as the measure of things (e.g. Hornung 1982a: esp. 100–8; for counter-arguments, see Baines 1985c: 72–5; Williams 1988: 35–46, 58–9). The principal meaning of the human figure is, however, probably not humanity in general, but the ideal representative or protagonist of 'human' action—the king—as well as the gods, whose only 'direct' iconography is human (see Williams, 1988; Kemp, Boyce, and Harrell 2000, for early statues of gods in human form). What seems a 'humanistic' and levelling feature is a complex, hierarchical one that should be understood in terms of its relations with alternative representational forms, such as the animal and emblematic (discussed below), rather than in terms of its superficially apparent content.

Between representation and writing

Early cursive and hieroglyphic writing was a limited instrument. Continuous language was not recorded; no more than a few words were written consecutively and they did not use linguistic syntax. Writing was adequate for some administrative purposes but not for encoding discourse or for any more than a few abstractions. Thus, pictorial representation and writing were not separate media; much could be expressed only by the linked use of both. Writing needed representation to fill out the detail of ideology and specific statement, while representation did not seek to convey through iconography matters that were better notated in writing. The bias toward the visual in presenting complex matters results in there being few textual sources for early Egyptian ideology, 'monumental' forms of which were in the mixed visual/verbal mode. There must have been a marked separation between oral discourse about ideology and these formulations. In addition, systematic constraints of decorum, which limited what could be represented and in what context, as well as what was later recorded in texts, result in there being no evidence for many central social and religious concerns (see Baines 1985c: 277–305; see now Ch. 1 here).

Even though there is relatively little stylistic disjunction between representation and writing, direct interplay between the two media, in which figures act as hieroglyphs or hieroglyphs as figures (Fischer 1973; 1986), is less common than is sometimes implied: conventions of scale and other details almost always keep the two separate, and no one confuses picture with script (as is true also in Mesoamerica). An emblematic mode of representation (or textual encoding) stands between normal representation and writing (Baines 1985c: 277–305); if the two other genres were not separate, such a bridging type could hardly exist. In its simplest form, in which its intermediate situation is clearest, the emblematic mode consists of partly representational figures, such as hieroglyphs or symbols to which arms are attached to indicate actions (Fig. 31). Extensions to these conventions show that depictions of cult images of deities, or of the king in animal form, belong in the same mode, which is fully integrated in the system of decorum.

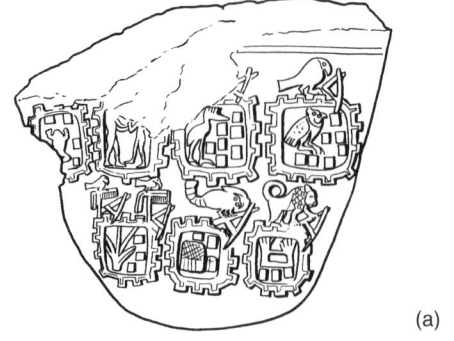
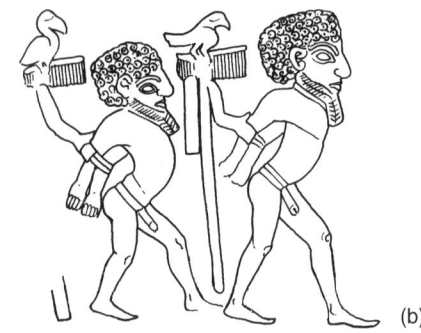

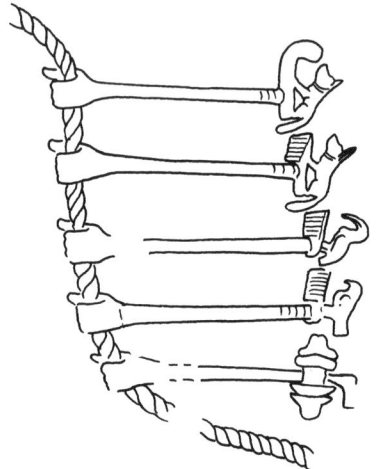

Fig. 31. Emblematic figures on palettes of dynasty 0, *c.*3100–3000 BCE. All siltstone, unknown provenance. After Baines (1985c: 43, fig. 12; drawings by Marion Cox).
(a) Cities Palette. Height *c.*19 cm. Cairo Museum, CG 14238.
(b) Battlefield Palette (detail). Detail *c.*12 cm high. Oxford, Ashmolean Museum, 1892.1171.
(c) Bull Palette (detail). Detail *c.*15 cm high. Paris, Louvre E 11255.

The essential early sources for representation and writing are a few monuments with relief decoration from the turn of the fourth millennium. These are siltstone 'palettes' of a design originally used for grinding pigments for painting the face or body (Figs. 30, 31, 38; Asselberghs 1961: pls. 44–96 [full series to 1960]), maceheads (Figs. 7, 32), and various ivory objects (e.g. Quibell 1900: pls. 5–16), as well as wood and bone tags of the 1st dynasty (*c.*2950–2800; e.g. Petrie 1900: pls. 10–17; 1901: pls. 2–12). Sculpture in the round was relatively rare (cf. Williams 1988) and not so advanced stylistically as relief, or as comparable representational features of elaborate stone vases (e.g. Fischer 1972), but some ivory pieces are of very high quality. Most representations are relatively small and were either dedicated in temples (Dreyer 1986: 11–58) or

Communication and display

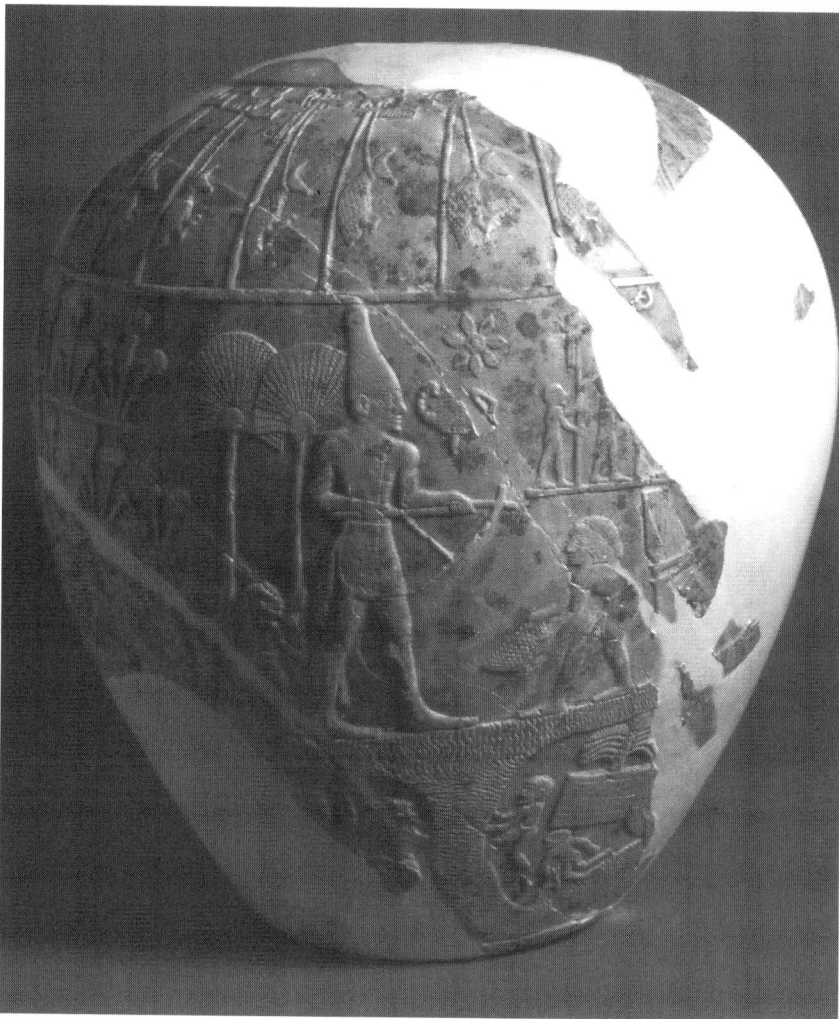

Fig. 32. The Scorpion Macehead from the Hierakonpolis Main Deposit. Limestone. Dynasty 0. Reconstructed height c.32.5 cm. Oxford, Ashmolean Museum E.3632. Courtesy Ashmolean Museum.

placed in tombs. Their style and composition is very close to that of later large-scale or colossal pieces—it is easy to mistake the size of Egyptian works—and they are conventionally called monuments (as I do here). 'Memorial' might be a more apt term, because many pieces ostensibly commemorate events, and the making of 'memorials' is one of the chief activities of the Egyptian king recorded when suitable textual contexts become available in the 4th dynasty (c.2550; Tawfik 1985; Laskowski 1998), but the pieces are monumental also in the sense that they ignore scale and create compositions that are both meaningful and impressive. 'Monuments' need not, however, be public, and the earliest known public pictorial compositions were set up outside Egypt (Williams 1986: 171–2 [conceivably a Nubian inscription]; Gardiner et al. 1952–5: I, pls. 1–4). Within Egypt itself, decorum may have been one of the constraints that led to their absence.

RESTRICTIONS ON THE SPREAD OF WRITING AND REPRESENTATION

Two essential restrictions limit the spread of a system like the Egyptian, whose complexity and incorporation of the elite technique of writing placed it outside the reach of most people. These restrictions are, first: the values it incorporates, which relate it almost exclusively to the elite, the king, and the gods, and are manifested in detail in the system of decorum; and second: the related use of other means of elite and royal display toward society as a whole and removal of access to art from all but the inner elite. Both of these are peremptory manifestations of the general reservation of works of art for central concerns in complex societies and civilizations—a reservation that renders the definition of what counts as art and the status of art as 'art' less problematic than has often been thought (e.g. Wolf 1957: 66–8), provided that an excessively narrow westernizing conception of art is not adopted (see more fully Ch. 14).

Values in representation

First, in terms of values the representational and iconographic system depicts and comments on the society's cosmos (so far as evidence goes, only the elite's cosmos). On the best known early monument, the Narmer Palette (Fig. 30), the mixed human/cows' heads at the top, together with the absence of a falcon above the patterned rectangle or *serekh* enclosing the king's name, demonstrate that the main relief areas show the 'world' or cosmos, above which is the sky, where the principal god Horus—the falcon—has his being, while the areas at the bottom present what is outside and 'beneath' the ordered world. This outside realm is not beyond royal intervention: the figure of a bull butting an enemy and an enclosure wall on one side represents the king, who for reasons of decorum is not shown in his human form in this context. He both pervades the ordered cosmos and influences the realm beyond. A contemporaneous miniature ivory cylinder presents similar distinctions in a highly sophisticated form (Fig. 8). The king is shown as a catfish, a powerful and ambivalent being also incorporated in his principal title, his Horus name, which signifies something like 'Mean Catfish' (Baines 1995a: 123–4). His—that is, the catfish's—human arms wield a long baton to smite enemies who are arranged in several registers and identified by a caption as Libyans. Above the king, a falcon facing in the opposite direction hovers in protection and holds out the hieroglyph for life. This falcon may be compared with the one in the main register of the Narmer Palette, which perches on a rebus for defeated countries and holds a rope securing the emblematic prisoner's head with a human arm. As is clearest in the rebus, both the falcons are indirect, emblematic representations of the god Horus, whose 'full' iconography is not attested from this period. The benefits of victory and life that they proffer to the king are those which the divine world gives to him and, through him, to humanity. In return, the king presents the fruits of his actions in the world, as well as the order and prosperity they bring, to the gods.

On most of these monuments the king is the only being shown at full scale in human form, and in some contexts he too is shown emblematically, as in the base area of the Narmer Palette and on the cylinder. In later reliefs from the inner areas of temples—the earliest extensive material is of the 5th dynasty (Borchardt et al. 1913)—gods in human form interact directly with the king; this is the core idiom in which exchanges between human and divine are shown. Some emblematic figures (e.g. Fig. 31) probably antedate the Narmer Palette. Thus, the emblematic mode came into being about the same time as writing, when pictorial representation was being reformed and defined as the third, and ideologically the most important, member of this interdependent set (much later, writing became somewhat more significant when its potential had increased). Discriminations of decorum in iconography, of which the emblematic mode forms an essential part, were therefore designed into the system from the beginning. In comparison with the conventions of slightly earlier palettes (e.g. Asselberghs 1961: pls. 65–7) and decorated pottery (e.g. Petrie 1921; Vandier 1952: 329–65; Asselberghs 1961: pls. 13–19; Hendrickx 2002), they leave little place on important monuments for humanity, whose radical exclusion has a later correlate in royal dominance of society as well as art and in the overpowering monuments of the pyramid age. Royal destiny and the destiny of society were identified with each other (Baines 1995a: 109–21). The force that made the elite espouse such a limited presentation was probably religious, at least in its principal aspects. The later Egyptians lived in a divine and human cosmos surrounded and threatened by disorder, and championed by the king (e.g. Hornung 1982a: 172–85). If this conception existed earlier, as is likely, its urgency may have legitimized the restriction and focus on the king.

The system of decorum should not be reduced to a narrowly religious phenomenon; it is the society's definition of what central concerns may be presented and represented, and it has general ideological and political meaning. Because much in religion was not depicted—such as most royal rituals and all temple rituals—one concomitant factor was that a great deal was retained in the oral sphere, where the restricted parts may have been safe from unwanted dissemination. This remained the case in later times when continuous texts were written. The exclusiveness of art is thus part of a wider exclusiveness. The limited cosmos that is depicted focuses on the king and emphasizes aggression (cf. Baines 2003a). Centuries were to pass before any significant number of non-royal people had major works of representational art among their monuments, and when they did, the subject matter of these works was quite separate from that of royal monuments.

Art and elite

The second restriction on the impact of representation and writing on society is in the use of other types of symbol by those in authority. The creation of the monumental style and context in late predynastic times was accompanied by other crucial changes in material culture. The Naqada II–III period (c.3500–3000), during which Egypt became culturally uniform, saw both the greatest development of predynastic prestige objects and the beginnings of their eclipse. The chief types were palettes (typologically the same as the Narmer Palette; Petrie 1921; Asselberghs 1961: pls. 42–96), maceheads (e.g. Barbara Adams 1974: pls. 5–6), stone vases (el-Khouli 1978), and decorated pottery. Of these, only stone vases survived into dynastic times. The decorated pottery is important here, because its themes, which centre on boats and various religious motifs (the boats too are likely to convey religious meanings), seem to go beyond what is known from later. Many people, probably members of elites, had access to representations which may be of rituals, possibly mortuary ones (the scenes have not been successfully interpreted). The later disappearance of palettes might relate to changing religious meanings of the pigments, which were made of valuable ores from the Eastern Desert and could have been restricted to certain groups of people or gods, but such an idea is problematic, because pigments continued to be used as cosmetics even though the objects on which they had originally been prepared ceased to be made. Maces, as symbols of individual martial values, are inappropriate to a centralized power. The king possessed and dedicated in temples the finest and largest maceheads ever made (Fig. 32; Asselberghs 1961: pls. 97–8; Adams 1974: pls. 1–4; on how these may have been displayed, see Whitehouse 1992, esp. 81), but these, too, ceased to be manufactured, and although the king holds a mace in countless reliefs of the dynastic period, maces were not significant objects (for 6th dynasty examples, see Quibell 1908: pl. 5; 1909: 19–20).

Thus, the king appropriated traditional symbols of individual independence and status, most of which subsequently disappeared. No representational materials were buried in normal graves, still less written ones. Members of the royal entourage of the 1st dynasty, who were buried around the royal tombs and mortuary cult areas at Abydos, might have crude stelae decorated with their names and a large sign representing a human being (Petrie 1900: pls. 30–6; 1901: pls. 26–30a), but elsewhere such objects are hardly known from before the end of the dynasty, in the finest case from one of the grandest non-royal tombs at Saqqara, belonging to an official named Merika (Fig. 18; see also Ch. 14, n. 14; Kemp 1967: 27 fig. 2). This stela is inferior in execution to royal works, although it is sophisticated in design and meaning (Baines 1999a: 25–9). As in later times, the location of a monument was almost as significant as its scale and quality. People of high status who were buried close to the king might have quite poor tombs and memorials.

This impoverishment of the non-royal record was accompanied by standardization. Most dynastic Egyptian pottery is uniform and almost devoid of aesthetic significance. Early Dynastic prestige materials included: stone vases, which were developed in virtuoso designs both before and after the beginning of the 1st dynasty; metal (e.g. Petrie 1901: pl. 9a; Emery 1949–58: I, pls. 4–10); ivory, from which many temple offerings were made; and, less impressive as works of art, faience (e.g. Quibell 1900: pls. 21–2; for these materials, Bruce Williams' dating, 1988, is too rigid; compare Whitehouse 1987, as well as much subsequent fieldwork). By the 1st dynasty, copper was used for many prestige containers, and for this purpose metal eventually ousted stone, whose use declined by the 3rd dynasty. Gold may have been relatively common but, as is to be expected, hardly any is preserved (for the 4th dynasty, see e.g. Reisner and Smith 1955).

The differentiation and privileging of certain forms and materials deprived most people of material artistic expression in any genre to which the elite would have accorded significance; here, pictorial representation was almost irrelevant. It is difficult to think ourselves into a world in which few people often see pictures, but the restriction of normative artistic expression and luxury objects to elites is common in many societies (and still applies to 'major' art outside museums). Those who used representation also used writing, although there must have been many literate people who had no access to representations. Display that was addressed to an audience beyond the elite could not always be couched in the system of writing and representation, whose chief message for others would have been that they could not understand it in more than general terms. The elite would naturally have seen the significance of that point, and the rest may also have comprehended it. The content of much early writing is the recording of taxation and other levies, which are hardly ever welcome, even if the symbol justifying the exaction is respected: writing is often an instrument of symbolic and executive authority rather than persuasion (compare Larsen 1988). Apart from strictly written documents, the scale of almost all early representations, including such pieces as royal tomb stelae (e.g. Fig. 17; Asselberghs 1961: pl. 1; Petrie 1900: frontispiece; 1901: pl. 31), is small and not suitable for addressing the people, who would not have had access to the places where they were sited.

Architecture

Instead of writing and representation, the chief form of more general display must therefore have been architecture. Royal Horus names (the *serekh*) depict an enclosure that forms the juncture between the world of the gods and the human world through the descent of the sky god Horus to 'inhabit' the king, who manifested Horus within the enclosure (Figs. 17, 33; Baines 1995a: 121–4). This image focuses on an architectural feature, the enclosure wall, which

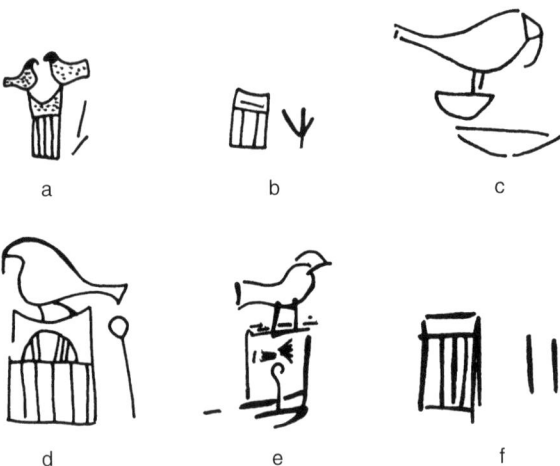

Fig. 33. Selected early examples of the *serekh*, from vase inscriptions of the Naqada III period. (a–b) earliest types; (c) Ro/Irihor; (d) Ka; (e) Narmer; (f) reign of Aha (1st dynasty). After Kaiser and Dreyer (1982: 263 fig. 14), redrawn by Marion Cox.

conveys its message to humanity through exclusion and dominates the landscape in which it is set. Enclosures themselves seem to have been uninscribed until more than a millennium later; even then it was an inner enclosure which was decorated (Arnold, Arnold, and Dorman 1988: 58–63, pls. 30–6). The motif of the *serekh* is attested among the oldest known hieroglyphs (Dreyer et al. 1998b: 130, 135 nos. 127–9, x181), and these enclosures may similarly have been among the first major brick structures in Egypt. At the beginning they may have been constructed of perishable materials, as has been suggested for their formal counterparts in Mesopotamia (Heinrich 1982: 4–14, figs. 1–43). Later they were of mud brick, plastered and painted white or perhaps with polychrome decoration. The largest structures standing from the Early Dynastic period, which are impressive by any standards, are the mortuary cult enclosures of 1st and 2nd dynasty kings (O'Connor 1989b; Hampson, Bennett, and Friedman 2000; earliest known examples, reign of Aha: Bestock in press). In addition, the new capital Memphis was named 'White Wall' or 'Wall' (Zibelius-Chen 1978: 39–43) and seems to have had such an enclosure or defining element.

The dominance of architecture conveyed in positive terms the same message of exclusion as did the inward-turning character of the system of writing and representation. Architecture was, however, slightly less value-laden than representation, because non-royal tombs of the highest-ranking members of the elite could be large and impressive, more so than those of the kings themselves (Kemp 1967). It is not known how they compared for size with palaces or temple enclosures. This relative freedom of non-royal tombs probably relates to the exclusive use of hallowed forms, materials, and sites for royal ones, while allowing the inner elite a medium of display, away from the rest of the elite, that was not so tightly restricted as monumental pictorial representation (see also Kaiser 1985b).

A SELF-SUSTAINING SYSTEM?

The communication and display of early works of art was virtually an internal matter for the gods, the king, and the elite. Until the Old Kingdom some centuries later, the elite appear to have been excluded from the most significant parts of the system. I consider at the end further aspects of this restricted system's place in its social context. First I review the positions of pictorial representation and writing, and of the fusion and mediation of the two, within the system.

An essential question is that of how specific the representations are: do they record actual events or are they generic? If the generic has a ritual function, it may fulfil it without particular reference and without relating to anyone beyond the king and the gods. In this respect, there is an apparent tension between pictorial records, which tend more toward the generic than the specific, and other material such as ceremonial tags with year names, which apparently record events. Records similar to these probably formed the basis of royal 'annals', which both preserved an ideal record of mainly ritual and royal events and acted as the point of reference when old documents were consulted in administration (Redford 1986; Wilkinson 2000). They had practical as well as ideological meaning, although all extant examples are probably grand, non-utilitarian pieces.

The palettes and maceheads, which are the main early reliefs, are slightly older than the tags. They too appear at first sight to record specific events. The Narmer Macehead (Fig. 7) fuses two possibilities by showing the royal *sed*-festival, a ritual of renewal in principle celebrated after thirty years of reign, with the enumeration of vast numbers of captives and a representation of offerings and a temple, in which the god to whom the fruits of royal success were to be dedicated would be worshipped (early evidence: Williams and Logan 1987). The figures for captives are, however, suspect, while many later depicted *sed*-festivals could not have occurred in reality (Hornung and Staehelin 1974). Thus, what is shown is a ritual of conquest allied to a prospective ritual that will bring benefits to the king, perhaps in the next life, and hence indirectly to society. For reasons of decorum, parts of the ritual which took place in a temple could not be shown pictorially, any more than the god could appear within the scenes, which include human beings and captives together with the king.

The same general point applies to the 'record' aspect of a monument like the Narmer Palette. There have been numerous attempts to identify the events it ostensibly shows, and one of these may have the correct answer, yet the chief purpose of the piece is not to record an event but to assert that the king dominates the ordered world in the name of the gods and has defeated internal, and especially external, forces of disorder (see further Ch. 5, n. 3; Baines 2003a). Whatever events were the ultimate model for the composition, they were probably some way back in time from the piece itself (as will apply to the cylinder, Fig. 8). Both the objects and the events they depicted were tokens of royal achievement. Ritual incorporated events and thus gave them full meaning, so that there was no necessary distinction between events and the celebration of the achieved order of the world (as noted already by Erik Hornung, 1957; 1966). The king's rule was ritual; in recording these two phenomena, representation fused them (Baines 1995a: 128–35). Similarly, ritual and repetitive occurrences dominated the year names and 'annals', assimilating transitory happenings to enduring meanings. Only in later times were there at all extensive written records of individual exploits. The events celebrated in the records were themselves ritualized, but more weakly.

Until later times, the near-total integration of representation and writing with ritual favoured a cyclical, non-specific position of records and of display, in which rulers participated in order to fulfil their role. This cyclical character does not exhaust the functions of records, but affects strongly those which are likely to be excavated. Between the palettes and maceheads and the later Early Dynastic period (that is, in the 1st–3rd dynasties), almost the only real evidence for kings' having projected their ritual role is in year tags. This gap in the record needs further investigation, but the appearance of a fuller royal/divine iconography toward the end of that time, for example on a granite doorjamb with a heraldic composition (Quibell 1900: pl. 2), implies the existence of lost monuments in which the iconographic tradition matured. The virtual separation of 'record' and iconography from specific events rendered the system self-sustaining so long as there was no great change in the potential of other media. Such a potential emerged gradually with the spread of continuous texts, and in a more limited way with extended records in the annals of the 4th–6th dynasties. Until that time, the fusion of writing and pictorial representation allowed the representational, and in a sense performative, aspect of the works of art to predominate.

CONCLUSION

Further aspects of communication and audience relate to the self-sustaining character of the system of writing and representation. This additional material also has implications for broader issues in the archaeological analysis of complex societies.

Although the communicative structure of early Egyptian writing and representation is not in doubt, and writing served important administrative functions, how far works of art meaningfully communicated with anyone beyond the gods is less clear. At every point, the apparent significance of works as statements that could be available to many was subverted by scale and accessibility, by the audience to which they were addressed, and by the omissions and formalizations in subject matter, which were such that what was not recorded was more central to the functioning of king and cult than what was. This restriction leaves the identity of the non-divine audience of the works unidentified, and this gap is acute because of the system's semiotic clarity.

The essential human audience must be the small elite involved in commissioning and producing the works, on which great resources were expended, and an explanation for the system's 'realism' must be sought among them (see Chs. 9 and 14). No adequate solution has been proposed for this problem, which has cross-cultural dimensions because of the evolution of numerous artistic traditions toward realism. This elite group's concern for a system that excluded them from being depicted is also problematic, and forms part of a wider problem of social access to knowledge, whose dimensions are beginning to be appreciated (cf. Baines 1990b). Such restrictions are common in small-scale societies, so that their existence in Egypt is not surprising, but they are at variance with some other aspects of Egyptian ideology in which, for example, kings are stated to proclaim their role publicly and to care for all in society (e.g. Baines 1998a: 28–41). A later religious analogy that may suggest how these conflicting aspects could be integrated ideologically while excluding much of the elite is the solar cult, whose central texts and institutions appear to have been kept 'secret' until relatively late times, perhaps in part because the matter was too portentous to be 'publicly' revealed (see notably Assmann 1995 [1983]: 16–37, who ascribes great antiquity to some of these conceptions).

Similar questions of audience apply to display. In earlier discussions (e.g. Ch. 2) I wrongly assumed that the display of the early elite and their appropriation of writing and representation could be taken for granted by the essential actors once the identity between elite and bureaucracy was appreciated. The essential form of display, however, was architecture, and it took centuries for the elite to supplement it to any extent with representation or writing (see also Ch. 4; compare Larsen 1988). Even royal reliefs were seldom placed in a public position, and here the communication the kings offered could have followed rather than led non-royal monuments. In addition, luxury aspects of material culture were probably important among the living, but hardly any evidence for them is preserved except from tombs. The crucial means—and to some extent the message—of display and differentiation was exclusion, as is fitting in a culture where representation and writing were very scarce resources.

Much of the core of high culture was in oral forms and in ritual. So long as continuous language was not written down, these domains retained their ideological precedence and now escape the archaeological record, while monumental representational forms only ever presented small excerpts from ritual. Writing and representation report minimally on the concerns of society as a whole, and only partially on those of the elite. They say hardly anything about social cohesion, a topic that is often absent from the Egyptian record, but their character and distribution make them the wrong place to look for expressions of such a concern. In the Early Dynastic period, relevant conceptions were probably confined to oral contexts. Here as in so many spheres, the distribution of evidence and evaluation of restrictions on it and gaps in it are vital to interpreting what remains. But although I suggest that the ultimate focus of ideology was oral, this gap in evidence devalues the significance of the recovered record only marginally. Architecture was visible, costly, and enduring, while the fused form of writing and representation created something of fundamental importance that could not have a close oral counterpart.

This material has broader implications for the evaluation of archaeological evidence, not just in Egypt. The Egyptian construction of a system of writing and monumental representation occurred in a relatively short period some time after the state was formed. Although the social transformations of the period of state formation were the ultimate stimulus for this surge of creativity, the two cannot be linked immediately; such a time lag should not be taken to imply a lack of connection (for other treatments of the transformation, see Kemp 2006: 60–110; Wengrow 2006). In essence, I have argued that the high-cultural system which came into being was in some respects tangential to the wider social context (see also Baines and Yoffee 1998). Its values, symbolism, and functions cannot be derived simply from its position in society; in their inward-turning character they are typical of the exclusivism of small groups that are not directly answerable to an audience. The legitimation I have suggested, of maintaining the cosmos against disintegration, need not have been thought about or accepted by all in the society.

In such a context, it could be misleading to read the broader archaeological record as showing the effects on society of these esoteric, artistically and semiotically ambitious products. For Egypt, such caution turns out to be unnecessary, because the restricted system has a negative counterpart in the deprivation and uniformity of the wider material culture. In other societies there might not be such a neat correspondence. Whether or not high culture sits easily within the record, archaeology cannot ignore something that absorbs so much of a society's resources and is the focus of so much of its prestige, even if the methods used for analysing the material may belong primarily to other disciplines.

14

On the status and purposes of ancient Egyptian art

INTRODUCTION

General

The definition and evaluation of works of art, and of art as a phenomenon, continue to vex archaeologists, among others. What is intuitively seen as art looms large in the material and textual record of recent millennia and responds ill to analyses that ignore either its elite character or its symbolic and aesthetic meanings. The oldest, Palaeolithic contexts in which such meanings are at issue have been discussed, for example, by Robert Bednarik (1992), P. G. Chase and H. L. Dibble (1992), and Iain Davidson (1992). Their discussion focuses on artefacts derived from what can only be non-complex societies; while their symbolism is crucial, their divisiveness and social status may not be. In addition to questions of symbolism, issues of definition and status are insistent for many complex societies, in part because art may be embedded in those societies in ways that many see as different from those of the contemporary world. These contrasts do not affect the prominence of artistic phenomena—however defined—in the record; so far as ancient and modern contexts can be compared, ancient artistic institutions often appear to be more prominent than analogous phenomena in today's societies.

In studying many societies, especially those approached through the material record, it is desirable to seek clarity—final agreement is beyond reach—in these matters of the definition, and still more of the status, of art. Ancient Egypt offers a paradigm example, both because artistic phenomena are so

Cambridge Archaeological Journal 4 (1994) 67–94. The argument of this chapter relates to, and in places intersects with, Norman Yoffee's and my comparative study, 'Order, legitimacy, and wealth in ancient Egypt and Mesopotamia', which was composed around the same time: Baines and Yoffee (1998).

salient in its preserved record and because of the pattern of modern discussion (for the ancient Near East, compare studies in Gunter 1990). The background within Egyptology is well illustrated by the opening of the first paper, by Friedrich Junge, in *Studien zur altägyptischen Kunstgeschichte*, which derives from a colloquium on Egyptian art history in 1987 (the author encapsulates a view rather than subscribes to it):

Strictly speaking, there can be no 'art history'—that is, academic documentation and interpretation of 'works of art' and study of the development of their motifs, forms, and styles—in our field, because, according to the general view, there are no Egyptian works of art, in the common understanding of a category of things distinct from other artefacts ... (Junge 1990: 1; trans. John Baines)

Egyptologists, especially the linguists among them, have observed that there was no indigenous Egyptian category of 'art', the nearest approach to such a thing being the word *ḥmt*, which is normally rendered 'craft'. Thus, the argument runs, not only can works of art not be identified as a distinct group, but the Egyptians had no notion of 'art'. The statement just quoted can be contrasted with an article by Rosemarie Drenkhahn on 'Artists and artisans in pharaonic Egypt', which uses a different approach and mode of reasoning to assert that:

The majority of the artefacts preserved from ancient Egypt are the products of artisans and artists who mastered techniques of working with, and giving a pleasing form to, such materials as wood, stone, metal, ivory, glass, leather, faience, and clay. ... Most people today assume automatically that these pieces are 'art'. (Drenkhahn 1995: 331)

My initial aims in this chapter are to suggest ways of bridging the gap between these two statements and to consider how a definition of the status and character of art can profitably be related to its social context. The first quotation above is a deliberately extreme formulation of a view most favoured by linguists, in part because of its correlation with arguments about the word *ḥmt*; it is unlikely to command wide acceptance. The formulation remains valuable, because it exemplifies the problems of reconciling largely philological evidence both with the chiefly artefactual basis for the position summarized in the second quotation and with approaches that focus on art as a social institution.

Theoretical context and definition

This is not the place for a detailed discussion of how to define art. What is relevant here is the widespread perception that art is a virtual universal, not because everyone is an artist or a connoisseur, but because most—perhaps all—societies exhibit phenomena of extremely diverse character that can be interpreted as art, despite problems of evaluation and disputes over what is and is not 'art'. Contrary to the first sentence of E. H. Gombrich's renowned *The story of art* (1972a: 4), I argue that there is 'such a thing as art'. Although some modern critical attitudes may suggest otherwise, art is a social more than an individual phenomenon, and works of art have their primary significance and interpretation in their originating society, as against the secondary aesthetic response of a modern viewer which Drenkhahn evokes in her acute formulation. The art historian and the iconologist need to seek an interpretive framework that is oriented toward the patrons, creators, and consumers of art in the producing society, as well as to the institution of art which they create and sustain. It seems hardly possible to arrive at a rigorous and generally acceptable definition of art; approaches such as that of Wollheim (1980) relate to different issues from those I address here. But this difficulty does not imply that art as a phenomenon does not exist, any more than the great difficulty linguists experience in defining the 'word' means that words do not exist. As in much humanistic study, there is an unavoidable circularity in identification and circumscription of the topic.

An initial weakness in the Egyptological view cited earlier relates to the linguistic argument derived from the word *ḥmt*. If a word for 'art' or 'craft' is identified and its meaning analysed, this may not help an investigation of the status of phenomena in the ancient society that should be called art. Instead, it may principally provide a foil for discussion of the modern term 'art', whose meaning itself changes. While familiar western meanings have parallels in classical antiquity, in themselves they hardly date further back than the Renaissance or even the 19th century. Such problems of fit between concepts and usages of different periods may be best met by adopting a middle ground.

To object to seeing Egyptian art as 'art' because the etymology or 'true' meaning of Egyptian *ḥmt* is 'craft' is in any case illogical. Etymology is not a good guide to usage and meaning; moreover, there are parallels, not least in western tradition, for an evolution from ideas of 'craft' to more value-laden ones of 'art'. In the reverse direction, the word *ḥmt* has usages parallel to those of western 'art', as when the skills of a doctor or lector priest are termed his *ḥmt* (e.g. Erman and Grapow 1929: 84), like the western 'physician's art'. However, since in such cases only the high prestige of the contexts leads one to render 'art' rather than 'craft', this alternative throws the burden of interpretation away from particular genres and back onto social factors. These analogies do not in themselves imply that the Egyptian word or concept had a spread of meaning comparable to those of 'art' in modern times, but rather leave the question open. Without wishing to pursue this issue further, I suggest that it is legitimate to use the extraneous category of 'art' to explore ancient material, provided that the term's fragility in any context is kept in mind and an institutionally based understanding is sought. Models of actors' perspectives on the institution of art should include the positions of both patrons and executants; the ancient public or audience is a much more problematic category. It is possible to approach these perspectives through extant works and their social context, rather than through descriptive texts or the analysis of ancient terminology.

The second Egyptological objection to employing the concept of art, presented by Friedrich Junge in the first quotation above, is that works of art did not form a single category or have a single function (I return to this issue below). The same, however, applies in essence to many or most forms of artistic production, although classical and western societies offer distractingly paradigmatic exceptions where a premium is placed on the artist and on high-value mobile works of art (I also return to this matter below). At a lower level, phenomena such as the material acquired in the contemporary world for its local or touristic interest also form exceptions. For many traditions, the fact that works have definite and various functions and can be analysed in terms of those functions is not seen as detracting from their status as 'works of art' or as lessening the desirability of studying them in artistic as well as functional terms. In any case, rather few categories of artefact have only one function. Architecture is essentially functional, while also being the premier art form for many societies.

Although it is impossible to define art to general satisfaction, some indication of what is meant here is needed. I suggest that ancient Egyptian works of art are products, created for any purpose, that exhibit a surplus of order and aesthetic organization which goes beyond the narrowly functional. Such a definition is not intended to be evaluative of quality but rather to point to ordering and aesthetic intent, and it hardly addresses genre or the cultural significance of works of art. It can, however, incorporate rituals and performing arts. In essence it is close to the characterization of Rosemarie Drenkhahn cited earlier. It is also probably compatible with the usage of ḥmt, but it focuses on the product rather than the skills which went into its making. The definition is partial in taking this focus and in appearing to neglect the social institutions that made, utilized, and valued the products. An awareness of this social dimension is necessary for a full definition, but it cannot easily be incorporated into a brief formulation.

This definition should be contrasted with two offered by Egyptologists. Both of these focus on pictorial representation. Junge (1990: 15–19) proposes that one thing which makes Egyptian representational works into 'art' is that practitioners were not engaged in a craft pursuit but in rendering an almost Platonic 'idea'. Although pictorial works tend to derive from one another more than to copy nature, and Junge's approach does not encompass this aspect, it does render some justice to the conceptual nature of representation. Yet such a nature characterizes many or most artistic traditions, while it is difficult to see in what way his position would bring ancient Egyptian and western art under a single rubric.[1] Roland Tefnin (1991b: 76–8), who concentrated on two-dimensional works, took a still more restrictive view, seeing as most strongly 'art' those works which exploit and make play with normal representational conventions to achieve unusual effects. In such a view, art would be most specifically materials that focus on metalevels of aesthetic discourse or engage in complex dialogue with tradition; this narrowing seems problematic to me.

These definitions respond to the elaborate and high-cultural character of artistic traditions in complex societies, but they hardly relate works to their use by patrons or to the commonality of purpose and style between architecture, representational art, and decorative arts. Furthermore, play with representational forms is also characteristic of strongly decorative traditions that are very different from that of Egypt; nor is it uniquely high-cultural. Thus, these definitions describe aspects of Egyptian art that can be paralleled in traditions and societies of many types. The centrality of a specific style to high-cultural traditions is nonetheless vital. A civilization and a style are nearly coextensive. A style is a crucial vehicle of discourse and of the maintenance of a society's identity. Development of and rupture with styles are matters of great importance. This role of style, which is easily perceived in Egypt, is less dominant in many later traditions.

SOCIAL CONTEXTS AND DIVISIONS

Art and exclusion

If the majority of the preserved Egyptian record has a deliberate aesthetic organization, and if definitions of art can accommodate that point, it is desirable to establish an interpretive framework that will incorporate this aesthetic character, and to set it within the ancient society and its values.

---

[1] Junge (1990, 19–25) proposes two further criteria, of 'reality' and 'beauty'. These may be specifically appropriate to Egyptian art, but although they address the function of works, again they are not very distinctive, and they do not address the commonality of character between Egyptian and other artistic traditions. The criterion of 'reality', however, can be related to the marked 'realism' of Egyptian representation (Ch. 9 §5), which it does not share, for example, with much Mesoamerican art or early Chinese traditions.

Status and purposes of ancient Egyptian art

The record focuses on monumental tomb complexes and temples. The materials used in both were generally more durable than those used in structures designed for the living. Tombs were sited where possible in the desert and thus have a disproportionate chance of survival. Although this bias in the sources is not accidental and says something about what mattered to the elite, tombs and temples do not exhaust the contexts in which art might be located. Other important but largely lost loci include palaces (e.g. O'Connor 1993; Baines 1995b) and the houses and estates of the elite;[2] fortresses, too, are highly patterned and not narrowly functional (cf. Trigger 1993: 75–7). Wherever static art was set up, mobile art was probably present and, at least in relation to Egyptian influence abroad (e.g. Teissier 1996), was evidently most important; yet it is very largely lost. Mobile art was accompanied by aesthetic genres of performance, for which pictorial and textual evidence, as well as architectural spaces and the manipulated environment, supply indirect evidence (see also below; Baines 2006a).

Characteristically Egyptian artistic culture of the dynastic period (from *c*.3000) transformed its prehistoric precursors, and the new art and culture were available only to the elite (Ch. 13). Not only was the transformed elite art specialized in its techniques, style, and iconography, it was also a typical art of a professional group of designers and executants. Its mode of execution, its choice of materials, which required great expenditure of resources and technical specialization, and its complex and complete integration of writing removed it from the purview of all but the elite, who could commission works or receive them as largesse and could in principle read what was written on them. The works' potential for imparting status could naturally have been independent of whether patrons comprehended them aesthetically or iconographically.

What cannot be established, and indeed seems unlikely, is that the life and even the death of those outside the elite—that is, of most people—included much that was aesthetically formed.[3] As in most complex societies, art was mainly of and for the elite, and it excluded the rest of society, who hardly had access to its products. So far as the non-elite subscribed to elite values, they were deprived of the potential to exploit artistic forms, partly by lack of

---

[2] El-Amarna, the capital of Akhenaten (*c*.1350–1340) and the principal site at which such houses have been recovered, is less informative than might be hoped because it was deserted deliberately rather than being abandoned in a hurry (for material, see e.g. Borchardt and Ricke 1980). The scarcity of evidence for wall paintings in elite houses, as against royal palaces, remains striking, and recent fieldwork has not altered the picture here.

[3] Contrast here the rather different, more encompassing, approach to the aesthetic that I now propose in Chapter 1. The point made here, that those outside the elite were aesthetically deprived, still holds.

wealth and partly by not being able to exploit its principal genres. In respect of genre, enduring artefacts that might have been typical of the non-elite seem to have been largely eliminated from the acknowledged repertory or to have been devalued in importance. The daily activities of the non-elite are unlikely to have included much that was artistic, except among those who made artistic products or served the elite. Whether distinctive artistic activities and traditions existed outside the elite can hardly be known. While the non-elite could have possessed artistic forms in perishable materials that leave no record and have used them in settlements that cannot be exploited by archaeology because sites in the floodplain are not accessible, the prestige attaching to elite-controlled materials and contexts makes it improbable that the elite would have valued any such things highly. A comparable phenomenon, which does seem to have existed, is that a few activities relating to certain areas of human activity and concern, such as fertility, lay outside standard high-cultural forms. Fertility figurines in various media, which depict generally nude women often with babies, do not conform to general representational conventions, yet their use appears to have been common to all archaeologically accessible strata of society (Pinch 1993: 198–234).

This issue can be formulated in terms of how far one can speak of 'two cultures' or of a counter-culture. Jan Assmann (e.g. 1991: 16–31) has proposed that there were 'two cultures' in Egypt, on the one hand the monumental, religious, and on the other hand the everyday, and that these were characterized by the use of stone or of mud brick and perishable materials respectively. He further asserts that this distinction is part of the Egyptian orientation toward permanence and toward the next world, and is thus especially characteristic of Egyptian civilization. Yet such privileging of particular forms and materials occurs in many societies; nor is it confined to complex ones. A selective privileging of architectural genres also has parallels in a number of civilizations. I suggest rather that the institutions on which Assmann focuses were even more socially exclusive than he implies, since they prescribed the correct cultural forms and materials as constituting societal values, as well as surrounding central cultural practices with a barrier of costly materials and of expertise. The only chance those outside the elite had to participate in artistic culture was by imitating the forms of their betters in materials and styles that were not appreciated. This barrier separating high culture from the rest was paralleled in a system of decorum that circumscribed the content of representational art and focused ultimately on the world of the gods.[4]

---

[4] Some aspects: Baines (1990b; see also Ch. 1 here). Gay Robins (e.g. 1993: 180–90) has extended the notion of decorum to gender, demonstrating the pervasiveness and subtlety of conventions that privileged men.

Thus, the elite appropriated resources, while restricting materially and symbolically what was available to others. Deprivation by poverty is typical of complex societies, but probably less characteristic of non-complex ones, where wealth, which tends to take the form of people as much as of things, often imposes on its possessor the obligation to exploit and disburse it for general consumption. In this sense, the phenomena considered by Assmann typify complex societies, which also exploit powerful means of creating value and social definition through style.

This specialization of artistic culture and aesthetic deprivation of the non-elite can be seen in various contexts. The basic living quarters in planned settlements attached to major constructions of the Old, Middle, and New Kingdoms (e.g. Hölscher 1934: pl. 2; 1951: 13–15) have an almost industrial uniformity in layout and style (for implications, see Kemp 1989: 111–80; 2006: 193–244; contrast Richards 1992: 37–46; 2005). Ceramics of most periods, which were used by everyone, had few aesthetic pretensions and were very seldom decorated. The elite could look to containers in metal, stone, and Egyptian faience (which may have been a rather more widely distributed luxury ware), whereas mass-produced pottery is virtually all that survives from other people. The strongly uniform ceramics suggest provision or organization by the centre or a strongly hegemonic non-high culture. This drab uniformity removed the aesthetic potential of a vital and universal material. The aesthetic devaluation of ceramics, as is found also, for example, in Mesopotamia, contrasts with their contemporaneous development in the rather less complex and centralized polities of Nubia and Sudan, where they remained aesthetically significant (see e.g. Bourriau 1981: 97–112; Nordström 2004).

This evidence addresses the non-elite only to a limited extent. Any aesthetic life the agricultural population outside national and regional centres may have enjoyed, perhaps largely in ephemeral media, is almost unknown. The evidence of pottery points toward their participation in universal forms, but hardly toward access to the more aesthetic manifestations of those forms (for a valuable range of material from religious contexts, see Pinch 1993). So far as they partook in central forms, they were culturally deprived by them.

Artistic genres and executants

The inevitable concentration of studies of art on central elite works has its full meaning only if the exclusivity of those works and their problematic relation with the remainder of society are borne in mind, especially where the legitimizing role of art is concerned. Drenkhahn continues the passage quoted above by noting the vast amount invested in 'artistic' production—including decorative arts as well as what are now perceived as the core genres—from the beginning of Egyptian history on. The proportion of resources dedicated to this purpose seems to have increased for several centuries in the early third millennium. The majority of works fall into the widely familiar categories of architecture, statuary, relief, and painting, just alluded to as 'core genres'. The order in which I have given these is, I think, also an order of relative significance in the culture. The range of major genres can be varied and supplemented for different periods and contexts. Noteworthy supplements to that range include stone vase production, both figured and plain, in late predynastic and early dynastic times (late fourth to early third millennium; el-Khouli 1978; Aston 1994), where it is significant that the hieroglyph for *ḥmt* 'art/craft' shows a drill used for producing stone vases: ↟ . At the time when the script was designed, this was a, or the, premier 'artistic' activity. Metal vessels then succeeded stone ones and became extremely important (e.g. Schäfer 1903; Radwan 1983; Insley Green 1987). Jewellery is another vital and slightly better attested genre (e.g. Aldred 1971; Wilkinson 1971). The latter two raise the problems, familiar from many ancient cultures, of how far the almost complete loss of metals and other precious materials distorts the archaeological and artistic record. The same applies still more to textiles, another salient genre that is poorly known from finds (although better than in many regions; see e.g. Vogelsang-Eastwood, 1993, whose presentation underplays the cultural significance of the material).

Decorative arts extend the role and functions of art to areas that cannot easily be assessed but were clearly significant. The use of much-recycled precious materials lessens the number of objects surviving, in comparison with such genres as statuary and stone vases. Decorative arts are pervasive in the funerary record (e.g. D'Auria, Lacovara, and Roehrig 1988; Brovarski, Doll, and Freed 1982), encompassing all but the most basic grave goods—of which relatively few seem to have been deposited; non-elite tombs are inevitably under-represented here, but also show a strong focus on amulets and jewellery. Furthermore, there was a general aestheticization of the life of the gods (for example in their cult images), of royalty, and of the elite (cf. Assmann 1991: 200–34), which extended through such categories as jewellery and furniture to clothing (whose value could be extremely high), cosmetics, perfumes, and performing arts. All these other artistic activities will have accentuated the division of the ruling group from other people, except insofar as some of those others made works of art, performed them, and in metaphorical and literal ways danced attendance on the more fortunate. An acknowledged characteristic of Egyptian artistic culture, which encourages those who study it to view it as a whole, is its consistency of style, from the largest work of architecture to the smallest piece of decorative art (e.g. Schäfer

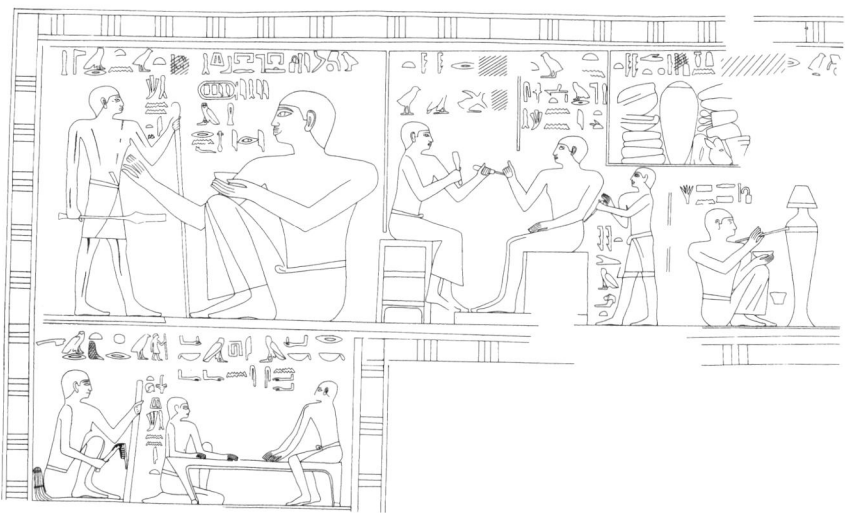

Fig. 34. Scenes of sculptors, painters, and carpenters making a bed and smoothing wood, in the tomb of Pepyankh Heny the Black at Meir, room A, north wall, west. 6th dynasty. After Blackman (1914–53: v, pl. 18).

1986 [1974]: 9–68). The consistency of art forms is part of the hegemony of elite culture and may not have furthered general social integration.

Decorative arts also affect modern perceptions of ancient artists. Drenkhahn (1976; 1995) argues, against Hermann Junker's study of the social position of Old Kingdom artists (1959), that the pattern of scenes showing artists and/or artisans (between whom it may not be advisable to distinguish), especially in non-royal tombs of the third millennium, shows that they were of similar status whether they were making beds and boxes or statues, and hence that neither the western-style 'artist' nor his aesthetically concerned patron existed. While some scenes may favour such a conclusion, caution is necessary. The argument could as well also be reversed, so that the cabinet maker would be an 'artist' almost as much as the sculptor in wood near whom he was shown in a tomb scene (e.g. Fig. 34). While this interpretation addresses a frequent commonality of technique and personnel among those who worked in the same media, it does not take into account questions of the design of major projects, of iconography, or of the general significance of artistic production and the amount of resources it absorbed.

A distinction can also be observed between sculptors and other craftsmen shown in these scenes: only the sculptors are frequently captioned with titles and personal names, and these identifications raise their status in relation to the others (Eaton-Krauss 1984: §§ 43, 44, 53–4, cat. 43–4). On a minimal reading, the sculptor who created the simulacrum through which the tomb owner was to exist in the next world had a more personal relationship with him and hence a higher status than the cabinet maker enjoyed. This point probably extends further, with the former's activity being seen as more broadly significant than the latter's. But this does not imply that the cabinet maker or jeweller was undervalued, because their professions were part of the same elite high-cultural complex as the sculptor's and shared his underlying aesthetic. Their products too could exhibit the highest levels of technical and artistic skill and should be accorded a commensurate value.[5]

What Drenkhahn's approach valuably highlights is that artists were not the free agents driven by ideas of originality and progress familiar from modern stereotypes. Those typically western conceptions are far from universal, and their absence in Egypt does not mean that there were no 'artists', or that there exists a single type of 'the artist', still less that there was no originality or change.[6] Clear evidence exists for a positive role for innovation (see e.g. Baines 1997: 215–16; Schneider 2003a), even though textual support deriving from those who created or supervised works of art is sparse (but see Dziobek 1992: 52–4). Apart from these difficulties of comparison, the evidence from non-royal tombs covers only a limited number of genres of artistic activity. The creation of major and large-scale stone statuary is seldom represented, and the design and decoration of temples and other major monuments not at all. For a variety of reasons, the preserved scenes are not suitable contexts for showing the most prestigious artistic activities, and so cannot provide evidence for the status of those activities and their executants. Nor can the role of the ultimate patron, the king, be seen in this material, which derives principally from the elite; few suitable royal contexts are preserved, and in any case restrictions of decorum make it unlikely that these things would have been widely depicted.

In its admirable aim to avoid imposing occidental categories on the ancient materials, an approach such as Drenkhahn's risks becoming reductive. If interpretation sticks closely to the preserved record, insufficient allowance

---

[5] One indication of the prestige of representations of jewellers is that they are shown a number of times as dwarfs, maintaining whom was a luxury of inner elite life. The notion that an individual might have his own jewellers' workshop is itself testimony to the importance of aesthetic matters and of this genre of 'decorative arts'. See Dasen (1993: esp. 118–22, discounting any imputed special 'magical' status of dwarfs in this context).

[6] The priest in charge of creating a statue is accorded a special, 'mystical' role during the ritual of opening the mouth, in a process that can be related to ideas of the artist (Fischer-Elfert 1998). 'Artistic temperament' is not confined to the west and may correlate with more general ideas of human creativity; see, for example, the study of Warren D'Azevedo (1973; see further D'Azevedo 1958), who also considered the balance between patron and executant in the production of aesthetic works.

may be made for the context and for the improbability that evidence for other relevant contexts would survive. The character of discourse in the ancient society may be underestimated. It is difficult to identify discourse directly comparable to that of western artists and commentators on art, and it can too readily be assumed that such things did not exist, as against the more likely possibility that they were not written down or that they took different forms from those of some other cultures. Here, the occurrence of comments about artists in the 14th century BCE cuneiform correspondence between the king of Egypt and Near Eastern rulers provides evidence from an international context that surely had counterparts within the individual cultures (Moran 1992: 19, no. 10, lines 29–42).

There is also the problem that writing about art is never easy; few of the greatest writings of most cultures are treatises on art. Visual art is best comprehended by viewing it and by doing it. Societies with a restricted range of written genres and subject matter may not develop a tradition of discursive writing about art; for Egypt it is hard to see where any such texts might belong. The character of Egyptian discourse about art was probably different from that of the modern West, but such discourse could still have had a comparable role or function, both among the elite and among the executants who created the works which sustained the traditions, and whose workshop continuity and regroupings will have affected development profoundly. In addition to citing specific evidence for such discourse (see below), I would allow more generally for its presence.

THE ROLE OF ART IN HISTORICAL DEVELOPMENTS

Discussion in society and social uses of art

Thus, one difficulty for scholars who approach Egyptian art from a theoretical and actor-oriented perspective has been the rarity of texts that provide evidence for attitudes to art or pointers to its intrinsic significance, coupled with clear evidence for non-artistic functions of works of art. This lack of explicit statements is part of a general difference between ancient Near Eastern and western styles of discourse: the former do not feature substantial amounts of mid-range theoretical discussion. Neither the lack of texts nor the presence of a function provides grounds for arguing that narrowly artistic concerns did not affect the production of the ancient works. Buildings, statuary, reliefs, and paintings had specific non-artistic functions, such as to act as temples or tombs, to be objects of veneration or means of persuasion, or to be vehicles through which a deceased person's identity would receive offerings. Such a line of reasoning would also be reductive. Words—and for some purposes especially the written word—are a problematic medium, yet scholars have tended to argue that since in surviving records people seldom formulated a topic in words, that topic did not exist or must have had a culturally idiosyncratic meaning or realization. In any case, the large gaps in the written record make it unwise to argue from silence. Furthermore, insistence on a single function for works ignores uses of them that may be neither directly aesthetic nor instrumental but are nevertheless significant, such as being the locus of display or competition within a group and a mark of division between groups. Multifunctionality is to be expected.

It is in any case possible to point to significant Egyptian discourse about works of art that focuses on their general positive and symbolic qualities, as against their narrow functionality. Maya Müller (1990) has collected passages describing works of architecture, including the graffiti of later visitors, which show an aesthetic appreciation that also assimilates them to ideal and quasi-cosmological canons that are closely paralleled in integral features of their buildings' decoration and inscription. These statements do not form a sophisticated critical vocabulary, but there is no reason why they should do so, any more than that would be expected of eulogies accompanying the opening of modern buildings or of the captions to picture postcards of them. Moreover, a few texts point toward more profound meanings (e.g. Assmann 1970), and the well-attested complex artistic uses of the past (e.g. Ch. 7 here; L. M. Leahy 1988: ch. 6; A. Leahy 1992) must have involved much discussion (see also below). Some of the most important works and contexts were subject to restrictions of knowledge and access that would have made them unsuitable for public discussion. The only text that presents an artist's skills is so obscure that it appears deliberately to allude to things without revealing them (Barta 1970a; see Baines 1990b: 8–9; Fischer-Elfert 2002).

The methodological scruples of theoreticians which I have discussed here have been generally ignored by Egyptologists who work with traditional methods and by many museum curators. These scholars categorize, analyse, and evaluate works in the central genres according to methods, generally similar to those used for numerous cultures, that are often grouped under the term 'connoisseurship'. While artistic traditions should not simply be lumped together and there is no reason for assuming that connoisseurship is a universal method, this intuitive approach points to an issue that is essentially the same as the one raised by Drenkhahn. Egyptian works of statuary and relief, as well as architecture, respond to traditional modes of art-historical analysis—more 'radical' ones have hardly been tried on them—whether or not their status and functions were different from those of superficially comparable works in other departments of the same museums. This argument from the cross-cultural comparability of genres again highlights the reductiveness of denying the status of 'art' on grounds of function. Function may differ in different cultures, but aspects of form and execution are nonetheless comparable.

The issue of function can be exemplified by reversing the argument about function and asking why the Egyptians used major works of art for 'utilitarian' purposes. Such a formulation emphasizes that those purposes are symbolic, not narrowly instrumental. It is hardly meaningful to ask whether the rituals performed upon a cult statue were directly causative, but the food placed before it was taken away and ultimately consumed by the priests, who must have known that the material nutrition it contained was available to them and was not consumed in the same way by the statues. The same point can be made about the supposed 'magical' and recreative function of statues (e.g. Russmann 1989: 3), or in another sense of buildings. These works underwent an 'opening of the mouth' ceremony in order to render them functionally effective (e.g. Blackman and Fairman 1946). In whatever way the actors may have comprehended this ritual, it need not have been completely different in kind from the consecration of a church, which makes it fit for its ceremonies but does not affect its status as a multifunctional and polysemous work of art that is comparable in this respect with the Egyptian one.

Thus, it seems justifiable to see Egyptian art as a phenomenon analogous in many ways with the art of other traditions. The centrality of the production of aesthetic objects to many periods of Egyptian history, notably some materially rich times that exhibit major cultural or political tensions, makes it worth reviewing the role of works of art in the discourse of the ancient elite. The importance of statuary and rare materials as early as the beginning of the fourth millennium can be illustrated by such objects as a statuette of lapis lazuli from Afghanistan found at Hierakonpolis (Porada 1980; this could have been made in the Near East or in Egypt). Three colossal statues of the god Min from Koptos (Fig. 35 shows one of them), which date to the late fourth millennium and were originally about four metres high, were probably set up outside a temple and thus suggest indirectly the presence of an imposing artistic and architectural context (e.g. Williams 1988; Dreyer 1995; contrasting interpretation: Kemp et al. 2000).

Among periods within Egyptian dynastic civilization that exemplify these issues are the formative time of dynasties 0–1 (c.3150–2800), which can be contrasted with the 3rd–4th dynasties and their development of pyramids and associated works of art and architecture (c.2650–2450); the 12th dynasty with its highly distinctive statuary (c.1940–1760); and the century or so from the time of Amenhotep III to that of Sety I (late 18th – early 19th dynasty,

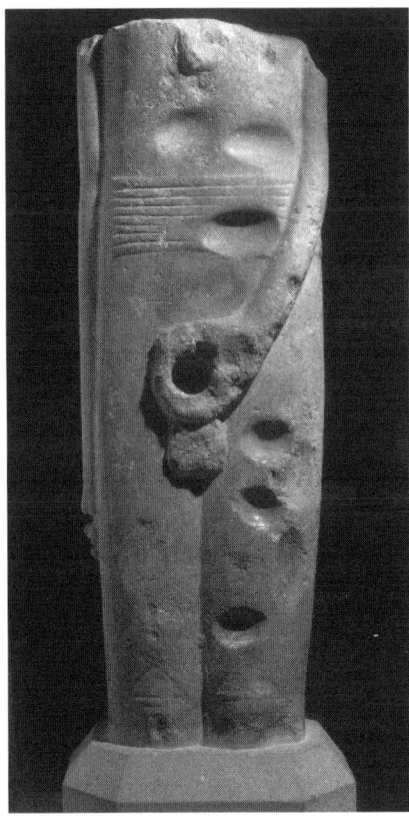

Fig. 35. Colossal statue of the god Min from Koptos. Limestone. Late fourth millennium, perhaps Naqada IIIa. Height of fragment 1.77 m. Oxford, Ashmolean Museum 1894.105e. Courtesy Ashmolean Museum.

c.1400–1275). Late period artistic modes (715–332), although generally less extravagant than earlier ones, display complex and significant relations with earlier traditions. The great temples of the Graeco-Roman period (320 BCE – c.200 CE) surviving in southern Upper Egypt document a vast expenditure of resources by culturally alien rulers on monuments of the traditional culture deep in the provinces. These periods, which I pass quickly in review in the following sections, can illustrate various aspects of the role of art.

Dynasties 0–1 and the 3rd–4th dynasties

(a) Defining styles and artists

The Egyptian state coalesced during the earliest of these periods. Around the time of political unification, there was a great transformation in artistic styles and content, leading to an iconographic definition of the Egyptian cosmos that set the pattern for later periods. During the 1st dynasty, large numbers of votive offerings were deposited in temples. Many were in precious materials also used for royal funerary equipment (materials such as gold are naturally seldom preserved). This production of elite objects must be very imperfectly represented by what is preserved; many others will have been deposited in lost locations. The architectural context, which would have conveyed vital meaning to people beyond the small numbers with access to temple sanctuaries, can hardly be reconstructed for this period (Friedman 1996: late predynastic case) and is much better known for mortuary complexes (e.g. O'Connor 1989b; Dreyer et al. 1990) than for temples (but see O'Connor 1992).[7]

What is most significant for art here is the chiefly iconographic formulation of ideology and cosmology (cf. Ch. 13). Although the hieroglyphic script was integral to pictorial compositions, it did not record continuous syntax until a century or two later, so that crucial meanings were conveyed through representational and architectural modes. While we cannot identify specific artists who created the works which embodied the new conventions, it seems inconceivable that an enterprise of such cultural importance as the definition of a style for the civilization and the encoding of its values was not under central direction and did not involve leading members of the society. At the core of the new system was the politically dominant figure of the king.

More can be said about artists and their position in the first pyramid age of the 3rd–4th dynasties, but some issues are disputed. The royal pyramid complexes exhibit comprehensive planning as works of art and, even on a minimal evaluation based on levels of craftsmanship, display standards of execution going far beyond the 'functional'. Techniques and styles evolved quite rapidly over a century or so, while most complexes exhibit major alterations in design, showing that there was ongoing engagement with their conception during construction. In the case of the 3rd dynasty Step Pyramid complex of Djoser (c.2650), we have the name of the likely designer or chief architect in the inscription on the front of a royal statue plinth found in the entrance, which names the 'master of sculptors' Imhotep (Fig. 36; Wildung 1977: 5–9; see also e.g. Junker 1959: 76–9). It is irrelevant here whether Imhotep carved the statue or rather supervised its production. What is relevant is that he had a quite exceptional status, as is shown by the fact that non-royal individuals are never otherwise named on royal statues. In exercising this privilege, he placed next to his name the title of chief sculptor

---

[7] The precise character of the Hierakonpolis Main Deposit, the principal group of this material, has since been questioned, and an alternative function for the location proposed, by Liam McNamara (in press). This change in the understanding of the context does not strongly affect the picture given here.

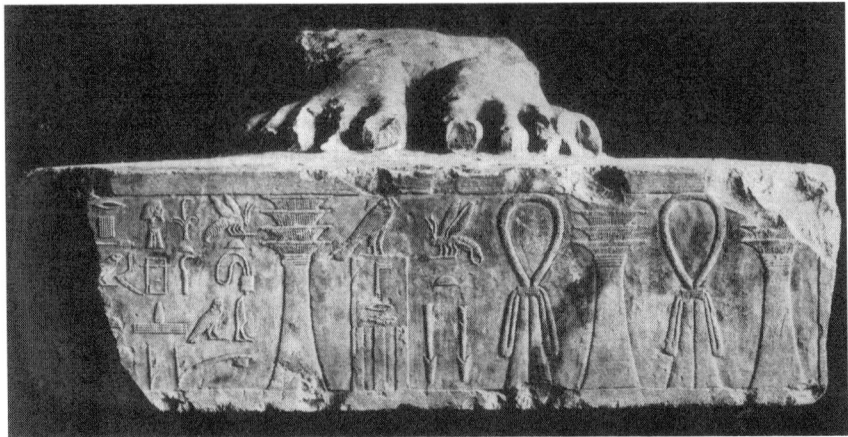

Fig. 36. Base from statue of Djoser, from the entrance colonnade of the Step Pyramid complex at Saqqara; the inscription on the left names the 'master of sculptors Imhotep'. 3rd dynasty. Painted limestone. Height 14.2 cm, width, 48.7 cm, depth 66.3 cm. Cairo Museum JdE 49889. After Firth, Quibell, and Lauer (1935: pl. 58).

and not that of an administrative office. Imhotep later became a culture hero, and may have been held, among other things, to have overseen a reform of Egyptian writing—and thus of artistic conventions—in the time of Djoser (Ch. 2 §1; opposite view: Wildung 1977: 88–9).

Although evidence for those who directed work on 4th dynasty pyramids is not so direct as with Imhotep, it can hardly be doubted that those undertakings, which will have involved much of the country's population indirectly or directly, were controlled by leading members of the elite. Some of these, who were the sons of kings, are known by name; their tombs at Giza were among the principal non-royal monuments of the necropolis, arranged to the east and west of the Great Pyramid.[8]

The projects for the pyramids display other artistic characteristics, of which I cite one. Between the Step Pyramid (e.g. Smith 1998: 26–34) and the mid-4th dynasty pyramid of Khephren at Giza, architectural vocabulary and style moved from adaptations in stone of earlier plant-based forms—themselves probably executed earlier in mixed media including mud brick—to a near-complete geometrical abstraction that a modern critic might see as exploiting the 'natural' properties of the stones. The new style lasted only two or three generations, being replaced in the 5th dynasty by a more representational one

---

[8] Strudwick (1985: 218 nos. 34, 96) cites evidence for 'overseers of all the king's works' from the 4th dynasty. Other Old Kingdom holders of that title were of the highest status, often viziers. For the statue of Hemiunu, who held that title, see Arnold and Ziegler (1999: 229–31 no. 44).

(e.g. Smith 1998: 49–52, 66–9). This double stylistic transformation cannot well be interpreted as a simple consequence of changes in religion and symbolism. Even if such changes played an important part, the transformation must have included an aesthetic component.[9] Such a development toward and away from austerity and abstraction has parallels, not least in the Modern movement with its epigone the Postmodern; it seems to be a natural way in which a tradition can develop and then move on again by returning to and developing older forms.

(b) Access to works of art

The 4th dynasty poses strongly the issue of access, and hence of audience. This applies even to vast pyramid complexes, but I review it in relation to statuary and relief. It too is relevant to many cultures.

One of the principal objections to seeing Egyptian creations as art has been the fact that many works were invisible in their final positions. Since they were not viewed and lacked an audience, it is implied, they could not be intended to be art. The 'reserve heads' of this period (Fig. 37), separate near-lifesized sculptures apparently lacking a context of installation and coming from the bottoms of tomb shafts, were subject to some ritual mutilation before they were deposited (Tefnin 1991a), while some of the 'slab stelae' forming the cult focus of elite tombs were walled up and made invisible—and hence are remarkably well preserved (e.g. Reisner 1942: 64–5; Smith 1998: 45 figs. 78–9; Arnold and Ziegler 1999: nos. 51–3; comprehensive study: Manuelian 2003). This walling-up is only the most striking of many invisible contexts in which sculpture and reliefs were placed.

To deny the status of art to these works is to rely too much on a single criterion. The context of patron and executant exists for such objects whether they are seen or not, and even whether they are to be conserved or destroyed. Moreover, while the uses to which these works were put often differed from those of modern times, such uses do not seem to have affected their appearance greatly. Apart from the mutilation of the reserve heads, two- and three-dimensional forms of objects destined to be seen are similar or identical to those which were to be invisible. This situation can be compared, almost at random, with the vast amount of sculptural and pictorial decoration in large medieval churches and cathedrals, much of it virtually invisible when completed and incorporating inscriptions that only the keenest-sighted among

---

[9] The variation in style does not seem to be technically motivated, although there was enormous technical change in the 3rd and 4th dynasties. Some much later buildings, notably the 'cenotaph' of Sety I at Abydos (c.1290; Frankfort 1930), seem to take up a 4th dynasty style, apparently without technical motivation.

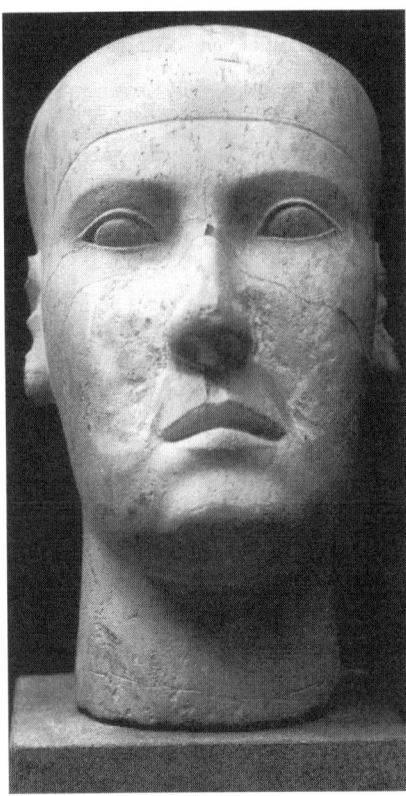

Fig. 37. Reserve head from Giza. Limestone. 4th dynasty. Height 30 cm. Museum of Fine Arts, Boston 14.718 (MFA negative C4362). Courtesy Museum of Fine Arts.

the literate few could have read.[10] In Egypt, invisibility also had little effect on the formation of traditions or on interactions of later periods with earlier works.

The issue of access also concerns the palettes (Figs. 30, 38) and maceheads (Figs. 7, 32) that embody the evolving state's ideology and cosmology and were dedicated in temples immediately before the 1st dynasty. These include works of the highest quality and technical mastery, whose relative merits are suggested by a comparison—across media—with the rather earlier and far cruder wall painting in Tomb 100 at Hierakonpolis, which probably itself belonged to a ruler (Quibell and Green 1902: pls. 75–9; see e.g. Williams and Logan 1987). The style and the technique of the palettes and maceheads were devised for their dimensions, context, and materials, and could not easily have had larger and more public counterparts, so that the pieces must be evaluated as the votive objects they appear to have been and not in relation to putative monumental propaganda works.

---

[10] Thus, for example, Norman Bryson's interpretation of these images as narrowly didactic (1981: 1–5) neglects the context in which they were located and the excess of means employed in relation to any such end.

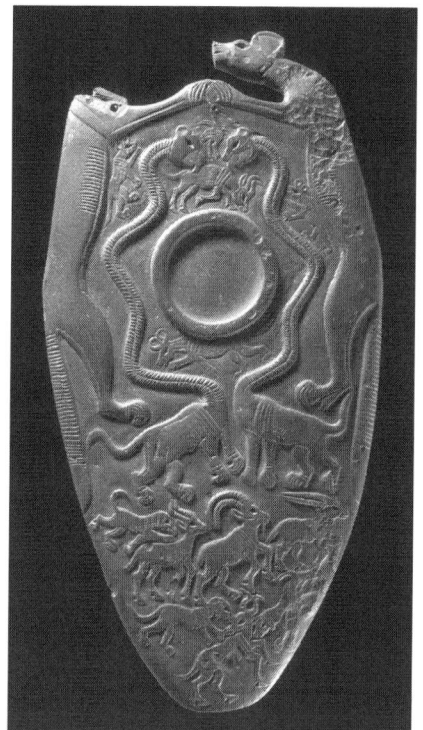 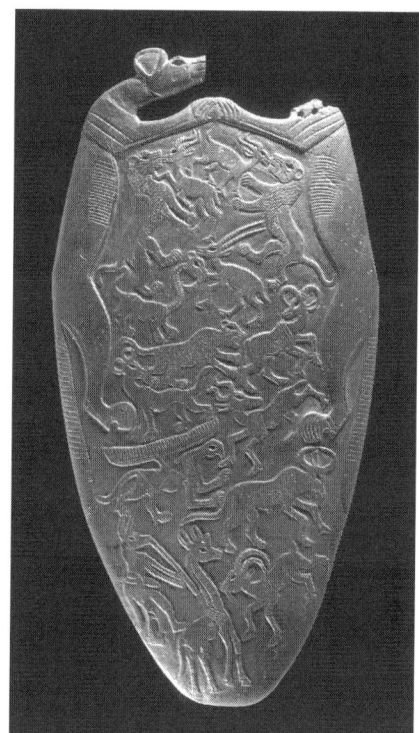

Fig. 38. The Two Dog Palette from the Hierakonpolis Main Deposit. Naqada III period. (*left*) Side with grinding depression ('recto'); (*right*) side with animal composition and flute player. Siltstone. Height 42.5 cm, width 22 cm. Oxford, Ashmolean Museum E.3924. Courtesy Ashmolean Museum.

Two implications of these finds are doubtless paralleled elsewhere. First, the divine audience as well as, to whom were dedicated votive offerings temple construction and decoration, was as integral to the objects' meaning as a human audience. Second, the artists were close to the ruling and commissioning elite, and the forms were developed between patrons and artists. Production for the gods paid due respect to them, as well as enhancing the status of the donor, principally the king. For the executant, the aim to produce works of high quality could apply equally to large or small pieces, whether destined to be visible or invisible, and might be exacted by the patron or donor in either case. Motivation toward excellence must, however, ultimately be internal to the executant, with whom it can also originate.[11]

---

[11] There are naturally cases where concealed work was less carefully done than what was more visible. This can be observed in many places in the temple of Sety I at Abydos.

The patron's and artist's search for quality does not explicate sufficiently the meaning of the works. The Narmer Palette (Fig. 30) crowns a development in which royal dominance, relations between the king and the gods, and the structure of cosmos and society were incorporated iconographically with the utmost sophistication (see also Ch. 13; Baines 2003a). The palette may stand on the margin of ideologically more central developments of temple relief and painting, in which the king was shown interacting with deities, both sides being depicted—as later—in human form at the same scale; but any such works that there may have been are lost.[12] The self-contained nature of the palette and its votive function may have required it to bridge symbolic domains and to condense a great deal of meaning. They do not alter its status as a work of art, but they do throw into relief the great weight of symbolism which it bears.

A striking aspect of the palettes and maceheads is that, despite their quite rapid evolution and centripetal role in the emergent state, they come at the end of a development, not at its beginning. With the 1st dynasty their production ceased, and preserved royal reliefs are confined to tomb stelae (e.g. Fig. 17; Lange and Hirmer 1968: pl. 6; Baines 1995a: fig. 3.12) and ivories, notably from the Hierakonpolis Main Deposit (e.g. Adams 1974; Whitehouse 1992). Reasons for this change probably include: developments in the use of materials, so that precious substances that are lost from the record began to carry meanings and implications of status previously associated with other media; the location of some artistic activities in lost contexts, principally temples and palaces within the floodplain; and, most importantly, a general restriction of the public contexts of art. The legitimizing functions of representational art could be complemented by other forms of display, including the increasingly monumental scale of architecture. Rituals, such as the sacrifice of retainers at 1st dynasty royal funerals,[13] demonstrated the power of king and state in the most peremptory fashion. Art appears to have become progressively restricted within the elite and to have acquired an introspective character that related it less to the wider society than was the case in some later periods. Few surviving pieces from the first two dynasties could clearly have functioned in social competition or have belonged to genres distributed throughout the elite. Competition and ranking can, however, be seen in architecture. The highest levels of society appear to have been strongly

---

[12] The earliest preserved temple reliefs date to the late 2nd and early 3rd dynasties. They appear to be fully within 'classical' Egyptian conventions. A provincial relief or stela tentatively dated to the 1st dynasty already exhibits many relevant features: Morenz (1994).

[13] See e.g. Dreyer (1990: 67). A number of further examples have since been found, notably around the 1st dynasty enclosures at Abydos. For a set of partly cross-cultural studies, see the themed issue of the journal *Archéo-Nil* 10 (2000), *Le sacrifice humain en contexte funéraire*, resumed and expanded as an edited book: Albert and Midant-Reynes (2005).

Status and purposes of ancient Egyptian art

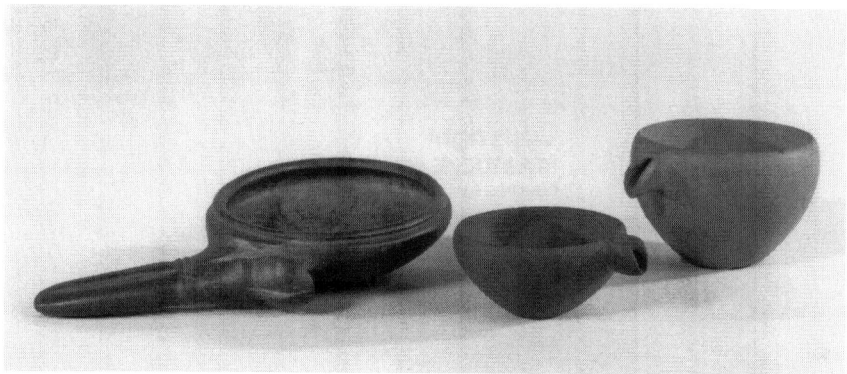

Fig. 39. Three stone vases, provenance unknown. Siltstone. 1st dynasty. Berlin, Ägyptisches Museum 13213, 12778, 12779. Courtesy Ägyptisches Museum Berlin.

stratified, with not more than one or two people at a time constructing the most elaborate tombs, notably in the Saqqara necropolis, next to the capital of Memphis.[14] There are more modest cemeteries with architecturally constructed tombs at a number of sites in the country, showing that wealth was not centralized to an extreme degree.

Thus, the 1st dynasty, rather like the 4th, appears to have restricted the range and use of significant works of representational art, and in a different way of architecture, to very few people. The stone vases characteristic of the period (e.g. Fig. 39; see el-Khouli 1978) do not affect this pattern significantly, because vast numbers were deposited in the tombs of the kings and of rather few others. What is striking in terms of categories of material is that the vases are much superior in execution to the rare preserved fragments of statuary, except for ivories (Fig. 40; see e.g. Quibell 1900: pls. 5–17); major stone sculpture seems not to have developed significantly until the later 2nd dynasty, notably with two statues of King Khasekhem (Fig. 41; parallel siltstone piece: Quibell 1900: pls. 40–1).[15] The skills which went into creating the palettes and maceheads may have been closely related to those used on vases, and the vases attained still

[14] One such tomb, belonging to an official named Merika who held the highest titles, also had wooden statues in a chapel, as well as a stela (Emery 1949–58: III, 10, pls. 27, 39; Kemp 1967: 26–30; see also Ch. 13 here). The attribution of this tomb is now questioned on a variety of grounds by Ellen Morris, David O'Connor (2005), and David Wengrow (2006: esp. 223–8); the very high status of Merika and the significance of his stela remain clear.

[15] Wood could have been important: see Emery (1949–58: III, 10, pl. 27). A life-size limestone half-kneeling statue of a man (king?) with a heavy wig from Hierakonpolis, of uncertain date but perhaps 1st dynasty, is unlike most later works in iconography, although parallels can be found: Quibell (1900: pl. ii, Cairo Museum JdE 32159); see also Fay (1999: 115–16, 146 figs. 57–8), who compares it with a statue of Amenemhat III. I am grateful to Marianne Eaton-Krauss for pointing this piece out to me and suggesting that it may show a king.

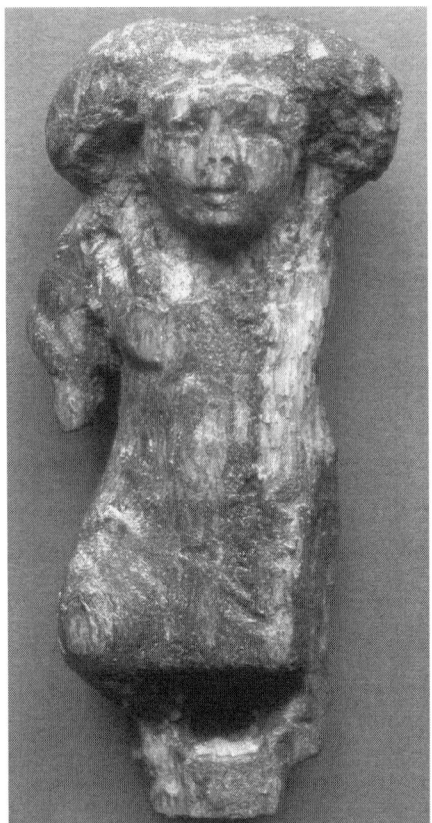 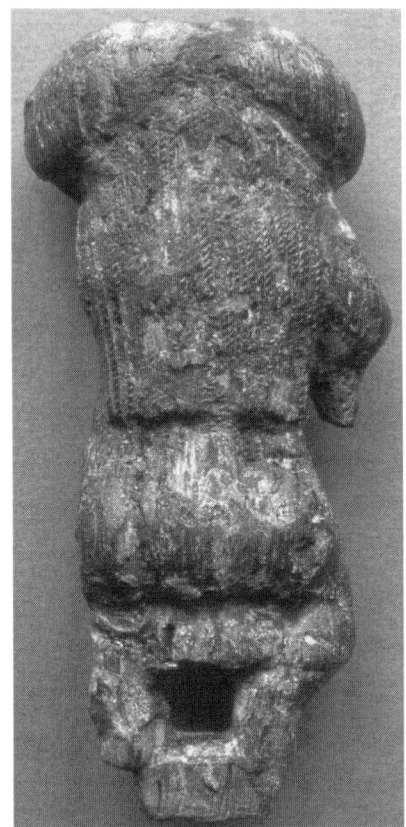

Fig. 40. Ivory statuette of a female dwarf from the Hierakonpolis Main Deposit. 1st dynasty (?). Height 13.3 cm. Oxford, Ashmolean Museum E.298. See Dasen (1993: 274 no. 106). Courtesy Ashmolean Museum.

higher levels after the palettes and maceheads ceased to be made, becoming the most significant mobile art preserved from the period and perhaps taking over traditions as well as executant personnel from other media. However, some inscriptions on stone vases from the Step Pyramid relate to their earlier use among the living, probably in temple rituals (e.g. Roth 1991: 145–95), reminding us that the range of preserved contexts is very incomplete. It seems thus that the vases must have been major symbolic resources for the cult, as well as being deposited as grave goods (in any case, objects like large granite vases can hardly have had a practical everyday use). Vast amounts of high-value goods were deposited in major early 1st dynasty tombs, in a practice that appropriated aesthetic value to the inner elite (see Ch. 4). Nothing points to a wide availability of aesthetic artefacts or practices outside the elite.

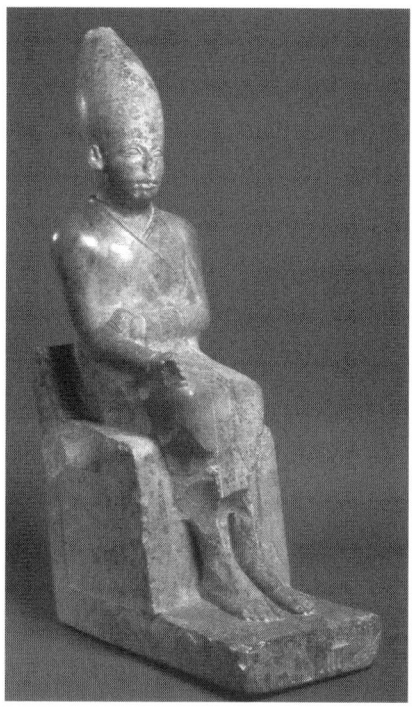

Fig. 41. Limestone statue of Khasekhem from the Hierakonpolis Main Deposit. 2nd dynasty. Height 63 cm, width of plinth 17 cm, depth 33 cm. Oxford, Ashmolean Museum E.517. Courtesy Ashmolean Museum.

12th dynasty royal statuary

Some of the most striking Egyptian images are the haggard figures of the late 12th century kings Senwosret III (Fig. 42) and Amenemhat III (Fig. 43). A fairly consistent stylistic development can be seen, from the statuary of Amenemhat I and Senwosret I at the beginning of the 12th dynasty to the time of Amenemhat III, after which evidence for royal works is sparse (Evers 1929; Aldred 1970; Tefnin 1992; Fay 1996). Some works of the first half of the dynasty, notably large hardstone statues but including at least one smaller one (Evers 1929: II, pl. xiii fig. 64), have more individual physiognomies than those of earlier times, and pieces from the entire dynasty have ears of exaggerated size. The highly individual features of Senwosret III and his successor nonetheless exhibit a marked change. Statues of the two can mostly be told apart on the basis of facial type. Both share the worn look, which is especially typical of Senwosret III; distinctions between them suggest that the kings' personal physiognomies contributed to the sculptural norm, but they do not demonstrate that an ideal of 'true' portraiture suddenly appeared (see further Ch. 9 §4, with refs.). As is shown by the marked contrast between the

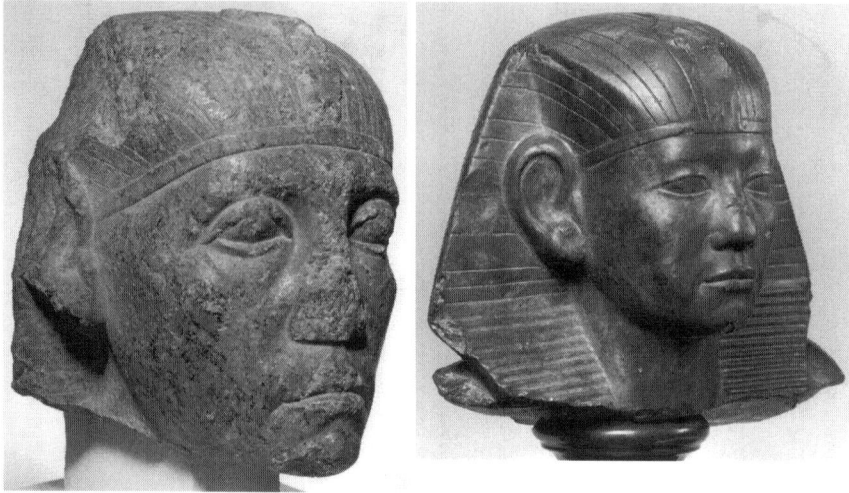

Fig. 42. (*left*) Over-lifesize head of Senwosret III, provenance unknown. Pink granite. 12th dynasty. Height 32.3 cm. Cambridge, Fitzwilliam Museum E.37.1930. Courtesy Fitzwilliam Museum.

Fig. 43. (*right*) Head of Amenemhat III, perhaps from the Aswan area. Dark shelly limestone. 12th dynasty. Height 11.6 cm. Cambridge, Fitzwilliam Museum E.2.1946. Courtesy Fitzwilliam Museum.

king's head and his body, which remains trim and muscular, the new type did not run counter to the principle that most people, and particularly kings, were shown in an idealizing and 'perfect' guise. This point applies strikingly to cases where the same facial type occurs on a sphinx. To modern eyes these create a strong contrast between the specificity of the face and the generality of the body. This apparent difference may illuminate by analogy the relation between body and face on anthropomorphic statuary: in some sense the worn facial type conveys an ideal.

This iconography, as one can appropriately term the facial treatment, should signify a quality of the king. The form has an evident analogy in the instruction texts of the period that are placed in the mouths of kings, notably the Instruction for Merikare and the Instruction of Amenemhat (e.g. Parkinson 1998: 212–34, 203–11), which emphasize the burdens of the king's office and the responsibility he must bear. Statues with the highly characterized faces come from temples (e.g. Naville 1907: pl. 19—four from a single temple), where this aspect of the king's role would be displayed to the gods, whereas only priests among humanity had access to inner areas; many examples are also quite small. But this 'intimate' interpretation should not be overstressed, because some of the same features occur in softened form on a perhaps more public colossal head (Romano 1979: no. 40), where such a treatment might perhaps seem surprising. The temple context can, however, be contrasted with a mortuary one, because a statue of Amenemhat III from his pyramid complex lacks the new features (e.g. Evers 1929: pls. 102–4; Lange and Hirmer 1968: pls. 114–15). The focus of this iconography appears therefore to be this-worldly.

This development can be viewed in two principal ways. As an approach to depicting the king's face, it could have originated near the beginning of the dynasty and have strengthened later. Alternatively, it could have been introduced under Senwosret III as a specific statement about the king's role and responsibility, and thus made an assertion about Senwosret III in particular. Roland Tefnin (1992) suggested that the iconography of royal eyes and ears signifies the king's responsible role in relation to humanity, and he integrated the facial presentation with the notion of royal 'propaganda', ascribing to it the same kind of meaning as I do (Tefnin 1991c; on the notion of propaganda, see further Baines 1996b). While this interpretation is tempting, the limitations on public access to the works restricts its focus so far that the term itself becomes problematic. It seems better to view the iconography as part of a dialogue between the king and gods on the one hand, and between the king and the elite group responsible for producing and giving meaning to statuary on the other. The latter could have consisted, in addition to the king himself, of officials in charge of furnishing temples and mortuary complexes and of the leaders of workshops. These people were presumably steeped in values, of which we can see another expression in literature, that formed part of the same overall high-cultural complex. It seems that they wished to incorporate those values into the king's sculptural image.

In this context of production within a small elite group of exacting royal and divine patrons, the works will have had a specifically artistic focus—a concern with visual form and its realization of meaning—while retaining a broad ideological significance. This focus can be seen in the influence exerted by the royal statuary. Many non-royal statues of the late 12th and 13th dynasties have similar casts of face to royal pieces. The royal style was disseminated to contexts where its iconographic implications could hardly have been the same, although its sober and serious qualities probably had their own value (see e.g. Vandier 1958: pls. 77–92; large group: Habachi 1985: pls. 50–109; see also Sourouzian 1991: pls. 48–52). Some owners may also have seen their position in their local communities as having elements in common with that of the king, but they could hardly have entertained his aspirations to a cosmic role. The tendency of the non-royal to follow the royal is widespread within and outside Egypt and is unsurprising. This case is nonetheless revealing, because a specific iconography changed in the course of dissemination into something that was mainly a prestigious association, rather than having all its royal meaning. Royal statuary was influential despite its general inaccessibility in its destined positions. Here, the large numbers of royal statues should be borne in mind: they must have been produced for many temples in a variety of sizes and types, and the most important temples contained numerous examples of them. Some of their influence may have passed directly through workshops, being stimulated either by members of the elite who were involved with them or by the sculptors themselves, who will have applied and spread their training and stylistic predilections broadly.

This dissemination and elaboration within a restricted context can be observed in many periods. The most striking example may be the development of temple relief and iconography in Ptolemaic and early Roman times (e.g. Sauneron and Stierlin 1978), when the ubiquitous hieroglyphic writing in the wall scenes was in a form very few could read, while the overall design and details of the interiors were largely invisible once they had been completed (as had always been the case).[16] Much of the motivation for these developments was religious, but aesthetic factors were also crucial (Baines 1997). In comparison with 12th dynasty royal statuary, the Graeco-Roman temple forms had relatively little impact in the world outside, in part because they were so highly specialized and in part because of a gradual withering of the indigenous elite.[17]

Both for the 12th dynasty and for Graeco-Roman temples, the institutional position of art should be borne in mind. Whereas the creation of enormous monuments such as the great pyramids self-evidently required huge resources and many people, the more regular pattern of production of statuary and relief involved high degrees of skill and of artistic decision and design on the part of smaller but still significant numbers of people. As might be expected, artistic and iconographic concerns were significant to the development of these genres at least as much as were concerns relating more closely to contexts of use. A straightforward notion of propaganda may not be appropriate for the interpretation of statuary and relief.

---

[16] Thus, the interpretation of Christian Leitz (2001: 341–2), who sees priestly personnel as absorbing the culture of the hieroglyphic inscriptions and scenes from being present in the temple, could only well apply to the lowest register of decoration (he suggests the first two, but this seems doubtful to me), and then only for good lighting conditions and people with excellent vision. It is another question whether a human audience was expected to read the inscriptions; I doubt whether that was their main purpose.

[17] Egyptian architectural forms were, however, widely influential in the Graeco-Roman world, but in free interpretations rather than close copies; see McKenzie (2007); briefly Baines (2004b: 39–40).

The late 18th dynasty

The third period I review briefly runs from the later 18th dynasty to the early 19th (c.1400–1275). This begins with the reign of Amenhotep III, during which more works of architecture and representational art were created than in almost any other (for the following, see Kozloff et al. 1992; O'Connor and Cline 1998). Unlike most kings, Amenhotep seems to have worked on projects at an undiminished or increased pace up to his death. Surviving works from his reign include royal and non-royal, as well as major and decorative forms; the great quantity preserved can be only a small fraction of what was created. Among the king's major undertakings was his stupendous mortuary temple, which was decorated with many hundreds of hardstone statues of himself (Fig. 44) and of deities (Fig. 45) and sacred animals (Bryan 1997). The temple may have been the largest single one built to date, and in front of it stood perhaps the largest transported statues in Egypt, the quartzite Memnon Colossi, which were carved in an extremely hard stone and brought hundreds of miles upstream to be set in position. These feats were recorded in inscriptions set up in the temple which presented them as being integrated into the design of the whole city of Thebes (Helck 1961: 195–9, 272–3). While these texts hardly

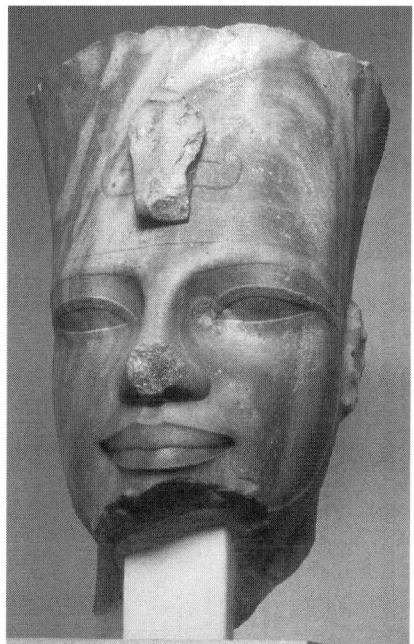

Fig. 44. Head from colossal statue of Amenhotep III, from his mortuary temple on the West Bank at Thebes. 18th dynasty. Quartzite. Height 1.31 m, width 1.02 m across top of crown. British Museum EA7. Courtesy British Museum.

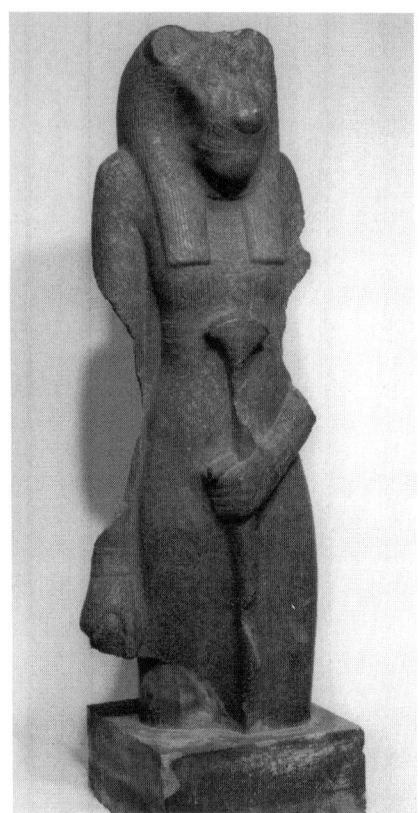

Fig. 45. Colossal statue of the goddess Sakhmet from the Mut temple complex at Karnak, probably first set up in the mortuary temple of Amenhotep III on the West Bank at Thebes. Granodiorite. 18th dynasty, reign of Amenhotep III. preserved height 1.98 m, width 48.7 cm. British Museum EA45. Courtesy British Museum.

address narrowly artistic concerns beyond general expressions of the temples' beauty and of the rich materials used in their construction and decoration, they do form an iconological commentary on their significance and thus supply some discourse—probably simple in comparison with its oral background—surrounding the king's whole project to remodel the country's religious capital and hence to extend a substantially aesthetic design beyond the core of temples and palaces (O'Connor in preparation).

The entire operation was organized by Amenhotep son of Hapu, a non-royal official who inscribed a version of the events on one of his statues (Helck 1961: 272–3). He had the highest non-royal status in the land and was granted the unprecedented privilege of a mortuary temple of his own (Wildung 1977: 286, with refs.). On the East Bank, opposite the king's mortuary temple, was the Luxor Temple, whose meaning seems to have focused on the kingship itself (Bell 1985). A hardstone stela of the twin brothers Suty and Hor, the 'architects' of that temple, is preserved (Edwards 1939: pl. 21). Several features of the stela, notably the innovative solar hymn, show that they were among the leading people of the age (Fecht 1967; Baines 1985b). Apart from this biographical flesh which can be added to the bones of the monuments and their builders, there was a high level of innovation in architecture, in the style of some statuary, and in the elaborate reliefs of non-royal tombs. Variety and quite rapid development in art parallel a great diversity in religious texts and support the assumption that the artistic changes form part of a wider ferment (Baines 1998b). Certain features looked to the past, for example in the performance of ancient rituals (Epigraphic Survey 1980: 43, pl. 28) and in the Middle Kingdom model for a major statue of Amenhotep son of Hapu (Fig. 46; Sourouzian 1991).

Art should be seen both as an essential medium through which these changes were formulated and as a goal: it was constitutive and not accessory. The ultimate purpose of Amenhotep III's projects may have been religious and political, being connected with solar religion and with raising the king's status in relation to people and to the gods. Such goals were realized through art and architecture, and ultimately in the king's grand remodelling of capital and

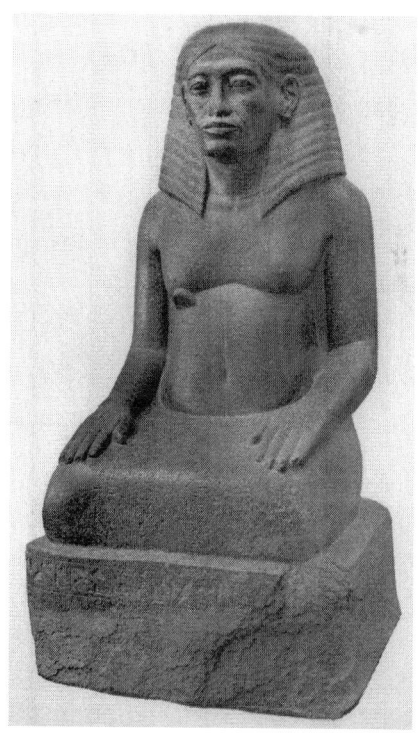

Fig. 46. Seated statue of Amenhotep Son of Hapu, pose and iconography inspired by Middle Kingdom models (nose area recarved in antiquity), from Karnak. Granodiorite. 18th dynasty, reign of Amenhotep III. Height 1.42 m. Cairo Museum CG 42127. After Legrain (1906: pl. 76).

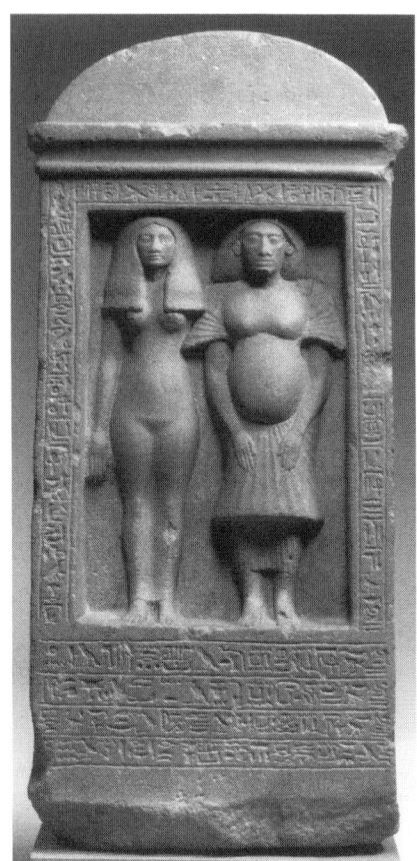

Fig. 47. Stela of the sculptor Bak and his wife Tahere, provenance unknown. Quartzite. 18th dynasty, reign of Akhenaten (Amarna period). Height 67 cm. Berlin, Ägyptisches Museum 1/63. Courtesy Ägyptisches Museum Berlin.

country as a divine cosmos with a superhuman royal protagonist (there is some evidence for the counterpart of all this in living ceremonial: Baines 2006a).

This prominence of art, and of people who can be termed artists, continued during the 'revolution' of Amenhotep III's successor Akhenaten. In a rock relief at Aswan, where they may have supervised the extraction of granite for statuary, the father-and-son sculptors Men and Bak commemorated their work for both kings, differentiating between the artistic styles of the two (Habachi 1965: 86 fig. 11; Krauss 1986: 18 fig. 8). Bak's own mortuary stela (Fig. 47; Krauss 1986) exemplifies the new style in a strong form. Later in the reign, the chief sculptor Thutmose, who occupied a large house compound at the new capital of el-Amarna, headed the studio which created numerous heads (e.g. Fig. 48), including the renowned Berlin bust of Nefertiti. The compound contained stabling for chariot horses—hardly a requirement for

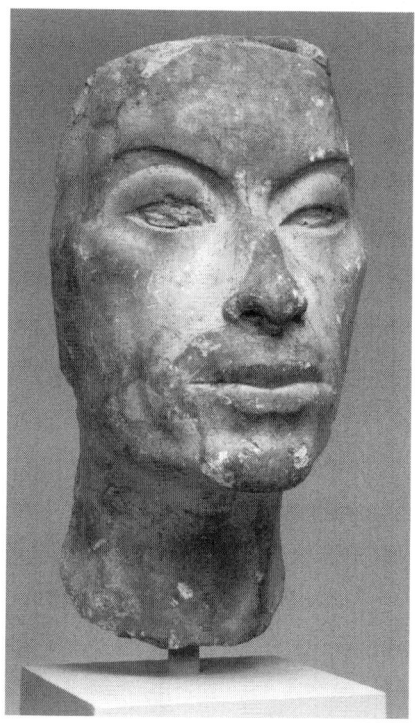

Fig. 48. Plaster head, possibly of the later King Aya, from the house compound of the sculptor Thutmose at el-Amarna. 18th dynasty, reign of Akhenaten (Amarna period). Berlin, Ägyptisches Museum 21350. Height 27 cm. Courtesy Ägyptisches Museum Berlin.

sculpting—and the object with the sculptor's name and titles that identified the tenant was an ivory horse blinker. In a city laid out for ceremonial chariot journeys to and from the suburbs where the king resided overnight (O'Connor in preparation), a chief royal sculptor could ride the streets on a richly caparisoned chariot alongside other members of the elite.[18]

Men, Bak, and Thutmose are important also because they came at the beginning and end of Akhenaten's radical artistic style. Men and Bak were active through its formative period, whereas the works from Thutmose's studio show a softening and a partial return to a traditional manner. Since Akhenaten was not himself an artist, he must have relied on people like these to make a reality of his ideas, and they in turn probably had a decisive impact on the particular direction of artistic development. The graffito of Men and Bak states that the king had instructed them personally, and this has sometimes been taken literally, but Rolf Krauss has demonstrated (1986: 40–2) that

---

[18] For the horse blinker, see Krauss (1983). On housing and status at el-Amarna, see Crocker (1985); Tietze (1985; 1986); Shaw (1992).

such statements are conventional in inscriptions of builders and architects—the earliest related text dates to the Old Kingdom (Roccati 1982: 181–6) and an instance is known from el-Amarna itself—and so need not show anything distinctive about Akhenaten. What is said is likely to contain some truth, if only by coincidence, since Akhenaten must have indicated that he wanted radically new artistic forms and may have influenced their direction, as well as quite probably selecting the artists who oversaw their production.

Where Amenhotep III and Akhenaten agreed, or more probably took things for granted, was in using artistic production to formulate and propagate their differing ideas. The scale of Amenhotep III's works hardly diminished under Akhenaten; nor did standards, at least in statuary. But, just as small-scale works of dynasty 0 like the palettes do not seem to have addressed a wider audience, even the colossal and relatively public—or at least highly visible—structures of Amenhotep III were ultimately aimed only at those who could visit the temples, or in their greatest dissemination at those who would partake in the life and ceremonies of the capital (see also Baines 2006a). They may not have had much message for the people of the country as a whole. There is no strong sense in which they were propagandistic to the widest public, although such propaganda would be hard to identify and might not be expressed in art. (There may be a case for seeing the comparably grandiose projects of Ramesses II in the following century as being more oriented toward a public.) What they do show is that radical change necessarily involved the artistic forms which were part of the civilization's definition.

Art remained significant for religious and other change when Akhenaten's reforms were rejected after his death, but not in a straightforward way. The almost immediate return to traditional forms has an obvious symbolism, but for at least a generation styles continued to be influenced by Akhenaten. Some developments in style and in the rendering of nature before and during the time of Akhenaten (e.g. Russmann 1980) were not lightly abandoned, and artists—like most modern interpreters—may not have seen them as specific to the ideas which were being repudiated. But under Sety I ($c.$1292–1279), when the rejection of Akhenaten and the return to enriched traditional forms culminated (Fig. 49), there was a generally stronger contrast with the styles of Akhenaten than at the end of the 18th dynasty (e.g. Calverley and Broome 1933–59; Hornung 1991). In his relatively short reign, Sety constructed and decorated many major works, notably temples and his tomb, continuing the artistic focus of Amenhotep III in particular (not addressed specifically by Peter Brand, 2000). The principal difference, and one that is in keeping with the aims of Sety I, is that his art was not strongly innovative. His military reliefs constitute an important exception here (Epigraphic Survey 1986). Sety's artistic achievements are noteworthy also in the context of the numerous

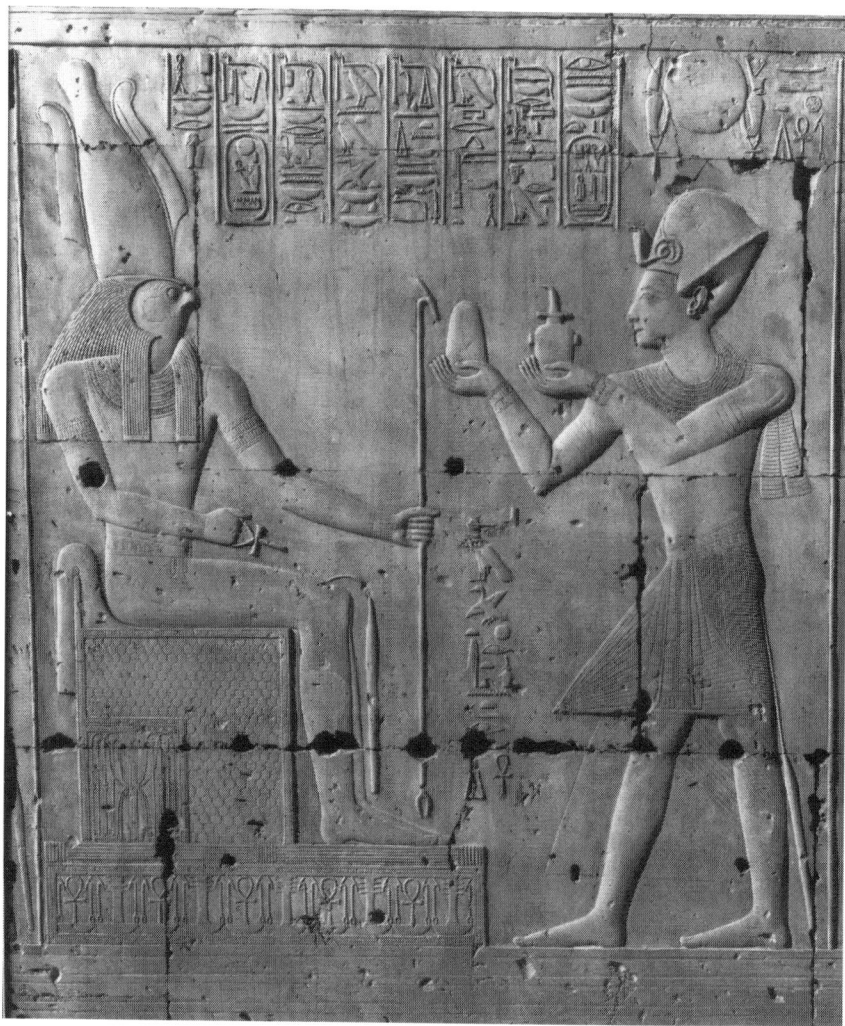

Fig. 49. Relief of Sety I offering to Ptah-Sokar, north wall of the Hall of Sokar and Nefertem in his temple at Abydos. 19th dynasty. Photograph by Amice M. Calverley. Courtesy Egypt Exploration Society.

military campaigns that he conducted (see e.g. Murnane 1990), which might have meant that he had fewer resources to devote to art than rulers in periods of peace. This expenditure is a measure of the continuing centrality of art, which was not an adjunct of other activities and purposes but a partly autonomous institution with its own patterns of development.

The Late and Graeco-Roman periods

The times of stability and prosperity between 700 and 300 were fewer than in earlier epochs. Only small numbers of major monuments survive from the period, in large part because they were concentrated in the Nile Delta, where preservation is poor. The relevance of this period to the argument here is especially in its uses of tradition (see also Loprieno 2003b). A 'revivalist' artistic style began to appear in the late 8th century, before there was any lasting political change or reunification of the country's fragmented territories (A. Leahy 1992; see also Russmann 1974). The extent of revival in the later 25th and 26th dynasties and focus on the past was, however, much greater than earlier, and it encompassed many spheres (see e.g. Brunner 1970; Neureiter 1994, both with problematic interpretations), including the reuse of ancient royal titularies, texts, and language (Manuelian 1993), and more generally a return to a rather more austere style characteristic of much earlier periods and not of the preceding late New Kingdom (*c*.1200–1070) and Third Intermediate Period (*c*.1070–730).

In art, the striking feature of this revival is the use, principally in its initial phase, of models a from wide range of periods. There are examples of the copying of standing monuments both in temple relief (e.g. Baines 1973) and in non-royal monuments, of the combination of different styles in single pieces (e.g. Manuelian 1985: 110–12), and of the commissioning by the rich of statues of themselves in a variety of styles (e.g. Leclant 1961: pls. 1–33; Bothmer 1969 [1960]: nos. 13–14). Copies on Roman period papyri of Middle Kingdom tomb inscriptions that were known in situ in the 19th century CE show such material interchanging with the stream of literary tradition (Baines 1992a: 254 with n. 41; Osing and Rosati 1998: 55–100; Kahl 1999: 268–70). Some of these features have more limited parallels from earlier periods, as with the statue of Amenhotep son of Hapu cited earlier, but their extent is new, as is their rather more public and self-conscious character. These are exemplified in an inscription in the tomb of Ibi at Thebes which invites the reader not just to read it out but also to copy it (Kuhlmann and Schenkel 1983: 71–3). This tomb is also striking for its decoration, sections of which were closely based on the 6th dynasty tomb (more than 1500 years older) of a namesake at Deir el-Gabrawi, about 300 kilometres to the north.[19] It would not have been very taxing to make suitable recordings of the old reliefs; what is remarkable is that the

---

[19] Kuhlmann and Schenkel (1983). The scepticism of Friedrich von Bissing (1926) about the connection was, I think, incorrect, being based on the notion of exact copying rather than reuse and adaptation of motifs and compositions. Parallels between the two tombs are strong enough to make coincidence very unlikely. See also Kemp (2006: 372–3).

later Ibi knew about the older tomb. Unless this was a matter of chance, it implies that someone had a detailed knowledge of not very prominent ancient provincial monuments. Even if it was chance, the fact would remain that such tombs were being explored. Although there is no evidence for art exhibitions or museums—analogous phenomena may occur elsewhere in the ancient Near East (Roaf 1992; Cooper 1990; Beaulieu 1989: 138–41)—these practices come close to them in their deliberate seeking out of ancient works.

The example of Ibi is one of many. The Late period use of the artistic past involved a more explicit and varied recourse than in earlier times, but not necessarily a fundamental difference in approach. It implies the presence of attitudes and treatments that can be paralleled in artists' methods in many cultures; the classical tradition, both in ancient Rome and thereafter, is the obvious European example. Artistic use of the past in Egypt is a visible analogy for the verbal practices of criticism whose absence from the record many scholars have taken to suggest that a sense of 'art' was lacking—while continuing tacitly to analyse the works themselves as art. As will be clear, I believe that their action is correct and that they are wrong to have such scruples. Such uses of the past leave space for a considerable measure of innovation, as is visible notably in 4th century tomb reliefs (e.g. Fig. 50; see L. M. Leahy 1988). A crucial point here is that, whether or not such developments were prompted by, or intended to incorporate, other ideological

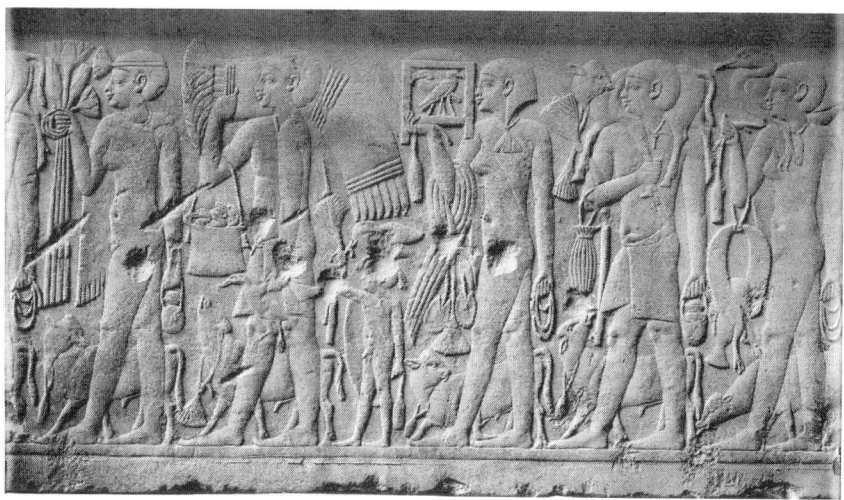

Fig. 50. Group of offering bearers on the lintel relief of Tjanefer from Heliopolis. Limestone, raised relief. 30th dynasty. Height 30.5 cm, total width 1.14 m. Cairo Museum JdE 29211. After Maspero (1907: pl. 34); see also L. M. Leahy (1988: no. 77).

matters, their formulation was artistic. The culture and tradition of art created an aesthetic domain that referred to itself in the first instance for its meaning, and was able to articulate its discourse in terms of differential recourse to past models, to more or less contemporaneous ones, or to a conscious mixture of the two.

Thus, while recourse to the past was a broad phenomenon, it is likely to have contributed to the insulation of the institution of art from other cultural activities. This separation has clear social implications. Those who can comprehend the use of old styles are a small, learned minority, in this case probably a smaller group than in the New Kingdom. Only they count as truly competent to judge; in their own eyes, only they count at all. Despite the use of divergent models, the social divisiveness of art becomes more evident than the cohesiveness it offers by sustaining a single cultural definition. These tendencies probably reached their high point in temples of the Graeco-Roman period (Fig. 51), some of whose inscriptions are almost literally indecipherable. These esoteric creations received massive patronage and were deeply serious in intent. They were very complex works of art, and in considerable measure their raison d'être was in their artistic character. In the long term, a situation emerged in which traditional artists were answerable only to a small indigenous priestly elite, and through them to the rulers. In one way, this is everything artists can ask for. In the end, however, it may be the death of art because too many people may come to see a specific form of it as dispensable or abhorrent. In Egypt this happened during the late

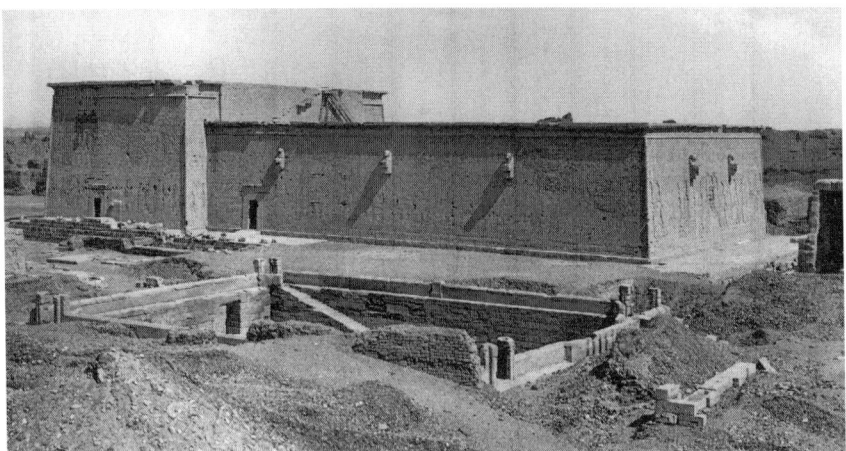

Fig. 51. View of the temple complex of Hathor and Isis at Dendara, from west. 1st century BCE – 2nd century CE. After Chassinat (1934: pl. xxv).

Roman period. When Christianity came, it too worked through art, necessarily rejecting traditional Egyptian style and subject matter along with the religion and civilization of which they had been an essential component.

CONCLUSION: THE INSTITUTION OF ART

The significance of art can be seen in many facets of Egyptian civilization, and is commensurate with the preponderance of aesthetically formed material in the record. Art served the ordered cosmos, which was celebrated on behalf of the gods and which humanity, as represented by the king, and the gods defended against the forces of chaos. Art defined, encapsulated, and perpetuated that cosmos. At the same time it served the perpetual destinies of ruler and inner elite and circumscribed their lifestyles in relation to the rest of society. The focus of artistic production on these central activities, many of them secret and exclusive, reinforced and legitimized the position of art, which in turn legitimized religious dedications together with much of the underlying division in society, in a mutually sustaining cycle. In this context, the role of hieroglyphic writing in art is important (Fischer 1986; Ch. 13 here). Writing brought representational forms together with verbal high culture, while also limiting access to that culture by incorporating it in a style of writing available only to a minority even of the literate, most of whom used the cursive form of hieratic. The reinforcing cycle of official religion and art also favoured the internal, self-regarding focus of both. What mattered in maintaining the order of things was to sustain the activity of the small group who commissioned, designed, and perhaps executed the works of art within the context of elite high culture. Only those involved comprehended the activities and their significance fully. A wider legitimation for their position is one that is general to elites: on behalf of society they assume responsibility for portentous matters and appropriate the necessary resources. This role for the elite in maintaining traditions is indeed formulated explicitly in religious and literary texts of the Graeco-Roman period (Derchain 1990: 25–8).

Within continuing artistic culture, the uses of tradition reinforce this focus on the elite and their artistic interests. There is ample evidence from Egypt for artistic change, variation, and innovation, so that interpretations of the fundamental aim of artistic conventions as being to maintain 'invariance' do not take an actor's perspective.[20] The perpetual dialogue with the past and

---

[20] Davis (1989); Assmann (1992: 169–74); see further Baines (1997: 217–18).

the use of different past models with diverse implications characterize an artistic discourse that is internally self-sustaining and exploits this characteristic to assert its significance both to itself and to the wider society. This internal discourse, which provides an analogy within the culture for the relative insulation of Egyptian civilization from its surroundings, is both a legitimation of art and a way in which artists create a context in which only their own concerns matter. As such, it is a typically professional phenomenon.

Professions, both ancient and modern, are exclusive and assume that only their members can judge the validity of what they do, avoiding recourse to a wider constituency. This characterization applies strongly to the Egyptian elite, and hence to the status of the art whose production they organized and which they or their masters, the king and the gods, consumed. The elite was a professional class, a group of administrators rather than a nobility, and in principle if not in practice lacking an independent source of wealth. Artists might be designers and supervisors, or possibly executants, who were part of that central group, or they could be subordinate artisans who worked for them. Either way, they depended principally on the king and the elite, and far less on the rest of society. Their livelihood came from state or elite incomes that were appropriated from producers to the centre by way of taxes, rents, or levies of labour (see e.g. Janssen 1975b). The artists had little constituency in the wider society. As people who did not wield supreme power in the state, they have left little individual trace in the record. Similarly, evidence bearing upon the grandees of many other periods and cultures hardly includes material about artists (contrast here Takeshi Inomata's archaeological findings of elite artistic activity at the Maya site of Aguateca, 2001).

The split between the groups involved in artistic production and consumption on the one hand, and the rest of society on the other, is complemented by the scarcity of artistically formed evidence from outside the elite. The scale of many artistic undertakings was so great that a large proportion of the population must have been affected by them. Such people often have little control over what is imposed on them, but they must have participated more or less willingly in these activities, and to a considerable degree they must have accepted the importance of what was done, that is in effect, its official legitimations. To that extent, the works and the institution of art will have exerted persuasive power over everyone. The archaeological record of the First Intermediate period (c.2150–2000), in which there was a proliferation of crude but characteristically artistic forms among a larger group than in centralized periods (e.g. Seidlmayer 1990; Dunham 1937), supports the assumption that artistic forms had such power. The tomb stelae and statuary of this period served a traditional elite function, and inherited artistic forms were in principle adopted with the function. Similarly, votive bronzes, the numbers of which proliferated in the Late period, and which were probably dedicated by a relatively broad social group, remained within established artistic conventions, although with widely varying levels of artistic execution (e.g. Roeder 1956).

The forms created in the first few dynasties continued to constitute much of the architectural and visual definition of the Egyptian cosmos and society; no alternative was available. This indissociable identification of art and civilization, which is a measure of the significance of art in Egypt, says something important about the role of art, rather than showing that so multifunctional and multifarious a phenomenon cannot be termed 'art'.

References

Adams, Barbara (1974). *Ancient Hierakonpolis* and *Ancient Hierakonpolis: supplement* (Warminster: Aris & Phillips).
Adams, William Y. (1977). *Nubia: corridor to Africa* (London: Allen Lane).
—— (1985). 'Doubts about the "lost pharaohs"'. *Journal of Near Eastern Studies* 44: 185–92.
Albert, Jean-Pierre, and Béatrix Midant-Reynes (eds.) (2005). *Le sacrifice humain en Egypte ancienne et ailleurs*, Etudes d'Egyptologie 6 (Paris: Soleb).
Aldred, Cyril (1970). 'Some royal portraits of the Middle Kingdom in ancient Egypt'. *Metropolitan Museum Journal* 3: 27–50.
—— (1971). *Jewels of the pharaohs: Egyptian jewellery of the dynastic period* (London: Thames & Hudson).
Alexanian, Nicole (1998). 'Die Reliefdekoration des Chasechemui aus dem sogenannten Fort in Hierakonpolis'. In Nicolas Grimal (ed.), *Les critères de datation stylistiques à l'Ancien Empire*, Bibliothèque d'Etude 120 (Cairo: Institut Français d'Archéologie Orientale) 1–29.
Allam, Schafik (1968). 'Sind die nichtliterarischen Schriftostraka Brouillons?' *Journal of Egyptian Archaeology* 54: 121–8.
Allen, James P. (2003). A new Middle Kingdom biographical inscription. Paper presented at American Research Center in Egypt Annual Meeting, Atlanta, April 2003.
—— (2005). *The art of medicine in ancient Egypt*, exhibition catalogue, Metropolitan Museum of Art (New York and New Haven: Metropolitan Museum of Art; Yale University Press).
Allen, T. G. (1974). *The Book of the Dead, or, Going Forth by Day: ideas of the ancient Egyptians concerning the hereafter as expressed in their own terms*, Studies in Ancient Oriental Civilization 37 (Chicago: Oriental Institute of the University of Chicago).
Altenmüller, Hartwig (1972). *Die Texte zum Begräbnisritual in den Pyramiden des Alten Reiches*, Ägyptologische Abhandlungen 24 (Wiesbaden: Otto Harrassowitz).
—— (1973). 'Bemerkungen zum Hirtenlied des Alten Reiches'. *Chronique d'Egypte* 48: 211–31.
—— (1984–5). 'Das "Sänftenlied" des Alten Reiches'. *Bulletin de la Société d'Egyptologie de Genève* 9/10: 15–30.
—— (1998). *Die Wanddarstellungen im Grab des Mehu in Saqqara*, Deutsches Archäologisches Institut, Abteilung Kairo, Archäologische Veröffentlichungen 42 (Mainz: Philipp von Zabern).
Amenta, Alessia (2002). 'The Egyptian tomb as a House of Life for the afterlife?' In Rosanna Pirelli (ed.), *Egyptological essays on state and society*, Università degli Studi di Napoli 'L'Orientale', Dipartimento di Studi e Richerche su Africa e Paesi Arabi, Serie Egittologica (Naples: n.p.) II, 13–26.

Ames-Lewis, Francis, and Anka Bednarek (eds.) (1992). *Decorum in Renaissance narrative art: papers delivered at the annual conference of the Association of Art Historians, London, April 1991* (London: Department of History of Art, Birkbeck College).

Andreu, Guillemette (ed.) (2002). *Les artistes de pharaon: Deir el-Médineh et la Vallée des Rois*, exhibition catalogue (Paris and Turnhout: Réunion des musées nationaux; Brepols).

Andrews, Carol A. R. (1990). *Catalogue of demotic papyri in the British Museum IV, Ptolemaic legal texts from the Theban area* (London: British Museum Publications).

Anthes, Rudolf (1941). 'Werkverfahren ägyptischer Bildhauer'. *Mitteilungen des Deutschen Instituts für Ägyptische Altertumskunde in Kairo* 10: 79–121.

Appadurai, Arjun (1981). 'The past as a scarce resource'. *Man* NS 16: 201–19.

Arnett, William S. (1982). *The predynastic origin of Egyptian hieroglyphs: evidence for the development of rudimentary forms of hieroglyphs in Upper Egypt in the fourth millennium B.C.* (Washington, DC: University Press of America).

Arnheim, Rudolf (1974). *Art and visual perception: a psychology of the visual eye*, new version (Berkeley etc.: University of California Press).

Arnold, Dieter (1962). *Wandrelief und Raumfunktion in ägyptischen Tempeln des Neuen Reiches*, Münchner Ägyptologische Studien 2 (Berlin: Bruno Hessling).

—— (1991). *Building in Egypt: pharaonic stone masonry* (New York and Oxford: Oxford University Press).

Arnold, Dieter, Dorothea Arnold, and Peter Dorman (1988). *The pyramid of Senwosret I*, Metropolitan Museum of Art Egyptian Expedition, South Cemeteries of Lisht 1 (New York: Metropolitan Museum of Art).

Arnold, Dorothea (1991). 'Amenemhat I and the early twelfth dynasty at Thebes'. *Metropolitan Museum Journal* 26: 5–48.

—— (2005). 'The architecture of Meketre's slaughterhouse and other early twelfth dynasty wooden models'. In Peter Jánosi (ed.), *Structure and significance—thoughts on ancient Egyptian architecture* (Vienna: Akademie der Wissenschaften) 1–75.

Arnold, Dorothea, and Christiane Ziegler (eds.) (1999). *Egyptian art in the age of the pyramids*, exhibition catalogue, Metropolitan Museum of Art (New York: Metropolitan Museum of Art).

Asselberghs, Henri (1961). *Chaos en beheersing: documenten uit het aeneolitisch Egypte*, Documenta et Monumenta Orientis Antiqui 8 (Leiden: E. J. Brill).

Assmann, Jan (1969). *Liturgische Lieder an den Sonnengott: Untersuchungen zur altägyptischen Sonnenhymnik* I, Münchner Ägyptologische Studien 19 (Berlin: Bruno Hessling).

—— (1970). *Der König als Sonnenpriester: ein kosmographischer Begleittext zur kultischen Sonnenhymnik*, Abhandlungen des Deutschen Archäologischen Instituts, Abteilung Kairo 7 (Glückstadt: J. J. Augustin).

—— (1975). *Zeit und Ewigkeit im alten Ägypten*, Abhandlungen der Heidelberger Akademie der Wissenschaften, philosophisch-historische Klasse 1975, 1 (Heidelberg: Carl Winter, Universitätsverlag).

Assmann, Jan (1977a). 'Das ägyptische Zweibrüdermärchen (Papyrus d'Orbiney): eine Textanalyse auf drei Ebenen am Leitfaden der Einheitsfrage'. *Zeitschrift für Ägyptische Sprache und Altertumskunde* 104: 1–25.

—— (1977b). *Das Grab der Mutirdis*, Archäologische Veröffentlichungen des Deutschen Archäologischen Instituts, Abteilung Kairo 13 (Mainz: Philipp von Zabern).

—— (1977c). 'Die Verborgenheit des Mythos in Ägypten'. *Göttinger Miszellen* 25: 7–43. Reprinted in Assmann, *Ägyptische Geheimnisse* (2004) 31–57.

—— (1977d). 'Fest des Augenblicks—Verheissung der Dauer: die Kontroverse der ägyptischen Harfnerlieder'. In Jan Assmann, Erika Feucht, and Reinhard Grieshammer (eds.), *Fragen an die altägyptische Literatur: Studien zum Gedenken an Eberhard Otto* (Wiesbaden: Dr Ludwig Reichert) 55–84.

—— (1980). 'Die "Loyalistische Lehre" Echnatons'. *Studien zur Altägyptischen Kultur* 8: 1–32.

—— (1982). 'Parallelismus membrorum'. In Wolfgang Helck and Wolfhart Westendorf (eds.), *Lexikon der Ägyptologie* (Wiesbaden: Otto Harrassowitz) IV, 900–10.

—— (1983a). 'Das Doppelgesicht der Zeit im altägyptischen Denken'. In *Schriften der Karl-Friedrich von Siemens Stiftung* 6 (Munich: Oldenburg) 189–23; reprinted in Assmann, *Stein und Zeit* (1991) 32–58.

—— (1983b). 'Schrift, Tod und Identität: das Grab als Vorschule der Literatur im alten Ägypten'. In Aleida Assmann, Jan Assmann, and Christof Hardmeier (eds.), *Schrift und Gedächtnis: Beiträge zur Archäologie der literarischen Kommunikation* (Munich: Wilhelm Fink) 64–93; reprinted in Assmann, *Stein und Zeit* (1991) 169–99.

—— (1985). 'Gibt es eine Klassik in der ägyptischen Literaturgeschichte? Ein Beitrag zur Geistesgeschichte der Ramessidenzeit'. *Zeitschrift der Deutschen Morgenländischen Gesellschaft, Supplement* 6: 35–52.

—— (1989). *Maât: l'Egypte pharaonique et l'idée de justice sociale*, Conférences, Essais et Leçons du Collège de France (Paris: Julliard).

—— (1990). *Ma'at: Gerechtigkeit und Unsterblichkeit im Alten Ägypten* (Munich: C. H. Beck).

—— (1991). *Stein und Zeit: Mensch und Gesellschaft im alten Ägypten* (Munich: Wilhelm Fink).

—— (1992). *Das kulturelle Gedächtnis: Schrift, Erinnerung und politische Identität in frühen Hochkulturen* (Munich: C. H. Beck).

—— (1995) [1983]. *Egyptian solar religion in the New Kingdom: Re, Amun and the crisis of polytheism*, trans. Anthony Alcock (London and New York: Kegan Paul International [revision of Assmann, *Re und Amun*, 1983]).

—— (1996). 'Kulturelle und literarische Texte'. In Antonio Loprieno (ed.), *Ancient Egyptian literature: history and forms*, Probleme der Ägyptologie 10 (Leiden: E. J. Brill) 59–82.

—— (1999). 'Cultural and literary texts'. In Gerald Moers (ed.), *Definitely: Egyptian literature; proceedings of the symposion "Ancient Egyptian literature: history and forms", Los Angeles, March 24–26, 1995*, Lingua Aegyptia, Studia Monographica 2 (Göttingen: Seminar für Ägyptologie und Koptologie) 1–15.

Assmann, Jan (1999) [1975]. *Ägyptische Hymnen und Gebete*, Orbis Biblicus et Orientalis, 2nd edn. (Fribourg and Göttingen: Universitätsverlag; Vandenhoeck & Ruprecht).
—— (2004). *Ägyptische Geheimnisse* (Munich: Wilhelm Fink).
Aston, Barbara G. (1994). *Ancient Egyptian stone vessels: materials and forms*, Studien zur Archäologie und Geschichte Altägyptens 5 (Heidelberg: Heidelberger Orientverlag).
Aston, Barbara G., James A. Harrell, and Ian Shaw (2000). 'Stone'. In Paul T. Nicholson and Ian Shaw (eds.), *Ancient Egyptian materials and technology* (Cambridge: Cambridge University Press) 5–77.
Aufrère, Sydney (1991). *L'univers minéral dans la pensée égyptienne*, Bibliothèque d'Etude 105, 2 vols. (Cairo: Institut Français d'Archéologie Orientale).
Backhaus, Werner, Reinhold Kliegl, and John Simon Werner (eds.) (1998). *Color vision: perspectives from different disciplines* (Berlin and New York: Walter de Gruyter).
Badawy, Alexander (1968). *A history of Egyptian architecture* III, *From the eighteenth dynasty to the end of the twentieth dynasty, 1580–1085 B.C.* (Berkeley and Los Angeles: University of California Press).
Baer, Klaus (1962). 'The low price of land in ancient Egypt'. *Journal of the American Research Center in Egypt* 1: 25–45.
Bagley, Robert W. (2004). 'Anyang writing and the origin of the Chinese writing system'. In Stephen D. Houston (ed.), *The first writing: script invention as history and process* (Cambridge: Cambridge University Press) 190–249.
—— (2005). 'The prehistory of Chinese music theory'. *Proceedings of the British Academy* 131: 41–90.
Bagnall, Roger S., and Bruce W. Frier (1994). *The demography of Roman Egypt*, Cambridge Studies in Population, Economy, and Society in Past Time 23 (Cambridge: Cambridge University Press).
Baines, John (1973). 'The destruction of the pyramid temple of Saḥureˁ'. *Göttinger Miszellen* 4: 9–14.
—— (1974). Review of H. A. Groenewegen-Frankfort, *Arrest and movement* (1951; 1972 reprint). *Journal of Egyptian Archaeology* 60: 272–6.
—— (1975). Egyptian religious personifications: a study of representational evidence. Doctoral dissertation: University of Oxford.
—— (1976). 'Temple symbolism'. *Royal Anthropological Institute News* 15: 10–15.
—— (1978). Review of Erik Iversen, *Canon and proportions in ancient Egyptian art*, 2nd edn. (1975). *Journal of Egyptian Archaeology* 64: 189–91.
—— (1982). 'Interpreting Sinuhe'. *Journal of Egyptian Archaeology* 68: 31–44.
—— (1983). 'Literacy and ancient Egyptian society'. *Man* NS 18: 572–99; = Ch. 3 here.
—— (1984a). 'Interpretations of religion: logic, discourse, rationality'. *Göttinger Miszellen* 76: 25–54.
—— (1984b). 'Schreiben' [article in English]. In Wolfgang Helck and Wolfhart Westendorf (eds.), *Lexikon der Ägyptologie* (Wiesbaden: Otto Harrassowitz) V, 693–8.
—— (1985a). 'Color terminology and color classification: ancient Egyptian color terminology and polychromy'. *American Anthropologist* 87: 282–97; = Ch. 11 here.

Baines, John (1985b). 'Egyptian twins'. *Orientalia* 54: 461–82.

—— (1985c). *Fecundity figures: Egyptian personification and the iconology of a genre* (Warminster: Aris & Phillips; Chicago: Bolchazy-Carducci).

—— (1985d). 'Schäfer's mottoes and the understanding of representation'. *Journal of Egyptian Archaeology* 77: 194–6; = Ch. 10 here.

—— (1985e). 'Theories and universals of representation: Heinrich Schäfer and Egyptian art'. *Art History* 8: 1–25; = Ch. 9 here.

—— (1986). 'The stela of Emhab: innovation, tradition, hierarchy'. *Journal of Egyptian Archaeology* 72: 41–53.

—— (1988a). 'An Abydos list of gods and an Old Kingdom use of texts'. In John Baines, T. G. H. James, Anthony Leahy, and A. F. Shore (eds.), *Pyramid studies and other essays presented to I. E. S. Edwards*, Occasional Publications 7 (London: Egypt Exploration Society) 124–33.

—— (1988b). 'Literacy, social organization and the archaeological record: the case of early Egypt'. In John Gledhill, Barbara Bender, and Mogens Trolle Larsen (eds.), *State and society: the emergence and development of social hierarchy and political centralization*, One World Archaeology 4 (London: Unwin Hyman) 192–214; = Ch. 4 here.

—— (1989a). 'Ancient Egyptian concepts and uses of the past: 3rd to 2nd millennium BC evidence'. In Robert Layton (ed.), *Who needs the past? Indigenous values and archaeology*, One World Archaeology (London: Unwin Hyman) 131–49; = Ch. 7 here.

—— (1989b). 'Communication and display: the integration of early Egyptian art and writing'. *Antiquity* 63: 471–82; = Ch. 13 here.

—— (1990a). 'Interpreting the Story of the Shipwrecked Sailor'. *Journal of Egyptian Archaeology* 76: 55–72.

—— (1990b). 'Restricted knowledge, hierarchy, and decorum: modern perceptions and ancient institutions'. *Journal of the American Research Center in Egypt* 27: 1–23.

—— (1991a). 'Egyptian myth and discourse: myth, gods, and the early written and iconographic record'. *Journal of Near Eastern Studies* 50: 81–105.

—— (1991b). Review of Whitney Davis, *The canonical tradition in ancient Egyptian art* (1989). *Antiquity* 65: 170–1.

—— (1991c). 'Society, morality, and religious practice'. In Byron E. Shafer (ed.), *Religion in ancient Egypt: gods, myths, and personal practice* (Ithaca and London: Cornell University Press) 123–200.

—— (1992a). 'Merit by proxy: the biographies of the dwarf Djeho and his patron Tjaiharpta'. *Journal of Egyptian Archaeology* 78: 241–57.

—— (1992b). 'Open palms'. In International Association of Egyptologists (ed.), *Sesto congresso internazionale di egittologia: atti* ([Turin]: Società Italiana per il Gas) I, 29–32.

—— (1994). 'On the status and purposes of ancient Egyptian art'. *Cambridge Archaeological Journal* 4: 67–94; = Ch. 14 here.

—— (1995a). 'Origins of Egyptian kingship'. In David O'Connor and David P. Silverman (eds.), *Ancient Egyptian kingship*, Probleme der Ägyptologie 9 (Leiden: E. J. Brill) 95–156.

Baines, John (1995b). 'Palaces and temples of ancient Egypt'. In Jack M. Sasson, John Baines, Gary Beckman, and Karen S. Rubinsohn (eds.), *Civilizations of the ancient Near East* (New York: Charles Scribner) I, 303–17.

—— (1996a). 'Classicism and modernism in the literature of the New Kingdom'. In Antonio Loprieno (ed.), *Ancient Egyptian literature: history and forms*, Probleme der Ägyptologie 10 (Leiden: E. J. Brill) 157–74.

—— (1996b). 'Contextualizing Egyptian representations of society and ethnicity'. In Jerrold S. Cooper and Glenn Schwartz (eds.), *The study of the ancient Near East in the 21st century: proceedings of the William Foxwell Albright Memorial Conference* (Winona Lake, Ind.: Eisenbrauns) 339–84.

—— (1996c). 'Myth and literature'. In Antonio Loprieno (ed.), *Ancient Egyptian literature: history and forms*, Probleme der Ägyptologie 10 (Leiden: E. J. Brill) 361–79.

—— (1997). 'Temples as symbols, guarantors, and participants in Egyptian civilization'. In Stephen Quirke (ed.), *The temple in ancient Egypt: new discoveries and recent research* (London: British Museum Press) 216–41.

—— (1998a). 'Ancient Egyptian kingship: official forms, rhetoric, context'. In John Day (ed.), *King and Messiah in Israel and the Ancient Near East: proceedings of the Oxford Old Testament seminar*, Journal for the Study of the Old Testament, Supplement Series 270 (Sheffield: Sheffield Academic Press) 16–53.

—— (1998b). 'The dawn of the Amarna age'. In Eric H. Cline and David O'Connor (eds.), *Amenhotep III: perspectives on his reign* (Ann Arbor: University of Michigan Press) 271–312 (bibliography 3–71).

—— (1999a). 'Forerunners of narrative biographies'. In Anthony Leahy and W. John Tait (eds.), *Studies on ancient Egypt in honour of H. S. Smith*, Occasional Publications 13 (London: Egypt Exploration Society) 23–37.

—— (1999b). 'On *Wenamun* as a literary text'. In Jan Assmann and Elke Blumenthal (eds.), *Literatur und Politik im pharaonischen und ptolemäischen Ägypten: Vorträge der Tagung zum Gedenken an Georges Posener 5.–10. September 1996 in Leipzig*, Bibliothèque d'Etude 127 (Cairo: Institut Français d'Archéologie Orientale) 209–33.

—— (1999c). 'Prehistories of literature: performance, fiction, myth'. In Gerald Moers (ed.), *Definitely: Egyptian literature; proceedings of the Symposium 'Ancient Egyptian literature: history and forms', Los Angeles, March 24–26, 1995*, Lingua Aegyptia, Studia Monographica 2 (Göttingen: n.p.) 17–41.

—— (1999d). 'Scrittura e società nel più antico Egitto'. In Francesco Tiradritti (ed.), *Sesh: Lingue e scritture nell'antico Egitto—inediti dal Museo Archeologico di Milano*, exhibition catalogue (Milan: Electa) 21–30; = Ch. 5 here.

—— (2000). 'Stone and other materials in ancient Egypt: usages and values'. In Christina Karlshausen and Thierry De Putter (eds.), *Pierres égyptiennes ... Chefs-d'œuvre pour l'Eternité*, exhibition catalogue, Faculté Polytechnique de Mons (Mons: n.p.) 29–41; = Ch. 12 here.

—— (2001). 'Colour use and the distribution of relief and painting in the Temple of Sety I at Abydos'. In W. Vivian Davies (ed.), *Colour and painting in ancient Egypt* (London: British Museum Press) 145–57.

Baines, John (2003a). 'Early definitions of the Egyptian world and its surroundings'. In Timothy Potts, Michael Roaf, and Diana Stein (eds.), *Culture through objects: ancient Near Eastern studies in honour of P. R. S. Moorey* (Oxford: Griffith Institute) 27–57.

—— (2003b). 'On the genre and purpose of the "large commemorative scarabs" of Amenhotep III'. In Nicolas Grimal, Amr Kamel, and Cynthia May Sheikholeslami (eds.), *Hommages à Fayza Haikal*, Bibliothèque d'Etude 138 (Cairo: Institut Français d'Archéologie Orientale) 29–43.

—— (2003c). 'Research on Egyptian literature: background, definitions, prospects'. In Zahi Hawass and Lyla Pinch Brock (eds.), *Egyptology at the dawn of the twenty-first century: proceedings of the Eighth International Congress of Egyptologists, Cairo, 2000* (Cairo and New York: American University in Cairo Press) III, 1–26 (responses 27–47).

—— (2004a). 'The earliest Egyptian writing: development, context, purpose'. In Stephen D. Houston (ed.), *The first writing: script invention as history and process* (Cambridge: Cambridge University Press) 150–89 (bibliography 354–94).

—— (2004b). 'Egyptian elite self-presentation in the context of Ptolemaic rule'. In William V. Harris and Giovanni Ruffini (eds.), *Ancient Alexandria between Egypt and Greece*, Columbia Studies in the Classical Tradition 26 (Leiden: E. J. Brill) 33–61 (bibliography 269–89).

—— (2004c). 'Modelling sources, processes, and locations of early mortuary texts'. In Susanne Bickel and Bernard Mathieu (eds.), *D'un monde à l'autre: Textes des Pyramides et Textes des Sarcophages*, Bibliothèque d'Etude 139 (Cairo: Institut Français d'Archéologie Orientale) 15–41.

—— (2006a). 'Public ceremonial performance in ancient Egypt: exclusion and integration'. In Takeshi Inomata and Lawrence Coben (eds.), *Archaeology of performance: theaters of power, community, and politics* (Lanham, Md.: AltaMira) 261–302.

—— (2006b). 'Display of magic in Old Kingdom Egypt'. In Kasia Szpakowska (ed.), *Through a glass darkly: magic, dreams, and prophecy in ancient Egypt* (Swansea: Classical Press of Wales) 1–32.

—— in preparation-a. Body as language: ancient Egyptian bodies, divine to demonic.

—— in preparation-b. *Les biographies de l'Egypte ancienne: monuments, images et textes* (Paris: Cybèle).

Baines, John, and Christopher Eyre (1983). 'Four notes on literacy'. *Göttinger Miszellen* 61: 65–96; = Ch. 3 here.

Baines, John, Julian Henderson, and Richard L. Jaeschke (1989). 'Techniques of decoration in the Hall of Barques in the temple of Sethos I at Abydos'. *Journal of Egyptian Archaeology* 75: 13–30.

Baines, John, and Peter Lacovara (2002). 'Burial and the dead in ancient Egyptian society: respect, formalism, neglect'. *Journal of Social Archaeology* 2: 5–36.

Baines, John, and Jaromir Malek (2000). *Cultural atlas of ancient Egypt*, rev. edn. (New York: Facts on File).

Baines, John, and R. B. Parkinson (1997). 'An Old Kingdom record of an oracle? Sinai Inscription 13'. In Jacobus van Dijk (ed.), *Essays on ancient Egypt in honour of Herman te Velde*, Egyptological Memoirs 1 (Groningen: Styx) 9–27.

Baines, John, and Norman Yoffee (1998). 'Order, legitimacy, and wealth in ancient Egypt and Mesopotamia'. In Gary M. Feinman and Joyce Marcus (eds.), *Archaic states* (Santa Fe: School of American Research Press) 199–260 (bibliography 353–419).

Bakir, A. M. (1970). *Egyptian epistolography from the eighteenth to the twenty-first dynasty*, Bibliothèque d'Etude 48 (Cairo: Institut Français d'Archéologie Orientale).

Barbotin, C., and J.-J. Clère (1991). 'L'inscription de Sésostris Ier à Tôd'. *Bulletin de l'Institut Français d'Archéologie Orientale* 91: 1–31.

Bard, Kathryn (1992). 'Origins of Egyptian writing'. In Renée Friedman and Barbara Adams (eds.), *The followers of Horus: studies dedicated to Michael Allen Hoffman*, Oxbow Monograph 20 (Oxford: Oxbow) 297–306.

Bardinet, Thierry (1995). *Les papyrus médicaux de l'Egypte pharaonique: traduction intégrale et commentaire*, Penser la Médicine (Paris: Fayard).

Barham, Lawrence S. (1998). 'Possible early pigment use in south-central Africa'. *Current Anthropology* 39: 703–10.

Barnett, Richard D. (1976). *Sculptures from the North Palace of Ashurbanipal at Nineveh (668–627 B.C.)* (London: British Museum Publications).

Barns, John W. B. (1948). 'Three hieratic papyri in the Duke of Northumberland's collection'. *Journal of Egyptian Archaeology* 34: 35–46.

Barta, Winfried (1970a). *Das Selbstzeugnis eines altägyptischen Künstlers (Stele Louvre C14)*, Münchner Ägyptologische Studien 22 (Berlin: Bruno Hessling).

—— (1970b). 'Der Königsring als Symbol zyklischer Wiederkehr'. *Zeitschrift für Ägyptische Sprache und Altertumskunde* 98: 5–16.

—— (1973). 'Bemerkungen zur Rekonstruktion des abydenischen Kultbildrituals'. *Mitteilungen des Deutschen Archäologischen Instituts, Abteilung Kairo* 29: 163–6.

—— (1978). 'Das Schulbuch Kemit'. *Zeitschrift für Ägyptische Sprache und Altertumskunde* 105: 6–14.

Basso, Keith B. (1980). Review of Jack Goody, *The domestication of the savage mind* (1977). *Language in Society* 9: 72–80.

Baud, Michel (1999). *Famille royale et pouvoir sous l'Ancien Empire égyptien*, Bibliothèque d'Etude 126, 2 vols. (Cairo: Institut Français d'Archéologie Orientale).

Baud, Michel, and Vassil Dobrev (1995). 'De nouvelles annales de l'Ancien Empire égyptien: une "Pierre de Palerme" pour la VIe dynastie'. *Bulletin de l'Institut Français d'Archéologie Orientale* 95: 23–92.

—— (1997). 'Le verso des annales de la VIe dynastie: Pierre de Saqqara-Sud'. *Bulletin de l'Institut Français d'Archéologie Orientale* 97: 35–42.

Baud, Michel, and Dominique Farout (2001). 'Trois biographies de l'Ancien Empire revisitées'. *Bulletin de l'Institut Français d'Archéologie Orientale* 101: 43–57.

Bavay, L. (1997). 'Matière première et commerce à longue distance: le lapis-lazuli et l'Egypte prédynastique'. *Archéo-Nil* 7: 79–100.

Bavay, Laurent, Thierry De Putter, Barbara Adams, Jacques Navez, and Luc André (2000). 'The origin of obsidian in predynastic and Early Dynastic Egypt'. *Mitteilungen des Deutschen Archäologischen Instituts, Abteilung Kairo* 56: 5–20.

Beard, Mary et al. (1991). *Literacy in the Roman world*, Journal of Roman Archaeology, Supplementary Series 3 (Ann Arbor: Journal of Roman Archaeology).

Beattie, John (1971). *The Nyoro state* (Oxford: Clarendon Press).
Beaulieu, Paul-Alain (1989). *The reign of Nabonidus, King of Babylon 556–539 B.C.*, Yale Near Eastern Researches 10 (New Haven and London: Yale University Press).
Beckerath, Jürgen von (1984). 'Bemerkungen zum Turiner Königspapyrus und zu den Dynastien der ägyptischen Geschichte'. *Studien zur Altägyptischen Kultur* 11: 49–57.
Bednarik, Robert G. (1992). 'Palaeoart and archaeological myths'. *Cambridge Archaeological Journal* 2: 27–43.
Beinlich, Horst (1991). *Das Buch vom Fayum: zum religiösen Eigenverständnis einer ägyptischen Landschaft*, Ägyptologische Abhandlungen 51, 2 vols. (Wiesbaden: Otto Harrassowitz).
Bell, Lanny (1985). 'Luxor Temple and the cult of the royal ka'. *Journal of Near Eastern Studies* 44: 251–94.
Belting, Hans, and Edmund Jephcott (1994). *Likeness and presence: a history of the image before the era of art*, trans. Edmund Jephcott (Chicago and London: University of Chicago Press).
Bender, M. Lionel (1983). 'Color term encoding in a special lexical domain: Sudanese Arabic skin colors'. *Anthropological Linguistics* 25: 19–27.
Bennet, John (2001). 'Agency and bureaucracy: thoughts on the nature and extent of administration in Bronze Age Pylos'. In Sofia Voutsaki and John Killen (eds.), *Economy and politics in the Mycenaean palace states: proceedings of a conference held on 1–3 July 1999 in the Faculty of Classics, Cambridge*, Cambridge Philological Society, Supplementary Volume 27 (Cambridge: Cambridge Philological Society) 25–37.
Berger-El Naggar, Catherine (2004). 'Des Textes des Pyramides sur papyrus dans les archives du temple funéraire de Pépy Ier'. In Susanne Bickel and Bernard Mathieu (eds.), *D'un monde à l'autre: Textes des Pyramides et Textes des Sarcophages*, Bibliothèque d'Etude 139 (Cairo: Institut Français d'Archéologie Orientale) 85–90.
Berlev, Oleg D. (1971). 'Les prétendus "citadins" au Moyen Empire'. *Revue d'Egyptologie* 23: 23–48.
Berlin, Brent, and Paul Kay (1991) [1969]. *Basic color terms: their universality and evolution*, reprint with revised preface and bibliography (Berkeley: University of California Press).
Bestock, Laurel in press. 'The evolution of royal ideology: new discoveries from the reign of Aha'. In Béatrix Midant-Reynes and Yann Tristant (eds.), *Egypt at its origins II, Proceedings of the international conference 'Origin of the State. Predynastic and Early Dynastic Egypt', Toulouse, 5–8th September 2005*, Orientalia Lovaniensia Analecta (Leuven: Peeters).
Bickel, Susanne (2003). '"Ich spreche ständig zu Aton": zur Mensch–Gott-Beziehung in der Amarna Religion'. *Journal of Ancient Near Eastern Religions* 3: 23–45.
Bickel, Susanne, Marc Gabolde, and Pierre Tallet (1998). 'Des annales héliopolitaines de la troisième période intermédiare'. *Bulletin de l'Institut Français d'Archéologie Orientale* 98: 31–56.
Bierbrier, M. L. (1975). *The late New Kingdom in Egypt (c.1300–664 B.C.): a genealogical and chronological investigation*, Liverpool Monographs in Archaeology and Oriental Studies (Warminster: Aris & Phillips).

Biggam, Carole P., and Christian J. Kay (eds.) (2006). *Progress in colour studies* I, *Language and culture* (Amsterdam and Philadelphia: John Benjamins).

Bissing, Friedrich Wilhelm von (1926). 'Das Verhältnis des Ibi-Grabes in Theben zu dem Ibi-Grabe von Deir el Gebrâwi'. *Archiv für Orientforschung* 3: 53–5.

Bisson de la Roque, Fernand (1937). *Tôd (1934 à 1936)*, Fouilles de l'Institut Français d'Archéologie Orientale 17 (Cairo: Institut Français d'Archéologie Orientale).

Björkman, Gun (1971). *Kings at Karnak: a study of the treatment of the monuments of royal predecessors in the early New Kingdom*, Acta Universitatis Upsaliensis, Boreas 2 (Uppsala and Stockholm: Almqvist & Wiksell).

Blacking, John (1995). *Music, culture, & experience: selected papers of John Blacking*, ed. Reginald Byron (Chicago and London: University of Chicago Press).

Blackman, A. M. (1914–53). *The rock tombs of Meir*, Archaeological Survey of Egypt 23–6, 28–9, 6 vols. (London: Egypt Exploration Fund/Society).

Blackman, A. M., and H. W. Fairman (1946). 'The consecration of an Egyptian temple according to the use of Edfu'. *Journal of Egyptian Archaeology* 32: 75–91.

—— (1949–50). 'The significance of the ceremony ḥwt bḥsw in the temple of Horus at Edfu'. *Journal of Egyptian Archaeology* 35: 98–112; 36: 63–81.

Blackman, Winifred S. (1927). *The fellāhīn of Upper Egypt* (London etc.: Harrap).

Bloch, Maurice E. F. (1968). 'Astrology and writing in Madagascar'. In Jack Goody (ed.), *Literacy in traditional societies* (Cambridge: Cambridge University Press) 278–97.

Blom-Böer, Ingrid (1994). 'Zusammensetzung altägyptischer Farbpigmente und ihre Herkunftslagerstätten in Zeit und Raum'. *Oudheidkundige Mededelingen uit het Rijksmuseum van Oudheden te Leiden* 74: 55–107.

Blumenthal, Elke (1982). 'Die Prophezeiung des Neferti'. *Zeitschrift für Ägyptische Sprache und Altertumskunde* 109: 1–27.

—— (1991). 'Die "Reinheit" des Grabschänders'. In Ursula Verhoeven and Erhart Graefe (eds.), *Religion und Philosophie im alten Ägypten: Festgabe für Philippe Derchain*, Orientalia Lovaniensia Analecta 39 (Leuven: Peeters) 47–56.

Boehmer, Rainer M., Günter Dreyer, and Bernd Kromer (1993). 'Einige frühzeitliche 14C-Datierungen aus Abydos und Uruk'. *Mitteilungen des Deutschen Archäologischen Instituts, Abteilung Kairo* 49: 63–8.

Bogoslovsky, Evgenii S. (1980). 'Hundred Egyptian draughtsmen'. *Zeitschrift für Ägyptische Sprache und Altertumskunde* 107: 89–116.

Bonnet, Charles, Matthieu Honegger, and Dominique Valbelle (2003). 'Kerma: rapport préliminaire sur les campagnes de 2001–2002 et 2002–2003'. *Genava* 51: 257–300.

Bonnet, Charles, and Dominique Valbelle (2005). *Des pharaons venus d'Afrique: la cachette de Kerma* (Paris: Citadelles & Mazenod).

Boone, Elizabeth Hill, and Walter D. Mignolo (eds.) (1994). *Writing without words: alternative literacies in Mesoamerica and the Andes* (Durham, NC, and London: Duke University Press).

Borchardt, Ludwig, Ernst Assmann, Alfred Bollacher, Oskar Heinroth, Max Hilzheimer, and Kurt Sethe 1913. *Das Grabdenkmal des Königs Śaȝḥu-Reʿ* II, *Die Wandbilder*,

Ausgrabungen der Deutschen Orient-Gesellschaft in Abusir 1902–1908, 7 (Leipzig: J. C. Hinrichs).

Borchardt, Ludwig, and Herbert Ricke (1980). *Die Wohnhäuser in Tell el-Amarna*, Ausgrabungen der Deutschen Orient-Gesellschaft in Tell el-Amarna 5, Wissenschaftliche Veröffentlichung der Deutschen Orient-Gesellschaft 91 (Berlin: Gebrüder Mann).

Borg, Alexander (ed.) (1999). *The language of color in the Mediterranean: an anthology on linguistic and ethnographic aspects of color terms*, Acta Universitatis Stockholmiensis: Stockholm Oriental Studies 16 (Stockholm: Almqvist & Wiksell).

Borghouts, J. F. (1978). *Ancient Egyptian magical texts*, NISABA, Religious Texts in Translation Series 9 (Leiden: E. J. Brill).

Bothmer, Bernard V. (1966–7). 'Private sculpture of dynasty XVIII in Brooklyn'. *Brooklyn Museum Annual* 8: 55–89.

—— (1969) [1960]. *Egyptian sculpture of the Late Period, 700 B.C. to A.D. 100*, reprint with addenda (New York: Arno Press).

Bottéro, Françoise (2004). 'Writing on shell and bone in Shang China'. In Stephen D. Houston (ed.), *The first writing: script invention as history and process* (Cambridge: Cambridge University Press) 250–61.

Bourdieu, Pierre (1979). *Algeria 1960: essays*, trans. Richard Nice, Studies in Modern Capitalism (Cambridge: Cambridge University Press).

—— (1984). *Distinction: a social critique of the judgement of taste*, trans. Richard Nice (London: Routledge & Kegan Paul).

Bourriau, Janine (1981). *Umm el-Ga{^c}ab: pottery from the Nile Valley before the Arab conquest*, exhibition catalogue, Fitzwilliam Museum (Cambridge: Cambridge University Press).

Bowman, Alan K., and Greg Woolf (eds.) (1994). *Literacy and power in the ancient world* (Cambridge: Cambridge University Press).

Boyaval, Bernard (1977). 'Tableau général des indications d'âge de l'Egypte gréco-romaine'. *Chronique d'Egypte* 52: 345–51.

Bradley, Richard (2002). *The past in prehistoric societies* (London: Routledge).

Brand, Peter James (2000). *The monuments of Seti I: epigraphic, historical and art historical analysis*, Probleme der Ägyptologie 16 (Leiden and Boston: E. J. Brill).

Bray, Warwick (1979). 'From village to city in Mesoamerica'. In P. R. S. Moorey (ed.), *The origins of civilization* (Oxford: Clarendon Press) 78–102.

Breasted, James Henry (1906). *Ancient records of Egypt* IV, *The twentieth to the twenty-sixth dynasties* (Chicago: University of Chicago Press).

Brenner, Athalya (1982). *Colour terms in the Old Testament*, Journal for the Study of the Old Testament, Supplementary Series 21 (Sheffield: J.S.O.T. Press).

Breyer, Francis Amadeus Karl (2002). 'Die Schriftzeugnisse des prädynastischen Königsgrabes U-j in Umm el-Qaab: Versuch einer Neuinterpretation'. *Journal of Egyptian Archaeology* 88: 53–65.

Brinkmann, Vinzenz, and Raimund Wünsche (eds.) (2004). *Bunte Götter: die Farbigkeit antiker Skulptur*, 2nd edn., exhibition catalogue, Staatliche Antikensammlungen und Glyptothek Munich, Ny Carlsberg Glyptotek Kopenhagen, and Musei Vaticani, 2003–04 (Munich: Staatliche Antikensammlungen und Glyptothek).

Brovarski, Edward J. (1987). 'Two Old Kingdom writing boards from Giza'. *Annales du Service des Antiquités de l'Egypte* 71: 27–52.

Brovarski, Edward J., Susan K. Doll, and Rita E. Freed (eds.) (1982). *Egypt's golden age: the art of living in the New Kingdom 1558–1085 B.C.*, exhibition catalogue, Museum of Fine Arts (Boston: Museum of Fine Arts).

Brown, Cecil H. (1984). *Language and living things: uniformities in folk classification and naming* (New Brunswick, NJ: Rutgers University Press).

Brunner, Hellmut (1957). *Altägyptische Erziehung* (Wiesbaden: Otto Harrassowitz).

—— (1970). 'Zum Verständnis der archaisierenden Tendenzen in der ägyptischen Spätzeit'. *Saeculum* 21: 151–61.

Brunner-Traut, Emma (1968). *Altägyptische Tiergeschichte und Fabel: Gestalt und Strahlkraft*, 2nd edn. (Darmstadt: Wissenschaftliche Buchgesellschaft).

—— (1977). 'Farben'. In Wolfgang Helck and Wolfhart Westendorf (eds.), *Lexikon der Ägyptologie* (Wiesbaden: Otto Harrassowitz) II, 117–28.

Bruno, Vincent J. (1977). *Form and color in Greek painting* (New York: Norton).

Bruyère, Bernard (1952). *Tombes thébaines de Deir el Médineh à décoration monochrome*, Mémoires Publiées par les Membres de l'Institut Français d'Archéologie Orientale 86 (Cairo: Institut Français d'Archéologie Orientale).

—— (1953). *Rapport sur les fouilles de Deir el Médineh (années 1948 à 1951)*, Fouilles de l'Institut Français d'Archéologie Orientale 26 (Cairo: Institut Français d'Archéologie Orientale).

Bryan, Betsy M. (1985). 'Evidence for female literacy from Theban tombs of the New Kingdom'. *Bulletin of the Egyptological Seminar* 6: 17–32.

—— (1997). 'The statue program for the mortuary temple of Amenhotep III'. In Stephen Quirke (ed.), *The temple in ancient Egypt: new discoveries and recent research* (London: British Museum Press) 57–81.

Bryson, Norman (1981). *Word and image: French painting of the Ancien Régime* (Cambridge: Cambridge University Press).

Buchberger, Hannes (1991). 'Ḥtp an *Ipw-rs.ti*—Der Brief auf dem Gefäss München ÄS 4313'. *Studien zur Altägyptischen Kultur* 18: 49–87.

Bucher, Paul (1932). *Les textes des tombes de Thoutmosis III et d'Aménophis II*, Mémoires Publiées par les Membres de l'Institut Français d'Archéologie Orientale 60 (Cairo: Institut Français d'Archéologie Orientale).

Budde, Dagmar (2000). *Die Göttin Seschat*, Kanobos: Forschungen zum Griechisch-römischen Ägypten 2 (Leipzig: Helmar Wodtke und Katharina Stegbauer).

Budge, E. A. Wallis (1910). *The Chapters of Coming Forth by Day or the Theban recension of the Book of the Dead* III, Books on Egypt and Chaldaea 30 (London: Kegan Paul, Trench, Trübner).

Burkard, Günter (1977). *Textkritische Untersuchungen zu ägyptischen Weisheitslehren des Alten und Mittleren Reiches*, Ägyptologische Abhandlungen 34 (Wiesbaden: Otto Harrassowitz).

Burkard, Günter (1980). 'Bibliotheken im alten Ägypten: Überlegungen zu Methodik ihres Nachweises und Übersicht zum Stand der Forschung'. *Bibliothek, Forschung und Praxis* 4: 79–115.

—— (1983). 'Der formale Aufbau altägyptischer Literaturwerke'. *Studien zur Altägyptischen Kultur* 10: 79–118.

—— (1993). *Überlegungen zur Form der ägyptischen Literatur: die Geschichte des Schiffbrüchigen als literarisches Kunstwerk*, Ägypten und Altes Testament 22 (Wiesbaden: Harrassowitz).

Burke, Peter (2001). *Eyewitnessing: the uses of images as historical evidence*, Picturing History (London: Reaktion).

Burkhardt, Adelheid, Elke Blumenthal, Ingeborg Müller, and Walter F. Reineke (eds.) (1984). *Urkunden der 18. Dynastie: Übersetzung zu den Heften 5–16*, Urkunden des Ägyptischen Altertums IV (Berlin: Akademie-Verlag).

Butzer, Karl W. (1976). *Early hydraulic civilization in Egypt: a study in cultural ecology*, Prehistoric Archaeology and Ecology (Chicago and London: University of Chicago Press).

Calverley, Amice M., and Myrtle F. Broome (1933–59). *The temple of King Sethos I at Abydos*, 4 vols. (London: Egypt Exploration Society and Oriental Institute Chicago).

Caminos, Ricardo A. (1954). *Late-Egyptian Miscellanies*, Brown Egyptological Studies 1 (London: Geoffrey Cumberlege, Oxford University Press).

—— (1977). *A Tale of Woe: from a hieratic papyrus in the A. S. Pushkin Museum of Fine Arts in Moscow* (Oxford: Griffith Institute).

Capart, Jean (1935). 'Les ex-libris d'Aménophis III'. *Chronique d'Egypte* 10: 23–5.

Cardona, Giorgio Raimondo (1981). *Antropologia della scrittura* (Turin: Loescher).

Carlotti, Jean-François (1995). 'Mise au point sur les dimensions et la localisation de la chapelle d'Hatchepsout à Karnak'. *Cahiers de Karnak* 10: 141–57.

Carr, David M. (2005). *Writing on the tablet of the heart: origins of literature and scripture* (New York: Oxford University Press).

Carter, Elizabeth, and Matthew W. Stolper (1984). *Elam: surveys of political history and archaeology*, University of California Publications: Near Eastern Studies 25 (Berkeley etc.: University of California Press).

Carter, Howard (1933). *The tomb of Tut·ankh·Amen* III (London: Cassell).

Caton-Thompson, Gertrude, and E. W. Gardner (1934). *The desert Fayum*, 2 vols. (London: Royal Anthropological Institute).

Cauville, Sylvie (1984). *Edfou*, Les Guides Archéologiques de l'Institut Français du Caire; Bibliothèque Générale 6 (Cairo: Institut Français d'Archéologie Orientale).

Černý, Jaroslav (1927). 'Le culte d'Aménophis Ier chez les ouvriers de la Nécropole Thébaine'. *Bulletin de l'Institut Français d'Archéologie Orientale* 27: 159–203.

—— (1929). 'Papyrus Salt 824 (Brit. Mus. 10055)'. *Journal of Egyptian Archaeology* 15: 243–58.

—— (1939). *Late Ramesside letters*, Bibliotheca Aegyptiaca 9 (Brussels: Fondation Egyptologique Reine Elisabeth).

Černý, Jaroslav (1942). 'Nouvelle série de questions adressées aux oracles'. *Bulletin de l'Institut Français d'Archéologie Orientale* 41: 13–24.

—— (1945). 'The will of Naunakhte and the related documents'. *Journal of Egyptian Archaeology* 31: 29–53.

—— (1973). *A community of workmen at Thebes in the Ramesside period*, Bibliothèque d'Etude 50 (Cairo: Institut Français d'Archéologie Orientale); 2nd edn. 2001.

—— (1976). *Coptic etymological dictionary* (Cambridge: Cambridge University Press).

—— (1978). *Papyrus hiératiques de Deir el-Médineh* I, ed. Georges Posener, Documents de Fouilles 8 (Cairo: Imprimerie de l'Institut Français d'Archéologie Orientale).

Černý, Jaroslav, and Alan H. Gardiner (1957). *Hieratic ostraca* I (Oxford: Oxford University Press for Griffith Institute).

Chafe, Wallace, and Deborah Tannen (1987). 'The relation between written and spoken language'. *Annual Review of Anthropology* 16: 383–407.

Charbonneaux, J. (1958). *Les merveilles du Louvre* I (Paris: Hachette).

Chase, P. G., and H. L. Dibble (1992). 'Scientific archaeology and the origins of symbolism: a reply to Bednarik'. *Cambridge Archaeological Journal* 2: 43–51.

Chassinat, Emile (1934). *Le temple de Dendara* I (Cairo: Institut Français d'Archéologie Orientale).

Cherpion, Nadine (1984). 'De quand date la tombe du nain Seneb?' *Bulletin de l'Institut Français d'Archéologie Orientale* 84: 35–51.

—— (1989). *Mastabas et hypogées d'Ancien Empire: le problème de la datation*, Connaissance de l'Egypte Ancienne 4 (Brussels: Connaissance de l'Egypte ancienne).

Ciałowicz, Krzysztof M. in press. 'The nature of the relation between Lower and Upper Egypt in the protodynastic period: a view from Tell el-Farkha'. In Béatrix Midant-Reynes and Yann Tristant (eds.), *Egypt at its origins* II, Proceedings of the international conference 'Origin of the State. Predynastic and Early Dynastic Egypt', Toulouse, 5–8th September 2005, Orientalia Lovaniensia Analecta (Leuven: Peeters).

Clagett, Marshall (1989). *Ancient Egyptian science: a source book* I, Knowledge and order, 2 vols. (Philadelphia: American Philosophical Society).

Clanchy, M. T. (1993) [1979]. *From memory to written record: England 1066–1307*, 2nd edn. (Oxford and Malden, Mass.: Blackwell).

Clarke, Somers, and R. Engelbach (1930). *Ancient Egyptian masonry: the building craft* (London: Humphrey Milford, Oxford University Press).

Cole, Michael, and Sylvia Scribner (1974). *Culture and thought: a psychological introduction* (New York: Wiley).

Colinart, Sylvie (2001). 'Analysis of inorganic yellow colour in ancient Egyptian painting'. In W. Vivian Davies (ed.), *Colour and painting in ancient Egypt* (London: British Museum Press) 1–4.

Collier, Mark, and Stephen Quirke (2002). *The UCL Lahun papyri: letters*, BAR International Series 1083 (Oxford: Archaeopress).

Collins, James (1995). 'Literacy and literacies'. *Annual Review of Anthropology* 24: 75–93.

Collombert, Philippe, and Laurent Coulon (2000). 'Les dieux contre la mer: le début du "papyrus d'Astarté" (pBN 202)'. *Bulletin de l'Institut Français d'Archéologie Orientale* 100: 193–242.

Collon, Dominique (1995). *Ancient Near Eastern art* (London: British Museum Press).

Conklin, Harold C. (1973). 'Color categorization (review article on Berlin and Kay, *Basic color terms*)'. *American Anthropologist* 75: 931–42.

Cooney, John D. (1960). 'Glass sculpture in ancient Egypt'. *Journal of Glass Studies* 2: 11–43.

Cooper, Jerrold S. (1989). 'Writing'. In Eric Barnouw (ed.), *International Encyclopaedia of Communications* (New York and Oxford: Oxford University Press) 4: 321–31.

—— (1990). 'Mesopotamian historical consciousness and the production of monumental art in the third millennium BC'. In Ann C. Gunter (ed.), *Investigating artistic environments in the ancient Near East* (Washington, DC: Smithsonian Institution) 39–51.

—— (2004). 'Babylonian beginnings: the origin of the cuneiform writing system in comparative perspective'. In Stephen D. Houston (ed.), *The first writing: script invention as history and process* (Cambridge: Cambridge University Press) 71–99 (bibliography 354–94).

Crawford, Dorothy J. (1980). 'Ptolemy, Ptah and Apis in Hellenistic Memphis'. In Willy Peremans (ed.), *Studies on Ptolemaic Memphis* (Leuven: n.p.) 3–42.

Crawford, Dorothy J.: see also Thompson.

Cressy, David (1980). *Literacy and the social order: reading and writing in Tudor and Stuart England* (Cambridge: Cambridge University Press).

Cribiore, Raffaella (1996). *Writing, teachers, and students in Graeco-Roman Egypt*, American Studies in Papyrology 36 (Atlanta: Scholars Press).

—— (2001). *Gymnastics of the mind: Greek education in Hellenistic and Roman Egypt* (Princeton and Oxford: Princeton University Press).

Criscuolo, Lucia (1978). 'Ricerche sul *Komogrammateus* nell'Egitto tolemaico'. *Aegyptus* 58: 3–101.

Crocker, Piers T. (1985). 'Status symbols in the architecture of el-ᶜAmarna'. *Journal of Egyptian Archaeology* 71: 52–65.

Crump, Thomas (1981). *The phenomenon of money* (London: Routledge and Kegan Paul).

Damerow, Peter (1999). *The origins of writing as a problem of historical epistemology*, downloadable as pdf from http://www.mpiwg-berlin.mpg.de/en/forschung/preprints.html; online: http://cdli.ucla.edu/pubs/cdlj/2006/cdlj/2006_01.html.

Dasen, Véronique (1993). *Dwarfs in ancient Egypt and Greece*, Oxford Monographs in Classical Archaeology (Oxford: Oxford University Press).

—— in press. 'Autour du portrait romain: marques identitaires et anomalies physiques'. In Agostino Bagliani Paravicini (ed.), *Le portrait: la représentation de l'individu*, Nature, Sciences and Medieval Societies, Micrologus Library 16 (Florence: Micrologus).

Daumas, François (1956). 'La valeur de l'or dans la pensée égyptienne'. *Revue de l'Histoire des Religions* 149: 1–17.

—— (1968). 'Les propylées du temple d'Hathor à Philae et le culte de la déesse'. *Zeitschrift für Ägyptische Sprache und Altertumskunde* 95: 1–17.

—— (1969). *Dendara et le temple d'Hathor: notice sommaire*, Recherches d'Archéologie, de Philologie et d'Histoire 29 (Cairo: Institut Français d'Archéologie Orientale).

—— (1973). 'Derechef Pépi Ier à Dendara'. *Revue d'Egyptologie* 25: 7–20.

D'Auria, Sue, Peter Lacovara, and Catharine Roehrig (1988). *Mummies and magic: the funerary arts of ancient Egypt*, exhibition catalogue, Museum of Fine Arts (Boston, Mass.: Museum of Fine Arts).

Davidson, Iain (1992). 'There's no art to find the mind's construction in offence'. *Cambridge Archaeological Journal* 2: 52–7.

Davidson, Iain, and William C. McGrew (2005). 'Stone tools and the uniqueness of human culture'. *Journal of the Royal Anthropological Institute* 11: 793–817.

Davies, Nina M., and Alan H. Gardiner (1936). *Ancient Egyptian paintings*, vols. I–II plates, III text (Chicago: University of Chicago Press).

—— (1962). *Tutᶜankhamūn's painted box* (Oxford: Griffith Institute).

Davies, Norman de Garis (1903–8). *The rock tombs of el Amarna*, Archaeological Survey of Egypt 13–18, 6 vols. (London: Egypt Exploration Fund).

—— (1927). *Two Ramesside tombs a Thebes*, Robb de Peyster Tytus Memorial Series 5 (New York: Metropolitan Museum of Art).

—— (1933). *The tomb of Nefer-ḥotep at Thebes*, The Metropolitan Museum of Art Egyptian Expedition (New York: Metropolitan Museum of Art).

—— (1943). *The tomb of Rekh-mi-Rēᶜ at Thebes*, The Metropolitan Museum of Art Egyptian Expedition 11 (New York: Metropolitan Museum of Art).

Davies, W. Vivian (1987). *Egyptian hieroglyphs*, Reading the Past (London: British Museum).

—— (ed.) (2001). *Colour and painting in ancient Egypt* (London: British Museum Press).

Davies, W. Vivian, and Renée F. Friedman (1998). *Egypt* (London: British Museum Press).

Davis, Alyson M. (1985). 'The canonical bias: young children's drawings of familiar objects'. In N. H. Freeman and M. V. Cox (eds.), *Visual order: the nature and development of pictorial representation* (Cambridge: Cambridge University Press) 202–13.

Davis, Whitney M. (1984). 'Canonical representation in Egyptian art'. *Res* 4: 20–46.

—— (1989). *The canonical tradition in ancient Egyptian art.*, Cambridge New Art History and Criticism (Cambridge: Cambridge University Press).

D'Azevedo, Warren L. (1958). 'A structural approach to esthetics: toward a definition of art in anthropology'. *American Anthropologist* 60: 702–14.

—— (1973). 'Sources of Gola artistry'. In Warren L. D'Azevedo (ed.), *The traditional artist in African societies* (Bloomington: Indiana University Press) 282–340.

de Buck, Adriaan (1961). *The Egyptian Coffin Texts* VII, The University of Chicago, Oriental Institute Publications 87 (Chicago: University of Chicago Press).

De Putter, Thierry (1997). 'Ramsès II, géologue? Un commentaire de la stèle de Manshiyet es-Sadr, dite "de l'an 8"'. *Zeitschrift für Ägyptische Sprache und Altertumskunde* 124: 131–41.

Dean-Jones, Lesley (2003). 'Literacy and the charlatan in ancient Greek medicine'. In Harvey Yunis (ed.), *Written texts and the rise of literate culture in ancient Greece* (Cambridge: Cambridge University Press) 97–121.

DeBoer, Warren R. (2005). 'Colors for a North American past'. *World Archaeology* 37: 66–91.

Dedrick, Don (1998). *Naming the rainbow: colour language, colour science, and culture*, Synthese Library 274 (Dordrecht and London: Kluwer Academic).

Dedrick, Don, Robert E. MacLaury, and Galina Paramei (eds.) (2007). *Anthropology of color: interdisciplinary multilevel modeling* (Amsterdam: John Benjamins).

DeFrancis, John (1989). *Visible speech: the diverse oneness of writing systems* (Honolulu: University of Hawaii Press).

DeMarrais, Elizabeth, Chris Gosden, and Colin Renfrew (eds.) (2004). *Rethinking materiality: the engagement of mind with the material world*, McDonald Institute Monographs (Cambridge: McDonald Institute for Archaeological Research).

Demsky, Aaron (1985). Alan R. Millard, 'An assessment of the evidence for writing in ancient Israel; with response by Aaron Demsky'. In *Biblical archaeology today: proceedings of the international congress on biblical archaeology, Jerusalem, April 1984* (Jerusalem: Israel Exploration Society etc.) 301–12; 349–53.

Depauw, Mark (1997). *A companion to Demotic studies*, Papyrologica Bruxellensia 28 (Brussels: Fondation Egyptologique Reine Elisabeth).

—— (1999). 'Demotic witness-copy-contracts'. *Revue d'Egyptologie* 50: 67–105.

Derchain, Philippe (1975). 'Le lotus, la mandragore et le perséa'. *Chronique d'Egypte* 50: 65–86.

—— (1990). 'L'auteur du Papyrus Jumilhac'. *Revue d'Egyptologie* 41: 9–30.

—— (1997). 'Des usages de l'écriture: réflexions d'un savant égyptien'. *Chronique d'Egypte* 72: 10–16.

Derchain-Urtel, Maria Theresia (1974). 'Die Schlange des "Schiffbrüchigen"'. *Studien zur Altägyptischen Kultur* 1: 83–104.

Dieleman, Jacco (2005). *Priests, tongues, and rites: the London–Leiden magical manuscripts and translation in Egyptian ritual (100–300 CE)*, Religions in the Graeco-Roman World 153 (Leiden and Boston: Brill).

Dobrovits, Aladár (1937). 'Harpokrates: Probleme der ägyptischen Plastik'. In *Emlékkonyv Dr. Mahler Ede ... /Dissertationes in honorem Dr. Eduard Mahler ... /Jubilee volume in honour of Edward Mahler ...* (Budapest: János Arany) 72–122.

—— (1959). 'Le problème de la frontalité dans la sculpture égyptienne et grecque'. *Acta Antiqua Academiae Scientiarum Hungaricae* 7: 39–43.

Dodson, Aidan (1988). 'Egypt's first antiquarians'. *Antiquity* 62: 513–17.

Dominicus, Brigitte (1994). *Gesten und Gebärden in Darstellungen des Alten und Mittleren Reiches*, Studien zur Archäologie und Geschichte Altägyptens 10 (Heidelberg: Heidelberger Orientverlag).

Donadoni Roveri, Anna Maria, and Francesco Tiradritti (1998). *Kemet: alle sorgenti del tempo*, exhibition catalogue (Milan: Electa).

Donker van Heel, Koen, and B. J. J. Haring (2003). *Writing in a workmen's village: scribal practice in Ramesside Deir el-Medina*, Egyptologische Uitgaven 16 (Leiden: Nederlands Instituut voor het Nabije Oosten).

Dorman, Peter F. (2002). *Faces in clay: technique, imagery, and allusion in a corpus of ceramic sculpture from ancient Egypt*, Münchner Ägyptologische Studien 52 (Mainz: Philipp von Zabern).

Drenkhahn, Rosemarie (1976). *Die Handwerker und ihre Tätigkeiten im alten Ägypten*, Ägyptologische Abhandlungen 31 (Wiesbaden: Otto Harrassowitz).

—— (1995). 'Artists and artisans in pharaonic Egypt'. In Jack M. Sasson, John Baines, Gary M. Beckman, and Karen S. Rubinsohn (eds.), *Civilizations of the ancient Near East* (New York: Scribners) I, 331–43.

Dreyer, Günter (1986). *Elephantine VIII, Der Tempel der Satet, die Funde der Frühzeit und des Alten Reiches*, Deutsches Archäologisches Institut, Abteilung Kairo, Archäologische Veröffentlichungen 39 (Mainz: Philipp von Zabern).

—— (1987). 'Ein Siegel der frühzeitlichen Königsnekropole von Abydos'. *Mitteilungen des Deutschen Archäologischen Instituts, Abteilung Kairo* 43: 33–43.

—— (1995). 'Die Datierung der Min-Statuen aus Koptos'. In *Kunst des Alten Reiches: Symposium im Deutschen Archäologischen Institut Kairo am 29. und 30. Oktober 1991*, Deutsches Archäologisches Institut, Abteilung Kairo, Sonderschrift 28 (Mainz: Philipp von Zabern) 49–56.

Dreyer, Günter, Joachim Boessneck, Angela von den Driesch, and Stefan Klug (1990). 'Umm el-Qaab: Nachuntersuchungen im frühzeitlichen Königsfriedhof, 3./4. Vorbericht'. *Mitteilungen des Deutschen Archäologischen Instituts, Abteilung Kairo* 46: 53–90.

Dreyer, Günter, Eva-Maria Engel, Ulrich Hartung, Thomas Hikade, Eva Christiana Köhler, and Frauke Pumpenmeier (1996). 'Umm el-Qaab: Nachuntersuchungen im frühzeitlichen Königsfriedhof, 7./8. Vorbericht'. *Mitteilungen des Deutschen Archäologischen Instituts, Abteilung Kairo* 52: 11–81.

Dreyer, Günter, Ulrich Hartung, Thomas Hikade, Eva Christiana Köhler, Vera Müller, and Frauke Pumpenmeier (1998a). 'Umm el-Qaab: Nachuntersuchungen im frühzeitlichen Königsfriedhof, 9./10. Vorbericht'. *Mitteilungen des Deutschen Archäologischen Instituts, Abteilung Kairo* 54: 77–167.

Dreyer, Günter, Ulrich Hartung, and Frauke Pumpenmeier (1998b). *Umm el-Qaab I, Das prädynastische Königsgrab U-j und seine frühen Schriftzeugnisse*, Deutsches Archäologisches Institut, Abteilung Kairo, Archäologische Veröffentlichungen 86 (Mainz: Philipp von Zabern).

Dreyer, Günter, and Werner Kaiser (1980). 'Zu den kleinen Stufenpyramiden Ober- und Mittelägyptens'. *Mitteilungen des Deutschen Archäologischen Instituts, Abteilung Kairo* 36: 43–59.

Drioton, Etienne (1952). 'Une mutilation d'image avec motif'. *Archiv Orientální* 20: 351–55.

Dubery, Fred, and John Willats (1983). *Perspective and other drawing systems* (London: Herbert Press).
Dumont, Louis (1970). *Homo hierarchicus: the caste system and its implications*, trans. Mark Sainsbury; Nature of Human Society (London: Weidenfeld & Nicolson).
Duncan-Jones, R. P. (1977). 'Age-rounding, illiteracy and social differentiation in the Roman Empire'. *Chiron* 7: 333–53.
—— (1979). 'Age-rounding in Graeco-Roman Egypt'. *Zeitschrift für Papyrologie und Epigraphik* 33: 169–77.
Dunham, Dows (1937). *Naga-ed-Dêr stelae of the First Intermediate period*, Museum of Fine Arts, Boston (London: Humphrey Milford, Oxford University Press).
—— (1938). 'The biographical inscriptions of Nekhebu in Boston and Cairo'. *Journal of Egyptian Archaeology* 24: 1–8.
Dunham, Dows, and William Kelly Simpson (1974). *The mastaba of Queen Mersyankh III, G 7530–7540*, Giza Mastabas 1 (Boston: Department of Egyptian and Ancient Near Eastern Art, Museum of Fine Arts).
Dunnell, Robert C., and Robert J. Wenke (1980). 'Culture and scientific evolution: some comments on "The decline and rise of Mesopotamian civilization"'. *American Antiquity* 45: 605–9.
Duthie, R. K. (1985). 'The adolescent's point of view: studies of forms in conflict'. In N. H. Freeman and M. V. Cox (eds.), *Visual order: the nature and development of pictorial representation* (Cambridge: Cambridge University Press) 101–20.
Dziobek, Eberhard (1992). *Das Grab des Ineni, Theben Nr. 81*, Deutsches Archäologisches Institut, Abteilung Kairo, Archäologische Veröffentlichungen 68 (Mainz: Philipp von Zabern).
Eaton-Krauss, Marianne (1984). *The representations of statuary in private tombs of the Old Kingdom*, Ägyptologische Abhandlungen 39 (Wiesbaden: Otto Harrassowitz).
—— (2003). 'A source for the portraits of Sesostris III and Amenemhet III'. *Göttinger Miszellen* 194: 17–19.
Eckmann, Christian, and Saher Shafik (2005). *"Leben dem Horus Pepi": Restaurierung und technologische Untersuchung der Metallskulpturen des Pharao Pepi I. aus Hierakonpolis*, Römisch-Germanisches Zentralmuseum Mainz, Forschungsinstitut für Vor-und Frühgeschichte, Monographien 59 (Mainz and Bonn: Verlag des Römisch-Germanischen Zentralmuseums; Habelt).
Edel, Elmar (1953). 'Inschriften des Alten Reichs II, Die Biographie des *Kȝj-gmjnj* (Kagemni)'. *Mitteilungen des Instituts für Orientforschung der Deutschen Akademie der Wissenschaften zu Berlin* 1: 210–26.
—— (1955–64). *Altägyptische Grammatik*, Analecta Orientalia 34, 39, 2 vols. (Rome: Pontificium Institutum Biblicum).
—— (1961–4). *Zu den Inschriften auf den Jahreszeitenreliefs der 'Weltkammer' aus dem Sonnenheiligtum des Niuserre*, Nachrichten der Akademie der Wissenschaften in Göttingen, philologisch-historische Klasse 1961, 1963, 3 vols. (Göttingen: Vandenhoeck & Ruprecht).
—— (1984). *Die Inschriften der Grabfronten der Siut-Gräber in Mittelägypten aus der Herakleopolitenzeit: eine Wiederherstellung nach den Zeichnungen der Description de*

l'Egypte, Abhandlungen der Rheinisch-Westfälischen Akademie der Wissenschaften 71 (Opladen: Westdeutscher Verlag).

Edel, Elmar, and Steffen Wenig (1974). *Die Jahreszeitenreliefs aus dem Sonnenheiligtum des Königs Ne-user-Re*, Staatliche Museen zu Berlin, Mitteilungen aus der Ägyptischen Sammlung 7 (Berlin: Akademie-Verlag).

Edwards, I. E. S. (1939). *Hieroglyphic texts from Egyptian stelae etc. in the British Museum* VIII (London: British Museum).

——— (1971). 'The Early Dynastic period in Egypt'. In I. E. S. Edwards, C. J. Gadd, and N. G. L. Hammond (eds.), *Cambridge Ancient History* 3rd edn. I: 2, *Early history of the Middle East* (Cambridge: Cambridge University Press) 1–70.

——— (1985). *The pyramids of Egypt*, rev. edn. (Harmondsworth: Penguin).

Egberts, A. (1995). *In quest of meaning: a study of the ancient Egyptian rites of consecrating the meret-chests and driving the calves*, Egyptologische Uitgaven 8, 2 vols. (Leiden: Nederlands Instituut voor het Nabije Oosten).

Eichler, Eckhard (1991). 'Untersuchungen zu den Königsbriefen des Alten Reiches'. *Studien zur Altägyptischen Kultur* 18: 141–71.

Eisenstein, Elizabeth L. (1993) [1979]. *The printing press as an agent of change: communications and cultural transformations in early modern Europe* (Cambridge: Cambridge University Press).

——— (1993) [1983]. *The printing revolution in early modern Europe*, Canto (Cambridge: Cambridge University Press).

el-Amir, Mustafa (1959). *A family archive from Thebes* (Cairo: General Organization for Government Printing Offices).

el-Khouli, Ali Abd el-Rahman Hassanain (1978). *Egyptian stone vessels, predynastic period to dynasty III: typology and analysis*, 3 vols. (Mainz: Philipp von Zabern).

el-Saghir, Mohammed (1991). *Das Statuenversteck im Luxortempel*, Antike Welt 22, special issue; Zaberns Bildbände zur Archäologie 8 (Mainz: Philipp von Zabern).

Emery, Walter B. (1938). *The tomb of Hemaka*, Service des Antiquités de l'Egypte, Excavations at Saqqara (Cairo: Government Press, Bulâq).

——— (1939). *Ḥor-Aha*, Service des Antiquités de l'Egypte, Excavations at Saqqara (Cairo: Government Press, Bulâq).

——— (1949–58). *Great tombs of the first dynasty*, vol. I: Service des Antiquités de l'Egypte, Excavations at Saqqara 1 (Cairo: Government Press); vols. II–III (London: Egypt Exploration Society).

——— (1961). *Archaic Egypt* (Harmondsworth: Penguin).

Endesfelder, Erika (1979). 'Zur Frage der Bewässerung im pharaonischen Ägypten'. *Zeitschrift für Ägyptische Sprache und Altertumskunde* 106: 37–51.

Engelbach, R. (1934a). 'A foundation scene of the second dynasty'. *Journal of Egyptian Archaeology* 20: 183–4.

——— (1934b). 'The quarries of the western Nubian desert: a preliminary report'. *Annales du Service des Antiquités de l'Egypte* 34: 65–74.

Enmarch, Roland (2005). *The dialogue of Ipuwer and the Lord of All* (Oxford: Griffith Institute).

Epigraphic Survey, the (1980). *The tomb of Kheruef: Theban Tomb 192*, Oriental Institute Publications 102 (Chicago: The Oriental Institute of the University of Chicago).
—— (1986). *The battle reliefs of King Sety I*, Reliefs and Inscriptions at Karnak 4, Oriental Institute Publications 107 (Chicago: The Oriental Institute of the University of Chicago).
Epron, Lucienne, François Daumas (senior), and Henri Wild (1939–66). *Le tombeau de Ti*, Mémoires Publiés par les Membres de l'Institut Français d'Archéologie Orientale du Caire 65, 3 vols. (Cairo: Institut Français d'Archéologie Orientale).
Erichsen, Wolja (1933). *Papyrus Harris I: hieroglyphische Transkription*, Bibliotheca Aegyptiaca 5 (Brussels: Fondation Egyptologique Reine Elisabeth).
Erman, Adolf, and Hermann Grapow (1928). *Wörterbuch der ägyptischen Sprache* II (Leipzig: J. C. Hinrichs).
—— (1929). *Wörterbuch der ägyptischen Sprache* III (Leipzig: J. C. Hinrichs).
—— (1930). *Wörterbuch der ägyptischen Sprache* IV (Leipzig: J. C. Hinrichs).
Evers, Hans Gerhard (1929). *Staat aus dem Stein: Denkmäler, Geschichte und Bedeutung der ägyptischen Plastik während des Mittleren Reiches*, 2 vols. (Munich: Bruckmann).
Eyre, Christopher (1979). 'A "strike" text from the Theben necropolis'. In G. A. Gaballa, Kenneth A. Kitchen, and John Ruffle (eds.), *Glimpses of ancient Egypt: studies in honour of H. W. Fairman* (Warminster: Aris & Phillips) 80–91.
—— (1980). Employment and labour relations in the Theban necropolis in the Ramesside period. Doctoral Dissertation: University of Oxford.
—— (1993). 'Why was Egyptian literature?' In *Sesto Congresso Internazionale di Egittologia: Atti* (Turin: Società Italiana per il Gas) II, 115–20.
—— (2000). 'The performance of the Peasant'. In Andrea M. Gnirs (ed.), *Reading The Eloquent Peasant: proceedings of the international conference held at the University of California, Los Angeles, March 27–30, 1997* = Lingua Aegyptia 8 (Göttingen: Seminar für Ägyptologie und Koptologie) 9–25.
Eyre, Christopher, and John Baines (1989). 'Interactions between orality and literacy in ancient Egypt'. In Karen Schousboe and Mogens Trolle Larsen (eds.), *Literacy and society* (Copenhagen: Akademisk Forlag) 91–119.
Fairman, H. W. (1958). 'A scene of the offering of truth in the temple of Edfu'. *Mitteilungen des Deutschen Archäologischen Instituts, Abteilung Kairo* 16: 86–92.
Fairservis, Walter A. (1983). *Hierakonpolis—the graffiti and the origins of Egyptian writing*, The Hierakonpolis Project: Occasional Papers in Anthropology 2 (Poughkeepsie NY: Vassar College).
Fakhry, Ahmed (1961). *The monuments of Sneferu at Dahshur* II, *The valley temple* I, *The temple reliefs*, Ministry of Culture and National Orientation: Antiquities Department of Egypt (Cairo: General Organization for Government Printing Offices).
Faulkner, Raymond O. (1969). *The ancient Egyptian Pyramid Texts translated into English* (Oxford: Clarendon Press).
—— (1973). *The ancient Egyptian Coffin Texts* I (Warminster: Aris & Phillips).

Faulkner, Raymond O. (1978). *The ancient Egyptian Coffin Texts* III (Warminster: Aris & Phillips).
—— (1985). *The ancient Egyptian Book of the Dead* (London: British Museum Publications).
Fay, Biri (1996). *The Louvre Sphinx and royal sculpture from the reign of Amenemhat II* (Mainz: Philipp von Zabern).
—— (1999). 'Royal women as represented in sculpture during the Old Kingdom part II: uninscribed sculptures'. In Christiane Ziegler and Nadine Palayret (eds.), *L'art de l'Ancien Empire égyptien: actes du colloque organisé au musée du Louvre par le Service culturel les 3 et 4 avril 1998*, Louvre Conférences et Colloques (Paris: Documentation Française) 99–147.
Fecht, Gerhard (1965). *Literarische Zeugnisse zur 'persönlichen Frömmigkeit' in Ägypten: Analyse der Beispiele in den ramessidischen Schulpapyri*, Abhandlungen der Heidelberger Akademie der Wissenschaften, philosophisch-historische Klasse 1965: 1 (Heidelberg: Carl Winter, Universitätsverlag).
—— (1967). 'Zur Frühform der Amarna-Theologie: Neubearbeitung der Stele der Architekten Suti und Hor'. *Zeitschrift für Ägyptische Sprache und Altertumskunde* 94: 25–50.
—— (1972). *Der Vorwurf an Gott in den 'Mahnworten des Ipuwer': zur geistigen Krise der Ersten Zwischenzeit*, Abhandlungen der Heidelberger Akademie der Wissenschaften, philosophisch-historische Klasse 1972: 1 (Heidelberg: Carl Winter, Universitätsverlag).
—— (1973). 'Ägyptische Zweifel am Sinn des Opfers'. *Zeitschrift für Ägyptische Sprache und Altertumskunde* 100: 6–16.
—— (1982). 'Prosodie'. In Wolfgang Helck and Wolfhart Westendorf (eds.), *Lexikon der Ägyptologie* (Wiesbaden: Otto Harrassowitz) IV, 1127–54.
—— (1990). *Metrik des Hebräischen und Phönizischen*, Ägypten und Altes Testament 19 (Wiesbaden: Harrassowitz).
Feucht, Erika (1984). 'Ein Motiv der Trauer'. In Friedrich Junge (ed.), *Studien zu Sprache und Religion Ägyptens zu Ehren von Wolfhart Westendorf* (Göttingen: n.p.) II, 1103–8.
—— (1995). *Das Kind im alten Ägypten: die Stellung des Kindes in Familie und Gesellschaft nach altägyptischen Texten und Darstellungen* (Frankfurt and New York: Campus).
Finnegan, Ruth H. (1981). 'Literacy and literature'. In Barbara Lloyd and John Gay (eds.), *Universals of human thought: some African evidence* (Cambridge: Cambridge University Press) 234–55.
—— (1988). *Literacy and orality: studies in the technology of communication* (Oxford: Basil Blackwell).
—— (1992). *Oral traditions and the verbal arts: a guide to research practices*, ASA Research Methods in Social Anthropology (London: Routledge).
Firth, Cecil M., James Edward Quibell, and Jean-Philippe Lauer (1935). *The Step Pyramid*, Service des Antiquités de l'Egypte, Excavations at Saqqara, 2 vols. (Cairo: Institut Français d'Archéologie Orientale).

Fischer, Henry George (1959). 'An example of Memphite influence in a Theban stela of the eleventh dynasty'. *Artibus Asiae* 22: 240–52.

—— (1961). 'The Nubian mercenaries of Gebelein during the First Intermediate period'. *Kush* 9: 44–80.

—— (1963). 'Varia aegyptiaca'. *Journal of the American Research Center in Egypt* 2: 17–51.

—— (1972). 'Some emblematic uses of hieroglyphs, with particular reference to an Archaic ritual vessel'. *Metropolitan Museum Journal* 5: 5–23.

—— (1973). 'Redundant determinatives in the Old Kingdom'. *Metropolitan Museum Journal* 8: 7–25.

—— (1976a). 'Archaeological aspects of epigraphy and palaeography'. In Ricardo A. Caminos and Henry George Fischer (eds.), *Ancient Egyptian epigraphy and palaeography* (New York: Metropolitan Museum of Art) 29–50.

—— (1976b). *Varia*, Egyptian Studies 1 (New York: Metropolitan Museum of Art).

—— (1977a). 'Gaufürst'. In Wolfgang Helck and Wolfhart Westendorf (eds.), *Lexikon der Ägyptologie* (Wiesbaden: Otto Harrassowitz) II, 408–17.

—— (1977b). *The orientation of hieroglyphs* I, *Reversals*, Egyptian Studies 2 (New York: Metropolitan Museum of Art).

—— (1986). *L'écriture et l'art de l'Egypte ancienne: quatre leçons sur la paléographie et l'épigraphie pharaoniques*, Collège de France, Essais et Conférences (Paris: Presses Universitaires de France).

Fischer-Elfert, Hans-Werner (1986). *Die satirische Streitschrift des Papyrus Anastasi I: Übersetzung und Kommentar*, Ägyptologische Abhandlungen 44 (Wiesbaden: Otto Harrassowitz).

—— (1998). *Die Vision von der Statue im Stein: Studien zum altägyptischen Mundöffnungsritual*, Schriften der Philosophisch-historischen Klasse der Heidelberger Akademie der Wissenschaften 5 (Heidelberg: Carl Winter, Universitätsverlag).

—— (2002). 'Das verschwiegene Wissen des Irtisen (Stele Louvre C 14): zwischen Arcanum und Preisgabe'. In Jan Assmann and Martin Bommas (eds.), *Ägyptische Mysterien? Kulte/Kulturen* (Munich: Wilhelm Fink) 27–35.

Fisher, Marjorie M. (2001). *The sons of Ramesses II*, Ägypten und Altes Testament 53, 2 vols. (Wiesbaden: Harrassowitz).

Fitzenreiter, Martin (2001). 'Grabdekoration und die Interpretation funerärer Rituale im Alten Reich'. In Harco Willems (ed.), *Social aspects of funerary culture in the Egyptian Old and Middle Kingdoms: proceedings of the symposium held at Leiden, 6–7 June, 1996*, Orientalia Lovaniensia Analecta 103 (Leuven, Paris, and Sterling VA: Peeters) 67–140.

Foster, John L. (1993). *Thought couplets in* The Tale of Sinuhe: *verse text and translation, with an outline of grammatical forms and clause sequences and an essay on the tale as literature*, Münchener Ägyptologische Untersuchungen 3 (Frankfurt am Main and New York: Peter Lang).

Frandsen, Paul John (1992). 'The letter to Ikhtay's coffin: O. Louvre inv. no. 698'. In R. J. Demarée and Arno Egberts (eds.), *Village voices: proceedings of the symposium*

'Texts from Deir el-Medîna and their interpretation', Leiden, May 31 – June 1, 1991, CNWS Publications 13 (Leiden: Centre of Non-Western Studies) 31–49.

—— (1998). 'On the avoidance of certain forms of loud voices and access to the sacred'. In Willy Clarysse, Antoon Schoors, and Harco Willems (eds.), *Egyptian religion, the last thousand years: studies dedicated to the memory of Jan Quaegebeur*, Orientalia Lovaniensia Analecta 85 (Leuven: Peeters) II, 975–1000.

—— (2000). 'On the origin of the notion of evil in ancient Egypt'. *Göttinger Miszellen* 179: 9–34.

—— (2001). '*Bwt* in the body'. In Harco Willems (ed.), *Social aspects of funerary culture in the Egyptian Old and Middle Kingdoms: proceedings of the symposium held at Leiden, 6–7 June, 1996*, Orientalia Lovaniensia Analecta 103 (Leuven, Paris, and Sterling, Va.: Peeters) 141–74.

Franke, Detlef (2003). 'The Middle Kingdom offering formulas: a challenge'. *Journal of Egyptian Archaeology* 89: 39–57.

Frankfort, Henri (1996). *The art and architecture of the ancient Orient*, revised by Michael Roaf and Donald Matthews; Pelican History of Art, 5th edn. (New Haven and London: Yale University Press).

Frankfort, Henri, Adriaan de Buck, and Battiscombe Gunn (1930). *The cenotaph of Seti I at Abydos*, Egypt Exploration Society, Memoir 39, 2 vols. (London: Egypt Exploration Society).

Freed, Rita E. (ed.) (1987). *Ramses II: the great pharaoh and his time*, exhibition catalogue (Denver: Denver Museum of Natural History).

Freed, Rita E., Sue D'Auria, and Yvonne Markowitz (eds.) (1999). *Pharaohs of the sun: Akhenaten, Nefertiti, Tutankhamen*, exhibition catalogue (Boston: Museum of Fine Arts; Bulfinch Press/Little Brown).

Freeman, N. H., and M. V. Cox (1985). *Visual order: the nature and development of pictorial representation* (Cambridge: Cambridge University Press).

Friedl, Erika (1979). 'Colors and culture change in Southwest Iran'. *Language in Society* 8: 51–68.

Friedman, Florence D. (1998). *Gifts of the Nile: ancient Egyptian faience*, exhibition catalogue, Rhode Island School of Design ([London]: Thames & Hudson).

Friedman, Renée (1996). 'The ceremonial centre at Hierakonpolis: Locality HK29A'. In A. Jeffrey Spencer (ed.), *Aspects of early Egypt* (London: British Museum Press) 16–35.

Frood, Elizabeth in press. *Biographical texts from Ramessid Egypt*, Writings from the Ancient World (Atlanta: Scholars Press).

Gaballa, G. A. (1977). *The Memphite tomb chapel of Mose* (Warminster: Aris & Phillips).

Gage, John (1995). 'Colour and culture'. In Trevor Lamb and Janine Bourriau (eds.), *Colour: art and science* (Cambridge: Cambridge University Press) 175–94.

Gage, John, Andrew Jones, Richard Bradley, Kate Spence, E. J. W. Barber, and Paul S. C. Taçon (1999). 'What meaning had colour in early societies?' *Cambridge Archaeological Journal* 9: 109–26.

Gardiner, Alan H. (1911). *Egyptian hieratic texts* I (Leipzig: J. C. Hinrichs).

Gardiner, Alan H. (1932). *Late-Egyptian stories*, Bibliotheca Aegyptiaca 1 (Brussels: Fondation Egyptologique Reine Elisabeth).
—— (1935). *Chester Beatty Gift*, Hieratic Papyri in the British Museum, 3rd series, 2 vols. (London: British Museum).
—— (1937). *Late-Egyptian miscellanies*, Bibliotheca Aegyptiaca 7 (Brussels: Fondation Egyptologique Reine Elisabeth).
—— (1938). 'The House of Life'. *Journal of Egyptian Archaeology* 24: 157–79.
—— (1946). 'Davies' copy of the great Speos Artemidos inscription'. *Journal of Egyptian Archaeology* 32: 43–56.
—— (1947). *Ancient Egyptian onomastica*, 3 vols. (Oxford: Clarendon Press).
—— (1948). *Ramesside administrative documents* (London: Geoffrey Cumberlege, Oxford University Press, for Griffith Institute, Oxford).
—— (1955a). *The Ramesseum papyri* (Oxford: University Press for Griffith Institute).
—— (1955b). 'A unique funerary liturgy'. *Journal of Egyptian Archaeology* 41: 9–17.
—— (1957). *Egyptian grammar, being an introduction to the study of hieroglyphs*, 3rd edn. (London: Oxford University Press for Griffith Institute, Oxford).
—— (1959). *The Royal Canon of Turin* (Oxford: Griffith Institute).
Gardiner, Alan H., T. E. Peet, and Jaroslav Černý (1952–5). *The inscriptions of Sinai*, 2 vols., vol. II by Jaroslav Černý, 2nd edn. (London: Egypt Exploration Society).
Gardiner, Alan H., and Kurt Sethe (1930). *Egyptian letters to the dead, mainly from the Old and Middle Kingdoms* (London: Egypt Exploration Society).
Gasse, Annie (1992). 'Les ostraca hiératiques littéraires de Deir el-Medina: nouvelles orientations de la publication'. In R. J. Demarée and Arno Egberts (eds.), *Village Voices: proceedings of the Symposium 'Texts from Deir el-Medîna and their interpretation', Leiden, May 31 – June 1, 1991*, CNWS Publications 13 (Leiden: Centre of Non-Western Studies) 51–70.
—— (2000). 'Le K2, un cas d'école?' In R. J. Demarée and Arno Egberts (eds.), *Deir el-Medina in the third millennium AD: a tribute to Jac. J. Janssen*, Egyptologische Uitgaven 14 (Leiden: Nederlands Instituut voor het Nabije Oosten) 109–20.
Gauthier, Henri (1912). *Le livre des rois d'Egypte* II, Mémoires de l'Institut Français d'Archéologie Orientale 18 (Cairo: Institut Français d'Archéologie Orientale).
Geertz, Clifford (1983) [1976]. 'Art as a cultural system'. In Clifford Geertz, *Local knowledge: further essays in interpretive anthropology* (New York: Basic Books) 94–120.
Gillam, Robyn A. (1995). 'Priestesses of Hathor: their function, decline and disappearance'. *Journal of the American Research Center in Egypt* 32: 211–37.
Gimbel, David Nelson (2002). The evolution of visual representation: the elite art of Early Dynastic Lagaš and its antecedents in Late Uruk period Sumer and predynastic Egypt. Doctoral dissertation: University of Oxford.
Giveon, Raphael (1974). 'A second relief of Sekhemkhet in Sinai'. *Bulletin of the American Schools of Oriental Research* 216: 17–20.
Glanville, S. R. K. (1931). 'Records of a royal dockyard of the time of Tuthmosis III: Papyrus British Museum 10056'. *Zeitschrift für Ägyptische Sprache und Altertumskunde* 66: 105–21.

Glanville, S. R. K. (1932). 'Scribes' palettes in the British Museum, Part I'. *Journal of Egyptian Archaeology* 18: 53–61.

Glassner, Jean-Jacques (2003). *The invention of cuneiform: writing in Sumer*, trans. Zainab Bahrani and Marc Van De Mieroop (Baltimore and London: Johns Hopkins University Press).

Gödecken, Karin Barbara (1976). *Eine Betrachtung der Inschriften des Meten im Rahmen der sozialen und rechtlichen Stellung von Privatleuten im Alten Reich*, Ägyptologische Abhandlungen 29 (Wiesbaden: Otto Harrassowitz).

Goebs, Katja (2002). 'A functional approach to Egyptian myth and mythemes'. *Journal of Ancient Near Eastern Religions* 2: 227–59.

—— (2007). *Crowns in Egyptian funerary literature: royalty, rebirth, and destruction* (Oxford: Griffith Institute).

Goedicke, Hans (1967). *Königliche Dokumente aus dem Alten Reich*, Ägyptologische Abhandlungen 14 (Wiesbaden: Otto Harrassowitz).

—— (1970). *Die privaten Rechtsinschriften aus dem Alten Reich*, Beihefte zur Wiener Zeitschrift für die Kunde des Morgenlands 5 (Vienna: Notring).

—— (1971). *Re-used blocks from the pyramid of Amenemhet I at Lisht*, Metropolitan Museum of Art, Egyptian Expedition 20 (New York: Metropolitan Museum of Art).

Goethe, Johann Wolfgang von (1962) [1804]. 'Polygnots Gemälde in der Lesche zu Delphi'. In, *Schriften zur Kunst*, II, Gesamtausgabe, Abteilung 2, vol. 17 (Stuttgart: Cotta) 79–106.

Goldwasser, Orly (1991). 'On dynamic canonicity in Late Egyptian: the literary letter and the personal prayer'. *Lingua Aegyptia* 1: 129–41.

—— (1995). 'On the conception of the poetic form—a love letter to a departed wife, Ostracon Louvre 698'. In Shlomo Izre'el and Rina Drory (eds.), *Language and culture in the Near East*, Israel Oriental Studies 15 (Leiden: E. J. Brill) 191–205.

Gomaà, Farouk (1973). *Chaemwese, Sohn Ramses' II. und Hoherpriester von Memphis*, Ägyptologische Abhandlungen 27 (Wiesbaden: Otto Harrassowitz).

Gombrich, E. H. (1966). 'The Renaissance conception of artistic progress and its consequences'. In E. H. Gombrich, *Norm and form: studies in the art of the Renaissance* (London: Phaidon) 1–10.

—— (1972a). *The story of art*, 12th edn. (London: Phaidon).

—— (1972b). *Symbolic images: studies in the art of the Renaissance* (London: Phaidon).

—— (1975). 'Mirror and map: theories of pictorial representation'. *Philosophical Transactions of the Royal Society of London* B: *Biological Sciences* 270: 119–49.

—— (1977) [1960]. *Art and illusion: a study in the psychology of pictorial representation*, 5th edn. (Oxford: Phaidon).

—— (1983). Review of William H. Peck and John G. Ross, *Drawings from ancient Egypt* (1978). *Journal of Egyptian Archaeology* 69: 192–3.

—— (1986) [1974]. 'Foreword'. In Heinrich Schäfer, *Principles of Egyptian art*, ed. Emma Brunner-Traut, trans. and ed. John Baines (Oxford: Griffith Institute) ix–x.

Gonda, J. (1975). *Vedic literature (Saṃhitās and Brāhmaṇas)*, History of Indian Literature 1:1 (Wiesbaden: Otto Harrassowitz).

Goneim, M. Zakaria (1957). *Horus Sekhem-khet: the unfinished step pyramid at Saqqara* I, Service des Antiquités de l'Egypte: Excavations at Saqqara (Cairo: Institut Français d'Archéologie Orientale).

Goody, Jack (1977). *The domestication of the savage mind* (Cambridge: Cambridge University Press).

—— (1986). *The logic of writing and the organization of society* (Cambridge: Cambridge University Press).

—— (2000). *The power of the written tradition*, Smithsonian Series in Ethnographic Enquiry (Washington and London: Smithsonian Institution Press).

—— (ed.) (1968). *Literacy in traditional societies* (Cambridge: Cambridge University Press).

Goody, Jack, and Ian Watt (1968) [1963]. 'The consequences of literacy'. In Jack Goody (ed.), *Literacy in traditional societies* (Cambridge: Cambridge University Press) 27–68.

Gophna, Ram (1976). 'Egyptian immigration into southern Canaan during the first dynasty?' *Tel Aviv* 3: 31–7.

—— (1978). ' ͨEn-Besor: an Egyptian staging post in the northern Negev'. *Expedition* 20:4: 4–7.

Görsdorf, Jochen, Günter Dreyer, and Ulrich Hartung (1998). '^{14}C dating results of the archaic royal necropolis Umm el-Qaab at Abydos'. *Mitteilungen des Deutschen Archäologischen Instituts, Abteilung Kairo* 54: 169–75.

Gough, Kathleen (1968a). 'Implications of literacy in traditional China and India'. In Jack Goody (ed.), *Literacy in traditional societies* (Cambridge: Cambridge University Press) 70–84.

—— (1968b). 'Literacy in Kerala'. In Jack Goody (ed.), *Literacy in traditional societies* (Cambridge: Cambridge University Press) 133–60.

Goyon, Jean-Claude, and Claude Traunecker (1980). 'Documents de l'allée des processions'. *Cahiers de Karnak* 6, 1973–1977: 129–52.

Graefe, Erhart (1981). *Untersuchungen zur Verwaltung und Geschichte der Institution der Gottesgemahlin des Amun vom Beginn des Neuen Reiches bis zur Spätzeit*, Ägyptologische Abhandlungen 37, 2 vols. (Wiesbaden: Otto Harrassowitz).

—— (1990). 'Die gute Reputation des Königs "Snofru"'. In Sara Israelit-Groll (ed.), *Studies in Egyptology presented to Miriam Lichtheim* (Jerusalem: Magnes Press) II, 257–63.

Grand Palais, Galeries nationales du (1982). *Naissance de l'écriture: cunéiformes et hiéroglyphes*, exhibition catalogue (Paris: Ministère de la Culture, Editions de la Réunion des musées nationaux).

Grandet, Pierre (1994–99). *Le Papyrus Harris I (BM 9999)*, Bibliothèque d'Etude 109, 3 vols. (Cairo: Institut Français d'Archéologie Orientale).

Grapow, Hermann (1956). *Kranker, Krankheit und Arzt: Grundriss der Medizin der Alten Ägypter* III (Berlin: Akademie-Verlag).

Grapow, Hermann, et al. (1954–73). *Grundriss der Medizin der Alten Ägypter*, 9 vols. (Berlin: Akademie-Verlag).

Green, Lorna (2001). 'Colour transformations of ancient Egyptian pigments'. In W. Vivian Davies (ed.), *Colour and painting in ancient Egypt* (London: British Museum Press) 43–8.

Green, M. W. (1981). 'The construction and implementation of the cuneiform writing system'. *Visible Language* 15: 345–72.

Griffith, F. Ll. (1898). *The Petrie Papyri: hieratic papyri from Kahun and Gurob*, 2 vols. (London: Bernard Quaritch).

—— (1909). *Catalogue of the demotic papyri in the John Rylands Library Manchester*, 3 vols. (Manchester and London: Manchester University Press; Bernard Quaritch; Sherratt and Hughes).

Grimal, Nicolas-Christophe (1980). 'Bibliothèques et propagande royale à l'époque éthiopienne'. In Jean Vercoutter (ed.), *Institut Français d'Archéologie Orientale, livre du Centenaire*, Mémoires Publiés par les Membres de l'Institut Français d'Archéologie Orientale 104 (Cairo: Institut Français d'Archéologie Orientale) 37–48.

Groenewegen-Frankfort, H. A. (1951). *Arrest and movement: an essay on space and time in the representational art of the ancient Near East* (London: Faber and Faber); several reprints.

Guglielmi, Waltraud (1973). *Reden, Rufe und Lieder auf altägyptischen Darstellungen der Landwirtschaft, der Viehzucht, des Fisch- und Vogelfangs vom Mittleren Reich bis zur Spätzeit*, Tübinger Ägyptologische Beiträge 1 (Bonn: Rudolf Habelt).

Gundlach, Rolf (1977). 'Goldgewinnung'. In Wolfgang Helck and Wolfhart Westendorf (eds.), *Lexikon der Ägyptologie* (Wiesbaden: Otto Harrassowitz) II, 734–8.

Gunter, Ann C. (ed.) (1990). *Investigating artistic environments in the ancient Near East* (Washington, DC: Smithsonian Institution).

Habachi, Labib (1965). 'Varia from the reign of King Akhenaten'. *Mitteilungen des Deutschen Archäologischen Instituts, Abteilung Kairo* 20: 70–92.

—— (1985). *Elephantine IV: the sanctuary of Heqaib*, Archäologische Veröffentlichungen des Deutschen Archäologischen Instituts, Abteilung Kairo 33, 2 vols. (Mainz: Philipp von Zabern).

Haeny, Gerhard (1971). 'Zu den Platten mit Opfertischszene aus Heluan und Giseh'. In *Aufsätze zum 70. Geburtstag von Herbert Ricke*, Beiträge zur Ägyptischen Bauforschung und Altertumskunde 12 (Wiesbaden: Franz Steiner) 143–64.

Hagen, Margaret A. (1985). 'There is no development in art'. In N. H. Freeman and M. V. Cox (eds.), *Visual order: the nature and development of pictorial representation* (Cambridge: Cambridge University Press) 59–77.

—— (1986). *Varieties of realism: geometries of representational art* (Cambridge: Cambridge University Press).

Hallo, William W., and William Kelly Simpson (1971). *The ancient Near East: a history* (New York etc.: Harcourt Brace Jovanovich).

Hamada, A. (1938). 'A stela from Manshîyet es-Sadr'. *Annales du Service des Antiquités de l'Égypte* 38: 217–30.

Hampson, Nick, Neill Bennett, and Renée Friedman (2000). 'Mapping the Fort and more'. *Nekhen News* 12: 20–1.

Hanke, Rainer (1959). 'Beiträge zum Kanonproblem'. *Zeitschrift für Ägyptische Sprache und Altertumskunde* 84: 113–19.
Hardin, Clyde L. (1998). 'Basic color terms and basic color categories'. In Werner Backhaus, Reinhold Kliegl, and John Simon Werner (eds.), *Color vision: perspectives from different disciplines* (Berlin and New York: Walter de Gruyter) 207–17.
Hardin, Clyde L., and Luisa Maffi (eds.) (1997). *Color categories in thought and language* (Cambridge: Cambridge University Press).
Hardin, Kris L. (1993). *The aesthetics of action: continuity and change in a West African town*, Smithsonian Series in Ethnographic Enquiry (Washington, DC, and London: Smithsonian Institution Press).
Haring, Ben (2000). 'Towards decoding the necropolis workmen's funny signs'. *Göttinger Miszellen* 178: 45–58.
—— (2003). 'From oral practice to written record in Ramesside Deir el-Medina'. *Journal of the Economic and Social History of the Orient* 46: 249–72.
Harris, J. R. (1961). *Lexicographical studies in ancient Egyptian minerals*, Deutsche Akademie der Wissenschaften, Institut für Orientforschung, Veröffentlichung 54 (Berlin: Akademie-Verlag).
Harris, Rivkah (1975). *Ancient Sippar: a demographic study of an Old-Babylonian city (1894–1595 B.C.)*, Uitgaven van het Nederlandsch historisch archeologisch Instituut te Istanbul 36 (Istanbul: Nederlandsch Instituut).
Harris, William V. (1989). *Ancient literacy* (Cambridge, Mass., and London: Harvard University Press).
—— (1983). 'Literacy and epigraphy, I'. *Zeitschrift für Papyrologie und Epigraphik* 52: 87–111.
Harvey, Stephen (1994). 'Monuments of Ahmose at Abydos'. *Egyptian Archaeology* 4: 3–5.
Havelock, Eric A. (1982). *The literate revolution in Greece and its cultural consequences* (Princeton: Princeton University Press).
Hawkins, J. D. (1979). 'The origin and dissemination of writing in western Asia'. In P. R. S. Moorey (ed.), *The origins of civilization* (Oxford: Clarendon Press) 128–66.
Hayes, William C. (1953). *The scepter of Egypt: a background for the study of the Egyptian collections in the Metropolitan Museum of Art* I, *From the earliest times to the end of the Middle Kingdom* (New York: Harper with Metropolitan Museum of Art).
—— (1959). *The scepter of Egypt: a background for the study of the Egyptian antiquities in the Metropolitan Museum of Art* II, *The Hyksos period and the New Kingdom (1675–1080 B.C.)* (New York: Harper).
Haymes, Edward R. (1973). *A bibliography of studies relating to Parry's and Lord's oral theory*, Publications of the Parry Collection, Documentary Series 1 (Cambridge, Mass.: Harvard University Press).
Hébrard, Jean (2002). 'The writings of Moïse (1898–1985): birth, life, and death of a narrative of the Great War'. *Comparative Studies in Society and History* 44: 263–92.
Heinrich, Ernst (1982). *Die Tempel im alten Mesopotamien: Typologie, Morphologie und Geschichte*, Deutsches Archäologisches Institut, Denkmäler Antiker Architektur 14, 2 vols. (Berlin: Walter de Gruyter).

Helck, Wolfgang (1952). 'Die Bedeutung der ägyptischen Besucherinschriften'. *Zeitschrift der Deutschen Morgenländischen Gesellschaft* 102: 39–52.

—— (1955a). 'Eine Stele des Vizekönigs Wśr-Śt.t'. *Journal of Near Eastern Studies* 14: 22–31.

—— (1955b). *Urkunden der 18. Dynastie Heft 17*, Urkunden des Ägyptischen Altertums 4 (Berlin: Akademie-Verlag).

—— (1956a). *Untersuchungen zu Manetho und den ägyptischen Königslisten*, Untersuchungen zur Geschichte und Altertumskunde Ägyptens 18 (Berlin: Akademie-Verlag).

—— (1956b). *Urkunden der 18. Dynastie Heft 18*, Urkunden des Ägyptischen Altertums 4 (Berlin: Akademie-Verlag).

—— (1957). *Urkunden der 18. Dynastie Heft 19*, Urkunden des Ägyptischen Altertums 4 (Berlin: Akademie-Verlag).

—— (1958). *Urkunden der 18. Dynastie Heft 21*, Urkunden des Ägyptischen Altertums 4 (Berlin: Akademie-Verlag).

—— (1960). 'Die soziale Schichtung des ägyptischen Volks im 3. und 2. Jahrtausend v. Chr'. *Journal of the Economic and Social History of the Orient* 2: 1–36.

—— (1961). *Urkunden der 18. Dynastie: Übersetzung zu den Heften 17–22*, Urkunden des Ägyptischen Altertums: Deutsch (Berlin: Akademie-Verlag).

—— (1963). 'Entwicklung der Verwaltung als Spiegelbild historischer und soziologischer Faktoren'. In Sergio Donadoni (ed.), *Le fonti indirette della storia egiziana*, Studi Semitici 7 (Rome: Università di Roma, Centro di Studi Semitici) 59–80.

—— (1968). *Geschichte des alten Ägypten*, Handbuch der Orientalistik 1:1:3 (Leiden and Cologne: E. J. Brill [extensively revised reprint 1981]).

—— (1970). *Die Prophezeiung des Nfr.tj*, Kleine Ägyptische Texte (Wiesbaden: Otto Harrassowitz).

—— (1971). *Die Beziehungen Ägyptens zu Vorderasien im 3. und 2. Jahrtausend v. Chr.*, Ägyptologische Abhandlungen 5, 2nd edn. (Wiesbaden: Otto Harrassowitz).

—— (1972). 'Zur Frage der Entstehung der ägyptischen "Literatur"'. *Wiener Zeitschrift für die Kunde des Morgenlands* 63–4: 6–26.

—— (1974a). *Altägyptische Aktenkunde des 3. und 2. Jahrtausends v. Chr*, Münchner Ägyptologische Studien 31 (Munich and Berlin: Deutscher Kunstverlag).

—— (1974b). *Die altägyptischen Gaue*, Beihefte zum Tübinger Atlas des Vorderen Orients B5 (Wiesbaden: Dr Ludwig Reichert).

—— (1974c). 'Die Bedeutung der Inschriften J. Lopez, Inscripciones rupestres Nr. 27 and 28'. *Studien zur Altägyptischen Kultur* 1: 215–25.

—— (1974d). 'Bemerkungen zum Annalenstein'. *Mitteilungen des Deutschen Archäologischen Instituts, Abteilung Kairo* 30: 31–5.

—— (1975). *Wirtschaftsgeschichte des alten Ägypten im 3. und 2. Jahrtausend v. Chr.*, Handbuch der Orientalistik 1:1:5 (Leiden: E. J. Brill).

—— (1977). *Die Lehre für König Merikare*, Kleine Ägyptische Texte (Wiesbaden: Otto Harrassowitz).

—— (1982). 'Palette (Schreib-)'. In Wolfgang Helck and Wolfhart Westendorf (eds.), *Lexikon der Ägyptologie* (Wiesbaden: Otto Harrassowitz) IV, 656–8.

Helck, Wolfgang (1983). *Historisch-biographische Texte der 2. Zwischenzeit und neue Texte der 18. Dynastie*, Kleine Ägyptische Texte, 2nd edn. (Wiesbaden: Otto Harrassowitz).
—— (1984). *Die Lehre des Djedefhor und die Lehre eines Vaters an seinen Sohn*, Kleine Ägyptische Texte (Wiesbaden: Otto Harrassowitz).
—— (1985a). 'Gedanken zum Ursprung der ägyptischen Schrift'. In Paule Posener-Kriéger (ed.), *Mélanges Gamal eddin Mokhtar*, Bibliothèque d'Etude 97 (Cairo: Institut Français d'Archéologie Orientale) I, 395–408.
—— (1985b). 'Politische Spannungen zu Beginn des Mittleren Reiches'. In *Ägypten: Dauer und Wandel. Symposium anlässlich des 75 jährigen Bestehens des Deutschen Archäologischen Instituts, Kairo, am 10. und 11. Oktober 1982*, Deutsches Archäologisches Institut, Abteilung Kairo, Sonderschrift 18 (Mainz: Philipp von Zabern) 45–52.
—— (1990). *Thinitische Topfmarken*, Ägyptologische Abhandlungen 50 (Wiesbaden: Otto Harrassowitz).
Hendrickx, Stan (2002). 'Checklist of predynastic "Decorated" pottery with human figures'. *Cahiers Caribéens d'Egyptologie* 3/4: 29–50.
Henige, David (1981). 'Generation-counting and late New Kingdom chronology'. *Journal of Egyptian Archaeology* 67: 182–4.
Hermann, Alfred (1940). *Die Stelen der thebanischen Felsgräber der 18. Dynastie*, Ägyptologische Forschungen 11 (Glückstadt and New York: J. J. Augustin).
—— (1969). 'Farbe'. In *Reallexikon für Antike und Christentum* (Stuttgart: Hiersemann) VII, 358–447.
Hibbard, Howard (1966). *Bernini* (Harmondsworth: Penguin).
Hinton, Howard (1973). 'Natural deception'. In E. H. Gombrich and Richard L. Gregory (eds.), *Illusion in nature and art* (London: Duckworth) 96–159.
Hölscher, Uvo (1934). *The excavation of Medinet Habu* I, *General plans and views*, Oriental Institute Publications 21 (Chicago: University of Chicago Press).
—— (1951). *The excavation of Medinet Habu* IV, *The mortuary temple of Ramses III, part II*, Oriental Institute Publications 55 (Chicago: University of Chicago Press).
Hopkins, Keith (1980). 'Brother–sister marriage in Roman Egypt'. *Comparative Studies in Society and History* 22: 303–54.
Hornung, Erik (1957). 'Zur geschichtlichen Rolle des Königs in der 18. Dynastie'. *Mitteilungen des Deutschen Archäologischen Instituts, Abteilung Kairo* 15: 120–33.
—— (1966). *Geschichte als Fest: zwei Vorträge zum Geschichtsbild der frühen Menschheit*, Libelli 246 (Darmstadt: Wissenschaftliche Buchgesellschaft). Eng. trans.: 'History as celebration', in Hornung, *Idea into image: essays on ancient Egyptian thought* (New York: Timken 1991) 147–64, trans. Elisabeth Bredeck from the altered reprint in Hornung, *Geist der Pharaonenzeit* (Zurich: Artemis 1989) 147–63.
—— (1967). *Das Amduat: die Schrift des verborgenen Raumes* III, *Die Kurzfassung; Nachträge*, Ägyptologische Abhandlungen 13 (Wiesbaden: Otto Harrassowitz).
—— (1971). 'Politische Planung und Realität im alten Ägypten'. *Saeculum* 22: 48–58.
—— (1979). *Das Totenbuch der Ägypter*, Die Bibliothek der Alten Welt, Der Alte Orient (Zurich: Artemis).
—— (1982a). *Conceptions of god in ancient Egypt: the one and the many*, trans. John Baines (Ithaca, NY: Cornell University Press).

Hornung, Erik (1982b). *Der ägyptische Mythos von der Himmelskuh: eine Ätiologie des Unvollkommenen*, Orbis Biblicus et Orientalis 46; 2nd edn. 1991 (Fribourg and Göttingen: Universitätsverlag; Vandenhoeck & Ruprecht).
—— (1984) [1972]. *Ägyptische Unterweltsbücher*, Die Bibliothek der Alten Welt, der Alte Orient, 2nd edn. (Zurich and Munich: Artemis).
—— (1990). *The Valley of the Kings: horizon of eternity*, trans. David Warburton (New York: Timken).
—— (1991). *The tomb of Pharaoh Seti I/Das Grab Sethos' I.* (Zurich and Munich: Artemis).
—— (1999). *The ancient Egyptian books of the afterlife*, trans. David Lorton (Ithaca, NY, and London: Cornell University Press).
Hornung, Erik, and Elisabeth Staehelin (1974). *Studien zum Sedfest*, Aegyptiaca Helvetica 1 (Geneva: Edition de Belles-Lettres).
Horton, Robin (1967). 'African traditional thought and western science'. *Africa* 37: 50–71, 155–87.
Houston, Stephen D. (1994). 'Literacy among the Pre-Columbian Maya: a comparative perspective'. In Elizabeth Hill Boone and Walter D. Mignolo (eds.), *Writing without words: alternative literacies in Mesoamerica and the Andes* (Durham, NC, and London: Duke University Press) 27–49.
—— (2000). 'Into the minds of ancients: advances in Maya glyph studies'. *Journal of World Prehistory* 14: 121–201.
—— (2004a). 'The archaeology of communication technologies'. *Annual Review of Anthropology* 33: 223–50.
—— (ed.) (2004b). *The first writing: script invention as history and process* (Cambridge: Cambridge University Press).
—— et al. in preparation. *Veiled brightness: a history of Maya color.*
Houston, Stephen D., John Baines, and John Bennet (eds.) in preparation. *Disappearances of writing* (London: Equinox).
Houston, Stephen D., John Baines, and Jerrold Cooper (2003). 'Last writing: script obsolescence in Egypt, Mesopotamia, and Mesoamerica'. *Comparative Studies in Society and History* 45: 430–79.
Hudson, Michael, and Cornelia Wunsch (eds.) (2004). *Record-keeping, standardization, and the development of accounting in the ancient Near East*, International Scholars Conference on Ancient Near Eastern Economies 4 (Bethesda: CDL Press).
Hunger, Hermann (1968). *Babylonische und assyrische Kolophone*, Alter Orient und Altes Testament 2 (Kevelaer and Neukirchen-Vluyn: Butzon & Bercker; Neukirchener Verlag).
Inomata, Takeshi (2001). 'The power and ideology of artistic creation: elite craft specialists in Classic Maya society'. *Current Anthropology* 42: 1–52.
Insley Green, Christine (1987). *The temple furniture from the sacred animal necropolis at North Saqqâra, 1964–1976*, Excavation Memoir 53 (London: Egypt Exploration Society).
Iversen, Erik (1963). 'Horapollon and the Egyptian conceptions of eternity'. *Rivista degli Studi Orientali* 38: 177–86.

Iversen, Erik, with Yoshiaki Shibata (1975). *Canon and proportions in Egyptian art*, 2nd edn. (Warminster: Aris & Phillips).

Jacquet-Gordon, Helen (1962). *Les noms des domaines funéraires sous l'Ancien Empire égyptien*, Bibliothèque d'Etude 34 (Cairo: Institut Français d'Archéologie Orientale).

Jaeger, Bertrand (1982). *Essai de classification et datation des scarabées Menkhéperrê*, Orbis Biblicus et Orientalis, Series Archaeologica 2 (Fribourg and Göttingen: Universitätsverlag; Vandenhoeck & Ruprecht).

Jäger, Stephan (2004). *Altägyptische Berufstypologien*, Lingua Aegyptia, Studia Monographica 4 (Göttingen: Seminar für Ägyptologie und Koptologie).

Jahoda, Gustav (1981a). 'Drawing styles of schooled and unschooled adults: a study in Ghana'. *Quarterly Journal of Experimental Psychology* 33: 133–43.

—— (1981b). 'Pictorial perception and the problem of universals'. In Barbara Lloyd and John Gay (eds.), *Universals of human thought: some African evidence* (Cambridge: Cambridge University Press) 25–45.

James, T. G. H., and M. R. Apted (1953). *The mastaba of Khentika called Ikhekhi*, Archaeological Survey of Egypt 30 (London: Egypt Exploration Society).

Jansen-Winkeln, Karl (1994). *Text und Sprache in der 3. Zwischenzeit: Vorarbeiten zu einer spätmittelägyptischen Grammatik*, Ägypten und Altes Testament 26 (Wiesbaden: Harrassowitz).

—— (1996). *Spätmittelägyptische Grammatik der Texte der 3. Zwischenzeit*, Ägypten und Altes Testament 34 (Wiesbaden: Harrassowitz).

—— (1997). 'Die Hildesheimer Stele der Chereduanch'. *Mitteilungen des Deutschen Archäologischen Instituts, Abteilung Kairo* 53: 91–100.

Janssen, J. J. (1960). 'Nine letters from the time of Ramesses II'. *Oudheidkundige Mededelingen uit het Rijksmuseum van Oudheden te Leiden* NS 41: 31–47.

—— (1975a). *Commodity prices in the Ramessid period: an economic study of the village of necropolis workmen at Thebes* (Leiden: E. J. Brill).

—— (1975b). 'Prologemena to the study of Egypt's economic history in the New Kingdom'. *Studien zur Altägyptischen Kultur* 3: 127–85.

—— (1975c). 'The rules of legal proceeding in the community of necropolis workmen at Deir el-Medina'. *Bibliotheca Orientalis* 32: 290–7.

—— (1977). 'Khaᶜemtore, a well-to-do workman'. *Oudheidkundige Mededelingen uit het Rijksmuseum van Oudheden te Leiden* 58: 221–32.

—— (1978). 'The early state in Egypt'. In Henri J. M. Claessen and Peter Skalník (eds.), *The early state*, New Babylon: Studies in the Social Sciences 32 (The Hague: Mouton) 213–34.

—— (1980). 'Absence from work by the necropolis workmen of Thebes'. *Studien zur Altägyptischen Kultur* 8: 127–52.

—— (1992). 'Literacy and letters at Deir el-Medîna'. In R. J. Demarée and Arno Egberts (eds.), *Village voices: proceedings of the symposium 'Texts from Deir el-Medîna and their interpretation', Leiden, May 31 – June 1, 1991*, CNWS Publications 13 (Leiden: Centre of Non-Western Studies) 81–94.

—— (1990). *Late Ramesside letters and communications*, Hieratic Papyri in the British Museum 6 (London: British Museum Press for the Trustees of the British Museum).

Janssen, J. J., and P. W. Pestman (1968). 'Burial and inheritance in the community of necropolis workmen at Thebes'. *Journal of the Economic and Social History of the Orient* 11: 137–70.

Jardine, Lisa (1997). *Worldly goods: a new history of the Renaissance* (London: Papermac).

Jasim, Sabah Abboud, and Joan Oates (1986). 'Early tokens and tablets in Mesopotamia: new information from Tell Abada and Tell Brak'. *World Archaeology* 17: 348–62.

Jeffreys, David J., and Ana Tavares (1994). 'The historic landscape of Early Dynastic Memphis'. *Mitteilungen des Deutschen Archäologischen Instituts, Abteilung Kairo* 50: 143–73.

Jenkins, Nancy (1980). *The boat beneath the pyramid: King Cheops' royal ship* (London: Thames & Hudson).

Jéquier, Gustave (1936–40). *Le monument funéraire de Pépy II*, Service des Antiquités de l'Egypte, Fouilles à Saqqarah, 3 vols. (Cairo: Institut Français d'Archéologie Orientale).

Jernudd, Björn H., and Geoffrey M. White (1983). 'The concept of basic colour terms: variability in For and Arabic'. *Anthropological Linguistics* 25: 61–81.

Johnson, Janet H. (1998). 'Women, wealth and work in Egyptian society of the Ptolemaic period'. In Willy Clarysse, Antoon Schoors, and Harco Willems (eds.), *Egyptian religion, the last thousand years: studies dedicated to the memory of Jan Quaegebeur*, Orientalia Lovaniensia Analecta 84 (Leuven: Peeters) II, 1393–1421.

Junge, Friedrich (1973). 'Zur Fehldatierung des sog. Denkmals memphitischer Theologie, oder Der Beitrag der ägyptischen Theologie zur Geistesgeschichte der Spätzeit'. *Mitteilungen des Deutschen Archäologischen Instituts, Abteilung Kairo* 29: 195–204.

—— (1977). 'Die Welt der Klagen'. In Jan Assmann, Erika Feucht, and Reinhard Grieshammer (eds.), *Fragen an die altägyptische Literatur: Studien zum Gedenken an Eberhard Otto* (Wiesbaden: Dr Ludwig Reichert) 275–84.

—— (1985). 'Sprachstufen und Sprachgeschichte'. *Zeitschrift der Deutschen Morgenländischen Gesellschaft*, Supplement 6: 17–34.

—— (1990). 'Versuch zu einer Ästhetik der ägyptischen Kunst'. In Marianne Eaton-Krauss and Erhart Graefe (eds.), *Studien zur ägyptischen Kunstgeschichte*, Hildesheimer Ägyptologische Beiträge 29 (Hildesheim: Gerstenberg) 1–25.

Junker, Hermann (1929). *Gîza I: Die Maṣtabas der IV. Dynastie auf dem Westfriedhof*, Akademie der Wissenschaften in Wien, philosophisch-historische Klasse, Denkschriften 69:1 (Vienna and Leipzig: Hölder, Pichler, & Tempsky).

—— (1934). *Gîza II: Die Maṣtabas der beginnenden V. Dynastie auf dem Westfriedhof*, Akademie der Wissenschaften in Wien, philosophisch-historische Klasse (Vienna and Leipzig: Hölder, Pichler, & Tempsky).

—— (1939). 'Pḥrnfr'. *Zeitschrift für Ägyptische Sprache und Altertumskunde* 75: 63–84.

—— (1941). *Gîza V*, Akademie der Wissenschaften in Wien, philosophisch-historische Klasse, Denkschriften 71 (Vienna and Leipzig: Hölder, Pichler, & Tempsky).

—— (1959). *Die gesellschaftliche Stellung der ägyptischen Künstler im Alten Reich*, Österreichische Akademie der Wissenschaften, philosophisch-historische Klasse, Sitzungsberichte 233, 1 (Vienna: Rudolf M. Rohrer).

Justi, Carl (1923). *Winckelmann und seine Zeitgenossen*, 3 vols., 3rd edn. (Leipzig: Vogel).

Kadish, Gerald E. (1973). 'British Museum writing board 5645: the Complaints of Kha-Kheper-Reᶜ-Senebu'. *Journal of Egyptian Archaeology* 59: 77–90.

—— (1978–9). 'The scatophagous Egyptian'. *Journal of the Society for the Study of Egyptian Antiquities* 9: 203–17.

Kahl, Jochem (1994). *Das System der ägyptischen Hieroglyphenschrift in der 0.–3. Dynastie*, Göttinger Orientforschungen 4: Ägypten 29 (Wiesbaden: Harrassowitz).

—— (1999). *Siut–Theben: zur Wertschätzung von Traditionen im alten Ägypten*, Probleme der Ägyptologie 13 (Leiden: E. J. Brill).

—— (2001). 'Hieroglyphic writing during the fourth millennium BC: an analysis of systems'. *Archéo-Nil* 11: 103–34.

—— (2003a). 'Die frühen Schriftzeugnisse aus dem Grab U-j in Umm el-Qaab'. *Chronique d'Egypte* 78: 112–35.

—— (2003b). 'Zwei änigmatische Relieffragmente aus Beit Khallaf'. In Anke Ilona Blöbaum, Jochem Kahl, and Simon D. Schweitzer (eds.), *Ägypten–Münster: kulturwissenschaftliche Studien zu Ägypten, dem Vorderen Orient und verwandten Gebieten; donum natalicium viro doctissimo Erharto Graefe sexagenario ab amicis collegis discipulis ex aedibus Schlaunstrasse 2/Rosenstrasse 9 oblatum* (Wiesbaden: Harrassowitz) 149–66.

Kaiser, Werner (1964). 'Einige Bemerkungen zur ägyptischen Frühzeit III: Die Reichseinigung'. *Zeitschrift für Ägyptische Sprache und Altertumskunde* 91: 86–125.

—— (1985a). 'Ein Kultbezirk des Königs Den in Sakkara'. *Mitteilungen des Deutschen Archäologischen Instituts, Abteilung Kairo* 41: 47–60.

—— (1985b). 'Zur Entwicklung und Vorformen der frühzeitlichen Gräber mit reich gegliederter Oberbaufassade'. In Paule Posener-Kriéger (ed.), *Melanges Gamal eddin Mokhtar*, Bibliothèque d'Etude 97 (Cairo: Institut Français d'Archéologie Orientale) II, 25–38.

—— (1990). 'Zur Entstehung des gesamtägyptischen Staates'. *Mitteilungen des Deutschen Archäologischen Instituts, Abteilung Kairo* 46: 287–99.

—— (ed.) (1967). *Ägyptisches Museum Berlin* (Berlin: Staatliche Museen Preussicher Kulturbesitz).

Kaiser, Werner, and Günter Dreyer (1982). 'Umm el-Qaab: Nachuntersuchungen im frühzeitlichen Königsfriedhof, 2. Vorbericht'. *Mitteilungen des Deutschen Archäologischen Instituts, Abteilung Kairo* 38: 211–69.

Kákosy, László (1964a). 'Ideas about the fallen state of the world in Egyptian religion: decline of the golden age'. *Acta Orientalia Academiae Scientiarum Hungaricae* 17: 206–16.

—— (1964b). 'Urzeitmythen und Historiographie im alten Ägypten'. In E. C. Welskopf, et al. (ed.), *Neue Beiträge zur Geschichte der alten Welt I: Alter Orient und Griechenland* (Berlin: Akademie-Verlag) 57–68.

Kammerzell, Frank (2001). '"... within the Altar of the Sun"—an unidentified hieroglyph and the construction of the sun temple *nḫn-rᶜw*'. *Lingua Aegyptia* 9: 153–64.

Kamrin, Janice (1999). *The cosmos of Khnumhotep II at Beni Hasan*, Studies in Egyptology (London and New York: Kegan Paul International).

Kanawati, Naguib (1977). *The Egyptian administration in the Old Kingdom: evidence on its economic decline* (Warminster: Aris & Phillips).

—— (1980). *Governmental reforms in Old Kingdom Egypt* (Warminster: Aris & Phillips).

—— (1981). 'The living and the dead in Old Kingdom tomb scenes'. *Studien zur Altägyptischen Kultur* 9: 213–25.

—— (1999). 'Some iconographic peculiarities in the Teti cemetery'. In Christiane Ziegler and Nadine Palayret (eds.), *L'art de l'Ancien Empire égyptien: actes du colloque organisé au musée du Louvre par le Service culturel les 3 et 4 avril 1998*, Louvre Conférences et Colloques (Paris: Documentation Française) 281–310.

Kaplony, Peter (1963). *Die Inschriften der ägyptischen Frühzeit*, Ägyptologische Abhandlungen 8, 3 vols. (Wiesbaden: Otto Harrassowitz).

—— (1968). 'Eine neue Weisheitslehre des Alten Reiches (Die Lehre des $M\underline{tt}j$ in der altägyptischen Weisheitsliteratur)'. *Orientalia* 37: 1–62, 339–45.

—— (1969). 'Das Hirtenlied und seine fünfte Variante'. *Chronique d'Egypte* 44/87: 27–59.

—— (1975). 'Beit Challaf'. In Wolfgang Helck and Eberhard Otto (eds.), *Lexikon der Ägyptologie* (Wiesbaden: Otto Harrassowitz) I, 686.

—— (1977–81). *Die Rollsiegel des Alten Reichs*, Monumenta Aegyptiaca 2–3, 2 vols. in 3 (Brussels: Fondation Egyptologique Reine Elisabeth).

Kaplony-Heckel, Ursula (1971). *Ägyptische Handschriften* I, Verzeichnis Orientalischer Handschriften in Deutschland 19 (Wiesbaden: Franz Steiner).

—— (1974). 'Schüler und Schulwesen in der ägyptischen Spätzeit'. *Studien zur Altägyptischen Kultur* 1: 227–46.

Kay, Paul (1975). 'Synchronic variability and diachronic change in basic color terms'. *Language in Society* 4: 257–70.

Kay, Paul, and Luisa Maffi (1999). 'Color appearance and the emergence and evolution of basic color lexicons'. *American Anthropologist* 101: 743–60.

Kay, Paul, and Chad K. McDaniel (1978). 'The linguistic significance of the meanings of basic color terms'. *Language* 54: 610–46.

Kay, Paul, and Terry Regier (2003). 'Resolving the question of color naming universals'. *Proceedings of the National Academy of Sciences* 100: 9085–9.

Kees, Hermann (1943). 'Farbensymbolik in ägyptischen religiösen Texten'. *Nachrichten von der Akademie der Wissenschaften in Göttingen, philologisch-historische Klasse* 11: 413–79.

Keller, Cathleen A. (1981). 'The draughtsmen of Deir el-Medina: a preliminary report'. *Newsletter of the American Research Center in Egypt* 115: 7–21.

—— (2001). 'A family affair: the decoration of Theban Tomb 359'. In W. Vivian Davies (ed.), *Colour and painting in ancient Egypt* (London: British Museum Press) 73–93.

Kemp, Barry J. (1966). 'Abydos and the royal tombs of the first dynasty'. *Journal of Egyptian Archaeology* 52: 13–22.

—— (1967). 'The Egyptian 1st dynasty royal cemetery'. *Antiquity* 41: 22–32.

Kemp, Barry J. (1977). 'The early development of towns in Egypt'. *Antiquity* 51: 185–200.
—— (1989). *Ancient Egypt: anatomy of a civilization* (London and New York: Routledge).
—— (2006). *Ancient Egypt: anatomy of a civilization*, 2nd edn. (London and New York: Routledge).
Kemp, Barry J., Andrew Boyce, and James Harrell (2000). 'The colossi from the early shrine at Coptos in Egypt'. *Cambridge Archaeological Journal* 10: 211–42.
Kemp, Martin (1984). 'Seeing and signs: E. H. Gombrich in retrospect'. *Art History* 7: 228–43.
Kessler, Dieter (1982). 'Nekropolen: Frühzeit und AR, 1.–6. Dyn.' In Wolfgang Helck and Wolfhart Westendorf (eds.), *Lexikon der Ägyptologie* (Wiesbaden: Otto Harrassowitz) IV, 395–414.
Kitchen, Kenneth A. (1975). *Ramesside inscriptions, historical and biographical* I (Oxford: B. H. Blackwell).
—— (1979). *Ramesside inscriptions, historical and biographical* II (Oxford: B. H. Blackwell).
—— (1980). *Ramesside inscriptions, historical and biographical* III (Oxford: B. H. Blackwell).
—— (1993a). *Ramesside inscriptions, translated and annotated: Translations* I, *Ramesses I, Sethos I and contemporaries* (Oxford: Blackwell).
—— (1993b). *Ramesside inscriptions, translated and annotated: Notes and comments* I, *Ramesses I, Sethos I and contemporaries* (Oxford: Blackwell).
—— (1996). *Ramesside inscriptions, translated and annotated: Translations* II, *Ramesses II, royal inscriptions* (Oxford: Blackwell).
Klasens, Adolf (1975). 'Abu-Roasch'. In Wolfgang Helck and Eberhard Otto (eds.), *Lexikon der Ägyptologie* (Wiesbaden: Otto Harrassowitz) I, 24–5.
Klein, Jacob (1981). *The royal hymns of Shulgi: man's quest for immortal fame*, Transactions of the American Philosophical Society 71:7 (Philadelphia: American Philosophical Society).
Knox, Bernard M. W. (1968). 'Silent reading in antiquity'. *Greek, Roman and Byzantine Studies* 9: 421–35.
Koefoed-Petersen, Otto (1950). *Catalogue des statues et statuettes égyptiennes*, Publications de la Glyptothèque Ny Carlsberg 3 (Copenhagen: n.p.).
Köhler, E. Christiana (2000). 'Excavations in the Early Dynastic cemetery at Helwan: a preliminary report of the 1998/99 and 1999/2000 seasons'. *Bulletin of the Australian Centre for Egyptology* 11: 83–92.
Kohn, Marek, and Steven Mithen (1999). 'Handaxes: products of sexual selection?' *Antiquity* 73: 518–26.
Korostovtsev, Mikhaïl (1947). 'Stèle de Ramsès IV d'Abydos'. *Bulletin de l'Institut Français d'Archéologie Orientale* 45: 155–73.
Kozloff, Arielle P., Betsy M. Bryan, and Lawrence M. Berman (1992). *Egypt's dazzling sun: Amenhotep III and his world*, exhibition catalogue (Cleveland: Cleveland Museum of Art; Indiana University Press).

Krauss, Rolf (1983). 'Der Bildhauer Thutmose in Amarna'. *Jahrbuch Preussicher Kulturbesitz* 20: 119–32.

—— (1985). *Sothis- und Monddaten: Studien zur astronomischen und technischen Chronologie Altägyptens*, Hildesheimer Ägyptologische Beiträge 20 (Hildesheim: Gerstenberg).

—— (1986). 'Der Oberbildhauer Bak und sein Denkstein in Berlin'. *Jahrbuch der Berliner Museen* 28: 5–46.

Krauss, Rolf (with H. Newesely) (1983). 'Der Bildhauer Thutmose in Amarna'. *Jahrbuch Preussicher Kulturbesitz* 20: 119–32.

Kroeber, Burkhart (1970). Die Neuägyptizismen vor der Amarnazeit: Studien zur Entwicklung der ägyptischen Sprache vom Mittleren zum Neuen Reich. Doctoral dissertation: University of Tübingen.

Kroeper, Karla, and Dietrich Wildung (1985). *Minshat Abu Omar: Münchner Ostdelta Expedition, Vorbericht 1978–1984*, Schriften aus der Ägyptischen Sammlung 3 (Munich: Karl M. Lipp).

—— (1994–2000). *Minshat Abu Omar: ein vor- und frühgeschichtlicher Friedhof im Nildelta*, 2 vols. (Mainz: Philipp von Zabern).

Kromer, Karl (1978). *Siedlungsfunde aus dem frühen Alten Reich: österreichische Ausgrabungen 1971–1975*, Österreichische Akademie der Wissenschaften, philosophisch-historische Klasse, Denkschriften 136 (Vienna: Verlag der Österreichischen Akademie der Wissenschaften).

Kuhlmann, Klaus Peter, and Wolfgang Schenkel (1983). *Das Grab des Ibi, Obergutsverwalters der Gottesgemahlin des Amun (Thebanisches Grab Nr. 36)* I, Deutsches Archäologisches Institut, Abteilung Kairo, Archäologische Veröffentlichungen 15, 2 vols. (Mainz: Philipp von Zabern).

Lacau, Pierre (1909). *Stèles du Nouvel Empire* I, Catalogue Général des Antiquités Egyptiennes du Musée du Caire (Cairo: Institut Français d'Archéologie Orientale).

—— (1913). 'Suppressions et modifications de signes dans les textes funéraires'. *Zeitschrift für Ägyptische Sprache und Altertumskunde* 51: 1–64.

—— (1921–22). 'Les statues "guérisseuses" dans l'ancienne Egypte'. *Académie des Inscriptions et Belles-lettres, Fondation Eugène Piot, Monuments et Mémoires* 25: 189–209.

—— (1949). *Une stèle juridique de Karnak*, Supplément aux Annales du Service des Antiquités de l'Egypte, Cahier 13 (Cairo: Institut Français d'Archéologie Orientale).

Lacau, Pierre, and Henri Chevrier (1956–69). *Une chapelle de Sésostris Ier à Karnak*, Service des Antiquités de l'Egypte, 2 vols. (Cairo: Institut Français d'Archéologie Orientale).

Lacau, Pierre, and Jean Philippe Lauer (1959–61). *La Pyramide à Degrés* IV, *Inscriptions gravées sur les vases*, Service des Antiquités de l'Egypte, Fouilles à Saqqarah (Cairo: Institut Français d'Archéologie Orientale).

—— (1965). *La Pyramide à Degrés* V, *Inscriptions à l'encre sur les vases*, Service des Antiquités de l'Egypte, Fouilles à Saqqarah (Cairo: Institut Français d'Archéologie Orientale).

Lafages, Catherine (1992). 'Royalty and ritual in the Middle Ages: coronation and funerary rites in France'. In John G. Peristiany and Julian Alfred Pitt-Rivers (eds.), *Honor and grace in anthropology*, Cambridge Studies in Social and Cultural Anthropology 76 (Cambridge: Cambridge University Press) 19–49.

Lamb, Trevor, and Janine Bourriau (eds.) (1995). *Colour: art and science* (Cambridge: Cambridge University Press).

Landsberger, Benno (1967). 'Über Farben im Sumerisch-Akkadischen'. *Journal of Cuneiform Studies* 21: 139–73.

Lange, Julius (1899). *Darstellungen des Menschen in der älteren griechischen Kunst* (Strasbourg: Heitz).

Lange, Kurt, and Max Hirmer (1968). *Egypt: architecture, sculpture, painting*, 4th edn. (London: Phaidon).

Larché, François (1998). 'Reconstruction of the barque shrine of Tuthmosis IV at Karnak'. *Egyptian Archaeology* 13: 19–22.

Larsen, Mogens Trolle (1987). 'The Babylonian lukewarm mind: reflections on science, divination and literacy'. In Francesca Rochberg-Halton (ed.), *Language, literature and history: philological and historical studies presented to Erica Reiner*, American Oriental Series 67 (New Haven: American Oriental Society) 203–25.

—— (1988). 'Literacy and social complexity'. In John Gledhill, Barbara Bender, and Mogens Trolle Larsen (eds.), *State and society: the emergence and development of social hierarchy and political centralization*, One World Archaeology (London: Unwin Hyman) 173–91.

Laskowski, Piotr (1998). 'Some remarks on the dedication formula $jr.n = f m\ mnw = f$'. *Göttinger Miszellen* 167: 77–81.

Lauer, Jean-Philippe (1936). *La Pyramide à Degrés: l'architecture*, Service des Antiquités de l'Egypte, Fouilles à Saqqara, 2 vols. (Cairo: Institut Français d'Archéologie Orientale).

Le Roy Ladurie, Emmanuel (1975). *Montaillou, village occitan de 1294 à 1324* (Paris: Gallimard); English: *Montaillou: Cathars and Catholics in a French village, 1294–1324*, trans. Barbara Bray (London: Scholar Press 1978).

Leahy, Anthony (1992). 'Royal iconography and dynastic change 750–525 BC: the blue and cap crowns'. *Journal of Egyptian Archaeology* 78: 223–40.

Leahy, Lisa Montagno (1988). Private tomb reliefs of the Late period from Lower Egypt. Doctoral dissertation: University of Oxford.

Leclant, Jean (1961). *Montouemhat, Quatrième Prophète d'Amon, Prince de la Ville*, Bibliothèque d'Etude 35 (Cairo: Institut Français d'Archéologie Orientale).

Lefebvre, Gustave (1923–4). *Le tombeau de Petosiris*, Service des Antiquités de l'Egypte, 3 vols. (Cairo: Institut Français d'Archéologie Orientale).

—— (1949). *Romans et contes égyptiens de l'époque pharaonique* (Paris: Adrien-Maisonneuve).

Legrain, Georges (1906). *Statues et statuettes de rois et de particuliers* I, Catalogue Général des Antiquités Egyptiennes du Musée du Caire (Cairo: Institut Français d'Archéologie Orientale).

Legras, Bernard (2002). *Lire en Egypte, d'Alexandre à l'Islam* (Paris: Picard).

Lehner, Mark E. (1985). 'The development of the Giza necropolis: the Khufu project'. *Mitteilungen des Deutschen Archäologischen Instituts, Abteilung Kairo* 41: 109–43.
—— (1997). *The complete pyramids* (London: Thames & Hudson).
—— (2002). 'The pyramid age settlement of the Southern Mount at Giza'. *Journal of the American Research Center in Egypt* 39: 27–74.
Leitz, Christian (2001). *Die Aussenwand des Sanktuars in Dendara: Untersuchungen zur Dekorationssystematik*, Münchner Ägyptologische Studien 50 (Mainz: Philipp von Zabern).
Lepsius, C. Richard n.d.-a. *Denkmaeler aus Aegypten und Aethiopien..., Abtheilung II, Denkmaeler des Alten Reichs*, III, pls. 1–81 (Berlin: Nicolai).
—— n.d.-b. *Denkmaeler aus Aegypten und Aethiopien..., Abtheilung III, Denkmaeler des Neuen Reichs*, V, pls. 1–90 (Berlin: Nicolai).
Lesko, Leonard H. (1990). 'Some comments on ancient Egyptian literacy and literati'. In Sarah Israelit-Groll (ed.), *Studies in Egyptology presented to Miriam Lichtheim* (Jerusalem: Hebrew University) II, 656–67.
—— (1994). 'Literature, literacy, and literati'. In Leonard H. Lesko (ed.), *Pharaoh's workers: the villagers of Deir el Medina* (Ithaca and London: Cornell University Press) 131–44, 185–8.
Lichtheim, Miriam (1945). 'The songs of the harpers'. *Journal of Near Eastern Studies* 4: 178–212.
—— (1971–2). 'Have the principles of ancient Egyptian metrics been discovered?' *Journal of the American Research Center in Egypt* 9: 103–10.
—— (1973). *Ancient Egyptian literature: a book of readings* I, *The Old and Middle Kingdoms* (Berkeley etc.: University of California Press).
—— (1976). *Ancient Egyptian literature: a book of readings* II, *The New Kingdom* (Berkeley etc.: University of California Press).
—— (1980). *Ancient Egyptian literature: a book of readings* III, *The Late period* (Berkeley etc.: University of California Press).
—— (1988). *Ancient Egyptian autobiographies chiefly of the Middle Kingdom: a study and an anthology*, Orbis Biblicus et Orientalis 84 (Fribourg and Göttingen: Universitätsverlag; Vandenhoeck & Ruprecht).
Light, Paul (1985). 'The development of view-specific representation considered from a socio-cognitive standpoint'. In N. H. Freeman and M. V. Cox (eds.), *Visual order: the nature and development of pictorial representation* (Cambridge: Cambridge University Press) 214–30.
Lippert, Sandra Luisa (2004). *Ein demotisches juristisches Lehrbuch: Untersuchungen zu Papyrus Berlin P 23757 rto*, Ägyptologische Abhandlungen 66 (Wiesbaden: Harrassowitz).
Liverani, Mario (1979). *Three Amarna essays*, trans. Matthew L. Jaffe, Sources and Monographs on the Ancient Near East 1, 5 (Malibu: Undena).
—— (2004) [1974]. 'Rib-Adda, righteous sufferer'. In Mario Liverani, *Myth and politics in ancient Near Eastern historiography*, ed. Zainab Bahrani and Marc Van De Mieroop, Studies in Egyptology and Ancient Near East (London: Equinox) 97–124.

Loeben, Christian E. (1997). Popular and other cults of royal statues of the New Kingdom: some Theban evidence. Paper presented at the Glanville Seminar, Cambridge, 1997.

Loprieno, Antonio (1995a). 'Ancient Egyptian and other Afroasiatic languages'. In Jack M. Sasson, John Baines, Gary M. Beckman, and Karen S. Rubinsohn (eds.), *Civilizations of the ancient Near East* (New York: Charles Scribners) IV, 2135–50.

—— (1995b). *Ancient Egyptian: a linguistic introduction* (Cambridge: Cambridge University Press).

—— (1996a). 'Linguistic variety and Egyptian literature'. In Antonio Loprieno (ed.), *Ancient Egyptian literature: history and forms*, Probleme der Ägyptologie 10 (Leiden: E. J. Brill) 515–29.

—— (2003a). 'Temps des dieux et temps des hommes en ancienne Egypte'. In Vinciane Pirenne-Delforge and Öhnan Tunca (eds.), *Représentation du temps dans les religions: actes du colloque organisé par le Centre d'Histoire des Religions de l'Université de Liège*, Bibliothèque de la Faculté de Philosophie et Lettres de l'Université de Liège 286 (Geneva: Droz) 123–41.

—— (2003b). 'Views of the past in Egypt during the first millennium BC'. In W. John Tait (ed.), *'Never had the like occurred': Egypt's view of its past*, Encounters with Ancient Egypt (London: UCL Press) 139–54.

—— (ed.) (1996b). *Ancient Egyptian literature: history and forms*, Probleme der Ägyptologie 10 (Leiden: E. J. Brill).

Lord, Albert Bates (2000) [1960]. *The singer of tales*, ed. Stephen Mitchell and Gregory Nagy, Harvard Studies in Comparative Literature 24, 2nd edn. (Cambridge, Mass., and London: Harvard University Press).

Lucas, Alfred, revised by J. R. Harris (1962). *Ancient Egyptian materials and industries*, 4th edn. (London: Edward Arnold).

Lucy, John A., and Richard A. Shweder (1979). 'Whorf and his critics: linguistic and non-linguistic influences on color naming'. *American Anthropologist* 81: 581–615.

Lüddeckens, Erich (1943). 'Untersuchungen über religiösen Gehalt, Sprache und Form der ägyptischen Totenklagen'. *Mitteilungen des Deutschen Instituts für Ägyptische Altertumskunde in Kairo* 11: 1–188.

—— (1960). *Ägyptische Eheverträge*, Ägyptologische Abhandlungen 1 (Wiesbaden: Otto Harrassowitz).

Luft, Ulrich (1976). '"Seit der Zeit Gottes"'. *Studia Aegyptiaca* 2: 47–78.

—— (1978). *Beiträge zur Historisierung der Götterwelt und der Mythenschreibung*, Studia Aegyptiaca 4 (Budapest: n.p.).

—— (1992). *Das Archiv von Illahun*, Hieratische Papyri aus den Staatlichen Museen zu Berlin – Preussischer Kulturbesitz 1 (Berlin: Akademie Verlag).

Lyons, John (1995). 'Colour in language'. In Trevor Lamb and Janine Bourriau (eds.), *Colour: art and science* (Cambridge: Cambridge University Press) 194–224.

Macadam, M. F. Laming (1949). *The temples of Kawa* I, *The inscriptions*, 2 vols. (London: Geoffrey Cumberlege, Oxford University Press, for Griffith Institute, Oxford).

Machinist, Peter (1986). 'On self-consciousness in Mesopotamia'. In S. N. Eisenstadt (ed.), *The origins and diversity of Axial Age civilizations*, SUNY Series in Near Eastern Studies (Albany, NY: State University of New York Press) 193–202, 511–18.

—— (2003). 'The voice of the historian in the ancient Near Eastern and Mediterranean world'. *Interpretation* 57: 117–37.

MacLaury, Robert E. (1997). *Color and cognition in Mesoamerica: constructing categories as vantages* (Austin: University of Texas Press).

—— (1999). 'Basic color terms: twenty-five years after'. In Alexander Borg (ed.), *The language of color in the Mediterranean: an anthology on linguistic and ethnographic aspects of color terms*, Acta Universitatis Stockholmiensis, Stockholm Oriental Studies 16 (Stockholm: Almqvist & Wiksell) 1–37.

Macramallah, Rizkallah (1935). *Le mastaba d'Idout*, Service des Antiquités de l'Egypte, Fouilles à Saqqarah (Cairo: Institut Français d'Archéologie Orientale).

Maguire, Henry (1996). *The icons of their bodies: saints and their images in Byzantium* (Princeton: Princeton University Press).

Malaise, Michel (1981). 'Inventaire des stèles égyptiennes du Moyen Empire porteuses de représentations divines'. *Studien zur Altägyptischen Kultur* 9: 259–83.

—— (1984). 'Les représentations de divinités sur les stèles du Moyen Empire'. In *Orientalia J. Duchesne-Guillemin emerito oblata*, Hommages et Opera Minora 9 = Acta Iranica 23 (Leiden: E. J. Brill) 393–420.

Malek, Jaromir (1982). 'The original version of the Royal Canon of Turin'. *Journal of Egyptian Archaeology* 68: 93–106.

—— (2003). *Egypt: 4000 years of art* (London: Phaidon).

Mann, Charles C. (2005). 'Unraveling khipu's secrets'. *Science* 12 August 2005: 1008–9.

Manniche, Lise (1982). 'The body colours of gods and men in inlaid jewellery and related objects from the tomb of Tutankhamun'. *Acta Orientalia* 43: 5–12.

Manning, J. G. (2003). *Land and power in Ptolemaic Egypt: the structure of land tenure* (Cambridge: Cambridge University Press).

Manuelian, Peter der (1985). 'Two fragments of relief and a new model for the tomb of Montuemhet at Thebes'. *Journal of Egyptian Archaeology* 71: 98–121.

—— (1993). *Living in the past: studies in archaism of the Egyptian twenty-sixth dynasty*, Studies in Egyptology (London: Kegan Paul International).

—— (1998). 'The problem of the Giza slab stelae'. In Heike Guksch and Daniel Polz (eds.), *Stationen: Beiträge zur Kulturgeschichte Ägyptens, Rainer Stadelmann gewidmet* (Mainz: Philipp von Zabern) 115–34.

—— (2003). *Slab stelae of the Giza necropolis*, Publications of the Pennsylvania–Yale Expedition to Egypt 7 (New Haven and Philadelphia: Peabody Museum of Natural History; University of Pennsylvania Museum).

Marcus, Joyce (1976). 'The origins of Mesoamerican writing'. *Annual Reviews in Anthropology* 5: 35–67.

Mariette, Auguste (1869). *Abydos, description des fouilles exécutées sur l'emplacement de cette ville* I (Paris: Franck–Vieweg).

Marr, David (1982). *Vision: a computational investigation into the human representation and processing of visual information* (San Francisco: Freeman).

Martin, Geoffrey Thorndike (1971). *Egyptian administrative and private-name seals, principally of the Middle Kingdom and Second Intermediate period* (Oxford: Griffith Institute).

—— (1985). *The tomb-chapels of Paser and Ra^cia at Saqqâra*, Excavation Memoir 52 (London: Egypt Exploration Society).

—— (1989). *The Memphite tomb of Ḥoremḥeb, Commander-in-Chief of Tut^cankhamūn I, The reliefs, inscriptions, and commentary*, Excavation Memoir 55 (London: Egypt Exploration Society).

Maspero, Gaston (1907). *Le Musée Egyptien: recueil des monuments et de notices sur les fouilles d'Egypte* II (Cairo: Institut Français d'Archéologie Orientale).

Mathieu, Bernard (1988). 'Etudes de métrique égyptienne I: le distique heptamétrique dans les chants d'amour'. *Revue d'Egyptologie* 39: 63–82.

—— (1991). 'Etudes de métrique égyptienne II: contraintes métriques et production textuelle dans l'*Hymne à la crue du Nil*'. *Revue d'Egyptologie* 42: 127–41.

—— (1994). 'Etudes de métrique égyptienne III: une innovation métrique dans une "litanie" thébaine du Nouvel Empire'. *Revue d'Egyptologie* 45: 139–54.

—— (1996). *La poésie amoureuse de l'Egypte ancienne: recherches sur un genre littéraire au Nouvel Empire*, Bibliothèque d'Etude 115 (Cairo: Institut Français d'Archéologie Orientale).

—— (1997). 'Etudes de métrique égyptienne IV: le tristique ennéamétrique dans l'hymne à Amon de Leyde'. *Revue d'Egyptologie* 48: 109–63.

Mattha, Girgis, and George R. Hughes (1975). *The demotic legal code of Hermopolis West*, Bibliothèque d'Etude 45, 2 vols. (Cairo: Institut Français d'Archéologie Orientale).

Mauss, Marcel (1954) [1950]. *The gift*, trans. Ian Cunnison, from *Essai sur le don* [1925], using the version in Marcel Mauss, *Sociologie et anthropologie*, foreword by E. E. Evans-Pritchard (London: Cohen & West).

Maxwell-Stuart, P. G. (1981). *Studies in Greek colour terminology*, 2 vols. (Leiden: E. J. Brill).

McCarthy, Blythe (2001). 'Technical analysis of reds and yellows in the tomb of Suemniwet, Theban Tomb 92'. In W. Vivian Davies (ed.), *Colour and painting in ancient Egypt* (London: British Museum Press) 17–21.

McDowell, Andrea G. (1992). 'Awareness of the past in Deir el-Medîna'. In R. J. Demarée and Arno Egberts (eds.), *Village voices: proceedings of the symposium 'Texts from Deir el-Medîna and their interpretation'*, Leiden, May 31 – June 1, 1991, CNWS Publications 13 (Leiden: Centre of Non-Western Studies) 95–109.

—— (1996). 'Student exercises from Deir el-Medina: the dates'. In Peter der Manuelian (ed.), *Studies in honor of William Kelly Simpson* (Boston: Department of Ancient Egyptian, Nubian, and Near Eastern Art, Museum of Fine Arts) II, 601–8.

—— (1999). *Village life in ancient Egypt: laundry lists and love songs* (Oxford: Oxford University Press).

—— (2000). 'Teachers and students at Deir el-Medina'. In R. J. Demarée and Arno Egberts (eds.), *Deir el-Medina in the third millennium AD: a tribute to Jac.*

J. Janssen, Egyptologische Uitgaven 14 (Leiden: Nederlands Instituut voor het Nabije Oosten) 217–33.

McKenzie, Judith S. (2007). *The architecture of Alexandria and Egypt, c.300 BC – AD 700*, Pelican History of Art (New Haven: Yale University Press).

McKitterick, Rosamond (1989). *The Carolingians and the written word* (Cambridge: Cambridge University Press).

—— (ed.) (1990). *The uses of literacy in early mediaeval Europe* (Cambridge: Cambridge University Press).

McMullen, Ramsey (1982). 'The epigraphic habit in the Roman Empire'. *American Journal of Philology* 103: 233–46.

McNamara, Liam in press. 'The revetted mound at Hierakonpolis and early kingship: a reinterpretation'. In Béatrix Midant-Reynes and Yann Tristant (eds.), *Egypt at its origins* II, *Proceedings of the international conference 'Origin of the State. Predynastic and Early Dynastic Egypt', Toulouse, 5–8th September 2005*, Orientalia Lovaniensia Analecta (Leuven: Peeters).

Meeks-Favard, Christine (1991). *Le temple de Behbeit el-Hagara: essai de reconstitution et d'interprétation*, Beihefte zu den Studien zur Altägyptischen Kultur 6 (Hamburg: Helmut Buske).

Mekhitarian, Arpag (1954). *Egyptian painting*, The Great Centuries of Painting ([Geneva]: Skira).

Meskell, Lynn (2004). *Object worlds in ancient Egypt* (Oxford: Berg).

Meyer, Elizabeth A. (1990). 'Explaining the epigraphic habit in the Roman empire: the evidence of epitaphs'. *Journal of Roman Studies* 80: 74–96.

Meyer, Gudrun (1990). 'Das Hirtenlied in den Privatgräbern des Alten Reiches'. *Studien zur Altägyptischen Kultur* 17: 235–84.

Meyer, Klaus-Heinrich (1974). 'Kanon, Komposition und "Metrik" der Narmerpalette'. *Studien zur Altägyptischen Kultur* 1: 247–65.

Michalowski, Kazimierz, Jean-Pierre Corteggiani, and Alessandro Roccati (1994). *L'art de l'Egypte*, 2nd edn. (Paris: Citadelles & Mazenod).

Michalowski, Piotr (1990). 'Early Mesopotamian communicative systems: art, literature, and writing'. In Ann Gunter (ed.), *Investigating artistic environments in the ancient Near East* (Washington: Smithsonian Institution Press) 56–69.

—— (1994). 'Early literacy revisited'. In Deborah Keller-Cohen (ed.), *Literacy: interdisciplinary conversations* (Cresskill, NJ: Hampton Press) 49–70.

Midant-Reynes, Béatrix (1987). 'Contribution à l'étude de la société prédynastique: le cas du couteau "ripple-flake"'. *Studien zur Altägyptischen Kultur* 14: 185–284.

Millar, Fergus (1977). *The emperor in the Roman world (31 BC – AD 337)* (London: Duckworth).

Millard, Alan R. (1985). 'An assessment of the evidence for writing in ancient Israel; with response by Aaron Demsky'. In *Biblical archaeology today: proceedings of the international congress on biblical archaeology, Jerusalem, April 1984* (Jerusalem: Israel Exploration Society etc.) 301–12, 349–53.

—— (1986). 'The infancy of the alphabet'. *World Archaeology* 17: 390–9.

Millet, Nicholas B. (1990). 'The Narmer Macehead and related objects'. *Journal of the American Research Center in Egypt* 27: 53–9.

Mills, A. J. (1979). 'Dakhleh Oasis project: report on the first season of survey, October–December 1978'. *Journal of the Society for the Study of Egyptian Antiquities* 9: 163–85.

Mitchell, John (1990). 'Literacy displayed: the use of inscriptions at the monastery of San Vincenzo al Volturno in the early ninth century'. In Rosamond McKitterick (ed.), *The uses of literacy in early mediaeval Europe* (Cambridge: Cambridge University Press) 186–225.

Mithen, Steven (2005). *The singing neanderthals: the origins of music, language, mind and body* (London: Weidenfeld & Nicholson).

Moran, William L. (1992). *The Amarna letters* (Baltimore and London: Johns Hopkins University Press).

Morenz, Ludwig D. (1994). 'Zur Dekoration der frühzeitlichen Tempel am Beispiel zweier Fragmente des archaischen Tempels von Gebelein'. In Rolf Gundlach and Matthias Rochholz (eds.), *Ägyptische Tempel—Struktur, Funktion und Programm: Akten der ägyptologischen Tempeltagungen in Gosen 1990 und in Mainz 1992*, Hildesheimer Ägyptologische Beiträge 37 (Hildesheim: Gerstenberg) 217–38.

—— (1996). *Beiträge zur Schriftlichkeitskultur im Mittleren Reich und in der 2. Zwischenzeit*, Ägypten und Altes Testament 29 (Wiesbaden: Harrassowitz).

—— (2002). 'Die Götter und ihr Redetext: die ältestbelegte Sakral-Monumentalisierung von Textlichkeit auf Fragmenten der Zeit des Djoser aus Heliopolis'. In Horst Beinlich (ed.), *5. Ägyptologische Tempeltagung: Würzburg, 23.–26. September 1999*, Ägypten und Altes Testament 33: 3 (Wiesbaden: Harrassowitz) 137–58.

—— (2004). *Bild-Buchstaben und symbolische Zeichen: die Herausbildung der Schrift in der hohen Kultur Altägyptens*, Orbis Biblicus et Orientalis 205 (Fribourg and Göttingen: Academic Press Fribourg; Vandenhoeck & Ruprecht).

Morgan, Teresa (1998). *Literate education in the Hellenistic and Roman worlds*, Cambridge Classical Studies (Cambridge: Cambridge University Press).

—— (1999). 'Literary education in classical Athens'. *Classical Quarterly* 49: 46–61.

Morison, Stanley (1972). *Politics and script: aspects of authority and freedom in the development of Graeco-Latin script from the sixth century B.C. to the twentieth century A.D.*, ed. Nicholas Barker, the Lyell Lectures 1957 (Oxford: Clarendon Press).

Morphy, Howard, and Morgan Perkins (2006). 'The anthropology of art: a reflection on its history and contemporary practice'. In Howard Morphy and Morgan Perkins (eds.), *The anthropology of art: a reader* (Oxford: Blackwell) 1–32.

Moussa, Ahmed M., and Hartwig Altenmüller (1977). *Das Grab des Nianchchnum und Khnumhotep*, Old Kingdom Tombs at the Causeway of King Unas at Saqqara excavated by the Department of Antiquities; Deutsches Archäologisches Institut, Abteilung Kairo, Archäologische Veröffentlichungen 21 (Mainz: Philipp von Zabern).

Müller, Maya (1990). 'Die ägyptische Kunst aus kunsthistorischer Sicht'. In Marianne Eaton-Krauss and Erhart Graefe (eds.), *Studien zur ägyptischen Kunstgeschichte*, Hildesheimer Ägyptologische Beiträge 29 (Hildesheim: Gerstenberg) 39–56.

Murnane, William J. (1990). *The road to Kadesh: a historical interpretation of the battle reliefs of King Sety I at Karnak*, Studies in Ancient Oriental Civilizations 42, 2nd edn. (Chicago: Oriental Institute of the University of Chicago).

Murray, Helen, and Mary Nuttall (1963). *A handlist to Howard Carter's catalogue of objects in Tutᶜankhamūn's tomb*, Tutᶜankhamūn's Tomb Series 1 (Oxford: Oxford University Press for Griffith Institute).

Murray, Oswyn (1980). *Early Greece* (Brighton: Harvester Books).

Naguib, Saphinaz-Amal (1990). *Le clergé féminin d'Amon thébain à la 21e dynastie*, Orientalia Lovaniensia Analecta 38 (Leuven: Peeters).

Narasimhan, R. (1991). 'Literacy: its characterizations and implications'. In David R. Olson and Nancy Torrance (eds.), *Literacy and orality* (Cambridge: Cambridge University Press) 177–97.

Naville, Edouard (1907). *The XIth dynasty temple at Deir el-Bahari* I, Egypt Exploration Fund, Memoir 28 (London: Egypt Exploration Fund).

—— n.d. *The temple of Deir el Bahari*, 6 vols. (London etc.: Egypt Exploration Fund).

Nettl, Bruno (1983). *The study of ethnomusicology: twenty-nine issues and concepts* (Urbana: University of Illinois Press).

Neugebauer, Otto, and Richard A. Parker (1960–9). *Egyptian astronomical texts*, Brown Egyptological Studies 3, 5, 6. 3 vols. in 4 (London: Lund Humphries for Brown University Press, Providence, RI).

Neureiter, Sabine (1994). 'Eine neue Interpretation des Archaismus'. *Studien zur Altägyptischen Kultur* 21: 219–54.

Nims, Charles F., and Richard C. Steiner (1983). 'A paganized version of Psalm 20:2–6 from the Aramaic text in demotic script'. *Journal of the American Oriental Society* 103: 261–74.

Nissen, Hans Jörg, Peter Damerow, and Robert K. Englund (1993). *Archaic bookkeeping: early writing and techniques of the economic administration in the ancient Near East*, trans. Paul Larsen (Chicago and London: University of Chicago Press).

Nordström, Hans-Åke (1972). *Neolithic and A-Group sites*, Scandinavian Joint Expedition to Sudanese Nubia 3 (Stockholm etc.: Scandinavian University Books).

—— (2004). 'Pottery production'. In Derek A. Welsby and Julie R. Anderson (eds.), *Sudan ancient treasures: an exhibition of recent discoveries from the Sudan National Museum* (London: British Museum Press) 248–73.

O'Connor, David (1969). 'Abydos and the University Museum: 1898–1969'. *Expedition* 12,1: 28–39.

—— (1989a). 'City and palace in New Kingdom Egypt'. *Cahiers de Recherche de l'Institut de Papyrologie et Egyptologie de Lille* 11: 73–87.

—— (1989b). 'New funerary enclosures (*Talbezirke*) of the Early Dynastic period at Abydos'. *Journal of the American Research Center in Egypt* 25: 51–86.

—— (1992). 'The status of early Egyptian temples: an alternative theory'. In Renée Friedman and Barbara Adams (eds.), *The followers of Horus: studies dedicated to Michael Allen Hoffman 1944–1990*, Egyptian Studies Association Publication 2, Oxbow Monograph 20 (Oxford: Oxbow) 83–98.

O'Connor, David (1993). 'Mirror of the cosmos: the palace of Merneptah'. In Rita E. Freed and Edward Bleiberg (eds.), *Fragments of a shattered visage: the proceedings of the international symposium on Ramesses the Great*, Monographs of the Institute of Egyptian Art and Archaeology 1 (Memphis, Tenn.: Memphis State University) 167–98.

—— (1995). 'The social and economic organization of ancient Egyptian temples'. In Jack M. Sasson, John Baines, Gary Beckman, and Karen S. Rubinsohn (eds.), *Civilizations of the ancient Near East* (New York: Charles Scribner) I, 319–29.

—— (2000). 'Society and individual in early Egypt'. In Janet E. Richards and Mary Van Buren (eds.), *Order, legitimacy, and wealth in ancient states*, New Directions in Archaeology (Cambridge: Cambridge University Press) 21–35.

—— (2005). 'The ownership of elite tombs at Saqqara in the first dynasty'. In Khaled Daoud et al. (eds.), *Studies in Honor of Ali Radwan*, Supplément aux Annales du Service des Antiquités de l'Egypte, Cahier 34 (Cairo: Supreme Council of Antiquities) I, 223–31.

—— in preparation. *City and cosmos in ancient Egypt*, Studies in Egyptology and the Ancient Near East (London: Equinox).

O'Connor, David, and Eric H. Cline (eds.) (1998). *Amenhotep III: perspectives on his reign* (Ann Arbor: University of Michigan Press).

O'Keeffe, Katherine O'Brien (1990). *Visible song: transitional literacy in Old English verse*, Cambridge Studies in Anglo-Saxon England 4 (Cambridge: Cambridge University Press).

Olson, David R., and Nancy Torrance (eds.) (1991). *Literacy and orality* (Cambridge: Cambridge University Press).

Omlin, Joseph A. (1973). *Der Papyrus 55001 und seine satirisch-erotischen Zeichnungen und Inschriften*, Catalogo del Museo Egizio di Torino I:3 (Turin: Edizioni d'arte Fratelli Pozzo).

Ong, Walter J. (1982). *Orality and literacy: the technologizing of the word*, New Accents (London: Methuen).

Oppenheim, A. Leo (1977) [1964]. *Ancient Mesopotamia: portrait of a dead civilization*, ed. Erica Reiner, 2nd edn. (Chicago: University of Chicago Press).

Osing, Jürgen (1975). 'Alte Schriften'. In Wolfgang Helck and Eberhard Otto (eds.), *Lexikon der Ägyptologie* (Wiesbaden: Otto Harrassowitz) I, 149–54.

—— (1976). *Der spätägyptische Papyrus BM 10808*, Ägyptologische Abhandlungen 33 (Wiesbaden: Otto Harrassowitz).

—— (1998). *Hieratische Papyri aus Tebtunis* I, The Carlsberg Papyri 2, CNI Publications 17, 2 vols. (Copenhagen: Museum Tusculanum Press).

Osing, Jürgen, and Gloria Rosati (1998). *Papiri geroglifici e ieratici da Tebtynis* (Florence: Istituto papirologico G. Vitelli).

Otto, Eberhard (1954). *Die biographischen Inschriften der ägyptischen Spätzeit*, Probleme der Ägyptologie 2 (Leiden: E. J. Brill).

—— (1957). 'Zwei Bemerkungen zum Königskult der Spätzeit'. *Mitteilungen des Deutschen Archäologischen Instituts, Abteilung Kairo* 15: 192–207.

—— (1964–6). 'Geschichtsbild und Geschichtsschreibung im alten Ägypten'. *Die Welt des Orients* 3: 161–76.

Otto, Eberhard (1969). 'Das "Goldene Zeitalter" in einem ägyptischen Text'. In *Religions en Egypte hellénistique et romaine*, Bibliothèque des Centres d'Etudes supérieures spécialisées, travaux du Centre d'Etudes supérieures spécialisé d'histoire des religions de Strasbourg (Paris: Presses Universitaires de France) 93–108.

—— (1977). 'Zur Komposition von Coffin Texts Spell 1130'. In Jan Assmann, Erika Feucht, and Reinhard Grieshammer (eds.), *Fragen an die altägyptische Literatur: Studien zum Gedenken an Eberhard Otto* (Wiesbaden: Dr Ludwig Reichert) 3–18.

Panofsky, Erwin (1991) [1927]. *Perspective as symbolic form*, trans. Christopher S. Wood (New York and Cambridge, Mass.: Zone Books; MIT Press).

Pantalacci, Laure (1996a). 'Fonctionnaires et analphabètes: sur quelques pratiques administratives observées à Balat'. *Bulletin de l'Institut Français d'Archéologie Orientale* 96: 359–67.

—— (1996b). 'Un été à Sérabit el-Khadim (encore sur l'inscription de Horourrê (Sinaï n° 90))'. *Göttinger Miszellen* 150: 87–91.

Parker, Richard A. (1950). *The calendars of ancient Egypt*, The Oriental Institute of the University of Chicago, Studies in Ancient Oriental Civilization 26 (Chicago: University of Chicago Press).

—— (1962). *A Saite oracle papyrus from Thebes in the Brooklyn Museum*, Brown Egyptological Studies 4 (Providence, RI: Brown University Press).

Parkinson, R. B. (1991a). *The Tale of the Eloquent Peasant* (Oxford: Griffith Institute).

—— (1991b). *Voices from ancient Egypt: an anthology of Middle Kingdom writings* (London: British Museum Press).

—— (1996). '*Khakheperreseneb* and traditional belles lettres'. In Peter der Manuelian (ed.), *Studies in Honor of William Kelly Simpson* (Boston: Department of Ancient Egyptian and Near Eastern Art, Museum of Fine Arts) II, 646–54.

—— (1998). *The Tale of Sinuhe and other ancient Egyptian poems, 1940–1640 BC*, Oxford World's Classics (Oxford: Oxford University Press).

—— (1999). 'Two or three literary artefacts: British Museum EA 41650/47896, and 22878–9'. In W. Vivian Davies (ed.), *Studies in Egyptian antiquities: a tribute to T. G. H. James*, British Museum Occasional Paper 123 (London: British Museum) 49–57.

—— (2002). *Poetry and culture in Middle Kingdom Egypt: a dark side to perfection*, Egyptology and Ancient Near Eastern Studies (London and New York: Continuum).

—— (2004). 'The history of a poem: Middle Kingdom literary manuscripts and their reception'. In Günter Burkard, Manfred Görg, Alfred Grimm, and Alexandra Verbovsek (eds.), *Kon-Texte: Akten des Symposions 'Spurensuche—Altägypten im Spiegel seiner Texte' München 2. bis 4. Mai 2003*, Ägypten und Altes Testament 60 (Wiesbaden: Harrassowitz) 51–63.

—— in preparation. *Among other histories: ancient Egyptian expressive culture* (Oxford: Blackwell).

Parsons, Talcott (1964). 'Evolutionary universals in society'. *American Sociological Review* 29: 339–57.

—— (1966). *Societies: evolutionary and comparative perspectives*, Foundations of Modern Sociology (Englewood Cliffs, NJ: Prentice-Hall).

Pattanayak, D. P. (1991). 'Literacy: an instrument of oppression'. In David R. Olson and Nancy Torrance (eds.), *Literacy and orality* (Cambridge: Cambridge University Press) 105–8.
Peden, A. J. (2001). *The graffiti of pharaonic Egypt: scope and roles of informal writings (c.3100–332 B.C.)*, Probleme der Ägyptologie 17 (Leiden and Boston: Brill).
Peet, T. Eric (1930). *The great tomb-robberies of the twentieth Egyptian dynasty*, 2 vols. (Oxford: Clarendon Press).
Pestman, P. W. (1961). *Marriage and matrimonial property in ancient Egypt: a contribution to establishing the legal position of the woman*, Papyrologica Lugduno-Batava 9 (Leiden: E. J. Brill).
—— (1982). 'Who were the owners, in the "Community of Workmen", of the Chester Beatty papyri?' In R. J. Demarée and J. J. Janssen (eds.), *Gleanings from Deir el-Medîna*, Egyptologische Uitgaven 1 (Leiden: Nederlands Instituut voor het Nabije Oosten) 157–72.
Peterson, Bengt E. J. (1973). *Zeichnungen aus einer Totenstadt = Medelhavsmuseet Bulletin 7–8* (Stockholm: n.p.).
Petrie, W. M. Flinders (1892). *Medum* (London: David Nutt).
—— (1900). *The royal tombs of the first dynasty, 1900* I, Egypt Exploration Fund, Memoir 18 (London: Egypt Exploration Fund).
—— (1901). *The royal tombs of the earliest dynasties, 1901* II, Egypt Exploration Fund, Memoir 21 (London: Egypt Exploration Fund).
—— (1913–14). *Tarkhan*, British School of Archaeology in Egypt and Egyptian Research Account, 19th year, 2 vols. (London: School of Archaeology in Egypt, and Bernard Quaritch).
—— (1921). *Corpus of prehistoric pottery and palettes*, British School of Archaeology in Egypt and Egyptian Research Account, 23rd year, 1917 (London: British School of Archaeology in Egypt etc.).
Petrucci, Armando (1993). *Public lettering: script, power, and culture*, trans. Linda Lappin (Chicago and London: University of Chicago Press).
—— (1995). *Writers and readers in medieval Italy: studies in the history of written culture*, trans. Charles Radding (New Haven and London: Yale University Press).
—— (1998). *Writing the dead: death and writing strategies in the western tradition*, Figurae (Stanford: Stanford University Press).
Pfuhl, Ernst (1923). *Malerei und Zeichnung der Griechen*, 3 vols. (Munich: F. Bruckmann).
Philips, Allan K. (1977). 'Horemheb, founder of the XIXth dynasty? O. Cairo 25646 reconsidered'. *Orientalia* 46: 116–21.
Phillips, Jacke (1994). 'The composite sculpture of Akhenaten: some initial thoughts and questions'. *Amarna Letters* 3: 58–71.
Phillips, W. A., M. Inall, and E. Lauder (1985). 'On the discovery, storage and use of graphic descriptions'. In N. H. Freeman and M. V. Cox (eds.), *Visual order: the nature and development of pictorial representation* (Cambridge: Cambridge University Press) 122–34.

Piacentini, Patrizia (2002). *Les scribes dans la société égyptienne de l'Ancien Empire* I, *Les premières dynasties; les nécropoles memphites*, Etudes et Mémoires d'Egyptologie (Paris: Cybèle).

Piankoff, Alexander (1954). *The tomb of Ramesses VI*, Egyptian Religious Texts and Representations 1, Bollingen Series 40, 2 vols. (New York: Pantheon Books).

—— (1957). *Mythological papyri*, Egyptian Religious Texts and Representations 3, Bollingen Series 40, 2 vols. (New York: Pantheon Books).

Pieper, Max (1929). *Die grosse Inschrift des Königs Neferhotep in Abydos*, Mitteilungen der Vorderasiatisch-Ägyptischen Gesellschaft 32:2 (Leipzig: J. C. Hinrichs).

Pierce, Richard Holton (1972). *Three demotic papyri in the Brooklyn Museum: a contribution to the study of contracts and their instruments in Ptolemaic Egypt*, Symbolae Osloenses, Supplement 24 (Oslo: Universitetsforlaget).

Pinch, Geraldine (1993). *Votive offerings to Hathor* (Oxford: Griffith Institute).

Pirenne, M. H. (1970). *Optics, painting and photography* (Cambridge: Cambridge University Press).

Pitchford, Nicola, and Carole P. Biggam (eds.) (2006). *Progress in colour studies* II, *Psychological aspects* (Amsterdam and Philadelphia: John Benjamins).

Podemann Sørensen, Jørgen (1989). 'Divine access: the so-called democratization of Egyptian funerary literature as a socio-cultural process'. In Gertie Englund (ed.), *The religion of the ancient Egyptians: cognitive structures and popular expressions*, Boreas 20 (Stockholm: Almqvist & Wiksell) 109–25.

Pollitt, J. J. (1974). *The ancient view of Greek art: criticism, history, and terminology* (New Haven: Yale University Press).

—— (1990). *The art of ancient Greece: sources and documents*, 2nd edn. (Cambridge: Cambridge University Press).

Porada, Edith (1980). 'A lapis lazuli figurine from Hierakonpolis in Egypt'. *Iranica Antiqua* 15: 175–80.

Porter, Bertha, and Rosalind L. B. Moss (1960). *Topographical bibliography of ancient Egyptian hieroglyphic texts, reliefs, and paintings* I, *The Theban necropolis Part 1, Private tombs*, 2nd edn. (Oxford: Clarendon Press).

—— (1972). *Topographical bibliography of ancient Egyptian hieroglyphic texts, reliefs, and paintings* II, *Theban temples*, 2nd edn. (Oxford: Griffith Institute, Ashmolean Museum).

Posener, Georges (1957). 'Le conte de Néferkarè et du Général Sisené (Recherches littéraires, VI)'. *Revue d'Egyptologie* 11: 119–37.

—— (1976). *L'Enseignement Loyaliste: sagesse égyptienne du Moyen Empire*, Centre de Recherches d'Histoire et de Philologie II, Hautes Etudes Orientales 5 (Geneva: Droz).

Posener-Kriéger, Paule (1973). 'Les papyrus de l'Ancien Empire'. In *Textes et langages de l'Egypte pharaonique: cent cinquante années de recherches 1822–1972—Hommage à Jean-François Champollion*, Bibliothèque d'Etude 64 (Cairo: Institut Français d'Archéologie Orientale) II, 25–35.

—— (1975). 'Les papyrus de Gébélein: remarques préliminaires'. *Revue d'Egyptologie* 27: 211–21.

Posener-Kriéger, Paule (1976). *Les archives du temple funéraire de Néferirkarê-Kakaï (les papyrus d'Abousir): Traduction et commentaire,* Bibliothèque d'Etude 65, 2 vols. (Cairo: Institut Français d'Archéologie Orientale).

—— (1983). 'Les nouveaux papyrus d'Abousir'. *Journal of the Society for the Study of Egyptian Antiquities* 13: 51–7.

—— (1986). 'Old Kingdom papyri: external features'. In M. L. Bierbrier (ed.), *Papyrus: structure and usage,* Occasional Paper 60 (London: British Museum) 25–41.

Posener-Kriéger, Paule, and Jean Louis de Cenival (1968). *The Abu Sir papyri,* Hieratic Papyri in the British Museum, 5th series (London: British Museum).

Postgate, J. N. (1977). *The first empires,* The Making of the Past (Oxford: Elsevier-Phaidon).

Postgate, Nicholas, Tao Wang, and Toby A. H. Wilkinson (1995). 'The evidence for early writing: utilitarian or ceremonial?' *Antiquity* 69: 459–80.

Potter, M. C. (1975). 'Meaning in visual search'. *Science* 187: 965–6.

Potts, Alex (1994). *Flesh and the ideal: Winckelmann and the origins of art history* (New Haven and London: Yale University Press).

Pratt, Francis (1985). 'A perspective on traditional artistic practices'. In N. H. Freeman and M. V. Cox (eds.), *Visual order: the nature and development of pictorial representation* (Cambridge: Cambridge University Press) 32–58.

Préaux, Claire (1943). 'Les Egyptiens dans la civilisation hellénistique de l'Egypte'. *Chronique d'Egypte* 18: 148–60.

Pritchard, James B. (ed.) (1969). *The ancient Near East: supplementary texts and pictures relating to the Old Testament* (Princeton, NJ: Princeton University Press).

Quack, Joachim Friedrich (2001). 'Ein neuer Versuch zum Moskauer literarischen Brief'. *Zeitschrift für Ägyptische Sprache und Altertumskunde* 128: 167–81.

—— (2005). *Einführung in die altägyptische Literatur* III, *Die demotische und gräko-ägyptische Literatur,* Einführung und Quellentexte zur Ägyptologie 3 (Münster: LIT).

Quibell, James Edward (1898). *El Kab,* Egyptian Research Account 1897 (London: Bernard Quaritch).

—— (1900). *Hierakonpolis* I, Egyptian Research Account Memoir 4 (London: Bernard Quaritch).

—— (1908). *Excavations at Saqqara (1906–1907),* Service des Antiquités de l'Egypte (Cairo: Institut Français d'Archéologie Orientale).

—— (1909). *Excavations at Saqqara (1907–1908),* Service des Antiquités de l'Egypte (Cairo: Institut Français d'Archéologie Orientale).

—— (1913). *The tomb of Hesy,* Service des Antiquités de l'Egypte, Excavations at Saqqara (1911–1912) (Cairo: Institut Français d'Archéologie Orientale).

—— (1923). *Archaic mastabas,* Service des Antiquités de l'Egypte, Excavations at Saqqara (Cairo: Institut Français d'Archéologie Orientale).

Quibell, James Edward, and F. W. Green (1902). *Hierakonpolis* II, Egyptian Research Account Memoir 5 (London: Bernard Quaritch).

Quirke, Stephen (2001). 'Colour vocabularies in Ancient Egyptian'. In W. Vivian Davies (ed.), *Colour and painting in ancient Egypt* (London: British Museum Press) 186–92.

Quirke, Stephen, and Jeffrey Spencer (eds.) (1992). *The British Museum book of ancient Egypt* (London: British Museum Press).
Rabbitt, Patrick (1984). 'The control of attention in visual search'. In Raja Parasuraman and D. R. Driver (eds.), *Varieties of attention* (New York: Academic Press) 273–91.
Radwan, Ali (1969). *Die Darstellungen des regierenden Königs und seiner Familienangehörigen in den Privatgräben der 18. Dynastie*, Münchner Ägyptologische Studien 21 (Berlin: Bruno Hessling).
—— (1983). *Die Kupfer- und Bronzegefässe Ägyptens: von den Anfängen bis zum Beginn der Spätzeit*, Prähistorische Bronzefunde II:2 (Munich: C. H. Beck).
Ransom Williams, Caroline (1932). *The decoration of the tomb of Per-Nēb: the technique and the color conventions*, Metropolitan Museum of Art, Department of Egyptian Art, Publications 3 (New York: Metropolitan Museum of Art).
Ray, John D. (1976). *The archive of Hor*, Texts from Excavations 2 (London: Egypt Exploration Society).
—— (1986). 'The emergence of writing in Egypt'. *World Archaeology* 17: 307–16.
—— (1994a). 'How demotic is Demotic?' *Egitto e Vicino Oriente* 17: 251–64.
—— (1994b). 'Literacy and language in Egypt in the Late and Persian periods'. In Alan K. Bowman and Greg Woolf (eds.), *Literacy and power in the ancient world* (Cambridge: Cambridge University Press) 51–66.
Rea, John R. (1978). *The Oxyrhynchus papyri*, 56, Graeco-Roman Memoir 65 (London: Egypt Exploration Society).
Redford, Donald B. (1984). 'The meaning and the use of the term *gnwt* "annals"'. In Friedrich Junge (ed.), *Studien zu Sprache und Religion Ägyptens zu Ehren von Wolfhart Westendorf* I, *Sprache* (Göttingen: n.p.) 327–41.
—— (1986). *Pharaonic king-lists, annals, and day-books: a contribution to the study of the Egyptian sense of history*, SSEA Publication 4 (Mississauga, Ont.: Benben).
—— (1997). 'Textual sources for the Hyksos period'. In Eliezer D. Oren (ed.), *The Hyksos: new historical and archaeological perspectives*, University Museum Monograph 96 (Philadelphia: University Museum, University of Pennsylvania) 1–44.
—— (2000). 'Scribe and speaker'. In Ehud Ben Zvi and Michael H. Floyd (eds.), *Writings and speech in Israelite and ancient Near Eastern prophecy*, SBL Symposium Series 10 (Atlanta: Society of Biblical Literature) 145–218.
Reents-Budet, Dorie, et al. (1994). *Painting the Maya universe: royal ceramics of the Classic period*, exhibition catalogue, Duke University Museum of Art (Durham, NC, and London: Duke University Press).
Regier, Terry, Paul Kay, and Richard S. Cook (2005). 'Focal colors are universal after all'. *Proceedings of the National Academy of Sciences* 102: 8386–91.
Reintges, Chris forthcoming. 'Traits of orality in the ancient Egyptian Pyramid Texts'. In Fredrik Hagen et al. (eds.), *Literary-linguistic approaches to narrative*, Orientalia Lovaniensia Analecta (Leuven: Peeters).
Reisner, George Andrew (1931). *Mycerinus: the temples of the Third Pyramid at Giza* (Cambridge, Mass.: Harvard University Press).

Reisner, George Andrew (1932). *A provincial cemetery of the pyramid age, Naga-ed-Dêr*, University of California Publications in Egyptian Archaeology 6 (Oxford: University Press, John Johnson).
—— (1942). *A history of the Giza Necropolis* I, 2 vols. (Cambridge, Mass., and London: Harvard University Press; Humphrey Milford, Oxford University Press).
Reisner, George Andrew, and William Stevenson Smith (1955). *A history of the Giza Necropolis* II, *The tomb of Hetep-heres the mother of Cheops* (Cambridge, Mass.: Harvard University Press).
Renger, Johannes (1967). 'Untersuchungen zum Priestertum in der altbabylonischen Zeit, 1. Teil'. *Zeitschrift für Assyriologie und Verwandte Gebiete* 58: 110–88.
Reuterswärd, Patrik (1958). *Studien zur Polychromie der Plastik* I, *Ägypten*, Acta Universitatis Stockholmiensis: Stockholm Studies in the History of Art 3, 1 (Stockholm: Almqvist & Wiksell).
Richards, Janet E. (1992). Mortuary variability and social differentiation in Middle Kingdom Egypt. Doctoral dissertation: University of Pennsylvania.
—— (2005). *Society and death in ancient Egypt: mortuary landscapes of the Middle Kingdom* (Cambridge: Cambridge University Press).
Richards, Janet E., and Mary Van Buren (eds.) (2000). *Order, legitimacy, and wealth in ancient states*, New Directions in Archaeology (Cambridge: Cambridge University Press).
Rickal, Elsa (2005). Les épithètes dans les autobiographies de particuliers du Nouvel Empire égyptien. Doctoral dissertation: Université de Paris IV Sorbonne.
Ricœur, Paul (1981). 'The model of the text: meaningful action considered as a text'. In Paul Ricœur, *Hermeneutics and the human sciences: essays on language, action, and interpretation*, trans. and ed. John B. Thompson (Cambridge and Paris: Cambridge University Press; Editions de la Maison des Sciences de l'Homme) 197–221.
Riefstahl, Elizabeth (1951). 'An Egyptian portrait of an old man'. *Journal of Near Eastern Studies* 10: 65–73.
Ritner, Robert Kriech (1993). *The mechanics of ancient Egyptian magical practice*, Studies in Ancient Oriental Civilization 54 (Chicago: The Oriental Institute of the University of Chicago).
Roaf, Michael (1992). Survivals and revivals in the art of the ancient Near East. Seminar paper, University of Oxford.
Robertson, Martin (1959). *Greek Painting*, The Great Centuries of Painting (Geneva: Skira).
—— (1975). *A history of Greek art*, 2 vols. (London: Cambridge University Press).
Robertson, Merle Greene (1983). *The sculpture of Palenque* I, *The Temple of the Inscriptions* (Princeton: Princeton University Press).
Robins, Gay (1982). 'The length of the forearm in canon and metrology'. *Göttinger Miszellen* 59: 61–75.
—— (1983). 'Natural and canonical proportions in ancient Egyptians'. *Göttinger Miszellen* 61: 17–25.
—— (1986). *Egyptian painting and relief*, Shire Egyptology (Princes Risborough: Shire Publications).

Robins, Gay (1993). *Women in ancient Egypt* (London: British Museum Press).
—— (1994). *Proportion and style in ancient Egyptian art* (Austin and London: University of Texas Press; Thames & Hudson).
—— (2005). 'Cult statues in ancient Egypt'. In Neal H. Walls (ed.), *Cult image and divine representation in the ancient Near East* (Boston: American Schools of Oriental Research) 1–12.
Robins, Gay, and Charles C. D. Shute (1982). 'Determining the slope of pyramids'. *Göttinger Miszellen* 57: 49–54.
—— (1985). 'Mathematical bases of ancient Egyptian architecture and graphic art'. *Historia Mathematica* 12: 107–22.
—— (1987). *The Rhind Mathematical Papyrus: an ancient Egyptian text* (London: British Museum Publications).
Roccati, Alessandro (1980). 'Il bilinguismo interno dell'Egitto'. *Vicino Oriente* 3: 77–84.
—— (1982). *La littérature historique sous l'Ancien Empire égyptien*, Littératures Anciennes du Proche-Orient (Paris: Editions du Cerf).
Rochemonteix, Maxence de (1892). *Le temple d'Edfou* I, Mission Archéologique Française au Caire, Mémoires 10 (Paris: Leroux).
—— (1894) [1885]. 'Le temple égyptien'. In Maxence de Rochemonteix, *Œuvres diverses*, Bibliothèque Egyptologique 3 (Paris: Leroux) 1–38. First published in *Revue Internationale de l'Enseignement* 7: 2: 19–38.
Roeder, Günther (1956). *Ägyptische Bronzefiguren*, Staatliche Museen zu Berlin, Mitteilungen aus der Ägyptischen Sammlung 6, 2 vols. (Berlin: n.p.).
Romano, James F. (1979). *The Luxor Museum of Ancient Egyptian Art: catalogue* (Cairo: American Research Center in Egypt).
Rosch (Heider), Eleanor (1972). 'Universals in color naming and memory'. *Journal of Experimental Psychology* 93: 10–20.
Rössler-Köhler, Ursula (1986). 'Totenklage'. In Wolfgang Helck and Wolfhart Westendorf (eds.), *Lexikon der Ägyptologie* (Wiesbaden: Otto Harrassowitz) VI, 657–8.
Roth, Ann Macy (1991). *Egyptian phyles in the Old Kingdom: the evolution of a system of social organization*, Studies in Ancient Oriental Civilization 48 (Chicago: The Oriental Institute of the University of Chicago).
—— (2001). 'Opening of the Mouth'. In Donald B. Redford (ed.), *The Oxford encyclopedia of ancient Egypt* (New York: Oxford University Press) II, 605–9.
—— (2002). 'The meaning of menial labor: "servant statues" in Old Kingdom serdabs'. *Journal of the American Research Center in Egypt* 39: 103–21.
Rothe, Russell D., George Rapp Jr., and William K. Miller (1996). 'New hieroglyphic evidence for pharaonic activity in the Eastern Desert of Egypt'. *Journal of the American Research Center in Egypt* 33: 77–104.
Roullet, Anne (1972). *The Egyptian and Egyptianizing monuments of Imperial Rome*, Etudes Préliminaires aux Religions Orientales dans l'Empire Romain 20 (Leiden: Brill).
Russell, Josiah C. (1966). 'The population of medieval Egypt'. *Journal of the American Research Center in Egypt* 5: 69–82.

Russmann, Edna R. (1973). 'The statue of Amenemope-em-hat'. *Metropolitan Museum Journal* 8: 33–46.

—— (1974). *The representation of the king in the XXVth dynasty*, Monographies Reine Elisabeth 3 (Brussels and Brooklyn: Fondation Egyptologique Reine Elisabeth; The Brooklyn Museum).

—— (1980). 'The anatomy of an artistic convention: representation of the near foot in two dimensions through the New Kingdom'. *Bulletin of the Egyptological Seminar* 2: 57–81.

—— (1989). *Egyptian sculpture: Cairo and Luxor* (Austin: University of Texas Press).

Ryholt, Kim (2005). 'On the contents and nature of the Tebtunis temple library: a status report'. In Sandra Lippert and Maren Schentuleit (eds.), *Tebtunis und Soknopaiu Nesos: Leben im römerzeitlichen Fajum, Akten des internationalen Symposions vom 11. bis 13. Dezember 2003 in Sommerhausen bei Würzburg* (Wiesbaden: Harrassowitz) 141–70.

—— (2006). *The Petese stories* II, The Carlsberg Papyri 6, CNI Publications (Copenhagen: Carsten Niebuhr Institute of Near Eastern Studies; Museum Tusculanum Press).

Saad, Zaki Youssef (1947). *Royal excavations at Saqqara and Helwan (1941–1945)*, Supplement to Annales du Service des Antiquités de l'Egypte, Cahier 3 (Cairo: Institut Français d'Archéologie Orientale).

—— (1951). *Royal excavations at Helwan (1945–1947)*, Supplément aux Annales du Service des Antiquités de l'Egypte, Cahier 14 (Cairo: Institut Français d'Archéologie Orientale).

—— (1957). *Ceiling stelae in second dynasty tombs from the excavations at Helwan*, Supplément aux Annales du Service des Antiquités de l'Egypte, Cahier 21 (Cairo: Institut Français d'Archéologie Orientale).

Saad, Zaki Youssef, and J. Frank Autry (1969). *The excavations at Helwan: art and civilization in the first and second Egyptian dynasties* (Norman: University of Oklahoma Press).

Saenger, Paul (1982). 'Silent reading: its impact on late medieval script and society'. *Viator* 13: 367–414.

—— (1997). *Space between words: the origins of silent reading*, Figurae (Stanford: Stanford University Press).

Sahlins, Marshall (1977). 'Colors and cultures'. In Janet L. Dolgin, David S. Kemnitzer, and David M. Schneider (eds.), *Symbolic anthropology* (New York: Columbia University Press) 165–80. Originally published in *Semiotica* 16 (1976) 1–22.

Sainte Fare Garnot, Jean (1938). *L'appel aux vivants dans les textes funéraires, des origines à la fin de l'Ancien Empire*, Recherches d'Archéologie, de Philologie et d'Histoire 9 (Cairo: Institut Français d'Archéologie Orientale).

Sakkarah Expedition, the (1938). *The mastaba of Mereruka*, University of Chicago, Oriental Institute Publications 31, 39, 2 vols. (Chicago: University of Chicago Press).

Saleh, Mohamed, and Hourig Sourouzian (1987). *The Egyptian Museum, Cairo: official catalogue* (Mainz and Cairo: Philipp von Zabern; Egyptian Antiquities Organization).

Salomon, Frank (2004). *The cord keepers: khipus and cultural life in a Peruvian village*, Latin America Otherwise (Durham, NC: Duke University Press).

Samuel, Alan E., W. K. Hastings, Alan K. Bowman, and Roger S. Bagnall (1971). *Death and taxes: ostraka in the Royal Ontario Museum* I, American Studies in Papyrology 10 (Toronto: A. M. Hakkert).

Saunders, Barbara A. C. (2000). 'Revisiting *Basic color terms*'. *Journal of the Royal Anthropological Institute* 6: 81–99.

Saunders, Barbara A. C., and J. van Brakel (1997). 'Are there nontrivial constraints on colour categorization?' *Behavioral and Brain Sciences* 20: 167–228.

Sauneron, Serge (1989). *Un traité égyptien d'ophiologie*, Bibliothèque Générale 11 (Cairo: Institut Français d'Archéologie Orientale).

Sauneron, Serge, and Henri Stierlin (1978). *Die letzten Tempel Ägyptens: Edfu und Philae* (Zurich: Atlantis).

Sauneron, Serge, and Jean Yoyotte (1959). 'La naissance du monde dans l'Egypte ancienne'. In *La naissance du monde*, Sources Orientales 1 (Paris: Editions du Seuil) 17–91.

Scamuzzi, Ernesto n.d. *Museo egizio di Torino* (Turin: Pozzi).

Schäfer, Heinrich (1902). *Ein Bruchstück altägyptischer Annalen*, Abhandlungen der Preussischen Akademie der Wissenschaften 1902, Anhang (Berlin: Georg Reimer).

—— (1903). *Die altägyptischen Prunkgefässe mit aufgesetzten Randverzierungen: ein Beitrag zur Geschichte der Goldschmiedekunst*, Untersuchungen zur Geschichte und Altertumskunde Ägyptens 4:1 (Leipzig: J. C. Hinrichs).

—— (1963). *Von ägyptischer Kunst: eine Grundlage*, 4th edn., ed. Emma Brunner-Traut (Wiesbaden: Otto Harrassowitz).

—— (1986) [1974]. *Principles of Egyptian art*, ed. Emma Brunner-Traut, transl. and ed. John Baines, revised reprint (Oxford: Griffith Institute). 1st German edn. 1919, 4th edn. 1963.

Scheidel, Walter (2001). *Death on the Nile: disease and the demography of Roman Egypt*, Mnemosyne Supplements: History and Archaeology of Classical Antiquity 228 (Leiden: Brill).

Schele, Linda, and Mary Ellen Miller (1986). *The blood of kings: dynasty and ritual in Maya art*, exhibition catalogue, Kimbell Art Museum, Fort Worth (London: Sotheby's).

Schenkel, Wolfgang (1963). 'Die Farben in ägyptischer Kunst und Sprache'. *Zeitschrift für Ägyptische Sprache und Altertumskunde* 88: 131–47.

—— (1965). *Memphis. Herakleopolis. Theben. Die epigraphischen Zeugnisse der 7.–11. Dynastie Ägyptens*, Ägyptologische Abhandlungen 12 (Wiesbaden: Otto Harrassowitz).

—— (1972). 'Zur Relevanz der altägyptischen "Metrik"'. *Mitteilungen des Deutschen Archäologischen Instituts, Abteilung Kairo* 28: 103–7.

—— (1975). 'Die Gräber des p^3-$\underline{t}nf$-j und eines Unbekannten in der thebanischen Nekropole (Nr. 128 und Nr. 129)'. *Mitteilungen des Deutschen Archäologischen Instituts, Abteilung Kairo* 31: 127–58.

Schenkel, Wolfgang (1976). 'The structure of hieroglyphic script'. *Royal Anthropological Institute News* 15: 4–7.

—— (1978). *Die Bewässerungsrevolution im alten Ägypten*, Deutsches Archäologisches Institut, Abteilung Kairo (Mainz: Philipp von Zabern).

—— (1983). 'Wozu die Ägypter eine Schrift brauchten'. In Aleida Assmann, Jan Assmann, and Christof Hardmeier (eds.), *Schrift und Gedächtnis*, Beiträge zur Archäologie der Literarischen Kommunikation 1 (Munich: Fink) 45–63.

—— (2007). 'Color terms in ancient Egyptian and Coptic'. In Don Dedrick, Robert E. MacLaury, and Galina Paramei (eds.), *Anthropology of color: interdisciplinary multilevel modeling* (Amsterdam: John Benjamins).

Schipper, Bernd Ulrich (2005). *Die Erzählung des Wenamun: ein Literaturwerk im Spannungsfeld von Politik, Geschichte und Religion*, Orbis Biblicus et Orientalis 209 (Fribourg and Göttingen: Academic Press; Vandenhoeck & Ruprecht).

Schlott-Schwab, Adelheid (1981). *Die Ausmasse Ägyptens nach altägyptischen Texten*, Ägypten und Altes Testament 3 (Wiesbaden: Otto Harrassowitz).

Schmandt-Besserat, Denise (1977). 'An archaic recording system and the origin of writing'. *Syro-Mesopotamian Studies* 1:2: 1–32.

—— (1978). 'An early recording system in Egypt and the ancient Near East'. In Denise Schmandt-Besserat (ed.), *Immortal Egypt*, Invited Lectures on the Middle East at the University of Texas, Austin (Malibu: Undena) 5–12.

—— (1981). 'From tokens to tablets: a re-evaluation of the so-called "numerical tablets"'. *Visible Language* 15: 321–44.

—— (1992). *Before writing*, 2 vols. (Austin: University of Texas Press).

Schmitz, Bettina (1980). 'Königssohn'. In Wolfgang Helck and Wolfhart Westendorf (eds.), *Lexikon der Ägyptologie* (Wiesbaden: Otto Harrassowitz) III, 626–30.

Schneider, Hans (1977). *Shabtis*, Catalogue of the National Museum of Antiquities at Leiden 2, 3 vols. (Leiden: Rijksmuseum van Oudheden).

Schneider, Thomas (2003a). 'Foreign Egypt: Egyptology and the concept of cultural appropriation'. *Ägypten und Levante* 13: 155–61.

—— (2003b). 'Texte über den Syrischen Wettergott aus Ägypten'. *Ugarit-Forschungen* 35: 605–27.

Schniedewind, William M. (2004). *How the Bible became a book: the textualization of ancient Israel* (Cambridge: Cambridge University Press).

Schofield, R. S. (1968). 'The measurement of literacy in pre-industrial England'. In Jack Goody (ed.), *Literacy in traditional societies* (Cambridge: Cambridge University Press) 311–25.

Schott, Erika (1977). 'Die Biographie des Ka-em-Tenenet'. In Jan Assmann, Erika Feucht, and Reinhard Grieshammer (eds.), *Fragen an die altägyptische Literatur: Studien zum Gedenken an Eberhard Otto* (Wiesbaden: Dr Ludwig Reichert) 443–461c.

Schott, Siegfried (1950). *Hieroglyphen: Untersuchungen zum Ursprung der Schrift*, Akademie der Wissenschaften und der Literatur (Mainz), Abhandlungen, geistes- und sozialwissenschaftliche Klasse 1950, 24 (Wiesbaden: Franz Steiner).

Schott, Siegfried (1952). *Das schöne Fest vom Wüstentale: Festbräuche einer Totenstadt*, Akademie der Wissenschaften und der Literatur (Mainz), Abhandlungen, geistes- und sozialwissenschaftliche Klasse 1952, 11 (Wiesbaden: Franz Steiner).

Scoditti, Giancarlo M. G. (1982). 'Aesthetics: the significance of apprenticeship on Kitawa'. *Man* NS 17: 74–91.

Scott, Gerry D. (1989). *The history and development of the ancient Egyptian scribe statue*. Doctoral dissertation: Yale University.

Scribner, Sylvia, and Michael Cole (1981). *The psychology of literacy* (Cambridge, Mass.: Harvard University Press).

Seele, Keith C. (1959). *The tomb of Tjanefer at Thebes*, Oriental Institute Publications 86 (Chicago: University of Chicago Press).

Seidl, Erwin (1937). *Demotische Urkundenlehre nach den frühptolemäischen Texten*, Münchener Beiträge zur Papyrusforschung und Antiken Rechtsgeschichte 27 (Munich: C. H. Beck).

—— (1968). *Ägyptische Rechtsgeschichte der Saiten- und Perserzeit*, Ägyptologische Forschungen 20, 2nd edn. (Glückstadt: J. J. Augustin).

Seidlmayer, Stephan Johannes (1990). *Gräberfelder aus dem Übergang von Alten zum Mittleren Reich: Studien zur Archäologie der Ersten Zwischenzeit*, Studien zur Archäologie und Geschichte Altägyptens 1 (Heidelberg: Heidelberger Orientverlag).

—— (1996). 'Town and state in the early Old Kingdom: a view from Elephantine'. In A. Jeffrey Spencer (ed.), *Aspects of early Egypt* (London: British Museum Press) 108–27.

Seipel, Wilfried (ed.) (1992). *Gott—Mensch—Pharao: viertausend Jahre Menschenbild in der Skulptur des Alten Ägypten; Künstlerhaus, 25. Mai bis 4. Oktober 1992; eine Ausstellung des Kunsthistorischen Museums Wien, Wien, Kunsthistorisches Museum, 1992*, exhibition catalogue (Vienna: Kunsthistorisches Museum).

Sethe, Kurt (1906). *Urkunden der 18. Dynastie* I, Urkunden des Ägyptischen Altertums 4:1 (Leipzig: J. C. Hinrichs).

—— (1907). *Urkunden der 18. Dynastie* III, Urkunden des Ägyptischen Altertums 4:3 (Leipzig: J. C. Hinrichs).

—— (1908). *Die altaegyptischen Pyramidentexte*, 2 vols. (Leipzig: J. C. Hinrichs).

—— (1926). 'Ein Prozessurteil aus dem alten Reich'. *Zeitschrift für Ägyptische Sprache und Altertumskunde* 61: 67–79.

—— (1928a). *Ägyptische Lesestücke zum Gebrauch im akademischen Unterricht: Texte des Mittleren Reiches*, 2nd edn. (Leipzig: J. C. Hinrichs).

—— (1928b). *Dramatische Texte zu altägyptischen Mysterienspielen*, Untersuchungen zur Geschichte und Altertumskunde Ägyptens 10 (Leipzig: J. C. Hinrichs).

—— (1933). *Urkunden des alten Reiches*, Urkunden des Ägyptischen Altertums 1:1, 2nd edn. (Leipzig: J. C. Hinrichs).

Sethe, Kurt, and Wolja Erichsen (1935). *Historisch-biographische Urkunden des Mittleren Reiches*, Urkunden des Ägyptischen Altertums 7:1 (Leipzig: J. C. Hinrichs).

Shaw, Ian (1992). 'Ideal homes in ancient Egypt: the archaeology of social aspiration'. *Cambridge Archaeological Journal* 2: 147–66.

Shaw, Ian, and Tom Heldal (2003). 'Rescue work in the Khafra quarries at Gebel el-Asr'. *Egyptian Archaeology* 23: 14–16.

Shedid, Abdel Ghaffar, and Matthias Seidel (1991). *Das Grab des Nacht: Kunst und Geschichte eines Beamtengrabes der 18. Dynastie in Theben-West* (Mainz: Philipp von Zabern).

Shinnie, Peter L. (1967). *Meroe: a civilization of the Sudan*, Ancient Peoples and Places (London: Thames & Hudson).

Shore, A. F., and H. S. Smith (1960). 'A Demotic embalmers' agreement (Pap. dem. B.M. 10561)'. *Acta Orientalia* 25: 277–94.

Shortland, Andrew J. (2000). *Vitreous materials at Amarna: the production of glass and faience in 18th dynasty Egypt*, BAR International Series 827 (Oxford: Archaeopress).

Silverman, David P. (1991). 'Texts from the Amarna period and their position in the development of Ancient Egyptian'. *Lingua Aegyptia* 1: 301–14.

—— (2000). 'The threat-formula and biographical text in the tomb of Hezi at Saqqara'. *Journal of the American Research Center in Egypt* 37: 1–13.

Simpson, R. S. (1996). *Demotic grammar in the Ptolemaic sacerdotal decrees*, Griffith Institute Monographs (Oxford: Griffith Institute).

Simpson, William Kelly (1974). *The Terrace of the Great God at Abydos: the offering chapels of dynasties 12 and 13*, Publications of the Pennsylvania–Yale Expedition to Egypt 5 (New Haven and Philadelphia: Peabody Museum; University Museum).

—— (1977). 'Amor dei: *ntr mrr rmt m t3 w3* (Sh. Sai. 147–148) and the embrace'. In Jan Assmann, Erika Feucht, and Reinhard Grieshammer (eds.), *Fragen an die altägyptische Literatur: Studien zum Gedenken an Eberhard Otto* (Wiesbaden: Dr Ludwig Reichert) 493–8.

—— (1978). *The mastabas of Kawab, Khafkhufu I and II*, Giza Mastabas 3 (Boston: Department of Egyptian and Ancient Near Eastern Art, Museum of Fine Arts).

—— (ed.) (1973). *The literature of ancient Egypt*, 2nd edn. (New Haven and London: Yale University Press).

—— (ed.) (2003). *The literature of ancient Egypt: an anthology of stories, instructions, stelae, autobiographies, and poetry*, 3rd edn. (New Haven: Yale University Press).

Small, Jocelyn Penny (1997). *Wax tablets of the mind: cognitive studies of memory and literacy in classical antiquity* (London: Routledge).

Smith, H. S. (1958). 'Another witness-copy document from the Fayyum'. *Journal of Egyptian Archaeology* 44: 86–96.

Smith, H. S., and W. John Tait (1984). *Saqqara demotic papyri* I, Texts from Excavations 7 (London: Egypt Exploration Society).

Smith, John D. (1977). '*The singer or the song?* A reassessment of Lord's "oral theory"'. *Man* 12: 141–53.

Smith, William Stevenson (1949). *A history of Egyptian sculpture and painting in the Old Kingdom*, 2nd edn. (London: Geoffrey Cumberlege, Oxford University Press, for Museum of Fine Arts, Boston).

—— (1998). *The art and architecture of ancient Egypt*, revised by William Kelly Simpson. Pelican History of Art, 3rd edn., revised version (New Haven and London: Yale University Press).

Smither, Paul C. (1942). 'An Old Kingdom letter concerning the crimes of Count Sabni'. *Journal of Egyptian Archaeology* 28: 16–19.

Smither, Paul C. (1945). 'The Semnah despatches'. *Journal of Egyptian Archaeology* 31: 3–10.

So, Jenny F. (2000). *Music in the age of Confucius* (Washington, DC: Freer Gallery of Art and Arthur M. Sackler Gallery).

Sourouzian, Hourig (1991). 'La statue d'Amenhotep fils de Hapou, âgé, un chef-d'œuvre de la XVIIIe dynastie'. *Mitteilungen des Deutschen Archäologischen Instituts, Abteilung Kairo* 47: 341–55.

Spalinger, Anthony John (2001). 'Calendars'. In Donald B. Redford (ed.), *The Oxford encyclopedia of ancient Egypt* (New York: Oxford University Press) I, 224–7.

—— (2005). *War in ancient Egypt: the New Kingdom*, Ancient World at War (Malden, Mass., and Oxford: Blackwell).

Spanel, Donald (1988). *Through ancient eyes—Egyptian portraiture: April 21 – July 31, 1988, an exhibition* (Birmingham, Ala.: Birmingham Museum of Art).

Spencer, A. J. (1980). *Early Dynastic objects*, Catalogue of Egyptian Antiquities in the British Museum 5 (London: British Museum Publications).

Spiegel, Joachim (1957). 'Zu der Kunstentwicklung der zweiten Hälfte des Alten Reiches'. *Mitteilungen des Deutschen Archäologischen Instituts, Abteilung Kairo* 15: 225–61.

—— n.d. [1935]. *Die Idee vom Totengericht in der ägyptischen Religion*, Leipziger Ägyptologische Studien 2 (Glückstadt and Hamburg: J. J. Augustin).

Spiegelberg, Wilhelm (1929). 'Note on the feminine character of the New Empire'. *Journal of Egyptian Archaeology* 15: 199.

Stadelmann, Rainer (1962). 'Ein bemaltes Hausmodell in der Ägyptischen Sammlung der Universität Heidelberg'. *Mitteilungen des Deutschen Archäologischen Instituts, Abteilung Kairo* 18: 54–8.

—— (1985). *Die ägyptischen Pyramiden: vom Ziegelbau zum Weltwunder* (Darmstadt: Wissenschaftliche Buchgesellschaft).

Staehelin, Elisabeth (1977). 'Hautfarbe'. In Wolfgang Helck and Wolfhart Westendorf (eds.), *Lexikon der Ägyptologie* (Wiesbaden: Otto Harrassowitz) II, 1068–72.

Steiner, Deborah Tarn (1994). *The tyrant's writ: myths and images of writing in ancient Greece* (Princeton: Princeton University Press).

Steiner, Richard C., and Charles F. Nims (1984). 'You can't offer your sacrifice and eat it too: a polemical poem from the Aramaic text in demotic script'. *Journal of Near Eastern Studies* 42: 89–114.

—— (1985). 'Ashurbanipal and Shamash-shum-ukin: a tale of two brothers from the Aramaic text in demotic script, Part I'. *Revue Biblique* 92: 60–81.

Steinmann, Frank (1974). 'Die Schreibkenntnisse der Kopten nach den Aussagen der Djeme-Urkunden'. In Peter Nagel (ed.), *Studia coptica*, Berliner Byzantinische Studien 45 (Berlin: Akademie-Verlag) 101–10.

Stock, Brian (1983). *The implications of literacy: written language and models of interpretation in the eleventh and twelfth centuries* (Princeton: Princeton University Press).

—— (1990). *Listening for the text: on the uses of the past*, Parallax: Re-visions of Culture and Society (Baltimore: Johns Hopkins University Press).

Street, Brian V. (1984). *Literacy in theory and practice*, Cambridge Studies in Oral and Literate Culture 9 (Cambridge: Cambridge University Press).

—— (ed.) (1993). *Cross-cultural approaches to literacy*, Cambridge Studies in Oral and Literate Culture 23 (Cambridge: Cambridge University Press).

Stricker, B. H. (1944). 'De indeeling der egyptische taalgeschiedenis'. *Oudheidkundige Mededelingen uit het Rijksmuseum van Oudheden te Leiden* 25: 14–51.

Strudwick, Nigel (1985). *The administration of Egypt in the Old Kingdom: the highest titles and their holders*, Studies in Egyptology (London etc.: KPI).

—— (2005). *Texts from the pyramid age*, Writings from the Ancient World (Atlanta: Society of Biblical Literature).

Sun, Richard K. (1983). 'Perceptual distances and the basic color term encoding sequence'. *American Anthropologist* 85: 387–91.

Sweeney, Deborah (1998). 'Women and language in the Ramesside period or, Why women don't say please'. In Christopher Eyre (ed.), *Proceedings of the Seventh International Congress of Egyptologists, Cambridge, 3–9 September 1995*, Orientalia Lovaniensia Analecta 82 (Leuven: Peeters) 1009–17.

Tacke, Nikolaus (2001). *Verspunkte als Gliederungsmittel in ramessidischen Schülerhandschriften*, Studien zur Archäologie und Geschichte Altägyptens 22 (Heidelberg: Heidelberger Orientverlag).

Tait, W. John (1977). *Papyri from Tebtunis in Egyptian and Greek (P. Tebt. Tait)*, Texts from Excavations 3 (London: Egypt Exploration Society).

—— (1991). 'P. Carlsberg 230: eleven fragments from a demotic herbal'. In Paul John Frandsen (ed.), *Demotic texts from the collection*, The Carlsberg Papyri 1; CNI Publications 15 (Copenhagen: Museum Tusculanum Press) 47–92.

—— (ed.) (2003a). *'Never had the like occurred': Egypt's view of its past*, Encounters with Ancient Egypt (London: UCL Press).

—— (2003b). 'The "Book of the Fayum": mystery in a known landscape'. In David O'Connor and Stephen Quirke (eds.), *Mysterious lands*, Encounters with Ancient Egypt (London: UCL Press: Institute of Archaeology) 183–202.

—— forthcoming.'The nuts and bolts of Demotic narrative'. In Fredrik Hagen et al. (eds.), *Literary-linguistic approaches to narrative*, Orientalia Lovaniensia Analecta (Leuven: Peeters).

Tambiah, Stanley Jeyaraja (1970). *Buddhism and the spirit cults in north-east Thailand*, Cambridge Studies in Social Anthropology 2 (Cambridge: Cambridge University Press).

Tarn, W. W. (1948). *Alexander the Great* I (Cambridge: Cambridge University Press).

Taube, Karl (2000). *The writing system of ancient Teotihuacan*, Ancient America 2 (Barnardsville, NC, and Washington, DC: Center for Ancient American Studies).

Tawfik, Sayed (1985). 'Der Palermostein als frühester Beleg für die Weihformel'. In Paule Posener-Kriéger (ed.), *Mélanges Gamal Eddin Mokhtar*, Bibliothèque d'Etude 97 (Cairo: Institut Français d'Archéologie Orientale) II, 309–13.

Taylor, Insup, and David R. Olson (eds.) (1995). *Scripts and literacy: reading and learning to read alphabets, syllabaries, and characters*, Neuropsychology and Cognition 7 (Dordrecht and Boston: Kluwer).

te Velde, Herman (1986). 'Scribes and literacy in Ancient Egypt'. In H. L. J. Vanstiphout et al. (eds.), *Scripta signa vocis: studies about scripts, scriptures, scribes, and languages in the Near East, presented to J. H. Hospers by his pupils, colleagues, and friends* (Groningen: Forsten) 253–64.

—— (1988). 'Egyptian hieroglyphs as linguistic signs and metalinguistic informants'. *Visible Religion* 6: 169–79.

Teeter, Emily (1997). *The presentation of Maat: ritual and legitimacy in ancient Egypt*, Studies in Ancient Oriental Civilizations 57 (Chicago: Oriental Institute of the University of Chicago).

Tefnin, Roland (1983). 'Une statue de reine British Museum et Karnak et les paradoxes du portrait égyptien'. *Journal of Egyptian Archaeology* 69: 96–107.

—— (1984). 'Discours et iconicité dans l'art égyptien'. *Göttinger Miszellen* 79: 55–69.

—— (1991a). *Art et magie au temps des pyramides: l'énigme des têtes dites 'de remplacement'*, Monumenta Aegyptiaca 5 (Brussels: Fondation Egyptologique Reine Elisabeth).

—— (1991b). 'Eléments pour une sémiologie de l'image égyptienne'. *Chronique d'Egypte* 66: 60–88.

—— (1991c). 'Statuaire royale de la 12e dynastie: la cohérence des signes'. In *Sixth International Congress of Egyptology: abstracts of papers* (Turin: Organizing Secretariat) 382–3.

—— (1992). 'Les yeux et les oreilles du Roi'. In Michèle Broze and Philippe Talon (eds.), *L'atelier de l'orfèvre: mélanges offerts à Ph. Derchain* (Leuven: Peeters) 147–56.

Teissier, Beatrice (1996). *Egyptian iconography on Syro-Palestinian cylinder seals of the Middle Bronze Age*, Orbis Biblicus et Orientalis, Series Archaeologica 11 (Fribourg and Göttingen: University Press; Vandenhoeck & Ruprecht).

Terrace, Edward L. B. (1968). *Egyptian paintings of the Middle Kingdom* (London: George Allen and Unwin).

Thomas, Rosalind (1989). *Oral tradition and written record in classical Athens*, Cambridge Studies in Oral and Literate Culture 18 (Cambridge: Cambridge University Press).

—— (1992). *Literacy and orality in ancient Greece*, Key Themes in Ancient History (Cambridge: Cambridge University Press).

Thompson, Dorothy J. (1994). 'Literacy and power in Ptolemaic Egypt'. In Alan K. Bowman and Greg Woolf (eds.), *Literacy and power in the ancient world* (Cambridge: Cambridge University Press) 67–83.

Thompson, Dorothy J.: see also Crawford.

Tietze, Christian (1985). 'Amarna: Analyse des Wohnhäuser und soziale Struktur der Stadtbewohner'. *Zeitschrift für Ägyptische Sprache und Altertumskunde* 112: 48–84.

—— (1986). 'Amarna (Teil II): Analyse der ökonomischen Beziehungen der Stadtbewohner'. *Zeitschrift für Ägyptische Sprache und Altertumskunde* 113: 55–78.

Tornay, Serge (ed.) (1978). *Voir et nommer les couleurs*, Recherches Thématiques 2 (Nanterre: Laboratoire d'Ethnologie et de Sociologie Comparative).

Trigger, Bruce G. (1976). *Nubia under the pharaohs*, Ancient Peoples and Places (London: Thames & Hudson).
—— (1993). *Early civilizations: ancient Egypt in context* (Cairo: American University in Cairo Press).
—— (2004). 'Writing systems: a case study in cultural evolution'. In Stephen D. Houston (ed.), *The first writing: script invention as history and process* (Cambridge: Cambridge University Press) 150–89 (bibliography 354–94). Originally published in *Norwegian Archaeological Review* 31 (1998) 39–62.
Turner, Victor W. (1966). 'Colour classification in Ndembu ritual'. In Michael Banton (ed.), *Anthropological approaches to the study of religion*, Association of Social Anthropologists Monograph 3 (London: Tavistock) 47–84.
Turton, David (1980). 'There's no such beast: cattle and colour naming among the Mursi'. *Man* NS 15: 320–38.
Ucko, Peter J., and Andrée Rosenfeld (1967). *Palaeolithic cave art* (London: Weidenfeld & Nicholson).
Urton, Gary (2005). 'Khipu archives: duplicate accounts and identity labels in the Inka knotted string records'. *Latin American Antiquity* 16: 147–67.
Vachala, Břetislav (2003). 'Das älteste Liebeslied?' In Nicole Kloth, Eva Pardey, and Karl Martin (eds.), *Es werde niedergelegt als Schriftstück: Festschrift für Hartwig Altenmüller zum 65. Geburtstag*, Studien zur Altägyptischen Kultur, Beiheft 9 (Hamburg: Buske) 429–31.
—— (2004). *Abusir* VIII, *Die Reliefs aus der Ptahschepses-Mastaba in Abusir*, trans. Wolf B. Oerter, Excavations of the Czech Institute of Egyptology (n.p.: Roman Mišek-Set Out for Czech Institute of Egyptology).
Valbelle, Dominique (1985). *'Les ouvriers de la Tombe': Deir el-Médineh à l'époque ramesside*, Bibliothèque d'Etude 96 (Cairo: Institut Français d'Archéologie Orientale).
Valbelle, Dominique, and Charles Bonnet (1996). *Le sanctuaire d'Hathor, maîtresse de la turquoise: Sérabit el-Khadim au Moyen Empire* (Paris and Aosta: Picard; Musumeci).
Van De Mieroop, Marc (2004). *A history of the ancient Near East, c.3000–323 BC*, Blackwell History of the Ancient World (Malden, Mass., and Oxford: Blackwell).
van den Boorn, G. P. F. (1988). *The duties of the vizier: civil administration in the early New Kingdom*, Studies in Egyptology (London: KPI).
van den Brink, Edwin C. M. (1992). 'Corpus and numerical evaluation of the "Thinite" potmarks'. In Renée Friedman and Barbara Adams (eds.), *The followers of Horus: studies dedicated to Michael Allen Hoffman*, Oxbow Monograph 20 (Oxford: Oxbow Books) 265–96.
van den Brink, Edwin C. M., and Thomas Evan Levy (eds.) (2002). *Egypt and the Levant: interrelations from the 4th through the early 3rd millennium BCE*, New Approaches to Anthropological Archaeology (London: Leicester University Press).
van Minnen, Peter (1998). 'Bookish or boorish: literature in Egyptian villages in the Fayum in the Graeco-Roman period'. *Journal of Juristic Papyrology* 28: 99–184.
Vandersleyen, Claude (1971). *Les guerres d'Amosis, fondateur de la XVIIIe dynastie*, Monographies Reine Elisabeth 1 (Brussels: Fondation Egyptologique Reine Elisabeth).

Vandersleyen, Claude (1982). 'Porträt'. In Wolfgang Helck and Wolfhart Westendorf (eds.), *Lexikon der Ägyptologie* (Wiesbaden: Otto Harrassowitz) IV, 1074–80.

Vandersleyen, Claude, et al. (1975). *Das alte Ägypten*, Propyläen Kunstgeschichte 15 (Berlin: Propyläen).

Vandier, Jacques (1950). *Moᶜalla: la tombe d'Ankhtifi et la tombe de Sébekhotep*, Bibliothèque d'Etude 18 (Cairo: Institut Français d'Archéologie Orientale).

—— (1952). *Manuel d'archéologie égyptienne* I:1, *Les époques de formation, la préhistoire* (Paris: Picard).

—— (1958). *Manuel d'archéologie égyptienne* III, *Les grandes époques, la statuaire*, 2 vols. (Paris: Picard).

Verner, Miroslav (1979). 'Neue Papyrusfunde in Abusir'. *Revue d'Egyptologie* 31: 97–100.

Vernus, Pascal (1996). 'Langue littéraire et diglossie'. In Antonio Loprieno (ed.), *Ancient Egyptian literature: history and forms*, Probleme der Ägyptologie 10 (Leiden: E. J. Brill) 555–64.

Vittmann, Günther (1995). 'Die Autobiographie der Tathotis (Stele Wien 5857)'. *Studien zur Altägyptischen Kultur* 22: 283–323.

—— (1998). *Der demotische Papyrus Rylands 9*, Ägypten und Altes Testament 38, 2 vols. (Wiesbaden: Harrassowitz).

Vleeming, Sven P. (1981). 'La phase initiale du démotique ancien'. *Chronique d'Egypte* 56: 31–48.

Vleeming, Sven P., and J. W. Wesselius (1982). 'An Aramaic hymn from the fourth century B.C.' *Bibliotheca Orientalis* 39: 501–9.

—— (1985). *Studies in Papyrus Amherst 63: essays on the Aramaic texts in Aramaic/demotic Papyrus Amherst 63*, I (Amsterdam: Juda Palache Instituut).

Vogelsang-Eastwood, Gillian (1993). *Pharaonic Egyptian clothing*, Studies in Textile and Costume History 2 (Leiden and New York: E. J. Brill).

Volten, Aksel (1945). *Zwei altägyptische politische Schriften*, Analecta Aegyptiaca 4 (Copenhagen: Einar Munksgaard).

von der Way, Thomas, and Klaus Schmidt (1985). 'Bericht über den Fortgang der Untersuchungen im Raum Tell el-Faraᶜin/Buto'. *Mitteilungen des Deutschen Archäologischen Instituts, Abteilung Kairo* 41: 269–91.

von Wattenwyl, André, and Heinrich Zollinger (1979). 'Color-term salience and neurophysiology of color vision'. *American Anthropologist* 81: 279–88.

Vycichl, Werner (1984). *Dictionnaire étymologique de la langue copte* (Leuven: Peeters).

Waddell, W. G. (1940). *Manetho*, Loeb Classical Library (Cambridge, Mass., and London: Harvard University Press; Heinemann).

Walbank, F. W. (1981). *The Hellenistic world* (Brighton: Harvester Books).

Wald, Paul (1978). 'Clôture sémantique, universaux et terminologies de couleur'. In Serge Tornay (ed.), *Voir et nommer les couleurs*, Recherches Thématiques 2 (Nanterre: Laboratoire d'Ethnologie et de Sociologie Comparative) 121–38.

Warburton, David (2004). 'The terminology of ancient Egyptian colours in context'. In Liza Cleland, Karen Stears, and Glenys Davies (eds.), *Colour in the ancient Mediterranean world*, BAR International Series 1267 (Oxford: Hedges) 126–30.

Ward, William A. (1977). 'Neferhotep and his friends: a glimpse at the lives of ordinary men'. *Journal of Egyptian Archaeology* 63: 63–6.

—— (1981). 'Lexicographical miscellanies II'. *Studien zur Altägyptischen Kultur* 9: 359–73.

Weber, Manfred (1969). Beiträge zur Kenntnis des Schrift- und Buchwesens der alten Ägypter. Doctoral Dissertation: University of Cologne.

Weeks, Kent R. (1970). The anatomical knowledge of the ancient Egyptians and the representation of the human figure in Egyptian art. Doctoral dissertation: Yale University.

—— (1979). 'Art, word, and the Egyptian world view'. In Kent R. Weeks (ed.), *Egyptology and the social sciences* (Cairo: American University in Cairo Press) 59–81.

Wengrow, David (2006). *The archaeology of early Egypt: social transformations in North-East Africa, 10,000 to 2650 BC*, Cambridge World Archaeology (Cambridge: Cambridge University Press).

Wenig, Steffen (1967). *Die Frau im alten Ägypten* (Leipzig: Edition Leipzig).

Wente, Edward F. (1961). 'A letter of complaint to the vizier To'. *Journal of Near Eastern Studies* 20: 252–7.

—— (1967). *Late Ramesside letters*, The Oriental Institute of the University of Chicago, Studies in Ancient Oriental Civilization 33 (Chicago: University of Chicago Press).

—— (1980). 'The Gurob letter to Amenophis IV'. *Serapis* 6: 204–15.

—— (1982). 'Mysticism in pharaonic Egypt?' *Journal of Near Eastern Studies* 41: 161–79.

—— (1985). 'A new look at the viceroy Setau's autobiographical inscription'. In Paule Posener-Kriéger (ed.), *Mélanges Gamal Eddin Mokhtar*, Bibliothèque d'Etude 97 (Cairo: Institut Français d'Archéologie Orientale) II, 347–59.

—— (1990). *Letters from ancient Egypt*, Writings from the Ancient World 1 (Atlanta: Scholars Press).

Westendorf, Wolfhart 1965–77. *Koptisches Handwörterbuch* (Heidelberg: Carl Winter, Universitätsverlag).

—— (1966). *Papyrus Edwin Smith: ein medizinisches Lehrbuch aus dem alten Ägypten*, Hubers Klassiker der Medizin und der Naturwissenschaften 9 (Bern and Stuttgart: Huber).

White, John (1987). *The birth and rebirth of pictorial space*, 3rd edn. (London: Faber & Faber).

—— (1993). *Art and architecture in Italy, 1250–1400*, Pelican History of Art, 3rd edn. (New Haven and London: Yale University Press).

Whitehouse, Helen (1987). 'King Den in Oxford'. *Oxford Journal of Archaeology* 6: 257–67.

—— (1992). 'The Hierakonpolis ivories in Oxford: a progress report'. In Renée Friedman and Barbara Adams (eds.), *The followers of Horus: studies dedicated to Michael Allen Hoffman 1944–1990*, Egyptian Studies Association Publication 2, Oxbow Monograph 20 (Oxford: Oxbow Books) 77–82.

Whitley, James (1997). 'Cretan laws and Cretan literacy'. *American Journal of Archaeology* 101: 635–61.

Wilcke, Claus (2000). *Wer las und schrieb in Babylonien und Assyrien: Überlegungen zur Literalität im Alten Zweistromland*, Sitzungsberichte der Bayerischen Akademie der Wissenschaften, philosophisch-historische Klasse 2000:6 (Munich: Bayerische Akademie der Wissenschaften).

Wildung, Dietrich (1969). *Die Rolle ägyptischer Könige im Bewusstsein ihrer Nachwelt I, Posthume Quellen über die Könige der ersten vier Dynastien*, Münchner Ägyptologische Studien 17 (Berlin: Bruno Hessling).

—— (1975). 'Besucherinschriften'. In Wolfgang Helck and Eberhard Otto (eds.), *Lexikon der Ägyptologie* (Wiesbaden: Otto Harrassowitz) I, 766–7.

—— (1977). *Imhotep und Amenhotep: Gottwerdung im alten Ägypten*, Münchner Ägyptologische Studien 36 (Munich and Berlin: Deutscher Kunstverlag).

Wilkinson, Alix (1971). *Ancient Egyptian jewellery* (London: Methuen).

Wilkinson, Toby A. H. (1999). *Early dynastic Egypt* (London: Routledge).

—— (2000). *Royal annals of ancient Egypt: the Palermo Stone and its associated fragments*, Studies in Egyptology (London: KPI).

Willats, John (1985). 'Drawing systems revisited: the role of denotation systems in children's figure drawings'. In N. H. Freeman and M. V. Cox (eds.), *Visual order: the nature and development of pictorial representation* (Cambridge: Cambridge University Press) 78–100.

—— (1997). *Art and representation: new principles in the analysis of pictures* (Princeton: Princeton University Press).

Willems, Harco (2001). 'The social and ritual context of a mortuary liturgy of the Middle Kingdom (*CT* spells 30–41)'. In Harco Willems (ed.), *Social aspects of funerary culture in the Egyptian Old and Middle Kingdoms: proceedings of the symposium held at Leiden, 6–7 June, 1996*, Orientalia Lovaniensia Analecta 103 (Leuven, Paris, and Sterling, Va.: Peeters) 253–372.

Williams, Bruce Beyer (1986). *Excavations between Abu Simbel and the Sudan frontier I, The A-Group royal cemetery at Qustul: Cemetery L*, Oriental Institute Nubian Expedition 3 (Chicago: The Oriental Institute of the University of Chicago).

—— (1987). 'Forbears of Menes in Nubia: myth or reality?' *Journal of Near Eastern Studies* 46: 15–26.

—— (1988). 'Narmer and the Coptos colossi'. *Journal of the American Research Center in Egypt* 25: 35–59.

Williams, Bruce Beyer, and Thomas J. Logan (1987). 'The Metropolitan Museum knife handle and aspects of pharaonic imagery before Narmer'. *Journal of Near Eastern Studies* 46: 245–85.

Wilson, John A. (1948). 'The oath in ancient Egypt'. *Journal of Near Eastern Studies* 7: 129–56.

—— (1951). *The burden of Egypt: an interpretation of ancient Egyptian culture* (Chicago: University of Chicago Press). [Later editions entitled *The culture of ancient Egypt*.]

Wilson, Penelope (1997). *A Ptolemaic lexikon: a lexicographical study of the texts in the temple of Edfu*, Orientalia Lovaniensia Analecta 78 (Leuven: Peeters; Departement Oosterse Studies).

Winlock, Herbert Eustis (1955). *Models of daily life in ancient Egypt, from the tomb of Meket-Rēᶜ at Thebes*, Publications of the Metropolitan Museum of Art Egyptian Expedition 18 (Cambridge, Mass.: Harvard University Press for Metropolitan Museum of Art).

Winter, Erich (1968). *Untersuchungen zu den ägyptischen Tempelreliefs der griechisch-römischen Zeit*, Österreichische Akademie der Wissenschaften, philosophisch-historische Klasse, Denkschriften 98 (Vienna: Hermann Böhlaus Nachfolger).

Winter, Irene J. (1981). 'Royal rhetoric and the development of historical narrative in Neo-Assyrian reliefs'. *Studies in Visual Communication* 7, 2: 2–38.

Witkowski, Stanley R., and Cecil H. Brown (1977). 'An explanation of color nomenclature universals'. *American Anthropologist* 79: 50–7.

—— (1981). 'Lexical encoding sequences and language change: color terminology systems'. *American Anthropologist* 83: 13–27.

Wittkower, Rudolf (1977). *Sculpture: processes and principles* (London: Allen Lane).

Wolf, Walther (1957). *Die Kunst Ägyptens: Gestalt und Geschichte* (Stuttgart: Kohlhammer).

Wollheim, Richard (1980). *Art and its objects: with six supplementary essays*, 2nd edn. (Cambridge: Cambridge University Press).

Wood, Ananda E. (1985). *Knowledge before printing and after: the Indian tradition in changing Kerala* (Delhi: Oxford University Press).

Wood, Wendy (1978). 'A reconstruction of the reliefs of Hesy-Re'. *Journal of the American Research Center in Egypt* 15: 9–24.

Wreszinski, Walter (1923–35). *Atlas zur altägyptischen Kulturgeschichte*, II (Leipzig: J. C. Hinrichs).

Yates, Frances Amelia (1966). *The art of memory* (London: Routledge & Kegan Paul).

Yoffee, Norman (1979). 'The decline and rise of Mesopotamian civilization: an ethnoarchaeologial perspective on the evolution of social complexity'. *American Antiquity* 44: 5–35.

—— (1980). 'Honk if you know Darwin: brief reply to Dunnell and Wenke'. *American Antiquity* 45: 610–12.

—— (2000). 'Law courts and the mediation of social conflict in early Mesopotamia'. In Janet E. Richards and Mary Van Buren (eds.), *Order, legitimacy, and wealth in ancient states*, New Directions in Archaeology (Cambridge: Cambridge University Press) 46–63.

—— (2005). *Myths of the archaic state: evolution of the earliest cities, states, and civilizations* (Cambridge: Cambridge University Press).

Yoffee, Norman, Roger Matthews, Bruce G. Trigger, Philip L. Kohl, David Webster, and Katharina Schreiber (2005). 'Review feature: *Myths of the archaic state*'. *Cambridge Archaeological Journal* 15: 251–68.

Youtie, Herbert Chayyim (1973). '*Ἀγράμματος* [Agrammatos]: an aspect of Greek society in Egypt' and '*Βραδέως γράφων* [Bradeōs graphōn]: between literacy and illiteracy'. In Herbert Chayyim Youtie, *Scriptiunculae* (Amsterdam: Adolf M. Hakkert) II, 611–27; 629–51.

Youtie, Herbert Chayyim (1981). ''Ὑπογραφεύς [Hupographeus]: the social impact of illiteracy in Graeco-Roman Egypt' and 'Because they did not know letters'. In Herbert Chayyim Youtie, *Scriptiunculae posteriores* (Bonn: Rudolf Habelt) I, 179–99; 255–62.
Yoyotte, Jean (1951). 'Le martelage des noms royaux éthiopiens par Psammétique II'. *Revue d'Egyptologie* 8: 215–39.
Yunis, Harvey (2003a). 'Introduction: why written texts?' In Harvey Yunis (ed.), *Written texts and the rise of literate culture in ancient Greece* (Cambridge: Cambridge University Press) 1–14.
—— (ed.) (2003b). *Written texts and the rise of literate culture in ancient Greece* (Cambridge: Cambridge University Press).
Žába, Zbyněk (1956). *Les maximes de Ptaḥḥotep* (Prague: Editions de l'Académie Tchécoslovaque des Sciences).
Zauzich, Karl-Theodor (1968). *Die ägyptische Schreibertradition in Aufbau, Sprache und Schrift der demotischen Kaufverträge aus ptolemäischer Zeit*, Ägyptologische Abhandlungen 19, 2 vols. (Wiesbaden: Otto Harrassowitz).
—— (1980). 'Kommt das Alphabet aus dem Hieratischen?' *Zeitschrift der Deutschen Morgenländischen Gesellschaft, Supplement* 4: 76–80.
Zeidler, Jürgen (1993). 'Zur Frage der Spätentstehung des Mythos in Ägypten'. *Göttinger Miszellen* 132: 85–109.
Zibelius-Chen, Karola (1978). *Ägyptische Siedlungen nach Texten des Alten Reiches*, Beihefte zum Tübinger Atlas des Vorderen Orients B 19 (Wiesbaden: Dr Ludwig Reichert).

Index

Note: a page reference in italics indicates a figure or table.
Museums are indexed under the cities in which they are located.

abnormal hieratic script 34, 69, 75–8, 141, 149
Abu Rawash, cemeteries 102
Abusir:
  papyri from 141
  funerary temple of Sahure 275
  tombs 66
Abydos:
  evidence for early writing 99
  evidence for sacrifice of retainers 318 n. 13
  inscriptions from 72, 102, 121; kinglist 188, 198
  stelae from 124, 134–5, 291; stela of Amenhotep II 22; stela of King Wadj (Djet) 101, *134*, *135*; stela of Nefer *134*, 248 n. 13; stela of Neferhotep I 79, 80, 195
  tags from 129; from Tomb U-j 118, *119*, 148; tag of Aha *124*; tag of Narmer 122 n. 3, 124
  temple of Ramesses II 250 n. 20
  temple of Sety I 23, 81, 91, 249 n. 16, 274, 315 n. 9, 317 n. 11, *331*
  Tomb U-j 98 n. 1, 100 n. 3, 121 n. 1, 122 n. 2; inscribed pots from 118, *120*, 122, 148; tags from 118, *119*, 148
  tombs 101, 102, 105, 183, 184; *see also* Tomb U-j (*above*)
  Umm el-Qaaab, cemetery: inscribed bowls from *132*; seals from 125, *127*, *130*, 137, *138*, *139*; stelae from *134*, *134*
access to works of art 315–20
  see also elite; non-elite
accounting, and origins of writing 35–7
administrative uses of writing 46, 49, 100, 101, 115, 128–30, 141
  at Deir el-Medina 43, 71, 90–1, 93
  and origins of writing 35–7, 282–3
aesthetics:
  and material culture 4–5, 14
  see also art
Afghanistan, lapis lazuli from 265, 311
Aha:
  serekh of 292
  tag of *124*
Ahmose 197, 198

battle reliefs from reign of 229 n. 32
palette with cartouche of 80
Akhenaten:
  art and artists in reign of 271, 328–30
  religious reforms 48 n. 32, 60–1
  use of purple quartzite 276
  written language reforms 157
  see also Amarna period; el-Amarna
Akhtai (chantress of Amun) 86
Akkadian language *see* Mesopotamia, languages
Alexandria 65, 69
alphabets 12
Amarna period:
  solar cult 24, 276
  stone use 276
  visual arts 24, 191, 224 n. 22, 229, 230
  see also Akhenaten, el-Amarna (site)
Amduat ('Book of the hidden space') 54–5, *164*
Amenemhab 161
  tomb at Thebes 26–7, *27*
Amenemhat I 81, 189
  Instruction of King Amenemhat 82, 189, 322
  pyramid temple at el-Lisht 194
  statuary 321
Amenemhat III:
  pyramid complex 195 n. 15
  statuary 319 n. 15, 321–4, 322
Amenhotep I 197, 199, 273
Amenhotep II 19–20, 26
  letter to Usersatet 79, 82
  stela with hymn to 22
  tomb 163, *164*
Amenhotep III:
  architectural and artistic projects 325–8, 330
  glazed 'ex libris' of 80
  statuary 224 n. 22, *325*, 325
  temple at Wadi el-Sebua 251
  use of purple quartzite 276 n. 8
  see also Thebes, mortuary temple of Amenhotep III
Amenhotep Son of Hapu 275, 326, 327, *327*, 332

America, pre-Columbian *see* Andean pre-Columbian empires; Inka empire; Maya; Mesoamerica; Teotihuacán
amulets 26, 280, 306
Amun:
 blue body colour 252
 cult of 70, 86, 168
Andean pre-Columbian empires 147
 see also Inka empire
animals:
 animal stories and fables 161
 in early Egyptian art 219, 283, 284–5
Ankhtify, tomb of 101
annals 38, 40, 98, 125, 183–4, 186, 294, 295
 Palermo Stone (annal stone) 125, *126*, 127–8, 135, 183
 see also kinglists
anorthosite gneiss 272–3, 275
'antiquity', concept of 185, 186, 187, 193, 194, 196, 197
 see also past, concepts and uses of
Anubis, enlarged hieroglyph of, in 4th dynasty tombs 109 n. 5
archaism 55, 192–4
 see also past, concepts and uses of
architecture:
 elite and non-elite 304, 305
 as means of display, early Egyptian 292–3, 296, 297
 stone: domains of use and symbolism 265–72; symbolic and structural uses 273–5
 texts about 269–71, 310
art:
 aesthetics and material culture 4–5, 14
 decorum 14–29
 definitions 299–302
 integration of art and writing 281–97
 restriction to elite 9, 13–14, 288, 290–2, 295–7, 303–5, 335–7
 role in historical developments 309–35
 Schäfer's theories 207–35, 236–9
 social contexts and divisions 302–9; art and exclusion 302–5; artistic genres and executants 305–9
 social uses 6, 309–12
 status and purposes 298–337
 see also pictorial representation; representation, visual; sculpture
artificial irrigation, date of first 65–6, 113
artists and craftsmen 307–8, *307*, 312–15, 317–18, 328–30, 334, 336

Assurbanipal 83, 230
Assyrian palace reliefs 230
Astarte and the Sea, Tale of 155
astronomical texts 41, 54
Aswan, quarries near 265, 276, 328
Asyut 72
Aya 81
 head ?of *329*

Bak (sculptor) 328, 329–30
 stela of Bak and Tahere 328, *328*
banquet scenes *see* mortuary banquet scenes
barque shrines 273, *274*
battle scenes 229–30
Battlefield Palette 286
Behbeit el-Hagar, temple of Isis 273
Beit Khallaf, tombs 105
belles lettres 83, 145, 149, 158, 168, 187, 189, 191
Berlin, Ägyptisches Museum *319*, 328–9
Berlin and Kay, colour encoding sequence 233, 234, 240–62, *241*
Bernini, Gianlorenzo 193
biographical inscriptions 40–1, 87, 114, 140, 156, 163
Bir Mueilha, inscription 277
black granite *see* granodiorite
blue frit 248, 263, 271
Book of the Dead 38 n. 5, 80, 181
Book of Gates 60
'Book of the hidden space' (Amduat) 54–5, *164*
Book of Kemyt 48, 140
Book of Two Ways 38 n. 5
Boston, Museum of Fine Arts 316
Brooklyn oracle papyrus 76–7
Buhen, stela ?from 79
Bull Palette 218 n. 11, 286
Butehamun (scribe) 70, 85, 86, 92, 153
Buto, votive deposits? 102
bwt, concept of 19

Cairo, Egyptian Museum 22, 284, 286, 314, *327*, *333*
calcite (Egyptian alabaster/travertine) 271, 272, 273, 276
calendars 41, 54, 181
Cambridge, Fitzwilliam Museum 322
canon of proportions 218–19, 227, 283–4
'canonical' representation 219 n. 13, 284
cartouches 18, 80, 137
catfish, Narmer shown as *123*, 289
cemeteries, as source for population estimates 65–7

Index

centralization in early Egypt 38–40, 95–116
ceramics *see* faience; pottery; terracotta
Chester Beatty papyri 92–3, 199
China:
  ancient China 5
  Chinese script/writing 12, 283 n. 1
Cities Palette 286
Classical/Middle Egyptian language *34, 47,*
    48–9, *49,* 149, 152, 156, 157, 174
  Graeco-Roman usage 157–8, 253 n. 24
clothing:
  iconography and depiction of 25–8, 255–6
  see also textiles
Coffin Texts 150, 151, 252 n. 23
colour:
  symbolism 243, 244–5, 246, 247, 251, 252–3,
    260–1
  terminology and classification 234–5,
    240–62; colour encoding sequence 233,
    234, 240–62, *241*
  see also pigments; polychromy
Complaints of Khakheperresonbe 196
copper:
  sources 278
  technology and use 112, 113, 264, 291
Coptic language *34, 47,* 56 n. 50, 149, 156
  colour terms 244, 262
  dialects in 46, 157
  Old Coptic 162
craftsmen 307–8, *307*
'crossword' inscriptions 47 n. 30
cryptography 47, 72
cursive hieroglyphic script 48, 140–2, 144–5
  dating 34
  text genres 46, 48, *49*
cursive script *34*
  cursive forms of hieratic *34,* 149, 335; *see
    also* hieratic script
  cursive signs on blocks and tiles, 3rd
    dynasty 131–3
  demotic cursive script 47, 282
  origins and early use 99–100, 120, 122, 141,
    145, 150, 281–2, 285
  relationship with pictorial art 281–2, 283, 285
  see also cursive hieroglyphic script
cylinder of Narmer 123, *123,* 289, 294

Dahshur:
  pyramid complexes 20–1, 105, 106, 108;
    Bent Pyramid 106; mortuary temples of
    Snofru 105, 106
  tombs 66, 107, 108
dance, evidence for 151

decorum 14–29, 304
Deir el-Gabrawi, tomb of Ibi 332–3
Deir el-Bahri:
  mortuary temples 197
  statue of Thutmose III from 272 n. 4
Deir el-Medina:
  education at 92, 140, 173–4
  literacy 50, 89–94, 172–4
  ostraca from 68, 88, 174
  scribes 76, 86, 89–94
  texts from 43, 71, 90–1, 93, 155; legal
    texts 76, 169–70; list of rulers 198
  tomb of Ipy 24
deities *see* gods
Demotic herbal 162
Demotic language *34, 47, 49,* 156, 158, 162
demotic script *34,* 69–70, 141, 149, 163
  demotic cursive script 47, 282
  text genres 46, *49*
  witnessing and signing
    documents 75–8, 87
Demotic tales 155, 161, 162
  Myth of the Sun's Eye 161
  Setna Khaemwese, tales of 81–2, 86, 87
Dendara, temple complex of Hathor
  and Isis 273, *334*
Destruction of Humanity 191
dialects 46, 101, 157
Dialogue of Ipuwer and the Lord of All 153,
  167, 190–1
Dime 162, 170
Diodorus Siculus 65
'directional straightness', rule of 221–2
Dispute of a Man with His Ba 199
divine adoratrices 84, 85, 89
Djet *see* Wadj
Djoser 39, 104, 105, 191, 193, 198
  chapel of, at Heliopolis 104, 138–9, *139*
  see also Saqqara, Step Pyramid of Djoser
drapery *see* clothing
draughtsmen, at Deir el-Medina 91–2, 93
Drenkhahn, Rosemarie, on Egyptian art 299,
  300, 301, 305–6, 307, 308
dress *see* clothing
Duris of Samos 237
dwarfs 308 n. 5, *320*
dynasties:
  dynasty 0 *see* Predynastic period
  1st–3rd dynasties *see* Early Dynastic period
  4th–8th dynasties *see* Old Kingdom
  9th–11th dynasties *see* First Intermediate
    period
  11th–13th dynasties *see* Middle Kingdom

dynasties: (cont.)
    18th–20th dynasties see New Kingdom
    21st–25th dynasties see Third Intermediate
        period
    25th–30th dynasties see Late period

Early Dynastic period:
    development of writing 36–9, 59, 99–105
    role of art in historical
        developments 312–20
Edfu, temple of Horus, granite naos 266,
    268, 273
education 44–5, 49
    at Deir el-Medina 92, 140, 173–4
    of princes 45, 81–2, 154
    training of scribes 44–5, 46, 48, 49, 140,
        153, 174
Egyptian alabaster see calcite
'Egyptian blue' see blue frit
Egyptian faience see faience
Egyptian language 121, 156
    Egyptian in Greek letters 34, 56 n. 50, 149
    spoken and written compared 47
    see also Classical/Middle Egyptian
        language; Late Egyptian language; Old
        Egyptian language; Demotic language
el-Amarna 90, 276, 303 n. 2, 330
    house and studio of Thutmose 328–9, 329
    see also Amarna
el-Lisht, pyramid temples 194, 195 n. 15
Elam, origins of writing 36
electrum 269, 270, 277
Elephantine, votive deposits 102
elite:
    restriction of artistic culture to 9, 13–14,
        288, 290–2, 295–7, 303–5, 335–7; see also
        decorum
    restriction of writing to 9–10, 13–14, 70–3,
        95–116, 288, 291–2; see also literacy
    size of 73–5
    see also non-elite
Elkab 105
    tomb of Paheri 72
Eloquent Peasant, Tale of the 19, 82, 188–9
emblematic mode of representation 16, 122,
    285, 286, 289
enclosures, depicted by royal Horus
    names 292–3
Ethiopia:
    Mursi language 247
    obsidian from 265

faience 225 n. 24, 263, 271, 276, 277, 291, 305

symbolism 244
tiles, signs on 131
Fayyum 38 n. 5, 69, 70, 162, 170
fertility figurines 304
First Intermediate period, literacy in 68
flint, technology and use 112, 264
folklore elements in literary texts 41, 53, 59
foreshortening 208, 215, 221, 223, 225, 227,
    230, 231–3, 235
    in Greek art 209–10, 232, 238
frit see blue frit
funeral processions, gender roles 168
funerary laments 167–8

galena (lead ore), mining 277
Gebel Ahmar, quarries 276
Gebel el-Silsila, quarries 274
Gebel el-Zeit, galena mines 277
Gebelein:
    papyri from 128
    relief from 136, 137
gemstones 263
gender issues see women
gestures, iconographic conventions as pointer
    to importance of oral forms 166–7
gilding see gold
Giza:
    limited use of copper 113
    pyramid complexes 20–1, 105, 106, 108, 187,
        193; Great Pyramid 54, 185, 186; pyramid of
        Khephren 314; town associated with
        pyramid construction 107; valley temple
        of Rekhaef (Khephren), statue from 272–3
    'reserve head' from 316
    tombs 66, 107–8, 193, 314
glass 263, 271, 277
    inlay 271, 277, 278
gneiss see anorthosite gneiss
gods:
    deities on non-royal stelae 21–2, 22, 23
    literate deities 43 n. 19, 87–8
    see also Amun; Anubis; Hathor; Horus;
        Osiris; Sakhmet; Seshat; solar cult; Thoth
Goethe, Johann Wolfgang von 236, 238–9
gold:
    gilding 266, 269, 270, 271, 272 n. 4
    sources 265, 277
    symbolism 244
    technology and use 264, 291
Gombrich, E. H., Art and illusion 207, 231,
    232, 235
Graeco-Roman period:
    Egyptianizing Roman statues 238

languages and scripts: Classical/Middle
  Egyptian 157–8, 253 n. 24; Egyptian in
  Greek letters 34, 56 n. 50, 149; *see also*
  Greek language; Greek script
literacy 49, 69, 94; and orality 162
role of art in historical
  developments 332–5
temples 273, 324, 334
use of colour 247, 252
use of stone 263–4
writing 48, 49
graffiti 72, 109, 133, 310, 329–30
granite 266, 269, 270, 272, 273, 274, 275, 276
granodiorite 266, 270, 273, 274
Great Pyramid (in medieval Arabic poem) 179
Greece:
  art: archaic painting and sculpture 221,
    229, 230, 234, 256; artistic theory 236–8;
    classical art 224, 232, 234–5, 237–8, 246,
    257; colour terminology and use 234,
    246, 251, 257; foreshortening 209–10, 232,
    238; Hellenistic art 224, 225, 234, 237,
    254 n. 28, 257; perspective 209, 210, 232,
    238; 'pre-Greek' representation
    (Schäfer) 209
  writing, origins and development 60, 61–2,
    97–8, 176–7
Greek language in Egypt 34, 43, 47, 48, 49, 50,
  69, 75, 77, 78, 157, 170
literacy among Greek speakers 49, 94
Greek script 34, 47, 152
  Egyptian in Greek letters 34, 56 n. 50, 149

hands, iconographic conventions as pointer to
  importance of oral forms 167
Hardjedef 81
Haremhab 81, 157, 198–9, 200
  statue of 272 n. 4
  tomb at Saqqara 167
harpists' songs 61, 160, 167, 199–200
  Harpist's Song from the Tomb of King
    Inyotef 167, 199
Hathor, cult of 168, 276, 277
Hatnub, quarries 276
Hatshepsut:
  barque shrine at Karnak 273, 274
  inscriptions 157, 197
  mortuary temple at Deir el-Bahri 197
Hebrew language, Old Testament 154, 159,
  243 n. 2
Heliopolis:
  chapel of Djoser 104, 138–9, 139
  relief of Tjanefer from 333

royal reliefs 104
stela of Ramesses II perhaps from 277
Hellenistic art 224, 225, 234, 237, 254 n. 28, 257
Helwan, cemetery 102, 105, 129, 134–5
Herdsman's Song (Old Kingdom) 53 n. 43,
  168
Herdsman's Story (Middle Kingdom) 191
Hermopolis 158
  demotic legal code from 48 n. 32
Herodotus 52, 187, 196
Hezyre 102
  tomb of 43, 105, 106, 131
Hierakonpolis 99
  'decorated tomb' (Tomb 100) 216, 217–18
  ivories from 318, 320
  lapis lazuli statuette from 311
  maceheads from *see* Narmer, macehead;
    Scorpion Macehead
  palettes from 317; *see also* Narmer,
    palette of
  statue of Khasekhem from 321
  temple reliefs from 137, 138
  Tomb 100 ('decorated tomb') 316
  votive deposits 102, 313 n. 7
  wooden statue from 319 n. 15
  see also Narmer, cylinder of
hieratic script 12–13, 34, 92, 140–2, 145
  cursive form 34, 149, 335
  in Late period 69
  origins 140–2, 281–2
  text genres 46, 48, 49
  training in writing 48
  'verse points' 159
  witnessing and signing documents 75–8
  see also abnormal hieratic script; demotic
    script
hieroglyphic script 11–13, 34, 46, 140–2, 145
  cryptography 47
  decrease in size of signs 67
  and literacy 48, 91
  origins and early use 99, 122, 127–8, 135,
    137–42, 281–3, 285
  relationship with pictorial art 281–3, 285,
    313, 335
  sign for ḥmt 306
  stone vase in form of two hieroglyphs 43,
    131, 133
  text genres 46, 48, 49
  see also cursive hieroglyphic script;
    emblematic mode of representation
historical texts, scripts used for 46
history, Egyptian concept of *see* past, concepts
  and uses of

ḥmt, meaning of 299, 300, 301, 306
Hor, archive of 71
Hori, satirical letter of 45 n. 27
Horus:
  falcon emblem 288, 289
  'following of' 125, 184
  temple at Edfu, granite naos 266, *268*, 273
  wedjat eye 21, 22
Horus names (*serekh*) 18, 20, 121, 135, 288–9, 292–3, *292*
Horus and Seth, tale fragment (Middle Kingdom) 191
Horus and Seth, Tale of 43 n. 19
Horus-and-Seth name, Khasekhemwy 138, *138*, *139*
'house of life' 45
human figure:
  canon of proportions 218–19, 227, 283–4
  colour conventions 246, *247*
  as focus of social representation 6
  iconography of clothing 25–8, 255–6
  nudity, and decorum 27
  Schäfer on 210
  three-dimensional representation 222–3; portraiture 224–5, 321–2; royal statuary, 12th dynasty 321–4
  two-dimensional representation 216–18, 220, 228–9, 255, 283–5
hunting scenes 229–30
hymns 41, 93, 154

Ibi, tombs of 154, 332–3
iconography:
  of clothing 25–8, 255–6
  conventions of, as pointer to importance of oral forms 166–7
  patterns of, and decorum 16
Idut (queen) 86 n. 16
Illahun 158
'illustrated books' 38
  see also Book of the Dead; underworld books
Imhotep (Imuthes) 39, 43 n. 18, 102, 104, 105, 133
  and Step Pyramid of Djoser 313–14, *314*
Imti, stela of *129*
Imuthes *see* Imhotep
India:
  ancient 58, 154
  caste system 15
Inka empire 58, 118, 147
inlays:
  faience 271

glass 271, 277, *278*
green and blue stone 243 n. 3, 250
semi-precious stones 271
inscriptions:
  biographical 40–1, 87, 114, 140, 156, 163
  'crossword' 47 n. 30
  royal *see* royal inscriptions
  on statues in temples 152
institutionalization, role of writing 169–70
instruction texts 188, 322
  for Kagemni 187 n. 6
  of Khety 50, 52, 153
  of King Amenemhat 82, 189, 322
  Loyalist Instruction 72
  for Merikare 60 n. 56, 79, 82, 154, 188–91, 194, 196, 322
  of Ptahhotep 153, 187
  for the Vizier 71
  see also Tale of the Eloquent Peasant
invisibility *see* access
Inyotef, tomb of 167, 199
Ipuwer 153, 167, 190–1
Ipy, tomb of at Deir el-Medina 24
Ireteru, tomb of 84
Irihor *see* Ro/Irihor
irrigation, date of first artificial 65–6, 113
Isis and Re (text) 191
ivory objects, early Egyptian 286, 291, 318, 319, *320*
  cylinder of Narmer 123, *123*, 289, 294
  tags 100, 124–5
Izezi 187
  letter to Senedjemib Inti 78, 79

Japanese script 12
jewellery 276, 280, 306
  jewellers 308
Josephus 65
Junge, Friedrich, on Egyptian art 299, 301–2

Ka, *serekh* of *292*
Kagemni, Instruction for 187 n. 6
Kamose, stelae of 157
Kanais, temple, inscriptions of Sety I 277
Kaninisut, tomb of 67
Karnak:
  barque shrines 273, *274*
  statue of Amenhotep Son of Hapu from *327*
  stela 75
  temple of Amon-Re 197
  temple of Mut 270, *326*

Index

Kawab (son of Khufu) 81
Kemyt, Book of 48, 140
Khaemwese 81–2, 196
  see also Setna Khaemwese, tales of
Khakheperresonbe, Complaints of 196
Khasekhem, statues 319, *321*
Khasekhemwy:
  Horus-and-Seth name 138, *138*, 139
  year name 264
Khephren, pyramid and valley temple at Giza 272–3, 314
Khety 189
  Instruction of Khety 50, 52, 153
khipu (Andean and Inka record-keeping system) 58, 147
Khufu (Cheops) 81
  mortuary temple of 105, 185
kinglists 181, 184, 188, 198
kings:
  literacy 43–4, 78–83, 100
  right to petition in writing or appear in person before 71
Koptos, colossal statues of Min from 311, *312*
Kushite statues 272 n. 4

laments, funerary 167–8
Lange, Julius, 'law of frontality' 221
language:
  aesthetic aspects 5
  colour terminology *see* colour, terminology and classification
  dating of forms and languages 34
  relationship with visual representation 7–9
  relationship with writing 6–7, 10, 156–8
  spoken *see* orality
  syntactic language, introduction of 16, 137–44
  see also Classical/Middle Egyptian language; Coptic language; Demotic language; Egyptian language; Greek language; Hebrew language; Late Egyptian language; Mesopotamia, languages; Mursi language; Ndembu language; Old Egyptian language; Semitic languages
lapis lazuli 248, 252–3, 263, 264, 269 n. 1, 271, 311
  sources 265
  symbolism 244
  ultramarine from 260
Late Egyptian language 34, 47, 49, 149, 157, 174, 199
Late Egyptian miscellanies 92

Late period:
  literacy 69
  role of art in historical developments 332–5
law *see* legal texts
lead *see* galena
lector priests 51, 93
legal texts 39, 57, 59, 169–70
  marriage agreements 163
  scripts used for 46
  wills 57, 76, 165, 169–70
  see also witnessing and signing documents
Leiden letter to the dead 86
Leonardo da Vinci 232 n. 37
letters and letter-writing 39–40, 78, 101, 143
  letters addressed to 'your scribe' 44, 153
  letters to the dead 86
life-expectancy 66, 73–5
limestone 266, 270, 272, 274–5
Linear B 37
literacy:
  cognitive aspects 53–62
  definitions 63–4, 147–8
  Deir el-Medina 50, 89–94, 172–4
  in early Egypt 95–116, 130–1
  of kings 43–4, 78–83, 100
  levels of 50
  nature of reading public 51–3
  numbers of literate 49–50; literate group as proportion of population 64–78, 88, 94, 172–3
  orality and 146–71
  origins and development 35–43
  scribal equipment in tombs as evidence for 80, 85, 90, 131, 173
  and status 43–5, 131
  of women 57, 83–9, 93, 94, 151–2, 173
  see also scripts; texts; writing
literalism, in visual art *see* realism
literary texts 19, 40, 41, 42, 49, 59, 109, 199, 335
  concepts and uses of the past 187–91, 196
  from Deir el-Medina 93
  educational use 174
  and evidence for literacy of kings 82–3
  from Fayyum, in Greek and Egyptian 170
  folklore elements 41, 53, 59
  scripts used for 46, 48, 49
  structure and style 56
  from tombs 51
  see also instruction texts; royal inscriptions
London, British Museum *132*, *134*, *165*, *326*
love poetry 41, 61, 87, 88–9, 159–60, 161
Loyalist Instruction 72

Luxor Temple 326–7
Lysippus 237

maat, concept of 19–20
maceheads 101, 135–6, 286, *287*, 290–1, 294, 316–18
   Narmer Macehead 122–3, *123*, 137, 294
Maghara, turquoise mines 276
magical texts 40, 41, 56–7, 93, 149–50, 154, 155, 157
   scripts used for 49
   see also Pyramid Texts; Coffin Texts
Maidum, tombs 105, 107
Manetho 39, 104, 125, 198
Manshiyet el-Sadr, stela from 277 n. 11
mark, signing with 93
marriage agreements 163
material culture:
   and aesthetics 4–5, 14
   emergence of 4–5
   and writing 4–10
mathematical texts 41, 54, 188
Maya, writing and pictorial representation 118, 131, 147, 261, 336
Mayyati (Meritaten), princess 85–6
medical texts 41, 54, 93, 106, 188
Mehu, tomb at Saqqara *267*
Meir, tombs 193
   of Pepyankh Heny the Black 192, *307*
Meketre, Middle Kingdom house models 18
Memphis:
   capital at 103, 183, 194
   cemeteries 66, 103
   chief priest of 158
   early enclosure at 293
   letters from 173
   urban centre, archaeological evidence 111
'Memphite theology' 80
Men (sculptor) 328, 329–30
Menes, cult of 198
Menkheperre scarabs 48
Mentuhotep *see* Nebhepetre Mentuhotep
Mereruka, tomb of 192, 193
Meresankh III, tomb of 151–2
Merika, tomb and stela at Saqqara 135, *136*, 291, 319 n. 14
Merikare, Instruction for 60 n. 56, 79, 82, 154, 188–91, 194, 196, 322
Meritaten *see* Mayyati
Meroitic alphabet 38
Mesoamerica:
   writing and pictorial representation 229 n. 31, 281, 283, 285
   see also Maya; Teotihuacán
Mesopotamia:
   ceramics 305
   languages 30; colour terms 242–3, 247, 253, 261
   literacy 83
   metrical forms 159
   political and social organization 58, 96
   sculpture 223 n. 20, 229 n. 31
   temple enclosures 293
   women in 88
   writing: origins 9–10, 36, 99, 121–2, 176; development 42, 97–8, 100, 118, 129–30, 146–7, 148, 176, 281
metals:
   casting 225–6
   usages and values 263, 264, 277–8, 306
   see also copper; gold
Metjen 102
metrical forms, in Egyptian texts 42, 56, 158–9
Middle Egyptian *see* Classical/Middle Egyptian language
Middle Kingdom:
   concepts and uses of the past 187–91, 193–200
   decorum 23
   development of writing 40–1, 59
   literacy 68
   painted colours 249
   royal statuary, 12th dynasty 321–4
Milan, cathedral 275
mining 277–8
Minshat Abu Omar 99
Mit Rahina, colossus of Ramesses II at 272 n. 4
Montuemhat, tomb of 69
mortality *see* life-expectancy
mortuary banquet scenes, in New Kingdom tombs 27, 88, 168
mortuary texts 154
   see also Pyramid Texts; Coffin Texts
Mose, legal text of 75
Mursi language (Ethiopia) 247
music:
   aesthetic aspects 5
   evidence for 151, 161, 168
   see also harpists' songs; Herdsman's Song
Mutirdis, tomb of 85 n. 15
Myth of the Sun's Eye 161

Nag el-Deir:
   cemeteries 105 n. 4
   coffins from 68
   naoi 266, *268*, 273, 277 n. 11

Naqada, tombs 102
Narmer:
  cylinder of 123, *123*, 289, 294
  macehead 122–3, *123*, 137, 294
  palette of 101, 217, 283, *284*, 288–9, 290, 294, 318; hieroglyphs 121, 122
  serekh of 292
  tag of 122 n. 3, 124
Naunakhte, will of 169–70
Ndembu language (Zambia) 245
Nebet (queen), as vizier 84
Nebhepetre Mentuhotep 194, 198
  mortuary temple at Deir el-Bahri 197
Nebka (?—king), cartouche of 137
Nectanebo I 266
Nefer:
  stela of *134*, 248 n. 13
  tomb of 67
Neferhotep I, stela of 79, 80, 195
Neferkare and Sisene (tale) 187
Neferti, Prophecy of 79, 82, 83, 187 n. 6, 189
Nefertiti, bust of 328
Neolithic art and culture 4, 106, 180
Neskhons, transfer document of 165
New Kingdom:
  colours in paint 249–52
  concepts and uses of the past 195–200
  decorum 21–5
  development of writing 41–3, 49, 59, 60–1
  literacy 68
  role of art in historical developments, late 18th dynasty 325–31
New York, Metropolitan Museum of Art *133*
Niankhsakhmet, texts of 25, 28, 248, 254 n. 26
Ninetjer, seals of 139
non-elite:
  evidence for artistic culture 303–5, 306
  evidence for writing 103, 114–15
  see also elite
non-perspective art *see* perspective
notaries 77
Nubia 79, 98, 116, 197, 288
  A-Group culture 111–12
  ceramics 113, 305
  gold from 277
  stone from 272
  viceroy of 79, 82
nudity, and decorum 27

obelisks 275
obsidian 265
offering bearers, representations of 223, 223 n. 19, 225, 263–4, *333*

offering lists, on stelae 128, *129*, 135
Old Coptic *see* Coptic language
Old Egyptian language 34, *47*, 48–9, 156
Old Kingdom:
  decorum 20–1
  development of writing 39–40, 59, 105–10
  literacy 66–8
  painted colours 247–9
  role of art in historical developments, 4th dynasty 312–20
onomastica 41, 127, 162
'opening of the mouth' ceremony 151, 308 n. 6, 311
orality:
  and literacy 146–71
  oral and written 'texts' 142–4
  written and spoken language 46, *47*, 48, 158–61
Osiris, and concept of time 181
ostraca 41, 68, 88, 104, 153, 161, 174
Oxford, Ashmolean Museum *123*, *132*, *286*–7, *311*, *317*, *320*–1

Paheri, tomb at Elkab 72
paint:
  changing set of colours 247–52
  painted imitations of valued stone 266, 270
  painted pottery, early Egyptian 112–13
  painted relief 255
  painted stone statues 272–3
  see also colour; pictorial representation; pigments; polychromy
Palaeolithic art and culture 5, 233, 255 n. 29, 298
Palermo, Museo Archeologico Regionale di Palermo *126*
Palermo Stone (annal stone) 125, *126*, 127–8, 135, 183
Palestine:
  origins of north-west Semitic writing 97–8
  trade with 102
palettes:
  decorated siltstone, early Egyptian 121, 135–6, 216, *286*, *286*, 289, 290, 294, 316–18; Bull Palette 218 n. 11, *286*; Narmer Palette *see* Narmer, palette of; Two Dog Palette *317*
  as evidence for paint usage 250 n. 19, 290
  in tombs, as evidence for literacy 80, 85, 90
papyrus, invention and early use 37, 100, 115, 128
Paris, Musée du Louvre *134*, *286*
past, concepts and uses of 38, 55, 179–201, 310

periods and 'history', Middle and New
    Kingdoms 195–200
  in visual arts 191–5, 197–8, 327, 332–4, 335–6
  see also annals; year names
Payankh (general and high priest of Amun) 70
Pehernefer 102
pens see scribal equipment
Pepy I:
  copper statues 264
  mortuary temple at Saqqara 141
Pepy II, mortuary complex at Saqqara 194
Pepyankh Heny the Black,
    tomb at Meir 192, 307
performance:
  indirect evidence for 303
  orality and 150–1, 152, 153, 154–5, 156, 160,
    161, 162–3, 166–8
Peribsen, seals of 130, 137, 138, 139
perspective 208, 227, 231, 232–3, 234, 235, 251
  in Greek art 209, 210, 232, 238
Petamenope, tomb of 69
Petosiris (priest of Hermopolis) 158
  tomb at Tuna el-Gebel 225 n. 23
petrified wood, statues 266
phonograms 11, 121 n. 1
pictorial representation (two-dimensional
    representation):
  restriction to elite 13–14
  theories of representation 208, 214–21;
    'realism' and its implications 227–31
  see also colour; foreshortening; human
    figure; perspective; polychromy;
    representation
pigments 5, 244 n. 5, 246, 247–54, 260, 261
  use of, evidence of palettes 250 n. 19, 290
  see also blue frit; paint
Plato:
  on dangers of writing 44, 108
  on proportion in art 236–7, 238
Pliny, Natural History 237–8
poetry 158–60
  love poetry 41, 61, 87, 88–9, 159–60, 161
polychromy 234, 240–62
Polygnotus 236, 238
population size 64–6
  life-expectancy 66, 73–5
  literate group as proportion of total
    population 64–78
portraiture, in sculpture 224–5, 321–2
pottery:
  aesthetic devaluation 305
  early Egyptian, painted/decorated 112–13,
    216, 289, 290

potmarks 131, 133
signs on, as early writing 99–100, 118, 120,
    122, 131, 133, 148
Predynastic period, dynasty 0:
  role of art in historical
    developments 312–20
  writing 99–104, 121–3
princes, education of 45, 81–2, 154
projective systems in drawing 227, 232–3
  see also perspective
Prophecy of Neferti 79, 82, 83, 187 n. 6, 189
proportions, canon of 218–19, 227, 283–4
pseudoglyphs (Maya) 131
Psherenptah (chief priest of Memphis) 158
Ptahhotep, Instruction of 153, 187
Ptolemaic period see Graeco-Roman period
Pyramid Texts 42, 67, 106, 140, 141, 149, 150–1,
    156, 195
pyramids 105, 106, 113, 279, 313–15
  see also Dahshur; el-Lisht; Giza; Saqqara

quarrying, stone 265, 274, 276, 279, 328
  quarry marks, 3rd dynasty 104, 131
quartzdiorite 270
quartzite 266, 269, 270, 273, 275–6

Ramesses I 81, 198–9
Ramesses II 81–2, 200, 330
  colossus of, from Mit Rahina 272 n. 4
  mortuary temple at Thebes 200
  stela of, from Heliopolis 277
  temple at Abydos 250 n. 20
Ramesses III 81, 200, 278
Ramesses V 71
Ramesseum papyri 141
reading:
  and oral forms 152–6
  reading aloud 45, 49 n. 33, 153–6;
    recitation 45, 150, 151
realism, in visual art 208, 227–31, 302 n. 1
recitation, evidence for 45, 150, 151
religious/ritual texts:
  cognitive aspects 55–6
  colour symbolism 244
  from Deir el-Medina 93
  earliest 42, 104, 140
  scripts used for 46, 48, 49, 140, 141
representation, visual:
  emblematic mode 16, 122, 285, 286, 289
  and language 7–9
  restrictions on spread 288–93
  Schäfer's theories 207–35, 236–9
  and style 283–5

three-dimensional *see* sculpture
two-dimensional *see* pictorial
  representation
see also art
Reqaqna 105 n. 4
'reserve heads', 4th dynasty
  315, *316*
Rib-Adda of Byblos, letters of 71
ritual texts *see* religious/ritual texts
Ro/Irihor:
  inscribed pottery of 99–100
  serekh of 292
rock crystal 271
Roman period *see* Graeco-Roman period
royal inscriptions 19, 40–1, 59, 79, 82, 157,
  182, 188
royal names:
  cursive notations, late predynastic
    period 120–1
  Middle Kingdom 23
  see also Horus names; year names
royal reliefs 104, *136*, *137*, 296, 318
royal statuary, 12th dynasty 321–4

sacred and profane, and decorum 18–20
Sahure:
  reliefs of 123
  temple at Abusir 275
Sakhmet, statues of, from mortuary temple
    of Amenhotep III 270, *326*
sandstone 269, 270, 273, 274–5
silicified *see* quartzite
Saqqara:
  manuscripts of Demotic tales
    from 162
  mortuary complex of Pepy II 194
  mortuary temple of Pepy I 141
  pottery from 112
  signs on blocks and tiles from 131–3
  stelae from 102, 129, 135, *136*, 291, 319 n. 14
  Step Pyramid of Djoser 184–5, 195 n. 15,
    313–14; ostracon from 104; statue plinth
    naming Imhotep 313–14, *314*; stone vases
    beneath 131, 184–5, 320
  Step Pyramid of Sekhemkhet 104
  stone vase in form of two hieroglyphs
    ? from 43, 131, *133*
  tombs 66, 102, 105, 107, 108, 129, 183, 192,
    193, 319; of Haremhab 167; of Mehu 267;
    of Merika 135, *136*, 291, 319 n. 14; papyrus
    roll from 128
sarcophagi, writing on 140
see also Coffin Texts

scarabs:
  cryptography 47
  Menkheperre 48
'scenes of daily life', in tombs, 5th–6th
    dynasty 220
Schäfer, Heinrich 207–35, 236–9
schools 44–5, 49
see also education
Scorpion Macehead 101, *287*
scribal equipment, in tombs, as evidence for
    literacy 80, 85, 90, 131, 173
scribes:
  career and status 43–4, 50, 52, 80–1, 172
  at Deir el-Medina 76, 86, 89–94
  equipment *see* scribal equipment
  female 84
  letter recipients addressed as 'your
    scribe' 44, 153
  pictured in Old Kingdom tombs 67
  proportion in village communities 70
  statues of 44, 223 n. 19
  training 44–5, 46, 48, *49*, 140, 153, 174
  village scribes, Greco-Roman 50, 50 n. 35,
    70, 90
  and witnessing and signing of
    documents 76, 77–8
scripts 11–13, 34, 46–9
  see also abnormal hieratic script; cursive
    hieroglyphic script; cursive script;
    demotic script; Greek script; hieratic
    script; hieroglyphic script
sculptors 307–8, *307*, 328–30
sculpture:
  materials 225–6
  portraiture 224–5, 321–2
  preparatory drawings 222
  'realism' and its implications 227–31
  theories of representation 208, 210, 217, 221–7
  see also representation; statuary
seals and seal impressions (sealings), early
    Egypt 100, 101, 102, 124, 129, 131, 139
  from Abydos: 'dynastic seals' of 1st
    dynasty 125, *127*; seals of Peribsen *130*,
    137, *138*, 139
  use of stone 280
Sehetepibre, stela of 72
Sekhemkhet, step pyramid complex at
    Saqqara 104
semi-precious stones, inlays 271
Semitic languages 152, 156
semograms 11, 121 n. 1
Senedjemib Inti 78, 79
Senwosret I 188, 189, 195

Senwosret I (*cont.*)
  pyramid complex at el-Lisht 194, 195 n. 15
  statuary 321
  'White Chapel' of 197
Senwosret II, pyramid town of 51
Senwosret III:
  song cycle in praise of 158
  statuary 321–4, *322*
Serabit el-Khadim, temple of Hathor 276
serekh see Horus names
Seshat, goddess of writing 43 n. 19, 87–8
Sethnakhte 81
Setna Khaemwese, tales of 81–2, 86, 87
Sety I 81, 277, 330–1, *331*
  see also Abydos, temple of Sety I
Shabaka 80
Shipwrecked Sailor, Tale of the 160, 188
Shulgi, king of 3rd dynasty of Ur 83
signing documents *see* witnessing and signing documents
silicified sandstone *see* quartzite
Simut 161
Sinai:
  royal reliefs 104
  turquoise and copper mining 276, 278
Sinuhe, Tale of 155, 160, 168, 189
Sippar 88
Snofru:
  and Prophecy of Neferti 79, 189
  reign later seen as 'golden age' 187, 189, 198
  see also Dahshur, pyramid complex; Palermo Stone
social organization, early Egypt 95–116
solar cult:
  Amarna period 24, 276
  quartzite associated with 275–6
  secrecy 296
  see also Amun
songs 158
  see also harpists' songs; Herdsman's Song; music; poetry
sphinxes 322
spoken language *see* orality
statuary:
  12th dynasty royal 321–4
  inscriptions on statues in temples 152
  materials 264–5, 270, 271, 272–3, 319 n. 15
  'opening of the mouth' ceremony 151, 308 n. 6, 311
  'reserve heads', 4th dynasty 315, *316*
  scribe statues 44, 223 n. 19
stelae:
  deities on non-royal stelae 21–2, 22, 23
  'slab stelae' 107–8, 247 n. 9, 248, 315
  texts on 40, 79, 80, 134–5; appeals to the living 72; offering lists 128, *129*, 135; stela from mortuary temple of Amenhotep III at Thebes 269–71
stone:
  architecture: domains of use and symbolism 265–70; symbolic and structural uses 273–5
  inlays 243 n. 3, 250
  painted imitations of valued stone 266, 270
  sources 265, 272, 274–5, 276, 279; *see also* quarrying
  statuary 264–5
  symbolism of particular stones 275–8
  usages and values 263–80
  vases, early Egyptian 113, 217, 286, 290, 291, 319–20, *319*; beneath Step Pyramid of Djoser 131, 184–5, 320; in form of two hieroglyphs 43, 131, *133*; inscribed 100, 131, *132*, 184–5, 320; materials and technology 112, 272, 306
Sudan 36, 38
  ceramics 305
Sumerian language *see* Mesopotamia, languages
sun god *see* Amun; solar cult
surgical treatises 41, 54
Suty and Hor, stela at Luxor 326–7
syntactic language, introduction of 16, 137–44
Syria, origins of writing 97–8

tags:
  with earliest surviving writing, from Abydos, Tomb U-j 118, *119*, 148
  with information about goods 129
  with year names, early Egyptian 100, 122 n. 3, *124*–5, *124*, 127–8, 286, 294, 295
Taimhotep, stela of 167–8
Tale of Astarte and the Sea 155
Tale of the Eloquent Peasant 19, 82, 188–9
Tale of Horus and Seth 43 n. 19
Tale of the Shipwrecked Sailor 160, 188
Tale of Sinuhe 155, 160, 168, 189
Tale of Truth and Falsehood 87
Tale of the Two Brothers 37, 42 n. 16, 87
Tale of Wenamun 160
Tale of Woe 160
tales, Demotic *see* Demotic tales
Tarkhan, cemeteries 102
teaching *see* education; schools
Tebtunis 162, 170
technical texts 40, 59, 145
Tell el-Farkha 110 n. 7

Index

temple reliefs, decorum 23
temples as repositories of literary texts 51
Teotihuacán 58, 147
terracotta 225–6
textiles 306
  see also clothing
texts:
  definitions 42, 142–4
  on use of stone 263–4, 269–71
  types see architecture, texts on;
    astronomical texts; belles lettres;
    historical texts; 'illustrated books';
    instruction texts; legal texts; letters;
    literary texts; magical texts;
    mathematical texts; medical texts;
    mortuary texts; poetry; religious/ritual
    texts; technical texts; 'wisdom' texts
Teye (queen), glazed 'ex libris' of 80
Thebes:
  divine adoratrices 84, 85, 89
  letters and other documents from 85, 165, 166
  monuments of early 12th dynasty 194
  mortuary temple of Amenhotep
    III 269–71, 325–6, 325–6; Memnon
    Colossi 275–6, 325; stela from 269–71
  mortuary temple of Ramesses II 200
  temple of Medinet Habu, relief of Ramesses
    III 278
  tombs 22, 27, 68, 69; of Amenemhab 26–7,
    27; of Ibi 154, 332–3
  see also Deir el-Medina; Valley of the Kings
Third Intermediate period:
  development of writing 59
  literacy 68–9
Thoth:
  as literate deity 43 n. 19, 87
  as mythical inventor of language and
    writing 60
Thutmose (scribe) 70, 85, 92
Thutmose (sculptor) 328–9, 329
Thutmose I:
  decree proclaiming accession 155
  royal inscriptions 157
Thutmose III 161
  annals of 125
  barque shrine at Karnak 273
  Menkheperre scarabs 48
  statue from Deir el-Bahri 272 n. 4
  tomb 163
Thutmose IV:
  barque shrine at Karnak 273
  naos of 277 n. 11
Ti, tomb of 192

time, Egyptian concepts of 180–3
tin, mining 277
Titian, *Sacred and profane love* 27
Tjanefer, relief from Heliopolis 333
travertine see calcite
Truth and Falsehood, Tale of 87
Tuna el-Gebel, tomb of Petosiris 225 n. 23
Turin, Museo Egizio 136, 139
Turin kinglist ('Turin Canon') 198
turquoise 263, 269 n. 1, 271, 275, 276, 278
  symbolism 244
Tutankhamun 157
  battle scenes of 229–30
  tomb of, palettes and pens from 80, 85–6
Two Brothers, Tale of the 37, 42 n. 16, 87
Two Dog Palette 317

ultramarine 260
underworld books 38 n. 5, 91, 162–3
  see also Book of Gates
universals in visual art 205, 231–5, 255 n. 30
  colour categories 240–1, 255 n. 30, 258
Ur see Mesopotamia
Uruk see Mesopotamia
Usersatet, viceroy of Nubia 79, 82

Valley of the Kings:
  ostraca from 68
  tombs 163, 164
  see also Deir el-Medina
Varro 237
vases, stone see stone, vases
verse see poetry
vessels, stone see stone, vases
village scribes 50, 70, 90
visual arts see art; pictorial representation;
  representation; sculpture
Vizier, Instruction for the 71
viziers 71, 314 n. 8
  as authors of didactic texts 51
  women as 84

Wadi el-Sebua, temple of Amenhotep III 251
Wadi Hammamat, quarries and mines 276, 277
Wadj, King (Djet), stela of 101, 134, 135
wedjat eye 21, 22
Wenamun, Tale of 160
Westcar Papyrus, tale in 79, 81, 87, 187, 187 n. 6
wills 57, 76, 165, 169–70
Winckelmann, J. J. 236–9
winged disk 21–2, 22
'wisdom' texts 41

witnessing and signing documents 75–8, 87, 93
  witness-copy documents 76–7, 163, *165*
women:
  decorum and 304 n. 4
  divine adoratrices 84, 85, 89
  education 173
  literacy 57, 83–9, 93, 94, 151–2, 173
  and oral high culture 168
  in pictorial art, colour conventions 246, 247
  role at funerals 168
  as scribes 84
  as singers 168
  as viziers 84
  wills of 57
  as witnesses 77
wood:
  statuary 264–5, 319 n. 15
  tags, early Egyptian 100, 124, *124*, 286
writing:
  administrative uses *see* administrative uses of writing
  development and use: Early Dynastic period 123–42; social organization and 95–6, 113–15
  elite, restriction to 9–10, 13–14, 70–3, 95–116, 288, 291–2
  and material culture 4–10
  non-elite, evidence for 103, 114–15
  origins 35–43, 96–8, 118–23, 282–3; *see also* pottery, signs on
  relationship with language 6–7, 10, 156–8
  relationship with pictorial art 281–97, 335
  restrictions on spread 288–93
  as stimulus for change 57–62, 169–70
  see also literacy; scripts; texts

year names 124–5, 127–8, 135, 183, 264, 295
  tags with, early Egyptian 100, 122 n. 3, 124–5, *124*, 127–8, 286, 294, 295
  see also annals

Zambia, Ndembu language 245